THE FACES OF POWER

THE FACES
OF POWER

CONSTANCY AND CHANGE
IN UNITED STATES FOREIGN POLICY FROM
TRUMAN TO REAGAN

SEYOM BROWN

COLUMBIA UNIVERSITY PRESS

NEW YORK   1983

Chapters 1–20 originally appeared, in somewhat different form, in *The Faces of Power: Constancy and Change In United States Foreign Policy from Truman to Johnson* (1968); chapters 21–26 originally appeared, in somewhat different form, in *The Crises of Power: An Interpretation of United States Foreign Policy During the Kissinger Years* (1979).

Library of Congress Cataloging in Publication Data

Brown, Seyom.
The faces of power.

Includes bibliographical references and index.
1. United States—Foreign relations—1945–
I. Title.
E744.B78   1983   327.73   83-1861
ISBN 0-231-04736-3
ISBN 0-231-04737-1 (pbk.)

Columbia University Press
New York   Guildford, Surrey

Clothbound editions of Columbia University Press books are Smyth-sewn and printed on permanent and durable acid-free paper.

For Two Benjamins

CONTENTS

PART VII.
THE REAGAN ADMINISTRATION

PREFACE

This book is for public officials and laypersons concerned with the foreign policy of the United States as much as for students and scholars. In examining major foreign policy decisions and debates from the end of World War II to the present, I focus on the basic premises of U.S. policy makers about the country's international interests and purposes and about the power of the United States to protect and further these interests and purposes. The premises of policy need continual reexamination by decision makers and by the national constituency to whom the government is accountable. The ability of the United States to function successfully in the international arena depends not only on the accuracy of official views about U.S. interests and the world situation but also on the extent to which the populace shares and supports these views.

My professional career has provided me with special access to the premises of U.S. foreign policy. During the administrations of John F. Kennedy and Lyndon B. Johnson, I was on the research staff of the RAND Corporation, analyzing policy options for the Department of Defense and the Department of State; and from September 1967 through January 1969 (though formally still a "consultant"), I participated directly in the interagency policy process that was responsible for revising the guidance on national security policy. During the administrations of Richard M. Nixon and Gerald R. Ford, I was a Senior Fellow in Foreign Policy Studies at the Brookings Institution in Washington, D.C., where I conducted a monthly seminar with key policy-level staff of the executive agencies and the Congress dealing with national security and foreign affairs. And during the first two years of the Carter administration, I directed the U.S.–Soviet Relations Program of the Carnegie Endowment for International Peace, which included my chairing, along with Marshall Shulman (then the Secretary of State's principal adviser on Soviet policy), a study group of policy makers and analysts dealing with Soviet–American issues. Much of my reconstruction of the world views of decision makers from the Kennedy through the Carter administrations is based on such interactions with policy officials and their staffs. This kind of involvement with the Washington policy community has somewhat diminished since my coming to Brandeis University in 1978. This has allowed me to step back and view the policy-making scene with more detachment (and, I hope, objectivity) than I could have were I to be as actively participating as I was during the previous sixteen years.

My analysis of the premises of U.S. foreign policy makers of the Truman and Eisenhower administrations, though sensitized by my own Washington experience in recent years, is based primarily on the usual kind of scholarly investigation—mining their memoirs and public documentary records and assimilating the studies of academic specialists on these periods. Much of this research was reflected in the first edition of *The Faces of Power*. Since the writing of the first edition, more archival material has become available to scholars on the Truman and Eisenhower periods and is now reflected in a number of excellent historical studies. The studies I have relied on most in revising my chapters on these periods are John Lewis Gaddis, *The United States and The Origins of the Cold War, 1941–1947* (Columbia University Press, 1972); Daniel Yergin, *Shattered Peace: The Origins of the Cold War and the National Security State* (Houghton Mifflin, 1977); Michael A. Guhin, *John Foster Dulles: A Statesman and His Times* (Columbia University Press, 1972); Townsend Hoopes, *The Devil and John Foster Dulles* (Atlantic, Little, Brown, 1973); and Robert A. Divine, *Eisenhower and the Cold War* (Oxford University Press, 1981).

The Chapters on the Kennedy–Johnson era have benefited particularly from the material released in *The Pentagon Papers: The Defense Department History of United States Decisionmaking in Vietnam* (Beacon Press, 1971) and from Doris Kearns's illuminating psychological study, *Lyndon Johnson and the American Dream* (Harper & Row, 1976).

The chapters on Henry A. Kissinger's impact on U.S. foreign

policy are revisions of my 1978 publication *The Crises of Power: An Interpretation of United States Foreign Policy During the Kissinger Years* (Columbia University Press, 1979). That book was written before the appearance of Kissinger's memoirs, *The White House Years* (Little, Brown, 1979) and *Years of Upheaval* (Little, Brown, 1982), under the assumption that my analysis would be more cogent and fresh if it reflected what I knew from my Washington experience during the Kissinger years rather than if it attempted to respond to Kissinger's own reconstruction of events. Having read Kissinger's massive account (2804 pages and still a third volume to come!), I am convinced of the correctness of my original assumption. The memoirs are an often superbly written brief for the essential wisdom of virtually every move that Kissinger made while in office. The apparent candor and overwhelming detail tend to thrust the burden of proof on anyone who would presume to contradict their author. Were I to have waited to start writing until Kissinger had published his story, I might have felt compelled to support my analysis with thousands of pages of evidence and argumentation.

Readers of *The Crises of Power* will see that I continue to stand by the basic analysis in that essay. Where the Kissinger memoirs have some especially meaty confirmation of my interpretation, I indicate this to the reader; and where Kissinger presents arguments that appear to refute my analysis, I give him "equal time." But all in all, I have maintained my equal right to structure the telling of history and have resisted Kissinger's efforts to make the rest of us chant to his script and score.

Post-Kissingerian foreign policy, under the administrations of Jimmy Carter and Ronald Reagan, is the subject of parts VI and VII—where the analysis is developed almost entirely out of raw materials still largely unprocessed by other scholars.

The memoirs of the Carter years, by Carter himself, by his national security adviser, Zbigniew Brzezinski and by other administration officials, do not contain many new revelations beyond what already is in the public record. Carter's was a relatively open—perhaps too open—administration. The analyst's problem is not the absence of access to the private thoughts of the decision makers, but rather the abundant availability, at the time of decision, to journalists and nongovernmental analysts, of the considerations and reconsiderations of officials at many levels within the administration. Perspective can be maintained on this abundant record of apparent inconsistency by the recognition that statements simultaneously running off in many directions by Carter administration officials were the functional equivalent of Kissinger's artful ambiguity.

I anticipate that the most controversial part of my analysis will be the finding of basically coherent patterns in the Carter foreign policy. My overall assessment of Carter's performance departs considerably from the standard portrait—I would say caricature—of ambivalent self-contradictory ineptitude. I see in the Carter administration's record a rather faithful mirror of the legitimate gropings and uncertainties of the nation at large, in response to Vietnam and Watergate and the new international forces with which Kissinger had only begun to wrestle. Carter's efforts to manage the contradictory pressures of the period rather than to resolve them appear to me to have been a sounder approach than the efforts of his successors to push them back into a simple cold war mold.

My characterizations of the Reagan foreign policy are necessarily tentative, written while the administration's own reassessments of its initial stridency were just beginning, and are based, as yet, on highly fragmentary reporting and a good deal of reading between the lines of the often opaque rhetoric of the President and his Secretaries of State and Defense. During their first year and a half in office, the inclination of the principal foreign policy officials of the administration to contradict one another in public, even more than was the case with the Carter administration, compounded the problem of discerning solid outlines of policy beyond the initial ideological posturing. But the visible lack of consensus and constancy at the upper foreign policy echelons, reflected in the resignation of Secretary of State Haig and the appointment of George Schultz, is welcome, for it reveals a healthy recognition that practical policy cannot be derived simply from the ideological world view the Reaganites brought in with them.

These prefatory remarks are mirrored in the body of the book. More space is allotted to the present and very recent past than to the earlier periods. Historical distance, like physical distance to the observer of an Impressionist painting, clarifies the patterns and allows for more elegant characterization. The immediate is the most confusing, as the analyst still must work with largely undigested events and decisions whose interconnections have yet to be revealed.

The exposition, reflecting this, becomes more detailed and less definitive—laying out the complexity, as it were, in front of the reader—the closer it gets to the messy present.

As with the recent foreign policy it reconstructs, the writing in the present book is organically related to what came before. This edition continues to draw on insights of mentors who helped shape the earlier analysis—my erstwhile graduate teacher in American foreign policy and national security at the University of Chicago, later my colleague at the Johns Hopkins School of Advanced International Studies, Robert E. Osgood; and my colleague and tutor in policy analysis at the RAND Corporation, Alexander L. George, now professor of political science at Stanford University. By mentioning them again, I do not mean to suggest that the reputation for excellence that attaches to their work should be transferred to mine (I find the game some writers play of "virtue by association" distasteful). I merely want to continue to pay some of my still-outstanding intellectual debts.

However, I would like to be excused from the ritual of specifically thanking, in the preface, individuals from whom useful ideas and information have been obtained. My reasons are twofold. First, as alluded to above, it suggests an attempt to inflate one's veracity by name-dropping. Often, those cited have had a manuscript imposed on them which they regard as grossly deficient, but their names appear nevertheless in the obligatory list of those who have offered valuable criticism—creating the false impression that the author has incorporated their wisdom in the published work. Similarly with those one has interviewed, or merely chatted with (sometimes only at a cocktail party), the list of prestigious officials and experts in the preface is often a variety of academic social climbing—by the stroke of one's own pen, one becomes a peer of those with higher status. Second, such acknowledgment lists inevitably are hazardous to friendships and cordial associations. *Somebody* once talked to on the subject or shown the manuscript is going to be left out, and nothing afterward will remove the suspicion that this was an invidious exclusion. The only way around this risk, for a book like this which is based on hundreds of interchanges, would be to include all the names in my address and personal telephone book. (Perhaps I flatter myself that those excluded would care; but I do not wish to carry the burden of that anxiety.)

There are notes at the back of the book where important intellectual and informational borrowing can be precisely indicated. Narcissistic colleagues will, in any event, turn first to the index to see where they are cited.

Of course, if my analysis was directly and largely built on that of others, I would mention that here. This is not the case, except in the diffuse sense that ideas about the source and substance of policy are for the most part freely circulating currency among the Washington and academic cognoscenti, and thus it becomes impossible to separate one's own insights from this general knowledge.

Those who have in fact worked on this edition, however, are deserving of a special note of appreciation: Sandra Davis, Elizabeth Storch, and Hope Rulison provided research assistance. The technical burdens of manuscript preparation were carried by Bertha Mintz, Geralyn Spaulding, Lisa Robinson, and Matthew Morelock Brown.

Finally, I shall refrain from the usual poignant efforts at recompense for all the impositions inflicted on loved ones during the writing. My inflictions probably can never be redressed—certainly not by a flourish of emotional prose at the end of a preface.

INTRODUCTION
POWER WIELDED AND POWER PERCEIVED

Power lies in the eye of the beholder. Its different forms appeal to different people in different measure; we can agree on a broad definition, however: Power is the ability to affect the condition or behavior of something or someone.

The powerful are those who have large purposes and can accomplish them. This usually requires some degree of consent from others. The ability to induce consent from others is the essence of political power. But the ingredients of this ability, and their appropriate weights for each situation, cannot be set forth in a tidy formula.

The multifaceted and elusive nature of power is not always taken into account in talking of the power of nations. Too often national power is regarded in purely physical terms—the ultimate measure being the nation's potential to inflict destruction upon other nations. But the ability to destroy is only one of the attributes of power among nations, since the people to be affected have wills, and these wills may determine action in advance of physical force or despite it. The power of one individual or society over another is determined profoundly by the willingness of each to act in accordance with the desires of the other.

The actual resort to physical force in order to exercise power is often a sign of powerlessness in other means of influence. And in a contest between two men or nations equal in physical force, it will be the additional capabilities for affecting the human will that will determine who is the more powerful. Even those inferior in physical force have sometimes proven themselves superior in overall human power by virtue of their ability to sustain their wills and achieve their purposes against the desires of a physically superior adversary. As in the case of Gandhi, and Martin Luther King, this was done by modifying the will and purposes of the opponent.

Statesmen know that power, to be effective, must be respected, and that respect is accorded out of a compound of reasons—fear of the consequences of opposition, admiration of pratical accomplishments, admiration of essential qualities of being, and shared ethical premises. A nation's arsenal of power must have variety of it is to be perceived by other nations as worthy of respect. The most successful statesmen nurture a variegated inventory, and have been as reluctant to deplete its nonphysical as its physical components. They have known that one cannot predict which will be the critical ingredients of power in any future conflict of purposes—with traditional friends, implacable opponents, or the initially uncommitted. These other groups of people are the objects in the environment that may have to be influenced for a nation to accomplish its purposes. And they shall not be moved unless they will.

The premise that national power is a many-faceted thing informs the analysis in the pages of follow. My effort is to expose the premises of power held by those entrusted with wielding it internationally on behalf of the United States. The central question is: What means have our statesmen considered necessary and most appropriate to affect the international environment so as to realize the nation's basic purposes? My thesis is that the significant changes in foreign policy from Truman to Reagan are attributable more to changes in the premises of power than to changes in the concept of the nation's basic purposes. Where the analysis seems to exhibit a critical tone it will be the result of my evaluation that the premises of power held by our foreign policy makers or suggested by their actions were at the time overly focused on too narrow a set of attributes of the nation's strength and influence. The implied criticism in such cases is less of the purposes and values of the responsible officials than of their premises of power.

Of course any such analysis of the judgments of the nation's responsible policy makers is tentative and speculative. The public disclosures by officials of the considerations influencing their decisions are necessarily incomplete. Nor is there any logical formula by which one may infer, with a high degree of confidence, the basic assumptions underlying observed official behavior. Thus the analysis in the following pages should be understood to carry, attached to each proposition, the critical caveat: *assuming* the available record reflects, without essential gaps or distortions, the privately held premises of officials responsible for final decision. This caveat in itself is necessarily imprecise, since "the record" is not something set forth on parchment with major and subordinate clauses neatly numbered. The record comprises much unexplained behavior and statements emanating from many sources which often seem to contradict one another.

The search for the official premises of power does not stop with public documents or archival materials. It must go behind the words and between the lines to seek out the operational premises, those which operate when important decisions are made, those which *make the difference* at forks in the road. We can observe that certain roads have been taken rather than others, and we can hear the official explanations. But between the official explanations and the observed behavior there often remains a hazy area: the articulated premises do not lead inevitably to the actions taken; one cannot deduce the specific behavior from the stated premises, nor can one infer the premises backward from the particular actions. Many premises remain inarticulated, not necessarily out of any official design to hide them, but because space and time do not seem to permit a statement of their sometimes complicated interconnections, and also because actions by governments, no less than by individuals, are often the result of conditioned responses, of pre-programing, in which the actor "knows" what he should do but is unable to summon forward at the time the complete set of premises governing his immediate response. One of the jobs of the analyst of policy is to search out these "memory tapes" of the official bureaucracy so that we may all become aware of the underlying assumptions of our national acts and ask ourselves, ever anew, whether we buy these assumptions today.

Part I tries to ferret out the constant assumptions of United States foreign policy from Truman to Reagan. A central official assumption will be shown to be that the United States, if it is to realize its purposes must make sure that no potential adversary or combination of adversaries will gain sufficient power to impose their purposes upon us. In other words, the "balance of power" must not be tipped in our disfavor. Parts II through VIII will attempt to show how this assumption, however persistent, has produced significantly different foreign policies from Truman to Reagan. Part of the explanation for change will be traced to changing premises about the capabilities, intentions, and identity of those who would oppose what we want. But accompanying these changing premises, and informing them, is the more subtle, yet potentially more significant, fluctuation in the premises about power itself.

PART I

THE SOURCES
AND LIMITS
OF CONSTANCY

In its relations with other nations this country, from its very beginning as a republic, has had one overwhelming direction which it has gone and from which it has never varied.

DEAN ACHESON

A consistent and dependable national course must have a base broader than the particular beliefs of those who from time to time hold office.

JOHN FOSTER DULLES

For two centuries America's participation in the world seemed to oscillate between overinvolvement and withdrawal, between expecting too much of our power and being ashamed of it, between optimistic exuberance and frustration with the ambiguities of an imperfect world.

HENRY A. KISSINGER

1

THE IRREDUCIBLE
NATIONAL INTEREST
AND BASIC PREMISES
ABOUT WORLD CONDITIONS

National interest is more important than ideology.
JOHN F. KENNEDY

Between the lofty reiteration of traditional platitudes and the glib profession of radical alternatives are found the deepest and most persistent reasons for basic United States foreign policy—the irreducible national interest. These bedrock reasons of state have been the foundation of the foreign commitments and programs of all of the administrations described in this book.

Each President is bound by a historical, constitutional, and contemporary political obligation to service, first and foremost, at least two basic objectives of the national society: its physical survival; and the perpetuation of something called the American Way of Life—in the familiar words, "to secure the blessings of liberty to ourselves and our posterity." [1] Periodically, policy makers and laypersons have been drawn into a debate over the proposition "Better Dead than Red" or its converse. But the underlying popular mandate to the President, from the end of World War II to the present, has been clear: Make sure that such a choice never, in fact, has to be faced.

Place *both* survival and the maintenance of the basic American Way of Life ahead of all other objectives.

A third imperative, with almost as much compelling force upon the highest policy levels, is the injuction to promote the general welfare, or the economic well-being of the whole society. From the vantage point of the presidency, there is a good deal of political steam in the passion of the populace to have its liberties and to eat well too.

Official rhetoric from Truman to Reagan has attempted to show how the administration's actions derive from these constitutional and political imperatives: We seek today, as we did in Washington's time, claimed President Johnson, "to protect the life of our nation, to preserve the liberty of our citizens, and to pursue the happiness of our people. This is the touchstone of our world policy." [2] Such resounding claims are more than ritualistic bell-ringing. They are reflective of the fact that the least common denominator of political demand, from the national constituency at large, is that the President pursue *simultaneously* the nation's interest in its own survival and those conditions which allow for the perpetuation of its essential socioeconomic and political patterns.

When President Nixon and many of his immediate subordinates tried to bypass this basic mandate in the Watergate scandal and coverup—rationalizing their violation of civil liberties by the purported need to protect America from its enemies—they were compelled by public outrage to resign their high offices.

The concept of an irreducible national interest provides no specific guidance for its implementation. Its programmatic expressions vary from administration to administration, depending upon prevailing definitions of essential American liberties, notions of what the economy needs to function well, and current intelligence on the capabilities and intentions of foreign adversaries. But these fluctuations are constrained within each administration by the presidential impulse to lead the nation away from situations where ultimate choices between survival, liberty, and welfare have to be made. The central thread of continuity in U.S. foreign policy from Truman to Reagan is in large measure traceable to this popularly sustained impulse.

Another important reason for the continuity in foreign policy from Truman to Reagan has been the persistence of the view that the primary threats to this irreducible national interest are the expansion of Soviet power and another world war. The constancy as well as many of the changes in foreign policy that will be detailed in the following pages can be read as the theme and variations of the basic objective of avoiding one of these threats without beinging on the other. A third basic threat to the country's security and well-being was added in the 1970s: the possibility that the United States might be denied access to foreign sources of petroleum energy, on which it had become increasingly dependent. The preoccupations with Soviet power, war, and energy dependence have been reinforced by a number of premises about world conditions and what these conditions seem to require of the United States in order to perpetuate itself and its Way of Life.

PREMISES ABOUT SOVIET INTENTIONS AND CAPABILITIES

A rather solid consensus has prevailed at the top levels of government from Truman to Reagan that the Soviet Union is motivated (how strongly is a variable) to be the dominant world power, and eventually to fashion the world into a single political system based on the Soviet model. The premise that the Soviets are motivated only to secure their own society against outside interference has been bought only by a small minority of government officials since the Second World War. However, there has been considerable disagreement over the extent to which the actions of the Soviets to implement expansionist motives are constrained by Kremlin perceptions that such action may place the Soviet Union itself in danger and/or take away from its ability to achieve domestic economic and social goals. The détente policies initiated during the Nixon administration rested in part on the premise that the Soviets, having seen the futility of expansionist adventures, were anxious to turn their energies to domestic modernization tasks. Varying interpretations have been offered of the presumed Soviet constriction of their external power drive. Some analysts regard the Kremlin's interest in détente in the early 1970s as the result of the maturing of the Soviet Union and the emergence of a bureaucratic generation most interested in efficiency and political stability. Others are more skeptical, seeing it as simply an application of the Leninist strategem of "two steps forward, one step backward," the Kremlin's objective being to perpetuate the post-Vietnam retrenchment of America, during which time the Soviet Union would be building up its military power and strengthening its economic base for the next phase of hostile competition.

The varying assessments of Soviet intentions and capabilities, however, have taken place within the consensus at the top levels of government from Truman to Reagan that the Soviets should be contained at least within their existing sphere of control.

NEITHER RED NOR DEAD

Another critical premise underlying the observed constancy in foreign policy from Truman to Reagan has been that in another world war the United States would quickly become a prime target for mass destruction. Early in the period the technology of warfare, plus the obvious strategies deduced from the new technology, were seen to be bringing about a situation in which the United States could not become involved in war against its largest rival without thereby placing the lives of millions of American civilians in jeopardy. By 1948 there was consensus among United States scientists and military planners that it would be only a matter of a few years before the Soviet Union developed such a capability. In the interim the Soviet Union could compensate for its strategic inferiority vis-à-vis the United States (we could already reach the Soviet Union with weapons of mass destruction from our overseas bases) by holding "hostage" the urban populations of Western Europe. By the mid-1950s Soviet thermonuclear developments plus great improvements in their long-range strategic bomber fleet made the vulnerability of the continental United States in a world war an operating premise of military planners and top foreign policy officials. The avoidance of another world war was seen to be equal in importance to preventing the expansion of Communism. "Deterrence" became for a time the magic word, presumably eliminating the potential conflict in priority between preventing strategic attack on the United States and containing the Soviets. But the pursuit of peace could no longer be dismissed as mere rhetoric. World peace, meaning basically the avoidance of general war between the United States and the Soviet Union, had become irrevocably an *essential* policy objective—that is, a necessary means of preserving the irreducible national interest.

Yet prevailing premises about the distribution of internation
power since World War II would not allow the pursuit of worl
peace to take *precedence* over the containment of Communism. The
war had left the Soviet Union surrounded by "power vacuums" where
previously it had been hemmed in by constellations of great power.
The only source of great countervailing power now was the United
States. Therefore, the desire to prevent the extension of Soviet power
(assuming the Soviets wanted to expand the territorial basis of their
power) carried with it a responsibility fot the United States to make
its power available to dissuade or block the Soviets.

At the close of World War II, President Roosevelt tried to dissuade the Soviets from expanding by appeals to the spirit of the
Grand Alliance and, more concretely, by making "spheres of influence" accommodations with Stalin. Under the immediate postwar
assumption that the Soviets, requiring foreign capital for reconstruction, were anxious to maintain the goodwill of the West, the
Truman administration early tried by tough talk to pressure the Soviets into a more benign posture. But as it appeared that Stalin was
more anxious to take advantage of opportunities to expand his territorial base than to maintain the goodwill of the West, the Truman
administration soon began to seek means of redressing the local imbalances of power around the Soviet periphery. At first, these efforts were concentrated in economic and social measures to reconstruct wartorn Europe and Japan. But Soviet military power plays
against Iran, Turkey, Greece, and Czechoslovakia brought into
prominence at the White House level premises of the critical effect
of military balances, local and global, on the Soviets' propensity to
expand. The Berlin blockade of 1948 apparently sealed the case for
Truman, and Secretary of State Acheson was given the go-ahead to
make explicit in the North Atlantic Treaty the unequivocal commitment of United States military power to counter any Soviet attempts to exploit their military superiority in Europe. In exchange
for this commitment of American power the West Europeans were
expected to work urgently to build up their own military power, so
that the burden would not fall disproportionately on the United
States. The willingness to forego even our commitment to world
peace, if indeed that were necessary to prevent the Soviets from
forcibly adding unto themselves the vast power potential of Western
Europe, was by 1949 an explicit premise of United States foreign

policy. Such explicitness was possible with respect to Western Europe because its fall to the Soviets could be defined as tantamount to "surrender." The Soviets would become the dominant world power, and could eventually overpower the United States itself.

Thus, the "balance of power" became the critical concept for determining the priority to be given in any specific situation to containment of Soviet expansion or the avoidance of world war, should these two objectives appear impossible to pursue at the same time.

THE BALANCE OF POWER AS A NECESSARY BUT INSUFFICIENT CONCEPT

Each of the eight administrations analyzed in this book have agreed on at least this much: /Where the U.S.–Soviet balance of power itself was at stake and, by extention, therefore, the survival of the United States, there was no question of where the national interest would lie. In such situations, peace would have to give way temporarily to the active containment of the Soviet Union, even if the temporary breakdown of peace would place the United States in danger of direct attack./

The consensus extends just so far, however, for there have been substantial differences between and within the administrations over the meaning and ingredients of power and thus over the assessment of the balance of power in any situation. These differences will be explored in detail in the following chapters.

Nor have the basic premises provided sufficient advance guidance for policy in situations where the overall U.S.–Soviet military balance was not clearly and immediately at stake. If the Soviets were making only a limited grab, would it be worth a world war to frustrate them? What if another Communist nation were attempting to extend its power—would we, should we, equate such an attempt with a likely increase in Soviet international power? What should be the response to the coming to power of anti-American, but not necessarily pro-Soviet, regimes, especially in countries of high geopolitical significance, such as the oil producers in the Persian Gulf? The fact that the United States, through successive administrations, has not been able to answer such questions *in principle* in advance of unfolding situations has been in large measure responsible for some of the major foreign policy crises over the past three decades.

The decision not to bring U.S. coercive power to bear to prevent Mao Tse-tung's victory over Chiang Kai-shek; the expenditure of blood and treasure in Korea to rectify the gross miscalculation by the Soviets that the United States would not be willing to intervene there to oppose aggression; the Truman–MacArthur controversy; the great debate over "massive retaliation" vs. "flexible response," and particularly its expression in NATO policy; the Quemoy and Matsu crises of the 1950s; the Bay of Pigs, the Cuban missile crisis, and the chronic problem of how to deal with Castro; the Dominican military intervention of 1965; Vietnam; Soviet–American détente; SALT; "even-handedness" toward the Arabs and the Israelis; extracting the embassy hostages from Iran—all of these produced as much dissensus as consensus in the nation, precisely because of the existence of varied concepts of international "power."

There has been constancy at one very important level of analysis and policy. Premises of the irreducible national interest, and basic assumptions about world conditions, have given persistence to the two-pronged objective of attempting to prevent the expansion of Soviet control without getting into a third world war. As perceived by those responsible for the conduct of United States foreign policy, this has primarily meant influencing the Soviets not to try to expand their territorial base, and influencing other countries to pursue policies that would enhance their resistance to Soviet aggression and pressure. Since the early 1970s, there has also been consensus on the need to assure access to Perisan Gulf oil supplies.

The major issues have been over means, not objectives. The problem has been essentially a problem of *power.* The difficult question has been what *kinds* of power—what capabilities—are needed to accomplish the agreed-upon objectives of the nation. The varying answers given to this question by each of the administrations and by factions within the administrations will be analyzed in parts II through VII.

The objectives of containing the Soviet Union, preserving peace, and—the third geopolitical objective—assuring access to overseas oil do not exhaust the range of objectives animating United States for-

eign policy since the Second World War. These have been emphasized first because they have been generally accepted as essential to
the irreducible national interest of survival without fundamental
sacrifice in the American Way of Life. There has also been increasing recognition that threats to the American Way of Life inhere in
the instabilities of the international economy, and this has complicated attempts to derive a coherent foreign policy from the irreducible national interest. Finally, the nation has considered itself committed to interests of a more altruistic nature, and the story of the
fluctuations in foreign policy from Truman to Reagan includes attempts to reconcile the requirements of these altruistic interests with
the requirements of self-preservation; but even on these "ideological" issues, the major arbiter of choice has proven to be the calculation of the effects of alternative policies on the power of the United
States in the international arena.

2

MORAL PURPOSES
AND THE BALANCE-OF-POWER
CONSIDERATION

Our policy is designed to serve mankind.
JIMMY CARTER

The liberties and well-being of other peoples have been explicit concerns of United States foreign policy since the Second World War. Officials of the Truman administration regarded our sponsorship of the United Nations, the Truman Doctrine, the European Recovery Program, and Point IV as consistent with American idealism as well as self-interest. John Foster Dulles preached anti-Communism as a universal moral imperative. President Kennedy, unsentimental realist he is supposed to have been, sounded the trumpet for "a grand and global alliance" against the "common enemies of man: tyranny, poverty, disease, and war itself." His generation of Americans, said Kennedy, felt an obligation to work toward a "more fruitful life for all mankind" and to help the world's poor and destitute peoples "not because the Communists may be doing it, not because we seek their votes, but because it is right." [1] And there can be little doubt that Jimmy Carter believed he was giving voice to the American mainstream when he claimed that a commitment to human rights around the world would be a centerpiece of U.S. foreign policy: "I think it's compatible with our constitutional stance, the framework of our societal structure. It's something that appeals to our own people. It restores kind of a beacon light of something that's clean and decent and proper as a rallying point for us all in the democracies of the world." [2]

In the main, U.S. foreign policy leadership since the Second World War has been fortunate in the large measure of coincidence between the nation's self-interest and the nation's altruistic ideals. [3] With the rival superpower propounding a monolithic global society, the traditional American commitment to *national* self-determination, now enshrined in the United Nations Charter, could be used as an ideology to firm up the will of other peoples to resist absorption in the Communist bloc. And with Communist regimes propounding and acting upon the doctrine that a highly regimented populace unquestioningly carrying out policies made at the top is necessary for modernization, the doctrine that governments derive their just powers from the consent of the governed could be one of the most powerful weapons of containment—and possibly even liberation.

Yet at times the magnitude of assistance required to significantly help others pursue their freedom and welfare has appeared too costly. It was 1947 when President Truman proclaimed the doctrine that "it must be the policy of the United States to support free peoples who are resisting attempted subjugation by armed minorities or outside pressures." But the universally phrased doctrine was applied only in particular cases between 1947 and the summer of 1950. It was applied first in Greece and Turkey—the crisis situations which prompted the doctrine. And the $17 billion program for European economic recovery was portrayed as its required corollary. Under cover of the same principle, Berlin was sustained by the American airlift in 1948–49, and the United States committed itself to the defense of Western Europe by the North Atlantic Treaty. But during this same postwar period the administration did not attempt to apply the Truman Doctrine to events taking place in Eastern Europe or in China.

A Republic administration got its chance during the 1953 East German uprisings, and then again during the Hungarian crisis of 1956, to demonstrate how high a price it would be willing to pay to help "liberate" other peoples from the yoke of Communism. Again, there were certain impassible limits. A prudent reluctance to directly challenge the Soviet Union in its sphere of control also drastically circumscribed the Kennedy administration's response to the erection of the Berlin Wall in 1961, the Johnson administration's reaction to the Soviet invasion of Czechoslovakia in 1968, and the Reagan administration's sanctions against the Soviet Union in 1981– 82 for imposing martial law in Poland.

Even the forcible *expansion* of the Soviet sphere of control—their invasion of Afghanistan in December 1979—was allowed to stand as a fait accompli, with the Carter administration's responses limited to commercial sanctions, diplomatic reprimands, a revival of cold war rhetoric, and increases in the U.S. defense budget, because the costs and risks of immediately meaningful military countermoves were prohibitive.

The limits are set by the irreducible national interest—the survival of the American Way of Life *here*—and premises about world conditions directly affecting this interest. Our larger interests in the liberties and well-being of other peoples have been pursued where such action is perceived as required by, or supportive of, the basic national interest. We have also expanded energy and resources, in limited amounts, to support the liberties and well-being of other peoples, even though not prompted by calculations of self-interest, for the sufficient reason that "it is right." But there has been constancy over the period in presidential refusals to service these larger interests when the action required was perceived as contrary to policies deemed necessary to secure the blessings of liberty to *ourselves* and *our* posterity.

Thus, although the objective of containment of Communist expansion was often explained to the people as motivated by our deepest desires to preserve and expand the area of freedom, the ultimate calculations underlying decisions to oppose particular Communist provocations have been in terms of the consequences of the contemplated action or inaction for the physical security of the United States and the freedoms and economic well-being of citizens of the United States.

If the expected costs of United States intervention are very high, and the benefits problematical—as in Eastern Europe, China, Cuba during the Bay of Pigs, and Afghanistan—valor gives way, painfully, to inaction dictated by prudence. But where the consequences of inaction would almost certainly be a disadvantageous change in the global balance of power, meaning that the United States could lose the wherewithal to secure its own survival, decisions to counter the provocation with all that is required tend to be made, unflinchingly, even though the expected costs in human and material resources are high.

The persisting United States commitment to defend a Western presence in Berlin (even though the balance of military force there is against us) and President Kennedy's willingness to establish a very dangerous direct confrontation with the Soviets to compel a removal of their missiles from Cuba are examples of high risks taken in "the defense of freedom" *when* the global balance of power is thought to be at stake. I am not arguing that these decisions were inevitable. I do argue that such decisions are practically inevitable when a President feels the global balance of power is at stake, because a global imbalance against us is regarded as putting our survival at the mercy of our opponents. As there is no absolute measure of power, one President may see the global balance of power at stake in a situation where another may not. Thus the premises of power hald by the various administrations is a crucial variable in explaining the changes as well as the constancy in United States foreign policy.

The more controversial decisions have involved situations where there is a highly ambiguous or tenuous relationship perceived between the liberty and well-being of others and the global balance of power, and where programs thought capable of significantly helping those in need would be very costly.

Such considerations determined the acceptance at the close of the Korean War of a stalemate based on the status quo ante rather than a pressing for "victory" to allow the United Nations to administer nationwide elections and reunify the country. The original decision to intervene to reverse the North Korean drive to take over the whole country, even though this task might be costly for the United States, was undertaken out of a notion that to allow the Communists to succeed in their invasion would drastically undermine the non-Communist side of the power balance. A weighty ingredient of Western power, particularly as expressed in the new North Atlantic Treaty, was thought to be the faith of our alliance partners that the United States would honor its pledges to oppose aggression. Thus, indirectly, but rather clearly to the American leadership, U.S. security—dependent upon Western Europe being on the U.S. side of the balance of power—was seen to be threatened. Consequently, it was very important to oppose the North Koreans with whatever force was necessary to throw them back at least to the line of demarcation. As it began to look as if the United States could defeat them in the North too, without a significantly larger operation than was already under way, the U.S. objective was temporarily expanded to include the freedom and reunification of all of Korea. But the intervention of the Communist Chinese changed the calculations of the cost of implementing this larger interest, which, after all, was not seen to be required by balance of power considerations; indeed, the maintenance of the global balance was thought to require that the United States husband its resources for the possibility of a greater battle with the Soviet Union over Western Europe (chapter 5).

The lack of clarity over just which American interests were really involved did not prevent the Eisenhower administration from assisting in the overthrow of a Guatemalan government infiltrated by pro-Soviet Communists. But in this case, the assessment of costs to the United States was made out to be very small. On the other hand, the United States continued to tolerate the existence of not very "free" regimes and depressed standards of living in many of our southern neighbors, since these conditions did not at the time seem to affect the balance of power, and hence United States security, one way or the other. Moreover, until the Act of Bogotá in 1960, the Eisenhower administration defended U.S. inaction to support the political liberties and well-being of Latin Americans as consistent with the principle of "nonintervention" (self-determination) as expressed in the inter-American treaties. The doctrine of nonintervention got fuzzy again as Castro solidified his ties with Moscow. The Kennedy administration, inheriting the contingency plan of its predecessor, began what it thought was a low-level-of-effort counterinsurgency operation, somewhat on the Guatemalan model. But as a Communist regime in Cuba was not thought to be a crucial factor in the global balance of power, the operation was called off as soon as the costs of carrying it through were seen to have been vastly underestimated. Also, part of the uncalculated cost in the plan as originally handed to President Kennedy was the likely effect on the social reform elements in Latin America whom Kennedy was trying to court; and thus under Kennedy's premises of power, the global balance, if invoked at all as a consideration, might seem to be adversely affected even if the United States were successful in forcibly beinging down Castro.

The ambivalent United States reactions toward propsects of Communist successes in Indochina also illustrate the problems of policy when unclear global power considerations are cojoined with high costs of commitment. The United States assisted the French effort to keep all of Indochina out of Ho Chi Minh's hands, so long as this involved a relatively small expenditure of U.S. material resources. Later, as the French effort collapsed, the possibility that America might decide to intervene led Eisenhower to talk for a time as if the balance of power itself was at stake—a contention hotly disputed by many U.S. allies and by the opposition party in Congress. After the 1954 truce, an aid program was reinstituted for South Vietnam, for the ostensible purpose of bringing about conditions that would allow for eventual nationwide self-determination. But the principle of self-determination would have to be postponed until the population could be secured against coercion by Ho's agents. During the Kennedy administration there was reluctance to define the outcome of the continuing struggle between the Vietnamese Communists and non-Communists in stark balance of power terms. It was "their war," said Kennedy, although we would do all we reasonably could to help the non-Communist side. Furthermore, U.S. aid was conditioned on at least a minimum respect being shown for civil liberties by the South Vietnamese regime. Later, as help changed into direct United States involvement, carrying with it the implication of an unlimited commitment to the maintenance of a non-Communist South Vietnam, the Johnson administration once again defined the stakes of the conflict in global balance of power terms. Yet this definition remained under considerable dispute in the United States as the costs of implementing the commitment rose, and by the time the Nixon administration pulled all U.S. troops out of Vietnam in 1973, few Americans believed it made any real difference to American security that there soon would be a Communist government in Saigon.

The foreign assistance program as a whole has been operating right in the center of this hazy area, where often the relation of any specific component of the program to basic United States security interests is not at all clear, and therefore the diversion of domestic resources to such foreign ends is disputed by interest groups within and without the government who would like comparable amounts diverted to them.

The Eisenhower administration, avoided a systematic policy dialogue on the relationships between foreign aid, the character of recipient regimes, political liberty, and basic United States interests by making foreign assistance, for the most part, the reward of military alignment. If economic and military assistance was necessary to assure the alignment and security of an ally, no additional rationale was necessary. It was sufficient to argue that, dollar for dollar, X amount given to the recipient allies would result in more military manpower and firepower for the non-Communist world than if that same amount were added to the United States military budget.

It remained for the Kennedy administration to push a fresh set of premises on the relationship between assistance from the United States, socioeconomic reform, political democracy, and our own security (see part IV). Enthusiasm in the White House still had to deal with sluggishness in a Congress responsive to parochial demands, and skepticism from career administrators and diplomats more comfortable in dealings with foreign "Establishment" types than with the bristling revolutionary nationalists of the nonaligned world. The Alliance for Progress and the manifest interest by Kennedy in the new leaders of Africa produced no significant changes in the scale of the overall foreign assitance effort, nor any major reallocation of disbursements within the program. But even if the visible effects of the new orientation to foreign assistance were still primarily on the symbolic level, the joining by Kennedy of concerns for the liberties and well-being of others with an appreciation of international power relationships struck a responsive chord in the country's growing constituency of business leaders and professionals with an active interest in world affairs.

By the end of the Johnson administration, however, the liberal Democratic disillusionment with all kinds of intervention ("no more Vietnams") led to congressional gutting of foreign assistance programs.

Nixon and Kissinger, with their realpolitik approach, returned to a selective emphasis on supposedly reliable military allies, often in the form of military equipment transfers (especially *sales* to recipients, like the Shah of Iran, who could easily pay for the weapons). But Kissinger began to realize that a truly nonideological realpolitik required the United States to identify itself with egalitarian pressures or else lose out to the Soviet Union in the competition for global influence. This calculation was reflected in his shift in 1977, at the Seventh Special Session of the United Nations, to a more positive response to the Third World demands for a new international economic order (See chapter 25).

The Carter administration revived the "social justice" rationale of the Kennedy approach to foreign assistance; but the post-Vietnam popular and congressional resistance to substantial commitments of U.S. resources to foreign countries kept this "progressive" policy mainly at the level of rhetoric.

Ronald Reagan, rejecting (in principle) governmental interventions in the international as well as the domestic economy, attempted to reverse the allegedly "socialistic" distortions of the market that were produced by direct governmental aid for economic development in the Third World. The United States government, under a leadership recommitted to the virtues of private enterprise and to the classical economic vision of worldwide economic growth brought about by the operation of a global free market, might still help to provide temporary seed money in the form of low-interest loans to stimulate private investment, but the major goal would be to get the government out of the business of development economics. Official U.S. assistance, once again, would be almost exclusively an adjunct of the renewed military alliance–building strategy.

For reasons of traditional sentiment and for the hard-headed consideration of not allowing the Soviets to parade as the sole sponsors of anticolonialism, the Truman administration and its successors have felt it necessary to identify the United States with the principle of self-determination. But these genuine efforts to support the new nationalisms of the Third World have been circumscribed by the emphasis given to the securing of the *military* components of the global balance of power. The military potential of a revived Western European technology, a girdle of military allies to prevent easy expansion by the Communist powers, and a system of far-flung bases to bring U.S. strategic striking power within reach of the Soviet heartland were regarded as priority objectives. As these assets were, in many cases, to be provided by nations with overseas dependencies, some deference to the sensibilities and the material interests of the colonial powers was thought to be a requirement of U.S. statecraft.

Fortunately, for this purpose, the ideology of national sovereignty embodied in the United Nations Charter cut two ways: it provided a rationale for mobilizing efforts to combat Communist subversion and overt aggression; it also provided the legal excuse for refusing to take sides in disputes which fell under the "domestic jurisdiction" of another nation.

Moreover, the United States has a vital interest, professed and real, in reducing the resort to violence as a means of bringing about change. But it by no means has been clear *who* in any given anticolonial uprising, say Algeria, is relying most on violence—those defending the existing system of public order, or those trying to overthrow it. In such circumstances the inclination of the U.S. government has been to straddle the fence.

With the liquidation of the old colonial empires, this dilemma has become less central to U.S. foreign policy. It emerged again as late as 1982, however, as the Argentinians, in the name of anticolonialism, attempted to forcibly wrest the Falkland Islands away from Britain. (The Argentine case was weakened by the fact that a majority of the islanders were English-speaking settlers who definitely considered themselves British.) After an initial attempt at "evenhanded" mediation, the Reagan administration threw its support behind the British effort to militarily dislodge the Argentine troops that had seized control of the islands, the administration's rationale being that the Argentinians were the first to use force.

Even where the resort to military violence is not the issue, each of the postwar administrations, in attempting to fashion concrete policies out of the various "human rights" the United States claims to stand for, has been bedeviled by the potential contradictions between:

1. The rights of national societies to determine in their own way their own form of government (a pluralistic world society; Articles I and II of the UN Charter);

2. The political and civil rights of each human being (the Universal Declaration of Human Rights, Part II; the Helsinki Accords, Basket III; Jimmy Carter's human rights policy);

3. The right of all national societies to exist in an economic condition sufficient to provide at least the rudimentary amenities of life to their peoples (the United Nations Charter on Economic Rights and Duties; the Brandt Commission Report); and

4. The right of all individual human beings to at least a subsistence level of physical sustenance (the World Bank's "human needs" emphasis in development financing).

Which of these rights should be put *first?* In much official rhetoric they are placed side by side, with the implication that they can and ought to be pursued *simultaneously.* This is a natural extrapolation from the American experience, where the demand for self-government was made by men committed to the rights of individuals, and an egalitarian social ethos grew in an environment of abundance.

But many of the poorer nations of the world are run by oligarchies anxious to hold on to their social and material privileges. Economic assistance to such nations without "political strings" attached has sometimes resulted in an increase in a nation's per capita productivity and income; but often it has also perpetuated a system of social injustice. Yet the United States has not been inclined to *intervene,* by withholding or withdrawing economic assistance until major social reforms are first implemented. The Alliance for Progress made a move in this direction, but gingerly.

In other nations there is a commitment to egalitarianism with a vengeance, in which the property rights and civil liberties are trod under heel. Yet with traditional American optimism, U.S. policy makers have been receptive to claims that such suspensions of constitutional processes are only temporary, and may—in some cases—be the necessary price for rapid socioeconomic development. They have been less willing to grant the benefit of the doubt to Communist as opposed to non-Communist reformers (such as the Shah of Iran). But even Communist regimes have been increasingly regarded as fit commercial partners and occasionally even aid recipients, so long as they refrain from interfering in the affairs of other countries.

The hopeful "answer" to the potentiality for contradiction between the various altruistic political, social, and economic interests of the United States—the insistence that all of these ought to be pursued simultaneously—has rarely worked out in practice. In attempting to apply this typically American solution to the problems of Third World development, Truman, Eisenhower, Kennedy, Johnson, Nixon, Ford, Carter, and Reagan have run up against the hard realization that in most of the poorer nations of the world the human and material resources make for very uneven patterns of progress. In most cases an absolute insistence that development in political procedures, civil liberties, social reform, and economic productivity go hand-in-hand would constitute a moralistic criterion defeating progress in any of these areas. A more pragmatic attitude, variously groped for by each of the eight administrations of the period, has been difficult to sell to the Congress. The legislature, acting as the broker for constituent domestic interests jealous of any diversion of resources to foreign objectives, needs either a grand moral crusade or a clear and present danger to the nation to forge a consensus in back of altruistic acts. Unable to provide the former, for the reasons just alluded to, the executive, from Truman to Reagan, has had to fall back on the national security rationale in order to be granted the wherewithal to influence other nations in directions consistent with American values.

As sincere as any administration has been in professing our larger commitment to the well-being and liberties of all peoples, all have tended to decide major foreign policy questions, ultimately, in terms of the irreducible national interest: How will a given action or program affect the *power of the United States* to secure its way of life for at least its own people? What actions and programs are required in order to keep the *power of potential adversaries* below a level at which they could force the United States to choose between its survival and its way of life?

The limiting criteria for decision have remained essentially constant.

But such constancy only sets the boundary to the story. International "power" is a many-faceted thing. The successive Administrations and factions within them have varied in their premises of power—the essential ingredients and most appropriate uses.

PART II

THE TRUMAN ADMINISTRATION

Do not be deceived by the strong face, the look of monolithic power that the Communist dictators wear before the outside world. Remember that their power has no basis in consent.

HARRY S. TRUMAN

The course we have chosen . . . involves building military strength, but it requires no less the buttressing of all other forms of power—economic, political, social, and moral.

DEAN ACHESON

3

THE SHATTERING OF
EXPECTATIONS

Force is the only thing the Russians understand.
HARRY S. TRUMAN

United States officials emerged from the Second World War in awe of the physical power nations had been able to develop, but with little confidence in the power of nations unilaterally to exercise the self-control required to channel their tremendous physical capabilities to constructive as opposed to destructive purposes. Throughout the government, there was wide consensus that the survival of civilization required the strengthening of international institutions and also, but with somewhat less conviction, the eventual reduction of the amount of destructive power in the hands of individual nations.

To translate these hopes into reality would require the kind of statesmanship which, in the past, had run afoul of strong American attachments to the value of self-reliance. Remembering the fate of Woodrow Wilson's sponsorship of the League of Nations, the administration started early this time to fully prepare the public, and particularly the opposition party leadership, for the premises on which the new postwar diplomacy would be based. Delegations to the founding conferences for the United Nations were carefully selected on a bipartisan basis. And, in an appeal to the patriotic, the successful wartime cooperation between members of the Grand Alliance against the Axis Powers was held up as the embryo from which the new organs of international cooperation would evolve.

The premise of continued cooperation among members of the Grand Alliance had two faces: its internal-governmental aspect, where it was viewed as the *most desirable condition* for managing the postwar world; and its public aspect, where the premise of big-power cooperation was viewed as a *prediction* that the presumed harmony would last.

The popular myth that Harry S. Truman, upon assuming the presidency on April 12, 1945, at the time of Franklin D. Roosevelt's death, inherited a set of idealistic beliefs from the Roosevelt administration about Soviet–American postwar cooperation is not borne out by historical research. Rather, FDR, in negotiating with Generalissimo Joseph Stalin at the Big Three meetings in Teheran (December 1943) and Yalta (February 1945), operated from premises very similar to the realpolitik notions of Prime Minister Winston Churchill. Despite differences in style and nuance between the Briton and the American, both viewed Stalin as interested primarily in the security of the Soviet Union, and secondarily in exploiting opportunities for an expansion of Soviet control in the direction of the Mediterranean and the Near East. Both Western statesmen sought to relieve Stalin's paranoid fears—of wartime Anglo-American collusion to weaken Russia and of postwar capitalist encirclement—by granting the Soviet Union a sphere of predominant influence in Eastern Europe and special awards in the Far East (including the Kurile Islands and lower Sakhalin from Japan, an "independent" outer Mongolia, and partial control or leases of key railway networks and ports in northeast China). In return, Stalin was supposed to accept British and American spheres of predominant influence outside of these areas. The basic bargain having been struck, the Big Three could then manage, through consultation, other conflicts over secondary issues, since none of their vital security interests would be threatened. The new United Nations organization would work on the basis of this essential East–West modus vivendi—an assumption carried into the structure and voting arrangements of the UN itself. [1]

At his Big Three meeting with Stalin and top British statesmen at Potsdam in the summer of 1945, Truman did little more than endorse this basic realpolitik deal worked our earlier with Stalin by FDR and Churchill.[2]

There was to be a basic shift in assumptions away from the Churchill/Roosevelt spheres-of-influence approach and toward what became known as "containment." And this took place at the top levels of the Truman administration a good year before they were revealed to the public in the Truman Doctrine in 1947. The general public got its ideas on the administration's assumptions about international relations during the first two postwar years from the official rhetoric which for the most part conveyed a set of more optimistic expectations:

1. The expectation that important international disputes would be settled by reasoned debate leading to an expression of majority will through the United Nations;

2. The expectation that in important international disputes the Big Five (the United States, the Soviet Union, Britain, France, and China) usually would find themselves on the same side—i.e., the veto would be an exceptional, rather than a frequently used, device,

3. The expectation that any required sanctions against international lawbreakers would be organized by this international community.

The real nature of the shift in the operating assumptions of early postwar foreign policy was hidden from the public—the shift from the Yalta view that "we can do business with Uncle Joe" to Truman's confidentially held perspective of 1946 that "force is the only thing the Russians understand."

In less than a year as President, Truman came to believe that the Soviets would expand as far as they could, that they were highly motivated to dominate the world, and would aggressively exploit all opportunities to enlarge their sphere of control unless effective countervailing power was organized to stop them. But prior to 1947, Truman felt that a candid presentation to the public of the internal government perception of the Soviet drive for power ascendancy might shock the country into total abandonment of the laborious effort to build up international institutions. This would be tragic, since such institutions, if strengthened by support of most of the peoples of the globe, were truly regarded as the *best* long-term hope

for peace. Yet without such candor, the public and their representatives in the Congress would probably not approve the stopgap military and economic measures that might be necessary to induce the
Soviets to keep their end of the postwar bargain to become constructive participants in the building of a world order acceptable to a
majority of nations.

The effort by Truman's subordinates to reconcile the President's
fears of shattering public expectations with his belief that standing
up to the Russians now might be a precondition for the eventual
realization of these expectations is the central story of the Truman
administrations's early gropings toward a coherent foreign policy.

TOWARD CONTAINMENT

Truman recalls that during the first weeks of his presidency he
gave much weight to the analysis of Soviet policies conveyed to him
by Averell Harriman, at that time the United States ambassador to
the Soviet Union. Harriman was urging a reconsideration of our
policy toward the Soviet Union, fearing that to some extent existing
policy might be the product of illusions that the Soviets shared our
commitments to an international order based on peaceful national
self-determination.

As recounted in Truman's *Memoirs,* the gist of the Harriman
analysis as of April 1945 was that Stalin was misinterpreting our
generosity and our desire to cooperate as a signal that the United
States would do nothing to prevent the extension of Soviet control
over her neighbors. The Soviets, reported Harriman, had no wish
to break with the United States, as they needed our aid for their
program of postwar reconstruction; but Stalin would not hesitate to
push his political frontiers westward if he felt he could do so without serious political challenge. We had to disabuse Stalin of his
illusion of American softness, counseled Harriman. We could be
firm with the Soviets without running serious risks, since they could
not afford to alienate their only source of help.[3]

Truman claims to have bought this evaluation at this early date,
and was disposed to follow Harriman's advice that the way to exert
a positive influence on Soviet policy was to be tough with them on
specific postwar issues as they arose. The assumption was, as Truman put it, "anyway the Russians needed us more than we needed

them."[4] The Soviets, presumably because of their economic needs, had more to lose than to gain by the collapse of great-power amicability. We wished to preserve an atmosphere of United States–Soviet cooperation because this was the key to an effective universal collective security system, which in turn, it was hoped, would induce more responsible Soviet behavior. It was not yet considered necessary or desirable to be able to force a general showdown with the Soviet Union over any specific issue, in the sense of pointing explicitly or implicitly to the military power at our disposal.

When Truman had his first high-level "confrontation" with Soviet diplomats Molotov and Gromyko at the White House on April 23, 1945, and used language that, according to Admiral Leahy, was "blunt" and "not at all diplomatic," he was evidently still leading from a perceived position of presumed *economic* leverage.[5]

The very next day Secretary of War Stimson wrote an urgent note to the President, requesting "a talk with you as soon as possible on a highly secret matter. . . . It . . . has such a bearing on our present foreign relations . . . that I think you ought to know about it without much further delay." The Secretary of War met with the President on April 25 and told him of the nuclear development program, and that in four months a completed weapon would be ready. The discussion with Stimson, reports Truman, centered on the effect the atomic bomb might likely have on our future foreign relations.[6]

The bomb was henceforth to be very much a part of Truman's overall calculus of the balance of military power *behind* his diplomacy, both for ending the war with Japan and bargaining with the Soviets over the postwar arrangements. He knew now that if it became necessary to lay all of his cards on the table in a confrontation with Stalin, he could soon do so from a unique position of strength. But the President was evidently unwilling at this stage—although recent scholarship shows he was pressued hard to do so[7]—to make the bomb a visible and immediate part of his bargaining cards in current diplomatic negotiations. At Potsdam in July he could have done so (having received news of the successful Alamagordo test while the conference was in session), but still chose to rely on the Harriman strategy of catering to the Soviet's expected hunger for our economic assistance.

After his face-to-face encounter with Stalin at Potsdam, Truman began to lean toward those in his administration who believed that a diplomacy characterized mainly by firm *verbal* expressions of disapproval would not disabuse the Soviets of their appetite for expansion. "I'm tired of babying the Soviets," Truman told Secretary of State Byrnes in January 1946. The past nine months had been filled with what he saw as a series of Soviet power plays.

The Soviet Union's failure to implement the Yalta provisions for freely elected regimes in Eastern Europe was only part of the story, which the President now recounted to his Secretary of State with evident exasperation: the actual disposition of military forces, sheer physical control, was the critical fact for the Soviets in subsequent negotiations over the future of Europe. Under the circumstances, confessed the President, we were "almost forced" to agree at Potsdam to Russian occupation of eastern Poland and the compensatory occupation by Poland of German territory east of the Oder River. "It was a high-handed outrage." The situation in Iran was another case in point—Iran of *all* places! The friendship of Iran had been critical for Russia's survival in the war; the United States had conducted a major supply operation to Russia through Iran. Without these supplies furnished by the United States, maintained Truman, Russia would have been shamefully defeated. Yet now Russia was stirring up rebellion and keeping troops on the soil of Iran.

Evidently, the original Harriman analysis that the Soviets would respond positively to our blunt talk was inadequate. Stalin, according to Truman's personal reading of events, obviously placed a higher value on expanding the Soviet sphere of control than on maintaining good relations with the United States. The threat of decisive action had to be added to the blunt talk: "Unless Russia is faced with an iron fist and strong language another war is in the making," concluded the President. "Only one language do they understand—'how many divisions have you?' I do not think we should play compromise any longer." [8]

These developing perceptions of Soviet aims were very much a part of the 1946 Acheson–Lilienthal report to the President on the international control of atomic energy, which became, in effect, the plan presented to the United Nations Commission by Bernard Baruch in June. In contrast to the Soviet plan, which put destruction of existing weapons stockpiles before inspection and controls, the United States plan demanded *prior* establishment of a comprehensive international inspection and control apparatus with access to and authority over all relevant national facilities, including plants where raw materials could be converted into fissionable materials. Moreover, the veto was not to apply to the operations of international control authority. Truman's instructions to Baruch unambiguously outlined the considerations that were to be kept paramount: It was in our interest to maintain our present advantage; thus we should attempt to gain a system of reliable international control that would effectively prevent the Soviets from proceeding with their own atomic weapons development program. And under no circumstances should we "throw away our gun" until we were sure that others could not arm against us.[9]

If President Truman and a few of his official intimates had an early perception of the dominant means by which the emerging political conflict with the Soviet Union would be waged, they were not ready in late 1945 and 1946 to make it the explicit central premise of our foreign policy. To do so would have required a major reversal of the rapid postwar military demobilization already in full gear. It would have shattered the public's expectations, reflected in the congressional agenda, that the priority business before the nation was to convert to a peacetime economy. James Forrestal's notes of a combined State–War–Navy meeting of October 16, 1945, recount that "it was agreed by all present that . . . it was most inadvisable for this country to continue accelerating the demobilization of our Armed Forces at the present rate." The Secretary of War contended the situation was of such gravity that "the President ought to acquaint the people with the details of our dealing with the Russians and with the attitude which the Russians have manifested throughout."[10]

Appeals to the President for governmental candor with the people about the international situation were made during the next few months by Secretaries Forrestal, Ickes, and others.[11] But Truman apparently needed more than individual instances of Soviet belligerence in order to go before the American people and tell them, brutally, that their fondest hopes for returning to the pursuit of happiness were based on false premises. Even as the increasing newspaper reports of Soviet totalitarianism at home and expansion abroad became a part of the public consciousness, Truman's public posture toward Soviet belligerence continued to stress the mobilization of "world opinion" in back of the principles of the United Nations Charter—issue by issue, situation by situation.

Governmental conceptions of the emerging struggle with the Soviet Union are supposed to have been given new cohesion and direction in February 1946 by George Kennan's eight-thousand-word cable from Moscow. The essentials of the Soviet grand design, the motives (rational and irrational) behind their imperialistic policies, and the meaning of their style of diplomacy were analyzed in historical and psychological depth, and with great cogency (see below, pp. 43–44, for a fuller account). Here was the authoritative and coherent analysis of the Soviet threat that many within the administration, particularly Forrestal, were looking for. But there is no evidence that these early reports from Kennan contained, either explicitly or by logical implication, the concrete policy prescriptions Forrestal wanted the President to champion. Kennan did urge, like Forrestal and his colleagues, the importance of having the public "educated to the realities of the Russian situation." And he discounted any deterioration in Russian–American relations that might result from such a campaign. Yet he saw no urgency for paying particular attention to the *military* components of power. "Gauged against the Western world as a whole . . ." observed Kennan, "the Soviets are still [this was early in 1946] by far the weaker force. Thus their success will really depend upon the degree of cohesion, firmness, and vigor which the Western world can muster." [12]

If Truman's *Memoirs* are accurate, he personally, as early as the winter of 1945–46, saw the Russian pressures on Iran and Turkey as an immediate threat to the global balance of power. Russia's failure to withdraw her armies from Iran stemmed from her central geopolitical interests in Iranian oil and control of the Black Sea Straits. Russian possession of Iranian oil, the President was convinced, would seriously alter the world's raw material balance, and would be a blow to the economy of Western Europe. But the power play in Iran was also directly related to the demands the Soviets had been making on Turkey for special privileges and territorial concessions. Turkey had been resisting these demands, but would be in a much weaker position to resist if she were outflanked on the east by Russian armies or a Russian puppet state. [13]

Truman saw Svoiet ambitions in Turkey revealed starkly in their proposals to put the Black Sea Straits under joint Turkish–Russian defense. Recalling his own studies of Middle Eastern history, the President recognized in the present Communist thrust a continuation of Czarist Russian attempts to gain control of the strategic exits to the Mediterranean Sea. If they were to succeed now, he deduced, it would only be a question of time before Greece and the whole Near and Middle East fell to the Soviets.[14]

"Domino Theory"

There is evidence that this is more than a retrospective reconstruction by Truman of his perceptions at the time. His January 1946 letter to Byrnes expressing exasperation at the way the Soviets were throwing their weight around contained a bald geopolitical evaluation of Soviet aims: "There isn't a doubt in my mind," he wrote less than a year after the close of the Second World War, "that Russia intends an invasion of Turkey and seizure of the Black Sea Straits to the Mediterranean."[15]

Moreover, Truman did begin to "show the flag" in 1946 in his dealings with the Russians on Middle Eastern issues. The battleship *Missouri* was sent to Istanbul to demonstrate support for Turkey's refusal to accede to Soviet demands for joint control over the Straits. Truman has divulged, though not until many years later, that he sent Stalin an ultimatum on the issue of Soviet troops in Iran, informing him that the United States would send troops in if the Russians did not got out, and that he had ordered preparations for the movement of American ground, sea, and air forces.[16] But however effective these moves were as gambits in the management of the particular crisis situations, they were not yet presented to the public as parts of a grand strategy toward the Soviet Union, in which the American military potential would be consciously and more or less continuously displayed in back of diplomatic efforts to moderate Soviet behavior.

Nor was the administration ready to openly embrace the balance of power ideas Winston Churchill was then advancing. When the British leader delivered his sensational "Iron Curtain" speech in March 1946, with President Truman sitting on the platform, the premises he advanced about Soviet motives and behavior were already widely shared in U.S. policy-making circles. But the main policy conclusion he drew, that there ought to be a long-term Anglo-American alliance against the Soviets, was still not acceotable to the highest levels in the American government.

THE TRUMAN DOCTRINE

An early moment of truth was to come shortly for United States policy makers. The February 1947 note from the British government, informing the United States that drastic economic conditions in England made it necessary for the United Kingdom to withdraw all support from Greece by the end of March, provided the need—and the opportunity. The President's top political and military advisers were of the opinion that it was only the presence of British troops in Greece since the war that had prevented that faction-ridden nation from being swept into the Soviet orbit. The prevailing view within the State Department was that unless the tottering Greek government received immediate assurances of large-scale military and financial aid the regime would lose all authority and confidence of the people, and the increasingly successful Communist guerrillas would grab control of the country as public disorder mounted. Truman translated the local situation into the starkest global terms: If Greece fell to the Communists, Turkey would become highly vulnerable to Soviet power plays and subversion. Inevitably, the entire eastern Mediterranean would be sealed behind the Iron Curtain. [17]

To save the situation this time more than a White House decision—which had been sufficient for deploying the Navy and sending blunt diplomatic notes in the earlier Turkey and Iran crises—was required. Large-scale economic and military assistance, to be directly administered by American officials, would need congressional authorization and special appropriations. But Republican majorities had just taken control of both houses, and, according to Speaker Joe Martin, were determined to fulfill election promises for a 20 percent across-the-board reduction in income taxes with a collateral reduction in government spending. Administration forces, having suffered badly in the congressional elections, were disposed to regard the Republican spokesmen as, for once, being in tune with popular sentiment. "Now that an immediate peril is not plainly visible," Secretary of State Marshall told an academic audience, "there is a natural tendency to relax and return to business as usual, politics as usual, pleasure as usual. Many of our people have become indifferent to what I might call the long-term dangers to national security." [18]

The stage was set. The national executive considered matters of high national interest to be at stake. But in order to service these interests it would have to ask the nation at large to reorder its priorities. Such a political context (rather than the logic of the international situation) prompts a democratic leadership to call upon the nation for reexamination of existing premises and stimulates it to promulgate new doctrine.

For the public this effort at basic revision of the national premises was associated with Truman's address to the Congress on March 12, 1947, requesting assistance for Greece and Turkey—the so-called "Truman Doctrine." But for many in the administration responsible for foreign diplomatic, economic, and military programs Truman's formal request of Congress was only the exposed tip of an iceberg of massive intellectual and bureaucratic activity.

The seminal statement for conceptualizing and catalyzing the new orientation was probably neither Truman's address nor Secretary of State Marshall's at Harvard a few months later, but Under Secretary of State Acheson's effort to educate the bipartisan group of congressional leaders Truman summoned to the White House on February 27, 1947.

According to a State Department official who was present, the leadoff presentation by Secretary Marshall went very badly. Marshall, rather than expounding on the central strategic importance of Greece and Turkey (a subject on which he was very well versed), conveyed the impression that the reasons for extending aid to Greece and Turkey flowed essentially from humanitarian impulses toward these countries and loyalty to Britain. Many of the congressional leaders present were not at all impressed, being preoccupied at the moment with reducing taxes.

Acheson got Marshall's attention and was given the floor. In bold strokes, he displayed for the congressmen the view of Soviet Middle Eastern strategy that for more than a year had prevailed at the White House and top State Department levels. The Under Secretary described the continuing Soviet pressures on Turkey for territorial cessions and for military and naval bases in the Turkish Straits, which if granted would mean "the end of Turkish independence." Soviet pressures on Iran were portrayed as "encircling movements" also apparently focused on the Straits. It was only because the Turks, with strong diplomatic backing from Britain and the United States, had stood up to the Russians that these moves had failed for the time being. As a result, the Communists were currently concentrating their pressure on Greece, Acheson explained, where all reports indicated that the Communist insurgents would succeed in seizing control "within a matter of weeks" unless the government of Greece received prompt and large-scale aid.

This was obviously more than helping the British salvage their interests, said Acheson, building up to his main message. The substance and tone of this message are best rendered in the account of the State Department official whose account is the basic public source for the White House meeting of February 27:

> Only two great powers remain in the world, Acheson continued, the United States and the Soviet Union. We had arrived at a situation unparalleled since ancient times. Not since Rome and Carthage had there been such a polarization of power on this earth. Moreover, the two great powers were divided by an unbridgeable ideological chasm. . . . And it was clear that the Soviet Union was aggressive and expanding. For the United States to take steps to strengthen countries threatened with Communist subversion was not to pull British chestnuts out of the fire; it was to protect the security of the United States—it was to protect freedom itself. For if the Soviet Union succeeded in extending its control over two-thirds of the world's surface and three-fourths of its population, there could be no security for the United States, and freedom anywhere in the world would have only a poor chance of survival. The proposed aid to Greece and Turkey was not therefore a matter of bailing out the British, or even of responding on humanitarian grounds to the need of a loyal ally. It was a matter of building our own security and safeguarding freedom by strengthening free peoples against Communist aggression and subversion. We had the choice, he concluded, of acting with energy to meet this situation or losing by default. [19]

Here, full-blooded, were the central premises of what came to be called the cold war: the two-way polarization of the international system around two great powers; an unbridgeable idological hostility between the two groupings, with the group led by the United States committed to individual liberty and a pluralistic international system, and the group led by the Soviet Union committed to totalitarian statism and a monistic international system organized on the Soviet model; and an intention by the Soviet-led grouping to impose its way of life on the rest of the world.

From these premises it was deduced that any allowance of an extension of Soviet control over additional areas, even if they were limited extentions, would not reduce Soviet aggressiveness, but, on the contrary, would stimulate further aggressiveness by adding to the material and political resources with which the Soviets hoped to impose their will. The policy implications for the United States-led grouping were clear: a balance of power had to be maintained against the Soviet-led grouping, and the intention to apply this power, wherever and to whatever extent necessary, to prevent any further extension of Soviet control had to be unambiguous.

President Truman's address before Congress on March 12, 1947, asking for $400,000,000 in military and economic aid to Greece and Turkey was based on these premises, but he deliberately refrained from making them as explicit as Acheson had done in the private session. A number of statements that emphasized military–strategic considerations were deleted from one of the last drafts of the speech upon the recommendation of Acheson. His view is reported to have been that too much emphasis on the military–strategic considerations might be alarming to the American people, who were not accustomed to thinking in these terms in time of peace. The emphasis in the public approach was to be on the global ideological conflict, and on the economic assistance needed by governments friendly to the United States to successfully combat subversion: [20]

I believe [Truman told the nation] that it must be the policy of the United States to support free peoples who are resisting attempted subjugation by armed minorities or by outside pressures.

I believe that we must assist free peoples to work out their destinies in their own way.

I believe that our help should be primarily through economic and financial aid which is essential to economic stability and orderly political processes.

The free peoples of the world look to us for support in maintaining their freedoms.

If we falter in our leadership, we may endanger the peace of the world—and we shall surely endanger the welfare of our own nation. [21]

THE MARSHALL PLAN

The Marshall Plan for the economic recovery of Europe, announced just four months after the promulgation of the Truman Doctrine, was also conceived of by Truman and Acheson as a geopolitical counterthrust to Soviet-sponsored subversion of the West, but it was sold to the public largely as a compound of humanitarian largesse and enlightened economic statesmanship, the latter proceeding from the premise that an economically healthy Europe was a precondition for the world trade required by an expanding United States economy. It was a conscious policy decision to underplay the global balance-of-power considerstions.

Between Truman's address to Congress in March 1947 and Marshall's speech at Harvard in June, the Moscow conference of foreign ministers adjourned in recognized failure to make any progress in resolving the East–West discord over the future of Germany and Austria. "The Americans came home from Moscow," Walt Rostow recalls, "firm in the conclusion that the United States should never again negotiate from a base of weakness. . . . The picture of Europe was one of mammoth slow-moving crisis. There was a growing awareness that something big had to be done in Europe to avoid a disaster to the American interest; that a substantial program of economic aid addressed constructively to the problems of economic recovery was required to deal with the multiple threats to the Eurasian power balance."[22] Secretary of State Marshall reported to the country over the radio that "disintegrating forces are becoming evident. The patient is sinking while the doctors deliberate. . . . action cannot await compromise through exhaustion."[23]

In a then-secret memorandum, George Kennan and the Policy Planning Staff recognized that "the communists are exploiting the European crisis and . . . further communist successes would create serious danger to American security." But they advised Secretary of State Marshall that

American effort in aid to Europe should be directed not to the combating of communism as such but to the restoration of the health and vigor of European society. It should aim, in other words, not to combat communism, but the economic maladjustment which makes European society vulnerable to exploitation by any and all totalitarian movements and which Russian communism is now exploiting.[24]

And significantly, there was a brief separate section at the end of the memorandum advising that

Steps should be taken to clarify what the press has unfortunately come to identify as the "Truman Doctrine," and to remove in particular two damaging impressions which are current in large sections of American public opinion. These are:
    a. That the United States approach to world problems is a defensive reaction to communist pressure and that the effort to restore sound economic conditions in the other countries is only the by-product of this reaction and not something we would be interested in doing if there were no Communist menace.

b. That the Truman Doctrine is a blank check to give economic and military aid to any area of the world where the Communists show signs of being successful. It must be made clear that the extension of American aid is essentially a question of political economy in the literal sense of the term and that such aid will be considered only in cases where the prospective results bear a satisfactory relationship to the expenditure of American resources and effort.[25]

This advice was heeded by the Secretary of State. Launching the program for European recovery at Cambridge on June 5, 1947, he claimed, "Our policy is directed not against any country or doctrine but against hunger, poverty, desperation and chaos." And the offer to join in the cooperative effort was made to *all* European nations.[26] There was considerable disagreement over this formulation. Indeed, many in the United States government and Western Europe were relieved when Stalin prevented the East European states from joining the effort. But the offer to all European nations was genuinely made by Marshall and those like him in the State Department who had a multifaceted view of the relevant balance of power considerations: they felt that the revival of Western European economic vigor, which was based in large measure on manufacturing, would be facilitated by the raw material resources that once again could be tapped in the East European areas. East Europe in turn could provide a market for the West's manufactured goods. To maintain an advantageous balance of power against the Soviet Union the West needed a strong Western Europe; it did not require an unhealthy Eastern Europe. Moreover, there were some in the United States government who felt that an Eastern Europe largely dependent for its own well-being upon economic relations with the West would be less subject to total Soviet control.[27]

But such questions became academic as the Soviet Union moved even more swiftly during the summer of 1947 to transform the lands it had occupied militarily into dependent units of a tightly integrated economic and political system. The last hopes for some preserve of Western liberalism in Eastern Europe died in February 1948 when the Communist leadership in Czechoslovakia, backed by Soviet armed might, demanded, and was granted, full powers of government.

Meanwhile the public dissemination in the summer of 1947, through the medium of *Foreign Affairs* magazine, of George Kennan's analysis of Soviet grand strategy, and his concept of "containment" as a countervailing grand strategy of the West,[28] provided the missing link for policy-oriented intellectuals who were trying to piece together the real basis, as distinct from the surface rationale, for the Truman Doctrine and the Marshall Plan. Kennan's coherent analysis and prescriptions were, of course, only one of a number of alternative formulations of the emerging official premises about United States–Soviet relations. In some accounts of United States cold war policy the "X" article is treated as the official position of the government. This is incorrect. Many of its premises continued to be debated within the highest levels of the administration. But it did take the public wraps off of a core set of beliefs around which there was already an operating consensus among the responsible decision makers: the Soviet's "unfriendliness of purpose," as Kennan put it, was "basic." It proceeded from the inner structure of Soviet-Russian society. Soviet policies over the foreseeable future would reflect "no real faith in the possibility of a permanent happy coexistence of the Socialist and Capitalist worlds, but rather a cautious, persistent pressure toward the disruption and weakening of all rival influence and rival power." Consequently, "if the Soviet government occasionally sets its signatures to documents which would indicate the contrary, this is to be regarded as a tactical maneuver permissible in dealing with the enemy." Moreover, the Soviets, believing in the ultimate triumph of their cause, were as patient as they were relentless. "The Russians look forward to a duel of infinite duration." The implications for American policy needed to be faced: "Sporadic acts" of standing up and talking tough to the Russians were not enough, even if they seemed to produce temporary Soviet retreats. "The main element of any United States policy toward the Soviet Union must be that of a long-term, patient but firm and vigilant containment of Russian expansive tendencies." This policy would require "the adroit and vigilant application of counterforce at a series of constantly shifting geographical and political points, corresponding to the shifts and maneuvers of Soviet policy." [29]

4

1948–1950: INTERNAL DIALOGUE ON THE COMPONENTS OF THE BALANCE OF POWER

God knows I am fully aware of the terrific task which this country faces if it is to keep a free economy and a free society. But to . . . deny Marshall the cards to play, when the stakes are as high as they are, would be a grave decision.

JAMES S. FORRESTAL

Kennan's article displayed important premises about Soviet intentions on which there was an emerging consensus among Truman administration officials. Nor was there any important disagreement with the policy consequences of these premises as broadly formulated by Secretary of State Marshall in a report to the Cabinet in early November 1947. Marshall stated, according to Forrestal's account, "that the objective of our policy from this point on would be the restoration of the balance of power in both Europe and Asia and that *all actions would be viewed in the light of this objective.*" [1]

There was still a significant lack of consensus on the *components* of either Kennan's "counterforce" or the "balance of power" that Marshall wanted "restored." The administration was divided, broadly, between those who regarded the industrial strength of the United States, based on a sound economy, as the weightiest ingredient in the global balance, and those who regarded the extension of Soviet control over new areas of the globe the most important factor. In the pre–Korean War period, the Bureau of the Budget, the Council of Economic Advisers, and the White House staff tended to stress domestic economic considerations, whereas State and Defense tended to emphasize stopping the Soviets.

But even among those who were most oriented toward a global, geopolitical view of the power rivalry with the Soviet Union there was an important divergence of premises concerning both the components of the balance of power and of the American strategies required to stop Soviet expansion. The divergent points of view in 1947–48 clustered around Secretary of State Marshall and Secretary of Defense Forrestal.

Marshall's most passionate commitment now was to the success of the European Recovery Program. But he did concede that a militarily strong Western Europe was essential to right the global balance of power and provide the means locally to dissuade the Russians from attempting an easy fait accompli, either by political subversion or military aggression. Western Europe itself could not contain the Soviets in a major war, but it could provide the front line of defense. The United States would have to come to the direct aid of Europe in any such war, but, as in the Second World War, the full weight of American power would be felt in the later stages of the war as mobilization went into high gear. Marshall favored universal military training in the United States to provide the base for such mobilization should it ever be required, and to signal in advance the refusal of the United States to tolerate Soviet aggression; but he did not view Soviet aggression as sufficiently imminent to require a major increment to ready forces-in-being. Even in response to the Soviet provocations around Berlin in the spring of 1948, and the blockade of 1948–49, Marshall pressed for priority to be given to *European* rearmament. Marshall, of course, was sensitive to the strong political motivations in the White House and Congress for keeping the lid on expenditures, and very likely saw UMT plus European rearmament—neither of which would require any sudden major increases in the U.S. budget—as compatible with continued congressional financing of the multibillion dollar project for rebuilding Europe's economy just getting under way.[2]

Secretary of Defense Forrestal gave priority to the rearmament of the United States as the most effective means of preserving the balance of power against the Soviet Union. To procrastinate on the buildup of an effective United states military posture would be to "deny Marshall the cards to play" in current crisis situations.[3] Strengthening European military capabilities was important, but Forrestal was skeptical of the Europeans' ability to sustain their level of effort on economic reconstruction and simultaneously build the kind of military establishments needed to balance Soviet military power to Europe. In the meantime—he wrote in late 1947—under current budget allocations, reflecting the existing policy of assisting European recovery before American rearmament, we were taking a "calculated risk." That risk involved reliance on the American *strategic* advantage, consisting of American productive capacity, the predominance of American sea power, and the exclusive possession of the atomic bomb. But the last factor, he warned, would have an "indeterminate" duration. "The years before any possible power can achieve the capabilities to attack us with weapons of mass destruction are our years of opportunity."[4] It was clear that had Forrestal been given his way he would have attached greater urgency to a buildup of a balanced United States military posture, which did not bank too heavily on either the perpetuation of the atomic monopoly or the rapid attainment of a level of recovery in Europe which would allow Europeans to assume the major burden of sustaining the balance on the continent.[*]

This difference between Marshall and Forrestal over the components of effective international power was in fact resolved in favor of Marshall by the White House and the Bureau of the Budget. Considerations of domestic political economy rather than a systematic analysis of the capabilities needed to carry out the nation's foreign policy commitments seemed to determine the executive choice to stick with military budgets well below $15 billion a year, until the Korean emergency revised the prevailing priorities.

---

[*]There was yet another consideration that may have weighed heavily with Forrestal. In contrast to the services over which he presided (as the first Secretary of Defense), Forrestal appeared to be more interested in a general increase in the military budget and capabilities than in the implementation of any particular strategic doctrine. He seemed to regard some of the esoteric strategic debates of the military as responses to low budget ceilings, and the consequent need to convince their political benefactors that security could be had only through the provision of capabilities required by their particular functions. Apart from this specious quality, these debates were a severe source of embarrassment to Forrestal's attempts to achieve harmony within the Defense establishment. Higher budgets would put him in a position to mitigate the intensity of interservice rivalry.

Actually, a systematic appraoisal *was* called for by the President and undertaken by a special State–Defense task force months before the North Korean invasion of South Korea. The Soviet blockade of Berlin during 1948–49 and the collateral negotiations of the North Atlantic Treaty had focused attention in the State Department and the White House on the limitations of the usable military power at the disposal of the West in case of major conflict in Europe. The Soviet atomic bomb detonation in August 1949, three years ahead of United States intelligence estimates, gave immediacy to alarms Forrestal had been sounding on the temporary nature of our strategic advantage. And the final fall of China to Mao Tse-tung the next month, placing the bulk of the Eurasian heartland under Communist control and raising the spectre of a division of the world's population into two halves, was suddenly seen by many in the administration, as it could not be when only hypothetical, as an immense strategic fact of life. The convergence of these events with the need for Truman to say yes or no to an H-bomb program produced a requirement for some kind of coherent doctrine on our military capabilities, just as the withdrawal of the British from Greece in 1947 produced the need for a doctrine on our intentions. Truman's decision in January 1950 to give the green light, tentatively, to the H-bomb program was accompanied by a directive to the Secretaries of State and Defense to make a comprehensive review of United States foreign and defense policies in light of the developments just mentioned. [5]

In the process of preparing the general strategic appraisal called for by Truman, a dialogue on the components of the global balance of power, analogous to that conducted between Marshall and Forrestal in the 1947–48 period, was now reenacted within the State Department between George Kennan and Paul Nitze.

Kennan laid greater stress on the nonmilitary components of the bipolar struggle, and felt that the Soviets had such a great reluctance to become involved in a major war against the United States that the most important fact in the strategic equation was a clear *resolve* by the United States not to tolerate piecemeal opportunistic extensions of Soviet control. Translating this into military terms was difficult, and apparently uncongenial to Kennan. However, he is reported to have urged the organization of mobile, quickly deployable United States task forces which could be rushed to the scene of "brushfire" conflicts and thus confront the Soviets with the choice of desisting from their provocation or engaging the United States in a military clash which might expand to a major war. Kennan's analysis of the Soviets convinced him that when confronted with such a stark choice the Soviets would back down. Kennan thus did not feel that a general rearmament program was necessary. Moreover, rearmament would stimulate further the undesirable focusing of national energies on the cruder means of waging the cold war, in opposition to flexible and subtler forms of diplomacy and stress on improving the quality of life of the Western nations.

Paul Nitze, who was given responsibilities for effecting greater liaison between State and Defense when Acheson became Secretary of State in January 1949, gave greater weight than did Kennan to the overall balance of military force between the Soviets and the United States. As Director of the Policy Planning Staff in 1950, and chairman of the *adhoc* study group which produced the strategic paper requested by the President, Nitze's views were critical in shaping the advanced planning concepts being developed at the time. Kennan retained major influence as State Department Counselor, and his knowledge of the Soviet Union was influential in the deliberations of the study group. But Nitze was known to have the full support of Secretary Acheson, who was taking the study very seriously. Forrestal was no longer at Defense, and his economy-minded successor, Louis Johnson, was a weak Secretary who provided little support or guidance to Defense Department participants in the study. Any initiative, or major departures in overall strategic planning, then, would be responsive to the momentum generated by Nitze in fulfilling Truman's desire for a new strategic appraisal.

Nitze felt that the nation's military planning was seriously constrained by the strict budgetary limits imposed by the White House and the Bureau of the Budget. In light of the emergence of a Soviet nuclear striking capability, the United States would need not only to improve its massive destructive capabilities (as was contemplated in the H-bomb program) but also to balance the Soviet capabilities for conventional war. These ideas emerged as major premises in NSC-68 (the paper's file number upon referral to the National Security Council).

But they were only a part of a set of premises designed to give coherence to national security policy. For the first time since the war, military planning concepts were tied to an explicit body of assumptions about the political and technological state of the world. On the basis of an analysis of Soviet economic strengths and weaknesses, the study projected that in four years the Soviets would have a nuclear capability sufficient to neutralize the function of the United States nuclear capability for deterring local wars. Moreover, the Soviets would build this capability without any diminution in their local war capability. Thus, by 1954, if the West did not take significant compensating measures, the balance of military power would have shifted in favor of the Soviets. When this happened economic and technical assistance would be insufficient to contain Soviet expansion.

A challenge to prevailing premises about the U.S. economy was also leveled by the Nitze group. They argued that the nation could well afford to devote 20 percent of the gross national product to national security purposes as compared with the 5 percent then being spent. In budget terms, defense expenditures could, and ought to, rise to possibly as high as $60 billion a year, from the $15 billion then programmed. Nitze and his staff economist, Robert Tufts, had an important ally in Leon Keyserling of the President's Council of Economic Advisers. (Keyserling had been consistently urging "expansionist" policies against the views of the Council's Chairman, Edwin Nourse. Nourse had resigned in October 1949, and from then on, first as acting Chairman, and as Chairman from May 1950, Keyserling dominated the Council and was an increasingly persuasive force throughout the administration.)[6] In retrospect it is not possible to say whether this alliance of Nitze and Acheson at State and Keyserling's Council of Economic Advisers would have been able to move Truman away from his natural economic conservatism and political responsiveness to "welfare" demands, and provide a convincing presidential rationale for *implementing* NSC-68, had the Korean invasion not taken place in June 1950.

Acheson had begun to lay the groundwork with his talks in February 1950 on the need to create "situations of strength" vis-à-vis the Soviet Union prior to attempting any kind of global settlement (as was then being suggested by Churchill). But as yet these declarations did not go much beyond making the aspiration explicit to wider public audiences.[7] An implementation of the aspiration through a diversion of a larger portion of the nation's resources to affect the global balance of military power was still not administration policy. Truman understood that such a shift in the allocation of resources would have to rest on popular consent; and the people, he believed, did not yet appreciate the current function of the military balance of power in global diplomacy.

The Communist North Koreans, by suddenly taking advantage of a local disparity of military power on June 24, 1950, finally gave Truman a sufficient basis for asking the people to approve militarily "rational" national security policies worked out by his professional foreign policy advisers.

5

THE PRIMACY OF
BALANCE-OF-POWER
CONSIDERATIONS DURING
THE KOREAN WAR

Instead of weakening the rest of the world, they [the Communists] have solidified it. They have given a powerful impetus to the military preparations of this country and its associates in and out of the North Atlantic Treaty Organization.

DEAN ACHESON

NSC-68 became the conceptual framework on which the rapid expansion of United States armed forces was hung during the first months of the Korean War. Before the war was over military spending had reached a peak of $50 billion a year. The 1,461,000 men in the United States armed forces in June 1950 were more than doubled in two years, with the Army accounting for the largest increase. As compared with 48 Air Force wings in 1950, the Korean Armistice in 1953 left the United States with nearly 100 wings, with another 50 expected to come into the inventory over the coming four-year period. The Navy was floating 671 ships on the eve of hostilities in 1950, and over 1100 by the summer of 1952.[1] But merely from the fact that administration spokesmen before Congress defended their early Korean War budgets with reference to NSC-68, and from the fact that there was an across-the-board doubling of military capabilities, it cannot be inferred that the original premises advanced by the Nitze group about the emerging balance of power now constituted the doctrinal bases of the Truman administration's new basic national security policy. The Korean War rapidly began to generate its own priority requirements, and the critical question put by members of Congress to any budget proposal was: How does this help us in Korea?

On the more conceptual military planning level, the Korean War heightened differences rather than produced a consensus. For some the Korean War confirmed the thesis that the Western alliance needed permanent and large-scale conventional armies to deter the Communists from future aggression. This view was reflected most clearly in the NATO force goals formulated during the Korean War, the high point of aspiration being the February 1952 Lisbon ministerial meeting which set the number of divisions to be ready and/or deployable for a European conflict at ninety-six. But the Korean experience also gave stimulus to advocates of the doctrinal antithesis: namely, that Korea was a model of how *not* to fight a war; that to allow the Communists to engage the United States in conventional land warfare was to allow them to choose the grounds and weapons most favorable to them; that the superior mode of warfare for the technologically advanced West was strategic, relying mostly upon air power to strike deep at the sources of enemy power with weapons of mass destruction; that the way to preserve the balance of power (as the Soviets built up their strategic capabilities) was not to dissipate our resources in an effort to redress the imbalance in armed manpower, but to enhance our capabilities for strategic warfare. The resolution of these antithetical military doctrinal reactions to the Korean War had to await a change in administrations.

Yet the Korean War—the way it was fought by the United States, and the force-posture planning decisions made at the time—left a material and institutional legacy of programs-in-being not significantly different from those implied in NSC-68. And programs-in-being tend to shape fundamental policy premises just as much as, if not more than, premises tend to shape programs. The perpetuation of existing programs often becomes a psychological, no less than bread-and-butter, commitment for those with the responsibility for their administration. The fact of the matter was that the Korean War *institutionalized* a set of operational (though not necessarily intellectually held) premises:

1. The Soviet Union would resort to military expansion if it were not checked by visible countervailing military power.

2. Local imbalances of military power which favored the Soviets or a Soviet satellite would lead to further "Koreas."

3. The most appetizing local imbalance to the Soviets was in Central Europe.

4. The global balance of power would shift in favor of the Soviets if they were able to swallow the rest of Central Europe, namely, West Germany and Austria. No other area on the periphery of the Communist world, except for the Greco-Turkish flanks (which were already being buttressed) had such a critical function for the balance of power. The next most critical area on the Soviet periphery was Japan.

5. But while attending to the power ratios focused on the prime military-industrial regions, the United States must not neglect local imbalances in secondary and tertiary areas. The capability and clearly communicated will to defend whatever area the Communist powers might choose to attack, regardless of its intrinsic geopolitical weight in the overall balance, was necessary to prevent the Communists from picking and choosing easy targets for blackmail and aggression. And a number of small territorial grabs *could* add up to a critical alteration of the global balance. Moreover, our failure to defend one area would demoralize nationals in other such localities in their will to resist the Communists. Even in Western Europe people would wonder under what circumstances we might consider them dispensable.

Similar premises, to be sure, antedated the Korean War. But their existence, even in the person, say, of Secretary of State Acheson, did not make them the basis of government policy. It took the Korean conflict to give "validity" to these premises—not in the sense of proving their correctness, but in making them the assumptions on which important wartime and planning decisions were reached.

The overriding fear in the White House was not simply that the loss of the Korean peninsula would encourage the Soviets to embark on further aggressions. Rather, it was that the Soviets were embarked, *now*, on some pattern of military aggression to pin down the resources of the United States in peripheral battles, and then to move, when the right moment arrived, virtually unopposed into Western Europe.

In his *Memoirs* Truman divulges how the strategic (United States–Soviet) situation limited his flexibility in the tactical (Korean) campaign. It was his intention, Truman recalls, to take all necessary measures to push the North Koreans back behind the 38th parallel. But he was unwilling to commit the United States so deeply in Korea that we would not have the resources to handle other situations.[2] The strategic prize was Western Europe, with its skilled manpower and industrial infrastructure. Truman was convinced that Europe was still at the center of the Soviet design for world domination, and he, for one, was not going to allow our attention to be diverted from this dominant feature of the global power contest.[3]

When the Communist Chinese armies intervened, the prospect of becoming bogged down in a huge war in Asia became more immediate, particularly in light of pressures from General MacArthur to attack the Communist staging bases in Manchuria, even at the risk of a general war with China. The administration's view was articulated by Dean Acheson at a November 28, 1950, meeting of the National Security Council. The Soviet Union was behind every one of the Chinese Communist and North Korean moves, said the Secretary of State. We were in competition with the Soviets all around the globe. Thus Korea was a world matter, not merely a regional matter. If we were to lose sight of this fact, he warned, and allowed Russia to trap us on the Asian mainland, we would risk sinking into a bottomless pit.[4]

The American Secretary of State presented a similar case to the British a few weeks later during the President's Washington conferences with Prime Minister Attlee. The central enemy was not China, stressed Acheson, but the Soviet Union. The aggression by the North Koreans was not a local, spontaneous maneuver. It was a part of the larger Communist design to get us preoccupied in Asia so the Russians could have a free hand in Europe. We must not and would not distort our global priorities.[5]

This Europe-first emphasis was of course congenial to the British, who were, if anything, afraid that the United States might have already become overcommitted to an increasingly costly Asian conflict, and might engage in rash action—such as nuclear bombardment of China. Attlee kept on raising reservations about the value of attempting to defend Formosa. Acheson thereupon was forced to refine the Europe-first emphasis, by pointing to strategic interdependencies among the various forward positions then being sustained. He explained to the British leaders that, apart from how we might feel about Chiang Kai-shek, we could not, for geopolitical

reasons, allow Formosa to fall into Communist hands. The fall of
Formosa would raise severe problems for us in Japan and in the
Philippines, contended Acheson; and these countries, being the sites
of our bases for conductiog operations in the theater, had become
essential to our survival as a Pacific power. [6]

General Marshall, present during one of these exchanges, added
his weight to the strategic evaluation of Formosa: it was of no particular strategic importance in our hands, but it would be of disastrous importance if it were held by an enemy. [7]

But if hard choices did have to be made in Asia, there was little
doubt that priority would have to be accorded the defense of Japan.
Such an eventuality was in the minds of the Joint Chiefs during the
bleakest days following the Chinese intervention. In the third week
of December 1950 they suggested to Truman that consideration
ought to be given to ways of withdrawing from Korea "with honor"
in order to protect Japan. [8]

The administration's view of the global geopolitical interests and
risks involved in the Korean struggle ran head on with General
MacArthur's view that decisive military victory in the theater of
operations was of overriding importance. But this very intensity of
the disagreement between Truman and MacArthur had the effect
of producing within the administration a greater self-awareness of
its own objectives and the policies it deemed necessary to implement
them.

The much-quoted testimony of General Bradley (to extend the
fighting in the mainland of Asia would "involve us in the wrong
war, at the wrong place, at the wrong time, and with the wrong
enemy" [9]) capsules the operational effects on the prosecution of the
war itself of the premise that the Soviets really had their military
sights focused on Western Europe. The effects on future-oriented
military planning and alliance diplomacy were no less significant.
As Truman telegraphed MacArthur near the final stages of their
controversy: "In reaching a final decision about Korea, I shall have
to give constant thought to the main threat from the Soviet Union
and the need for a rapid expansion of our armed forces to meet this
great danger." [10]

The Europe-oriented consequences of these premises were visible
in the rapid efforts to transform NATO from a security-guarantee
pact into an international regional theater army, most heavily de-

ployed at the spot of critical vulnerability in the global balance: the Central European front. This in turn meant that our European diplomacy was to be oriented toward gaining acceptance from the North Atlantic alliance partners of the rearmament of West Germany. And the rearmament of West Germany, in its turn, would require—largely to reassure the French—a United States commitment to the principle of supranational (or "integrated") commands, in which the German units would be unable to take independent action.[11]

Although the stimulus of the Korean crisis was short-lived and, by late 1951, the Europeans returned to their pre-1950 emphasis on economic recovery, an institutional framework was created for redressing the Central European balance in a future conflict. A Supreme Commander over allied forces was created, and provided with a large international (NATO) staff and planning organization, for the purpose of implementing NATO directives on force posture and strategy. A major responsibility was accorded to Germany for providing troops for a "forward defense" under a multination command directly subordinate to the Supreme Allied Commander (Eisenhower). An American military presence—not just bases for the strategic arm, but an overseas army in the forward defense apparatus—was accepted by United States planners as necessary for the indefinite future. (There was some ambiguity with respect to the function and eventual size of these overseas United States deployments, however. Both General Eisenhower and Secretary of Defense Marshall, in urging congressional authorization for an additional four divisions for Europe in 1951, attempted to delimit their function as largely that of a catalyst for European contributions to a forward ground defense force, in which the Europeans were expected to assume the major burden.)

Moreover, the United States view of the altered scale of priorities, now giving first place to the military components of the power balance, was made explicit to recipients of Marshall Plan assistance. Further economic assistance was to be made contingent upon the alliance partner's conscientious attempt to fulfill its NATO rearmament obligations.[12] By 1951, the European Recovery Program was formally subordinated to "security" considerations under the omnibus Mutual Security Act.

The *way* the United States fought the Korean War—particularly our willingness to allow sanctuary status to Communist China even after she became an active belligerent—did confirm and sharpen the preexisting official premise that mainland Asia was a secondary weight in the balance of global power as compared with Western Europe. But the fact that we were willing to fight a high-cost war to keep South Korea out of Communist hands also gave impetus to the emerging realization that the power contest could be won or lost in the secondary theaters when there was a stalemate in the primary theaters.

The Korean War thus marked a globalization of containment in terms of operational commitments as well as rhetoric. The United States finally "intervened" physically in the Chinese Civil War by interposing the Seventh Fleet between Mao Tse-tung's forces and Chiang's last island fortresses. Despite our anticolonial protestations, we now put our money behind the French efforts to suppress the Ho Chi Minh Communist-nationalist insurgency in Indochina. And although the United States *formally* intervened in Korea under a United Nations mandate (by virtue of the absence of the Soviet delegate from the Security Council at the time the votes were taken), henceforth our plans and public commitments and material undertakings would no longer convey to our global adversaries the impression that we would hesitate to act unilaterally. As with Europe, Article 51 (the self-defense provision) of the UN Charter now became the operative legal instrumentality of our "collective security" arrangements in the secondary as well as the primary theaters.

The globalization of containment—the notion that practically all pieces of territory now had significant, if not decisive, weight in the power balance, that the reputation for being willing to defend each piece was a critical ingredient of our maintenance of allies and deterrence of enemies—rested on solid bipartisan support. The Republican challenge was not to these fundamental assumptions. Rather, it was a charge that the Truman administration was first of all too late and then too restrained in countering the threat of Communism in Asia.

The forum for the partisan rallying was the 1951 Senate investigation of Truman's recall of General MacArthur from his command.[13] It was here, for the first time, that the bipartisan Europe-first policy was made the subject of a great debate between the two parties. It was only now that Secretary of State Acheson's January

1950 statement omitting South Korea from our "defense perimeter" in the western Pacific was held up to scorn by the opposition (who neglected to note that General MacArthur had traced a similar line in March 1949), the charge being that Acheson's statement constituted an "invitation" to Stalin to attack.[14] It was now that it became a Republican article of party faith that the Truman administration, out of nearsightedness as to the ultimate power stakes involved, "lost" China to the Communists.

But this breakdown in the domestic consensus over where the stakes in the global power balance lay was a *retrospective* cleavage.

In 1948 no prominent United States politician or China expert rose to challenge Secretary of State Marshall's assessment that:

China does not itself possess the raw material and industrial resources which would enable it to become a first-class military power within the foreseeable future. The country is at present in the midst of a social and political revolution. Until this revolution is completed—and it will take a long time—there is no prospect that sufficient stability and order can be established to permit China's early development into a strong state.[15]

Nor had the critics of the Truman administration's China policies been willing to go so far as to support United States *combat* operations against Mao in 1948 and 1949 when it became clear that military assistance alone would not suffice. Only marginal increments in aid were offered by members of Congress in the China Aid Act of 1948. The statement of Representative Walter Judd (one of Chiang's staunchest supporters) was typical: "Not for one moment has anyone contemplated sending a single combat soldier in. . . . So it is important to make clear when we speak of military aid . . . it is supplies, training, and advice, nothing further."[16]

This had been the period when our rapid postwar military demobilization was in high gear. It was the same atmosphere that led Truman to defer approval of the NSC-68 recommendations, even though he appreciated their strategic soundness.

When the Korean War allowed Republicans and Democrats alike to loosen the purse strings a bit for military rearmament, many in the opposition party, now urging a decisive victory in Korea, and willing to follow MacArthur into a general war with China, were ready to claim superior wisdom from having been Mao haters since the middle 1940s. This was virtue through hindsight only. Their new charges that the Truman administration had been overly feeble in its approach to the China problem a few years back were re-garded by administration policy makers as gratuitous. These charges conveniently overlooked the fact that the critics themselves cooper-ated in the enfeeblement process. General Marshall later recalled how he was pressed ad nauseam in the early postwar period to give the Communists hell. "I am a soldier and know something about the ability to give hell," he told a Pentagon audience. "At that time, my facilites for giving them hell . . . was [sic] 1⅓ divisions over the entire United States. That's quite a proposition when you deal with somebody with over 260 and you have 1⅓." [17]

Significantly, Marshall did not count among his hell-giving facil-ities the atomic bomb. If there was to be a military contest with the Chinese Communists, the bomb apparently was of little military utility, nor evidently could it be used as a threat to forestall coun-terintervention by the Soviets. This was also a part of the atmo-sphere of the times—especially with respect to any official contem-plation in public of its use against Asians so soon after Hiroshima and Nagasaki.

However, the Korean War also eroded this constraint on United States calculations of usable power in conflict situations. Truman did not unequivocally rule out the use of the bomb. [18] And the Ei-senhower administration went further in actually hinting that it would have to resort to nuclear weapons if the war resumed due to a breakdown in peace negotiations.

If the NSC-68 planners had their way, Korea would have marked the transition to a new era of higher peacetime military budgets, aimed centrally at rectifying local imbalances of power between the Communist and non-Communist nations. The Eisenhower admin-istration also felt it was beholden to a popular mandate against fur-ther Koreas. And alterations in the existing local military imbal-ances would be an essential requisite for the maintenance of our global commitments and preventing Soviet miscalculations such as Korea. But the plans of the Truman administration for rearmament were seen to be incompatible with the conventional Republican phi-losophy of reduced government expenditures.

The most appropriate kind of military power for implementing our now globalized "containment" policy was to remain the primary subject of policy-level debate. But for at least another ten years, the policy itself (however much the Republicans disliked associating themselves with the word), and the premise that an advantageous military balance of power was its essential prerequisite, was taken as fact in official Washington.

The weight of the non-Communist nations in the global balance of power was to be defined, predominantly, as the product of three variables: United States military forces-in-being, United States industrial–economic strength, and the indigenous military-forces-in-being of allies of the United States. Significantly, the *economic* strength of other non-Communist nations was not to be directly taken into account, in terms of requiring significant outlays by the United States. To the extent that balance-of-power considerations would suppress other considerations in United States foreign policy, policies whose rationale was the socioeconomic development of other nations would receive only marginal attention by top United States decision makers.

PART III

THE EISENHOWER ERA

Occasional pages of history do record the faces of the "Great Destroyers" but the whole book of history reveals mankind's never-ending quest for peace, and mankind's God-given capacity to build.

It is with the book of history, and not with isolated pages, that the United States will ever wish to be identified.

DWIGHT D. EISENHOWER

I don't expect other nations to love us. . . . But I do expect them to respect us. . . . This means that we abide by our commitments, that we speak only of what we can do, and do what we speak of.

JOHN FOSTER DULLES

6

A NEW LOOK FOR LESS
EXPENSIVE POWER

*We keep locks on our doors; but we do not have an armed guard in every home.
We rely principally on a community security system so well equipped to punish
any who break in and steal that, in fact, would-be aggressors are generally deterred. That is the modern way of getting maximum protection at bearable cost.*
JOHN FOSTER DULLES

In one important respect the Korean War simplified the policy
dilemmas of the Truman administration. It gave the maintenance of
a balance of power against the Soviet Union and China top spot
among previously competing foreign policy objectives, and it gave
primacy to the military components of power. Yet the Truman administration left office without resolving the competing doctrines of
effective military power put forward by the military strategists.

The Eisenhower administration retained the predominantly military definition of the power balance instituted during the later Truman years; but it carried the process of simplification even further
by selecting one of the competing strategic doctrines—and the most
narrowly specialized one, at that—as the concept that would guide
the allocation of national resources to meet the perceived external
threats to the nation. The military definition of the power balance
was leavened somewhat, however, by the prominence given in the
Eisenhower administration to the nation's economic health as a critical factor in sustaining the global balance. But here too, the poli-

ticoeconomic doctrines which prevailed in the White House tended toward a simplification and narrowing of the premises governing the choice of overseas programs.

The Eisenhower administration early came to different conclusions about the necessary military ingredients for maintaining the balance of power than did the preceding administration. The latest views of the Truman administration were passed on to the incoming administration in the National Security Council Document 141, a report prepared specially for guidance during the transition, and signed by Secretary of State Acheson, Secretary of Defense Lovett, and mutual security administrator Harriman. The report apparently sustained the NSC-68 premise (see above, pp. 49–50) that a balanced military establishment, including substantial limited-war forces, was necessary in the face of the anticipated Soviet long-range strategic nuclear capability. So there were no realistic prospects for reduced budgets after the Korean War. Indeed, serious planning to take cognizance of the Soviet strategic threat would require *increases* of about $7 billion to $8 billion yearly, largely concentrated in new systems of air defense for the continental United States. The paper also claimed that expanded programs of military and economic assistance were needed in the Far East, the Middle East, and Africa.[1] Eisenhower's basic reaction to this paper was that it ignored the "connection between national security and fiscal responsibility."[2]

The President, unlike some members of his Cabinet, and the Republican leadership in the Congress, claimed to be unwilling to buy the more extreme proposition that *first* place should be given to reducing taxes and balancing the budget through reduction of government expenditures. Eisenhower recalls telling the "astounded and upset" Senator Taft of the inability of the new administration to scale down by more than $9 billion the fiscal 1954 budget inherited from the Truman administration because any further reduction would "endanger the security of the United States":

I deeply respected Senator Taft's views and his dedication to the nation's welfare, but I could not agree that the country should have, or wanted, a tax cut ahead of a balanced budget or a balanced budget ahead of national security. In answer to Senator Taft I took time to review the international situation and this country's global strategy. I referred to the dangers in Iran and pointed out that Western

Europe and the oil of the Middle East must in no circumstances fall to Communism. I reminded him of the alarming news of a new Communist invasion of Laos and the continuing wars in Korea and Vietnam. . . . I did not agree that the proposed budget would ruin Republicans in 1954. . . . "Regardless of the consequences," I said, "the nation's military security will take first priority in my calculations."[3]

Eisenhower was stung by charges from influential Democrats, journalists, scholars, and army generals that his New Look defense policy put domestic economic considerations ahead of national security; and he later devoted a chapter in the first volume of his memoirs to a refutation of those charges. Eisenhower's main contention was that he was providing more security at less cost. He would stand as a military man on the force posture he was designing, and the strategy for its use. He was concerned only to eliminate *unnecessary* cost: "The brave statement 'America can afford anything it needs for national security' was and is true. . . . But I also emphasized that America could not afford to waste money in any area, including the military, for anything that it did *not* need."[4] Moreover, "long-term security required a sound economy." National security could not be measured in terms of military strength alone. "The relationship between military and economic strength is intimate and indivisible."[5]

However, the Eisenhower administration's premises concerning the ingredients of domestic economic strength were essentially the premises of the Taft wing of the Republican Party; George Humphrey at the Treasury Department, Charles Wilson at the Defense Department, Sinclair Weeks at the Commerce Department, Arthur Burns at the Council of Economic Advisers, and Gabriel Haugue, the President's administrative assistant responsible for economic affairs, constituted a formidable phalanx of economic conservatism. The programmatic expression of their economic philsosphy appealed to the more homespun philosophy of thrift and solvency that governed Eisenhower's approach to the federal budget. Balanced budgets, fiscal and monetary checks to avoid inflation, tax reductions, and, underlying these, a restoration of the "free market" economy with a minimum of government interference were defined as the ingredients of economic strength.[6] If the relationship between military and economic strength was "intimate and indivisible"—as Eisenhower preached—then he might yet be convinced that a good deal of the military programs in being were sapping America's strength.

Eisenhower's search for a strategic concept that would satisfy both terms of this great equation (reduced government expenditures, and military security in the face of expanding Soviet capabilities) had begun shortly after the November 1952 election, and continued with intensity, at various levels in the administration, for fifteen months, until it emerged full-blown in the spring of 1954.[7]

The notion that defense budget economies could be effected by concentrating on strategic airpower was being urged by the Churchill government during 1951 and 1952. The concept propounded was very similar to that being urged by the United States Air Force since 1948: namely, that strategic air power was now the decisive element in warfare and deterrence, its function being to break the back of enemy power and will at their source. All other capabilities were subsidiary, and, to the extent the other capabilities took away from the resources necessary to maintain strategic superiority over the Soviets, these other capabilities were wasteful. Such strategic monism went against the grain of the balanced defense concepts developed in NSC-68 and implemented on an emergency basis during the Korean War; but they fit in handily with the Republican attempt to exploit popular discontent and confusion with the frustrating military stalemate in Korea. In a *Life* magazine article of May 19, 1952, John Foster Dulles presaged the doctrine which was worked out more fully later by writing of an "instant massive retaliation" capacity as one that provided the United States with the means of taking "action of our own choosing" in contrast to Korea-type engagements where terrain and means were chosen by the enemy.

Eisenhower, at this early stage, still fresh from his NATO role, where it was his job to convince the allies of the necessity for building a significant "forward defense" capability in Europe, did not take too readily to such strategic *avant-gardism*. The presidential candidate is reported to have insisted that the phrase "retaliatory striking power" be stricken from the Republican platform, where it appeared at Dulles' suggestion. However, the general was somewhat enamored of the idea of a mobile strategic reserve based in the United States as the concept for organizing the United States contribution to alliance defense, with the forward positions sustained initially by the forward countries themselves. This hope for allied assumption of the major forward defense burdens had been somewhat dampened by his exposure, as Supreme Allied Commander under NATO, to the economic difficulties the Europeans were encountering in raising and provisioning their armies. As yet, though, Eisenhower himself had propounded no discernibly coherent strategic concept which could serve as an alternative to the programs of the Truman administration.

The initial approach to a new concept is supposed to have begun in earnest in December, before inauguration, as Eisenhower assembled his new Cabinet aboard the U.S.S. *Helena*, on his way back from a trip to Korea. Eisenhower posed the problem: a prolongation of the defense programs then under way would have serious consequences for the American way of life. A free economy with minimal government interference in the life of the citizens would be supplanted by a "garrison state." And the draw upon the resources and finances of the nation would likely lead to serious inflation which would do major harm to the economy. Admiral Radford (soon to be selected by Eisenhower as Chairman of the Joint Chiefs of Staff) and Dulles offered suggestions for effecting savings by more efficient deployment and use of the technologies of atomic-age warfare. Radford is said to have argued that United States military power was overextended—especially in Asia, where it could be pinned down. Instead, he favored a "mobile strategic reserve" based in or near the continental United States. Major reliance for initial local defense would be on indigenous forces. Dulles used the opportunity to argue the virtues of a United States posture based primarily on massive strategic striking power whose function would be to *deter* the Russians instead of trying to contain them all around their extensive perimeter.

These ideas evidently made an impact on Eisenhower, but they were not yet sufficiently gelled to constitute a base for resolution of budgetary issues in the spring of 1953. With a passion to effect dramatic slashes in the Truman holdover budget for fiscal 1954, budget director Dodge, with the President's blessing, instructed all departments to effect downward adjustments of existing program levels. The Department of Defense was informed that it was expected to effect reductions of some $4 billion for the forthcoming fiscal year, with a view toward an additional $6 billion reduction for fiscal 1955. The means by which the reductions were to be effected was apparently of little interest to the Bureau of the Budget—that was the business of the defense people; but reductions there must be. Not surprisingly, the Joint Chiefs of Staff reported back to the National Security Council that reductions down to the contemplated ceilings would dangerously effect national security. The civilian officials of the Department of Defense thereupon took matters into their own hands, and largely through not letting any new contracts in 1954 were able to effect paper reductions (actually deferred decisions) to a level somewhat in line with White House requests.

Clearly, a continuation of such leveling off and reduction in expenditures would requre a major revision in the concepts by which the military were then generating their requirements.

One of the earliest of the concepts developed at the White House–NSC level was announced by the President at the end of April 1953. This was the so-called long-haul basis for military planning, which, presumably, was to substitute for the previous administration's method of planning toward some selected "crisis year" or "year of maximum peril." Under this "new" concept a broad base for effecting mobilization when and if needed was to be substituted for high military manpower levels; and an industrial–technological base capable of supporting expanded production schedules was to be maintained along with research and development in new systems, instead of attempting to fulfill specific production goals tagged to some specific year, only to be faced with inventories of technologically obsolete weapons. Actually, the "old" system was not the caricature it was made out to be by the new administration. The target years were meant primarily as a stimulus—as a way of dramatizing the adverse consequences to the global balance of power if corrective action was not well under way by then; and this in no way implied that the provision of mobilization, industrial and research bases for expansion and innovation was to be given short shrift.

The effect of the announcement of the long-haul concept seems to have been primarily to deflate somewhat the sense of urgency underlying existing defense budget levels. This was, of course, part of the effect intended. "It has been coldly calculated by the Soviet leaders," explained Eisenhower, ". . . by their military threat to force upon America and the free world an unbearable security burden leading to economic disaster." [8]

Needless to say, the announcement was very well received in NATO circles, where the NATO Council in its April 1953 session agreed to Dulles' suggestions for a slowdown in the NATO buildup. This was merely a formal recognition of the slackening that had already been taking place in Europe during the previous year; but now their economy-mindedness was dignified as giving emphasis to long-term quality ahead of short-term quantity. [9]

A more drastic revision of strategic concepts was still needed, however, to legitimize the reduced national security expenditures made necessary by the goal of a balanced budget. The vehicle was to be a broad examination of the grand strategy of the United States conducted for the President during the spring and summer of 1953 by three task forces under the overall direction of Under Secretary of State Walter Bedell Smith and Robert Cutler, the President's special assistant for national security affairs. Each task force was to explore the implications of one of three alternative grand strategies: (1) continuation of "containment"; (2) global deterrence by the threat of nuclear punishment; and (3) "liberation" of Communist-held areas through economic, paramilitary, and psychological warfare methods. The National Planning Board of the National Security Council was to integrate the best ideas of the three groups into a single coherent policy paper.

The resulting document, labeled NSC-162, was a reasonably coherent policy paper, but a failure insofar as its purpose was to provide the administration with a new concept that would allow for major reductions in defense expenditures. The policy of containing the Soviet Union—with essentially the kind of balanced forces recommended by the previous administration—was to be retained, but apparently somewhat greater reliance might be placed on strategic air power for deterrence. The Soviet threat was painted as harshly as ever and likely to continue over the long term. The Soviet hydrogen explosion in August underlined earlier fears that the Soviets would soon have the capacity to hit the United States with a massive nuclear strike. As a consequence, NSC-162 was unable to recommend a reduction in military forces, ground forces included. National security, in the years ahead, would have to take priority over all policy objectives. [10]

Meanwhile, the newly selected Joint Chiefs of Staff, with Admiral Radford as Chairman, had also been conducting a study under orders of the President, who had made firm his expectation that they would give due weight to domestic economic considerations. Their paper, presented in late summer 1953, purported to be a statement of general premises which should guide further detailed planning. The critical premises here, in contrast to those of NSC-162, were a combination of those advanced by Dulles and Radford aboard the *Helena* the previous December. The Joint Chiefs of Staff were unanimous in their opinion that United States military forces were overextended, and that the local defense of potentially threatened areas such as Korea and Germany should be the primary responsibility of indigenous forces backed by United States sea and air power. United States force-posture planning should concern itself primarily with two primary functions: defense of the continental United States against strategic bombardment, and the maintenance of a massive retaliatory capability. Mobility, efficiency, and readiness should be stressed for the nonstrategic forces and reserves.[11]

Yet in attempting to carry out these premises in the form of substantial budgetary reductions for fiscal 1955, the Joint Chiefs of Staff found little in their respective service programs that they could bring themselves to cut. In the National Security Council meetings in the fall of 1953, Treasury Secretary Humphrey (very much a Taft Republican) and budget director Dodge indicated profound disappointment with the estimates presented by the Defense Department. Admiral Radford reacted at this point by insisting that the only way substantial reductions could be effected would be as a result of a basic decision by the administration on the *kind* of war to be planned for. If the military planners knew that permission would be forthcoming to use nuclear weapons whenever it was militarily advantageous to do so, then there could be substantial dollar savings, since current planning was on the basis of preparing simultaneously for brushfire and limited conventional wars, conventional wars on the Second World War model, limited nuclear wars, general nuclear wars, and various combinations of these. Apparently, this argument now made an impact on the entire Cabinet, including the President.

By the end of October 1963 there was a consensus on the Radford line, and the President approved a formal paper, NSC-162/2, which specified the critical assumptions of guidance for planners throughout the military establishment: it was decreed that the military commanders could count on using nuclear weapons, tactical and strategic, when militarily required; and it was implied that the President would issue the appropriate weapons release orders upon request from the commanders in the field. Force-posture planning was to proceed on this basis, and on the basis that the fundamental objective of national security was to *deter* Soviet aggression—a function primarily of the massive strategic retaliatory capability of the United States. To the extent that it was necessary to counter local aggression, greater reliance would have to be placed on indigenous allied forces; concurrent with these local buildups there could be some return of United States overseas forces to the United States.[12]

Here, finally, was the set of premises which allowed the Joint Chiefs of Staff to take their "New Look" at the overall level of military spending, and the allocation of resources within the total military budget. The document they submitted in December 1953 refined somewhat the general politicostrategic ideas of NSC-162/2. The massive retaliatory power of the United States was seen as a deterrent to *major* aggression, and as a means of fighting general war. Local limited aggression was still a distinct possibility, for which the bulk of the locally deployed ground forces ought to be provided by our allies; but an "educational" effort was needed to convince the allies that such a specialization of functions would benefit everyone. United States ground forces in forward areas in Europe and Asia would eventually be reduced; and our participation in local defense operations would be mainly through tactical air and sea power, and quickly deployable mobile ground units—these functions, presumably, to be built around the new concepts of tactical atomic warfare. The recommended force-posture implementations of these concepts were to begin, on an interim basis, with the fiscal 1955 budget and mature by fiscal 1957, resulting in a 25 percent drop in military manpower, and a reduction in the nearly $50 billion annual defense bill to a level under $35 billion.

It was only after the internal administrative tug-of-war had been resolved that the New Look was dressed up in a neat package for public display by the Secretary of State and the President. However, the public versions—particularly Dulles'—do distill from the potpourri of considerations that went into its formulation the rather simplified new orientation toward the global balance of power.

As Dulles explained on January 12, 1954, to the Council on Foreign Relations:

It is not sound military strategy permanently to commit U.S. land forces to a degree that leaves us no strategic reserves.

It is not sound economics, or good foreign policy, to support permanently other countries; for in the long run, that creates as much ill will as good will.

Also, it is not sound to become permanently committed to military expenditures so vast they lead to "practical bankruptcy."

                    .   .   .

We need allies and collective security. Our purpose is to make these relations more effective, less costly. This can be done by placing more reliance on deterrent power, and less dependence on local defensive power.

                    .   .   .

Local defense will always be important. But there is no local defense which alone will contain the mighty land power of the Communist world. Local defense must be reinforced by the further deterrent of massive retaliatory power. A potential aggressor must know that he cannot always prescribe the battle conditions that suit him. Otherwise, for example, a potential aggressor, who is glutted with manpower, might be tempted to attack in confidence that resistance would be confined to manpower.

Under the previous policy, maintained the Secretary of State, our military leaders could not be selective in building our military power. We needed to be ready to fight in the tropics, Asia, the Near East, and Europe, by sea, land, and air. Such a strategy, he insisted, "could not be continued for long without grave budgetary, economic and social consequences."

In order for the nation's military planning to be put on a more rational basis, said Dulles, it was necessary for the President to make this basic policy decision which he, Dulles, was now announcing to the world: namely, that henceforth this nation would "depend primarily upon a great capacity to retaliate, instantly, by means and at places of our own choosing." Now our military establishment could be shaped to fit *our* policy, instead of having to try to be ready to meet the enemy's many choices: "That permits us a selection of means instead of a multiplication of means. As a result, it is now possible to get, and share, more basic security at less cost." [13]

In one important respect, Dulles had seriously overstated the planning premises agreed upon within the administration. He had talked of the massive retaliation capacity as if it were to be the primary military means of defense for the entire free community, neglecting to stress adequately the role of indigenous local forces in blocking aggressions during their initial stages. This led to the widespread impression that United States policy had narrowed the choices of the non-Communist world into either accepting local Communist aggressions or turning every local aggression into general nuclear war. Dulles and other administration officials were hard pressed to explain that they had no such extreme policy in mind,[14] and that local defense capabilities would still be important to deny the enemy easy territorial grabs. Moreover, these local forces could be buttressed quickly by rapid deployments from the central mobile reserve here in the United States. The Communist powers would now know, however, that they could not count on drawing the United States into a purely local encounter with a limitation on the weapons employed. The choice would be ours as to when and where to respond with weapons of mass destruction. Backing away from the denigration of a strategy of readiness to fight in all theatres, that appeared in the Dulles speech, administration spokesmen explained that programmed reductions in United States military manpower levels were the result of improved local defense capabilities in NATO and the Far East, and the development of tactical nuclear weapons which, it was assumed, would reduce ground manpower requirements.

7

COMMITMENTS AND COERCION: DULLES' PSYCHOLOGY OF POWER

The free nations have adopted and implemented two interrelated policies for collective security. The first policy is to give clear warning that armed aggression will be met by collective action. The second policy is to be prepared to implement this political warning with deterrent power.

JOHN FOSTER DULLES

In his "massive retaliation" speech before the Council on Foreign Relations Dulles had undoubtedly resorted to hyperbole. In failing to give sufficient stress to the role of indigenous military forces he underplayed that which he was later to be accused of overplaying. Indeed, Dulles personally was much more interested in this means of enhancing the non-Communist side of the balance than in the diplomatic exploitation of advanced weaponry.

Dulles believed in the virtues of alliance building for reasons that went beyond the purely military calculus of power. Unity of purpose and coordination of policy were no less important in his view as attributes of strength. The cement for effecting such cohesion was thought to be a shared ideology and economic and military interdependence. But in the areas of the Eisenhower administration's most feverish alliance-building activity—the wide arc through the Middle East and Southeast Asia that connects Europe to Japan, and hems in the Communist Eurasian heartland—there was thought to be little basis for cultivating strong economic ties.[1]

In the first place, the administration, in its determined effort to reduce all but the most essential expenditures, was in no mood to begin new programs of foreign assistance unless these could be shown to be directly related to crucial United States national security requirements. Second, the Eisenhower Cabinet was skeptical of the ability of the new nations to make productive use of purely economic assistance. Consequently, the dominant basis of Eisenhower–Dulles appeals for military aid between 1953 and 1956 was that of the supposed comparative economic advantage to the United States of relying on indigenous local forces rather than United States military manpower in order to contain Communist military expansion.

This narrow basis for alliance building underlay Dulles' signing up of Pakistan and Iraq as recipients of United States military assistance in 1953–54, in the face of outraged opposition from the Arab states and India, and his fashioning of the Southeast Asia Treaty Organization during a period of increasingly self-conscious neutralism in Asia.

The efforts to sign up military allies in the Middle East, particularly, illustrate the way in which the policy of containment had become submerged in the effort to add overseas weights to the military balance—a departure from the pre–Korean War days when instances of military assistance to countries on the Communist periphery were defined as stopgap emergency efforts, while the most important contributions expected from these peripheral countries were serious strides in their own socioeconomic development.

The military balance-of-power emphasis to containment in the Middle East was, as in Western Europe, stimulated by the Korean War. The Truman administration had always regarded the Middle East as of strategic significance; and in the early 1950s its special attributes—the source of two-thirds of the West's oil reserves, the Suez Canal, and the location of important British military bases— were seen as immediately vital should there be a global test of strength. The United States, joined by Britain, France, and Turkey, tried to induce the Arabs to participate in a Middle East Defense Command. But Egypt and the other Arab States had defined the effort as a plot by the imperialist powers to reestablish control of the area. Their fingers burned in this attempt, Truman and Acheson fell back on the Point IV approach, offering technical assistance without "strings" in the hope of maintaining a basis for friendly association.

Dulles, however, was not to be dissuaded by these past failures to fill the Middle Eastern military vacuum. The premises of the New Look gave a new imperative to the organization of indigenous military capabilities. The Middle East may be complicated, but certainly not unmanageable to the skilled diplomatist. In 1953 Dulles made a trip to the area, sounding out, with offers of economic and military assistance, current receptivity to a Middle East Defense Command. Colonel Nasser's unequivocal rejection of the scheme, on the grounds that the new nationalist leaders in the area would be committing political suicide if they entered into external defense alliances, only prompted Dulles to try an end run:

Many of the Arab League countries are so engrossed with their quarrels with Israel or with Great Britain or France [observed Dulles] that they pay little heed to the menace of Soviet Communism. However, there is more concern where the Soviet Union is near. In general, the northern tier of nations shows awareness of the danger.[2]

The most receptive countries were Turkey (already a loyal member of NATO, but concerned, on its own account, with being outflanked on the East by its historic rival) and Pakistan (hardly concerned over Soviet aggression, but willing to exploit the cold war to redress its local imbalance with India). The United States could make direct deals with these two widely separated nations; but the nations between—Iran and Iraq—would be less likely to risk antagonizing their Arab neighbors. The trick was to blur the American role in the Turko-Pakistani association, and then on their own have these nations establish a mutual security arrangement with their neighbors, Iran and Iraq.

In February 1954 the United States military assistance agreement with Pakistan was announced; it was defined only as an arrangement for handling arms aid, without any formal alliance obligations. Paralleling these negotiations with the United States, Pakistan and Turkey entered into a treaty of friendship and cooperation for security, pledging to study means of cooperating to defend against external aggression, and inviting other states in the area to become associated with this effort. Overt initiatives to bring Iraq into the "northern tier" arrangements were Turkey's responsibility. The United States had already effected a bilateral military aid agreement with Premier Jamali; but, again, this involved no formal commit-

ments to participate in collective regional defense. The Turkish–
Iraqi agreement signed at Baghdad in February 1955 was very similar in terms to the previous year's agreement between Turkey and
Pakistan; now, however, a more concerted attempt was made to draw
in other states. The Iraqi leadership, quite openly in competition
with Egypt for influence among the Arab states, was anxious to
increase its regional bargaining power by extracting the maximum
assistance from the West. Britain accepted the invitation to transform its previously bilateral base agreements with Iraq into a part
of this expanding regional security system—now called the Baghdad
Pact. Pakistan's adherence was a foregone conclusion. The next big
plum was Iran. In 1954 there was still much political instability
after the deposition of the anti-Western Mossadegh regime; an obvious pro-Western alignment might reignite the extremist fires. But
by the fall of 1955 the Shah felt more secure politically, and was
particularly anxious to qualify for the assistance benefits of pact
membership in order to modernize his army. [3]

The result was a local bipolarization of the Middle East, with the
north organized into the Baghdad Pact, and the south dominated
(through subversion and threat, as well as common ideology and
friendship) by Egypt. The new situation was very much the outcome of Dulles' efforts, but he was unwilling to become completely
associated with his own handiwork. Financial and military support,
and participation in the work of pact subcommittees, yes; but full
membership, no. Perceiving Soviet attempts to exploit the local bipolarization, Dulles felt the necessity of preserving some residue of
United States influence with Nasser. Thus the simplification that
had been taking place in United States diplomacy—attempting to
maintain the balance of power by a somewhat indiscriminate adding
of military allies—was beginning to produce its own complications.

The American-sponsored proliferation of alliances in the Middle
East overlapped the similar effort in Asia to redress the Communist
advantage in military manpower by getting signatures to a multilateral Southeast Asian treaty.

The deteriorating French position in Indochina was the immediate stimulus to the attempt to multilateralize, put some military flesh
on, and give an indigenous cast to the existing pattern of special
relationships between some of the local states and the United States,
Britain, and France. Dulles and Eisenhower had been urging a

Southeast Asian "NATO" since 1953. The full-fledged push now
was in part the result of the military lessons of the Indochina conflict: the tactical irrelevance of United States strategic power, the
unavailability of United States ground forces, and the lack of trained
indigenous forces. And in part the new momentum for a local treaty
association was an expression of the growing perception that resistance to Communism requires support of the indigenous peoples affected, and that this would not be forthcoming if the anti-Communist resistance bore the stigma of colonialism.

The administration had been claiming that a Communist victory
in Indochina would have serious consequences for the global balance of power. To the American people, Eisenhower dramatized the
strategic considerations underlying his desire to help the French by
comparing Indochina to the first of a row of dominoes, which if
knocked over would topple the whole row.[4] To Prime Minister
Churchill, in an urgent note requesting the British to join us and
the *ad hoc* construction of a Southeast Asian collective defense force,
the President wrote:

If . . . . Indochina passes into the hands of the Communists the ultimate effect on
our and your global strategic position with the consequent shift in the power ratios
throughout Asia and the Pacific could be disastrous.[5]

But however disastrous the consequences of a Communist victory
in Indochina, Eisenhower felt that the consequences to our global
power position could be even *more* disastrous if the United States
took up the major military burden of saving the area.

Various schemes for bringing United States military power into
play were being advanced by Admiral Radford and Secretary Dulles.
The leading option was an air strike from carriers of the U.S. Seventh Fleet. Eisenhower tended to agree with the majority of the
Joint Chiefs of Staff that, in purely military terms, this would not
significantly help the French situation on the ground. Yet he admitted to feeling "there was some merit in the argument that the psychological effect of an air strike would raise French and Vietnamese
morale and improve, at least temporarily, the entire situation."[6] The
real barrier, as far as the President was concerned, was the unwillingness of other countries to associate themselves with us in this or
any other military intervention on the side of the French. Dulles,
having failed to arrive at a common basis for action with Eden,

appears at one point to have been willing to go it alone.[7] But Eisenhower claims to have maintained a consistent position throughout that "there would be no intervention without allies." As Eisenhower explained to General Alfred Gruenther, then NATO Supreme Commander:

> No Western power can go to Asia militarily, except as one of a concert of powers, which concert must include local Asiatic peoples.
>
> To contemplate anything else is to lay ourselves open to the charge of imperialism and colonialism—or at the very least—of objectionable paternalism.[8]

At the climax of the 1954 crisis, with the French under siege at Dienbienphu, the point of no return for a presidential choice from among unpalatable alternatives—negotiate from a position of weakness or unilateral United States intervention—had been reached. On April 29, in a strategy huddle with his top advisers, Eisenhower interposed his military judgment to dispose of all further discussion of United States forcible intervention:

> I remarked [recounts Eisenhower] that if the United States were, unilaterally, to permit its forces to be drawn into conflict in Indochina and in a succession of Asian wars, the end result would be to drain off our resources and weaken our over-all defensive position.[9]

Henceforth, the task remained for diplomacy to salvage as much of the situation as possible.

Although Dulles would not put his signature to the resulting Geneva accords (which could be read as giving legitimacy to the extension of Communist control that had occurred), the administration expected a worse outcome than the one the Communists accepted: the allowance (albeit temporary) of a non-Communist government for the southern half of the country. The dire consequences to the power balance which had been forecast were, it could be claimed, predicated on the fall of the whole of Indochina.

Thus, the local balance of power could still be consolidated if the non-Communist countries in the region worked fast enough in responding to the challenge. Dulles immediately concentrated his efforts once again, committing the prestige of the United States to the construction of a Southeast Asian mutual defense pact to be based primarily on indigenous capabilities. The result was an agreement somewhat short on the provision of capabilities and somewhat unconvincing in its purpose of giving an indigenous, noncolonial cast to anti-Communism.

The Southeast Asia Collective Defense Treaty, dated September 8, 1954, required only *consultation* among its signatories in case one of them were the victim of armed attack or subversion. Each member "recognizes that aggression . . . in the treaty area against any of the Parties . . . would endanger its own peace and safety," but each member pledged no more than to "act in that event to meet the danger in accordance with its constitutional processes" (Article IV). The list of signatories to the treaty was revealing in itself: the United States, France, Britain, Australia, New Zealand, Thailand, the Philippines, and Pakistan. At the most the treaty provided, as Eisenhower claimed, "a moral, legal, and practical basis for helping our friends of the region." At the least, SEATO merely formalized preexisting power relationships in Asia, neither significantly adding to nor subtracting from the three-way balance between the Communists, the anti-Communists, and the nonaligned.

Actually, Dulles and Eisenhower were already beginning to lose any illusions they might have had that formally committed military allies were one of the most relevant factors in the global balance of power. If anything, SEATO was a face-saving monument to the obsolescence of that simpler conception. Yet, along with the Baghdad Pact, it reinforced the "pactomania" stereotype of Dullesian diplomacy. More significantly, these early solemn agreements acted later as a constraint on attempts to implement more flexible premises about the functions of nationalism and nonalignment in Asia.

The enrichment of the Eisenhower administration's premises about the ingredients of effective international power in Asia was reflected by the Formosa Straits crisis of 1954–55. The ink was still wet on the SEATO treaty when the Chinese Communists opened their bombardment of the offshore islands remaining in the hands of the Chinese Nationalists. The failure of the Communists to launch their threatened invasions of Quemoy and Matsu (they did take the Ta-chen) was proudly attributed by Dulles to those very factors of power with which he was most identified, and for which he was most criticized: formal military alliances, threats of strategic reprisal in response to limited enemy probes, and a willingness to convert a seemingly marginal objective into a life and death matter for our side if this appeared necessary to maintain the objective.

And characteristically, for Dulles, the form, more than the material substance, of power received his closest attention.

SEATO was inapplicable to the defense of Taiwan (Formosa) and the offshore islands defined by the administration as contingently necessary to Taiwan's defense. For one, Taiwan was neither a member of the treaty organization nor covered by the treaty provisions, since there was considerable divergence of policy toward the whole China question among the signatories. All United States moves in the crisis had to be undertaken under the authority of bilateral agreements between the United States and the Republic of China on Taiwan. More important, the definition of the conflict by the United States as vital, involving essential strategic interests of the entire free world, was unacceptable to most of our allies. Yet Dulles attempted to give credit to the spirit, if not the letter, of the multi-nation regional security arrangement:

Its [Communist China's] almost unlimited manpower would easily dominate, and could quickly engulf, the entire area, were it not restrained by the mutual security structure which has been erected. But that structure will not hold if it be words alone. Essential ingredients are the deterrent power of the United States and our willingness to use that power in response to a military challenge. [10]

In a news conference on March 15, 1955, the Secretary was asked to indicate how he expected to apply United States military power to the defense of the offshore islands or other points in the Far East and Southeast Asia. "U.S. policy," he replied, "is not to split that power up into fragments." It was rather to preserve the ability to "use our full power." The most effective contribution the United States could make to the defense of the area was by our "strategic force with a high degree of striking power by sea and air." [11]

Eisenhower has disclosed in his memoirs that such public hints of strategic retaliation, however vague, were regarded within the administration as more than merely threats. A few days before making the above remarks to the press, Dulles had returned from a two-week Asian trip and reported to the President that the Chinese were determined to capture Taiwan. Gaining Quemoy and Matsu would not end their determination.

"If we defend Quemoy and Matsu," advised Dulles, "we'll have to use atomic weapons. They alone will be effective against mainland airfields."

"To this I agreed," recounts Eisenhower. And in response to Dulles' estimate of "at least an even chance" of war growing out of the situation, Eisenhower recalls that "I merely observed that if this proved to be true it would certainly be recognized that the [war] would not be of our seeking." [12]

To take an even risk of general war with Communist China with such equanimity, Eisenhower had to be convinced of two propositions: that the issue involved was of major importance to the global position of the United States, and that Soviet Russia would refrain from direct involvement. These were the essential propositions of John Foster Dulles. Eisenhower showed his concurrence in two messages to Winston Churchill during the height of the crisis. Never was the Dullesian style and substance more evident.

On the vitalness of the interests at stake:

We believe that if international Communism should penetrate the island barrier in the Western Pacific and thus be in a position to threaten the Philippines and Indonesia immediately and directly, all of us, including the free countries of Europe, would soon be in far worse trouble than we are now. Certainly the whole region would soon go.

. . .

Only a few months back we had both Chiang and a strong, well-equipped French Army to support the free world's position in Southeast Asia. The French are gone—making it clearer than ever that we cannot afford the loss of Chiang unless all of us are to get completely out of that corner of the globe. This is unthinkable to us—I feel it must be to you.

On the consequences of a failure to stand firm:

There comes a point where constantly giving in only encourages further belligerency. I think we must be careful not to pass that point in our dealings with Communist China.

. . .

We must show no lack of firmness in a world where our political enemies exploit every sign of weakness, and are constantly attempting to disrupt the solidarity of the free world's intentions to oppose their aggressive practices.

And finally, in discounting the likelihood of Soviet intervention:

I do not believe that Russia wants war at this time—in fact, I do not believe that even if we became engaged in a serious fight along the coast of China, Russia would want to intervene with her own forces. She would, of course, pour supplies into China in an effort to exhaust us and certainly would exploit the opportunity to separate us from your country. But I am convinced that Russia does not want, at this moment, to experiment with means of defense against the bombing that we could conduct against her mainland. [13]

The fact that the Chinese Communists decided not to attack after all was for Dulles proof of his premises of power and vindication of his strategic concepts. Emmet Hughes quotes the Secretary of State as claiming, "Of all the things I have done, the most brilliant of all has been to save Quemoy and Matsu." [14] This pride was reflected in the controversial "brink of war" interview he gave late in 1955 to James Shepley of *Life* magazine:

The ability to get to the verge without getting into the war is the necessary art. If you cannot master it you inevitably get into war. If you try to run away from it, if you are scared to go to the brink you are lost. We've had to look it square in the face—on the question of getting into the Indo-China war, and on the question of Formosa. We walked to the brink and we looked it in the face. We took strong action. [15]

Dulles claimed that in all of these situations the ultimate decisions were the President's, which undoubtedly was the case. He also claimed that "the President never flinched for a minute on any of these situations. He came up taut." [16] Again, this may very well have been the case, once the alternatives had been narrowed. But Dulles' intended implication that he and Eisenhower had identical premises about the most effective means of dealing with the nation's opponents bears further examination.

8

WAGING PEACE:
THE EISENHOWER FACE

Quite naturally . . . [John Foster Dulles and I] agreed that a determined pursuit of peace with justice should be . . . the foremost objective of the American government. Such an objective . . . could reasonably be pursued, we knew, only if the United States spoke from a position of power.

But the needed power would have to comprehend not only military strength, the age-old single criterion of civilizations long since reduced to rubble, but moral and economic strength as well.

DWIGHT D. EISENHOWER

The international posture of the United States during Eisenhower's first term cannot be shown to have flowed directly from the premises of power of Secretary Dulles—neither as consistently as is claimed by his adulators nor as unrelentingly as is charged by his detractors. The policy flexibility (or ambivalence) during the early Eisenhower years seems less attributable to any revision of premises by the Secretary than to the fact that the President had very different attitudes on the prominence to be given coercive tools of power in our diplomacy. [1]

The greatest source of Eisenhower's power—in a personal sense—was that he was so well liked. His inclination as a world statesman was to transfer his likeableness to the nation which made him its leader, to make the personal style the national image.

The observation by Eisenhower's speech writer, Emmet Hughes, that there was a "deep conflict of premises" between the President and his Secretary of State [2] refers primarily to the disagreement about the best means for influencing men and nations.

Both men were apparently aware of the difference from the beginning of their relationship. Dulles put the matter delicately in a private conference before their official association began: "With my understanding of the intricate relationships between the peoples of the world and your sensitivities to the political considerations involved, we will make the most successful team in history." [3] And in one sense they did; the teamwork aspect of their relationship was impeccable. Eisenhower, in awe of Dulles' diplomatic credentials, gave his Secretary of State an unusual amount of authority in policy formulation and implementation, while Dulles, in awe of Eisenhower's tremendous domestic popularity and international prestige, was scrupulously deferential and loyal to the President's convictions, to the extent they were expressed in any particular policy.

However, as both the record and the memoirs of the period suggest, Dulles was much more industrious in translating his own predilections into policy than those of the President. And since such translation of general approach into particular diplomatic moves was, in the Eisenhower administrative fashion, the Secretary's job, not his, the President's general approach often remained unarticulated (in policy as well as speech) while the Secretary's policy premises were well attended. Readers of Eisenhower's own memoirs must fill in a great deal between the lines to glean the essentials of this relationship. With the exception of one or two instances, such as Eisenhower's questioning of Dulles' abruptness in withdrawing the Aswan Dam assistance (see below, p. 103), we are exposed to no differences of opinion. Eisenhower records the version of their relationship which he would like to stand:

It was said . . . that he [Dulles] sought not only to be influential in the conduct of foreign affairs, but to be responsible only to his own convictions and inclinations. What his critics did not know was that he was more emphatic than they in his insistence that ultimate and personal responsibility for all major decisions in the field of foreign relations belonged exclusively to the President, an attitude he meticulously maintained throughout our service together. He would not deliver an important speech or statement until after I had read, edited, and approved it; he guarded constantly against the possibility that any misunderstanding could arise between us. It was the mutual trust and understanding, thus engendered, that enabled me, with complete confidence, to delegate to him an unusual degree of flexibility as my representative in international conferences, well knowing that he would not in the slightest degree operate outside the limits previously agreed between us. The association was particularly gratifying to me because of the easy partnership we developed in searching for the answer to any complex problem. But although behind closed doors we worked as partners, he in all our conversations lived his conviction that he was the adviser, recognizing that the final decision had to be mine.[4]

Sherman Adams too claims that "the Secretary of State never made a major move without the President's knowledge and approval"; but he goes on to make the revealing observation that "the hard and uncompromising line the United States government took toward Soviet Russia and Red China between 1953 and the early months of 1959 [was] more a Dulles line than an Eisenhower one."[5]

Each of the prominent "peace" initiatives of the period was generated and formulated by special assistants or staff aides to the President, not by Dulles, in contrast to the usual pattern.

According to the principal drafter (Hughes), Eisenhower's April 1953 "Chance for Peace" address to the American Society of Newspaper Editors went against Dulles' grain. But because the Secretary of State knew how impatient the President was to follow through on a hunch that a dramatic peace probe in the wake of Stalin's death was worth a try, Dulles only objected obliquely to the address. To those working on the speech, Dulles spoke plainly:

. . . there's some real danger of our just seeming to fall in with these Soviet overtures. It's obvious that what they are doing is because of outside [Western] pressures, and I don't know anything better we can do than keep up these pressures right now.[6]

Dulles' view of the power struggle between the Communist and non-Communist worlds conformed quite closely to what a game theorist would call a "zero-sum" game: that is, anything which could be rated as a plus for one's opponents, such as an increase in their military power, general power potential, or even economic well-being, should be regarded as a minus for oneself—and vice versa. Eisenhower, on the other hand—and this is what worried Dulles—was anxious to reduce the costs and risks of the contest to the United States by finding opportunities for *mutual* gain: by searching for "non-zero-sum" relationships.

Eisenhower's biggest frustrations at this time came from trying to reduce government expenditures. If only the huge burden of arms spending could be reduced significantly, then budgets could be balanced, taxes could be reduced, and private enterprise could flourish with less government interference! To Eisenhower's way of thinking, these effects would in turn lead to a revival of the American spirit of individual initiative which was the basic source of our national strength.

Possibly the new Soviet leaders had analogous problems. Eisenhower recalls that his "hope" was that "perhaps the time had arrived when the Soviet leaders had decided, because of the discontent of their subjects, to turn their factories to producing more goods for civilian use and thus to raise the living standards of the Soviet population." [7]

Dulles' hope was in the other direction—that the gap between the desires of the Soviet people and the policies of the Soviet regime would become so wide that the Soviet Union would eventually collapse. Dulles could, and did, finally go along with the peace probe Eisenhower and his White House advisers were preparing in April 1953, and banked on the result's being an intensification of the gap between popular aspiration in the Communist countries and Politburo policy. His most optimistic view of the speech seems to have been that it might be a good weapon of political warfare.

But Eisenhower appears to have meant it when he pleaded publicly with the Soviet leaders for "a few . . . clear and specific acts . . . of sincere intent" (such as a finalization of the Korean armistice, and the conclusion of an Austrian peace treaty) so as to strengthen "world trust." Out of this could grow "political settlements for the other serious issues between the free world and the Soviet Union," and, concurrently, "the reduction of the burden of armaments now weighing upon the world." This last, Eisenhower truly wanted the Soviet leaders to realize, was his deepest aspiration. The core of the speech, and the part to which Eisenhower gave greatest emphasis, tried to convey his appreciation of the mutual benefits to be derived from substantial disarmament:

Every gun that is made, every warship launched, every rocket fired signifies, in the final sense, a theft from those who hunger and are not fed, those who are cold and are not clothed.

The world in arms is not spending money alone.

It is spending the sweat of its labors, the genius of its scientists, the hopes of its children.

The cost of one modern heavy bomber is this: a modern brick school for more than 30 cities.

It is two electric power plants, each serving a town of 60,000 population.

It is two fine, fully equipped hospitals.

It is some 50 miles of concrete highway.

We pay for a single fighter plane with a half million bushels of wheat.

We pay for a single destroyer with new homes that could have housed more than 8,000 people. [8]

Non-Dullesian premises also underlay the Atoms for Peace proposal, presented before the United Nations on December 8, 1953. This venture, too, which Eisenhower referred to as "my second major speech in the field of foreign relations," [9] found Dulles on the sidelines. The idea appears to have been very much Eisenhower's own. The President had been gloomy over the early drafts by his special assistant C. D. Jackson for an "Operation Candor" speech on the destructive power of thermonuclear weapons. The Soviet hydrogen explosion in August 1953 only reinforced Eisenhower's conviction that some way had to be found to dampen the tension and suspicion which had now evolved into an ever-more lethal, expensive phase of the arms race. He was disappointed that nothing concrete had come of his speech to the newspaper editors. "I began to search around," Eisenhower wrote to a friend, "for any kind of an idea that could bring the world to look at the atomic problem in a broad and intelligent way and still escape the impasse to action created by Russian intransigence in the matter of . . . inspection." [10]

While vacationing in Denver the idea occurred to the President that the United States and the Soviet Union could each donate fissionable material to the United Nations from their respective stockpiles, and the donations could be diverted to peaceful projects under international supervision. This would not be disarmament, but "my purpose was to promote development of mutual trust, a trust that was essential before we could hope for success in the . . . [major] disarmament proposals." To generate such trust it was important:

to get the Soviet Union working with us in a noncontroversial phase of the atomic field. . . . If we were successful in making even a start, it was possible that gradually negotiation and cooperation might expand into something broader; there was hope that Russia's own self-interest might lead her to participate in joint humanitarian efforts. [11]

Eisenhower delegated the major responsibility for translating this idea into action to General Robert Cutler, his special assistant for national security affairs; Admiral Lewis Strauss, Chairman of the Atomic Energy Commission; and C. D. Jackson. Dulles, busy with a round of diplomatic conferences, was brought in only during the last-minute drafting efforts on the UN speech. But this was not really his cup of tea. "An idealistic venture like the Atoms-for-Peace plan was hardly the sort of thing that would fire the imagination of a man like Dulles anyway," divulges Sherman Adams. "He gave it his tacit approval, but he had some doubts about it." [12]

Eisenhower was to be disappointed again at the lack of a positive Soviet response to his proposals, and nine months later turned Atoms for Peace into a project for joint Western cooperation in research on the peaceful uses of atomic energy. Eventually, Eisenhower could take credit for the creation of the International Atomic Energy Agency, which the Soviets did join, for the exchange of nuclear information and limited inspection over the nuclear energy facilities of member nations without weapons programs. But the tension-reducing and trust-building functions of the original proposal were eclipsed by more dramatic events of 1954—the Indochina conflict, the formation of the Asian and Middle Eastern military alliances, the acceptance of a rearmed West Germany in the Atlantic defense system—all of which were conducted in the Dulles style and reflected his premises.

Dulles inherited the Acheson attitude that there were in fact no significant negotiable issues between the Soviets and us. Each side, for the foreseeable future, was likely to adhere to the position "what's mine is mine; what's yours is negotiable." From the standpoint of the United States the potentially negotiable issue was the Soviet illegal absorption of Eastern Europe, or at least a critical segment of that problem: the division of Germany. But both Secretaries of State were convinced that a condition for Soviet willingness to sacrifice some of their control would be a global imbalance of power clearly favoring the West. Acheson does not seem to have had confidence in the emergence of such a condition of obvious Western superiority. Dulles, at least in his rhetoric, looked forward to an advantageous balance of power developing as a result of the collapse of the Soviet economy and social system. Meantime, however, it was essential to maintain the military strength of the West to deter the Soviets from attempting to alter the balance of power in their favor.

To these premises Dulles added the corollary that some amount of East–West tension was an important condition for the maintenance of Western power. As he confided to a State Department colleague:

> If there's no evident menace from the Soviet bloc our will to maintain unity and strength may weaken. It's a fact, unfortunate though it be, that in promoting our programs in Congress we have to make evident the international communist menace. Otherwise such programs as the mutual security one would be decimated.
>
> The same situation would probably prevail among our allies [as a result of a détente]. They might feel that the danger was over and therefore they did not need to continue to spend large sums for defense. [13]

The Soviets, Dulles believed, were aware of this susceptibility of the Western democracies and were trying to exploit it. Their calls for negotiations, for relaxation of tensions, for disarmament agreements, were a "Trojan horse" technique to defeat efforts at European rearmament—particularly the integration of a rearmed Germany into the Western bloc, as in the European Defense Community.

However, Dulles found that other political leaders in the Western alliance (with the possible exception of Adenauer) felt compelled—partly for domestic political considerations—to make a convincing display of peace initiatives before asking their peoples to support major rearmament. From 1953 to 1955, Churchill, and then Eden, was a leading advocate of a big-power summit meeting. The administration maintained its position that the Soviets would first have to show by deeds, not by promises, that they were interested in serious attempts to reduce tension. As an example of a sincere deed, Dulles and Eisenhower on a number of occasions mentioned Soviet agreement to an Austrian peace treaty. Suddenly, in the spring of 1955, the Soviets reversed their earlier intransigence on Austria and agreed to a mutual withdrawal of troops, demilitarization, neutralization, and a political system contemplating a non-Communist regime. Dulles was apparently surprised and temporarily thrown off balance by the demands for a summit, now increasingly heard from most capitals. [14]

The Secretary of State quickly regained his footing by suggesting that the Soviets' willingness to pay the entry price (the Austrian treaty) for a summit meeting was due to the success of his diplomacy. "It is clear we are seeing the results of a policy of building unity and strength within the free world," he said in his May 24, 1955, press conference. "This policy has produced a radical change in Soviet policy, illustrated by new Soviet attitudes toward Austria and Yugoslavia."[15]

Now, in order to continue to play the role of man out front in alliance diplomacy vis-à-vis the Soviets, Dulles took an active part during the next few months in clearing the path to the summit. It is doubtful, however, that he believed the Soviets had made a shift in grand strategy. If anything, the Austrian treaty was a tactical retreat, and Dulles was determined that it should be shown as such. He was skeptical of any important agreements occurring at the summit, particularly on the key question of Germany; but for that very reason Dulles felt it important to have the matter of Germany a prominent part of the agenda. Soviet unwillingness to barter control of East Germany would be exposed, and Adenauer could then convincingly reply to critics of his rigid policy that the Soviets were not really interested in a reunified Germany even if it were neutral.[16]

Although Eisenhower appreciated Dulles' reluctance to have the President drawn into a high-level charade of mutual accommodation and cordiality with the Soviets, once it was decided to go to the summit Eisenhower's inclinations again found an opportunity for expression. "Unlike Dulles, who entertained no such high hopes," writes Sherman Adams, "Eisenhower went to Geneva seeking to make the meeting a solid beginning of a move toward world disarmament."[17]

Adams' characterization of Eisenhower's purposes and expectations may be a slight exaggeration. The President had been somewhat disillusioned in his optimism by the Soviets' lack of positive response to his Atoms for Peace plan; and, in light of this, particularly angered at the Russian pose as the champion of peace and disarmament. A month before the conference, Eisenhower wrote in confidence to his friend Swede Hazlett: "Personally, I do not expect any spectacular results from the forthcoming 'Big Four' conference."[18] But, in contrast to Dulles, he was unworried about the possibility that the Soviets were engaged in a "Trojan horse" tactic to compel the West to let down its guard. If Soviet tactical considerations required a temporary reduction of tensions, Eisenhower seemed concerned only that the Soviets not attempt to take all the credit for the improved atmosphere. Especially in the field of disarmament negotiations the Soviet should not be able to make all the grandstand plays, as they had been doing recently. Although not particularly hopeful of immediate results, the President was at least determined that this time the propaganda battle would not be won by the Soviets.

Eisenhower did agree with Dulles that in his attempt to convince world opinion that the United States was making a major effort toward peace, he should not create overly high expectations in the American people which would then be followed by extreme disillusionment. Even so, in his address to the nation on the eve of his departure for the conference the former general transformed his peace "probe" into a crusade; and this one, like the others he had led, he must *win:*

If we look at . . . [the] record we would say, "Why another conference? What hope is there for success?" Well now the first question I ask you. "Do we want to do nothing? Do we want to sit and drift along to the inevitable end in such a contest of war or increased tensions?"

Pessimism never won any battle, he reminded his listeners.

But also missing from the previous conferences, said Eisenhower, was "an honest intent to conciliate, to understand, to be tolerant, to see the other fellow's viewpoint as well as we see our own." We must change the spirit in which these conferences are conducted, he urged.

Finally, there was emerging "a terrific force"—the common desire for peace on the part of the people of all the world—"to which I believe all the political leaders of the world are beginning to respond." Throughout the world prayers for peace were ascending. These prayers, said the President, could achieve "a very definite and practical result at this very moment":

Suppose, on the next Sabbath day . . . America, 165 million people of us, went to our accustomed places of worship and, crowding those places, asked for help, and by so doing demonstrated to all the world the sincerity and depth of our aspirations for peace.
This would be a mighty force.[19]

This demonstrative, symbolic aspect of Eisenhower's speeches for peace also appears to have been the aspect which most appealed to him in the "open skies" plan he dramatically unveiled at Geneva.

Again, this plan was conceived by a group more directly responsive to Eisenhower and his slant on the ways of influencing men and nations than to the Dulles line. A panel of governmental and outside experts headed by Nelson Rockefeller, then special assistant to the President on foreign policy, had been meeting at Quantico Marine base to study various positions which the United States might take at the forthcoming summit conference. The Rockefeller group's terms of reference were very much Eisenhower's: the Soviets were almost sure to offer a disarmament plan at Geneva, and the United States could not afford to appear any less interested in arms control, especially in light of the rising pacifist and neutralist sentiments in Europe. According to the journalist who was given the privilege of writing the "inside" story on the open skies plan, the problem facing the Quantico group was "how the United States could retain its nuclear power but still make it clear for all to see that its purpose was peace." [20] Both of these demands might be met, the panel decided, if the President were to revive and present in a fresh expanded version some of the ideas for mutual aerial inspection and exchange of military information which had appeared in the "control" provisions of United States arms reduction proposals, starting with the Baruch Plan. This time mutual aerial inspection would be presented as a desirable way to reduce the likelihood of surprise attack. The President received the Quantico recommendations on June 10, 1955, and read them with enthusiasm. Dulles was less enthusiastic, but not opposed. After careful discussion, the plan was held in suspension, pending developments at the conference. [21]

When Bulganin tried to attract attention to Soviet disarmament proposals on the first days of the conference Rockefeller pressed Eisenhower to seize the initiative. Eisenhower sought the counsel of Anthony Eden, who immediately saw the virtues of the proposal. It was decided that the President himself would present the idea to the conference, but exactly when was held in abeyance. [22] The search was for the best moment of maximum impact. Everybody in the United States delegation knew the President was going to make some particularly important statement, wrote James Reston from Geneva. "Photographers were alerted ahead of time for the briefing. Plans were made to publicize his remarks." [23] The situation was made for the grand gesture, and particularly for the Eisenhower personality.

As if seized by an inspiration, in the middle of reading from his

prepared remarks to the July 21 meeting of the conference, the
President took off his glasses, placed them on the table, faced Bulganin and Khrushchev, and said extemporaneously:

Gentlemen, since I have been working on this memorandum to present to this
conference, I have been searching my heart and mind for something that I could
say here that could convince everyone of the great sincerity of the United States in
approaching his problem of disarmament. I should address myself for a moment
principally to the delegates from the Soviet Union, because our two great countries
admittedly possess new and terrible weapons in quantities which do give rise in
other parts of the world, or reciprocally, to the fears and dangers of surprise attack.

I propose, therefore, that we take a practical step, that we begin an arrangement, very quickly, as between ourselves—immediately. These steps would include:

To give to each other a complete blueprint of our military establishments, from
beginning to end, from one end of our countries to the other; lay out the establishments and provide the blueprints to each other.

Next, to provide within our countries facilities for aerial photography to the
other country—we to provide you the facilities within our country, ample facilities
for aerial reconnaissance, where you can make all the pictures you choose and take
them to your own country to study; you to provide exactly the same facilities for us
and we to make these examinations—and by this step to convince the world that
we are providing as between ourselves against the possibility of great surprise attack, thus lessening danger and relaxing tension. Likewise we will make more
easily attainable a comprehensive and effective system of inspection and disarmament, because what I propose, I assure you, would be but a beginning.[24]

The Soviets, possibly sensing the gesture's emotional impact, possibly caught off guard, and quite evidently anxious to allow as much
"relaxation of tension" as possible to emerge from the conference,
held back their negative response. Contrary to their usual practice,
the Moscow papers reprinted the text of the President's speech.
Even on the sensitive question of Germany, the Soviets accepted a
rather ambiguously worded joint statement that could be interpreted, loosely, as willingness to accept the Western proposals as
terms of reference for forthcoming detailed discussions to be held
by the foreign ministers in October.

In Eisenhower's final statement at Geneva before the conference
adjourned on July 23 he told the assembly, "It has been on the
whole a good week." In his judgment, he said, "the prospects of a
lasting peace . . . are brighter. The dangers of the overwhelming
tragedy of modern war are less."[25] Sherman Adams recalls when
the White House staff welcomed the President back to Washington,

"he spoke to us with feeling that he had accomplished some real good." And the next day the President told congressional leaders that the Russians seemed to be changing their tactics toward us.[26]

The October foreign ministers' meeting confirmed for Dulles his view that there was really nothing to negotiate about, once having descended from the pleasant atmospherics of the summit to the bedrock of incompatible cold war objectives. On the matters of Germany, and European security, there was no desire on the part of the Soviets in 1955 to trade their de facto control for paper guarantees that a reunited Germany would be rearmed and "neutral" (Germany was no Austria). Nor was there enthusiasm on the part of Dulles or Adenauer to trade the presumed stability of the present German situation (resulting from a tight integration of the Federal Republic into the NATO apparatus) for the highly volatile political crosscurrents that would be loosed if reunification, under an Austria-type formula, were an immediate prospect. Schemes for local military "disengagement" were no less suspiciously viewed by the two superpowers. The Soviets were afraid of loosening their main means of keeping the satellites in check. But even if the Soviets should seriously want a mutual thinning out of forces along the Iron Curtain, from the Dulles perspective, this would seriously weaken the overall Western diplomatic position in Europe which now, more than ever, depended upon a large German military contribution to NATO. The reduction of Western military strength could only follow a general political settlement in Europe; it should never be countenanced as a means for "reducing tensions." "Open skies" was flatly rejected by the Soviets as another Western scheme for espionage; thus it never had to undergo the hard scrutiny (its effect upon the credibility of United States strategic doctrines, for example) Dulles would have felt compelled to give it were it truly negotiable.

This return to the more rigid level of East–West interaction was to Eisenhower a "disillusionment," a "grievous disappointment," which he attributed to "Soviet duplicity." But one of his purposes, he felt, had been fulfilled. "The record was established: All could now see the nature of Soviet diplomatic tactics as contrasted with those of the Free World." In addition,

peoples had been given a glowing picture of hope and, though badly blurred by the Soviets, at least the outlines of the picture remained. Moreover . . . the cordial atmosphere of the talks . . . never faded entirely. Indeed, the way was opened for some increase in intercourse between East and West—there began, between the United States and Russia, exchanges of trade exhibitions, scientists, musicians and other performers; visits were made by Mikoyan and Kozlov to the United States, and returned, by Vice President Nixon and my brother Milton, to the Soviet Union and Poland. These were small beginnings, but they could not have transpired in the atmosphere prevailing before Geneva.[27]

The Geneva episode, more than any other event during the Eisenhower presidency, illustrated Eisenhower's sourness with the coercive tools of power of the thermonuclear age and a diplomacy premised upon their readiness for use. The kind of influence he wanted to wield, personally, and as the symbol of the nation, was influence over others derived from their confidence in our goodwill and mutual affection. If the people of the world could only know our sincere purposes they would come to trust and like us—and ultimately their rulers (even in Communist countries) would follow suit. This was the underlying secret of power.

9

COMPLICATING THE PREMISES: SUEZ AND HUNGARY

The cement of fear is not so strong to hold us together as it was to bring us together.

JOHN FOSTER DULLES

While Dulles was pointing with pride at his success in deterring the Communists through the organization and skillful manipulation of the *military* ingredients of the balance of power, the Soviets and Chinese were pushing the competition into new channels. The administration, however reluctant it was to do so, would need to develop a more complex conception of the requirements for maintaining the balance.

Chou En-lai's emergence as the champion of coexistence at the Afro-Asian Conference held in Bandung, April 18–24, 1955, has been hailed by a Dulles biographer as a "notable victory for the Dulles policy of deterrence as tested at the brink of war." [1] Other analysts are more cautious about the cause and effect relationship, and point to the fact that the tapering off of Chinese pressure against Quemoy and Matsu merely *coincided* with Chou's attitude at the Bandung conference.

If Communist China's sweetness and light at Bandung was regarded as only the cowed performance of a country chastened by a brink-of-war confrontation with the United States, then the intelligence arms of the United States government must have been totally inept. There is, of course, no support for the notion that Eisenhower and Dulles were unaware of what was really going on—Dulles' self-serving rhetoric to the contrary. In fact, Dulles had conjectured to the President and leaders of Congress two weeks before Bandung that, with the Afro-Asian Conference in mind, the Communists might be trying to quiet the straits conflict so as to be accepted as a peace-loving nation.

Since 1953 the Soviets had been quite openly conducting a program of expanded trade and lending with the new nations. (China was of course not as active in the economic field; but this was still the period when, in American policy-making circles, the "Sino-Soviet Bloc" was thought to be practicing a largely coordinated strategy.) By 1956 the network of Communist bloc trade and credit agreements extended to practically every nonaligned country in the Middle East and Asia, and even to a few countries supposedly a part of the Dulles alliance system—namely, Pakistan, Iran, and Greece.

The problem was not so much one of *recognizing* the shift in Communist tactics to win friends and influence people through cooperative economic ventures instead of coercion as it was one of *what* to do about it. There was pressure within the administration as early as 1953–54, notably from mutual security administrator Harold Stassen and from Elsworth Bunker, ambassador to India, to expand United States economic assistance to additional nations, without making membership in an anti-Communist military pact the determining qualification for assistance.

However, in mid-1954, Stassen was replaced at the Mutual Security Administration by John Hollister, whose aim was to reduce foreign aid expenditures. And Dulles gave his newly appointed Under Secretary of State, Herbert Hoover, Jr., overall guidance of foreign economic policy. Innovation was effectively blocked. And orthodox premises were reasserted with even greater adamancy: namely, that economic aid to nations not militarily allied with the United States was an extravagance we could not afford; that such nations were essentially hostile to our purposes anyway, seeking to embarrass us, and to play off East against West for their own material gain; that many of these new nationalist regimes were more interested in following "Socialist" models of development, and thus had ideological leanings toward the "other side" in the cold war despite their protestations of nonalignment; and, finally, that even if we discounted these ideological incompatibilities and extended aid, most of the would-be beneficiaries lacked the administrative and technical talent, economic structure, and will to make significant gains with the additional capital.[2]

In late 1955 and early 1956, with Soviet salesmen in the under-developed areas becoming a familiar part of the international scene, Nixon and Nelson Rockefeller added their voices to Stassen's in urging a dramatic response by the United States. The same ortho-dox wall was encountered again.[3] But now the evidence of Soviet economic penetration, particularly in the Middle East, was more alarming. Dulles was specially worried, as he expressed to a Cabinet meeting on September 30, 1955, over the extent to which the "com-mercial" transactions were involving the provision of obsolete Soviet weapons to the Arab nations.[4] This time Eisenhower and Dulles asked Congress to increase the foreign aid program—then running at about $2.7 billion annually—to $4.9 billion. They also asked for limited authority, in the nature of contingency funds, to support large projects such as Nasser's Aswan Dam.

U.S. economic assistance was viewed primarily as a slush fund to entice the reluctant to "our side" in the bipolar struggle. However, the premise that the balance of power was essentially bipolar, or ought to be organized on a bipolar basis, was undermined drastically by the Suez and Hungarian crises in the fall of 1956.

The United States insistence that Israel, Britain, and France des-ist from their military intervention against Nasser was an embar-rassing eruption of the centrifugal tendencies which had long seethed beneath the surface of the Atlantic alliance. The premise that dif-ferences among the principal allies in NATO were marginal and mainly over tactical questions, involving how to implement the basic shared commitment to maintain a global balance of power against the Communist bloc, was now shattered. To differ over what was a sufficiently severe threat to require an act of war against a signifi-cant Middle Eastern power, and risk provoking direct Soviet coun-terintervention, was to differ over a central, not a marginal, issue.

By the time the Baghdad Pact efforts had reached their culmina-tion in 1955, the United States had already begun to act on assump-tions antithetical to those underlying its original sponsorship of this "northern tier" alliance system. This network of alliances was based on the premise that the goal of preventing Soviet absorption of the

Middle East was best served by building up the indigenous armies of those regimes willing to enter into formal alliance with the West. Nasser's response—the organization of a Pan-Arab alliance system and the bartering of Middle Eastern products for arms manufactured by Soviet Union satellites—shook the foundations of the existing United States approach to the Middle East.

The Soviets were seen to be leapfrogging the northern tier with such success that the administration feared Soviet absorption of the area to the south (including the oil pipelines and the Suez Canal) might occur without a single Communist soldier crossing an international boundary. And, ironically, this was happening through the very device that we had fashioned: the establishment of military-dependency relationships on the part of local regimes toward external big powers. The administration was still not ready to throw its established orientation overboard. But its policies increasingly evidenced ambivalence in attempting to demonstrate respect for the nationalisms of the area in order to avoid the local political alienation from the West which was easing the way for Soviet penetration.

This ambivalence was expressed in a series of United States moves in 1955–56 which alienated Britain and France, and contributed ultimately to their split with us over Suez. An early manifestation was the administration's embarrassed avoidance of formal identification with its own offspring, the Baghdad Pact. The British, who had joined the pact, felt betrayed by this turnabout, which Prime Minister Eden branded an American "failure to put its weight behind its friends in the hope of being popular with its foes." [5] (The British had recently agreed to liquidate their military base at Suez under the assumption that they could still focus military pressure on the area through the instrumentalities of the Baghdad Pact.) France had been disappointed throughout this period in United States unwillingness to demonstrate any sympathy for the French position in North Africa. But now, to add injury to insult, the United States in offering financial assistance to Nasser's billion-dollar development scheme, the Aswan Dam, was aiding an Egyptian regime which in turn was openly giving assistance to the Algerian rebel movement.

From Dulles' perspective, the British and French were the prisoners of their traditional colonial viewpoint as well as their current economic interests in the area. But the United States had the responsibility of keeping its eye on the ball: the East–West balance of power. If the struggle with the Communists for influence in the Middle East was assuming a new form, because of the growth of nationalism and the Soviet attempt to exploit its combustibility, then the United States would have to adjust its policies.

To our European allies, the American "adjustment" was crude, unsophisticated, and ultimately disastrous. First, the United States demonstrated a magnanimity to Nasser which the wily politician could only define as New World gullibility. Then, Eisenhower and Dulles, having finally come to the conclusion that Nasser was playing off the United States against the Soviets on the Aswan Dam project, canceled the project in such an abrupt, back-of-the-hand manner that Nasser was driven to nationalize the Suez Canal. In French and British eyes, this act—the catalyst of their subsequent military intervention—was an overreaction; it could have been avoided were Dulles not so anxious to humiliate Nasser for having taken the United States for a sucker.

Eisenhower subsequently had doubts that "we might have been undiplomatic in the way the cancellation [of Aswan financing] was handled"; and admitted that if the United States had "avoided a showdown on the issue, we would probably have deprived Nasser of a dramatic and plausible excuse for his subsequent actions affecting the Canal." But Dulles maintained that Nasser got the treatment he was asking for. [6]

But when, in response to Nasser's canal grab, others inflicted their own punishment on Egypt, Eisenhower and Dulles slapped them down. The motives of the administration in demanding that Israel, Britain, and France call off their military action were manifold and complex (indeed, so complex that the Europeans appeared to have genuinely miscalculated that the United States would support them).

On the one hand, the old policy of buying military allies through military assistance agreements had reached a point of diminishing return; and the denial of Soviet penetration into the remaining nonaligned areas required a willingess to back the national development efforts of the strident, sensitive, and unpredictable charismatic leaders around whom the new mass national parties tended to form.

On the other hand, if these a-plague-on-both-your-houses regimes

were to qualify for assistance, the relative value to our alliance partners of joining us in anti-Communist pacts was degraded.

The policies of the United States during the Suez crisis reflected
the fact that such considerations had come into play at the highest
levels of government, but also that they had not been resolved. First,
there was the wooing of the proud Egyptian nationalists from the
Soviet embrace; then came the public altercation in response to being
two-timed, with a fear of taking action that would drive Egypt and
its allies irreversibly into the arms of Russia. This last result would
disadvantageously affect the balance of power.

The British and the French, of course, cast their case *for* military
intervention in global balance of power terms and equated any exercise of allied restraint with the appeasement of Hitler prior to
1939.

The Europeans were thinking of their own economic well-being,
and equating this with the global balance of power. But Eisenhower
and Dulles felt that times had changed. Not only was the most
intense United States–Soviet competition shifting to non-European
areas, but the resilience of the European economies in the face of a
squeeze on their oil and commerce was not as enfeebled as the British and French were picturing it. "Foster felt that Anthony's fears
of being wholly deprived of Middle East oil were exaggerated," explains Eisenhower.[7] To assuage the fears of the Europeans, the
administration worked out an emergency oil pool plan by which the
French and British would be supplied by the United States and
other nations whose resources were not cut off by the Middle Eastern crisis. A permanent blocking of the Suez to French and British
commerce, and an indefinite denial to them of Middle Eastern supplies of fuel, might very well have serious consequences for the global
balance. The President and Dulles assured the Europeans that this
eventuality was a central consideration in all our efforts. The question was *how* to avoid such a consequence and, of equal importance
in United States calculations, how to do it without turning the entire Arab world against the West. "Obviously we were anxious to
sustain our continuing relations with our old and traditional friends,
Britan and France," writes Eisenhower. "But to us the situation
was not quite so simple as those two governments portrayed it."[8]

The debate between the United States and its principal allies over
the consequences of resorting to force against Nasser intensified

during the weeks leading up to the British and French military intervention. On October 5, Foreign Ministers Pinay and Lloyd met with Dulles and frankly urged the use of force, maintaining that only through bringing Nasser to his knees could Western prestige in Africa and the Middle East be restored. According to Eisenhower's account, "Foster disagreed vehemently . . . setting forth our conviction that Africa, the Middle East, and Asia would be inflamed against the West if we resorted *unnecessarily* to force." [9]

Exchanges of this nature continued between the three governments up to the last minute, when the British and French intervened with troops and planes, ostensibly to separate the Israelis and Egyptians, three days after the Israelis smashed into Egyptian positions in the Sinai. Eisenhower's last pleading cable to Eden remained unsent as on October 31 British planes based on Cyprus struck at Egyptian ports and communications centers. The cable, which Eisenhower quotes in part in his memoirs as an example of his thoughts at the time, stressed again the weight the United States was giving to the new anticolonial nationalisms:

I must say that it is hard for me to see any good final result emerging from a scheme that seems to antagonize the entire Moslem world. Indeed I have difficulty seeing any end whatsoever if all the Arabs should begin reacting somewhat as the North Africans have been operating against the French. [10]

The United States reaction, once military action had begun, was consonant with the position developed up to that time. The flat unwillingness to support the British, French, or Israeli action and the sponsorship of United Nations cease-fire and peacekeeping efforts were defended in Eisenhower's election campaign speeches, and in Dulles' addresses to the United Nations, as being required by our morally based adherence to the principles of nonaggression. However, in a letter to Winston Churchill on November 27, following the acceptance of a United Nations-controlled cease-fire, the President was more candid as to our overriding considerations:

Many months ago it became clear that the Soviets were convinced that the mere building of mighty military machines would not necessarily accomplish their purposes, while at the same time their military effort was severely limiting their capacity for conquering the world by other means, especially economic. . . . My point [in communications to Eden counseling against the use of force] was that since the struggle with Russia had obviously taken on a new tactical form, we had to be especially careful that any course of action we adopted should by its logic and justice command world respect, if not sympathy. [11]

The compelling concerns, it should be underlined, had been for the political repercussions of Western military intervention. But there also had been a certain degree of concern that the Soviets might make a direct military response. During the height of the crisis, Eisenhower and Allen Dulles, Director of the Central Intelligence Agency, were worried that the Soviets might try to stage fighter planes from Egypt. The President asked for high-altitude reconnaissance flights over Israel and Syria to see if Soviet planes and pilots had landed at Syrian bases. "Our people should be alert in trying to determine Soviet intentions," he told Dulles. "If the Soviets should attack Britain and France directly we would of course be in a major war." [12]

The President ordered the military to implement measures to "progressively achieve an advanced state of readiness." In general, however, these were regarded as precautionary signals to the Soviets that the United States would not be taken by surprise. Admiral Radford, in discussing the strategic military context with the President, observed that the Soviets would find it extremely difficult to undertake any military operations in the Middle East. "The only reasonable form of intervention would be long-range air strikes with nuclear weapons—which seems unlikely." [13]

Eisenhower was suspicious, however, that the Soviets might attempt some ruse to gain a military foothold in the area without running the high risks of direct provocation of the United States. He therefore rejected the Soviet proposal for joint police action by the Soviets and the United States as "unthinkable." The Soviets, Eisenhower told the White House staff on November 5, "seeing their failure in the satellites, might be ready to undertake any wild adventure . . . [they] are as scared and furious as Hitler was in his last days. There's nothing more dangerous than a dictatorship in that frame of mind." [14]

The existing military balance of power, based on United States superiority in strategic nuclear striking capabilities, gave the administration relative confidence that it could control the military dimensions of the conflict—largely by deterring Soviet military moves. But the military balance was seen to be largely irrelevant to the political dimensions of the conflict, and it was these political dimensions that could very seriously affect the global distribution of power.

The Suez crisis thus drove home, and made operational, the

premise that in the power struggle with the Soviets the sentiments of the new nationalist regimes were of critical importance. But as yet the policy implications were drawn primarily in the form of guidelines concerning what *not* to do for fear of alienating the non-aligned nationalists. Policies for positive action—for programs to strengthen the ability of these regimes to counter the socioeconomic sources of Communist subversion within their countries—required the acceptance of additional premises which were still unpalatable to the Eisenhower administration.

Another lesson of the crisis for the administration was that neither could the biggest weights on the Western side of the global balance of power be manipulated as if the alliance were a simple hierarchy with the United States at the apex, nor the movement of these weights be restricted to conflicts between the non-Communist and Communist worlds.

The nonhomogeneity of the opposing bloc was another prominent realization of this period. But again, the problem was what to do about it. The need to solve this problem in concrete policy terms, rather than with the sloganeering rhetoric used to cover lack of action during the Berlin uprisings of 1953, was finally forced upon the administration by the Hungarian uprising. The Eastern European crisis, too, was to have the effect of undermining the reliance by Dulles and Eisenhower on a rather limited set of coercive tools as our primary weights on the Western side of the global power balance.

Events in the Middle East complicated the premises about the utility of United States technological–military resources (reflected in the United States strategic posture, and military assistance to allies) for solidifying the anti-Communist side of the balance, and bringing this organized power more under United States direction.

The simultaneous events in Eastern Europe dramatically demonstrated the impotence of these military components for "offensive" operations, including the support of *diplomatic* efforts, to reduce the sphere of Soviet control. It is technically correct that in the rhetoric of the 1952 election Dulles and Eisenhower had explicitly disassociated their "liberation" policy from any incitements to armed revolt. "The people [in Eastern Europe] have no arms," said Dulles in a Chicago campaign speech, "and violent revolt would be futile; indeed it would be worse than futile, for it would precipitate massacre." [15] Yet implicit in Dulles' call to "activate the strains and stresses within the Communist empire so as to disintegrate it" was the premise that the Soviets might be dissuaded from a violent repression of such disintegrating tendencies out of a fear that the United States *might* feel compelled to take coercive countermeasures. And this in turn would have to be based on the premise that the balance of coercive power, on a global basis, was such that our implicit threat was credible.

The standard Republican attacks against the Roosevelt and Truman administrations were that the Democrats had been overly respectful of Soviet power. Their contention was that the Soviets could have been prevented from consolidating their control over the occupied countries of Eastern Europe if only the United States had been willing to bring its superior power to bear. This, of course, was the Republican line in hindsight only; since in the 1945–48 period no prominent Republican was advocating that the United States be willing to fight the Soviets on the East European question. But it was a tough line in 1952 despite the qualifications against the initiation of violence by the anti-Communist side. Republican campaigners around the country pointed to their platform promise to

end the negative, futile, and immoral policy of "containment" which abandons countless human beings to a despotism and Godless terrorism which in turn enables the rulers to forge the captives into a weapon for our destruction. . . . The policies we espouse will revive the contagious, liberating influences which are inherent in freedom. They will inevitably set up strains and stresses within the captive world which will make the rulers impotent to continue in their monstrous ways and mark the beginning of the end. Our nation will again become the dynamic, moral, and spiritual force which was the despair of despots and the hope of the oppressed. [16]

Campaign hyperbole or not, the premises were carried over into statements Dulles made early in his career as Secretary of State. From his new position of responsibility, in his first public address (January 27, 1953), he again sounded the clarion: "To all those suffering under Communist slavery . . . let us say: you can count on us." [17]

Stalin's death in March 1953, like the loosening of the lid of a steaming kettle, would seem to have compelled the administration to face up to the immediate *action* implications of its professed policy. Decisions made, and avoided, in the early months constituted an abandonment at the White House level of "liberation" as an operational policy, but the abandonment was concealed by the rhetoric.

Convincing pressure was brought to bear against neither the East Germans nor the Soviets to dissuade them from their violent suppression of the worker's uprisings in East Berlin and East Germany in June 1953. The allied commandants in Berlin protested "the irresponsible recourse to military force" by the Communist authorities, and demanded that "the harsh restrictions imposed upon the population be lifted immediately," but there was no significant coercive sanction implied in the context of these demands. [18]

The Secretary of State used the occasion of the Berlin uprisings to claim the correctness of his earlier writings that "the Communist structure is over-extended, over-riding, and ill-founded. It could be shaken if the difficulties that were latent were activated." But he also insisted he had been saying all along that "this does not mean an armed revolt which would precipitate a massacre." [19]

The Congress followed up with its concurrent resolution of August 3, 1953. The hollowness of its operative clause juxtaposed with its statement of conditions in the Soviet sphere came close to being a caricature of administration paralysis on this issue:

WHEREAS the Soviet regime being unable to win the allegiance of the people under its rule, knows no other method of achieving the compliance of the people to their dictatorship than by force of arms, terror, murder, imprisonment, reprisals and mass deportation; and

WHEREAS the cause of freedom cannot be contained and will eventually triumph; Now therefore, be it

Resolved, That the Congress commends and encourages the valiant struggle of these captive peoples for freedom. [20]

The only material encouragement offered by the United States during the crisis was the distribution of extra food to the East Berliners who flooded into West Berlin. The problem begging for decision, however, was whether the United States should prepare itself to act to greater effect in future contingencies of this sort, which, according to Dulles, were only just beginning.

The abandonment of "liberation" as an operational policy seems to have been made, with some consciousness, at a high level during this period. The grand-strategy task forces appointed by the White House in the spring of 1953 to explore the implications of alternative strategies and come up with recommendations included one group specifically assigned to the "liberation" alternative. In the initial terms of reference for this group the concept conveyed a "rollback" of existing Communist frontiers through political, psychological, and economic warfare programs, along with paramilitary measures. But when the reports of the groups were integrated into one document and presented to the President for approval in October 1953, no part of the "liberation" alternative was incorporated.[21] And it does not seem to have appeared again as a premise for grand-strategy planning during the Eisenhower years.

Yet the official, and officially blessed, propaganda agencies do not seem to have received the message clearly. Their role was critical in keeping alive and inflating expectations between 1953 and 1956 that the United States would somehow interpose against Soviet repressive measures during a period of major uprisings.

In the fall of 1956 the administration had neither the intention nor the capability of intervening in Poland or Hungary. It is possible that Khrushchev's willingness to strike a bargain with Gomulka over the degree of permissible Polish independence from the Soviet Communist Party was in part for fear of United States action if the Soviet Army should actually engage Gomulka's troops in battle. (Gomulka, at the climax of his dispute with the Soviet party, made it clear that if Soviet troops were brought in, as threatened, the whole nation would stand and fight. Khrushchev would have been rash to regard this merely as a bluff, since Gomulka had rallied the nation around him, including the police and the Army.)

But if fear that the administration might feel morally obligated to implement its "liberation" rhetoric was a factor in the Polish situation, it may have been removed prematurely from the Soviet calculus of risks to be incurred by violent repression of the Hungarian revolt. A series of administration statements from October 27 to October 31 seemed very anxious to indicate the United States had no intention of intervening. On November 4 the Soviets returned with 200,000 troops and 4,000 tanks to crush the revolt, reversing their October 30 decision to compromise. How the public posture of the administration was in fact read by the Soviets, and what real effect the statements, concurrent with the allied split over Suez, had on their calculation, cannot be known. It is known, however, that as far as Eisenhower and Dulles were concerned, American power was unable to affect the fate of the revolution.

Eisenhower recalls the administration's stark appraisal of the balance of usable force at the time:

> The launching of the Soviet offensive against Hungary almost automatically had posed to us the question of force to oppose this barbaric invasion.
>
> . . . I still wonder what would have been my recommendation to the Congress and the American people had Hungary been accessible by sea or through the territory of allies who might have agreed to react positively to the tragic fate of the Hungarian people. As it was, however, Britain and France could not possibly have moved with us into Hungary. An expedition combining West German or Italian forces with our own, and moving across neutral Austria, Titoist Yugoslavia, or Communist Czechoslovakia was out of the question. The fact was that Hungary could not be reached by any United Nations or United States units without traversing such territory. Unless the major nations of Europe would, without delay, ally themselves spontaneously with us (an unimaginable prospect), we could do nothing. [22]

The weight given by the administration to this essential appraisal of the military situation is corroborated by other writers. Drummond and Coblentz in their book on Dulles tell of a private State Department session at the height of the crisis at which the Secretary of State listed the following reasons against United States military intervention (theirs is a paraphrase, not a verbatim record):

> First, any attempt at limited intervention by the nearest available American troops in Southern Germany would result in their defeat and massacre by the massive Russian forces.
>
> Second, only a full-scale intervention would be feasible from a military viewpoint. It would risk a nuclear war with the Russians, and the American government was not prepared to take this risk on the Hungarian issue.
>
> Third, one of the many ghastly results of a full-scale intervention war would be the total annihilation, rather than the salvation, of Hungary, the country for whose sake the war would be undertaken. [23]

Dulles, according to Drummond and Coblentz, made clear that these considerations would equally have prevailed if the Suez crisis had not been in progress and if the Soviet Union had been the only aggressor on the world stage. [24]

In the aftermath of the Hungarian crisis the tone of administration public statements on Eastern Europe changed, as did the tenor of United States diplomacy.

There were a few lame recitals of the history of the "liberation" doctrine, recalling the exclusion of "armed revolts" as an American policy objective. But the talk of activating stresses and strains in the Soviet empire so as to bring about its disintegration disappeared from high administration statements.

The agitational content of both the official Voice of America and the unofficial Radio Free Europe (which was thought to be the main culprit in arousing expectations of American intervention) was cut down.

The most telling change was in the opening of economic relations on a selective basis with the European satellites. Using American experience with Tito since 1948 as the model, the new view was that trade and aid relationships advantageous to a particular Communist regime—Gomulka's Poland was the leading beneficiary of the new policy—could have the short-term result of lessening its need to be subservient to Moscow. In the longer term, greater economic independence in Eastern Europe might affect the global balance of power in our favor. Moreover, the side effects of demonstrating to the people of these areas that the United States had a concern for their well-being and the chance for increased exposure to Western values might indirectly act to moderate the totalitarian characteristics of these regimes.

Loud talk and the stick were, at least on an experimental basis, to give way to soft talk and the carrot as tools of power. The Soviets too, not only the satellites and Soviet-leaning neutrals, were to be approached in this vein.

This orientation again gave prominence to the Eisenhower face, as opposed to the Dulles face, of administration policy—the face associated with the President's welfare-not-warfare speech to the newspaper editors in 1953, with his Atoms for Peace proposal of the same year; and with the smiles, handshakes, and open skies of Geneva 1955.

10

SPUTNIK: NEW ATTENTION TO MATERIAL FACTORS OF POWER

I must say to you in all gravity that . . . it is entirely possible in the years ahead we could fall behind . . . unless we now . . . clearly identify the exact critical needs that have to be met. . . . This means selectivity in national expenditures of all sorts.

DWIGHT D. EISENHOWER

The two-year period from mid-1955 to mid-1957 saw United States policy makers beginning, fitfully, ambivalently to restructure their premises of power to take into account the military and political stalemate in Europe and the new force of self-assertive nationalism in the ex-colonial areas. The integration of a rearming West Germany into NATO, the 1955 Geneva summit meeting, and the Soviet suppression of the Hungarian uprising did more than reaffirm the Acheson–Dulles premise that there was no real basis for negotiation with the Soviet Union. These events also allowed for serious consideration of the hypothesis that henceforth neither the United States nor the Soviet Union had as an operational objective interference in one another's sphere of influence in Europe. The movement away from coercion to courtship in Communist bloc relations with the Bandung nations and the deference to Middle Eastern nationalism shown by the United States in opposition to the effort by Israel, Britain, and France to crush Nasser, also registered, in a halting fashion, a symbiotic mutual movement by the two superpowers away from grand strategies of coercive confrontation toward the acceptance of a mutual military standoff, and to nonmilitary modes of competition for the favor of the Third World.

But the dramatic Russian space achievements in the fall of 1957, and attempts by the Soviets to exploit diplomatically their potential military significance,[1] riveted American public and official attention, more than ever before, on the military–technological factors of power. From 1957 to 1960 the administration was increasingly pressed to answer opposition-party charges that it was letting the nation fall behind the Soviets in strategic military power *and* in the domestic economic and technological foundations for such power. The prospect of our losing in the socioeconomic competition to influence the developing nations was now also a part of the policy dialogue, and was reflected in the Mutual Security Administration's renewed emphasis on economic assistance. However, the major controversies surrounding administration decisions for the allocation of resources had to do with the best means of preventing the Soviets from surpassing us in strategic military power.

The administration's first public reactions to the Soviet orbiting of their 184-pound Sputnik I on October 4, 1957, were a model of studied nonchalance. The Soviet announcement on August 26 that they had launched an intercontinental ballistic missile had been greeted with skepticism. The satellite was more easily verified. The Soviets were congratulated for their scientific achievement, but its military implications were publicly deprecated.

In retrospect, Eisenhower recounts, more faithfully than he was willing to for the public at the time, the shock which pervaded the administration:

The size of the thrust required to propel a satellite of this weight came as a distinct surprise to us. There was no point in trying to minimize the accomplishment or the warning it gave that we must take added efforts to ensure maximum progress in missile and other scientific programs.[2]

When only a month later the Soviets launched Sputnik II, which carried a dog and many instruments, and was more than five times heavier than Sputnik I, the tremendous strides the Soviets had been making in technology required something more than sanguine recognition.

In the next few weeks science, technology, and their military applications received priority attention at the White House. The appointment of James R. Killian, president of the Massachusetts Institute of Technology, as special assistant for science and technology was announced, a new post described by the President as carrying "active responsibility for helping me to follow through in the scientific improvement of our defense." In addition, Eisenhower gave personal attention to the administrative bottlenecks in the missile program. He directed his Secretary of Defense (Neil McElroy) "to make certain that the Guided Missile Director is clothed with all the authority that the Secretary himself possesses," and announced other changes designed to eliminate overlapping and conflicting service jurisdictions in the rocket and missile programs. These actions were revealed in a major television address on science and defense four days after Sputnik II (the address had originally been scheduled for delivery a week later).

The President's main message was one of reassurance. It was right that the nation should feel concern in light of the Soviet accomplishments. Otherwise, we might become complacent and fall behind. But there was every reason for confidence that *existing* programs, with only marginal modifications, would continue to provide the nation with "both a sound defense and a sound economy." It was his conviction, he said, that "although the Soviets are quite likely ahead in some missile and special areas, and are obviously ahead of us in satellite development, as of today the over-all military strength of the Free World is distinctly greater than that of the Communist countries." He based this conclusion, said the President, on a number of important facts: we were well ahead of the Soviet Union in the nuclear field, both in quantity and quality. Our stock of nuclear weapons was sufficiently dispersed, so that if we were attacked first, "ample quantities would be available for instant retaliation." The United States missile program was well under way, with test shots of 3500 miles already accomplished; and because of our forward system of bases, ringing the Soviet Union, an intermediate-range missile would be "for some purposes, as good as an intercontinental missile." In addition to these offensive components, the nation was protected from direct attack by "a complex system of early warning radars, communication lines, electronic computers, supersonic aircraft, and ground-to-air missiles, some with atomic warheads." He also expressed confidence in the combined strength of the ground and naval forces of the United States and its allies. The essential approach of the so-called New Look for serving the nation's security was reaffirmed. It was important to maintain "selectivity" in defense spending, cautioned the President, otherwise we would neglect priorities and "ride off in all directions at once."[3]

The President's expressed confidence in the adequacy of existing premises and programs in the military sphere, which he said was "supported by trusted scientific and military advisers," was not shared at all by one group of prestigious advisers, whose secret report he had just received. The Gaither Committee report had been briefed to the President and the National Security Council on the morning of November 7. Although recommendations in the report were a direct challenge to the New Look, it was the hope of the committee that the shock of the Sputniks would be utilized by the President, somewhat as Truman had used the shock of the Communist attack in Korea, to mobilize public support in back of a larger and more diversified military program.

Though ostensibly secret, the major recommendations of the Gaither Committee, and the premises on which they were based, were known. Newspaper accounts and congressional speeches described the report in detail and leaders of the Democratic Party demanded its declassification.[4] The administration refused to release even a "sanitized" version; but among policy-oriented elites there was general agreement concerning its contents. The contemporaneous accounts have since been confirmed as being essentially accurate through comparison with Eisenhower's own account in the second volume of his memoirs.[5]

The Gaither Committee painted the United States as increasingly vulnerable to Soviet strategic power unless significant corrective action was taken, estimated as leading within a few years to annual defense expenditures of at least $8 billion above the current $38 billion. The Soviets were reported to be devoting 25 percent of their gross national product to defense, as compared with 10 percent for the United States. Thus, taking into account the greater American GNP, in absolute terms both countries were spending just about equal amounts. And on the basis of the more rapid Soviet rate of economic growth, the committee concluded that the Soviets would soon be spending more.

The committee had been charged originally with assessing the worthwhileness of a proposed $40 billion five-year program of blast-shelter construction. The committee quickly found that such evaluation required it to compare the returns expected against alternative uses of the money; and this in turn required a rather broadly based survey of the strengths and gaps in our overall military posture. It was concluded that a multibillion dollar program of population protection, whether through blast or fallout shelters (the committee did recommend the latter, but as a relatively low priority item), was not the best use of additional defense monies.

Rather, the most critical problem facing the United States, in the eyes of the Gaither Committee, was how to maintain an effective strategic retaliatory capability when, in the early 1960s, the Soviets would have an operational ICBM force. If no corrective action was taken, the Soviets, if they struck first, would be able to destroy the Strategic Air Command. The vulnerability of SAC, rather than its initial destructive capability, was the matter that should be receiving priority attention. Temporary remedies, such as increasing the number of planes on alert status, dispersal to a greater number of bases, and improvements in early warning, were recommended. An acceleration in the intermediate-range ballistic missile program was also urged. But these marginal manipulations of present programs would be insufficient to provide an adequate basis for security, warned the Gaither Committee.

Missiles with intercontinental ranges would have to become the foundation of the strategic force. This would have to be primarily designed as a "second-strike" force with attention given to its ability to survive a first strike. But the implications of such strategic planning had to be faced: namely, with survivable strategic capabilities on both sides, the non-Communist world would also need to be capable of fighting limited wars. However, for the limited-war capability to be significant, as opposed to that maintained by the Communists, the United States would have to maintain much larger ground forces and airlift capacity than planned for under the New Look.[6]

These proposals, leaked to the press, and given the dramatic context of Sputniks I and II and Soviet claims of an operational ICBM, could not have come at a worse time from the point of view of the administration. Eisenhower had failed during his first term to keep military expenditures under the New Look ceiling of $34 billion annually. Reluctantly, for the second term, a more realistic ceiling of $38 billion had been agreed upon. But the second term began amid a general price inflation, with the costs of gods and services purchased by the Defense Department rising faster than those of the economy as a whole. Defense Department officials were now telling Eisenhower that even *without* new programs, military expenditures during fiscal 1958 would rise to about $42 billion.[7] Rather than being able to balance the budget, the President would have to ask Congress to raise the statutory limit on the national debt!

In these circumstances Eisenhower was not at all pleased with the recommendations of the Gaither report, and looked more kindly on arguments which showed that with only marginal improvements in existing programs, and possibly even *more* selectivity than had yet been exercised, we could preserve the existing balance of strategic power against the Soviet Union. It also spurred his renewed interest in the Mutual Security program as a means of saving United States defense expenditures by providing for local defense capabilities with the cheaper-to-provision armies of allies.

Unlike the 1950 period, when Secretary of State Acheson helped provide the President with a grand-strategy rationale for devoting a larger portion of the nation's resources to military programs, the post-Sputnik period found the Secretary of State most effective in buttressing the President's effort to quiet the chorus of demands for greater military outlays. Eisenhower was now joined by Dulles in deprecating those who would overemphasize military factors in the balance of power. In a top-level meeting that considered the Gaither Report, Dulles noted that the committee had confined itself to military problems. "But the international struggle," he observed, "is not just military." The United States in overdevoting its resources to defense could lose the world economic competition. And, in a comment with significance for a whole set of New Look premises, Dulles pointed out that the Soviet Union had made its greatest seizures of territory and people "when only the United States had the atomic bomb."[8]

The implied denigration of the utility of United States military–strategic *superiority* in these remarks was more than polemical. Administration defense planners, fending off prods to spend more to keep ahead of the Russians in strategic striking power, had as early as 1956 accepted the essentials of mutual strategic deterrence as an operational guideline. As explained by Secretary of the Air Force Quarles in August 1956, looking a few years ahead:

[The] build-up of atomic power [on both sides of the Iron Curtain] . . . makes total war an unthinkable catastrophe for both sides.

. . .

Neither side can hope by a mere margin of superiority in airplanes or other means of delivery of atomic weapons to escape the castastrophe of such a war. Beyond a certain point, this prospect is not the result of *relative* strength of the two opposed forces. It is the *absolute* power in the hands of each, and the substantial invulnerability of this power to interdiction.[9]

Eisenhower was responsive to suggestions, from the Gaither Committee and other experts, that attention should be paid to maintaining at least this minimum deterrent against a massive Soviet strategic strike, and that hardening, mobility, and dispersal were important components of a survivable deterrent. However, he accepted the counsel that this could be done within existing expenditure levels, with possibly some alteration in priorities among various projects.

As in 1953, the President bristled at suggestions that he was sacrificing national security to economy considerations. But he adamantly refused to be stampeded by those whom he saw as converting every international crisis into larger appropriations for their pet projects:

The problem was not unfamiliar [Eisenhower recalls]. Our security depended on a set of associated and difficult objectives: to maintain a defense posture of unparalleled magnitude and yet to do so without a breakdown of the American economy.

"We must get people to understand that we confront a tough problem," I said, "but one that we can lick." We could not turn the nation into a garrison state.[10]

Although the President's first reaction to the Soviet space shots was to maintain that we were not in a space race with the Soviets, the United States space effort, centered in the Vanguard project, was accelerated on an emergency basis. The first results were none too happy, with launching pad failures televised before the entire world. Finally, on January 31, 1958, the United States entered space with the launching of Explorer I—an event which the Secretary of State hailed as having "reestablished the prestige of the United States."[11]

By the summer the race was in full momentum, with successful United States launches of Vanguard I, Explorer III, and Explorer IV. The Soviets continued to launch heavier satellites (Sputnik III, May 15, 1958, weighed 2900 pounds), but the United States could claim greater sophistication.

In the more immediately critical field of long-range ballistic missiles, the competition also began to be equalized by the end of 1958. While the 1500-mile Thors and Jupiters were readied for deployment in England, Italy, and Turkey, the administration called attention to every evidence of progress in its long-range Atlas and Titan projects. In November an Atlas was successfully tested on a 6300-mile course. The solid-propellant Minuteman ICBM entered its development phase, and the Polaris program for submarine-launched missiles was begun in earnest.

Yet the Administration had a difficult time in trying to restore confidence. During its last year and a half in office the growing body of defense-oriented intellectuals, journalists, and politicians were circulating and repeating the phrases "delicate balance of terror" and "missile gap." The thrust of the criticism directed at the administration was that it was overly complacent about the ability of the United States to maintain a retaliatory capability that was not vulnerable to destruction by a Soviet first strike. Journalists, claiming their reports were based on the estimates of high Defense Department officials, predicted a Soviet missile lead of three-to-one for the early 1960s. Administration spokesmen refused to talk "numbers" in public. They insisted that numerical estimates were not as important as the fact that there would be no "deterrent gap"—a vague concept meant to convey the notion that regardless of the forecast Soviet missile strength, the United States, while constructing its advanced ICBM force, would maintain a diversified capacity (based in part on manned bombers) to inflict unacceptable damage on the Soviet Union in a strategic exchange.

Science, technology, the rate of economic growth, and the esoteric calculus of strategic nuclear deterrence were the dominant terms with which national power was evaluated by administration defenders and critics during the later Eisenhower years. But underneath this dialogue, forces stubbornly resistant to such material factors of power continued to brew and erupt and undermine the peace on which the American pursuit of happiness depended.

11

CONDITIONED RESPONSES TO NEW CHALLENGES

What attracts attention are the aggressive probings of the Communists and the free-world reactions thereto. That gives the impression that our foreign policy consists primarily of reacting to Communist initiatives.

Nothing could be farther from the truth. The fact is that . . . we are building quietly but steadily . . . the solid foundations of an international order based upon justice and law as substitutes for force.

JOHN FOSTER DULLES

Dulles and Eisenhower, in opposing the military moves of Britain and France against Nasser in 1956, had taken a very large step in the direction of a United States foreign policy that attempted to work with, rather than against, neutralist nationalism. They expected applause from the Middle Eastern Nasserites, but instead seemed to be encountering jeers. Rather than having United States restraint interpreted by the Arabs as respect for their desire to be fully independent, United States insistence that force not be used was being defined by the Nasserites and the Soviets as the product of our fear of a Middle Eastern confrontation with the Soviets.

Now with Britain and France thoroughly humiliated in the eyes of the Arabs, and the Baghdad Pact allies more confused than ever as to United States objectives in the area, Dulles felt it essential to reassert the United States interest and intention of keeping the Middle East out of Communist hands. So instead of translating the events of 1956 into an invitation to the Soviets to cooperate in a mutual cold war "disengagement" from the Middle East, the administration redefined the area as a critical weight in the bipolar balance and reaffirmed the nation's resolve to do battle there to keep it on our side.

In his special message to the Congress on January 5, Eisenhower went even farther than had Truman in March 1947 in simplifying the United States interest in the Middle East as one of preventing this critical geopolitical region from falling under the control of the Soviets:

Russia's rulers have long sought to dominate the Middle East. That was true of the Czars and it is true of the Bolsheviks.

. . .

The reasons for Russia's interest in the Middle East are solely those of power politics. Considering her announced purpose of dominating the world, it is easy to understand her hope of dominating the Middle East.

Stressing its importance as a transportation and commercial link between the continents, and as a source of two-thirds of the world's oil deposits, the President painted the consequences of a Soviet domination of the area in global terms:

Western Europe would be endangered just as though there had been no Marshall Plan, no North Atlantic Treaty Organization. The free nations of Asia and Africa, too, would be placed in serious jeopardy. . . . All this would have the most adverse, if not disastrous, effect upon our own nation's economic life and political prospects. [1]

With the stakes this high, said the President, "Nothing is more necessary . . . than that our policy with respect to the defense of the area be promptly and clearly determined and declared." In the situation then existing "the greatest risk . . . is that ambitious despots may miscalculate. If power-hungry Communists should either falsely or correctly estimate that the Middle East is inadequately defended, they might be tempted to use open measures of armed attack." [2] The greatest insurance against the possibility of major war for control of the Middle East, contended the President, was a congressional reaffirmation of the vital American interest in the area, and a clear declaration by the Congress of its willingness to have the armed forces of the United States used to help Middle Eastern nations "requesting such aid, against overt armed aggression from any nation controlled by International Communism." [3] The President's address also contained requests for congressional authorization of economic and military assistance for regimes in the area to use for purposes of economic development and self-defense. But these were subordinate in emphasis to the request for the declaration of intent to employ United States armed forces directly against Communist encroachments in the Middle East.

The urgency of the need for a clear commitment by the United States to defend the Middle East against Communist aggression was presented in starkest outline by the Secretary of State before the congressional committees handling the proposed resolution:

Soviet ground, naval and air forces are stationed in the areas adjacent to the Middle East—Bulgaria, the Black Sea, the Ukraine, the Caucasus, and Central Asia. These Soviet forces are of a size and are so located that they could be employed at any time with a minimum of warning. This fact is nothing new. But today it takes on new implications.

There has been a change in the possible deterrent role of certain Western European nations. Until recently they provided a serious deterrent to Communist aggressions against the Middle East. But for a variety of reasons—psychological, financial, and political—this no longer meets the needs.

Another factor is evidence that the Communist rulers may now be thinking in terms of possible "volunteer" operations in the Middle East, such as the Chinese Communists perpetrated in Korea.

. . .

There is ample evidence of Communist infiltration into certain areas, particularly organized labor; and there are plottings of assassinations and sabotage to gain Communist ends. Local Communists have recently obtained small arms. . . . Arab refugees . . . are a special target for Communist propaganda.

Thus the Middle East area is at once endangered by potential military threats against which there is now no adequate deterrent, by a rapidly mounting financial and economic crisis, and by subversive efforts which seek advantage from exceptional opportunities arising out of recent events. This adds up to a new and grave danger. [4]

Dulles rejected charges that in focusing on the Communist threat he was misdirecting American efforts, which should rather be directed at the underlying causes of instability and hatred of the West. He contended that the administration was conducting a many-faceted approach to the Middle East, including an intensified program of economic assistance. The United States believed that no efforts should be spared to tackle the root causes of trouble in the area, said Dulles. "But we do not take the pessimistic view that, unless and until these problems can be solved, nothing can usefully be done to prevent the area from being taken over by international communism."[5]

Congress passed the joint resolution, henceforth referred to as the "Eisenhower Doctrine," essentially in the form and words requested by the administration. The Senate and the House of Representatives resolved

that the President be . . . authorized to cooperate with and assist any nation or group of nations in the general area of the Middle East desiring such assistance in the development of economic strength dedicated to the maintenance of national independence.

SEC. 2. The President is authorized to undertake . . . military assistance programs with any nation or group of nations of that area desiring such assistance. Furthermore, he is authorized to employ the armed forces of the United States as he deems necessary to secure and protect the territorial integrity and political independence of any such nation or group of nations requesting such aid against overt armed aggression from any nation controlled by international communism.[6]

The clumsiness of the instrument for dealing with the intricacies of the Middle East was soon apparent. But rather than asking for a refinement of congressional intention or refashioning a more flexible public rationale for its policies, the administration preferred to rest its case for its response to the unanticipated challenges of 1957 and 1958 on the familiar military containment premises of the Eisenhower Doctrine.

The first application of the military clause of the Eisenhower Doctrine could be viewed as a limited success. In April 1957 the Sixth Fleet was ordered to the eastern Mediterranean as a display of United States support for King Hussein of Jordan, then in severe political trouble following the king's dismissal of his pro-Nasser Prime Minister, Suleiman Nabulsi. Egypt and Syria were abetting the antiroyalist rebels, and to this extent the conflict was more than a purely domestic affair. With the local alignments against the king, his gambit—understandably—was to attempt to redress the balance by bringing in the cold war. King Hussein claimed that the independence and integrity of Jordan were threatened by "International Communism"; and the administration in Washington, conditioned to the clang of its own bell, poised itself to respond. In addition to the demonstrations by the Navy, $10 million of emergency aid was promptly granted to Jordan.[7] Egypt and Syria failed to intervene on the side of the rebels, nor did Israel move to preempt such intervention, which would have presented Washington with an even worse tangle. In administration circles, the rapid quieting down of the Jordanian crisis was attributed to the swiftness with which King Hussein was brought under the protective cover of the Eisenhower Doctrine.

A more plausible case of Communist exploitation of Middle Eastern instabilities occurred in Syria. The Soviets were equipping the Syrian army and, in conjunction with the visit of the Syrian Minister of Defense to Moscow in August 1957, announced large-scale credits for increased trade. The Syrians, meanwhile, were charging the United States with complicity in a plot to overthrow the government in Damascus. Three United States Embassy and attaché officials were expelled under allegations that they were involved in the subversive conspiracy. The Syrian Army chief of staff, whom Washington regarded as a political moderate, resigned, and his place was taken by a general thought to be a Communist. "The entire action was shrouded in mystery," recalled Eisenhower, "but the suspicion was strong that the Communists had taken control of the government."[8]

In the Jordanian crisis, the invocation of the Eisenhower Doctrine was simple; it involved only military demonstrations and emergency aid to a regime begging to be saved from Communist subversives. Now, however, although the Communist threat was less of a fiction, the invocation of the Eisenhower Doctrine might back the administration into a corner in which a failure by the United States to reverse the drift of political loyalties in Syria, by whatever means necessary, would undermine the credibility of United States commitments all over the world. The problem was that the means thought necessary for purging Syria of its Soviet-leaning leadership were likely to be very costly and involve risking war. Avoidance of direct United States intervention was based on the legal grounds that the Eisenhower Doctrine stipulated that United States intervention would come in response to a *request* from a threatened government, and also on the lack of sufficient information concerning the real loyalties of the Syrian regime.

To demonstrate the availability of United States military power in case of need, the Sixth Fleet was again ordered to the eastern Mediterranean; some United States aircraft were redeployed from Western Europe to Adana, Turkey; and the Strategic Air Command was alerted.[9] Deputy Under Secretary of State Loy Henderson was dispatched on a mission to sound out officials of Turkey, Lebanon, Jordan, and Iraq on their need for further military aid.

The Soviets were quick in attempting to turn the situation to their advantage. They accused the United States of planning, in collusion with Turkey, Israel, and others, to intervene militarily in Syria, citing the Henderson trip and the White House press release on his return as evidence. "As for the alleged existence of a danger that Syria will take aggressive action against neighboring states," said the Soviet Foreign Minister on September 10, "why doesn't the U.S. government raise this question in the U.N. Security Council if it has such fears?"[10] The United States was clearly being out-maneuvered, and had little recourse but to deflate the war scare that, it must be admitted, was partly of our own making.

Dulles, as dexterous in backing away from the brink as approaching it, used his September 10 press conference to signal the administration's final realization that it would do no good to make Syria the issue over which there would be a choosing up of sides in the Middle East: "There has been as yet no determination that Syria is dominated by international communism within the meaning of the Middle East resolution," explained the Secretary of State:

There have to be three findings before there is direct armed intervention by the United States. There has to be a finding by the President that one of the countries was dominated by international communism; secondly, there has to be an act of aggression by that country; third, there has to be a request by the country attacked for that aid. . . . And I might say at the present time I don't think it likely that those three things will occur.[11]

The malappropriateness of the kind of power the United States had been trying to apply in the Middle East was driven home once again during the Iraq–Lebanon crisis of 1958. Indeed the United States assistance to the panicky government in Lebanon was a dramatic example of impotence, not power.

The event which precipitated the presidential decision of July 14, 1958, to intervene with Marines in Lebanon was the bloody coup in neighboring Iraq that overnight transformed the West's only major Arab ally into a Soviet-leaning Nasserite regime, and, it was feared in those early days, possibly a Communist satellite of the Soviet Union. Yet our response—the Marine landing in Lebanon—was undertaken without any real hope of thereby undoing the coup in Iraq. Nor does it appear that the situation in Lebanon was deemed to require a direct American intervention, despite the renewed requests from pro-Western and Christian President Camille Chamoun to help him put down Nasserite threats to his regime.

In the President's public announcements on July 15, 1958, of his decision to dispatch United States Marines to Lebanon, the action was presented as a means for preserving the "independence and integrity" of Lebanon against "indirect aggression." The source of this indirect aggression was not identified, but there were strong suggestions that it was the United Arab Republic. There was no reference to "international communism" as the source of aggression, nor was the UAR painted as being "controlled by international communism." [12]

The success of the rebel movement in Lebanon would not in itself constitute an alteration in the balance of power, materially or geopolitically. But if the United States were again seen as standing by helpless, as it had in Syria, and as it had in Iraq, a profound psychological ingredient of the power of the non-Communist coalition—the reputation of its leader as one willing to take potentially costly action—would be disastrously undermined. Without a clear conception of what the consequences of action might be, it was nevertheless essential to *act*. The Dulles style was again ascendant. The face of power must exhibit the hard lines of courage and resolve. Without these, the capacity to move nations would be lost.

As it happened, the United States military intervention in Lebanon and the coordinated British intervention to help King Hussein of Jordan incurred less cost and risk than had been contemplated by Eisenhower and Dulles. The Soviets made their usual protests, sent their usual warnings to the Western allies, and made their usual appeals for a summit conference. Nasser, not at all anxious to have a Soviet presence substituted for a Western one, apparently assured the Soviets there would be no requirement for Soviet military intervention unless the Western powers invaded Iraq or the UAR. Moreover, the Egyptian leader kept his assistance to the Lebanese rebels to a minimum, and quickly threw his weight on the side of those who saw gains to be made from a political compromise inside Lebanon. The United States and the Soviet Union had little choice but to fall in behind an all-Arab resolution in the General Assembly affirming the obligation of the Arab states to respect each other's form of government, and asking the Secretary General to help arrange the withdrawal of foreign troops from Lebanon and Jordan. [13]

The administration was able to claim a major success by retrospectively defining our aims in the Lebanon affair as directed primarily toward keeping Nasser from swallowing up yet another Middle Eastern country, and by attributing Nasser's reluctance to intervene in force to the United States preemptive intervention. Eisenhower maintained that one result of the American action was a "definite change in Nasser's attitude toward the United States." Our behavior at the time of the Suez affair had presumably convinced the Egyptian that we would rarely, if ever, resort to force to support our friends or our principles. Now "he certainly had his complacency as to America's helplessness completely shattered." [14]

Eisenhower also claimed that the Lebanon operation was a demonstration—particularly to the Communists—of "the ability of the United States to react swiftly with conventional armed forces to meet small-scale, or 'brush-fire' situations." But he makes the curious point—curious in light of the difficulty he had in identifying the *source* of the "indirect aggression" in Lebanon—that he was now more than ever convinced that "if 'small wars' were to break out in several places in the world simultaneously, then we would not fight on the enemy terms and be limited to his choice of weapons. We would hold the Kremlin—or Peking—responsible for their actions and would act accordingly." [15]

However, beneath the surface of self-congratulation and reassertion of old strategic doctrine, the Middle East crises of 1957–58 exhibited to those at the helm of United States policy the inadequacy of the predominantly military approach to problems of subversion and "indirect aggression." President Eisenhower's address to the UN General Assembly on August 13, 1958, contained the harbinger of a new orientation toward the sources of effective power in, and over, the revolutionary nationalisms of the ex-colonial and developing areas. "We are living in a time," said the President, "when the whole world has become alive to the possibilities for modernizing their societies." The United States looked with favor upon this trend since "only on the basis of progressing economies can truly independent governments sustain themselves." The President proposed an Arab regional development plan, analogous to the Marshall Plan, to be formulated and managed by the Arab nations themselves, but to be financially and technically supported by the advanced nations. He was ready to pledge United States support now, contingent upon the Arab nations' ability to come up with a plan and willingness to devote their own resources to its implementation. But such an effort would not succeed, warned the President, unless there was simultaneously an elimination from the area of the chronic fear of violence and outside interference in the Arabs' internal affairs. To this end, the United States would support the creation of a United Nations peacekeeping force, so that nations of the area "will no longer feel the need to seek national security through spiralling military buildups. These lead not only to economic impotence but to war." [16]

Rather than focusing on a possible Soviet ground invasion of the Middle East, the new orientation was toward productively exploiting the nationalist ambitions of the Arab world. Economic assistance would no longer be conditioned on membership in the anti-Communist alliance system. Neutralism, and even overt anti-Western postures, would be viewed realistically in their own political contexts—as more often than not the necessary credentials for Third World political elites who would lead, rather than be swept away by, the mass demands, frustrations, and explosive anger that accompany the removal of colonial overlordship and the enfranchisement of the have-not elements of the population.

Logically, the recognition of the failure of past policies to harness the emotional steam of Third World nationalism, and the search for new tools, particularly economic ones, for channeling this energy toward tasks of internal development rather than external adventures, should have produced a revolution in United States policies for Asia, Africa, and Latin America. However, our policies in each of these areas had yet to undergo the crisis of impotence that faced us in the Middle East before the Eisenhower rhetoric of August 1958 would become the operational premises of our action programs on a global basis.

When the administration faced the prospect of a Communist takeover of Guatemala in 1954 by *political* means, Dulles' strategy, on the diplomatic front, had been to get the Latin Americans to make an exception to mutual pledges of nonintervention in the case of Communist regimes. The result of his efforts was the "Declaration of Solidarity for the Preservation of the Political Integrity of the American States Against International Communist Intervention," adopted at the Tenth Inter-American Conference in Caracas, Venezuela, in March 1954. (Guatemala voted against; Mexico and Argentina abstained.) The Caracas declaration condemned "the activities of the international communist movement as constituting intervention in American affairs," and declared

that the domination or control of the political institutions of any American State by the international communist movement, extending to this Hemisphere the political system of extra-continental power, would constitute a threat to the sovereignty and political independence of the American States, endangering the peace of America.[17]

Dulles wanted an expansion of the concept of "intervention" to cover political subversion, and this much he got. But he also wanted specific commitments for collective action against the Arbenz regime in Guatemala. In this the Latin treaty partners would not go along. They were not yet ready to define the situation in Guatemala as one in which the "international communist movement" had taken over a country. Nor were they willing to commit themselves to direct counterintervention when and if such a contingency materialized. A Communist takeover of an American republic would, in the language of Caracas, "call for a Meeting of Consultation to consider the adoption of appropriate action in accordance with appropriate treaties." But to prevent misinterpretation of what had and had not been agreed to, the Latin countries made sure the text of the resolution included the caveat that "this declaration . . . is designed to protect and not impair the inalienable right of each American State freely to choose its own form of government and economic system and to live its own social and cultural life."[18]

Unable to make use of the hemispheric collective security system for toppling the Arbenz regime, the Eisenhower administration took unilateral action—rather unconvincingly cloaked as aid to Honduras and Nicaragua under the bilateral mutual defense assistance pacts just negotiated.[19] The June 1954 invasion of Guatemala from Honduras by Castillo Armas with an army of one thousand men obviously encouraged and assisted by the United States government[20] was so successful, from a tactical point of view, that it discouraged fundamental reassessments in the White House of our approach to the growing militancy of the democratic left in Latin America. The United States apparently did have adequate power at its disposal to handle Communist insurgency or subversion in the hemisphere, if only we would follow the example shown by Dulles in the Guatemalan affair and, unsqueamishly, do what was required. "The rest of Latin America was not in the least displeased," opined Eisenhower.[21]

This being the perception at the highest levels in the administration of the dimensions of the Latin American "problem," there was only pro forma attention given to the appeals of others with ties to the President (such as Milton Eisenhower, Douglas Dillon, and Nelson Rockefeller) that we pay greater attention to the socioeconomic conditions creating a fertile field for Communist cultivation.

The shocked recognition that there was need of a deeply cutting reappraisal of U.S. foreign policy toward Latin America came with Castro's overthrow of the Batista regime on January 1, 1959, and the rapid transformation of revolutionary Fidelismo into a harsh totalitarianism as known Communists were given increased responsibility in the Cuban government. Before the year was out, the United States had subscribed $450 million to the new Inter-American Development Bank, and Washington had begun a sweeping policy review.[22]

By early 1960, recalled Eisenhower, the outcome of this policy review was still questionable, but there was "one thing we did know: Fidel Castro was a hero to the masses in many Latin American nations. They saw him as a champion of the downtrodden and the enemy of the privileged who, in most of their countries, controlled both wealth and governments." To counter the Castro *carisma* and the appeal of his programs of expropriation of foreign interests, land reform, and redistribution of the wealth, it would be necessary for the United States to pull out all the stops. The United States would have to demonstrate its concern for hemispheric development and reform in a more dramatic and convincing manner than heretofore. The personality and prestige of the President would have to be closely identified with these efforts. "I decided by early 1960," writes Eisenhower with cryptic understatement, "that the time had arrived for a presidential journey to South America."[23]

Upon his departure for South America the President addressed the nation and the world on the possible sources of misunderstanding between the United States and its neighbors to the south, and on his hopes for a better understanding of one another's purposes. The President observed that Latin Americans sometimes charged the United States with being "so preoccupied with the menace of Communist imperialism and the resulting problems of defense that . . . we neglect cooperation and progress within this hemisphere." But he hoped to make clear, said Eisenhower, that our great arsenals were for one purpose only: "the maintenance of peace, as important to Latin America as to us." And our Mutual Security Program, under which military assistance had been funneled to forty-two nations, "makes possible a forward defense for the greater security of all, including our neighbors to the South."

If the United States had been devoting a large portion of its resources to the building and maintenance of "an umbrella of military strength" for the free nations, Latin America should recognize that they, as much as anyone else, had been the beneficiaries. The balance of the speech was a self-congratulatory recitation of the extent of United States investments in Latin America, collective security commitments, and historic dedication to the principles of "nonintervention, mutual respect, and the juridical equality of states." There was only passing reference to the problems crying for new approaches—the lack of development capital, wide fluctuations in the prices for Latin American exports, the gulf between wealthy oligarchies and poor masses, and the depressed levels of health, housing, and education.[24]

When the President returned to the United States two weeks later, the tone and emphasis of his remarks had changed. He talked more about what yet needed to be done and less about what had already been accomplished; he particularly stressed the needs for development capital and more dependable export markets.

But there was still a skirting of the most touchy problem—internal socioeconomic reform, and the close association of the United States with regimes reputed to be resisting such reforms. The President's comments were indicative of the inability of his administration to revise some rather basic ideological premises:

On occasion I heard it said that economic advance in some American Republics only makes the rich richer and the poor poorer, and that the United States should take the initiative in correcting this evil. This is a view fomented by Communists but often repeated by well-meaning people.

If there is any truth in this charge whatsoever, it is not the fault of the United States. . . .

Moreover, when internal social reform is required, it is purely an internal matter.[25]

In his memoirs Eisenhower discloses that the statement just quoted apparently did not represent his latest thoughts on the relationship between social reform, economic development, and United States influence in Latin America. He claims to have perceived, while on his trip,

that the private and public capital which had flowed bounteously into Latin America had failed to benefit the masses, that the demand for social justice was still rising. . . . Upon my return home I determined to begin planning, and the plans would culminate eventually in historic measures designed to bring about social reforms for the benefit of all the peoples of Latin America.[26]

Evidently his trip had made him an ally of those within his administration, led by Douglas Dillon and Milton Eisenhower, who saw the dangers in a failure by the United States to identify itself with the forces of social reform. It was the premises of this group which now came to the fore, and provided United States policy with the first manifestation of the orientation that was to receive fuller elaboration and commitment in Kennedy's Alliance for Progress.

At Newport, on July 11, 1960, the Eisenhower face and voice were publicly identified with this new orientation: *change* is the law of life, he said. "Latin America is passing through a social and political transformation. Dictatorships are falling by the wayside. Moderate groups, seeking orderly reform, are contesting with dictators of both right and left who favor violence and authoritarianism." The choice had narrowed. It was now "social evolution or revolution." It was therefore "imperative that institutions be developed and strengthened sufficiently to permit the peoples' needs to be met through the orderly processes of change." Anticipating the proposals being prepared by Dillon for presentation to the forthcoming inter-American conference at Bogotá, the President listed those matters requiring the urgent attention of "every American nation": land reform, housing, and a wider share of the national product for the bulk of the population; the strengthening of institutions for mobilizing resources and promoting economic growth; and greater respect for human rights and the will of the people as expressed in democratic elections. "The United States will not, cannot stand aloof." [27]

These ideas were given expression in a new program drafted by Under Secretary of State Dillon, and presented to the special meeting of the economic ministers of the Organization of American States at Bogotá, September 5–13, 1960. Dillon conveyed the offer of the President, backed up by congressional authorization, of an immediate loan of $500 million for the purpose of inaugurating "a broad new social development program for Latin America." In addition to our steadily increasing programs of economic and industrial development, said Dillon, we must make a "conscious and determined effort to further social justice in our hemisphere." He brought with him to the conference a draft agreement for the establishment of an inter-American program of social and economic development envisioning

an overall improvement in the conditions of rural life, through better use of agricultural land, through better housing and community facilities, and through the modernization and improvement of education.

. . .

The agreement also envisages increased contributions to this effort by Latin American governments, particularly through the modernization of tax systems . . . and modernized credit institutions.

"In the light of existing social tensions," continued the Under Secretary to his Latin counterparts, it was obvious that "it is not enough only to construct modern factories, power plants, and office buildings." The benefits from these projects often did not reach down to the ordinary citizen quickly enough:

We must bring fresh hope to the less privileged people who make up such large portions of the populations in many countries of Latin America. We must help them to replace a hovel with a home. We must help them to acquire ownership of land and the means for its productive use.

The administering agency for the allocation of subscribed funds and for the evaluation of projects in conformity with agreed criteria would be the Inter-American Development Bank. As progress was made through joint and cooperative efforts, the United States would maintain its support with additional funds. [28]

The Act of Bogotá, adopted by the conference on September 13,

1960, incorporated the essential ideas of the Dillon proposal as they appeared in the detailed United States draft. As characterized by President Eisenhower:

"Non-intervention" had given way to a new idea—the idea that *all* American nations had an interest in ending feudalism, the vast hereditary gulf between rich and poor, the system that assured to a handful of families opulence without labor and condemned millions to near starvation without opportunity.[29]

In six short months the White House had moved a long way from its charge that such insidious ideas were "fomented by Communists," and from its insistence that social reform was "purely an internal matter."

The Latin American regimes, however, were not entirely pleased with the new shift in White House thinking. They did not mind the words about social and political reform; these were the standard ritual incantations of all Latin American politicians. What they were pressing for most—behind the scenes—they did not get: namely, guaranteed markets and price supports for their primary products.

Meanwhile the administration's policy toward Cuba, in reaction to Castro's increasing intransigence, had become steadily more rigid. Repeated attempts by the United States to conciliate Castro, to engage his regime in discussions on the diplomatic level concerning such matters as compensation for expropriated United States companies, met with repeated rebuffs and harangues. It does not appear to have been until about fifteen months after his takeover in January 1959, however, that the United States changed its approach from one of trying to reestablish normal relations to one whose goal was the destruction of the Castro regime. On March 17, 1960, President Eisenhower agreed to a CIA program for the training of Cuban exiles in Guatemala for a possible insurgency operation.[30] In July, the policy of coercion was exhibited publicly in the reduction and subsequent suspension by the United States of the importation of Cuban sugar. And just two weeks before relinquishing the presidency to John F. Kennedy, President Eisenhower broke off diplomatic relations with Cuba in retaliation for Castro's demands that the United States Embassy in Havana drastically reduce its staff. Even serious critics of the Eisenhower administration concede that the deterioration of relations after the Castro takeover was not by design of the United States, but a reaction to Castro's increasing pugnaciousness, concomitant with the solidification of his ties to the Soviet Union. Most would agree with Arthur Schlesinger that "the policy of the Eisenhower administration lacked both imagination and consistency, but it was certainly not one of purposeful hostility."[31]

Also, the White House now apparently believed its own words about the necessity of opposing dictators of the right as well as the left in Latin America. On August 20, 1960, the United States took a leading role at the San José, Costa Rica, meeting of OAS foreign ministers in the passage of a resolution condemning the Trujillo government's actions against Venezuela, and calling for a total blockade on the shipment of arms to Trujillo and a partial economic blockade. The United States promptly complied, cutting most of the Dominican Republic's sugar quota and breaking diplomatic relations with Trujillo.

When the Eisenhower administration left office, Latin America, the area of greatest lag in the appreciation of revolutionary nationalism as a significant factor in the global power balance, had become the field for the greatest experimentation with new tools and a new ideological stance for influencing global alignments.

The summer of 1958, when Washington was reviewing its Middle Eastern and Latin American policies, was the occasion for a renewal of the Chinese offshore island conflict, in the form of threatening deployments and shelling from the mainland. The administration responded as if, well conditioned by its response to the same challenge three years earlier, it knew the ropes. However, Eisenhower appeared more worried than Dulles. The Secretary of State seemed as convinced as before that a show of resolve not to give an inch to the Communists was required and would work. Eisenhower was not as confident that the risks—which he now saw as higher than in 1955—were worth the preservation of these tiny islands. The Formosa (Taiwan) Resolution, passed by Congress in the 1955 crisis, was supposed to give him discretion to defend or not to defend Quemoy and Matsu depending on his judgment as to whether their defense was necessary to the defense of Taiwan and the Pescadores. But now

Chiang Kai-shek had helped complicate the problem. Ignoring our military advice, he had for many months been adding personnel to the Quemoy and Matsu garrisons, moving them forward, nearer the mainland. By the summer of 1958, a hundred thousand men, a third of his total ground forces, were stationed on those two island groups. . . . It seemed likely that his heavy deployment to these foreward positions was designed to convince us that he was as committed to the defense of the offshore islands as he was to that of Formosa.[32]

The President was not at all pleased at being boxed in, especially in light of his reading of the changed global strategic situation, in which the Soviets had built up their nuclear striking force. "I did not doubt our total superiority," recalled Eisenhower, "but any large-scale conflict stimulated here was now less likely to remain limited to a conventional use of power." In addition to his fear that the Chinese Communists might consider *us* deterred by the prospect of a two-way nuclear war, the President took special note of the substantial buildup that had taken place over the past three years in Chinese Communist tactical air and artillery capabilities focused on the off-shore islands and Taiwan. Clearly the risks were higher than before. But this time, because of Chiang's forcing our hand, we had even less of an option not to fight even if the Communists made very limited moves directed only at the offshore islands.

Under the circumstances, Eisenhower felt that the United States had no other choice but to persuade the Communists that, regardless of the risks, we would actively intervene to throw back an assault, "perhaps using nuclear weapons." For he was still convinced that Taiwan should be kept out of Communist hands to sustain the anti-Communist balance in the Pacific area. If Taiwan fell, said an internal governmental memorandum signed by Eisenhower and Dulles,

Indonesia, Malaya, Cambodia, Laos, and Burma would probably come fully under Communist influence. U.S. positions in this area, perhaps even Okinawa, would probably become untenable, or unusable, and Japan with its great industrial potential would probably fall within the Sino-Soviet orbit. These events would not happen all at once but would probably occur over a period of a few years. The consequences in the Far East would be even more catastrophic than those which followed when the United States allowed the Chinese mainland to be taken over by the Chinese Communists.[33]

Again the strategy of looking determined, of having no alternative but to fight,[34] symbolized by deployments of the Seventh Fleet and destroyer escorts for Chiang's resupply operations, seemed to pay off. But the White House was not sure to what extent the Chinese Communist failure to test our will further was determined by the reluctance of the Soviets to give them promises of counterintervention against the United States.

At the conclusion of the 1958 crisis, Eisenhower was determined that he should not be caught in such a bind again. We would be willing to defend Taiwan, to be sure; but Dulles was instructed to make clear to Chiang that he should reduce his garrisons on the offshore islands. The United States would not be deprived of the decision as to when and if it should go to war should the Communists resume their campaign against Quemoy and Matsu. The Nationalists did thereafter reduce the size of their forces on the offshore islands, "but not to the extent I thought desirable," wrote Eisenhower.[35] It was also important, from Eisenhower's point of view, to make it clear to the rest of the world that the United States rejected force as an acceptable means of regaining the mainland. In this, the President seems to have been less concerned that the Communists would be driven to preemptive counteractions than with preventing the Communists from legitimizing their own threats of force. The whole world was watching, and for Eisenhower the opinions of mankind were to be reckoned in the balance of power.

Throughout the spring and summer of 1958, while the United States was embroiled in the Lebanon crisis in the Middle East and the offshore island confrontation with Communist China, the Soviets were gradually beginning to tighten the screws in Europe—combining administrative harassments of Western traffic to the city of Berlin with calls for a new summit conference to reduce tension.[36] The Warsaw Pact countries also renewed their campaign for a military disengagement from Central Europe.

The United States reactions were initially no more than a stale rehearsal of old positions: we would maintain our rights of access to Berlin; we would not be forced into a summit conference. If the Soviets were serious about reducing tension in Europe, they should be willing to undertake serious negotiations to reduce the sources of such tension—the most outstanding being the unnatural division of Germany. A summit conference would be useless unless there had been substantial progress made toward a resolution of the German problem at the working diplomatic levels. A basis for serious negotiations over the German question had been provided in the Geneva heads of government communiqué of July 1955—namely, reunification on the basis of free elections. But the Soviets had thus far not shown any willingness to negotiate according to those terms.

It seemed that the Soviets were evidently anxious to test the degree of new diplomatic leverage they had gained as a result of their space success and missile claims. Khrushchev announced on November 10, 1958, that the Soviet Union was committed to put an end to the Western occupation of Berlin and was ready to renounce its Potsdam Agreement obligation unilaterally if the West was unwilling to negotiate an end to the occupation status of Germany and Berlin. Then on November 27, the Soviet Union, in formal notes to the United States, Great Britain, and France, put a time limit of six months for the West to accept their proposals for a termination of the military occupation of Berlin and the "conversion of West Berlin into an independent political unit—a free city . . . demilitarized . . . that . . . could have its own government and run its own economic, administrative, and other affairs." This "free city" of West Berlin, according to the Soviet note, should be guaranteed in its status by the four powers, and possibly by the United Nations. But the immediately responsible nation would be the German Democratic Republic, in whose territory this free city would lie. Thus, in order to guarantee unhindered communications between the free city and the outside world, negotiations would have to be undertaken by the four powers with the GDR. The six-months deadline to effect such negotiations read like an ultimatum:

The Soviet Government proposes to make no changes in the present procedure for the military traffic of the USA, Great Britain, and France from West Berlin to the FRG for half a year. It regards such a period as fully sufficient to provide a sound basis for the solution of . . . Berlin's situation. . . .

If the above-mentioned period is not utilized to reach an agreement, the Soviet Union will then carry out the planned measures through an agreement with the GDR. It is envisaged that the German Democratic Republic, like any other independent state, must fully . . . exercise its sovereignty on land, water, and in the air. At the same time there will terminate all contracts still maintained between . . . the Soviet Union in Germany and . . . the USA, Great Britain, and France in questions pertaining to Berlin.[37]

The State Department's response to the Soviet proposals was, of course, negative. But this meant the United States had to face up to the likelihood that the Soviets, in six months, would carry out their threat to abrogate, unilaterally, their Berlin obligations; and this would mean, in turn, that the West would have to deal directly with the East German authorities on all questions of access to Berlin through GDR territory. By such a maneuver, the Soviets apparently hoped to force *us* to "recognize" the authority of the GDR, thereby legitimizing the division of Germany and presumably demoralizing the Federal Republic. Dulles attempted to provide some basis for sidestepping a "confrontation" by hinting in his November 26 press conference that we might have to deal with the GDR officials as "agents" of the Soviet Union.[38]

If a confrontation *were* to arise on this issue, if after the expiration of the six-months deadline the East German authorities were to attempt to exercise administrative controls on the access routes to Berlin and not let Western traffic through until we recognized their authority, what would be our response? Would we try to force our way through?

Until now, whenever the West had felt it necessary to threaten a physical challenge to Soviet administrative harassments on the access routes, the Soviets were able to cease the application of the particular procedure at issue without losing face. The Soviets would usually cover their retreat in advance by claiming that the procedures were made necessary by road repairs or some other temporary technicality.

But with a confrontation in the context of the Soviet ultimatum, the particular technical pretext might be infused for *both* sides with a high political content. The very real possibility that this time the East German officials, backed by the Soviets, would not retreat under U.S. threats to resort to physical means compelled the administration to reassess the balance of locally applicable force.

Assessing the local military situation, Eisenhower observed that it was "so lopsided as to be ridiculous." He was convinced that if the conflict entered a phase of actual military engagement, "our troops in Berlin would be quickly overrun, and the conflict would almost inevitably be global war." In a White House meeting, critics, particularly leaders of the Democratic Party in Congress, tried to paint this situation as a deficiency of New Look defense policies. But the President was no less adamant in insisting that an attempt to balance Soviet ground troops in Europe was a senseless policy:

"The Soviets are engaged in confronting the United States with a series of crises," I said. "The United States has a need for an efficient military system. But it has to be realized that if we program for the sum total of all recommendations for increasing military strength, the mounting burden would call for full mobilization," putting the nation on a wartime footing. I said that we could not have ground forces to match those that the Soviets could mobilize in Middle Europe.

. . .

I went on to say that we had no intention of opposing, with ground troops only, a full-out attack by a couple of hundred Soviet divisions, but that we would take care of the situation.

We would be in a third world war, and "for this type of war our nuclear forces were more than adequate." To Speaker Rayburn and Lyndon Johnson (then Senate majority leader) the President reiterated his confidence in United States strategic superiority: "In fact, I said, 'If we were to release our nuclear stockpile on the Soviet Union, the main danger would arise not from retaliation but from fallout in the earth's atmosphere.' " [39]

It was obviously necessary to put this confident face on this assessment of the balance of usable force; for, if we had no capabilities or intention of fighting a limited engagement for control of Berlin, the Soviets would have us over a barrel unless we could appear less fearful than they of a general nuclear war. "Possibly, we were risking the very fate of civilization on the premise that the Soviets would back down from the deadline when confronted by force," reflects Eisenhower. "Yet this to my mind was not really gambling, for if were not willing to take this risk we would be certain to lose." [40]

Yet in actual planning, as far as can be gleaned from Eisenhower's subsequent published description, Eisenhower was very careful to provide himself with alternative courses of action—even in the case of a Soviet refusal to back down. The basic contingency plan which the President approved in late January 1959, included these steps:

(a) A refusal to acquiesce in any substitution of East Germans for Soviet officials in checking the Western occupying powers movement to and from Berlin . . . ; (b) A decision to begin quiet military preparations in West Germany and Berlin prior to May 27, sufficient to be detected by Soviet intelligence but not sufficient to create public alarm; (c) Should there by any substitution of East German officials for Soviets, a small convoy with armed protection would attempt to go through, and if this convoy were stopped, the effort would be discontinued and the probe would fire only if fired upon; (d) transit would then be suspended and pressure would be brought to bear on the Soviets by publicizing the blockade and taking the matter to the United Nations Security Council and, if necessary, to the General Assembly. In these circumstances our further military preparations would be intensified by observable means such as the evacuation of dependents from West Berlin and possibly from all Germany; (e) In the event that this moral and other pressure was not sufficient, use of additional force would be subject to governmental decision.[41]

Meanwhile the West would agree, assuming the Soviets would drop their ultimatum, to engage in high-level discussions, but at the foreign ministers' level, not the summit. These discussions, according to the administration, were to provide the Soviets with the opportunity to back away from their November 1958 demands without losing face. Expectedly, the White House and State Department denied any intention to compromise Western rights in Berlin or to review their refusal to accord the Ulbricht regime any formal or symbolic recognition. Yet they did agree to the attendance of the GDR and the FRG at the forthcoming conference, though not as full participants.

Between January and May 11, 1959, the date of the convening in Geneva of the foreign ministers' meeting, the Soviets gave many indications of backing away from their rigid six-months deadline. This made it easier for the West to agree to participate in the foreign ministers' meeting, as it diluted the image of the United States being dragged to the conference table under the grip of an ultimatum.

At the start of the May meeting both sides dutifully repeated their mutually unacceptable solutions to the German question. The conference then proceeded to the Berlin issue where, uncharacteristically, the differences between the Western nations and the Soviet Union over future arrangements seemed to be narrowing. But the significant compromises were almost all on the side of the West in the direction of the Soviet position, rather than the other way around. The draft agreement handed by the Western foreign ministers to Gromyko on June 16 provided that (1) the United States, Britain, and France would limit the combined total of their forces in Berlin to 11,000 "and to continue to arm these forces only with conventional weapons." The draft agreement noted that "the Soviet Foreign Minister has made known the decision of the Soviet Government no longer to maintain forces in Berlin"; so the presumption was that only the materialization of this Soviet troop withdrawal would allow the Western governments to adhere to their limitation. On the surface this may have looked like a satisfactory quid pro quo; but even if it did come to pass, the Soviets would maintain overwhelming military superiority in the immediate environs of Berlin; (2) the "procedures" for controlling access to West Berlin, "without prejudice to existing basic responsibilities . . . may . . . be carried out by [East] German personnel" (it was stated that the access should be "free and unrestricted" and that "basic" responsibilities should remain in the hands of the four powers; but the legitimizing of operational control by the GDR was a major concession by the West); (3) measures should be taken "to avoid in both parts of Berlin activities which might either disturb public order or seriously affect the rights and interests, or amount to interference in the internal affairs, of others." (This curb on propaganda and intelligence activities cut hardest against Western operations and gave in to one of the persistent Soviet complaints against the West Berliners.)[42]

Some analysts have attributed the major concessions by the West to the fact that John Foster Dulles was no longer in charge of United States diplomacy,[43] having resigned on April 15 during the terminal phase of his illness and having died on May 24. But Secretary of State Herter was not representing a personal position. His was the administration position, worked out by high officials loyal to Dulles and Eisenhower and responsive to their recognition that the United States had coercive leverage in the Berlin situation only to the extent that the threat to initiate general nuclear war was believed by the Soviets. The point is that the administration did not *know* if it was believed by the Soviets; and in the event that it was not, lacking an advance indication of some willingness to modify our original negotiating position, concessions by the West at the time of a "confrontation" would have all the attributes of a surrender.

Paradoxically, the administration was saved the embarrassment of a Soviet acceptance of the Western proposals by Khrushchev's assumption that he could press his advantage to get even more. The Soviet leader had let the six-month "deadline" pass without turning over major Soviet Berlin responsibilities to the East Germans, explaining to Ulbricht that "conditions are not ripe as yet for a new scheme of things." Finding the West surprisingly malleable, at the June sessions in Geneva the Soviets extended their deadline for a year, but meanwhile intensified their intransigence at the conference to see if there was even more give in the Western position. This reduced the immediate risks to the Soviets of pressing the West too far too soon, while allowing for the possibility of greater rewards later.

Khrushchev must have been encouraged in the assumption that the West believed it was negotiating from a position of weakness when, before the close of the foreign ministers conference, he received a formal invitation from President Eisenhower to visit the United States. Another meeting at the summit, it will be recalled, had been built up as a *Soviet* objective; and now the United States was giving in to this also. The fruit on the tree must have appeared to be ripening fast.

Eisenhower had been consistently trying to deflect the growing popular clamor for a summit (considerably amplified by Prime Minister Macmillan's entreaties) with which the Soviets had identified themselves. As the prospect increased of a collapse of negotiations at the foreign ministers' meeting, Eisenhower reminded Macmillan of their agreement that substantive accomplishments at the foreign ministers' level would have to precede a summit conference. The President confided to his British colleague his fear that "if I surrendered on this point I would no longer have any influence with Khrushchev, who would, thereafter, consider me a 'pushover.' Indeed . . . I would myself interpret such an agreement as an exhibition of weakness." [44]

As Khrushchev pushed his campaign for a summit, Eisenhower thought he found "a device to break the stalemate" in an invitation for the Soviet leader to visit the United States on an "informal basis." This would be no "summit," there would be no "negotiations"; but an opportunity might be provided for an informal conversation on matters of mutual concern. [45]

This "informal conversation," held at Camp David, Maryland, on September 25 and 26, 1959, produced an agreement by Chairman Khrushchev to withdraw his time limit for a Berlin settlement in return for Eisenhower's agreement to a Big Four summit conference in 1960 during which the Berlin issue could be discussed. To purists in the delicate art of German-issue diplomacy, this was an American blunder. Clumsier yet was Eisenhower's press conference remark on September 28 that the Berlin "situation is abnormal." [46]

The standard Western formulation was supposed to be the *division of Germany* was abnormal.

The total breakdown of the 1960 summit, ostensibly over the U-2 reconnaissance issue, and the diplomatic hiatus produced by the impending change in United States leadership, saved the Eisenhower administration from further negotiations on the Berlin issue. Significantly, the Democrats, watching from the wings, resolved they would not let themselves be caught in a similar diplomatic confrontation without some redressing of the balance of local military capabilities in Europe.

PART IV

THE KENNEDY-JOHNSON YEARS

Too long we have fixed our eyes on traditional military needs, on armies pre-pared to cross borders, on missiles poised for flight. Now it should be clear that this is no longer enough—that our security may be lost piece by piece, country by country, without the firing of a single missile or the crossing of a single border.

JOHN F. KENNEDY

We still tend to conceive of national security almost entirely as a state of armed readiness: a vast, awesome arsenal of weaponry.

We still tend to assume that it is primarily this purely military ingredient that creates security.

We are still haunted by this concept of military hardware.

ROBERT S. MC NAMARA

12

PERCEIVED DEFICIENCIES IN
THE NATION'S POWER

Power is not a matter of arms alone. Strength comes from education, fertile acres, humming workshops and the satisfaction and pride of peoples.

DEAN RUSK

The state of the union leaves a lot to be desired, the new President informed the nation on January 30, 1961. "Our problems are critical. The tide is unfavorable. The news will be worse before it is better." With the help of more than twenty-five specialized task forces, assembled during and after the election campaign, he had been taking a close inventory of "our whole arsenal of tools," and had been discovering serious gaps—gaps which if not corrected would leave the nation with a deficiency of power for meeting the coming challenges to its very survival. And certainly without attention to the neglected components of our national power, we could not hope to advance beyond these immediate security needs and apply our resources to reduce the misery of others.

The New Frontier's initial analysis of the overall power position of the United States and those components of power requiring remedial attention offered little that was new to those who had kept up with the substance of the informed political dialogue in this country. It was essentially an amalgam of the ideas of two sets of Democrats-in-exile: the Truman Democrats and the Stevenson Democrats. What was strikingly new about the New Frontier was the vital fusion of the hardheaded cold war orientation of the first with the international idealism of the second. President Kennedy, given his practical frame of mind and wide intellectual grasp, was able to accept the analyses of both groups without offending either and fashion fresh programs in which both could see their views reflected.

The first order of business the new administration set for itself was to attend to the perceived deficiencies in the nation's power to protect its most vital interests. The gaps identified constituted a potpourri of the criticisms leveled at the Eisenhower administration by various Democratic spokesmen during the last few years.

There was the potential "missile gap" that congressional Democrats had been harping on since 1958. Kennedy joined in the charge with a major Senate speech in August of that year, systematically outlining the requirements of strategic deterrence. But the intelligence estimates handed over to the new administration on the United States–Soviet strategic balance showed the standard congressional Democratic charge of Republican neglect of the strategic arsenal to have been a vast exaggeration. Revised estimates which were being compiled on the basis of newly received information showed, if anything, a missile imbalance in our favor. Actually, the Kennedy administration found that its predecessor had done a pretty good job in translating the nation's technological resources into actual and projected instruments for the deterrence of stategic attack. The President's State of the Union message, and his defense budget message two months later, thus told of decisions to "step up" and "accelerate" the missile program, but no new concept for the strategic forces was advanced. Like their predecessors, President Kennedy and Secretary of Defense Robert McNamara accepted the planning premise for the design of the strategic force that there should be no *deterrent* gap, by which they meant that the force should be large enough to retaliate with "unacceptable damage" against an attacker or combination of attackers, even under the assumption that *we* had suffered a surprise strategic attack with all the weapons the enemy could launch. An alternative planning premise—namely, that deterence of attacks upon other areas, particularly Western Europe, required that the United States maintain a "first-strike" strategic force, capable of knocking out the Soviet's means of nuclear bombardment of the United States—appears to have been rejected in these early days and never to have been revived.* A more usable means of protecting our vital overseas interests against military attack was thought to lie in the improvement of local defense capabilities.

The perceived deficiency in the nation's ability to fight "limited," or nonnuclear wars was a rallying point for a wide spectrum of Democrats, however they might differ on other matters. The premise that this deficiency was a critical gap in the overall power of the non-Communist world as opposed to the Communist world had been standard with "security"-minded Truman exiles like Dean Acheson and Paul Nitze, both of whom had been pointing since 1949 to the dangers that would face the United States if we did not remedy this gap by the time the Soviets deployed an intercontinental nuclear capability.†

The "conventional" capabilities gap had also become a concern of Adlai Stevenson, Hubert Humphrey, and others who were urging greater United States efforts to control the arms race. This group, in the late 1950s, was increasingly pessimistic about the prospects for *dis*armament, but were strongly oriented toward "arms control" concepts that stressed a "stabilization" of the nuclear "balance of terror." They perceived that unless the non-Communist world could balance the capabilities of the Communist nations at lower levels of warfare, the United States would have to maintain an obvious superiority at the nuclear strategic level in order to dissuade the Communists from military adventures. And since the Soviets, it was believed, would never accept a position of strategic inferiority, there would be no end to the ever-more-lethal arms race unless a balance of forces could be achieved at the lower levels. As the Soviets were not about to scale down their local war capabilities, the only recourse for the West, therefore—a proposition reluctantly but realistically accepted by the Stevensonians—was to scale up.

Kennedy, characteristically, chose to sidestep the potential contradiction between the Nitze position, which urged superiority across the board, and the arms controllers' position, which sought parity

---

*However, see p. 151 for discussion of the refinements in planning premises for the strategic forces instituted by the Department of Defense under McNamara.

†See discussion of NSC-68, pp. 49–50 above. Nitze, the chief author of this prescient document, headed Kennedy's preinauguration task force on national security matters.

at all levels. He chose rather to stress their operational similarities as they came immediately to bear on the improvement of conventional capabilities.

The more precise case for the improvement of capabilities for nonnuclear warfare came by way of the Defense Department after the new administration had settled in, and it remained for the Secretary of Defense and his deputies to articulate the sharpened rationale (see the following chapter).

Analysts with an orientation toward military affairs are prone to pay most attention to the so-called Kennedy-McNamara "revolution" in military policy, as if it were the centerpiece of the Kennedy administration's foreign policy. But this is to confuse immediacy with high value. At the center of the Kennedy foreign policy was the premise that the competition between the Soviet Union and the United States was shifting to a new arena—the competition for influence over the direction of development in the poorer half of the globe; and it was with respect to this competition that we were in greatest danger of falling behind.

Kennedy's view that the Third World had now become the decisive field of engagement was shared by most of the Stevensonians, by Senate foreign policy leaders such as J. William Fulbright and Mike Mansfield, and by ever-renewable Averell Harriman. But the Europe-first emphasis remained strong among Truman State Department alumni, led by Acheson—still the idol of many seasoned top-level career diplomats in the State Department who had survived the Eisenhower–Dulles doldrums. When it came to programmatic expression of the new orientation, the burden of proof would fall on those arguing for allocating a larger proportion of our human and material resources to "containment" in the underdeveloped world. Two weeks before inauguration, the supporters of the new orientation received their most effective ammunition from an unexpected source.

Premier Khrushchev, in his historic foreign policy speech of January 6, 1961, displayed the Soviet grand-strategy rationale for focusing Soviet efforts on the underdeveloped areas: due to developments in the technology of warfare, "world wars" and "local wars" had become obsolete (they would lead to a nuclear holocaust destroying the workers as well as the capitalists) and therefore "unjust." The "just wars" of the contemporary period, the inevitable and necessary wars according to the Marxist-Leninist appraisal of the relation between social and material forces, were "wars of national liberation." The phrase was a catchall for anticolonial agitations, popular uprisings against established indigenous regimes, and actual guerrilla wars. Examples were the campaign of the FLN in Algeria for independence from France, the Castro takeover in Cuba, general efforts to mobilize the leftist forces in Latin America, and the insurgency in South Vietnam. "The Communists support just wars of this kind wholeheartedly and without reservations," said the Soviet leader. [1]

Here, in Kennedy's view, was an eminently realistic appraisal by the Soviets themselves of where their best opportunities for expansion lay. It conformed to the strategy shift attributed to the Soviets particularly by Walt Rostow—one of the first in Kennedy's circle of foreign policy advisers to make a serious pitch for a major United States counterinsurgency program. Arthur Schlesinger reports that Khrushchev's January 6 speech "made a conspicuous impression on the new President, who took it as an authoritative exposition of Soviet intentions, discussed it with his staff and read excerpts from it aloud to the National Security Council." [2]

The President was familiar with Mao Tse-tung's aphorism that power grows out of the barrel of a gun. But he knew there was more to guerrilla warfare than forming new commando-type units. He appreciated and liked to quote Mao's equally important aphorism: "Guerrillas are like fish, and the people are the water in which the fish swim. If the temperature of the water is right, the fish will thrive and multiply." [3] It was critically important to tend the temperature of the water—and as far in advance as possible.

The prophylactic aspects of counterinsurgency provided the link between those in Kennedy's advisory entourage who saw the balance of power primarily in terms of the distribution of coercive capabilities and those who emphasized the more benign components of international influence. When it was put in this frame of reference, Paul Nitze, Generals Maxwell Taylor and James Gavin, Walt Rostow, Roger Hilsman, Chester Bowles, Averell Harriman, John Kenneth Galbraith, and Adlai Stevenson could all agree on the necessity for a much larger program of long-term development aid to the many potential targets for Communist insurgency in Asia, the Middle East, Africa, and Latin America.

Having forged agreement that the purpose of foreign assistance was to affect the "temperature of the water" in the recipient countries—to assure those economic, social, and political conditions that are inhospitable to the growth of Communist movements—the next step was to assure application of foreign aid criteria designed by those with credentials in this type of oceanography. The dominant standard that had prevailed during the Eisenhower period, the degree of overt acquiescence on the part of regimes in power to the anti-Communist orientation of United States diplomacy, was now seen to be hopelessly inadequate. Kennedy accepted the need for a much more "technical"—and complicated—analysis for determining the utility of the kinds and amounts of assistance to go to any particular country. As senator and President-elect he sought the counsel of professionals, and they were not to be found within the government. He found them, again mainly New Deal–Fair Deal exiles (but professional economists all), encamped along the banks of the Charles River: Galbraith, Carl Kaysen, Edward S. Mason, David Bell, and Lincoln Gordon at Harvard; Rostow, Max Millikan, and P. N. Rosenstein-Rodan at the M.I.T. Center for International Studies.[4] Here, during the 1950s, were developed the propositions on economic assistance that became official government policy in the 1960s: namely, that operational criteria for evaluating the worth of any particular foreign aid program must be stated in terms of the socioeconomic modernization process; and the explicit objective of measures sponsored by the United States should be self-sustaining economic growth for each recipient nation. The concept and objective will be elaborated in chapter 14. For the present, it should be noted that the lack of such a concept and objective for determining the flow of foreign assistance to the poorer nations was considered by the new President as probably the most critical deficiency in the arsenal of tools by which we hoped to influence the international environment.

Kennedy's economist friends were contending that modernization and the development of greater constitutional democracy and social justice could go hand in hand; that, indeed, economic development required national planning and reliable administration, and these required the kind of political stability that was best sustained in a constitutional system providing for responsible government according to the consent of the governed. But Kennedy was also sensitive to the potential gap between the rational political-economy of his advisers and their Western-trained counterparts in the developing countries, on the one hand, and the combustible character of the "revolution of rising expectations," particularly when exploited by demagogues, on the other hand. He understood that part of the weakness of the United States in trying to influence the poorer nations from succumbing to totalitarian models for modernization was the lack of passion in the U.S. commitment to egalitarian aspects of social justice. We had been only halfhearted in our support for the kind of land reform and tax reform that would bring about the structural economic changes we knew were necessary for modernization. Our excuse, under previous administrations, had been that an open advocacy of such reform measures would constitute an interference in the domestic affairs of those smaller nations—that it was up to those nations, in their own way, however gradually, to take such social reform upon themselves without outside pressure. The effect of our self-denying ordinance, however, had been to identify the United States with status quo elements in these countries, and to provide social revolutionary elements with confirmation of their suspicion that the State Department was in cahoots with United States private interests who profited from privileges extended them by entrenched local oligarchies. It was from this concern that the Alliance for Progress evolved. As the President put it on the first anniversary of its launching:

> For too long my country, the wealthiest nation on a poor continent, failed to carry out its full responsibilities to its sister Republics. We have now accepted that responsibility. In the same way those who possess wealth and power in poor nations must accept their own responsibilities. They must lead the fight for basic reforms which alone can preserve the fabric of their own societies. Those who make peaceful revolution impossible will make violent revolution inevitable.
>
> These social reforms are at the heart of the Alliance for Progress. They are the precondition to economic modernization. And they are the instrument by which we assure to the poor and hungry, to the worker and the *campesino*, his full participation in the benefits of our development and in the human dignity which is the purpose of free societies.[5]

These are strong words. And there might be a problem in seeing that the expectations they might arouse of United States action in support of social reform did not outrun *our* ability to influence "those who possess wealth and power in poor nations." But, in Kennedy's view of where the stakes in the global struggle for power then lay, he had little choice but to reidentify the United States with the rising demands of the poor and the disenfranchised.

In order to respond to this challenge, the people of the United States would have to feel confident enough of their own productivity to allow for a diversion of effort to the needs of others. But, reported Kennedy, in his first presidential address to the Congress:

We take office in the wake of . . . three and one-half years of slack, seven years of diminished economic growth, and nine years of falling farm income.

. . .

Our recovery from the 1958 recession . . . was anemic and incomplete. Our Gross National Product never again regained its full potential. Unemployment never returned to normal levels. Maximum use of our national industrial capacity was never restored.

In short, the American economy is in trouble. The most resourceful industrialized country on earth ranks among the last in the rate of economic growth. [6]

Not only did this lagging state of our economy reduce our capacity and will to provide direct help to the poorer nations; it also reduced another very important aspect of our influence: our reputation for successful management of a largely free economy for the well-being of all our people. "We must show the world what a free economy can do," [7] admonished Kennedy, in recommending a set of economic measures to take up the slack.

Moreover, the United States was placed in a vulnerable diplomatic position with respect to other industrialized nations by its adverse balance of international payments, which Kennedy felt was partly the result of the sluggishness of the U.S. economy in competition with the dynamically expanding economies in Western Europe. "Our success in world affairs has long depended in part upon foreign confidence in our ability to pay," he said. [8] And to intimates he confided his anxiety that the payments deficit was "a club that de Gaulle and all the others hang over my head. Any time there's a crisis or a quarrel, they can cash in all their dollars and where are we?" [9]

For Kennedy, programs to "get the country moving again"—his antirecession measures of 1961, the Trade Expansion Act of 1962, and the tax cut of 1963—were as much required by global balance of power considerations as they were by considerations of domestic economic well-being. The continued productive growth of the United States was a value in itself, and to be pursued as part of the basic national interest. But it was also regarded as a means toward the more vigorous exercise of power internationally. Unlike the preceding administration, which seemed to view the requirements of domestic economic productivity as competitive with, and therefore a constraint upon, overseas commitments (we could not raise additional conventional forces because that might bankrupt us), the New Frontier felt that any gap between overseas commitments and the existing domestic economic base needed to sustain them was only an argument for expansion of the domestic economy. It was not an argument for reduced defense spending. A contraction in commitments or an unwillingness to provide the widest array of diplomatic and military tools to sustain these commitments would endanger U.S. security in the long run, and currently would further reduce America's ebbing global leadership.

Similarly, a continuance of reliance on protectionist devices in order to protect the home market from growing foreign competition would have adverse consequences on America's overall power on the international scene. "Economic isolation and political leadership are wholly incompatible," asserted Kennedy in urging the Congress to grant him the broad tariff-reducing authority requested in the administration's trade expansion bill of 1962:

If we are to retain our leadership, the initiative is up to us. The revolutionary changes which are occurring will not wait for us to make up our minds. The United States has encouraged sweeping changes in free world economic patterns in order to strengthen the forces of freedom. But we cannot ourselves stand still. If we are to lead, we must act. We must adapt our own economy to the imperatives of a changing world, and once more assert our leadership.[10]

Pervading most of President Kennedy's major recommendations to the Congress, for "domestic" no less than specifically foreign programs, was this notion of the power of *movement* itself. The key to leadership on the international scene was a creative exploitation of the currents of change. The surge by the new nations for a place in the sun, the social and economic egalitarianism of the newly enfranchised masses across the globe, and the unconquerable assertion of men that the object of government is to protect and extend the exercise of free choice—this was the very stuff of the new international politics. Leadership in this arena called for a renewal of the dynamics of the American experiment in freedom. Thus, our prestige abroad, our influence upon others—i.e., our power—were seriously weakened by the squalor of our cities, the crime on our streets, the overcrowding and low standards in many of our schools, our shortage of adequate health facilities and medical professionals, and most of all, by the "denial of constitutional rights to some of our fellow Americans on account of race." [11] We had to recapture, Kennedy felt, that pride and nerve to explore uncharted frontiers, without which the nation "would trend in the direction of a slide downhill into dust, dullness, languor, and decay." [12]

As much as to help in the spread of literacy and technical know-how, and to improve the American image abroad, the Peace Corps was directed at improving the quality of life here in the United States. The Peace Corps was typical of Kennedy's integrated and long-term approach to the problem of the nation's power, which would demand from the coming generation of leaders, no less than his own, a willingness to pay a price to secure the blessings of liberty. "A price measured not merely in money and military preparedness, but in social inventiveness, in moral stamina, and physical courage." [13]

President Kennedy's decision, after some hesitation, to stress the competitive nature of the space race with the Soviets, not just the potentials for cooperative scientific exploration, was very much a part of his concern to avoid a flabbiness of the national fiber. The scientific or potential military payoffs from trying to be "first" in space seem to have impressed him less than the intangible effects on the national spirit. Many of the welfare liberals who supported him down the line on other planks in his program cried "Moondoggle." His reply, best articulated in his September 1962 address at Rice University, reflected the New Frontier's intuition of where to probe for that critical vein of adventuresomeness which had once been, and could again be, a special source of national strength:

But why, some say, the moon? . . . And they may well ask, why climb the highest mountain? Why, thirty-five years ago, fly the Atlantic? Why does Rice play Texas? . . .

We choose to go to the moon in this decade, and do the other things, not because they are easy but because they are hard; because that goal will serve to organize and measure the best of our energies and skills. . . .

Many years ago the great British explorer George Mallory, who was to die on Mount Everest, was asked why did he want to climb it, and he said, "Because it is there."

Well, space is there, and . . . the moon and planets are there, and new hopes for knowledge and peace are there.[14]

13

ATTENDING TO THE MILITARY BALANCE

Nuclear and non-nuclear power complement eath other . . . just as together they complement the non-military instruments of policy. . . . I firmly believe that the non-nuclear buildup will—by improving and expanding the alternatives open to the Free World—reduce the pressures to make concessions in the face of Soviet threats.

ROBERT S. MC NAMARA

President Kennedy's emphasis on a variegated arsenal of power did not in any way lead him to the conclusion that, short of a major political settlement with the Communists, the United States could reduce substantially the amount of destructive power at its disposal. In fact, the thrust of his remarks on the nation's military posture, during his years in the Senate and during his presidential campaign, was that our forces were insufficient across the whole spectrum of warfare. If anything, a greater proportion of the national effort and product needed to be devoted to strengthening and maintaining our military tools than had been the case under Eisenhower.

The required diversion of resources, however, would not have to be away from other public programs, domestic or international; indeed, some of these would have to be expanded. Reallocations, to the extent they were necessary, would be away from private pursuits to public purposes. "Ask not what your country can do for you—ask what you can do for your country." Even so, the New

Frontier economists, unlike their immediate predecessors, did not believe that expanded government programs (with or without a compensatory tax increase) would slow private investment and consumption. Temporary imbalances in the federal budget, according to the new economics, were often a positive stimulus to the market economy. [1]

The assumption that efforts and resources devoted to the various aspects of the nation's power more often than not complemented each other, rather than detracted from each other, was an essential of the initial Kennedy approach toward the problem of defense spending. The notion of the nation bankrupting itself by an increase, say, of 20 percent in federal spending was regarded as an almost comical superstition. Kennedy's early instructions to Secretary of Defense McNamara reflected the newer pragmatism: "Develop the force structure necessary to our military requirements without regard to arbitrary or predetermined budget ceilings. And . . . having determined that force structure . . . procure it at the lowest possible cost." [2] The requirements came first.

Kennedy's general premises about the nation's military requirements were well developed before he assumed the presidency and were very much reflective of the "conventional wisdom" among Democrats involved in foreign policy matters. But the premises themselves were not the product of partisan politics, however they may have been invoked to that effect. They were the product of a number of strains of strategic thought that had now converged: the ideas generated by Paul Nitze and the Policy Planning Council in NSC-68, the 1960 document reflecting on the military planning implications of the soon-to-come Soviet intercontinental nuclear capability (see above, pp. 49–51); Air Force–RAND Corporation arguments for a survivable ("invulnerable") strategic retaliatory force (also favored by the Navy as the major rationale for the Polaris submarine-fired missile); the doctrine of "flexible response" put forward within the Eisenhower administration by Army Chiefs of Staff Matthew Ridgway and Maxwell Taylor in opposition to the strategic monism of Secretary of State Dulles and Admiral Radford; [3] the analysis of the possibilities for limited war in the thermonuclear age by scholars such as William Kaufmann, Robert Osgood, Henry Kissinger, and Bernard Brodie; [4] and the recommendations for a balanced defense posture appearing in the reports of the Gaither Committee and Panel

II of the Special Studies Project of the Rockefeller Brothers Fund.*

Most reputable American analysts of military policy, by the time of Kennedy's election, were in agreement on at least the following premises:

The temptation of the Soviets and the Chinese Communists to expand into new areas, and otherwise to impose their wills on the non-Communist nations, correlates inversely with their belief in the likelihood of effective counteraction by the leading non-Communist nations.

Effective counteraction, from the perspective of the Soviets and Chinese, would be that which imposes costs disproportionate to their anticipated gain.

The Soviets and Chinese determine the probability of such counteraction on the part of the leading non-Communist nations by attributing to them essentially the same calculus: counteraction will be taken by the non-Communists to the extent that the costs to the non-Communists of such action would be less than the costs of acquiescence in the Communist moves.

Deterrence being the product of these mutual assessments of one another's anticipated costs and gains, an effective strategy and military posture for the United States is one that comprises an ability to respond to each provocation with a degree of violence bearing some reasonable relationship to the value thought to be immediately at stake.

The willingness to incur the amount of destruction to the nation that would accompany total war is not a very believable deterrent threat unless it is posed as a counter to the threat of major direct aggression against U.S. home territory.

To deter provocations short of direct aggression upon the United States, we must therefore be prepared to do at least one of two things: (1) to respond effectively at levels of violence well below total war; (2) to define the costs of submitting to such provocations as intolerable as the costs we would incur in total war. The latter might work for some extraterritorial interests—for example, keeping

*See above, pp. 117–18, for recommendations of the Gaither Report. The Rockefeller Panel report, "International Security: The Military Aspect," was first published in January 1958, and then republished as a part of *Prospect for America: The Rockefeller Panel Reports* (New York: Doubleday, 1961).

Western Europe from falling to the Communists; but the Communists were unlikely to believe that every inch of territory in the non-Communist world had a comparable value. Conflicts over territorial objectives which during the cold war had developed a high emotional content for each side might be seen as involving essential psychological components of the overall balance of power. Berlin was one of these conflicts, and with less clarity so were the Chinese offshore islands. But even with respect to these values, the degree of the nation's psychological commitment could fluctuate. In such an eventuality, they might have to be surrendered to our opponents if we lacked effective capabilities for at least initial counteraction at lower levels of violence.

Thus, without capabilities across the entire spectrum of warfare, available for measured application and bearing some relation to the value at stake and the initial intensity of a provocation, firm diplomatic commitments might ultimately have to be restricted to that class of extraterritorial objectives clearly required by the global balance of power. The opportunities for enemy probes beneath the threshold of our clearly defined vital interests would grow accordingly. The non-Communist world would feel increasingly insecure as a result of the uncertainty of U.S. commitment to their defense, and the non-Communist world, including the United States, would become increasingly demoralized because of the recognition of the fickleness of these guarantees. The balance of power itself—composed in large measure of the *reputation* for power among the leading nations—would be seen to be shifting drastically against the United States. Such a situation would be ready-made for the kinds of miscalculation and irrationality that would bring on the dreaded thermonuclear holocaust.

A few concrete policy implications were drawn from these general strategic premises. U.S. strategic nuclear capability was to be designed primarily, if not exclusively, as a last resort, as an instrument of retaliation for a direct attack upon the United States. U.S. capabilities for limited war were to be expanded considerably.

But any number of questions remained, whose answers could not be logically deduced from the above: Would the downgrading of the function of the strategic nuclear forces for deterrence of limited conflicts mean that there would be no contingencies in which the

United States might be the first to use these weapons? If the strategic forces were to be primarily retaliatory weapons, what should be their targets? Under such concepts, what should be done in advance to deal with the possibility of strategic attack upon us despite our capabilities for retaliation? Did we want to limit "limited war" to nonnuclear weapons? If so, how did we propose to enforce such limitations? Did the concept of limiting war mean also localizing it? How would the European allies respond to strategies that seemed to reduce the possible costs to the superpowers of a future war over Europe *in* Europe? The President's early statements on his defense policies skirted many of these complicated issues.

In President Kennedy's March 26, 1961, special message to the Congress on the defense budget, there were a number of explicit, and definitely stressed, pledges "not to strike first in any conflict." And these statements were coupled with recommendations for improving the ability of our strategic nuclear forces to survive any attack and strike back with devastating retaliation. The President came closer in this message than any official spokesman before or afterward to enunciating a doctrine of no first use of strategic nuclear weapons, but he stopped just short of such an absolute unilateral inhibition. In light of subsequent statements by him and other members of his administration, the presumption is that his failure to dot the *i*'s and cross the *t*'s was deliberate. Kennedy undoubtedly understood the disadvantage to the West of pledging not to use its strategic nuclear forces unless the opponent did so first. If the opponent was the Soviet Union, and the battlefield was Central Europe, or, say, Iran, the Soviets would then be accorded military superiority, since the applicable forces would only be the local theater forces in which we were, by our own admission, inferior. The attribution of deliberate ambiguity to Kennedy on the matter of whether the United States would ever launch a strategic nuclear strike on the Soviets before they launched one on us is sustained by his insistence in the same early message that

our strategic arms and defense must be adequate to deter any deliberate nuclear attack on the United States *or our allies*—by making it clear to any potential aggressor that sufficient retaliatory forces will be able to survive a first strike and penetrate his defenses in order inflict unacceptable losses upon him.[5] (Emphasis added.)

How the United States might respond to a *non*-nuclear attack on friends or allies was left similarly vague. Clearly, the President was now recommending a major increase in airlift and sealift capacities, and in Army and Marine Corps personnel, in order to "increase our ability to confine our response to non-nuclear weapons." The ability to fight "limited wars" should be the "primary mission" of our overseas forces, he told the Congress.

But a potential opponent must know that "in the event of a major aggression that could not be repulsed by conventional forces," we will continue to be prepared "to take whatever action with whatever weapons are appropriate." He must know that our response will be "suitable, selective, swift, and effective."

Not unexpectedly, the emphasis on limited war was not received with enthusiasm by some of our partners in the North Atlantic Treaty Organization. Since the mid-1950s NATO military doctrine, planning, and programs had been based on the premise that any war in response to Soviet aggression upon Western Europe would be general nuclear war; there would be no serious attempt to repulse a major aggression by conventional means. To be sure, under the leadership of the NATO Supreme Commander, General Lauris Norstad, the automatic nuclear "trip wire" concept had been abandoned as too dnagerous, and in its place was put the concept of the "pause"—an initial response to an enemy probe with nonnuclear weapons to demonstrate our determination to resist, and to provide the enemy with time to decide that he had miscalculated our will; but this new doctrine of a flexible and measured response, coupled with budgetary recommendations for increasing nonnuclear capabilities, immediately aroused suspicions in Europe that in the face of the Soviet intercontinental strategic reach the Americans would regard even a war over Europe as a local war to be fought and won (or lost) in Europe without the United States being subject to devastation.[6] To the Europeans, quite naturally, a war for Europe was total war and they wanted the Soviets to know, in advance, that an attack upon Europe would be just as certainly an act of suicide as an attack upon the United States.

In the context of these growing doubts on the part of our NATO allies, the Kennedy administration sought for ways of reassuring them that nuclear weapons would continue to be available for the defense of the entire treaty area. The administration's main fear was that Germany would attempt to follow the lead of Britain and France and develop its own nuclear capability—one that while possibly too weak to serve by itself as a convincing deterrent to the Soviets would nonetheless make it virtually certain that no war over German soil would remain a limited war. Kennedy appreciated the concerns of his alliance partners, and regarded their leaders as patriotic men conscientiously pursuing their national interests. But his responsibility was to pursue United States national interest, and that seemed to require that the United States maintain control over the dimensions of conflict in the NATO area.

The campaign to reassure the European members of NATO was waged on two fronts: doctrinal elaborations of "flexible response" by McNamara and his subordinates to show that with its adoption by NATO, deterrence of Soviet provocations in Europe would be increased; and offers by the White House to "share" ownership and control of a part of the U.S. strategic arsenal.

The Berlin crisis of the spring and summer of 1961 (see below, pp. 223–33) provided the opportunity for the administration to demonstrate that a buildup of nonnuclear capabilities did not lessen Soviet fears of a general war, but, on the contrary, reinforced expectations on all sides that the United States would resist a Soviet attack with whatever force was necessary to do the job.

To deflect the growing suspicion that the United States was moving toward a "denuclearization" of Europe, the President, in his May 17, 1961, address before the Canadian Parliament, announced that the United States was now committing five Polaris nuclear missile submarines to the NATO Command "subject to any agreed NATO guidelines on their control and use." But anticipating that this would be insufficient—the submarines would still be under the operational command of the United States Navy and direct political control of the United States President—Kennedy took advantage of his Ottawa address to explicitly hold out "the possibility of eventually establishing a NATO sea-borne force, which would be truly multi-lateral in ownership and control, if this should be desired and found feasible by our Allies, *once NATO's non-nuclear goals have been achieved.*" (Emphasis added.)[7]

The purpose may have been reassurance, but imbedded as it was in the precondition of European increases in conventional fighting capabilities, the proposal for a Multilateral Force (the MLF), from its first mention, merely served to reinforce European anxieties. This early statement probably was one of the most forthright on the issue of nuclear sharing by the administration, representing its real position that flexible intra-alliance arrangements for the management of strategic nuclear weapons were possible as long as there was close agreement on strategy and tactics—this, of course, presupposing that such close agreement would be in terms of the Kennedy–McNamara doctrine, which would shift the burden of coercion in the most likely contingencies to locally applicable nonnuclear capabilities. The European members of NATO found such an ordering of priorities uncongenial: if there was to be an reorientation of NATO plans, deployments, and administrative arrangements, priority, in their view, should be given to the issue of who manages the "deterrent." First, the political control and military command arrangements of alliance strategic nuclear forces must be such as to give prior assurance that when these forces were needed for the defense of *European* soil the required decisions would be made. Then, and only then, could the Europeans agree that current arrangements for nearly automatic strategic retaliation should be supplanted by a flexible tactical fighting capability.

The MLF was a political control device and an arms control device. It was to be designed as a nonuse military system, with "fifteen fingers on the safety catch." From a military point of view, it could be considered an irrelevancy, costly only in the dollars and cents' worth of the United States contribution in vessels and weapons, but in no way compromising the essential vast arsenal of strategic nuclear power which would still remain under United States command and control. It was because of its presumed political virtues for holding Europe together that the project generated so much enthusiasm with State Department officials responsible for NATO affairs.

Following de Gaulle's veto of British entry into the European Economic Community, the State Department began more and more to use the promise of United States nuclear sharing with Europe under the MLF scheme as a goad to European efforts to form themselves into a true political union. (See below, pp. 261–69, for discussion of the role of European unity in the Kennedy foreign policy.) Statements by Secretary Rusk and Undersecretary Ball hinted at an eventual relinquishing of our absolute veto on any decision to use the weapons in the MLF *after* the Europeans had made "impressive strides" toward political unity, but this condition was never elaborated in detail.[8]

The President, while never very enthusiastic about the MLF as a military instrument or as a prod to European integration, evidently did see value in the *offer* of the NATO nuclear fleet, or anything similar anyone could come up with, as a way of deflecting, or at least deferring, West German desires to follow France into the nuclear club.[9] As it turned out, only the Germans were seriously interested; but this was not at all palatable to the White House, where there was sensitivity to the domestic and international political sentiment against anything that smacked of an exclusive military partnership between the United States and Germany, especially involving weapons of mass destruction.

Yet in the absence of an alternative for diverting the Germans and symbolizing the ideal of an "indivisible" strategic nuclear deterrent for all of NATO, the President stayed with it. The greatest pressure was directed toward the British. If they would join the scheme, it would avoid the label of a German–American enterprise, would stimulate other members of NATO to join, and, if coupled with a renunciation by Britain of its independent nuclear force, might reverse the anticipated trend toward the spread of nuclear weapons. Simultaneously, the independent nuclear weapons programs of France and Britain were deprecated by Washington, and the "credibility" of our pledges to use nuclear weapons, if necessary, on behalf of NATO's vital interests, was affirmed.

As put by Secretary of Defense McNamara, "relatively weak national nuclear forces" (he could only have been referring to those of Britain and France), when operating independently, are "dangerous, expensive, prone to obsolescence, and lacking in credibility as a deterrent." Such a force was likely to be vulnerable to destruction before being launched, and thus, "if a major antagonist came to believe there was a substantial likelihood of its being used independently, this force would be inviting a pre-emptive first strike against it." In the event of war, the Secretary contended, "the use of such a force against the cities of a major nuclear power would be tantamount to suicide, whereas its employment against significant military targets would have a negligible effect on the outcome of the conflict." [10]

By contrast, affirmed McNamara, "the United States nuclear contribution to the alliance is neither obsolete nor dispensable." And we would continue to make this power available to the defense of NATO interests on a global basis. Moreover, our strategic forces were sufficiently protected, powerful, and accurate to allow us to use them in a controlled and deliberate fashion against military targets at the outset of a general war, thus providing decision time for both sides before engaging in the ultimate folly of mutual population destruction. By spelling out this strategic concept a bit, McNamara was able to drive home his basic argument on behalf of centralized control of the nuclear capabilities of the alliance. To a June commencement audience, the Secretary of Defense breezily explained (his real intended audience was, of course, overseas):

> The U.S. has come to the conclusion that to the extent feasible, basic military strategy in a possible general nuclear war should be approached in much the same way that more conventional military operations have been regarded in the past. That is to say, principal military objectives, in the event of a nuclear war stemming from a major attack on the Alliance, should be the destruction of the enemy's military forces, not of his civilian population.
>
> The very strength and nature of the Alliance forces makes it possible for us to retain, even in the fact of a massive surprise attack, sufficient reserve striking power to destroy an enemy society if driven to it. In other words, we are giving a possible opponent the strongest imaginable incentive to refrain from striking our own cities.

In such a strategy, explained McNamara, there cannot be conflicting strategies on the part of the NATO allies, nor can there be more than one list of targets. The nuclear campaign would have to be based strictly on centralized direction and control. [11]

We were ready, and would continue to be ready, to fulfill our commitments to the alliance, whatever this might require, reiterated the Secretary of Defense, and the strategy of controlled strategic response "gives us some hope of minimizing damage" in the event of general nuclear war. But we should not try to avoid facing up to the fact—"the almost certain prospect"—that severe damage would be suffered in such a war.

Thus such a war should not be regarded as a desirable contingency under any circumstances, and we had to do all in our power to insure that lesser conflicts were controlled and stopped short of the commitment to battle of major force by either side. Because of the strength of the alliance, and the strategy we were enunciating, it was unlikely that any power would attempt to launch a massive attack, nuclear or conventional, on NATO. But for the kinds of conflicts, both political and military, most likely to arise in the NATO area, it was inappropriate, indeed unbelievable, that we should respond at the outset with nuclear weapons. The Soviet superiority in nonnuclear forces "is by no means overwhelming." Moreover, the NATO countries possessed a *potential* for successful defense even against the full Soviet nonnuclear potential. "We do not believe that if the formula, $E = mc^2$, had not been discovered, we should all be Communist slaves." [12]

If prior to these public remarks by the Secretary of Defense the Europeans only suspected that the doctrine of flexible response was to be used to justify the retention by the White House of tight control over the disposition of alliance forces, their remaining doubts were now resolved. General de Gaulle's most apocalyptic visions were seen to be not entirely fantastic ("who can say that if the occasion arises the two [the Soviet Union and the United States], while each deciding not to launch its missiles at the main enemy so that it should itself be spared, will not crush the others? It is possible to imagine that on some awful day Western Europe should be wiped out from Moscow and Central Europe from Washington"). [13]

McNamara's Ann Arbor address may well stand in the history of official strategic thought as a document of seminal theoretical importance, but as an effort at *political* persuasion it was crude, to say the least. It was as if a husband and wife were to try to solve some difference over household management by discussing what they would do in the event the two were lost at sea in a lifeboat with enough food for only one to survive. [14]

Kennedy's instinct was to avoid detailed discussion in public of remote future contingencies, but he was compelled to do so by the course of the ensuing intra-alliance debate over nuclear control. In his news conference of February 14, 1963, he was asked by a reporter whether the government was yet at the stage of making the actual decision to share command and control of nuclear forces with our European allies:

It is a very difficult area because the weapons have to be fired in 5 minutes, and who is going to be delegated on behalf of Europe to make this judgment? If the word comes to Europe or comes any place that we're about to experience an attack, you might have to make an instantaneous judgment. Somebody has to be delegated with that authority. If it isn't the President of the United States, in the case of the strategic force, it will have to be the President of France or the Prime Minister of Great Britain, or someone else. And that is an enormous responsibility. The United States has carried that responsibility for a good many years. . . .

Now, it is quite natural that Western Europe would want a greater voice. We are trying to provide that greater voice through a multilateral force. But it is a very complicated negotiation because, as I say, in the final analysis, someone has to be delegated who will carry the responsibility for the alliance.[15]

After McNamara's exposition of the need for absolute centralized control and before the statements by Kennedy, both men had come too close for their own equanimity to making decisions in a real and terribly immediate context, rather than in the hypothetical world of strategic theory. The Cuban missile crisis confirmed and refined their premises on the necessity for very tight and unified command arrangements under absolute political control, on the multiplication of risks of awful accidents of miscalculations which would accompany a spread of nuclear weapons to additional powers, and on the importance of denuclearizing the United States–Soviet competition.

It had been the President's hope that, having come so close to the fire over the issue of Soviet missiles in Cuba, the United States and the Soviet Union could cooperate in establishing a fresh tone to the language of diplomacy, resulting in the strategic nuclear balance being pushed into the background where it would still operate as a restraint-inducing factor, but not as a visible element of everyday international discourse. He had looked forward to the December 1962 meeting with Prime Minister Macmillan at Nassau as an opportunity to engage in a wide-ranging where-do-we-go-from-here dialogue in this mood of the Cuban aftermath. Undoubtedly, he would have liked the discussion of United States relations with Europe to have got back to economics—the British role in the Common Market, and a more open trading relationship—rather than defense. But out of the blue came Skybolt, a seemingly technical matter to the President when he reviewed McNamara's defense budget before preparing for his Carribean meeting.

Skybolt, a 1000-mile missile to be carried and launched from a manned aircraft, had been under close scrutiny by McNamara's economists and engineers and found wanting on "cost-effectiveness" grounds. If its $2.5 billion development costs were invested in other weapons system improvements, a greater increment to our military capabilities could be produced. The U.S. Air Force would, of course, be aggrieved at being denied its best hope of extending the role of manned strategic bombers into the missile age; but McNamara was confident of his ability to manage the generals. The Royal Air Force was also banking heavily on extending the life of its V-bombers through purchase of the American-produced missile, as agreed to by Macmillan and Eisenhower in 1960. However, McNamara's confidence that he could placate the British as well as the U.S. Air Force was a gross political miscalculation. The President, evidently unaware of the extent to which it was not only the RAF, but the British Ministry of Defense *and* the Prime Minister himself, whose prestige was staked on maintaining their "independent deterrent" with Skybolt, gave McNamara the go-ahead to work out some adjustment with British Defense Minister Thorneycroft.[16]

The "agreement" produced by the Nassau conference was a logical monstrosity and almost worthless as a military planning instrument for either government. But as a diplomatic communiqué meant to give the appearance of unity on fundamental issues where there was in fact irreconcilability, it was a masterpiece.

The only concrete agreement was that as a substitute for the Skybolt missile program, the United States would make available Polaris missiles for British submarines (the British would construct the submarines and nuclear warheads for the missiles). But lest it appear that the United States was now supporting an independent nuclear deterrent for Britain, it was provided that British forces developed under this plan will be "assigned as part of a NATO nuclear force and targeted in accordance with NATO plans" (Articles 6 and 8). These forces and at least equal United States forces "would be made available for inclusion in a NATO multilateral nuclear force" (Article 8). But in Article 7 the "multilateral force" was described as more of an end product of these endeavors, and presumably not identical with the "NATO nuclear force" described in Article 6, which was specifically designated as the command organization for the new force of Polaris carrying British submarines. Moreover, the British contribution to the so-called multilateral force was apparently to be taken back under British command in those very situations when it was most likely to be used!

The British Prime Minister made it clear that except where H.M.G. may decide that supreme national interests are at stake, these forces will be used for the purpose of international defense of the Western Alliance in all circumstances. (Article 8.)

If the British were wily in slipping that one in, the Americans could bring something home in the words of Article 10, where

the President and the Prime Minister agreed that in addition to having a nuclear shield it is important to have a non-nuclear sword. For this purpose they agreed on the importance of increasing the effectiveness of their conventional forces on a worldwide basis. [17]

Macmillan could return to London claiming a victory for the concept of an independent British deterrent, which, of course, the Labour Party was not going to let him get away with. Kennedy and McNamara could forget about Skybolt and leave the State Department to plod through the maze that might eventually lead toward some kind of NATO multilateral force.

But what would de Gaulle say? Almost as an afterthought, the conferees at Nassau extended an offer to de Gaulle to contract for Polaris missiles on terms "similar" to those offered the British. The French promptly and curtly, through their Minister of Information, rejected the offer, pointing out that France had neither the submarines nor the nuclear warheads for the Polaris missiles. Deliberately ignoring the rebuff, Kennedy instructed Ambassador Charles Bohlen to inform President de Gaulle that from our point of view all possibilities were still open for discussion. [18]

By the time Secretary McNamara appeared before the cognizant congressional committees in the early months of 1963 to defend his department's budget request for the coming fiscal year, de Gaulle had blasted the Anglo-American relationship (using Nassau as a telling exhibit) and had vetoed British entry into the Common Market. Macmillan was on the defensive for his handling of the Skybolt affair, and for his perpetuation of the fiction of nuclear independence while in fact agreeing to become even more dependent upon United States components for England's still-to-be-developed submarine force. Furthermore, Kennedy and Macmillan were both subjected to the charge that it was their ineptitude at Nassau that provoked de Gaulle into excluding Britain from the Common Market. Journalists were portraying the alliance as being in "disarray."

Many in Congress were ready to attribute all of these difficulties to the attempt by McNamara and Kennedy to shift NATO policy against the will of the Europeans, away from deterrence through the threat of all-out war to a posture that would allow substantial fighting to take place on European soil while the homelands of the Soviet Union and the United States were spared. The standard European argument that this would reduce the risks to the Soviets of an attack upon Western Europe, and thereby increase their temptation to attack, was reflected in questions thrown at the Secretary—particularly by senators and representatives who had in the past been staunch defenders of budgetary requests of the U.S. Air Force.

In defending administration policy and doctrine against these charges, McNamara went further than any previous spokesman of the government in elucidating official premises about the state of the existing military balance of power and about intentions for applying our power in future military conflicts. The intended audience for these remarks, quite clearly, was not only the congressional committee members and their constituents, but potential opponents *and* allies who might doubt our capabilities and resolve to live up to our commitments.

Under questioning, the Secretary of Defense maintained that our "current strategic superiority . . . does give us a war-winning nuclear capability, in the sense that we are confident that we can completely crush the Soviet Union if forced to do so." But he cautioned that this fact should not make us overlook the "increasing capability of the Soviet Union to make the United States pay a heavy price for such victories in terms of tens of millions of casualties."[19] Thus when he used the word "win" he meant it only in a special sense, which should be clearly understood:

We would win in the sense that their [the Soviet Union's] way of life would change more than ours [if the strategic forces of both sides were unleashed against each other] because we would destroy a greater percentage of their industrial potential and probably destroy a greater percentage of their population than they destroyed of ours.

Yet if we also calculated the destruction inflicted on Western Europe, the total amount in the West "would exceed that of the Soviet Union." His personal opinion, whichever calculation was made, was that "we cannot win a nuclear war, a strategic nuclear war, in the normal meaning of the word 'win.' "[20]

Members of Congress wanted to know if the Secretary's opinion that there could be no real winners in a strategic nuclear war meant that he were operating under a doctrine of "nuclear stalemate" or "mutual deterrence." And they pressed him to show how the United States could still deter the Soviets from attacking, especially in Central Europe, where the prize was big and the West was presumably still inferior on the ground, if we had convinced ourselves that strategic nuclear war, no matter how we tried to improve our capabilities, would still result in tens of millions of Americans dead.

McNamara rejected the terms "nuclear stalemate" and "mutual deterrence" as inaccurate descriptions of our operating strategy, which he kept insisting was to use whatever force was necessary to defend our vital interests. But he was not willing to *depend* upon our strategic forces for deterring all Soviet provocations, nor was he sufficiently certain that the Soviets would always get the message in advance concerning what interests of ours were so vital as to make us risk millions of fatalities in their defense. The important question is what enemy actions we can be certain our strategic forces will deter, and what enemy actions might require other kinds of ready responses to make deterrence work:

Now I feel quite certain that if the Soviets are rational, our strategic forces program will deter the Soviets from launching a first strike against this country.

I say that for the very simple reason that, if they did, we would utterly destroy them, and I mean completely destroy . . . the Soviet Union as a civilized nation.

Our strategic nuclear capability, however,

is not a deterrent force in the sense that it will deter all political and military aggression by the Soviets. It did not deter them from putting pressure on Berlin when we had a nuclear monopoly in the early part of the 1950's. It did not deter the Communists from invading Korea. It did not deter them from building a wall in Berlin. It did not deter the Communist . . . attempt to subvert Southeast Asia. . . . It did not deter their attempt to move offensive weapons systems into Cuba.[21]

By the time the Kennedy administration took office, he said, "it was clear that, unless we were willing to live under a constant threat of having to choose between nuclear holocaust and retreat, we required major improvements in our less-than-all-out war capabilities."[22]

The "general purpose forces," consequently, were being rapidly improved at a new high annual cost of over $19 billion. This included an expansion in manpower (the Army, with 11 divisions from the Eisenhower years, was now being maintained at 16 divisions); improved equipment and munitions; and, especially, mobility of the "tactical" forces of all three services, and the provision of new, more flexible and functionally integrated command structures, like the multiservice strike command.[23] These programs, McNamara explained, would provide the country with forces that "could, by nonnuclear means alone, counter a wide spectrum of Sino-Soviet bloc aggressions in regions other than Europe."

However, with regard to Europe, "the programmed U.S. forces, together with present forces of other NATO countries, would not be able to contain an all-out conventional Soviet attack without invoking the use of nuclear weapons."[24] It was this latter requirement—the necessity for reliance on nuclear weapons for balancing Soviet military power in Europe—that continued to give the administration trouble diplomatically and doctrinally.

Even if the Europeans were to accept the validity of flexible response, and therefore to take the "conventional option" seriously, even if they were to conscientiously fulfill their existing pledges to increase their manpower and equipment levels, still NATO could not contain and repulse a determined Soviet attempt to forcibly absorb Western Europe unless the United States was prepared to redress the local imbalance by turning the war into a global strategic war.

If this was indeed the situation in Europe, asked various senators, then why all the emphasis on strengthening nonnuclear capabilities in Europe? If the Soviets could beat us in all-out contest of nonnuclear forces, was it not rational for the Europeans to regard the American stress on the conventional option as futile, and not the best use of the West's resources? Reiterating the arguments Paul Nitze had used in connection with the Berlin buildup, McNamara explained that "the purpose of the increase in conventional forces is to deter certain *low-scale* forms of Soviet political and military aggression which they might be tempted to carry out were they not opposed by the type that are being strengthened."[25] (Emphasis added.)

The Secretary's congressional interrogators were not entirely convinced. Suppose the Soviets did try to overwhelm our admittedly inferior local forces:

SENATOR THURMOND. If we were fighting a conventional war and we were about to lose it, we would use tactical nuclear weapons, wouldn't we?

SECRETARY McNAMARA. I think a large-scale assault by the Soviet Union and its satellites forces against Western Europe would rather quickly require the use of tactical nuclear weapons in order to preserve the control of Western Europe in the hands of the West. Whether that could be limited to the use of tactical nuclear weapons is an open question in my mind.

McNamara's point was that NATO needed to be prepared to fight in this middle range of conflict between conventional war and strategic nuclear war, particularly to *deter* the Soviets from escalating to strategic nuclear war, and to that end the United States already had "thousands" of nuclear weapons in Europe. But it was important to discourage inflated expectations for the potential role of these tactical weapons in deterring, or repelling, a Soviet nonnuclear attack. As he explained to the House Armed Services Committee in his prepared remarks on the fiscal 1964 budget:

Nuclear weapons, even in the lower kiloton ranges, are extremely destructive devices and hardly the preferred weapons to defend such heavily populated areas as Europe. Furthermore, while it does not necessarily follow that the use of tactical nuclear weapons must inevitably escalate into global nuclear war, it does present a very definite threshold, beyond which we enter a vast unknown. [26]

Some senators pointed to what seemed to be an underlying premise of the whole strategy of flexible response, from its stress on a delayed resort to nuclear weapons through its notion of a city-avoiding nuclear exchange: namely, the premise of a similarly restrained Soviet Union, the notion that our opponent would accept the rules of warfare we wanted to impose.

McNamara was careful not to answer categorically these questions of likely Soviet behavior in a military conflict. Indeed, the very reason the United States was maintaining such a strong nuclear arsenal in Europe was to *deter* the Soviets from taking it upon themselves to cross the threshold into nuclear war.

With respect to the city-avoidance "option" in strategic nuclear war, again, our hope for Soviet restraint was not based on faith in their willingness to "play fair." It was based entirely on the premise that at the moment of truth, despite previous Soviet protestations to the contrary, they would still want to save the Soviet Union from complete devastation. By holding in reserve our vast potential to wipe out their cities, we would be saying: you have not yet lost

everything, but whether you do depends on your next move. Mc-
Namara was not willing to predict Soviet behavior, only to provide
Soviet leaders with an incentive to act more rationally. But this
would take advance planning, and he had to admit that, under present circumstances, neither the Soviets nor the United States had
the kind of forces-in-being that would allow them to fight a controlled strategic nuclear campaign as distinguished from an all-out
war. McNamara's most careful discourse on this complicated strategic problem was in response to a question by Congressman Leslie
Arends before the House Committee on Armed Services:

> I do think we should separate the discussion into two parts: one related to cir-
> cumstances today and the other related to possible circumstances in the future.
> Today we know that the great majority of the Soviet strategic forces, both their
> bombers and their missiles, are in soft [jargon for highly vulnerable] configurations.
> Under these circumstances it seems almost inconceivable to me that were the So-
> viets to attack the United States they would attack other than our cities, because
> they have no possibility of holding in reserve forces for later use against our cities
> with any expectation that those forces would survive a U.S. attack. . . .
> Now, turning to the future, it is possible, although I think not probable, that
> . . . Soviet attack might be directed primarily against our military installations.
> And were that to be the case, it might be advantageous to direct our retaliatory
> attack primarily against their military installations, thereby giving them an incen-
> tive to avoid an attack on our major urban areas. [27]

The point was not lost on the congressmen that McNamara's preferred strategic context seemed to be one in which both the Soviet
Union and the United States possessed highly invulnerable "reserve" strategic weapons. This meant, quite obviously, that he had
abandoned as desirable, let alone feasible, a United States first-strike
capability powerful enough to destroy the Soviet capability to inflict
unacceptable damage upon the United States.

This was precisely the premise of McNamara's statement to
Stewart Alsop in an interview published shortly after the Cuban
missile crisis. A nuclear exchange confined to military targets seemed
more possible, not less, he emphasized, "when *both* sides have a
secure second-strike capability. Then you might have a more stable
'balance of terror.' This may seem a rather subtle point, but from
where I'm sitting it seems a point worth thinking about." [28]

Senator Stuart Symington, a Secretary of the Air Force during
the Truman administration, was somewhat disturbed by Mc-
Namara's interview with Alsop, "I presume that means the sooner

they [the Soviets] have a second strike capability the better. That was the impression I got from the article." McNamara denied that this was a correct interpretation of his remarks. But it was necessary for us to adjust to the new emerging strategic situation in which the Soviets were in fact moving toward a relatively invulnerable missile force. The point of his comment to Alsop, he explained, was that "we should not assume that our position is worsening as they do that. As a matter of fact, it will put less pressure on them to carry out a pre-emptive strike in a period of crisis, and this is to our advantage." [29]

Senator Margaret Chase Smith was worried that the suggestion that we resign ourselves to the coming condition of essential strategic parity with the Soviets was likely to have "serious long-term effects on our national will, our courage and our determination to resist attacks on our way of life."

McNamara did grant that the questions raised by his predictions of increasing Soviet strategic power, and by the administration's response to this new strategic reality, did go "straight to the fabric of national will and determination." But what was it that sustained this national will and determination and most important, the perception by our opponents of our willingness to stand by our commitments? It was our *total* power as a nation, and this was not simply the measurement of our strategic nuclear effectiveness in all-out war as opposed to theirs (the ultimate unlikely contingency which, regardless of relative "margins of superiority," would be disastrous to both sides). The overall balance of power was what really mattered, and

I don't believe that any time in our lifetime they will reach parity with us in the total power of their system versus ours; particularly, I believe that if you include as an element of that power, the attraction and influence and effectiveness of our political system, but even for the moment excluding that and dealing only with their economic and military power, I don't foresee any situation in which they will reach parity with us. [30]

It was the Secretary of Defense's responsibility to speak in precise terms about the military balance and to elaborate the sometimes esoteric strategic doctrine that guided his budgetary decisions on the military posture. But his discussions of those matters were often revealingly matter-of-fact and dryly abstract, far removed from the everyday crisis preoccupations of the administration.

Yet those discussions were an essential background factor to diplomacy, and it was on occasion necessary for the President himself to bring them forward as a reminder to friends and foes alike that Americans were prepared, if driven to it, to pay the highest price in defending their values. The address the President proposed to deliver before the Dallas Citizens' Council on November 22, 1963, was to be one of these occasions. He was going to talk in detail about the various components of the nation's power, "ranging from the most massive deterrents to the most subtle influences."

This need to stay militarily powerful was only a part of the role, thrust upon us "by destiny rather than by choice," to be "the watchman on the walls of world freedom." But, the President was going to tell his audience at Dallas, to be truly worthy of the power and responsibility that was inevitably ours, we must "exercise our strength with wisdom and restraint," never in the pursuit of aggressive ambitions, and always in the pursuit of peace and goodwill toward men. "For as was written long ago: 'Except the Lord keep the city/the watchman waketh but in vain.' "[31]

14

NEW TOOLS FOR THE
NEW ARENA:
OPPORTUNITIES AND OBSTACLES

*To bring real economic progress to . . . the less developed world will require
. . . a fresh approach—a more logical, efficient, and successful long-term plan—
for American foreign aid. . . . I strongly urge its enactment . . . in full awareness of the many eyes upon us—the eyes of other industrialized nations, awaiting
our leadership for a stronger united effort—the eyes of our adversaries, awaiting
the weakening of our resolve in this new area of international struggle—the eyes
of the poorer peoples of the world, looking for hope and help, and needing an
incentive to set realistic long-range goals—and finally, the eyes of the American
people, who are fully aware of their obligations to the sick, the poor, and the
hungry, wherever they may live.*

JOHN F. KENNEDY

President Kennedy approached the problem of the economic underdevelopment of large portions of the non-Communist world with
a fervor reserved for no other element of public policy. Fresh innovation in policy rationale and programs were possible with respect
to the Third World.

The Truman and Eisenhower administrations had been concerned about those segments of mankind who, while not Communist, were by no means securely aligned in opposition to the spread
of Communism nor inclined toward the kinds of socioeconomic development able to sustain democratic political systems. But this con-

cern had been marginal to the Truman and Eisenhower foreign policies; Kennedy made it a central pillar of his.

The approach of the Truman administration to the economically backward societies had been primarily one of benevolent protection: we would help them help themselves in their own way through a low-key program of technical assistance; and we would organize whatever coercive responses were required to prevent the Communists from taking over these countries.

The Eisenhower administration had been pessimistic about significantly affecting socioeconomic conditions in the Third World, and concentrated on lining up existing regimes as military allies. As allies they could qualify for military assistance to build up their own military forces which could be used as forward barriers against attempts by the Communist nations to extend their realm, and as instruments of domestic social control.

In his pre–White House years, Kennedy turned most of his fire on the Eisenhower–Dulles approach to the Third World. The Middle East, particularly, had been the scene of "grave errors":

> We overestimated our own strength and underestimated the force of nationalism. . . . We gave our support to regimes instead of to people—and too often we tied our future to the fortunes of unpopular and ultimately overthrown governments and rulers.
>
> We believed that those governments which were friendly to us and hostile to the Communists were therefore good governments—and we believed that we could take unpopular policies acceptable through our own propaganda programs.
>
> . . .
>
> We must talk in terms that go beyond the vocabulary of the Cold War—terms that translate themselves into tangible values and self-interest for the Arabs as well as ourselves.
>
> It is not enough to talk only in terms of guns and money—for guns and money are not the basic need in the Middle East. It is not enough to approach their problems on a piecemeal basis. It is not enough to merely ride with a very shaky *status quo*. It is not enough to recall the Baghdad Pact or the Eisenhower Doctrine—it is not enough to rely on The Voice or America of the Sixth Fleet. These approaches have failed. [1]

For "terms that go beyond the vocabulary of the Cold War" Kennedy went to his Charles River economist friends (see above, p. 182). They were putting together a doctrine on the relationship between the structure of societies, the availability of external capital, and the modernization process. This was no academic exercise. Most of the economists had either been government officials, were now consultants to the government, or were participants in overseas technical assistance programs of private foundations. They ere primarily concerned with applications, and most particularly with affecting the foreign assistance program of the United States government. There were the expected intellectual disagreements among learned men of an inexact science; but there was a notable convergence on a set of propositions with important implications for concrete policy. [2]

The objective of assistance to the underdeveloped nations should be to help them achieve a condition in which economic growth is a normal and self-sustaining process within a democratic political system.

The attainment of a condition of self-sustaining growth for most of the underdeveloped nations will require fundamental modifications of the economic *and* noneconomic structures of their societies.

Procrastinating the fundamental societal modifications until popular demands for change have risen to a high pitch will likely lead to violent upheavals followed by totalitarian rule.

The required structural modifications can be accomplished peacefully if they are begun early, and are translated into carefully coordinated attacks on the particular roadblocks to modernization found in each nation.

Frequently occurring roadblocks are: (1) a lack of sufficient agricultural productivity beyond the subsistence level (sufficient productivity is an important source of investment capital formation); (2) a lack of sufficient investment in social overhead projects (transportation and communication networks especially); (3) the lack of indigenous specialists able to administer these development tasks and to train the rural population in modes of greater productivity; (4) the lack of literacy, which does not allow for the absorption of new values (including population control) and techniques by the population; and (5) the lack of sufficient commitment on the part of elites to greater economic egalitarianism and political democracy.

Since the need for various expensive projects will arise in advance of the market for them, the government in these countries, not the free market, will have to be the major determiner of investment during the early stages of economic growth.

But in many of these countries those people who run the government, who would be responsible for formulating and carrying out national development plans and negotiating for foreign assistance, are themselves very much attached to the existing social structure. Even in those nations where the top political leadership is personally committed to basic structural alterations of their societes (this is particularly likely in the new postcolonial societies where mass nationalist parties were the instruments of the independence movements), their continued authority may rest on the support of those groups in the society who still command the bulk of resources in the countryside, and who continue to staff the civil and military bureaucracies. These latter groups, for material and psychological reasons, may be reluctant to bring on the restructuring that would have to accompany true modernization.

As a source of desired investment capital and foreign exchange, the United States, other developed nations, and international development authorities can exercise some leverage over the otherwise sluggish pace of structural change by making performance in attacking the critical roadblocks to modernization the foremost criterion for continued economic assistance.*

Military or ideological alignment with the United States should not be a prominent criterion for the flow of assistance.

Many of the scholars involved in generating these propositions were now brought into the government—on the White House staff, the State Department, and as ambassadors to important underdeveloped countries (Galbraith as ambassador to India, Lincoln Gordon as ambassador to Brazil). From their point of view, and from Kennedy's, they had practically a carte blanche opportunity to reorganize the entire foreign assistance program, its personnel as well as its operational guidelines. All foreign assistance would henceforth come under the direction of one agency whose tasks and functions could be defined afresh. Moreover, a large new foreign aid program

---

* The Foreign Assistance Act of 1961 gave legislative sanction to the injection by the President of this criterion when negotiating development loans. The President, in the language of the act, was to take into account "the extent to which the recipient country is showing a responsiveness to the vital economic, political, and social concerns of its people, and demonstrating a clear determination to take self-help measures." (Title I, Sec. 201, *Foreign Assistance Act of 1961*, 87th Congress, 1st session, August 30, 1961.)

for Latin America was to be funded. In Latin America, because it had been largely ignored in the aid programs of the previous administrations, the new premises would have a proving ground, unencumbered by existing programmatic commitments.

In back of the dry premises of political economy was the competition between the West and the Communists for influence over the mode of modernization in the Third World. This, to the Kennedy administration, was the arena of most active, international competition, signaled by Khrushchev's emphasis on "wars of national liberation" (see above, pp. 153–54). The Soviets and the Chinese, deterred at the strategic level, and presumably also at the level of overt local aggression across international boundaries, were now seen to be exerting their most intense pressure beneath these levels. It was as if the United States had been involved with its major adversaries in a gross game of cold war *de*escalation. U.S. effectiveness in this game depended on an ability to block their gains at the next lower level, while sustaining the barriers already erected at the higher levels.

We were still involved in a competition for global strategic ascendancy. But the tactical requirements of success at this current low level demanded the utmost subtlety and skill, since the objects of the power competition by both sides were national societies undergoing rapid transitions in socioeconomic structure and values, where the only predictably persistent value was the emotionally charged commitment to *self*-determination. The most damaging epithet politicians in these countries could throw at one another was that of being some other nation's pawn.

President Kennedy's appreciation of, even empathy with, the highly insecure political base of the leaders of the developing nations was in back of his attempt to expunge cold war rhetoric, as much as possible, from the public rationale for foreign assistance. He responded positively to the suggestions from Walt Rostow, David Bell, and others to tone down the anti-Communist appeals appearing in the first draft of his March 1961 foreign aid message.[3] From the outset, however, he was the focal point of the tension between two "constituencies" of the foreign assistance program: the overseas recipients of assistance (whose Washington champions were the development economists in Kennedy's advisory entourage); and, opposing them, the neo-isolationist elements in the American electorate, in portions of the business community, and in segments of organized labor whose congressional brokers have traditionally coalesced to prune administration foreign assistance requests not carrying a simple "essential for national security" rationale. The President did have a basic national security rationale; but it was far from simple. He did see the need to ride with, rather than against, a good deal of the political turbulence in the recipient nations, even when it assumed anti-American, quasi-Marxist overtones; but he was too shrewd a domestic politician to assume that his tactical international apoliticism would get the needed appropriations out of Congress.

The contrary ideological requirements of the overseas recipients as opposed to the domestic provisioners bedeviled Kennedy throughout his Presidency, and explains the observed ambivalence in the public rationale of his foreign assistance program—with one tendency represented by the Alliance for Progress, and the other by the Clay report.

To be sure, the Alliance for Progress was very much a part of the grand strategy of the Kennedy administration for frustrating Communist penetration of the Third World. But this aspect of the Alliance's rationale was consciously underplayed in the public rhetoric.

As revealed by Arthur Schlesinger, Jr. (who was heavily involved as a consultant to Kennedy on Latin American affairs), the cold war was a pervasive part of the discussions in the White House on the Latin American aid program. Kennedy's interregnum task force on Latin America (chaired by Adolph Berle*) emphasized the Communist threat, describing it as "more dangerous than the Nazi-Fascist threat [to Latin America] of the Franklin Roosevelt period. . . ." The objective of the Communists, said the task force report, was "to convert the Latin American social revolution into a Marxist attack on the United States itself." As this revolution was "inevitable and necessary," the way to counter the Communist threat was to "divorce" the Latin American social transformation "from connection with and prevent its capture by Communist power politics." The United States needed to put itself clearly on the side of

---

* The interregnum task force on Latin America, in addition to Berle, included Richard Goodwin, Lincoln Gordon, Teodoro Moscoso, Arturo Morales-Carrion, Robert Alexander, and Arthur Whitaker.

the indigenous "democratic-progressive movements . . . pledged to representative government and economic reform (including agrarian reform) and resistance to entrance of undemocratic forces from outside the hemisphere." The truly democratic social reform groups "should be known to have the good will and support of the United States, just as every Communist group in Latin America is known to have the support of Moscow or of Peiping." It was also necessary for the United States to develop its capabilities for paramilitary and military counterinsurgency operations and to be prepared to offer effective military support to progressive regimes such as Betancourt's in Venezuela. But we should not try to "stabilize the dying reactionary situations."[4]

The aspect of the Berle report which surfaced in the full-blown Alliance for Progress was the insistence that the United States offer a hemisphere-wide long-range economic development plan, based on the kind of coordinated national planning urged by the Harvard and M.I.T. economists. This was the type of action required to avoid the spread of violent insurrectionary movements in Latin America and also to give credibility to United States professions of being on the side of those working for social justice and democracy.

After the Kennedy inauguration the momentum for a new departure to Latin American policy accelerated. Berle was appointed to head a reconstituted task force on Latin America in the Department of State, where he and Thomas Mann, the new Assistant Secretary for Inter-American Affairs, labored to give the earlier ideas operational content. One of their recommendations was that the President make a major address on United States policy toward Latin America, proposing a ten-year program of continental development.

Richard Goodwin, a member of the interregnum task force, Kennedy's staff man on Latin America during the campaign, and now a member of the White House staff, was given the responsibility for a first draft of the address. Goodwin responded to the challenge by gathering in all the ideas then adrift in Washington on what the content of a fresh approach toward Latin America ought to be. The time was ripe for major emphasis on Latin America (thanks especially to Castro's increasing alignment with Moscow); and there was a growing appreciation, cultivated by the President, that an economic development orientation in our foreign assistance program was our best long-term weapon of counterinsurgency in the hemisphere.

The problem was how to sell the economic propositions at home and in Latin America without injecting the cold war rationale, which would alienate the reformist elements in Latin America with whom we were trying to align ourselves.

The "solution," as exhibited in the President's proposal of March 13, 1961, for "a vast new ten-year plan for the Americas," was a coupling of the structural approach to economic development that had been advanced by the Charles River economists with the revolutionary idealism of Thomas Jefferson and Simón Bolívar. Kennedy christened the *Alianza* as the contemporary expression of the American revolution (North and South) for the rights of man:

Our nations are the product of a common struggle—the revolt from colonial rule.

.   .   .

The revolutions which gave us birth ignited, in the words of Thomas Paine, "a spark never to be extinguished." . . . we must remember that . . . the revolution which began in 1776 and in Caracas in 1811 . . . is not yet finished. Our hemisphere's mission is not yet completed. *For our unfulfilled task is to demonstrate to the entire world that man's unsatisfied aspiration for economic progress and social justice can best be achieved by free men working within a framework of democratic institutions.* [5]

The concrete steps "to complete the revolution of the Americas" were to be presented in detail at a ministerial meeting of the Inter-American Economic and Social Council. But the President's speech gave a preview of the socioeconomic standards which his administration would insist be applied in evaluating a potential recipient's commitments to the ideals of the unfinished hemispheric revolution. If the Latin American nations were ready to do their part to "mobilize their resources, enlist the energies of their people, and modify their social patterns so that all, and not just a privileged few, share in the fruits of growth," then the United States, "for its part, should help provide resources of a scope and magnitude sufficient to make this bold development plan a success." [6] Political freedom, said the President, had to accompany material progress, but political freedom must be accompanied by social change:

For unless necessary social reforms, including land and tax reform, are freely made, unless we broaden the opportunity of all our people, unless the great mass of Americans share in increasing prosperity, then our alliance, our revolution, our dream, and our freedom will fail. [7]

This approach, which was to be elaborated five months later at Punta del Este, was a product of the analysis of the New Frontiersmen that the weakest chink in the armor of the non-Communist world was the phenomenon of the entrenched oligarchy holding on to privilege in the face of rising demands for social justice. The approach of the Alliance for Progress was also based on the administration's fresh premises about which components of United States power were most appropriate for affecting the course of Third World development. Identifying the United States with the current of social revolution would give it a legitimacy in these countries that would draw responsible professional and middle-class elements into the reform movements, and thereby channel pressures into practical demands and nonviolent modes of agitation. Furthermore, by providing an agenda of practical reforms and insisting that governments in these countries make discernible progress in these directions in order to qualify for development loans, the United States would be providing significant pressure from above to complement and reinforce the popular pressures we were encouraging from below. Progressive regimes would be strengthened against conservative elements in their societies; and oligarchical regimes would be squeezed in an ever-tightening vise. Opportunist leaders would at least know where their bread was to be buttered.

If the Latin American nations took the necessary internal measures, Secretary of the Treasury Douglas Dillon told his fellow delegates at Punta del Este, they could reasonably expect their own efforts to be matched by an inflow of capital during the next decade amounting to at least $20 billion. The problem, he said, did not lie in a shortage of external capital, but "in organizing effective development programs so that both domestic and foreign capital can be put to work rapidly, wisely, and well." There were underlying principles to be adhered to: the loan recipients would have to dedicate larger proportions of their domestic resources to national development projects; integrated national programs for economic and social development would have to be formulated, setting forth goals and priorities to insure that available resources were used in the most effective manner; and such national development programs would have to be in accord with the right of all segments of the population to share fully in the fruits of progress.

   To implement these principles, said Dillon, difficult and far-reaching changes would have to be instituted by many of the Latin American nations:

It will require a strengthening of tax systems so that would-be evaders will know they face strict penalties and so that taxes are assessed in accordance with ability to pay. It will require land reform so that under-utilized soil is put to full use and so that farmers can own their own land. It will require lower interest rates on loans to small farmers and small business. It will require greatly increased programs of education, housing, and health.[8]

The assembled delegates of the Latin American republics, except for Cuba's Che Guevara, responded with enthusiasm to the United States initiative (U.S. spokesmen were careful, however, to point out that the United States was responding to the original Latin initiative for an Operation Pan America first proposed by Brazil's President Kubitschek in 1958), and pledged themselves in the Charter of Punta del Este to[9]

   • Direct their efforts immediately toward assuring that the rate of economic growth in any Latin American country was "not less than 2.5 percent per capita per year."
   • Arrive at "a more equitable distribution of national income, raising more rapidly the income and standard of living of the needier sectors of the population, at the same time that a higher proportion of the national product is devoted to investment."
   • Achieve more balanced economies, less dependent upon the export of a limited number of primary products.
   • Accelerate the process of "rational industrialization," with special attention to the development of capital-goods industries.
   • "Raise greatly the level of agricultural productivity . . . and to improve related storage, transportation, and marketing services."
   • "Encourage" comprehensive land reform programs, including the

effective transformation, where required, of unjust structures and systems of land tenure and use, with a view to replacing latifundia and dwarf holdings by an equitable system . . . so that, with the help of timely and adequate credit, technical assistance and facilities for the marketing and distribution of products, the land will become for the man who works it the basis of his economic stability.

   • Eliminate illiteracy and provide, by 1970, a minimum of six years of education for each school-age child, and to modernize and expand the entire educational system so as to provide the skilled personnel required during rapid economic development.

- Improve basic health services and disease prevention and control.
- Increase the construction of low-cost houses for low-income families.
- Maintain stable price levels.
- Promote regional economic integration, with a view to achieving ultimately a Latin American common market.
- Cooperate with other nations to prevent harmful effects from fluctuations in foreign exchange earned from exports of primary products, and to facilitate Latin American exports to foreign markets.

But it turned out to be an *Alianza* mainly at the level of verbalized aspiration. According to Ted Sorensen, the President, after a year or so of little progress, was disappointed:

. . . what disturbed him most was the attitude of that 2 percent of the citizenry of Latin America who owned more than 50 percent of the wealth and controlled most of the political-economic apparatus. Their voices were influential, if not dominant, among the local governments, the armies, the newspapers and other opinion-makers. They had friendly ties with U.S. press and business interests who reflected their views in Washington. They saw no reason to alter the ancient feudal patterns of land tenure and tax structure, the top heavy military budgets, the substandard wages and the concentrations of capital. They classified many of their opponents as "communists," considered the social and political reforms of the *Alianza* a threat to stability and clung tenaciously to the status quo.[10]

Moreoever, even when there was the will to reform, there appeared to be a conspiracy of history, natural phenomena, and elemental human forces against essential change. The desire to effect at least a 2.5 percent per capita rate of economic growth just did not conform to the facts. A 3 percent per annum increase in the gross national product was very impressive for a Latin American country, yet with population growth running at 2.5 to 3 percent, the per capita increase was usually all but wiped out even in the best of cases. The lack of Latin American economists with experience in integrated national economic planning was another factor making for sluggishness. By the end of 1962 only five countries were able to submit national development plans for review, and of these only those submitted by Mexico and Venezuela were competently done and within the spirit of the *Alianza*. The lack of sufficiently studied and engineered projects meant that the United States government was able to disburse only two thirds of the $1.5 billion it had already pledged for the first year and a half of the program.[11] Nor was the picture brightened by the worldwide drop in basic commodity prices—the major source of national income for most of the Latin American countries.

Was it all worth the effort anyway? Kennedy continued to think so, but without the earlier euphoria. He admitted that the Alliance for Progress "has failed to some degree because the problems are almost insuperable." In some ways, he said, "the road seems longer than it was when the journey started. But I think we ought to keep at it." [12]

A basic purpose of the Alliance, after all, had been to make it clear to all in the hemisphere, and hopefully elsewhere in the Third World, that the United States was not a status quo power working to preserve oligarchical privilege in the backward countries. It was to demonstrate, by putting money in back of the rhetoric, to whom and to what we were committed. It was to show that we were on the side of change in the direction of a more equitable distribution of wealth within nations and among nations, of greater participation by men and women in deciding upon the rules by which they would live, and of a more abundant and creative life for all human beings. And it was to convey the message that we were for all of these things not simply out of compassion for the less fortunate, but out of enlightened self-interest.

"Perhaps our most impressive accomplishment," said the President on the first anniversary of the Alliance for Progress, "has been the dramatic shift in thinking and attitudes which has occurred in our hemisphere":

> Already elections are being fought in terms of the Alliance for Progress. . . . Already people throughout the hemisphere—in schools and in trade unions, in chambers of commerce and in military establishments, in government and on the farms—have accepted the goals of the charter as their own personal and political commitments. For the first time in the history of inter-American relations our energies are concentrated on the central task of democratic development.
>
> This dramatic change in thought is essential to the realization of our goals. [13]

The problem was that the dramatic change in thought, if unaccompanied by meaningful changes in government programs in these countries, could create an even larger gap between popular demands and government responsiveness, with governments in turn attempting to stifle demand, and the discontented turning in their frustration to insurgency. Our strategy for effecting a "divorce" between Communist and non-Communist social reform movements, and making the latter more powerful by tangible evidence of the success of their programs, was based on the assumption that governments, under prodding by the United States, would respond to the mounting political pressure more quickly than they had in the past.

The prod, around which the Alliance for Progress was built, was the long-term low-interest loan program for development projects administered in accord with the guidelines set forth in the Charter of Punta del Este. But the diffusion of responsibility to internationally appointed technical experts for implementing the conditions in the charter made it difficult to use this tool as an instrument of reform. Governments could too easily blame their failure to gain the new external capital promised in the Alliance on the bureaucracy and red tape of the inter-American machinery, rather than on their own procrastination. And the United States could be accused of insisting upon complicated technical standards precisely for the reason that it would reduce the projects requiring U.S. financial support. Before the end of 1962 the governments of the Americas, through their delegates to the Inter-American Economic and Social Council, were recommending that "in order to prevent disappointment both on the part of the countries seeking assistance and of the financing institutions, both national and international, it will be advisable to make the conditions and operations of these institutions more flexible.[14]

Latin American diplomats also began to press with greater fervor for international commodity price stabilization agreements, arguing that the instability of their countries' foreign earnings, more than anything else, prevented the amount of domestic capital available for investment in development from being increased. This case was not entirely convincing to the administration, since there was a good deal of "surplus" domestic Latin American private money drawing interest in American and European banks. The people receiving money from the export of basic commodities were very often the same elements least interested in the social reform that would have to accompany true economic development in their countries.

The more conservative Latins, and United States interests unsympathetic to the national planning approach and emphasis upon public investment in the original conception of the Alliance, were able to point to the fact that there had been a decline in the flow of private capital to Latin America since Punta del Este. The obvious implication was that all the talk of dramatic social change, including drastic land and tax reforms, had raised the specter of confiscation of private holdings without sufficient compensation, harassment of foreign-subscribed private enterprise, and political instability leading to unpredictable radical economic experiments. "Taking into account the limitations to the availability of public funds," said the first-year evaluation report of the IA-ECOSOC, "it is clear that the objectives of the Alliance cannot be achieved without the full participation of the private sector and adequate measures must be taken to assure maximum contribution to growth by the private sector." [15] The forces for stability, recovering from the first shock of seeing the White House seriously identifying itself with the forces for change, had begun to regroup.

The President's response to the conservative counterattack was to show as much favor as possible to leaders like Betancourt and Mateos, and to point his finger at those Latin American forces who, in his view, constituted an alliance against progress:

No amount of external resources, no stabilization of commodity prices, no new inter-American institutions, can bring progress to nations which do not have political stability and determined leadership. No series of hemispheric agreements or elaborate machinery can help those who lack internal discipline, who are unwilling to make sacrifices and renounce privileges. No one who sends his money abroad, who is unwilling to invest in the future of his country, can blame others for the deluge which threatens to overcome and overwhelm him.

But the elements of lethargy, obstruction, and despair were not going to prevail this time, affirmed the President four days before his death. These forces should know that he was fully committed, and prepared for a long struggle. "Nothing is true except a man or men adhere to it—to live for it, to spend themselves on it, to die for it," he declaimed, quoting from a poem by Robert Frost. More important than money or institutions or agreements was this spirit of persistence in the face of great obstacles. [16]

Whatever the President's real assessment of the chances of implementing the goals of Punta del Este, the Alliance for Progress put forward the face of United States power the New Frontier preferred to emphasize, combining the features of modernity (the new science of development economics) with the gaze of fiery idealism (Tom Paine and Simón Bolívar). Underneath was the hard unsentimental assumption that anything less would allow the Communists to capture, with their "science" and their revolutionary ardor, the revolution of rising demands by the newly enfranchised poor of the Third World. The visage of social reformer, however, was not something put on simply as a cold war expedient. It was also thought to be the expression of our deeper and better selves, "for America at its best has never wholly lost a sense of the community of human destiny." [17]

The United States has a mixed tradition. Those who claim that altruistic motives are illegitimate considerations of foreign policy trace their lineage to George Washington's farewell address. The Constitution talks of securing the blessings of liberty to ourselves and our posterity; it says nothing of our obligation to extend these blessings to others. This view that the "irreducible national interest" (see part I, chapter 1) ought to be the *sole* determinant of foreign policy, not just the primary object of policy, had proven a powerful weapon in the hands of the opponents of economic development assistance since the Second World War. And the opponents, by virtue of their control of key appropriations committees, have held an effective veto over administration proposals. A President asking for an increase in foreign aid thus usually needs to use all of the instruments of leverage at his disposal. But as executive leverage is to some extent an expendable commodity, its use on a particular program has required that the case be made for that program's priority within the administration as well as to the public and the Congress, since other budget items also need White House backing. The strongest contention is that in the President's judgment program X is essential for national security.

The Kennedy administration, partly because of its analysis of the sensitivities of the new nations, partly because of its belief that the country was at its best when it gave vent to its altruistic traditions, was initially inclined not to make the national security rationale the be-all and end-all of foreign aid. But gradually, and tragically to some New Frontiersmen, the White House began to trim its approach back to this irreducible national interest as the Congress fell back into its habit of trimming the "fat" from foreign aid requests.

Congress went along with the essentials of the administration's program in 1961, creating the Agency for International Development, authorizing the Alliance for Progress and the funds requested for this new venture, and increasing the proportion of foreign assistance appropriations devoted to economic as opposed to military projects. But the next year, the counterattack was in full swing, led by Congressman Otto Passman, chairman of the House appropriations subcommittee on foreign aid.

In 1962, the President asked the Congress for a total of $4.9 billion for the various foreign assistance programs. As Congress began to axe the recommended economic development programs, Kennedy appealed to the legislators in the terms of his preferred public rationale: if we were truly for a world of independent self-reliant nations, if we really believed that weakness and dependence for national societies was not a proper environment for the development of political liberty and individual well-being, then in good conscience we could not reduce these foreign assistance programs any further.[18]

Insufficiently impressed, the Congress trimmed a full billion dollars off the President's request. There was great disappointment in the White House; AID's first chief, Foweler Hamilton, resigned. Schlesinger portrays Kennedy as "convinced that extreme measures were necessary to get the aid bill through Congress in 1963," and deciding upon "the familiar device of a blue-ribbon panel of bonded conservatives set up to cast a presumably cold eye on the aid effort and then to recommend its continuance as essential to the national interest."[19]

The panel was about as bonded a group as could be found. Designated "the Committee to Strengthen the Security of the Free World," it was chaired by General Lucius D. Clay, highly respected in banking and financial circles and famed for his cold war toughness toward the Soviets over Germany and Berlin. Fiscal responsibility was represented by Robert B. Anderson, Eisenhower's last Secretary of the Treasury, and before that Secretary of the Navy. Robert A. Lovett, a Secretary of Defense under Truman, and the man most identified in the public mind with the New York "establishment," could never be accused of fuzzy liberalism. Organized labor was represented by the militantly anti-Communist George Meany. Edward S. Mason, of the Harvard–M.I.T. economists circle, was added as an afterthought, but largely as a concession to some of the development economists who may not have appreciated the political gamesmanship of the President. The main economic development aura was provided by Eugene Black of the World Bank. Other members were Clifford Hardin, L. F. McCollum, Herman Phleger, and Howard Rusk.

If a blue ribbon was desirable for packaging the 1963 foreign aid proposals, the Clay committee was more than willing to provide the truest blue, in the form of a return to the strict national-security-only criterion that had kept economic development assistance to a trickle since the Korean War, and in its insistence that the "private sector" rather than government-owned enterprises should be the favored recipients of assistance. But rather than squaring the circle by arguing that the nation's security interest and interest in expanding overseas private investment would be best served by a long-term continuation of the level of effort the President was recommending, the committee did just the opposite:

We believe that we are indeed attempting too much for too many and that a higher quality and reduced quantity of our difficult aid effort in certain countries could accomplish much more. We cannot believe that our national interest is served by indefinitely continuing commitments at the present rate to the 95 countries and territories which are now receiving our economic and/or military assistance. Substantial tightening up and sharpened objectives in terms of our national interests are necessary.

. . .

For the present . . . we are convinced that reductions are in order in present military and economic assistance programs. Mindful of the risks inherent in using the axe to achieve quickly the changes recommended, the Committee recommends these reductions be phased over the next three years. [20]

The administration released the report reluctantly, in the knowledge that Clay's support was politically indispensable, even if only to salvage the 1963 bill after it was torn apart by Representative Passman and his friends. The Louisiana Democrat could not have been more pleased by the Clay report. And now cautious Republicans like Everett Dirksen and Charles Halleck could vote for cuts in the administration's aid program while wrapped in the mantle of establishment patriotism.

The "national security" standard, as wielded by the Congress, applying narrower concepts of security and the global balance of power, was in 1963 a keener instrument for whittling down than building up. The actual appropriations bill of $3.2 billion, a slash of $1.7 billion from Kennedy's original request, was the lowest since

1958, and the smallest percentage of U.S. gross national product allocated to foreign assistance since the start of the Marshall Plan.

In an administration that defined the Third World as the major arena of competition, this congressional action was interpreted as a severe curb on the diplomatic power of the United States.

The President, however, was not one to take such defeats without fighting back. If the case for foreign aid had to be made in terms of national security, then that was the way he would make the case. But the connection would have to be more clearly set forth than previously.

In a westward swing through the United States with Secretary of the Interior Udall in the fall of 1963, the President frequently departed from his major theme—the conservation of national resources—to talk about the preservation of the nation as a whole.

Except for his address during the Cuban missile crisis, probably the hardest-hitting basic national security speech of the President's career was made at the Mormon Tabernacle in Salt Lake City. It was the last week of September 1963. The Senate had ratified the nuclear test ban treaty. There was talk of détente with the Soviet Union. The President, aware that the audience to which he spoke would translate their mood of increasing isolationism into a disapproval of foreign economic assistance, drove home the connections between the security concerns of his audience, the global balance of power, and our array of foreign commitments. This largely extemporaneous address merits liberal quotation:

I know that many of you in this State and other States sometimes wonder where we are going and why the United States should be involved in so many affairs, in so many countries all around the globe.

.   .   .

I realize that the burdens are heavy and I realize that there is a great temptation to urge that we relinquish them, that we have enough to do here in the United States, and we should not be so busy around the globe. From the beginning of this country . . . we had believed that we could live behind our two oceans in safety and prosperity in a comfortable distance from the rest of the world.

.   .   .

I can well understand the attraction of those earlier days . . . but two world wars have shown us that if we . . . turn our back on the world outside . . . we jeopardize our economic well-being, we jeopardize our political stability, we jeopardize our physical safety.

.   .   .

Americans have come a long way in accepting in a short time the necessity of world involvement, but the strain of this involvement remains and we find it all over the country. . . . We find ourselves entangled with apparently unanswerable problems in unpronounceable places. We discover that our enemy in one decade is our ally the next. We find ourselves committed to governments whose actions we cannot often approve, assisting societies with principles very different from our own.

. . .

The world is full of contradiction and confusion, and our policy seems to have lost the black and white clarity of simpler times when we remembered the Maine and went to war.

. . .

The United States has rightly determined, in the years since 1945 under three different administrations . . . that our national security, the interest of the United States of America, is best served by preserving and protecting a world of diversity in which *no one power or no one combination of powers can threaten the security of the United States*. The reason that we moved so far into the world was our fear that at the end of the war, and particularly when China became Communist, that Japan and Germany would collapse, and these two countries which had so long served as a barrier to Soviet advance, and the Russian advance before that, would open up a wave of conquest of all Europe and all of Asia, and then *the balance of power turning against us we would finally be isolated and ultimately destroyed*. That is what we have been engaged in for 18 years, to prevent that happening, to prevent any one monolithic power having sufficient force to destroy the United States.

For that reason we support the alliance in Latin America; for that reason we support NATO . . . for that reason we joined SEATO. . . . And however dangerous or hazardous it may be, and however close it may take us to the brink on occasion, which it has, and however tired we may get of our involvements with these governments so far away, we have *one simple central theme of American foreign policy* which all of us must recognize, because it is a policy which we must continue to follow, and that is *to support the independence of nations so that one block cannot gain sufficient power to finally overcome us*. There is no mistaking the vital interest of the United States in what goes on around the world. . . .

If we were to withdraw our assistance from all governments who are run differently from our own, we would relinquish the world immediately to our adversaries.[21]

The New Frontier tried to transcend the vocabulary of cold war diplomacy, but found it had often to return to this vocabulary when addressing the American public in order to be granted the resources to develop more flexible programs for the Third World.

15

CASTRO, LAOS, THE CONGO: LIMITS ON THE COERCIVE POWER OF THE SUPERPOWERS

There is a limitation . . . upon the power of the United States to bring about solutions. . . . The problems are more difficult than I had imagined them to be.

JOHN F. KENNEDY

During the first nine months of his presidency, Kennedy was faced with a number of crises that seemed to many of his advisers to require a direct application of United States military power. In each of these situations he held back, confirmed anew in his premise that if the nation's military power was indeed powerful enough it need not be used, provided its leaders were sufficiently imaginative and facile in applying the varied instruments of influence at their disposal.

Kennedy was highly motivated to explore all means short of force, for he perceived the contagious nature of violence and appreciated the awful dimensions it could reach. He also saw the limitations of military power when used as an instrument of persuasion. These limitations were characterized to an academic audience on November 16, 1961: "We possess weapons of tremendous power—but they are least effective in combating the weapons most often used by freedom's foes: subversion, infiltration, guerrilla warfare, civil disorder." Yet, "we cannot, as a free nation, compete with our adversaries in tactics of terror, assassination, false promises, counterfeit mobs and crises." We had been cast in the role of "the most powerful defender of freedom on earth," but we were unable to perform that role "without restraints imposed by the very freedoms we seek to protect." Moreover, not everyone agreed with us in our definition of freedom and human dignity, nor did they possess the same will to defend it. "We send arms to other peoples—just as we send them the ideals of democracy in which we believe—but we cannot send them the will to use those arms or to abide by those ideals."

Kennedy would not have denied these premises nine months earlier, but neither would he have made them a central theme of a major address on public policy. At his inaugural he had exorted his nation to respond to the trumpet call of world leadership. He had cautioned, even in his exultation, that this was to be a "long twilight struggle," requiring great sacrifices, and no prospects of quick reward. But the mood had been one of great confidence in the ability of the new generation of American leaders to mobilize first the nation's and then the world's resources for the mammoth struggle "against the common enemies of man: tyranny, poverty, disease and war itself." Now it was in a considerably more chastened mood that the President counseled:

We must face the fact that the United States is neither omnipotent nor omniscient—that we are only 6 percent of the world's population—that we cannot impose our will upon the other 94 percent of mankind—that we cannot right every wrong or reverse each adversity—and that therefore there cannot be an American solution to every world problem. [1]

The Bay of Pigs fiasco was probably Kennedy's major chastening experience, but he did not come to these premises suddenly in the midst of that crisis. He had decided already in the cases of Laos and the Congo that the least desirable policy options were those that would require United States military intervention, and that we would have to accept barely tolerable outcomes (neutralization for Laos, a flimsy UN presence for the Congo) rather than solutions. The denouement of the Bay of Pigs took place during the Laotian and Congolese crises of 1961. On the one hand, it does seem to have reinforced his skeptical attitude toward plans based on the assumption that by the exercise of its military prowess the United States would control all of the critical variables in these messy political situations. "Thank God the Bay of Pigs happened when it did," he told Ted Sorensen. "Otherwise we'd be in Laos by now—and that would be a hundred times worse." [2] On the other hand, he was under tremendous pressure to compensate for the demonstration of United States impotence at the Bay of Pigs. As he confided to Walt Rostow, Eisenhower could survive the Communist successes in Indochina in 1954 because the blame fell on the French, but "I can't take a 1954 defeat today." [3]

Though the Bay of Pigs did not determine Kennedy's actions henceforth, it bears special examination as a crisis that made the President more keenly aware of the scope and limitations of the various facets of the nation's power. In this respect it was a more significant event than even the missile crisis of 1962; and certainly what he learned during the Bay of Pigs crisis was central to his evaluation of the various options presented to him for dealing with Cuban missiles (see pp. 233–41).

Kennedy's handling of the Laotian crisis was a product, but also a reinforcement, of his premise that it was of fundamental importance for the superpowers to avoid a direct military clash, and of the corollary that this would often require of both that they accept only tolerable outcomes rather than "solutions." These premises were rooted in an appreciation of the deep ideological gulf that separated the Communist and non-Communist nations, so that a victory for one side, such as a satellite in the Third World, could well be regarded by the other as "intolerable." In such situations, to press for victory could be very risky. The risk, Kennedy further appreciated, was shared by both sides, given the balance of thermonuclear capabilities, but was also difficult to control once a war was underway, since in the heat of battle the pressure to win could easily submerge the more limited objective of merely denying the opponent victory.

The objective of avoiding a direct military confrontation of the superpowers also dominated our considerations during the Congo civil wars of 1960–62. The Soviets were rushing in where angels feared to tread, with military assistance to some of the factions rebelling against the central Congolese government. Pessimistic about the ability of any external power to control the local situation, but unwilling to see the Soviets exploit the chaos unopposed, the Kennedy administration carried forward the Eisenhower administration's policy of keeping the Soviets out by putting the United Nations in. Nevertheless, events in the Congo compelled a degree of United States support for UN operations bordering on direct involvement. United States pronouncements and actions were carefully tailored in line with the assumption that expectations about who and what the United States supported in the Congo would critically influence internal Congolese politics. Not that we could determine or control the situation but, rather, that important local participants and potential outside meddlers knew that the balance of forces in the Congo depended upon the degree of support various factions could expect from the United States. As it turned out, things went our way more than we expected (see below, pp. 215–21), but not primarily because of what we did. The Congo crisis was not only another lesson to Kennedy on the limits of U.S. power; it was also a demonstration of the degree to which the Soviets are limited in their ability to exploit Third World instabilities.

President Kennedy hesitated, reversed himself, and was embarrassingly unsure of his footing during his effort to topple Castro in the spring of 1961. But from the outset he was constant, in his basic premise that fundamental United States interests would be ill-served if that effort were to involve the direct employment of our military power. This premise was a part of the ground rules for Central Intelligence Agency contingency planning, as originally approved by the Eisenhower administration. The condition that there would be no United States military intervention was explicitly a part of the understanding between the White House and the CIA, and was reiterated and stressed during the secret meetings in March and April between the new President and his chief military, diplomatic, and intelligence advisers.[4] This self-denying ordinance against the application of United States military power was reinforced in a pledge by Kennedy, just five days before the exile landing at the Bay of Pigs:

. . . there will not be, under any conditions, an intervention in Cuba by the United States Armed Forces. This government will do everything it possibly can, and I think it can meet its responsibilities, to make sure that there are no Americans involved in any actions inside Cuba.

The basic issue in Cuba is not one between the United States and Cuba. It is between the Cubans themselves. I intend to see that we adhere to that principle and as I understand it this administration's attitude is so understood and shared by the anti-Castro exiles from Cuba in this country.[5]

And it was this prohibition, in the "moment of truth" where he saw what in fact would be required to make the exile operation succeed, that led Kennedy to accept the terrible embarrassment and pain of allowing the 1400 Cuban exiles to be decimated by Castro's forces.

In everything that has thus far been divulged about the Bay of Pigs crisis, the evidence is that the President thought he had approved an operation whose success would *not* require the use of United States military forces. He accepted the intelligence of the CIA that Castro's hold over the people of Cuba was very unstable, and that the majority of the people, including presumably Castro's own army, would rise against him once a small force of exiles had established a beachhead. The President and his military advisers also accepted the CIA's intelligence on Castro's military forces, and the derived evaluation by the Joint Chiefs of Staff, that an insurrectionary beachhead could be established by the Cuban exiles, using the equipment already at their disposal, and without direct United States military support. And at the outside chance that the operation might not succeed militarily, it would have been conducted in such a low-key manner that the exiles presumably could disappear into the hills and reorganize themselves for a longer-term guerrilla operation without having to call on the United States to bail them out.[6]

On all of these critical intelligence and military operational premises the President discovered, after the assault was underway, that he was wrong. A good deal of what has been written about the Bay of Pigs explores the bases of these mistaken premises—poor advice, deliberate deception by operatives afraid to tell the President the truth for fear the whole thing would be called off (but possibly confident that once it was underway the President would be too heavily committed to reverse himself), the failure of the President to draw out advisers who had important doubts, and inexperience on Kennedy's part in knowing how to manage the vast military and intelligence bureaucracies.

Some people, looking back at the calamity, argue that better generalship on the administration's part would have saved the day: a less-vulnerable landing site should have been selected; the time of the exiles' air strikes should have been better; supplies of ammunition should have been dispersed rather than concentrated in a single ship which was sunk early in the campaign, and so on. Other critics dwell on the failure of the United States to become militarily involved even in a marginal way—but presumably the critical margin: if the United States had been willing to provide air cover, it is argued, the exiles could have at least established a beachhead from which a major insurgency could have then been mounted.

But as the facts came in, the President apparently was convinced that he and his subordinates had made more than a series of technical and marginal errors: the principal agencies and individuals involved in the planning and direction of the venture had cooperated in constructing a grossly uninformed depiction of the situation in Cuba. Different pictures of Castro's political and military strength were available from British intelligence, and even from the State Department, not to mention usually responsible American newspaper reporters.[7] Yet from those within his inner circle, the President received no thoughtful dissent to the most critical premises sustaining the consensus to go ahead, except that offered by Arthur Schlesinger. By Schlesinger's own account, he too was ineffectual in advancing counterarguments at meetings when they might have done the most good. Moreover, Schlesinger seems to have neglected to pinpoint the implication which later, in the midst of the operation, faced the President: namely, that there was no way of avoiding a direct and obvious and substantial United States military involvement if the objective was to take Cuba away from the Castroites.[8]

When the President, belatedly, realized that this indeed was the situation, he was able to quickly regain his perspective and evaluate the remaining options—take on Castro directly, or liquidate the Bay of Pigs operation—in terms of their implications for the global balance of power. When viewed in this context, liberated from preoccupation with the tactical factors, he knew what he had to do. He was well aware that he, personally, would be subjected to charges of cowardice, of callous disregard for the lives of the exiles on the beach, and of downright political inepititude; and that overseas these charges would be directed at the nation as a whole. During those critical hours, Kennedy confided to James Reston and Arthur

Schlesinger his conception of where the basic national interest lay.
In Schlesinger's account:

Kennedy seemed deeply concerned about the members of the Brigade. They were
brave men and patriots; he had put them on the beachhead; and he wanted to save
as many as he could. But he did not propose to send in the Marines. Some people,
he noted, were arguing that failure would cause irreparable harm, that we had no
choice now but to commit United States forces. Kennedy disagreed. Defeat, he
said, would be an incident, not a disaster. The test had always been whether the
Cuban people would back a revolt against Castro. If they wouldn't, the United
States could not by invasion impose a new regime on them. But would not United
States prestige suffer if we let the rebellion flicker out? "What is prestige?" Kennedy asked. "Is it the shadow of power or the substance of power? We are going to
work on the substance of power. No doubt we will be kicked in the can for the
next couple of weeks, but that won't affect the main business." [9]

The main business—the substance of power—what was it? The
main business was still, as it had been since the days of the Truman
Doctrine, preventing extensions of Communist control that would
constitute a significant change in the global balance of power, but
accomplishing containment of Communism, if at all possible, without a major war. We would risk war, even the survival of the United
States itself, were that necessary to prevent an imbalance of power
against us. But Kennedy, on this score, found himself in complete
agreement with the argument of Senator Fulbright, who during the
planning stages of the operation had protested, "The Castro regime
is a thorn in the flesh; but it is not a dagger in the heart." [10] If the
thorn could be extracted with a tweezer, that was one thing. It was
surely not worth hacking to pieces the tissue of hemispheric relations now being nurtured in the Alliance for Progress, nor worth a
major diversion of military resources at a time when trouble was
brewing in Laos, the Congo, and Berlin. Sorensen recounts the
President's calculations:

"Obviously," he [Kennedy] said later, "if you are going to have United States air
cover, you might as well have a complete United States commitment, which would
have meant a full-fledged invasion by the United States."

American conventional forces . . . were still below strength, and while an estimated half of our available Army divisions were tied down resisting guerrillas in
the Cuban mountains, the Communists could have been on the move in Berlin or
elsewhere in the world.

When the reports of the failure of the exile brigade demanded presidential action one way or the other,

he would not agree to the military-CIA request for the kind of open commitment of American military power that would necessitate, in his view, a full-scale attack by U.S. forces—that, he said, would only weaken our hand in the global fight against Communism over the long run. [11]

The global fight against Communism had been shifting to the new arena of competition for influence over the development process in the Third World. To allow ourselves to be panicked into a military intervention in the Americas would, if anything, be playing the game as the Communists wanted us to play it—in the stereotyped style of the hated colossus to the north. The real issue, Castro's betrayal of the ideals of the Cuban revolution, would be submerged in the escalation of battle and emotions. And the dichotomization between left and right, which always gives the Communists their biggest opportunities for exploiting indigenous revolutions, would block the new lines of communication Kennedy was trying to string with progressive reformist groups in Latin America, Africa, and Asia.

In his address before the American Society of Newspaper Editors on April 20, the President, while taking full responsibility for the disastrous outcome at the Bay of Pigs, tried to direct the nation's attention to the lessons of the episode. It is clearer than ever, he said, that we face a relentless struggle in every corner of the globe "in situations which do not permit our own armed intervention":

We dare not fail to see the insidious nature of this new and deeper struggle. We dare not fail to grasp the new concepts, the new tools, the new sense of urgency we will need to combat it—whether in Cuba or South Viet-Nam. And we dare not fail to realize that this struggle is taking place every day, without fanfare, in thousands of villages and markets—day and night—and in classrooms all over the globe.

Too long, he said, we had fixed our eyes on traditional military tools for maintaining the balance of power—on armies prepared to cross borders, on missiles posed for flight. "Now it should be clear that this is no longer enough." [12]

In dealing with Castro's Cuba, Kennedy from the outset of his planning rejected the use of substantial United States military power. The United States was initiating a change in the status quo, and could set the rules of engagement. In Laos the situation was quite different. Major opponents of the United States were trying to topple the status quo in their attempts to absorb Laos, and their decisions too would substantially determine the dimensions of the conflict.

Kennedy perceived that the question of *who* was trying to change the existing situation was a very important one in our evolving relations with the Soviet Union. The effects of a "war of national liberation," fomented and successfully managed by the Soviets or Chinese, would be considerable on the global balance of power—on its psychological "wave of the future" component affecting the expectations and alignments of men and nations. "The security of all Southeast Asia will be endangered if Laos loses its neutral independence," explained Kennedy in his March 23, 1961, news conference. "Its own safety runs with the safety of us all." Yet when pressed by a reporter to "spell out your views a little further" on the relationship of the security of Laos to the "security of the United States and to the individual American," the President rested his case on formal treaty commitments and on local geopolitical considerations:

Well, quite obviously, geographically Laos borders on Thailand, to which the United States has treaty obligations under the SEATO Agreement of 1954, it borders on South Vietnam . . . to which the United States has very close ties, and also which is a signatory of the SEATO Pact [actually, only covered by a separate protocol]. The aggression against Laos itself was referred to in the SEATO Agreement. So that, given this, the nature of the geography, its location, the commitments which the United States and obligations which the United States has assumed toward Laos as well as the surrounding countries—as well as other signatories of the SEATO Pact, it's quite obvious that if the Communists were able to move in and dominate this country, it would endanger the security of all and the peace of all of Southeast Asia. And as a member of the United Nations and as a signatory of the SEATO Pact, and as a country which is concerned with the strength of the cause of freedom around the world, that obviously affects the security of the United States. [13]

The possibility that he might not be putting the strength of his commitment to an independent Laos across to the people of the United States and to the Soviets worried the President, particularly after the Bay of Pigs. How could he convince them that he had not ruled out United States intervention against Communism in a tiny kingdom on the other side of the world while he had rejected intervention against a Communist regime ninety miles off our shores in our traditional sphere of influence and military control? [14] He was apparently unwilling to resort publicly to the bald "falling dominoes" arguments Eisenhower and Dulles invoked over Indochina in 1954 and Quemoy and Matsu in 1958. His problem was that anything short of that might not be sufficiently convincing to the Communists.

The President saw that his most important task was to convince the Soviets that he could not and would not accept a Communist takeover of Laos. If that ultimately required a larger diversion of United States resources and even a military engagement, the task of fully convincing the American people and the Congress would be formidable, but he would have to cross that bridge when he came to it. For the present, he was unwilling to whip up war fever over Laos that might then get out of hand and foreclose his immediate diplomatic objective of achieving a cease-fire in Laos and a neutralization agreement backed by the big powers.

One hope of the administration was to "collectivize" the commitment and any military response, just as the Eisenhower administration attempted when contemplating intervention in Indochina in 1954. Secretary of State Rusk argued for SEATO assumption of responsibility for intervention at the organization's annual ministerial meeting in Bangkok on March 27. But France was clearly against what it regarded as a resumption of the Indochina war; and Britain, actively engaged in the "honest broker" role of trying to persuade the Soviets to impose a cease-fire on the Communist Pathet Lao prior to the convening of the Geneva peace conference, felt its effectiveness would be compromised by voting for SEATO intervention. SEATO was immobile and served to confirm Mao's thesis that it was a paper tiger.[15] If there was to be any military intervention, the United States would have to assume full responsibility.

The United States commitment, and Kennedy's resolve to stick by it, had somehow to be conveyed to Khrushchev before the Soviets became overcommitted. Outwardly, they were as yet doing little more than airlifting military supplies to the Pathet Lao from Hanoi, but there was pressure on them, too, to increase their aid and possibly even to preempt a United States intervention by more direct involvement. It was here that the Kennedy administration made a shrewd guess as to the Soviets' real motivations in Laos at that particular time: it might very well be that the Soviets were not anxious to become involved in the Laotian insurgency, but felt they had to be the dominant backer of the Pathet Lao for fear of that role—and presence—falling to the Chinese Communists. If this premise about Soviet motives was true, then the Soviets might be seriously interested in a viable neutralization of Laos as a device to take the pressure off them to intervene, and as a buffer against Chinese southwestward expansion. Kennedy saw his job as convincing Khrushchev that whereas the U.S. commitment to prevent the Communists from overrunning Laos was absolute, even if that required a major military intervention by the United States, he was sufficiently appreciative of the Soviets' interests to accept their bona fides about neutralization.

There remained, of course, the difficult task of getting the Laotians to accept whatever settlement was worked out, since the terms of neutrality would obviously have to include stipulations as to the makeup of the Laotian regime. But at the time this was viewed as a subordinate problem to that of bringing the intentions of the superpowers together on the neutralization outcome.

"I want to make it clear to the American people and to all of the world," Kennedy had said at his March 23 press conference, "that all we want in Laos is peace, not war; a truly neutral government, not a cold war pawn; a settlement concluded at the conference table and not on the battlefield." [16] However for the Soviets to have as much clarity in their intentions, Kennedy understood that they might have to be given more than merely words; this was of course the meaning of the President's deployment of Marines to Thailand simultaneous with his protestations of sincere peaceful intent. In this respect, Kennedy was a traditional diplomatist—unsheathing the arrows while holding forth the olive branch. And this was exactly the posture the President felt was of greatest importance to display before Khrushchev in their meeting at Vienna that June, especially since the Bay of Pigs might have given him the erroneous impression that Kennedy was unwilling to send American boys into battle.

The gratest danger, Kennedy told Khrushchev at Vienna, was the possibility of miscalcuation by one side of the interests and policies of the other. [17] Such a miscalculation could lead to situations where, against the intentions and interests of both sides, they might find themselves embroiled in war against one another. One of the purposes of their conversations, then, was to reduce the uncertainty each might have about the other's vital interests and intentions, so that hopefully the United States and the Soviet Union would be able to survive their rivalry.

The "wars of national liberation," which the Soviet Premier had endorsed in January, were fraught with such possibilities for miscalculation, maintained Kennedy. Khrushchev insisted that the Soviet Union could not be held responsible for every popular uprising, even when it assumed a Communist coloring. If what Kennedy meant by urging that the superpowers should refrain from challenging each other's vital interests was that the Soviets should refuse to aid those progressive forces trying to rid themselves of capitalist-imperialist domination, then the President was only trying to get him to acquiesce in continued Western intervention. Khrushchev agreed there should be no interference by the superpowers in the Third World against the will of the peoples, especially in the context of the ability of the United States and the Soviet Union to destroy each other, but insisted that it was the United States that was interfering, not the Soviets.

Kennedy attempted to get Khrushchev to agree on the importance of preserving the existing balance of power. The equilibrium would be disturbed, he contended, if additional nations were brought into the Communist camp. The Soviet countered with the observation that if some African country were to go Communist it would be but a drop in the bucket on the Communist side, if that was how the balance was conceived. The point was that it was dangerous to oppose movements toward Communism in any country where it was an expression of the popular will. It was only such popular movements that the Soviets would support anyway. They knew that it was futile to send guerrilla troops into a country to support a movement not supported by the people. This was evidently something the Americans had not yet learned.

Much of this dialogue, though not mentioning Laos directly, would seem to have been a dialogue about Laos. Yet in those early conversations at Vienna, Khrushchev seemed to be attempting to avoid the issue whenever Kennedy tried to get down to specifics.

As it turned out, Khrushchev really had only one matter on which he was willing to agree and that was Laos—that is, the necessity for a mutual backing off from a military confrontation and the establishment of a neutral buffer state. But to get to this area of agreement too quickly would have been to avoid the opportunity to intimidate the young President by a more ideological discussion. There were other conflicts between them not subject to resolution, such as Berlin, and it was important, evidently, for Khrushchev to display his toughest side and the depth of his commitments, in order to ward off attempts by the new administration in Washington to probe for Soviet vulnerabilities. Kennedy did afterward admit to a rough time, but not to being intimidated.

When the discussion finally got around to Laos, Kennedy led the conversation away from the great issues to the practical problem of decreasing commitments on both sides and establishing a truly neutral and independent country. If a reduction of commitment was now a sincere American objective, then why the threat of sending in U.S. Marines? asked Khrushchev, possibly hoping to exact a pledge of nonintervention. Kennedy denied that any order had been issued to send in the Marines. But he would not play the game Khrushchev's way, and instead drove home the point that all this could be avoided if there were a genuine cease-fire, so that negotiations could begin in earnest. Khrushchev, apparently more readily than expected, did agree that a cease-fire should be the priority item, and that negotiations for an independent neutral Laos should proceed. For his part, the Premier would exert every influence over the Laotians to arrive at a settlement.

Kennedy would never know whether it was mainly the course of the Sino-Soviet conflict itself that led Khrushchev to cooperate to neutralize Laos, or whether it was the result of "getting the message" from Kennedy's intensified diplomatic campaign, and intelligence of military preparations and deployments.

The Seventh Fleet had been moved into the South China Sea. Helicopter-borne Marines had been alerted for deployment from Japan and Okinawa to Thailand, within quick assault range of the Laotian capital of Vientiane. Reporters wrote of intensive military planning in the administration, and suggested the planners were contemplating a spectrum of commitment from military advisers to a major assault. Sorenson recalls that Kennedy viewed the "leak" of the military planning as an aid in communicating his intentions to the Communists.[18]

The military deployments and planning were not just for show. Kennedy considered the direct employment of United States military force as *undesirable,* yet possibly necessary. He was unwilling to deny himself bold coercive moves to keep the Soviets and Chinese out of Southeast Asia; but he was highly skeptical of those who recommended such bold moves under the simple assumption that this would scare the Communists off. Moreover, his examination of the contingency plans presented to him by his military advisers, in the context of still-understrength U.S. conventional forces, and the festering Berlin, Cuban, and Congo crises, made him responsive to General MacArthur's advice that anyone who wanted to commit United States ground forces to the Asian mainland should have his head examined.[19]

The President had had his fingers burned by his uncritical acceptance of self-serving evaluations by the military during the planning sessions for the Bay of Pigs, and was now merciless in puncturing the optimism of their Laos scenarios. Sorensen's account reveals the sharp edge of the President's questioning and his underlying assumption that military means ought to be viewed as last-resort options:

The Chiefs had talked of landing and supplying American combat forces through Laotian airports (inasmuch as the kingdom is landlocked). Questioning now disclosed that there were only two usable airstrips even in good weather, that Pathet Lao control of the nearby countryside could make initial landing difficult, and that a Communist bombing of these airstrips would leave us no alternative but to bomb Communist territory.

If we use nuclear bombs, the President asked, where would it stop, how many other Communist movements would we have to attack, what kind of world would it be? No one knew. If we didn't use nuclear weapons, he asked, would we have to retreat or surrender in the face of an all-out Chinese intervention? The answer was affirmative. If we put more forces in Laos, he asked the Chiefs, would that weaken our reserves for action in Berlin or elsewhere? The answer was again in the affirmative. If neither the royal nor the administrative capital cities fell, and the cease-fire squabble was merely over where the truce was to be signed, would these risks be worthwhile? No one was sure.

Once in, how and when to get out? he asked. Why cannot air and naval power suffice? Do we want an indefinite occupation of an unenthusiastic, dark-skinned population, tying up our forces and not those of the Communists? Is this our best bet for a confrontation with Red China—in the mountains and jungles of its landlocked neighbor? Would forces landing in Vietnam and Thailand end up defending those regimes also?[20]

Fortunately, the diplomatic campaign displaced the urgent military planning, for a while at least, in the aftermath of the Kennedy–

Khrushchev meeting at Vienna. The Geneva negotiations, with Averell Harriman leading the United States delegation, took over a year—with infinite patience, and cajolery, exercised by both the Soviet Union and the United States in response to the maneuverings and tantrums of their respective Laotian counterparts. When the United States finally succeeded in bringing around the rightist Phoumi Nosavan (favored by the Eisenhower administration) to accept a secondary position in a government headed by the neutralist Souvanna Phouma, the Pathet Lao, whose candidate Prince Souphanouvong was also supposed to accept a Cabinet portfolio, reopened its military campaign. It was this open violation of the cease-fire that led Kennedy finally to move the Marines into Thailand, but this apparently only under the prodding of Harriman himself.[21] The Pathet Lao called off the new military push, as quickly as it had started, and negotiations resumed.

Finally, on June 12, 1962, Kennedy and Khrushchev simultaneously announced the good news each had received from Geneva that agreement on a coalition Laotian government had been reached. And the Declaration and Protocol on the Neutrality of Laos was solemnly signed on July 23 by the Geneva conference participants, an impressive array of the aligned and nonaligned: Burma, Cambodia, Canada, Communist China, North Vietnam, South Vietnam, France, India, Poland, Thailand, the Soviet Union, the United States, and the Kingdom of Laos itself.[22]

However, the mood of mutual congratulation swiftly turned again to one of mutual recrimination as the Laotian factions fought among themselves, and North Vietnam began to once again openly assist the Pathet Lao while using the corridor the latter controlled, the so-called Ho Chi Minh Trail, for supplying the Viet Cong in South Vietnam.

The conflict and its resolution, however messy, did provide useful lessons and precedents for the Kennedy administration, and hopefully for the Soviet Union as well. It demonstrated the paradoxical effect on the objectives of both occasioned by the almost unlimited destructive power at the disposal of each. The mere existence of such destructive potential could serve as a rationale, and indeed an honest motive, for one to refuse to intervene in third-area conflicts against the will of the other, and also to provide the pretext for mutual military withdrawal. To this extent the coercive power of the superpowers could be viewed as a stabilizer—making it mutually advantageous for each not to challenge the vital interests of the other. Yet at the same time, it could lead smaller, and still nonaligned, actors on the international stage to defy the will of either superpower, knowing full well that intervention by the defied superpower was forestalled by the threat of counterintervention by the other; or more unscrupulously, to bribe one superpower by hinting of alignment with the other. To this extent the mutual inhibition felt by the superpowers against intervention in third-area conflicts might be destabilizing, in the sense of permitting local conflicts to reach an incendiary stage in preference to intervening.

Under Kennedy's leadership the administration in Washington was at least cognizant of the uncertainties and did not demand answers or solutions, perceiving that such demand in the absence of a power to bring about solutions might be more dangerous that a groping adaptation to each situation as it arose. "We are taking a chance in all of southeast Asia," said Kennedy of his decision to support a shaky coalition government in Laos, "and we're taking a chance in other areas":

Nobody can make any predictions for the future, really, on any matter where there are powerful interests at stake. I think, however, we have to consider what our alternatives are, and what the prospects for war are if we fail in our present efforts. . . . So . . . there's no easy, sure answer for Laos. . . . And I can assure that I recognize the risks that are involved. But I also think we should consider the risks if we fail, and particularly of the possibility of escalation of a military struggle in a place of danger. [23]

It was a similar willingness to confront uncertainty, and live with it, that governed Kennedy's reactions to the Congo upheaval during this same period.

For many who were uncomfortable with uncertainty, and the lack of visible solutions, the best attitude toward the Congo crisis was "let Dag do it." Let the Secretary General bear the responsibility and also the onus for what, from all accounts, was a hopeless situation. For Eisenhower the appropriate reactions to "the whole sorry mess" had been "dismay and disgust." [24] The New Frontiersmen, however, seemed to regard the situation with all its Byzantine intrigue as a challenge to their own political agility.

The global balance-of-power considerations that governed the Eisenhower administration's basic decision for the Congo in the summer of 1960 remained for the most part the premises underlying the Kennedy administration's actions.

But so tangled had the situation in the Congo become—the United States seeming to support one Congolese faction one day, opposing it the next; the United Nations police action turning into a military operation against the attempt of the pro-Western Katanga Province to become an independent African state—that many in the Congress wondered if the administration had any conception left of where basic United States interests lay.

Secretary of State Rusk felt it necessary to set the record straight on why the United States supported the UN action in the first place. He reminded the cognizant Senate committee that Eisenhower's support of a UN presence for the Congo was primarily a means of keeping the Soviets out. The Congolese Army had mutinied during the first week of July 1960, immediately after the Congo became independent, whereupon Belgium announced the return of Belgian troops to protect the life and property of the Europeans still there. The Congolese government was outraged at the return of the Belgian military, and sought help from all quarters—the UN, the Soviet Union, and the United States.

The alternative to United Nations intervention, Rusk recalled, would have been violence and chaos, and a ready-made opportunity for Soviet exploitation, which the United States would have been compelled to counter. Thus, "if a direct confrontation of the great powers in the heart of Africa was to be avoided," it was necessary to establish a UN presence. "Looking back, gentlemen, it seems obvious now that this was the right choice." [25]

The requirements of preventing a great power confrontation during the early phase of the Congo crisis had been complicated, but did not take any fundamental rethinking of our premises about the nature of the global balance of power. The Soviet Union was pouring personnel, materials, and political agents into the Congo, hoping to establish a foothold in the center of Africa. This was truly an extension of the Soviet presence into a new area, and if they did succeed in establishing a loyal regime in the Congo, they would emerge as the only great power capable of calling the tune for the many new nations south of the Sahara. The result would not be merely "a drop in the bucket," as Khrushchev phrased it, but a new imperial momentum for the Soviets, bringing them eventually to the

Atlantic and putting them in command of the great, still-unexploited wealth of the vast African continent.

The objective of the United States was simple, before Kennedy assumed the presidency, and could be easily understood. We had to keep the Soviets out, but without getting in ourselves if at all possible. First, it was important to avoid a direct clash with the Soviets. Second, we wouldn't know what to do once in the Congo, anyway. We were unfamiliar with the intricacies of tribal relationships, and were not about to assume the obligations, politically and financially, for making the new Congo nation a showpiece of United States-sponsored development. All we wanted was a relatively stable authority in the Congo willing and able to resist Sovet overlordship. The United Nations presence was a device to preempt the Soviet military assistance which, presumably, was requested by the Kasavubu–Lumumba government in Leopoldville solely for the purpose of giving it the wherewithal to restore order and restore the authority of the central Congolese government. Thus, we supported the unprecedented granting of supranational functions to the Secretariat of the UN—that is, the mandate to establish domestic order within a nation, to act as if it were the national authority in the Congo until an indigenous authority could establish its power and legitimacy over the area.

We did not find it too difficult to dispense with our formal legalistic position in favor of the sovereignty of nations and the inability of the United Nations to act on domestic matters, particularly to take sides in favor of certain contending political factions within a nation. The balance of power was at stake, and we knew where our interests lay.

In the early phase of the crisis, the source of the threat to the balance of power was also the source of the threat to the authority of the central government—or, at least, this was our plausible definition of the meaning of the growing Soviet intervention. So the United States support of the UN police force and even the use of the United States Air Force for supplying materials to the UN operation and for flying in troops of the UN force was not a subject of major political controversy in the United States.

When Premier Lumumba objected to President Kasavubu's acceptance of the UN role, and the heavy indirect United States support, the nationalist Congo President dismissed his pro-Soviet Premier, who thereupon became the leader of an insurrection against the central government. Lumumba was captured and murdered, and Antoine Gizenga, his political heir, established himself in Stanleyville as the leader of the insurgency, hoping for major support from the Soviets. Then, in 1960, when the Soviets continued to supply the Gizenga elements with agents and materials, President Kasavubu closed the major airfields to all but United Nations traffic and ordered the Soviet and Czechoslovakian embassies to close.

The chaos once again seemed to have rapidly assumed an order of simplicity consistent with the balance-of-power premises that Eisenhower used to justify our support of the UN action, and most unfavorable to the Soviets' effort to capture an indigenous African nationalist regime through a low-cost, low-risk, policy of subversion. In order to establish their foothold, the Soviets would have to openly support an insurrection against the legitimate Congolese government, supported by UN forces with contingents from the nonaligned world operating under a mandate of the world organization.

The Soviets now turned their fire on Dag Hammarskjöld's management of the UN operation, and tried to create opportunities for Soviet vetoing of decisions within the Secretariat—the meaning of their notorious troika proposal. But they were clearly on the defensive, and swinging back wildly in their frustration.

During the fall of 1960 and spring of 1961 events in the Congo took a turn, largely self-generated, which denied the new administration in Washington the luxury of neatly fitting the crisis into the cold war context.

The troublemaker now was the clever ruler of Katanga Province, Moise Tshombe. Receiving major revenues from the Belgian-owned copper mines in Katanga, which made that province the wealthiest of any in the Congo, Tshombe saw the advantages of turning Katanga into a sovereign state, not having to dissipate its wealth throughout the poorer sections of the former Belgian colony. Not surprisingly, the Belgian copper interests, fearing the consequences of unstable—and possibly radical—rule from Leopoldville, encouraged Tshombe in his dreams of becoming a chief of state.

However, the UN operation and the viability of the central Congolese government would collapse if the legitimacy of Katanga's secession were granted. The Congo, after all, was only a potential nation; if each segment, whether because of tribal or economic reasons, was allowed the right to choose how long and under what conditions it would remain a part of the union, there would be no union. Hammarskjöld appreciated this, and certainly, remembering our own Civil War, the United States should have appreciated this. But there was a contrary ideology in the American ethos—self-determination. This unresolved contradiction was exploited by Tshombe and his Belgian-supported propagandists in the United States, so that the Kennedy administration was placed on the defensive in justifying its continued support of UN operations as they began to be directed primarily against the professedly anti-Communist Tshombe. Moreover, the Communist agents still active in the Congo were now most vocal in promoting the use of force against Tshombe to keep Katanga a part of the union. Hammarskjöld (soon to die in a plane crash in Africa and to be succeeded by U Thant) and Kennedy were caught in a bind, cynically exploited by Tshombe and his European supporters on one side and by the Communists on the other.

They knew that the United States was unwilling to intervene in the Congo, but also that it was reluctant to have the UN assume the management of a full-fledged combat operation against Katanga. To have the UN assume this role in such inauspicious circumstances would probably dash forever the hopes of gradually building up its peacekeeping functions through consensus of its member nations, and would probably make it more likely that other nations would support the Soviet scheme for injecting the veto into all major administrative functions of the world organization.

On the other hand, if the United Nations were unable to keep Tshombe in the Congolese union, that effort—the mobilization of African forces for an attack upon Tshombe—might fall by default to the Soviet-backed Gizenga. The cold war polarization of the Congo crisis would be resumed, but this time with the emotional issues unfavorable to the anti-Communists.

It was Kennedy's sensitivity to the emotional issues involved—which was a part of his orientation to the whole question of "power" in international relations—that led him to reject the counsel of United States neutrality on the Katanga issue. The United States had to side with the Congolese nationalists, supported as they were on this issue by the extremists, against the Katanga secession, or else the Soviets would be able to pose as the sole champions of the nationalists. As the UN operation was allowed to cross into that hazy area where the distinction between pacification and offensive combat operations breaks down, criticism mounted in the Congress and in Europe. Still Kennedy stood firm in his support of Hammarskjöld, and then U Thant. How far Kennedy was actually willing to go, being committed to the restoration of a unified Congo, no one knew. Schlesinger reports that during the summer of 1962 our ambassador to the Congo, Edmund Gullion (whose advice had been closely followed by the President), was suggesting that UN troops ought to be given the go-ahead to smash Tshombe's army. But in the White House, Carl Kaysen and Ralph Dungan were against a deeper American involvement, which would have been required, at least for logistic support, if major combat ensued.[26] Kennedy, naturally, was up to his stratagem of turning the coercive screws while fashioning tempting inducements. But this time, in Moise Tshombe he was dealing with a man who saw that time was on his side, and also a man who seemed to take a perverse delight in the amount of international mischief he was capable of causing. Tshombe would enter into "negotiations" with United States, British, Belgian, and UN diplomats, and then either break the "negotiations" off, or agree with broad smiles and proceed to stall. He was apparently bargaining for major concessions from the government in Leopoldville as the price for his return.

By December 1962 the UN, backed by the United States, was reaching the point where its inability to compel Katanga's reintegration was severely undermining the United Nations' authority, and pressures by the radical Africans for taking matters into their own hands was increasingly difficult to contain. U Thant was now asking for additional United States transport planes and equipment. Within the State Department he had supporters who were urging Kennedy to persuade the Secretary General to accept a squadron of United States fighter aircraft, to be flown by the U.S. Air Force, in support of a swift assault by UN forces against Tshombe's strongholds. The President, reports Sorensen, ruled against an immediate move of this sort, pending a survey by a military mission on the combat requirements for an effective defeat of Tshombe's forces. But he did approve U Thant's original request for additional logistics equipment.[27]

A few days before the new year, as a result of confused orders from UN headquarters, attributed by some to a communications foul-up, UN forces in the Congo, evidently provoked by some belligerent action by Katanga, took the offensive, sweeping into a central Katangese stronghold at Jadetville, and breaking the back of Tshombe's military resistance. The sophisticated Tshombe gracefully bowed to reality, and emerged a few months later as Prime Minister of the unified Congo—an outcome that must have put Kennedy's teeth on edge, with all his appreciation of historical irony. After all, Tshombe could have been the pretext for a major Communist insurgency campaign in the heart of Africa; and now it seemed that he might only have been playing for little more than personal glory.

Yet somehow the outcome, like that in Laos, was tolerable. Had Kennedy demanded more control and certainty over the outcome, he might either have washed his hands of the situation earlier, giving other parties a chance to exploit a collapsing UN effort, or intervened prematurely and then have been held responsible for the chaos which still exists.

These efforts to gain tacit Soviet cooperation in a policy of mutual nonintervention in the Third World were made in an experimental spirit. The President was aware of the major risk that a perception by other nations that the superpowers were afraid of becoming embroiled against one another might contribute to the belligerency of the smaller powers: expansionist nations like China and Indonesia; divided nations like Vietnam and Korea; nations with historic animosities, such as India and Pakistan; or the Arab countries and Israel.

Whether the pressure exerted by the superpowers against the "escalation" of local conflicts would win out against the propensity of the lesser powers to take matters into their own hands promised to be the big uncertainty of the coming decade.

16

BERLIN AND CUBAN MISSILES: DEFINING SPHERES OF CONTROL

. . . this secret, swift, and extraordinary buildup of Communist missiles—in an area well known to have a special and historic relationship to the United States and the nations of the Western Hemisphere . . . is a deliberately provocative and unjustified change in the status quo which cannot be accepted by this country if our courage and our commitments are ever to be trusted again by either friend or foe.

JOHN F. KENNEDY

It was over Berlin and the missiles in Cuba that President Kennedy displayed most clearly his appreciation of the central function played by military power as an arbiter of conflicting goals and wills in international relations. These two crises were also indicators of the gap existing between the reality of a two-sided organization of effective power in the international system and the hope for a pluralistic world based on self-determination. Berlin and Cuba compelled Kennedy, at least temporarily, to renew the bipolar concept as indeed the safer basis for coping with the fierce conflicts in a world armed with nuclear power and without a central system of law and order. He could still hope that on the basis of such a bipolar balance of power, sustained by each superpower's fear of the other's military prowess, a more peaceful phase of competition between the

Communists and non-Communists could begin. A period of peaceful competition, based initially on well-defined and mutually respected spheres of control, might *eventually* lead to depreciation of military power as the currency behind most international transactions, and to a less rigid international order.

Kennedy was keenly sensitive to the great instability of the bipolar balance of terror at its most immediate point of direct contact in Berlin. If he was wrong, in either encouraging the Soviets too much or provoking them too much, he might be wrong forever. It was easy for advisers to advise, but he bore the responsibility for action taken. Consequently, his steps were smaller, and more tentative, than many in his entourage might have liked.

United States official statements on Berlin early in 1961 were few and far between, but conveyed a stiffer posture on Berlin and Germany than had been displayed by the Eisenhower administration during the last round of negotiations in 1959 (see above, pp. 138–45). In the city, on March 8, 1961, Averell Harriman, the President's roving ambassador, explicitly disassociated the new administration from the Eisenhower administration's concessionary proposals of 1959. "All discussions on Berlin," he said, "must begin from the start." [1] At the same time Kennedy, through Ambassador Llewellyn Thompson, had sent a personal note to Premier Khrushchev suggesting a meeting between the two leaders to clear the air. The meeting was not to be for purposes of negotiation, but rather for each side to better understand the other's basic commitments so as to remove any chance of miscalculations that might lead to war.

As it turned out, the Soviet Premier was very tough on Berlin during their meeting, using language close to the tone of an ultimatum: a peace treaty recognizing East German jurisdiction over access to Berlin would be signed in December and wartime occupation rights would be ended. If the West tried to violate the sovereign rights of the Ulbricht regime, force would be met with force. It was up to the United States to choose whether there would be war or peace. [2] And at the close of their talks, Kennedy was handed an official Soviet *aide-mémoire,* somewhat less belligerent in tone, but clearly heralding a resumption of the Berlin conflict.

The Soviet *aide-mémoire* called for the immediate convening of a peace conference to "formally recognize the situation which has developed in Europe after the war, to legalize and consolidate the inviolability of existing German borders, [and] to normalize the situation in West Berlin." In the interests of achieving agreement rapidly, said the Soviets, it would not be necessary to tie the conclusion of a peace treaty to the formal recognition of the German Democratic Republic or the Federal Republic of Germany by all parties to the treaty. If the United States was not prepared to sign a joint peace treaty with the two Germanys, a peaceful settlement could be achieved on the basis of two separate treaties. But the peace treaty, or treaties, as the case might be, would have to contain the same kind of provisions on the most important points of a peaceful settlement.

The most important points to be settled, the Soviets made clear, involved the status of West Berlin. At present, said their *aide-mémoire,* "the Soviet Government does not see a better way to solve the West Berlin problem than by tranforming it into a demilitarized free city." This "free city" of West Berlin (East Berlin was by implication to remain under the complete control of the GDR) would have

unobstructed contacts with the outside world and . . . its internal regulations should be determined by the freely expressed will of its population. . . . Token troop contingents of the United States, the United Kingdom, France, and the U.S.S.R. could be stationed in West Berlin as guarantees of the free city.

This, of course, would mean "putting an end to the occupation regime in West Berlin, with all its implications": namely, the peace treaty or treaties which provided for the new status of West Berlin would establish clearly that any questions relating to the use of "communication by land, water or air within the territory of the G.D.R. would have to be settled solely by appropriate agreements with the G.D.R."[3]

The Soviets were proposing, in short, an agreement to legitimize the division of Germany, with East Berlin to be under the complete authority of the Ulbricht regime and West Berlin to become an international city. The Soviets and their allies would be given as much control over the administration of West Berlin as the United States and its allies. Moreover, access to this new international city—located within East Germany—would be controlled by the East German government. Clearly, for the West to make such an agreement would have been to capitulate to the essence of the demands

Khrushchev had been making with respect to Germany since 1958.

Why was Khrushchev renewing these demands with such vigor and confidence now? This question bothered President Kennedy and his associates in their post mortems on the Vienna conference. Did the Soviets feel emboldened by perceptions that the strategic nuclear balance finally was such as to make Communist local military superiority in Central Europe the only relevant factor of power behind the diplomatic bargaining? Had Kennedy's backing out of the Bay of Pigs adventure and backing away from a superpower showdown over Laos given Khrushchev the impression that the United States would be the first to swerve off the collision course?

The President, in his oral exchanges with the Soviet Premier at Vienna, seems to have sensed that Khrushchev might be capable of underestimating the Kennedy resolve and nerve under pressure. Kennedy was careful to choose the words and demeanor to disabuse him of such notions. Sorensen and Schlesinger both recount Kennedy's response to Khrushchev's final insistence that the decision to change the occupation status of West Berlin by December was irrevocable, whether the United States agreed or not. If that was the case, retorted the President, "it will be a cold winter."

It was also very important that the new Soviet demands, which were broadcast to all the world, were responded to publicly. If the Soviets were committing themselves before the public to move against our will, we must commit ourselves before that same public not to let them get away with it.

The President's instincts were to open up the Berlin issue to a wide set of alternatives, and for the United States, for a change, to set the terms of reference, rather than always reacting negatively to Soviet proposals. But he was unwilling to enter into negotiations with only the increasingly unbelievable "trip wire" military posture in Western Europe to back him up. Accordingly, he put his foreign policy advisers, including elder statesman Acheson, to work on developing an expanded list of political options while he put the Defense Department to work on increasing his military options.

As it turned out, his advisers found it easier to be creative when proposing military measures than when proposing political approaches. The State Department, designed more to implement and reiterate established policy premises than to generate new ones, responded characteristically: it took exasperatingly long to reply, but came up eventually with a remarkably thorough statement of our position on Berlin, which turned out to be little more than a marginally updated amalgam of positions developed in the 1950s. Acheson had more of substance to propose, but it was also designed primarily for strengthening our hand in preserving the status quo, rather than changing the status quo. Backed by Vice President Johnson, Acheson urged a presidential proclamation of national emergency. This could be accompanied by an immediate expansion of military manpower, including the calling up of reserves, a $5 billion increase in the defense budget, plus new taxation and standby controls on wages and prices. To openly prepare our people for the worst and visibly begin to make our economy ready for war would demonstrate to Khrushchev, more starkly than any manipulation of our military capabilities in the vicinity of Berlin, that the current Soviet threats were merely stimulating us to enhance our commitments and to more thoroughly involve the national honor in those commitments.

Acheson's national emergency package was opposed by powerful voices within the administration. Walter Heller and the Council of Economic Advisers were strongly against a tax increase at that time, and argued that there was a real danger of serious inflation resulting from the scare buying that would accompany the proclamation of emergency. Heads of the domestic departments were wary of the effects of the civilian welfare programs. And McNamara, Rusk, and even reputedly "tough" White House advisers like Henry Kissinger warned against unnecessarily bellicose reactions by the United States, which rather than indicating unflinching resolve might convey hysteria. Others on the White House staff were concerned that we not overemphasize the Berlin confrontation by devices like the proclamation, and thereby induce Khrushchev, for considerations of his own prestige, to respond in kind with arms increases and menacing postures in preparation for a showdown.

Kennedy rejected the suggestion for an immediate declaration of national emergency, but incorporated some of the major premises underlying the Acheson proposals into his own planning. He knew that words were not enough to dissuade the Soviets from an easy Berlin *fait accompli*. It was diplomatically unsound to enter into negotiations, with the Soviets assuming we were afraid of and unprepared to handle such a contingency. It was agreed that the military increase which the President had already ordered as a part of his general program for remedying the nation's military deficiencies should perhaps be accelerated under the impetus of the Berlin crisis to convince Khrushchev that his bluster could lead only to the firming up of our backbone. Nor did the President unequivocally reject the more extreme suggestions of a large-scale mobilization and a declaration of national emergency. These might yet have to be used; but they should not be used up so early in a crisis. Our grand strategy should be the classical one of arming to parley; we *wanted* the parley, and we wanted it to take place in an atmosphere conducive to calm deliberation on terribly complicated conflicts of interest. Showdowns could only revive the simplifications of the cold war, and possibly lead to hot war.

The President's television address on July 25 was designed to be both very tough and more reasonable than previous United States statements on the Berlin issue. We would not be pushed around, and were ready to resist with force, if need be, any unilaterally imposed changes in the status quo. But the status quo was not our objective.

Our presence in West Berlin, and access thereto, cannot be ended by any act of the Soviet government, the President told the world. It would be a mistake to consider Berlin, because of its location, as a tempting target: "I hear it said that West Berlin is militarily untenable. And so was Bastogne. And so, in fact, was Stalingrad. Any dangerous spot is tenable if men—brave men—will make it so." The city had become "the greatest testing place of Western courage and will, a focal point where our solemn commitments . . . and Soviet ambitions now meet in basic confrontation." Berlin was no less protected than the rest of us, "for we cannot separate its safety from our own."

He warned the Soviets not to make the dangerous mistake, which others had made, of assuming that the West was too soft, and too divided in the pursuit of narrow national interests, to fight to preserve its objectives in Berlin. Too much was at stake for the alliance as a whole: "For the fulfillment of our pledge to that city is essential to the morale and security of Western Germany, to the unity of Western Europe, and the faith of the entire Free World . . . in . . . our willingness to meet our commitments."

Accordingly, in addition to the supplementary defense buildup the

President had asked the Congress to approve in March, he was now asking for \$3.25 billion more—most of which would be spent on making certain that we have the capability-in-being to deploy rapidly to the Central European front without lessening our ability to meet our commitments elsewhere. The new measures included a tripling of the draft calls for the coming months, the ordering of duty of certain reserve and National Guard units, the reactivation of many deactivated planes and ships, and a major acceleration in the procurements of nonnuclear weapons.

It was unwise to call up or send abroad excessive numbers of troops, explained the President. But he wanted to make it clear that "while we will not let panic shape our policy," he was contemplating still more dramatic steps if the situation required them:

> . . . in the days and months ahead, I shall not hesitate to ask the Congress for additional measures, or exercise any of the executive powers that I possess to meet this threat to peace. . . . and if that should require more men, or more taxes, or more controls, or other new powers, I shall not hesitate to ask them.

In that message, however, he did request one additional item, separated from the others in his text, and related more to the overall preparedness of the nation than to the Berlin crisis. Yet it was this item—his request for a special appropriation of \$207 million for a new start on a Civil Defense shelter program—that came close to creating that national atmosphere of "panic" and overreaction likely to interfere with his efforts to direct attention in this country and the Soviet Union to political alternatives and away from military posturing.

Most of what followed this section in the President's July 25 address was anticlimactic—reversing the emphasis he had intended. The press played up the military measures, including the Civil Defense program, but gave comparatively scant attention to his offer "to consider any arrangement or treaty in Germany consistent with the maintenance of peace and freedom, and the legitimate security interests of all nations." The very carefully worded elaboration of this offer was all but ignored in United States news summaries:

> We recognize the Soviet Union's historical concern about their security in Central and Eastern Europe, after a series of ravaging invasions, and we believe arrangements can be worked out which will help to meet these concerns, and make it possible for both security and freedom to exist in this troubled area.

He had said that we were "ready to search for peace in quiet exploratory talks—in formal or informal meetings,"but the noisier measures got the headlines in the United States.[4] And it was these that dominated Khrushchev's reaction to the President's speech.

Khrushchev, a the time was discussing disarmament issues with John J. McCloy. He told McCloy in emotional tones that he was angered by the President's speech, and professed to find in it only an ultimatum akin to a preliminary declaration of war.

By this time, however, the refugee flow from East Berlin to West Berlin was seriously damaging Soviet prestige and the prodctive manpower resources of East Germany. Khrushchev may have welcomed an atmosphere of imminent explosion as the context for his sealing of the boundary between East and West Berlin just three weeks after the Kennedy address.

On August 7, the Soviet Premier delivered one of the most belligerent speeches of his career, linking "military hysteria" in the United States with an "orgy of revanchist passions" in West Germany, and warning the West against any intervention under the illusion that there could be anything like a limited war over Berlin. Khrushchev was bestowing honors on Cosmonaut Titov for his space feat, and used the occasion to make pointed allusions to the strategic power of the Soviet Union. "Any state used as a springboard for an attack upon the Socialist camp will experience the full devastating power of our blow." The territory of the United States would be crushed. Intervention, an act of war by the West, would be a suicidal act, spelling "death to millions upon millions of people."[5]

When the East Berlin sealing action was begun six days later, the specter of a thermonuclear holocaust had already been projected as its backdrop. The next move was up to the United States. We could regard it, as the Soviets were claiming, as a stabilizing device to bottle up the combustible passions on both sides of the boundary to within controllable confines. Or we could define it as a unilateral abrogation of established four-power responsibility for the city as a whole, and besides that a shameless denial of free choice to the Berliners, thus fitting into that category of action which the President insisted we would be forced to resist. Khrushchev was gambling on the vividness of the nuclear backdrop as the main barrier to Western action. But it was not such a terribly dangerous gamble for him, since the "wall" at first consisted of double strands of barbed

wire and other light barricades, backed up by elements of a motor-
ized division of the East German Army at critical crossing points.
Western counteraction, if it was to be physical, could have been in
the form of a symbolic cutting of the wire, or pushing over of some
obstacles. It need not have involved anything as dramatic as a bull-
dozing operation with tanks and cannon; and the next move would
have been up to the Soviets. Khrushchev still had many options.
His gamble, of course, was that *we* would not "overreact."

But he did more than simply gamble. The Soviets launched a
well-planned diplomatic campaign, calculated to provide the Western nations with a convincing political excuse for doing nothing. On
August 13, the Warsaw Pact countries issued a declaration against
"subversive activities directed from West Berlin" against the "socialist countries." The pact members accordingly were requesting
the East Germans

. . . to establish an order on the borders of West Berlin which will securely block
the way to the subversive activity . . . so that reliable safeguards and effective
control can be established around the whole territory of West Berlin, including its
border with democratic Berlin.

And then, in a deft attempt at limiting the issue: "It goes without
saying that these measures must not affect existing provisions for
traffic control on communications routes between West Berlin and
West Germany." [6]

The Ulbricht regime in its implementing decree, issued on the
same day, emphasized the point again: "As regards the traveling of
West Berlin citizens abroad along the communications lines in the
German Democratic Republic, former decisions remain valid." And
the decree stated explicitly that no former decisions on transit along
these routes were being revised.

On the afternoon of August 13, the United States Secretary of
State, after checking with the President at Hyannis Port, issued a
statement which, however caustic, signaled that the United States
got the message:

Having denied the collective right of self-determination to the peoples of East
Germany, Communist authorites are now denying the right of individuals to elect
a world of free choice rather than a world of coercion. The pretense that communism desires only peaceful competition is exposed: the refugees . . . have "voted
with their feet" on whether communism is the wave of the future.

Available information indicates that *measures taken thus far are aimed at residents of East Berlin and East Germany and not at the Allied position in West Berlin or access thereto.* (Emphasis added.) [7]

Rusk did claim that restrictions on travel between East Germany and Berlin were in direct contravention of the 1949 four-power agreements (signed at the conclusion of the Berlin blockade) and indicated that the appropriate diplomatic protests would be forthcoming. But there was not even a hint that the unilateral imposition of barriers across the city might constitute a fighting issue.

Many in the West were shocked and outraged at the Communist action. The West Berlin leaders who had foreseen the wall in the writing, as it were, felt themselves helpless and suddenly demoralized. Even Chancellor Adenauer at first maintained silence.

Kennedy sought advice from advisers at home and abroad, and found a solid consensus that there was not much we could do apart from issuing verbal protests. Sorensen recounts that "not one responsibile official in this country, in West Berlin, West Germany, or Western Europe—suggested that allied forces should march into East German territory and tear the Wall down." [8] The Mayor of Berlin, Willy Brandt, in a personal letter to President Kennedy, demanded actions of a retaliatory nature, such as a selective ban on imports from East Germany, a refusal to issue travel permits to East German officials wishing to travel to the West, and the taking over of the portion of the elevated railroad system in West Berlin that was still administered by the East. He also called for special actions to demonstrate renewed support by the United States for the West Berliners, many of whom felt that the West's failure to prevent the erection of the wall meant that the balance had been tipped in the Soviets' favor, and it was only a matter of time before the noose would be tightened around the entire city. Among the symbolic actions suggested by Brandt, four were adopted by the White House during the next few days:

a reinforcement of the allied garrison in West Berlin;
the appointment of General Lucius Clay as the American commandant;
a movement of allied troops along the Autobahn into West Berlin to demonstrate the continuing rights of Western access;
the dispatch of a high-level member of the United States Cabinet to the city (Vice President Johnson was Kennedy's choice).

The wall remained, and was reinforced with bricks and mortar. There were a number of incidents involving brutal treatment of refugees trying to escape, and a number of dangerous incidents, such as a confrontation of Soviet and American tanks across the barriers, and other rather daring demonstrations of resolve by General Clay.[9] West Berlin remained Western. And the allies continued to exercise their rights of access to the city while refusing to grant recognition to the East German regime. December 1961 came and went and the Soviets refrained from carrying out the unilateral actions threatened in their July *aide-mémoire*.

The situation seemed to be settling down to an uneasy, but basically stable, equilibrium, based on what now could be tacitly recognized as more clearly defined spheres of effective control. Meanwhile, the "search for peace—in quiet exploratory talks" that Kennedy had called for in his July address had got underway in the form of periodic meetings between Secretary Rusk and Soviet Foreign Minister Gromyko, and the Soviet and American ambassadors.

Kennedy was willing to live with the situation as it stood, coming around to the realization that a major global settlement was probably the necessary correlate of significant "movement" on the German question. As he put it to President Kekkonen of Finland, "Let the Soviet Union keep Germany divided on its present basis and not try to persuade us to associate ourselves legally with that division and thus weaken our ties to West Germany and their ties to Western Europe."[10]

Berlin and the other diplomatic crises of Kennedy's first year could be viewed as tests of the ground rules for coexistence that the President had propounded to Khrushchev during their conversations in Vienna: no action by either superpower to alter the existing balance of power and no attempt by either to interfere within the other's sphere of control. At Vienna there was what looked like mutual assent to these ground rules in principle, but considerable difference over how they might apply in practice. There was no objective definition of the balance of power, nor could the President and the Chairman assent unequivocably to the other's definition of *legitimate* spheres of control. The Soviet Union and the United States still differed importantly over ideology and objectives. The Berlin conflict was the product of these differences, not its cause. Neither side could agree simply to a maintenance of the "status quo." Moreover, with so many new nations experimenting with various types of regimes and still determining their interests and inclinations internationally, there was no such thing as even a de facto status quo in the Third World. Consequently there would be a series of tests in a volatile environment to determine who had effective power over what, and where in fact, at any point in time, the spheres of control lay.

The biggest test during Kennedy's presidency was to occur once again in the Caribbean, within the sphere of effective control of the United States, but now, according to the Soviets, part of the environment of dynamic change. From the Soviet point of view, there was no reason, in principle, why a Communist regime, aligned with the Soviet Union, should be regarded as an illegitimate penetration into the U.S. sphere of control. Khrushchev could easily interpret Kennedy's inhibitions at the time of the Bay of Pigs as the product of a realistic appraisal by the President that acceptable "spheres" have ideological more than geographic dimensions.

Kennedy, of course, was unworried about a Communist Cuba from a strictly geopolitical point of view. His objection to a Communist Cuba was ideological; it was on the grounds that Castro did not rule according to the voluntary consent of the governed that Kennedy regarded his regime as illegitimate. Kennedy's reluctance to apply United States military power to topple Castro was due to pragmatism, not cynicism. He was unwilling to make Castro a martyr to the Cuban people and to the rest of Latin America by sending in the Marines; the more effective method was to allow Castro to fashion his own noose, which would eventually be tightened by the Latins themselves.

What finally moved Kennedy to coercive action during the second Cuban crisis was the balance-of-power consideration. Khrushchev surely must have known that the President would be compelled to take countermeasures if it were clear that the global balance of power was being threatened. But this is probably why Khrushchev tried to confuse the issue, and, as a hedge, to keep his missile deployments to Cuba clandestine.[11] As it turned out, Kennedy had a clearer notion of the intangible *political* components of the balance of power than Khrushchev anticipated. In a retrospective reflection on the event, Kennedy characterized the Soviet missile deployment as

. . . an effort to materially change the balance of power . . . not that they were intending to fire them, because if they were going to get into a nuclear struggle, they have their own missiles in the Soviet Union. But it would have politically changed the balance of power. It would have appeared to, and appearances contribute to reality. [12]

It was of course significant that Khrushchev must have thought the President would be constrained from taking counteraction once the missiles became operational, and this continued to bother Kennedy:

What is of concern is the fact that both governments were so far out of contact, really. I don't think that we expected that he would put the missiles in Cuba, because it would have seemed an imprudent action for him to take, as it was later proved. Now, he obviously must have thought that he could do it in secret and that the United States would accept it. So that he did not judge our intentions accurately. [13]

Khrushchev had broken the ground rules. He had not merely penetrated our sphere of control, but he had done so in a manner that, if it had been allowed to stand as a fait accompli, would tip the global balance of power against us. Kennedy had been insisting publicly that the United States could not allow Cuba to become a base for Soviet "offensive" weapons. It was as much the fact of this drawing of the line in public as it was the actual military situation created by the Soviet deployments that underlay Kennedy's definition of the deployment as intolerable. Once the line had been so unequivocally drawn, for us to allow Khrushchev to defiantly step over it would have been to appear impotent against the Soviets' attempts to do as they pleased. This was the "appearance" that would have "politically changed the balance of power."

The administration seemed to fear that the consequences of this apparent change in the balance of power would be felt first in the form of a new Soviet squeeze play on Berlin. Khrushchev had lessened his pressure on Berlin the previous year at about the time it became generally known that recent Soviet missile claims had been greatly inflated, and that the United States still possessed overwhelming superiority in intercontinental strategic striking power. The deployment of missiles to Cuba, which might well appear to redress the balance by extending the Soviet strategic reach, could revive that margin of insurance against a United States strategic response which, presumably, was the necessary and sufficient condition for a Soviet probe in Berlin. Indeed, throughout the crisis,

Kennedy and his advisers were very much on edge in expectation of Soviet retaliation in Berlin for our exercising our superiority in the Caribbean (there was some thought that the symmetry of a blockade for a blockade would appeal to the Russians).* This anxiety was eased somewhat by the realization that Khrushchev had clearly indicated he would not reopen the Berlin issue until after the November congressional elections, which suggested that he did not feel safe enough to move on Berlin until the missiles became operational. Still Kennedy felt it necessary to warn the Soviets in his October 22 speech that "any hostile move anywhere in the world against the safety and freedom of peoples to whom we are committed, including in particular the people of West Berlin, will be met by whatever action is needed."[14]

Once the missiles were detected there was no question in the President's mind but that they would have to be removed. The question was how to attain their removal at the lowest cost in United States lives and Cuban lives without in the process bringing on a major war with the Soviet Union. For Kennedy, the corollary to the latter constraint was that we should not attempt to humiliate Khrushchev.

The notion that Cuban lives and Soviet face ought to constrain our plan of action guided the President in his narrowing of options. However, some members of his entourage did not appreciate or share the President's convictions on these boundary conditions. We know the course of action that was finally selected, and how the issue of the missiles (and bombers) was resolved. This course of action was by no means an inevitable derivation from an analysis of the irreducible national interest, the immediate threat posed by the Soviet deployments, and the balance of military capabilities on both sides.

Experienced presidential advisers with access to the same information as the President came to different conclusions about the actions necessary and most desirable to protect the basic national in-

---

*Arnold Horelick accepts as plausible the hypothesis that the Soviets had Berlin in mind when they decided to install the missiles, but he rejects the notion that there was danger the Soviets would retaliate in Berlin for our toughness over Cuba. His analysis of Soviet behavior and statements in this and other crises over the years leads him to put more credence in the speculation that the Soviets would be particularly reluctant to couple Berlin to a crisis atmosphere over Cuba. Soviet strategy has been to define its Berlin ploys as localized adjustments not worth a global confrontation. A Berlin crisis in the midst of the Cuban crisis would only make it easier for the United States to claim the Berlin issue was central and strategic.

terest and preserve the balance of power. Consequently, the intensive dialogue, actually decalogue, conducted by the President and his advisers during the period October 16–28, 1962, heightened the administration's self-awareness of the sometimes conflicting premises of power underlying its foreign policy, and contributed, in the form of a presidential choice, to a selection and sharpening of those premises which would govern administration policy henceforth.

A consideration which the President found he could not ignore, but which was easier for some of his advisers to bypass, was the moral character of our actions.

The arguments in behalf of restraint because of moral considerations were presented most strongly by George Ball and Robert Kennedy in opposing the resort to an air strike against the missiles—the option favored at first by most of Kennedy's special executive committee, including the Joint Chiefs of Staff. Ball argued that, regardless of the military outcome, a surprise attack would be against our best national traditions. The Attorney General supported Ball's stand, offering, "My brother is not going to be the Tojo of the 1960's." [15] Sorensen quotes Robert Kennedy as contending passionately that the sudden air strike would be "a Pearl Harbor in reverse, and it would blacken the name of the United States in the pages of history." [16] To knock out the Cuban missiles and aircraft capable of reaching the United States might mean killing 25,000 Cubans. Castro would become a martyr throughout Latin America, and the Cuban people would bear a grudge against us for decades.

These arguments, it should be noted, stressed the political value of action consistent with the presumed moral expectations of others, and of our own people. It rested on the premise that the reputation for moral restraint by a great power is an important element of political influence. It was apparently this line of reasoning that swayed a number of influential members of the executive committee away from the air strike. "I had wanted an air strike," recalls Douglas Dillon. "What changed my mind was Bob Kennedy's argument that we ought to be true to ourselves as Americans, that surprise attack was not in our tradition. Frankly, these considerations had not occurred to me until Bobby raised them so eloquently." [17] Robert Kennedy has claimed that the ideas which he voiced were really the President's, and has attributed them to his brother's "belief in what is right and what is wrong." [18]

But the detailed accounts of the deliberations during the thirteen days of the crisis show the President to have been less absolutely constrained by such an absolutist ethic than his younger brother later claimed.[19] The President was not willing to rule out an air strike, not even an invasion of Cuba, if that were what it would take to effect a removal of the "offensive weapons." His position seems to have been that these more costly actions (calculated in part in moral terms) should not be taken until the less costly alternatives had been exhausted. And he ultimately came around to the naval "quarantine" on weapons-carrying vessels as the least costly of potentially effective alternatives, which did not, by its adoption as the first move, prevent us from resorting to the higher cost and higher risk alternatives later. His was an ethic of pursuing the objective, but patiently, with means least destructive of human life, even though the objective might be more certainly and swiftly attained by alternative means if one did not worry about their destructive side effects.

Such moral questions were involved and taken very seriously by the President. But it would be a distortion to separate them explicitly from the other considerations which weighed heavily upon him. These considerations can be grouped under his general concern for "controlling the risks."[20]

The biggest risk, from the point of view of the President, was to do nothing, to accept the presence of Soviet strategic weapons in Cuba as the new status quo. The Soviets would have achieved a tremendous victory on which they would then surely capitalize to put the squeeze on Berlin or anywhere else that their objectives came into conflict. They would be prone to miscalculate the strength of our commitments and be more than ever tempted to take reckless actions that would compel us to respond in force, possibly at a level where the ability to keep things under control on either side would be severely destabilized.

If there were very high risks in doing nothing, there were also high risks in reacting too massively. The White House was not afraid of a "rational" Khrushchev, but a Khrushchev forced to eat humble pie in public was an unknown. It was important to keep the Soviets reality-oriented, to show them that we had the capability and the will to forcibly remove their local threat to our security if driven to it, and to provide them with a less-humiliating option than retreat under a public ultimatum. Nor was it thought desirable to put the Khrushchev pledges to protect Castro under too severe a test by actually invading Cuba. The choices narrowed rather quickly, therefore, to either the naval blockade or the air strikes, with the latter finally abandoned by the President—as an initial response, though not ruled out as the next step in case the blockade failed. The President's reasons, according to Abel, Sorensen, and Schlesinger—those reasons which he expressed to his assembled group of advisers[21]—were primarily on the grounds of the immediate risks of the air strike as opposed to the naval blockade. Thus, in Abel's account, in the final review of the alternatives, on October 21:

The President asked General Walter C. Sweeney, Commander of the Tactical Air Force, whether he could be certain that an air strike would take out all the Soviet missiles at one stroke. Sweeney replied that it should be possible to destroy some 90 per cent of them, though he could not guarantee 100 per cent effectiveness. A clean surgical operation, in short, was a military impossibility. The plan called for bombing Castro's military airports, as well as the missile bases, and several of these were in populated areas. Haunted by the thought that thousands of Cuban civilians might be killed, in addition to the Russians manning the missile sites, Kennedy once again vetoed the air strike. Even if only 10 per cent of the missile sites were to survive, he reasoned, they might be fired against the United States.[22]

The blockade, by contrast, offered Khrushchev the choice of avoiding an immediate military clash, by merely keeping his ships away. This would not settle the matter of the missiles already there, but it would, without a direct engagement, establish firmly our intention to maintain control in the Caribbean. Khrushchev could, of course, stall on the matter, but once he had turned away from challenging the blockade, the reality of our power would have been recognized. If Khrushchev under these circumstances were to make concessions, they would be temporary concessions to present realities, a tolerable posture for a Bolshevik; it would not have to look like a humiliating and irreversible defeat.

The strongest *public* remarks to Khrushchev were made in the President's dramatic October 22 radio-television address, divulging the fact that we knew the Soviet missiles were in Cuba, and outlining our initial low-level response. The only specific reference to a higher level military response was in connection with the hypothetical contingency of an actual launching of nuclear missiles from Cuban soil: "It shall be the policy of this Nation to regard any nuclear missile launched from Cuba against any nation in the Western Hemisphere as an attack by the Soviet Union on the United States, requiring a full retaliatory response upon the Soviet Union." [23] There was a deliberately vague reference in Kennedy's speech to further action, in addition to the blockade, if the missile preparations in Cuba continued, but nothing even approaching an ultimatum. It was only through *private* channels that the screws were tightened; and then, only in conjunction with our public acceptance of the formula: you remove the weapons under UN supervision; we will give assurances against invasion. We now know that Robert Kennedy, at the request of the President, when handing a copy of this formula to the Soviet ambassador, accompanied it with a very tough oral message: the point of escalation was at hand. Unless the President received immediate notice that the missiles would be withdrawn, we were in a position to take strong and overwhelming retaliatory action. [24] That was on Saturday, October 27, six days since the President's radio-television address demanding the removal of the missiles, one day after the receipt of the emotional and surprisingly contrite secret letter from Khrushchev, only hours after a second stronger Khrushchev letter, this one broadcast to the entire world.

There had still been no real confrontation of wills. The installation of the missile sites in Cuba, from components already there, had been continuing at a rapid pace. The naval quarantine was in force, but both sides had avoided a clear test: the President had taken his time in actually implementing the blockade. His speech was delivered Monday night. On Thursday morning, when the Navy hailed a Soviet tanker, Kennedy ordered it to be passed through without inspection, allowing for the possibility that the ship had not yet received its instructions from Moscow. [25] The Soviet cargo ships with their submarine escorts would have arrived Friday. The Navy was urging the President to go far out into the ocean to intercept the Soviets before they reached the Caribbean. But, backed by McNamara, he insisted that Khrushchev be given all possible time to communicate with his ships. The President did, however, find the opportunity to stop a ship to symbolically show our resolve: a dry-cargo freighter, owned by a Panamanian company, Lebanese registered, with a Greek crew, but sailing under a Soviet charter was halted and boarded at dawn Friday, found to be carrying only trucks and spare parts, and allowed to pass.[26] The Soviets, for their part, stopped the progress of their cargo ships, and had actually turned them back toward home port by Friday. But would they stop work on the missiles already in Cuba? And, once these were operational, would the Soviet Navy sail toward Cuba more confidently? Or would the Communists invoke a counterblockade around Berlin, where they had tactical superiority? As the President dispatched his brother with his final private ultimatum to Khrushchev, these doubts remained intense. Still, Kennedy stood his ground, and refused to be stampeded into the tempting chest-thumping postures urged upon him by some advisers.

Even after the Soviets agreed to dismantle the missiles in return for a U.S. pledge not to invade Cuba and a secret agreement to dismantle the obsolete U.S. missiles in Turkey, Kennedy insisted, as Sorensen describes it, that there was to be

. . . no boasting, no gloating, not even a claim of victory. We had won by enabling Khrushchev to avoid complete humiliation—we should not humiliate him now. If Khrushchev wanted to boast he had won a major concession [no U.S. invasion of Cuba] and proved his peaceful manner, that was the loser's prerogative.[27]

It is tempting to overdefine the resolution of the Cuban missile crisis as having reestablished clarity concerning the spheres in which each superpower was to exercise effective control. It is true that the Soviets were effectively kept from establishing an offensive military base in the Western hemisphere. But Castro was not about to accept anything like the "normalization" of relations with the neighboring superpower that the Soviet Union reimposed on Hungary and Poland in 1956 following the threat (which never materialized) of Western intervention in Eastern Europe. Castro would not even allow the UN to verify the dismantling of the Soviet missile sites, the contingency upon which our no-invasion pledge was conditioned. For three weeks Castro balked at returning to the Soviets their Ilyushin-28 bombers, which, like the missiles, were within range of the United States. This, not the inspection issue, became the outstanding problem between the United States and the Soviets. When finally the Soviets persuaded Castro to give up the bombers also, Kennedy lifted the naval quarantine, and talked in public with the Soviets as if the crisis was now completely resolved. This allowed the Soviets to portray the outcome as one establishing the legitimacy of the Castro regime, thanks to the Soviet missile ploy.

The United States for its part never explicitly affirmed the no-invasion pledge, but neither did we deny that we felt bound by it as a tacit agreement. Indeed, many of our actions and statements henceforth suggested that if only Castro would pledge not to export his revolution to other Latin American countries, we would be perfectly willing to establish normal relations with Cuba again, despite the fact that it was a Communist regime and an ally of the Soviet Union. The Communists thus were given an even greater claim to legitimacy in the Caribbean than they were willing to allow the West in Berlin.

Ambiguity remained, but the lines were holding, and had weathered their most serious threat. Henceforth attempts at interpenetration of one another's sphere would be more subtle, and far below the threshold of frontal challenge to the other's military dominance in areas of traditional hegemony.

Possibly also—but this would materialize more in the context of the nuclear test ban negotiations—there could be mutual agreement to refrain from actions, symbolic or material, designed to significantly alter the existing balance of coercive power.

17

THE TEST BAN: STABILIZING
THE BALANCE

On the Presidential Coat of Arms, the American eagle holds in his right talon the olive branch, while in his left he holds a bundle of arrows. We intend to give equal attention to both.

JOHN F. KENNEDY

The unwillingness of the United States to destroy the wall the Communists had built in the festering Berlin enclave and the unwillingness of the Soviet Union to run the blockade the United States had cast around Cuba had parallels that were perceived in the White House. The symmetrical aspects were disturbing and hopeful at the same time.

It was disturbing to have it again made clear that military force, the distribution of physical coercive capabilities, counted more than the nonmaterial factors—ideology, community, loyalty, and even kinship—in defining "power."

But the reassertion of the dominance of the impersonal factors of power, however cruel to those finding their demands factored out of the calculus, allowed for the beginning of a less jittery relationship. Each had demonstrated to the other a "rational" respect of the other's arsenal of massive destruction, each had respected the other's refusal to be dramatically undermined within its existing territorial sphere of dominance, and each had also demonstrated it was not about to allow lesser members of its ideological community to stampede it into an actual test of strength with its giant opponent.

Soviet behavior in the China–India border war, which took place concurrently with the Cuban crisis, also could be read as a sign that the Soviets had possibly reached a critical turning point in their global strategy. Instead of demonstrating solidarity with the Chinese Communists, and thereby attempting to gain some of the laurels for the ascendancy of Communist power in that theater, the Soviets maintained an icy neutrality in that conflict, and after the cease-fire entered into negotiations with India to augment their military assistance to the Nehru government. Policies of East–West confrontation were to be avoided in the Third World as well as in Europe; but this might require assisting in the creation of local balances of power so as not to require the direct intervention of either the Soviet Union or the United States on behalf of weaker parties, interventions which would lead to counterinterventions by the other superpower to prevent alterations in the overall balance.

The situation could be perceived as an equilibrium of sorts. Its maintenance, however, would depend upon the perpetuation of the belief by both of the giants that neither was positioning to topple the other.

A modicum of mutual trust was thus an important element in any program for stabilizing the equilibrium, at least trust in the other's good sense, and, at best (though this was still far in the distance), trust in the other's good intentions. The journey of a thousand miles, as stated in the Chinese proverb Kennedy quoted to Khrushchev in Vienna, starts with but a single step. Khrushchev had not been ready to take that step with Kennedy the previous year. He had explored the alternative path, with its lures of a quick and decisive victory in the Cuban missile deployment, and had almost tumbled into the abyss. Moreover, the President, in an admixture of good grace and prudence, had refrained from the temptation to push the opponent as he lost his balance. Would the Soviet leader's common sense lead him to a more positive response to a fresh invitation from the President? Both Kennedy and another seasoned politician, Prime Minister Macmillan, against the advice of some of their more "sophisticated" advisers, believed it was worth a try, and that the first step ought to be the much offered and much rejected nuclear test ban treaty.

There were clues that Khrushchev might be ready. He seemed to be pushing hard within his own camp to convert the events of October and November 1962 into lessons on the futility of a foreign policy based on military confrontations and an accelerating arms competition. On December 12, in a post mortem to the Supreme Soviet on the Cuban crisis, he accused the Albanians and the Chinese of wanting "to bring on a clash between the Soviet Union and the United States."

He could not agree with the irresponsible characterization of the United States as a "paper tiger," said Khrushchev: "If it is a 'paper tiger' . . . those who say this know that this 'paper tiger' has atomic teeth. It can put them to work; and it cannot be regarded frivolously." If during the Cuban crisis the Soviet Union had not shown the proper restraint, asked Khrushchev, if instead the Soviet Union had heeded "the promptings of the ultrarevolutionary loudmouths," what would have been the consequences?

We would have entered the stage of a new world war, a thermonuclear war. Our vast country would have withstood it, of course, but tens and tens of millions of people would have perished! And Cuba would have simply ceased to exist. . . . Other densely populated countries that do not have vast expanses . . . also would have perished completely. And even those who remained alive, and future generations too, would have suffered incredibly from the consequences of atomic radiation.

Was this the path of mankind's development outlined by Marx and Lenin?

There must be other modes of conducting the competition with the United States. The "sensible norms" of international relations should be strengthened, urged the Soviet Premier. It was necessary to show "more sobermindedness and a greater desire to remove the roadblocks that cause friction and create tension among states." It was necessary to manifest goodwill in the search for mutually acceptable solutions.

One of the areas in which new efforts had to be made to achieve mutually acceptable solutions, said Khrushchev, was in disarmament. And to that end, "We call upon the Western powers to remove the last barriers to an agreement on ending nuclear tests for all time to come." [1]

This time there appeared to be more than rhetoric involved in the Soviet call for an agreement. Khrushchev had been agitating within his party for some time for a greater concentration of resources and administrative attention to domestic economic problems, especially the shortfall in agricultural production. His November 19 speech to the Central Committee plenum outlining new party and administrative arrangements for attending to the domestic economy was read with care in Washington.[2] It had obviously been the product of much detailed study, analysis, and prolonged debate within the party hierarchy even before the Cuban missile crisis. But possibly to clinch his controversial program now, and solidify the party ranks behind him, Khrushchev needed concrete evidence that a modus vivendi with the United States was feasible.

Chairman Khrushchev's most recent special notes to the President contained what looked like quite sincere attempts to underline the seriousness of his pleas to finalize negotiations on the test ban. "This is a very propitious moment for doing so," he wrote in his December 19 letter. "The period of maximum crisis and tension in the Caribbean is behind us. We are now free to consider other urgent international matters, in particular a subject which has long been ripe for action—the cessation of nuclear tests."

The differences between the two sides, Khrushchev correctly pointed out, had narrowed to the question of how to confirm that suspicious seismic vibrations on the territories of the nuclear powers were not underground tests. Both were willing to rely on existing means of detection for determining violations in space and under water.

Every time the question of inspecting for underground tests had come up, the Soviets had accused the West of using the issue as a pretext for establishing a spy system on Soviet territory. The preferred Soviet formula during the past few years was to include underground tests in a comprehensive ban but to exempt these from inspection, relying instead on an unpoliced voluntary moratorium. In pre-Cuba negotiations at the Eighteen Nations Disarmament Conference in Geneva, in response to the Western scientific evidence that outside seismic detection systems could not identify disturbances below a certain magnitude, the Soviets had accepted the idea of a network of international seismic stations to be installed near the frontiers of the nuclear powers and in their territory. The apparatus in these stations was to be sealed, so as to preclude tampering, but they were not to be manned by international personnel.

The West continued to insist that such purely technical means of inspection would be insufficient, and that some degree of human verification would be essential.

Now, however, Khrushchev claimed to be making a further concession:

If . . . it should be considered necessary for foreign personnel to participate in such deliveries of apparatus to and fron automatic seismic stations, we could agree to this, taking measures, if required, to prevent such visits from being used for espionage purposes. Our proposal for automatic seismic stations thus includes elements of international control. This is an important gesture of goodwill on the part of the Soviet Union.

Having accepted the principle of on-site inspection, Khrushchev then proceeded to define the only outstanding issue between the two sides as being the number of on-site inspections to be permitted each year. "Very well: if this is the only obstacle to agreement, we are prepared to meet with you on this point in the interests of the noble and humane cause of ending nuclear weapons tests." Khrushchev urged that discussions to find an agreed number, already having begun between V. V. Kuznetsov for the Soviet Union and Arthur Dean for the United States, continue posthaste with the intention of coming to an agreement by the first of the year.[3]

Yet when it actually got down during the coming months to arriving at an agreed number of inspections, the Soviets seemed to be as recalcitrant as ever. The Soviets had started their post-Cuba negotiations on this issue with the announcement they would accept "two to three" inspections a year on their territory. The United States had been insisting that the minimum number it could now accept (and that due to progress in technical detection devices) was eight to ten. The "bargaining" was actually asymmetrical, since the Soviet maximum was an arbitrary barrier meant to "protect" against presumed espionage, whereas the Western minimum was professedly based on a scientific determination of the average amount of normal seismic disturbances each year below the threshold of intensity that could be picked up with the instruments. It was not unreasonable for the President to assume the Soviets had an acceptance price somewhat different from their asking price. But the Soviets broke off the tripartite talks that had been taking place in New York City during January 1963, without so much as a hint that they might be willing to strike for a middle ground between the Western minimum and their maximum. In April, after considerable debate among the President's advisers, the United States presented a revised minimum of seven, instead of eight to ten, to the Eighteen Nations Disarmament Conference; but the Soviets still wallowed in the mud of two to three, lacing their pronouncements in Geneva with innuendoes of lack of Western good faith.[4]

President Kennedy was losing hope, but felt he should still try. If Khrushchev's signals were confusing as to his real intentions, could it not also be that he was not completely sure of the meaning of those he was receiving. In April and May, through an exchange of letters with Khrushchev, Kennedy and Macmillan persisted in trying to convey the seriousness of their objective to negotiate a nuclear test ban, and both offered to send very senior representatives to Moscow to speak for them on this issue.

The President's position was reinforced in late May by the resolution introduced in the Senate by Thomas Dodd and Hubert Humphrey to put the Senate on record as favoring (1) an agreement to prevent nuclear testing in the atmosphere and under water (where adherence could be adequately verified without new arrangements), and (2) a pledged by the United States to refrain from further testing in these environments even in advance of a formal agreement so long as the Soviets also refrained from resuming their tests. Unlike the earlier unpoliced moratorium Eisenhower had agreed to, and Khrushchev had then violated without prior notice in 1961, this mutual abstention would not extend to underground tests in the absence of effective inspection machinery.* President Kennedy, according to Schlesinger, was somewhat concerned that a push for the limited ban now might undercut the narrowing of differences on the comprehensive ban, but was pleased to be able to point to a growing national consensus in favor of some antitesting agreement.[5]

A momentum was building up which the President was anxious to encourage. Sorensen was set to work on a first draft of a major speech about "peace," to be ready for delivery on June 10 at the President's commencement appearance at American University. "The President was determined to put forward a fundamentally new em-

---

*The proposed ban on atmospheric tests had been offered by the United States before, under Eisenhower in 1959 and under Kennedy in 1962. Both times it had been rejected by the Soviets as a hypocritical attempt to convince the world that the nuclear arms race was being halted, whereas in reality it was not.

phasis on the peaceful and the positive in our relations with the Soviets," recalls Sorensen. "He did not want that new policy diluted by the usual threats of destruction, boasts of nuclear stockpiles and lectures on Soviet treachery." [6]

Two days before Kennedy's American University address, Khrushchev replied in a sour letter that he would receive the high-level emissaries as proposed by the President and Prime Minister Macmillan. It is doubtful that Khrushchev knew he was significantly strengthening the President's hand, but the timing could not have been better. White House correspondents were briefed that the June 10 speech was of major importance. They were not to be disappointed. And, as it turned out, even Khrushchev was impressed.

The President used the American University rostrum to announce two important decisions: the agreement between Khrushchev, Macmillan, and him to have "high-level discussion" take place shortly in Moscow, "looking toward early agreement on a comprehensive test ban treaty"; and the decision by the United States government not to conduct further nuclear tests in the atmosphere so long as other states did not do so. "We shall not be the first to resume." If revealed matter-of-factly in a press conference, these decisions would have been regarded as significant, but not momentous. However, embedded as they were in a dramatic appeal to the nation to reexamine our attitudes toward the Soviet Union, the cold war, and peace itself, the impression was created of a turning point in United States–Soviet relations with far-reaching implications.

The Soviet Union and the United States, said the President, shared a common interest in relieving themselves of the heavy burden of armaments:

For we are both devoting massive sums of money to weapons that could be better devoted to combating ignorance, poverty, and disease. We are both caught up in a vicious and dangerous cycle in which suspicion on one side breeds suspicion on the other, and new weapons beget counterweapons.

Both sides, therefore, could be regarded as having "a mutually deep interest in a just and lasting peace and in halting the arms race," and "agreements to this end are in the interests of the Soviet Union as well as ours—and even the most hostile nations can be relied upon to accept and keep those treaty obligations, and only those treaty obligations, which are in their own interest."

Our primary long-range interest, maintained the President, was in an agreement for general and complete disarmament. The prospects for a treaty involving such a comprehensive agreement were of course still very dim. But we would continue to work on this effort.

Efforts should be concentrated on the one major area of negotiations where the end *was* in sight: the treaty to outlaw nuclear tests. With less equivocation than he was to display two months later in asking the Senate to ratify the treaty, the President catalogued a list of far-ranging implications:

The conclusion of such a treaty . . . would check the arms race in one of its most dangerous areas. It would place the nuclear powers in a position to deal more effectively with one of the greatest hazards which man faces . . . the further spread of nuclear arms. It would increase our security—it would decrease the prospects of war.

Anticipating criticisms at home, as well as driving home the solidity of his intentions to Khrushchev, the President dealt with the risks of noncompliance. He admitted that no treaty, however much it might be to the advantage of its signatories, however tightly it might be worded, could provide absolute security against the risk of deception and evasion, "but it can . . . offer far more security and far fewer risks than an unabated, uncontrolled, unpredictable arms race." [7]

The Soviets broadcast the speech with very little deletion and then rebroadcast it in its entirety. The full text was published in the Soviet press. But there was no immediate response from Khrushchev. Meanwhile, the President made preparations for a European trip to tend to one of the effects of the emerging United States–Soviet strategic standoff–namely, the ability of de Gaulle to sow doubt, particularly in the minds of the Germans, about the credibility of our pledges to bring our strategic capability into play to counter Soviet military provocations in Europe. (See chapter 18 for an elaboration.)

The Presidential rhetoric (and presumably the private assurances also) designed for West German ears would be somewhat at odds with the tone of the American University speech. There are few clues to indicate if the President and his advisers gave close attention to the apparent contradictions, or whether this was one of those cases where the position papers, having been written in different offices of the government, were never compared. It is possible, but one can only speculate, that a higher statecraft was at work during the summer of 1963: the assurances to the West Germans could be considered as guarantees by the United States to back them up in their conflicts with the Soviets in *hypothetical* situations, which would become more remote under conditions of East–West détente. To work toward the détente with the Soviets while, simultaneously, refurbishing our guarantees to the Germans was thus not a policy contradiction, unless the Soviets or the Germans chose to put that construction on it. Kennedy could reasonably expect that if the Soviets were truly interested in the test ban and other steps toward détente, they would not use our rhetoric toward Germany as a pretext for charging us with bad faith. After all, the Soviets also had their Germany to soothe, and ought to understand the requirements.

Khrushchev evidently did understand and also seemed to appreciate the symmetry involved. On July 2, one week after the President's ringing *Ich bin ein Berliner* reiterations of the identity of United States and West German security interests, the Soviet Premier was in East Berlin lambasting the West for trying to use a nuclear test ban as a means of obtaining access to the Socialist countries by "NATO intelligence experts." For that reason, the Soviet government was proposing a test ban that did not involve territorial inspection—that is, an agreement to ban all nuclear tests in the atmosphere, in outer space, and under water, setting aside the ban on underground tests. But this agreement should be combined with "the simultaneous signing of a nonaggression pact" between the NATO and Warsaw Pact countries, he insisted. [8]

Two weeks later the American delegation, headed by Averell Harriman, and the British delegation, headed by Lord Hailsham, began their negotiations with Khrushchev and Gromyko in Moscow.

The atmosphere in the city was electric, as the Soviets were just winding up a round of secret ideological talks with the Chinese Communists. The bitterness of the split between the two powers was explicitly displayed on July 14 in the form of an "open letter" by the Soviet Communist Party Central Committee to their new party organizations. The CPSU letter charged that the Communist Party of China was digressing more and more from the common line of the Communist movement on basic issues, particularly "the question of war and peace" and the "possibility of averting a world thermonuclear war." The Chinese comrades erred in not realistically appraising the consequences of the "radical, qualitative change of the means of waging war," contended the Soviets. They failed to take account of the fact that "the atomic bomb does not distinguish between imperialists and working people; it hits entire areas and therefore, for one monopolist, millions of workers would be destroyed." The struggle against world war, with its corollary of the peaceful coexistence of states with different social systems, argued the CPSU letter, was derived from this realistic appraisal of the balance of forces. In such a context, general disarmament, and lesser steps in that direction like the nuclear test ban treaty, should not be regarded as mere tactical expedients. They were the historically determined responsibility of any party which wanted to implement the precepts of Marxism-Leninism.[9]

Harriman seems to have shared the President's view that this time Khrushchev was not merely playing to the galleries in professing peaceful coexistence and deep interest in arms limitation measures. At this particular juncture, Khrushchev probably was as anxious as we were for some concrete agreement to result from the text ban negotiations. Betting on the correctness of this hunch, Harriman was steadfast in compelling Khrushchev to stick to the item where agreement was very near at hand—the three-environment test ban—and to defer negotiation on any nonagression treaty. But allowing for Khrushchev's need to show the other Communist countries that there was room to accomplish a great deal through negotiation as opposed to belligerency, Harriman permitted the implication to stand that we would take up the matter of a nonagression pact in subsequent discussions. Still, he was careful not to condition the test ban on any agreement to negotiate the matter.*

* Robert Kennedy, in recalling this period, gives much weight to the counsel of Harriman in buttressing the President's premises concerning the meaning of Soviet moves. In his forward to a collection of documents built around the theme of the American University speech, Senator Kennedy states that "after the Cuban nuclear confrontation . . . he [the President] felt the world was changed and that perhaps there would be less opposition to a renewed effort for agreement. This view was not shared in many quarters of the government, although

It took nine days of negotiation to agree on the final text of the Treaty Banning Nuclear Weapons Tests in the Atmosphere, in Outerspace, and Underwater, initialed in Moscow on July 25, 1963, by Andrei Gromyko, Averell Harriman, and Lord Hailsham. "Yesterday a shaft of light cut into the darkness," said Kennedy in his July 2 radio-television address announcing the conclusion of the treaty and explaining its meaning. It signaled not a victory for one side, but rather "a victory for mankind." It reflected "no concessions either to or by the Soviet Union." But he was anxious to avoid raising expectations of a sudden end to the cold war and the attendant risks of military conflict:

This treaty is not the millennium. It will not resolve all conflicts, or cause the Communists to forego their ambitions, or eliminate the dangers of war. It will not reduce our need for arms or allies or programs of assistance to others. But it is an important first step—a step towards peace—a step towards reason—a step away from war.

Looking toward the need to gain Senate ratification of the treaty, the President attempted to show where such a first step could lead as a way of generating a popular consensus for an affirmative vote, but mindful of the tendency of the American democracy to lower its guard at times of good feeling, he was careful to make a distinction between possible effects and predicted effects.

This treaty "can be a step towards reduced world tension and broader areas of agreement," said the President. Among the measures mentioned were a comprehensive treaty banning tests everywhere, controls on the numbers and types of armaments, controls on preparations for surprise attack, further limitations on the spread of nuclear weapons, progress toward general and complete disarmament ("our ultimate hope"), and even a mutual foreswearing of aggression, direct and indirect. As yet, however, there were no indications that the Soviet government was willing to accept the kind of inspection arrangements such agreements would require: "No one can predict with certainty, therefore, what further agreements, if any, can be built on the foundations of this one."

The President laid special emphasis on the treaty's potential for

it was shared by Averell Harriman, among others. Based on this view and on the encouragement received from Averell Harriman, President Kennedy made the speech at American University . . . from the American University speech and the efforts that followed came the nuclear test ban treaty." *Toward A Strategy of Peace,* edited by Walter C. Clemens, Jr. (Chicago: Rand McNally, 1965), pp. xiii–xiv.

helping prevent the spread of nuclear weapons to nations not yet possessing them. "This treaty can be an opening wedge in that campaign." It provided that none of the signatories would assist other nations to test in the prohibited environments. But the transference of completed weapons or their parts was not prohibited, nor were currently nonnuclear nations prohibited from producing weapons from the blueprints and test results of the nuclear nations. Kennedy could refer to such eventual comprehensive prohibitions only as a "great obligation" possibly now closer to implementation.

An immediate effect of the test ban treaty, if faithfully observed by at least the United States and the Soviet Union, would be to reduce the fears and dangers from radioactive fallout. But the President did not claim more than a marginal reduction.

Finally, the President directed the attention of his audience to the likely effects of the test ban treaty upon the nuclear strategic balance itself. With the assistance of the Secretary of Defense, this part of the case for the treaty had been very carefully prepared. The administration anticipated—and, as it turned out, correctly—that domestic opponents of the treaty would turn their fusillade on its implications for the United States–Soviet competition for military ascendancy. If the country was taking too many gambles with respect to the survivability of its nuclear deterrent, this would be prima facie grounds for the treaty's rejection. The Senate Preparedness Investigating Subcommittee, chaired by John Stennis of Mississippi, had been holding hearings on the military implications of various test ban alternatives since September 1962, and was expected to be sharpening its axe for this one. "Under this limited treaty," the President maintained:

The [still-permissible] testing of other nations could never be sufficient to offset the ability of our strategic forces to deter or survive a nuclear attack and to penetrate and destroy an agressor's homeland.

We have, and under this treaty will continue to have, the nuclear strength that we need. It is true that the Soviets have tested nuclear weapons of a yield higher than that which we thought to be necessary, but the hundred megaton bomb of which they spoke 2 years ago does not and will not change the balance of strategic power. The United States has chosen, deliberately, to concentrate on more mobile and more efficient weapons, with lower but entirely sufficient yield, and our security is, therefore, not impaired by the treaty I am discussing.

The President also attempted to anticipate the objections that would be raised about evasions, secret violations, and secret preparations for sudden withdrawal. These he admitted were possible, "and thus our own vigilance and strength must be maintained, as we remain ready to withdraw and resume all forms of testing, if we must." But he insisted that it would be a mistake to assume that there was any significant likelihood of the treaty being quickly broken. In terms of their own self-interest, the nations that initialed the treaty in Moscow and others whose accession was expected would be more likely to see the gains of illegal testing or evasion to be slight compared to their cost:

. . . For these nations too, and all nations, have a stake in limiting the arms race, in holding the spread of nuclear weapons and in breathing air that is not radioactive. While it may be theoretically possible to demonstrate the risks inherent in any treaty, and such risks in this treaty are small, the far greater risks to our security are the risks of unrestricted testing, the risk of a nuclear arms race, the risk of new nuclear powers, nuclear pollution, and nuclear war.

In closing, the President stressed once again that the "familiar places of danger and conflict" still require "all the strength and vigilance we can muster. Nothing could more greatly damage our cause than if we and our allies were to believe that peace has already been achieved," but

. . . history and our own conscience will judge us harsher if we do not now make every effort to test our hopes by action, and this is the place to begin. According to the ancient Chinese proverb, "A journey of a thousand miles must begin with a single step." [10]

It was a balanced appeal. It promised neither sudden gains nor the complete absence of risks. It was uncongenial to the President's style to play the demagogue. Besides, the President's experience probably told him that this was the best way to gain bipartisan support in the Congress.

Not surprisingly, in the debates and hearings directed toward Senate ratification, it was the potential military risks rather than anticipated political gains which received the most attention from critics and defenders alike. During those two months and administration's central arguments in behalf of the test ban moved from stressing its value as a first stop toward détente and peace to its utility as a means of preserving our strategic superiority.

The burden of the treaty's defense fell to McNamara. "The net of the relevant factors," he confidently pointed out, "is that the

U.S. nuclear force is manifestly superior to the Soviet Union's." The question was how this favorable situation would be affected by the test ban. "I can say that most of the factors will not be affected at all—not the accuracy of missiles, not variety of systems, not their dispersal or mobility, and not numbers." [11]

Critics, supporting their claims by testimony from distinguished nuclear physicists such as Edward Teller (the "father" of the H-bomb) and John Foster, Jr., director of the Lawrence Radiation Laboratory, had focused on these particular issues, as they were in fact the grey areas of legitimate scientific controversy. "From the evidence," intoned the report of Senator Stennis' Preparedness Investigating Subcommittee, "we are compelled to conclude that serious—perhaps even formidable—military and technical disadvantages to the United States will flow from the ratification of the treaty." [12]

In attempting to deal with the doubts raised by Edward Teller, Senator Stennis, and others, McNamara and his civilian and military associated in the Department of Defense presented facts to the Senate committees which, more than any previous presentation by the executive branch, disclosed the technical bases of the Kennedy administration's strategy and planning decisions for maintaining the nuclear strategic balance.

With respect to the suspected Soviet superiority in nuclear weapons exceeding fifty megatons, the Secretary of Defense granted the Soviet lead, and deferred to those experts who believed that the United States could not make significant improvements of the kind needed to catch up unless it were to resume nuclear testing in the atmosphere. These, to the best of his knowledge, were the facts. But what was their *military* significance? This was the relevant consideration in agreeing to the test ban agreement. For some years the Defense Department had been examining the possible uses of very high-yield weapons, such as the Soviets were apparently developing. These studies showed, according to McNamara, that there were two military disadvantages to deploying the higher-yield weapons as contrasted with deploying a large number of smaller weapons:

First . . . for most missions directed at military targets, we can achieve a higher confidence of kill by using two or three smaller weapons instead of one very large one; for a given resource input we achieve higher target destruction with our smaller systems.

Second, very high-yield warheads are relatively inferior as second-strike, retaliation, weapons; it is much more difficult and costly to make them survivable—to harden, camouflage or make mobile the huge missiles required to deliver these weapons.[13]

On the matter of whether a sufficient number of U.S. offensive weapons would be able to strike back after having absorbed the worst the Soviets could throw at us, McNamara was not at all troubled. With or without a continuation of tests in the atmosphere, "The U.S. strategic missile force is designed to survive, and it will survive." It was true that large-yield nuclear tests in the atmosphere would help us determine with greater precision the effects of nuclear explosions on hardened structures such as the silos housing our Minutemen missiles. This would only help to somewhat reduce the uncertainty of calculations based on past atmospheric tests and whatever underground testing was to continue. But where there were such uncertainties we would always err in our planning and deployments on the side of overcorrection:

We know, and the Soviets know, that in the event of a surprise Soviet first strike, at least a substantial proportion of our Minutemen will survive. Also, we and they know that the Polaris submarines at sea and many strategic aircraft will survive. We can say with assurance, therefore, that, even after a Soviet strike, the total surviving U.S. strategic nuclear force will be large enough to destroy the enemy.[14]

Some scientists, notably John Foster of Lawrence, felt that we did not know enough about the vulnerability of our weapons and their associated radars to other "blackout" phenomena, and that the Soviets, in their recent series of atmospheric tests, may have accumulated such information.[15] However, administration scientists claimed that this concern was ill-founded. Harold Brown, the Pentagon's director of defense research and engineering, maintained that the Soviet and American experience in determining the effects of such induced phenomena on the performance of nuclear weapons "appears to be comparable." Of course, he said, "the more we learned about it, the better we could do. But I want to make the point that this is a useful, but not vital piece of information."[16] It was not "vital" because, as the Chairman of the Joint Chiefs of Staff put it, "with regard to the immediate problems of the weapons systems we are contemplating, the general opinion is that we can attain these weapons even with the present uncertainties about this particular phenomenon."[17]

The same kind of criticism and rebuttal characterized the testimony about the implications of the test ban for the development of an antiballistic missile (ABM). Teller was concerned that in the absence of further testing to determine the effects of nuclear explosions on the defensive radars, it would be very difficult for us to develop a reliable ABM. Again, Harold Brown maintained that the United States and the Soviet Union were "roughly comparable" in knowledge in this field, with the United States possibly even somewhat ahead. More important, the ABM did not look like a good system to deploy anyway, since our calculations showed that even the most sophisticated systems would be ineffective (at the time they entered the inventory) against the improved offensive systems and "penetration aids" now under development.[18]

Even if we did decide to deploy an ABM system, said McNamara, by analysis of presently available data, and that obtained from underground testing, "we will be able to design around the remaining uncertainties." With or without a test ban, we could proceed with its development. But the "ABM problem is dominated by factors unrelated to the treaty."[19]

Finally, the Secretary of Defense contested the broadside assertion by some senators (notably Barry Goldwater and Richard Russell) that the overall effect of the treaty would be to preserve the Soviet lead in high-yield weaponry while permitting them to catch up with us in low-yield research through a diversion of their test activity underground. "We pay a price: they do not," said Goldwater.[20] The Secretary emphatically disagreed:

If testing continued indefinitely without limit as to test environment or size of yield, the most likely ultimate result would be technical parity between the United States and the U.S.S.R. . . .

But, by limiting Soviet testing to the underground environment, where testing is more difficult and more expensive and where the United States has substantially more experience, we can at least retard Soviet progress and thereby prolong the duration of our technological superiority. A properly inspected comprehensive test ban would, of course, serve this purpose still better.

This prolongation of our technological superiority will be a principal direct military effect of the treaty on the future military balance and I consider it a significant one (Emphasis added.)[21]

The administration's defense of the treaty against its critics was undoubtedly of educational value to the public and their representatives in Congress. Possibly it also helped to communicate to the Soviets the fact that our approach toward strategic weapons planning and strategies was based on security considerations, and not for aggressive purposes; but McNamara's championing of the atmospheric test ban as a means to prolong our military–technological superiority was ammunition for the more paranoid elements in the Communist world.

The dominance, which was probably inevitable, of military issues in the ratification debates gained the Kennedy administration its "first step" (The Senate ratified the treaty by a vote of 80 to 19), but it meanwhile put a gloomy pall on those who had sensed a straight path to significant arms reductions immediately ahead. The major premises in the President's American University speech seemed in retrospect as if they had been part of a discussion of some entirely different matter.

18

THE BREAKUP OF BLOCS:
THE DECLINE OF IDEOLOGY
AND CONTROL

Change is underway within the Communist world, as well as within the free world. Most of the smaller states of Eastern Europe are restoring, more and more, their historic ties with Western Europe and the United States. They are recovering their individuality and becoming less rigid in their internal policies. And these processes are visible within the Soviet Union too.

DEAN RUSK

Security for the superpowers required not only that they balance one another's military power, but that the supply of advanced armaments be kept in as few hands as possible. Such centralization of control within each alliance system was tolerable to all members so long as there was unity on the essential purposes for which action was most likely to be undertaken. But as hostility and the threat of war between the two major blocs of allies declined, each alliance member was able to rediscover its unique historical, geopolitical, national interests and rivalries. And the possibilities for these different interests requiring imcompatible strategies, even in interbloc conflicts, accelerated the loosening of bloc ties in the Communist and non-Communist worlds.

Mao's grievance against Khrushchev for the latter's insistence that the nuclear development program in China be conducted under close supervision from Moscow was severely aggravated during the Quemoy and Matsu crisis of 1958–59 when the Soviets failed to back up Communist Chinese actions with counterthreats against United States implied use of nuclear weapons. In the early 1960s, with Khrushchev and Kennedy insisting that the nonnuclear nations stop their own nuclear weapons development programs, the Chinese could see only collusion between the superpowers to support one another in the perpetuation of their hegemony over their respective allies. Marxist-Leninist ideology, which was supposed to put the interests of all proletarian movements first, was, according to the Chinese, being subordinated to Soviet self-interest. This charge was not without a melodious ring to other Communist parties—particularly in Eastern Europe, where there was serious resistance to the Soviet concept of economic specialization within a self-sufficient Communist trading area, which for most East European nations meant economic vassalage.

The United States was in the early 1960s quite well attuned to this bickering among the Communist nations. The question was how to exploit it to the advantage of our long-range interest in a reduction of Soviet imperialism, without driving the Soviets into a renewal of anti-Western belligerency and paranoia in order to reassert control in their own sphere.

Developments in our alliance system, and the problems these must have posed to Soviet strategists, were viewed by the Kennedyites as somewhat embarrassingly parallel. And it was not beyond some members of the alliance, notably de Gaulle with his penchant for caricature, to draw these parallels in bold strokes to a world audience. His apocalyptic visions, such as "some awful day" when "Western Europe should be wiped out from Moscow and Central Europe from Washington," while the two superpowers spared one another, were the currency of intellectual discussion in Europe and the undertone to diplomatic discussion in NATO.

De Gaulle was stating bluntly what Anthony Eden and Guy Mollet had implied as far back as the Suez crisis in 1956. Only temporarily had the threat of bloc vs. bloc war, in the post-Sputnik Berlin crisis, and then again in 1961, suppressed the subterranean strains. Even in the Berlin crises, allied unity was seen by some observers as merely a façade covering intense differences among the allies over military and diplomatic moves for various contingencies. Also during these years, the intensifying centrifugal pulls of national interest were sublimated in esoteric strategic debates over the timing and targeting of nuclear strikes.

Meanwhile, pariculraly at the substructures of economic and technological development, the currents for division were also eroding the bases of "the community," piously proclaimed by the supranational institution builders in NATO and Common Market headquarters. And the two major Western community institutions were themselves increasingly at cross-purposes, as the latent contradictions in their reasons for existence were exposed.

In the spring and early summer of 1962, with the Third World crises of the previous year no longer consuming so much of its energies, the Kennedy administration gave special attention to reasserting its leadership of the Atlantic Community within both the military and economic spheres. Experimental projects for a greater European nuclear role in the alliance were stressed for the former, and the vision of institutional innovation on a grand scale was projected for the latter.

Early in his presidency, Kennedy had affirmed his intention to commit to the NATO command the five Polaris submarines originally suggested by President Eisenhower.[1] The commitment of the missile-carrying submarines was confirmed by the President in his May 17, 1961, address to the Canadian Parliament (see above, pp. 166–67).

During the first half of 1962 private diplomatic discussions among the NATO members were held on what Secretary Rusk was now calling "a NATO nuclear deterrent" in preparation for the May ministerial session of the North Atlantic Council. There was expectation that some departure in the existing United States policy of keeping unto ourselves exclusive command and control of the alliance's nuclear forces (with the exception of the British V-bombers) might be announced at the May meeting. But evidently this expectation was premature. Subsequent clarifications by United States officials showed we had no intention of increasing the number of "fingers on the nuclear trigger." And apparently, within this condition of retaining control in Washington, the French found our proposed arrangements not at all attractive.

Expressing the French discontent, General de Gaulle, in his news conference pronunciamento of May 15, 1962, confirmed that France was now bringing its own atomic deterrent force into existence. "As regards the defense of France, the battle of Europe and even the world war as they were imagined when NATO was born, everything is now in question." The French atomic force "is changing and will completely change the conditions of our own defense, those of our intervention in faraway lands and those of the contribution that we would be able to make to safeguard our allies." France's defense, he intoned, for moral and political reasons had to "become once again a national defense." [2]

In President Kennedy's press conference two days later, the status of the disagreement with France was clarified. We believed the existing deterrent system for NATO provided adequate protection, said the President. Once nation after nation begins to develop its own deterrent, "You are moving into an increasingly dangerous situation." "If they [the French] choose to go ahead, of course they will go ahead, and General de Gaulle has announced they are going ahead." There was apparently nothing we could do or say that would dissuade him. However, with respect to the long-range future of the Atlantic Community, and the respective roles of each country within it, the discussions would continue.

Kennedy avoided the immediate temptation to express the full extent of his annoyance with de Gaulle, salvaging instead whatever measure of influence he might retain with the imperious Frenchman, and retaining in view of our other allies the demeanor of the leader who knows that his own ascendancy remains unshaken:

. . . I would say, speaking personally, that however difficult becomes this dialogue with General de Gaulle over . . . the Atlantic Community . . . I would think it would be a far more difficult situation if General de Gaulle were not as stalwart in his defense of the West. We do not look for those who agree with us, but those who defend their country and who are committed to the defense of the West. I believe General de Gaulle is. So we will get along. [3]

Despite the gracefulness, it *was* a serious rebuff the United States had suffered, and, at that, in reply to an intendedly magnanimous offer to give the Europeans a greater participatory role in planning and administering the nuclear strategy of the alliance. Temporarily, our efforts to reforge unity through a new momentum in military planning were stalemated.

The other arena of challenge to United States hegemony was that of international economics, to which the emphasis was quickly shifted. Here the momentum was in Europe. Even Great Britain had made application to join the Common Market, in a major reversal of her historic insular trading position, and at a sacrifice to her special Commonwealth relationships. The Kennedy administration had prodded the British in this direction, largely to open up the continental exclusiveness. But there was the risk that Britain would adapt to the protectionist pattern against America, rather than wedge an opening for American penetration.

There was yet opportunity for us to respond to the European economic movement creatively and augment our international influence while promoting our own economic health. The Reciprocal Trade Agreements Act was due to expire in mid-1962. The occasion of congressional action for its renewal could be turned into a major reconsideration of our position in the world economy: and analysis of our adverse balance of international payments in comparison with the dramatically improving balances on the part of members of the European Common Market, and the recommendation of a vigorous new United States trade policy designed to compete with and within the market. The administration's Trade Expansion Act had been prepared in late 1961 and presented to the Congress in January 1962; but now the time was at hand when a major push for its passage coincided with the need to redefine our attitude to an increasingly independent, and, if de Gaulle had his way, inward-looking, Europe.

On the same day he had replied to de Gaulle in his press conference, President Kennedy combined the themes of Atlantic partnership and trade expansion in his address to a national conference on trade policy. It is a "fact of history," he told the gathering of Congressmen and businessmen active in the trade field, "that responsibility and influence—in all areas, political, military, and economic—ultimately rise and fall together." He discounted the fears expressed in Europe that the United States might be abandoning its commitment to European security. But he also wanted to discount "fears . . . on this side of the Atlantic that the United States may be excluded from the councils and the markets of Europe." The "true course of history" was toward "Atlantic unity." He was striking out at the "limited visions and suspicions" on both sides of the Atlantic.

The President was groping for an idea, the Grand Design, that was to emerge full-blown, in all its glorious ambiguity, on July 4 in his ringing call for a "Declaration of Interdependence":

One hundred and eighty-six years ago, in the same hall from which he now spoke, Thomas Jefferson and his colleagues pledged their lives, their fortunes, their sacred honor in support of a declaration whose doctrine of national *independence* "remains the most powerful force anywhere in the world today."

But the idea of national independence had now reached its zenith: "With the passing of ancient empires, today less than 2 per cent of the world's population lives in territories officially termed 'dependent.' " Out of the power of the first idea, as in the American experience, was born its natural antithesis—which also resounded from this hall in Philadelphia across the world—the doctrine of the "indivisible liberty of all":

As this effort for independence, inspired by the American Declaration of Independence, now approaches a successsful close, a great new effort—for interdependence—is transforming the world about us. And the spirit of that new effort is the same spirit which gave birth to the American Constitution.

The new spirit was currently exhibiting the greatest momentum on the other side of the Atlantic. The United States, having for the past seventeen years aided this vast enterprise for European unity, looked upon this development with hope and admiration, said the President:

We do not regard a strong and united Europe as a rival but as a partner. . . . We believe that a united Europe will be capable of playing a greater role in the common defense, or responding more generously to the needs of the poorer nations, of joining with the United States and others in lowering trade barriers . . . and developing coordinated policies in all economic, political and diplomatic areas.

But this effort to form a more perfect union in Europe was only the first order of business of the grand effort to build the Atlantic partnership:

I will say here and now, on this Day of Independence, that the United States will be ready for a Declaration of Interdependence, that we will be prepared to discuss with a united Europe the ways and means of forming . . . a mutually beneficial partnership between the new union now emerging in Europe and the old American Union founded here 175 years ago.

It would be premature, said the President, to present in concrete detail the design of this emerging Atlantic partnership. Great edifices were not simply or cheaply built. They emerged cretively out of the practice and act of building. But "let the world know it is our goal."[4]

However vague the Grand Design, it did serve as an orienting goal and legitimating ideology for policies which, in the face of a decline in enthusiasm for anti-Communism as an orienting principle, were becoming increasingly difficult to defend. Under the Grand Design it was still possible to assert the requirement for a complete coordination of military planning within the NATO alliance, for a unified system of command and control, for a specialization of function according to capability and resources, for the United States to serve as nuclear "trustee" of the West, for a solid front on economic matters toward the Communist world—in short, but never stated so baldly, for the perpetuation of United States hegemony.

The Cuban missile crisis intervened, and diverted high-level discussion away from Atlantic community matters for a few months. Indeed, so compelling was the need for secrecy of deliberation, rapid dispatch of decisions made, and tight command and control, that allies were informed of all key decisions after the fact, rather than consulted while strategies were being formulated. The NATO heads of state understood and, in contrast to the sniping expressed in their parliaments and newspapers, gave President Kennedy every indication that they backed his tight control of the reins of decision during the crisis. De Gaulle openly pledged his complete support, and apparently fully approved of the premise of unilateralism exhibited by United States actions in the Caribbean crisis. After all, it confirmed his own thesis of self-mastery for the life-and-death decisions of the national unit. He only wanted the United States to accept that such national sovereignty was legitimate for others as well.

But for Kennedy the lessons, at least the immediate ones, of the Cuban missile crisis only strengthened conclusions that were diametrically opposed to de Gaulle's with respect to the international management of nuclear weapons. During his thoughtful radio-television conversation shortly after the Cuban missile crisis, the President was asked about his views on proliferation of nuclear weapons among our European allies. "We don't want six or seven separate nuclear powers diverting their funds to nuclear power," answered the President, but if they want to do it, "we are not stopping them." The question was whether we should help make France a nuclear power—"then Italy, then West Germany, then Belgium":

How does that produce security when you have ten, twenty, thirty nuclear powers who may fire their weapons off under different conditions? That isn't in our interest, or in my opinion in the interest of peace, or the interest of Western Europe.[5]

The day following the broadcast of these remarks, the President met with Prime Minister Macmillan in the Bahamas to negotiate the Nassau agreement, which was to make the British nuclear deterrent force ever-more dependent upon United States technical and material support, and provided for its incorporation into a NATO multilateral force (see above, pp. 172–73). The same type of association was offered to France.

De Gaulle seized the occasion to stage one of his tantrums: Britain was castigated in French diplomatic circles for perfidious double-dealing, of pretending its inclinations were toward continental association but meanwhile carrying on its "special relationship" with the United States. In January 1963, the French President abruptly halted the Brussels negotiations for Britain's entry into the Common Market, charging that her insular and maritime nature, plus her traditional trading linkages with diverse and distant countries, had made it impossible for Britain to accept the primary commitments to the six continental members of the market that membership would entail. Britain, he implied, was insisting upon unacceptable conditions, presumably the maintenance of Commonwealth trading preferences. If Britain now entered, she would probably be followed by the other members of her European Free Trade Association, with their own special extracontinental relationships. The European Community thus would be confronted with "all the problems" of Great Britain's economic relations with "a crowd of other states, and first of all with the United States." It was foreseeable, said the French President, that the cohesion of the European Community would not hold for long, and that:

In the end there would appear a colossal Atlantic Community under American dependence and leadership which would completely swallow up the European Community.

This is . . . not at all what France wanted to do and is doing, which is a strictly European construction.

Commenting on the Anglo-American agreement at Nassau as a basis for organizing the nuclear forces of the alliance, de Gaulle rejected it as having any utility for France or, for that matter, he implied, any self-respecting European power:

To turn over our weapons to a multilateral force, under a foreign command, would be to act contrary to . . . [the principles] of our defense and our policy. It is true that we too can theoretically retain the ability to take back in our hands [when supreme national interests were at stake] . . . our atomic weapons incorporated in the multilateral force. But how could we do it in practice during the unheard of moments of the atomic apocalypse? And then, this multilateral force necessarily entails a web of liaisons, transmissions and interferences within itself, and on the outside a ring of obligations such that, if an integral part were suddenly snatched from it, there would be a strong risk of paralyzing it, just at the moment, perhaps, when it should act.

Instead of the Atlantic relationships sponsored by the United States, France was now concentrating on the "more fruitful" rapprochement between France and Germany. "For the first time in many generations, the Germans and Gauls realize their solidarity." [6]

The State Department "theologians" (the name current during this period for United States officials who were fervent disciples of the European and Atlantic integrator, Jean Monnet) were only stimulated to greater proselytyzing by the high-level "confrontation" between the two "Grand Designs." De Gaulle's design was now openly pictured as reactionary—a return to the older pattern of historical national rivalries in Europe, the pattern which had led to two world wars—and dangerous in that it would encourage the spread of independent nuclear weapons, especially to West Germany, who, with her deep urges to reunite Germany, was capable of rash action. The President was persuaded to appoint a special mission, headed by ex-diplomat Livingston Merchant, to tour West European capitals in behalf of a revised multilateral nuclear force whose core owner-members were now to be Britain, West Germany, and the United States, along with any other NATO members who could be induced to join. France was written off as neither a necessary nor a desirable participant. This new MLF, a fleet of twenty-five missile-carrying surface ships, each manned by an international crew, was now presented as the "only alternative" to a presumed imminent German decision to build her own nuclear force under French tutelage.

The President allowed this kind of talk to go on, during the very same months he was making his major efforts to negotiate a nuclear test ban with the Soviets, perhaps to strengthen the impression that we were doing all we could to restrict the spread of nuclear weapons. It is doubtful that he was as highly motivated to actually launch the MLF as were the State Department Atlanticists; nor, apparently, did he think the Europeans would really want to join. Sorensen reports that "gradually in 1963 the MLF proposal fell from the top of the President's agenda toward the bottom." Moreover, "Kennedy had never looked upon either MLF or British entry into EEC as pillars of American policy." [7]

Chroniclers of the Johnson presidency portray him during his first year as the captive of pronouncements of the MLF zealots in the Department of State, who interpreted his lack of personal attention to this matter as approval of the preexisting formal policy line. Philip Geyelin's account suggests that public endorsements of the multilateral force by the President himself on April 20 and June 12, 1964, were probably in the nature of speech ingredients included as part of the standard recipe of foreign policy statements handed up from the bureaucracy. But Johnson, with his instinct for unfettered movement, swiftly cast off these prior commitments, when it came to making more specific decisions on the financing and composition of such a multilateral venture. [8]

The MLF was in fact abandoned, and left to die from presidential neglect, although in rhetoric it lingered for a while as the centerpiece of the United States concept of Atlantic partnership; and the virtual institution that had grown up around it in the State Department continued with artificial respiration (the Germans were insisting on the MLF, went the line) to keep up the pretense that the MLF was still everyone's hope for holding together an otherwise crumbling NATO.

A part of United States political strategy, of which the MLF was only a convenient instrument, was to keep the Federal Republic of Germany oriented toward us rather than de Gaulle. Every opportunity was taken, in rhetoric, in NATO force-planning sessions, in trade negotiations, to remind Germany that what she wanted most— protection against attack from the East, continued access to Berlin, eventual reunification, membership in international bodies, new trading opportunities—would be more likely to be advanced through her close ties with the United States than with France. We were pleased at the German–French reconciliation, we said, but not at all likely to respond kindly to German adopting a Gaullist "inward-looking" posture. The post-Adenauer regime of Ludwig Erhard and Gerhard Schroeder at first seemed to size up the situation in this way too; but as the French President began to intensify French–

Eastern European trading and cultural contacts, and to show greater cordiality to Moscow, to take specific steps, not just pontificating, toward weaving a greater Europe "from the Atlantic to the Urals," the post-Adenauer politicians of West Germany also began to search for opportunities to demonstrate "movement," away from the static NATO-first concepts propounded by the United States.

The frustrations suffered by the United States government in trying to begin the MLF and other devices of military "integration" as a means for consolidating the Atlantic partnership produced two contrary reactions in high policy circles.

The first, associated mainly with the Atlanticists in the Department of State, sought to counter the belief propounded by many of West Europeans, including the Germans, that the threat of war between the NATO and Warsaw Pact nations was now so unlikely as to render strict unity of command principles obsolete if not irrelevant. Reflecting the formulations of George Ball, Robert Schaetzel, and others in the State Department, Secretary Rusk reminded the spring 1964 meeting of the NATO Council that, although certain tensions in Europe appeared to have been somewhat relaxed and Communist tactics had been modified, "Communist objectives continue to pose a direct threat to the free world." We should not let NATO's success blind us to current dangers, he cautioned: "Certain of these dangers seem to have diminished; but they can reappear suddenly without warning. The need for a strong alliance of North Atlantic nations remains essential so long as basic Communist aims remain unchanged." [9]

The second reaction to our frustrations in NATO surfaced at first largely in the form of recommendations by prominent unofficial analysts of the Soviet Union and the cold war that we consider major alterations in our prevailing mode of containing Communist expansion in Europe. George Kennan resigned his ambassadorship to Yugoslavia in pique at the congressionally imposed restrictions on his attempts to establish flexible bilateral trading relationships with the Tito regime, and returned to argue with his colleagues at the Council on Foreign Relations on the need of fundamentally revising our premises on how to deal with the Communist world in its new phase of "polycentrism." [10] Before that same influential body in 1965, Professor Marshall Shulman argued that "the language and ideas of the Cold War are no longer adequate as a guide to international politics today." [11] And Zbigniew Brzezinski began to lecture and write extensively to officials and opinion leaders on the timeliness of a major new Western effort to increase economic and political ties across the Iron Curtain. [12]

Though differing in the details of their analyses and prescriptions, these prominent analysts gave voice to and advanced a common body of premises:

1. The so-called international communist movement was undergoing significant changes in its political structure, socioeconomic bases, and ideology that were not planned or dictated by its leaders, nor forecast in its ideology.

2. The tendencies within the Communist world which appeared to be gaining the upper hand over countervailing tendencies were (a) the decentralization of authority and power over resource allocation from the Communist Party of the Soviet Union to the national units; (b) decision making on major policy issues (for managing affairs within the Communist world and for relations with the non-Communist world) being transferred to the arena of interstate diplomacy—that is, Communist national leaders bargaining with other Communist national leaders, and away from reliance on decision making by the international party machinery; (c) independent, bilateral foreign relations between nations within the Communist world and by individual Communist nations with non-Communist nations, especially on matters of trade; and (d) powerful segments of bureaucracies and societies in the Communist nations (including the Soviet Union) becoming committed to the perpetuation of the kind of international East–West climate conducive to this decentralization toward national as opposed to "bloc" instrumentalities of decision.

3. If these tendencies were allowed to continue, it was possible to envision a transformation of international Communism from an aggressive centralized movement seeking world domination to heterogeneous Marxist parties attempting to implement their preferred concepts of state Socialism within their own countries.

4. None of this would guarantee a mitigation of the harsher aspects of totalitarian rule in these nations; indeed, the transition to national Communism from Soviet-controlled Communism could, in some cases, be accompanied by a tightening of political, intellectual, and artistic control. But the very fact of pluralism in the Communist world, of relief from exclusive dependency upon decisions made at the apex of a rigid hierarchy located in Moscow, and the opportunity for each nation to choose trading

and cultural partners in the non-Communist world, could in time lead to a greater pluralism, pragmatism, and genuine democracy within most national Communist societies.

5. These evolutionary tendencies were fully consistent with the central objective of U.S. foreign policy since 1947: namely, to contain Communism without in the process bringing on a third world war.

On this much there was agreement among Kennan, Shulman, and Brzezinski, and a growing coterie of Soviet specialists and foreign policy analysts, many of whom were consultants to the departments of State and Defense, and to the White House during the Kennedy years.

The question on which the growing consensus broke down was what the United States could and should do to encourage this evolution in the Communist world. Even before our heavy involvement in the shooting war in Vietnam, the official bureaucracy, more guarded against congressional censure than charges from academic friends of being wedded to obsolete policy premises, lumbered along with programs and rhetoric fashioned in the simpler good guys vs. bad guys phase of the cold war. Lacking concrete suggestions for altering existing policy, the official rhetoric, for the most part, noted the "hopeful signs" appearing in the Communist world, but held fast to the proposition that this merely demonstrated the correctness of our past policies, particularly with respect to the rebuilding, rearming, and coalescing of Western Europe under our leadership.

There were some exceptions to the official reiteration of standing formulas, however, which extended back to the Truman administration. The United States had aided and traded with Yugoslavia to strengthen Tito's ability to maintain his independence of the Soviet Union, even though in the early days U.S. policy makers were unimpressed with the differences between the Yugoslav Socialist system and the Stalinist model. After the East European crises of 1956, the United States moved quickly to provide economic assistance to Poland; Poland as well as Yugoslavia was extended "most-favored-nation" trading privileges. And during the late 1950s and early 1960s cultural exchanges with the East European countries were intensified, with ballets, symphony orchestras, and popular musical artists leading the East–West traffic.

But even these marginal policies for extending economic and cultural contacts across the Iron Curtain were met with a wall of congressional resistance, especially when they happened to enter the glare of publicity. The announcement of Tito's October 1963 visit to the United States produced a new wave of articles in magazines such as *U.S. News and World Report* on how the United States was spending billions on those who want to "bury capitalism." The arrival of Tito in Washington so soon after the ratification of the test ban had stirred fears that the White House was moving too fast on its "journey of a thousand miles."

President Kennedy's guarded handling of his decision to allow the Soviets to purchase United States wheat was a product of this perception that influential segments of Congress would only revive the "blood on their hands" accusations against international Communism if it were presented as a détente-enhancing transaction. The President resorted to justifying the wheat transaction as only a commercial undertaking, dictated primarily by national economic self-interest: it would result in savings to the taxpayer by reducing government-stored surpluses; it would be paid for in gold, and thereby help reduce our balance-of-payments deficit; it would allow us to enter a world market already being exploited by other agricultural exporting countries, many of whom were our allies.

In short, explained the President, this particular decision on sales of surplus wheat to the Soviets "does not represent a new Soviet-American trade policy. That must await the settlement of many matters." [13]

A pragmatic exploration of more economic and cultural bridges across the Iron Curtain was on the agenda at the time of John F. Kennedy's assassination. The wheat transaction with the Soviets was yet encountering congressional obstacles. The overcoming of these obstacles (such as the amendments to the 1964 Foreign Assistance Act denying the Export-Import Bank authority to guarantee loans to the Soviets to purchase the wheat) was a task to which President Johnson became committed—not so much out of conviction that the wheat sale was a good thing, but more as an early test case to establish his control over the Congress. In his successful push to defeat these legislative restrictions on his negotiating authority, the new President discovered that there was less of an emotional, popular opposition to fresh commercial transactions with the Communist countries than some congressmen were claiming.

Moreover, the President found considerable enthusiasm among the exporting segments of American industry for greater economic openings to the East, especially since the Canadians and West Europeans were rapidly expanding their commerce with the Communist world. Reflecting this growing sentiment in the business community, the United States Chamber of Commerce gave its endorsement to the efforts of Presidents Kennedy and Johnson to arrange for the sale of wheat to the Soviet Union and called for additional exploration of the possibilities for expanding East–West trade in nonstrategic goods. Organized labor at this point was more hostile to the idea of expanding East–West trade, fearing that the influx of cheap goods made by labor unable to increase its wages through collective bargaining would undercut American labor's ability to bargain for higher wages in the future.

The January 1964 issue of *Foreign Affairs* featured an article by George Kennan calling upon the Western nations to shape their policies in such a way as "to create advantages and premiums for efforts on the part of the satellite governments to extend their relations with Western countries." He urged his readers to recall that the original Marshall Plan concept deliberately left open the possibility of the extension of European economic arrangements to the entire continent, and that the failure of this grander scheme to materialize was due to the self-exclusion of the East European regimes. Now, if as a result of the evolution of interstate relations in the Communist bloc and the gradual loosening of their rigidly controlled economies and totalitarian social structures, the satellite regimes were willing to increase their economic relations with the West, should we not return to our original concept for a revived continent-wide European economy? Although it was too early to talk of a fundamental settlement of the issues dividing Europe, and of a mutual disengagement of military forces from the German demarcation zone, we ought to be doing what could be done to encourage ideological differentiation, polycentric tendencies, and the interpenetration of spheres in the hope that these would be accompanied by a reduction in the military bloc vs. military bloc legacy of the harsher days of the cold war. Ideally, at the end of the process lay the realization of the dream of the peaceful unification of all of Europe, and the revival of the great European civilization.

Seasoned diplomat Kennan admitted that "polycentrism may continue to develop, in spite of . . . the face which the West turns to the troubled and vacillating world of Communism." But if we fail to exploit creatively this historic opportunity for greater interaction, he warned, we risk alienating those "tens of millions of people in Communist countries who still look to the West with longing and with hope and who expect from it policies which take account of all the subtlety and contradiction of their position." More than anything else now these people want "contact with the outside world." This—not the continuation of a Western "quixotic commitment to a highly unlikely violent revolution"—was their hope for a relaxation of the severity under which they were forced to live.

Kennan was no longer in the government, nor could he claim to speak for the unofficial foreign policy establishment. But occasionally the relevance and basic truth of a position, if eloquently stated to those in power, will resound within the decision-making centers of the polity so that the purely academic becomes a political force by the fact of its clear and timely articulation. This was one of those times.

It was incumbent upon the Secretary of State to react constructively to the Kennan thesis. He could not ignore it, nor cavalierly rebut it. What Rusk did was to show, by his own thoughtful statement on Eastern Europe, that Kennan was actually describing a gradual policy evolution which the administration was fostering. "We have always considered it unnatural," the Secretary of State affirmed in his address of February 25, 1964,

for the diverse peoples of Eastern Europe, with their own talents and proud traditions, to be submerged in a monolithic bloc. We have wanted these peoples, while living in friendship with their Russian and other neighbors, to develop in accordance with their own national aspirations and genius.

This had been our objective, and beyond that we had also ardently hoped for the evolution within those nations of "open" societies capable of satisfying the basic human needs, including the enjoyment of individual freedom. However much these might be our objectives, explained the Secretary, our capacity to influence trends within the Communist world was very limited. This was particularly so during the period of Stalinist terror:

But in recent years an important new trend has been perceptible: some of the Communist governments have become responsive, in varying degrees, if not directly to the aspirations of their subjects, at least to kindred aspirations of their own. *The Communist world is no longer a single flock of sheep following blindly behind one leader.* (Emphasis added.)

In light of these recent trends, Rusk outlined the approach the administration favored for implementing "our policy to do what we can to encourage evolution in the Communist world toward national independence and open societies":

We favor more contacts between the peoples behind the Iron Curtain and our own peoples. We should like to see more Soviet citizens visit the United States. We would be glad to join in cooperative enterprises to further mankind's progress against disease, poverty, and ignorance.

And informing the particular applications of this general policy of encouraging peaceful contacts and cooperation, claimed the Secretary of State, was the conviction that "we can best promote these objectives by adjusting our policies to the differing behavior of different Communist states—or to the changing behavior of the same state."[14]

Rusk's speech was well received in this country and in Western Europe, with the exception of the West German government, which feared it might imply a move on the part of the Johnson administration toward diplomatic recognition of the Ulbricht regime.

President Johnson, evidently impressed by the lack of any significant outcry even from politicians with East European descendants prominent in their constituencies, also sounded the theme of East–West reconciliation. In a speech drafted by Brzezinski, then serving on the State Department's Policy Planning Staff, Johnson said that

we will continue to build bridges across the gulf which has divided us from Eastern Europe. They will be bridges of increased trade, of ideas, of visitors, and of humanitarian aid. We do this for four reasons: First, to open new relationships to countries seeking increased independence yet unable to risk isolation. Second, to open the minds of a new generation to the values and visions of the Western civilization from which they come and to which they belong. Third, to give freer play to the powerful forces of legitimate national pride—the strongest barrier to the ambition of any country to dominate another. Fourth, to demonstrate that . . . the prospects of progress for Eastern Europe lie in a wider relationship with the West.[15]

The President was clearly saying things that would again raise the West German government's fear of according legitimacy to the Communist regime in East Germany. But this time, he was prepared to take the offensive, tying "building bridges" to the reunification of Germany, but suggesting the former was a *means* to the latter, that reunification would not simply emerge full-blown in some grand negotiated settlement—which no one thought was really feasible anyway. America and Europe have achieved sufficient strength and self-confidence, contended the President, to follow a course based on hope and opportunity rather than hostility and fear.

Gradually, somewhat fitfully, the nation was moving toward the European policy Zbigniew Brzezinski had been advocating since 1961 and had been calling "peaceful engagement." This was an alternative to simple containment, which implied an indefinite perpetuation of a partitioned Europe, or to Acheson's negotiation from strength, which was predicated vaguely on some kind of Soviet submissive rollback of her Iron Curtain because of the overwhelming military superiority of the West, or to Dulles' "liberation" which assumed a collapse, possibly violent, of the Communist societies due to their internal contradictions. The policy of "peaceful engagement" assumed the capacity of Communist societies for evolution in the direction of greater pluralism internally and a more benign posture toward the outside world—if they were provided the proper environment and inducements to evolve in that manner.

The proper environment and inducements comprised:

The maintenance of Western military strength sufficient to deter Soviet provocations to Western interests (such as access to Berlin).

But abandonment of any posture, military or political, that conveys an intention of inducing a *defection* to the Western side by any of the current Soviet allies or economic partners east of the Elbe.

A shifting of our timetable for German reunification, making it the result of the mending of the split of Europe, rather than the precondition for a European settlement. This need not imply an acceptance for the time being of the legitimacy of the Ulbricht regime; but it did mean the abandonment of the rigid West German policy, reflected in the "Hallstein Doctrine" of refusing to have cordial relations with other states that recognized East Germany. It was important for West Germany to cultivate good relations with such states, particularly Poland and Czechoslovakia, in order to eventually isolate East Germany, and show the obsolescence of a Soviet policy based on Germany's perpetual division.

A vigorous expansion of economic ties and cultural contacts between the West and Eastern Europe, the latter always insisted upon as being the necessary concommitant of closer commercial relations. An increasingly free flow of people and ideas, not simply a narrow economic quid pro quo, should be the explicit aim of our trade policy; and thus we should bargain hard on credit extensions, most-favored-nation treatment, and the like to gain more openness in the East–West exchanges of literature, art, political journals and newspapers, intellectuals, scholars, and students. It would be such exchanges, not simply the alteration of material consumption patterns in the Communist countries, that would restore the vigor of the greater European civilization and render anachronistic the ideological division of the continent.

In 1965–66 the writings of Brzezinski and others; speeches by administration spokesmen; the formal introduction into Congress of an East–West trade bill; and a series of limited accords including an agreement on the peaceful uses of outer space, the opening of direct air flights to the Soviet Union, the removal of more than 400 nonstrategic items from export control, the allowance of commercial credits to all the East European nations except Albania and East Germany, the extension of consular and cultural exchange agreements with the Soviet Union, the upgrading of our Bulgarian and Hungarian legations to embassies, the beginning of formal discussions in NATO on ways to increase contacts with Eastern European countries—all of these signaled the early phases of an adjustment of United States policy premises to a more pluralistic world; a world where the cement of friendship is more than ideological orthodoxy, and where the dominant lines of institution building are determined by more than considerations of military security, a world where power is a measure of one's ability to contribute creatively to the welfare and development of all.

Yet this tendency was upstaged by the more dramatic events in the external relations of the nation during the same period. The headlines, the rhetoric, and the allocation of resources were focused on crises that called for, or at least so it seemed to the leaders, a visible resort to the coercive instruments of power.

19

THE VIETNAM AND THE DOMINICAN INTERVENTIONS

The world has changed and so has the method of dealing with disruptions of the peace. . . . As a matter of fact, some people urged me to hurry in the marines when the air became hot on a particular occasion recently. . . . The people of the world . . . prefer reasoned agreement to ready attack. And that is why we must follow the Prophet Isaiah many many times before we send the marines, and say, "Come now and let us reason together."

LYNDON B. JOHNSON

On two central planks of the Kennedy foreign policy—arms control and a reduction in the hostile aspects of the United States–Soviet competition—President Johnson seemed able to credibly honor his pledge of November 1963 to continue in the path of his predecessor. In these fields, as pointed out in previous chapters, the essential groundwork had been laid, the implementing dialogue had started, and the critical factor in the environment, the Soviet Union's willingness to reduce the coercive content of her diplomacy, augured well for a period of peaceful coexistence.

But it had not been a premise of the Kennedy foreign policy that the thawing of the icy confrontation in Europe and the suppression of military conflict would end the intense power competition between the Communist and non-Communist worlds. Rather, the locus and the modes would shift, but the power contest would persist.

Kennedy had often told the Soviets that if they would only be concerned with their own security and not with communizing the world, there would be no disagreements between them and us. But this had been offered more in the nature of a rhetorical point. He did not really expect a return to tranquility, if indeed there ever was such a condition in international relations. The power struggle, in international no less than domestic politics, was a fact of political life, especially between the giants. Kennedy had delighted in being President at a time when the United States was unequivocally a giant; while appreciating the terrible responsibility of his position, he obviously relished full participation in the game.

Lyndon Johnson, on the other hand, did not seem to bring with him to the White House any well-developed premises about the workings of the international political system, nor any particular enthusiasm for the diplomatic game. With Kennedy's key foreign policy lieutenants assisting him in the details of maintaining the détente and negotiating arms control agreements, Johnson could hope to devote his unique political skills to major innovations in domestic welfare policy. Foreign affairs were either an annoying distraction from his penchant for manipulating the domestic political system or, if anything, conducted in response to a domestic political alignment rather than to an international one.

To this extent Johnson could be expected to act very much in the tradition of American nationalism, striving to avoid complicated foreign entanglements, but, when finally nagged into international action, coming out of the domestic hearth with a roar, legitimizing brutish entry into the arena with sweeping moralisms and pronouncements on our indispensability for the survival of the right and just. This describes a *style* of behavior and public posturing; it shows Johnson a reluctant warrior in international politics and Kennedy, by contrast, a happy one. Much of an entertaining nature has been written about the difference in style between Kennedy and Johnson. Differences in style may make for a difference in substance, but what does the record reveal?

Two moves by Johnson warrant special analysis: his decision, or series of decisions, to involve the United States as an increasingly active military participant in the Vietnam War; and his decision to intervene in the Dominican Republic with United States troops to prevent "another Cuba."

INTO THE QUAGMIRE

Arthur Schlesinger, Jr., adviser to and sympathetic biographer of the Kennedys, and a critic of Johnson's policies in Vietnam, claims that "Kennedy had no intention of dispatching American ground forces to save South Vietnam." Schlesinger argues that President Kennedy's 1962 instruction to Secretary of Defense McNamara to start planning for a phased withdrawal of U.S. military personnel from Vietnam, which was originally to have been only a precautionary contingency plan, "was turning in 1963 into a preference." [1]

Kennedy's shift toward serious contemplation of a U.S. withdrawal was the product of his growing disillusion with the policies of the Diem regime in Saigon—especially Diem's ruthless suppression of the civil liberties of opponents, including the jailing of prominent Buddhist leaders. "In the final analysis it's their war," said Kennedy in September 1963, preserving his options to scale U.S. assistance up or down depending upon the extent to which the Diem government demonstrated the political as well as the military capability of sustaining its counterinsurgency effort. "We can help them, we can give them equipment, we can send our men there as advisers, but they have to win it—the people of Viet Nam—against the Communists." [2]

But the withdrawal option was effectively removed from Kennedy three weeks before his death by the cooperation of the U.S. ambassador, Henry Cabot Lodge, and other U.S. officials in Saigon with the anti-Diem elements in the South Vietnamese military who engineered the November 1, 1963, coup in which Diem and his brother Ngo Dinh Nhu were deposed and murdered. [3] Now the top officials of the U.S. government, although not directly responsible for the coup, and certainly not the murder of the Diems, felt, like traditional imperialists, implicated in the fate of their wards. After the coup, there could be no question of a U.S. pullout, at least not until the regime, with augmented U.S. help, was given a good chance to put the counterinsurgency effort back on track.

This was the situation Lyndon Johnson inherited on November 22, 1963, as he assumed the presidency after the assassination of John Kennedy. Until the Gulf of Tonkin crisis of August 1964, Johnson left the direction of Vietnam policy largely in the hands of

Secretary of Defense McNamara; but he did approve National Security Action Memorandum 288, authorizing preparations by the U.S. military "to be in a position on 72 hours' notice to initiate . . . Retaliatory Actions against North Vietnam, and to be in a position on 30 days' notice to initiate the program of 'Graduated Overt Military Pressure' against North Vietnam."[4] The President also approved, on McNamara's recommendation, stepped-up covert operations under Operations Plan 34-A, including intelligence collection and graduated "destructive undertakings" against North Vietnam. The 34-A operations, conducted with increasing intensity during the spring and summer of 1964, included commando raids by mercenaries hired by the South Vietnamese to blow up rail and highway bridges and coastal installations north of the 17th parallel, raids by Laotian-marked T-28 fighter-bombers on North Vietnamese and Pathet Lao troop concentrations in Laos, and U.S. naval intelligence-gathering patrols off the coasts of North Vietnam.[5]

The clash in the Gulf of Tonkin during the first week of August 1964, which resulted in the first overt U.S. military action in the Vietnam War and the famous Gulf of Tonkin Resolution that set the stage for the subsequent heavy U.S. intervention, was precipitated by the 34-A covert operations. During one of the amphibious commando raids against a group of coastal North Vietnam islands, the U.S. destroyer *Maddox* was in the area on an electronic intelligence-gathering mission and evidently was believed by the North Vietnamese to have been part of the coastal harassment operation. On August 2, when according to Pentagon testimony the *Maddox* was 23 miles from the coast and heading further into international waters, three North Vietnamese torpedo boats began a run at her. The *Maddox* sunk one of the PT boats with a direct hit from her five-inch guns, and the other two were damaged by aircraft from the carrier *Ticonderoga*, which was cruising to the south of the encounter.

President Johnson thereupon ordered another destroyer, the *C. Turner Joy,* to accompany the *Maddox* back into the gulf of Tonkin up to 11 nautical miles from the North Vietnamese coast and ordered a second aircraft carrier, the *Constellation,* to join the *Ticonderoga* to provide additional air cover. Plans were readied to bomb North Vietnam in the event of another attack on U.S. ships, and the administration dusted off a draft congressional resolution that it had prepared in May to gain legislative support for a commitment of U.S. armed forces to the Indochina conflict.

On August 4, North Vietnamese torpedo boats again made a run at the U.S. naval deployments. In response, in missions approved by the President, U.S. fighter-bombers from the *Ticonderoga* and *Constellation* struck four torpedo boat bases and an oil storage depot in North Vietnam. Johnson met with leaders of the Congress to inform them of his decision to retaliate against North Vietnam for what he claimed was an unprovoked attack against U.S. ships, and to enlist their support in passing what became known as the Gulf of Tonkin Resolution. [6]

On August 7, by a vote of 88 to 2 in the Senate and 416 to 0 in the House, the Congress resolved to "approve and support the determination of the President, as Commander in Chief, to take all necessary measures to repel any armed attack against the forces of the United States and to prevent further aggression"; and declared that "the United States is . . . prepared, as the President determines, to take all necessary steps, including the use of armed force, to assist any member or protocol state of the Southeast Asia Collective Defense Treaty requesting assistance in defense of its freedom." [7]

All the ingredients were now in place for a major and direct U.S. military intervention into the war in Southeast Asia. Detailed scenarios for systematic bombing of North Vietnam had been developed in the Pentagon. All that was needed was another attack on U.S. forces, either at sea or upon U.S. military bases in South Vietnam, *or* a formal request for military intervention from the government of South Vietnam, for the President to feel that he was acting legitimately—with the advice and consent of the Congress—in deciding to make the United States an active fighting ally of South Vietnam.

Although many of Johnson's political–military advisers were foaming at the bit of the presidentially imposed restraint, he was not about to be stampeded into the war, which now looked almost inevitable, until he had first validated his own mandate to rule in the presidential elections of 1964—particularly as his election victory would be best assured by making his Republican opponent, Barry Goldwater, appear to be the "warmonger." It was the Republicans, he charged, who were "eager to enlarge the conflict." "They call upon us to supply American boys to do the job that Asian boys should do." [8] As far as he was concerned, said the President,

I want to be very cautious and careful, and use it only as a last resort, when I start dropping bombs around that are likely to involve American boys in a war in Asia with 700,000,000 Chinese. So just for the moment I have not thought that we were ready for American boys to do the fighting for Asian boys. [9]

During the windup of the election campaign, he reiterated unequivocally, "We are not going to send American boys nine or ten thousand miles away to do what Asian boys ought to be doing for themselves." [10]

Even when the Vietcong, on November 1, 1964, in a surprise attack on the Bien Hao air base, killed five Americans, wounded seventy-six, and destroyed six B-57 bombers, Johnson continued to adhere to the escalation restraints, despite the view of principal administration foreign policy experts that the Bien Hao attack was at least as serious as the Gulf of Tonkin incident and therefore deserving our military reply.

It was only after the 1964 votes were in that Johnson operationalized as policy the premise that the Vietnam conflict was the current flash point of the global conflict between the Communist and non-Communist worlds—the major corollary being that as leader of the non-Communist side the United States had to assume full responsibility for assuring that the Communists did not win. The American commitment, the price the nation would be willing to pay, was henceforth to be unqualified and open-ended. The implications began to be revealed in a series of events and decisions during the first half of 1965.

On February 7 a reprisal raid was undertaken by United States fighter-bombers on North Vietnamese military barracks areas north of the 17th parallel in response to Vietcong mortar attacks on United States installations earlier in the day, particularly at the Pleiku airstrip, where 7 Americans were killed, 109 wounded, and at least 20 aircraft destroyed or damaged. We have every reason to believe, McNamara explained to reporters, "that the attack on Pleiku, Tuyhoa, and Nhatrang was ordered and directed and masterminded directly from Hanoi." Under Secretary of State George Ball backed him up in the joint State–Defense Department press conference on the day of the raids. There is no question, said the diplomat (reputed to be the leading administration "dove" on Vietnam), that "this was a deliberate, overt attempt by the regime in Hanoi to test the will of the South Vietnamese Government . . . and the Government of the United States." This was a situation in which "we could not fail to respond without giving a misleading signal to the . . . regime in Hanoi" as to the strength of our purpose.[11]

The basis of the administration's conviction that Hanoi was masterminding the campaign in the South obviously needed further elaboration. Accordingly, on February 28, the State Department issued its so-called White Paper entitled "Aggression from the North: The Record of North Vietnam's Campaign To Conquer South Vietnam."[12] The sixty-four-page text, released to all news media, claimed to contain "massive evidence of North Vietnamese aggression." It did document an increase, especially during 1964, of military aid from the North, in the form of weapons and key advisory personnel; but it was certainly no more massive than our increase in "supporting assistance" to Saigon during the same period.

The "advisers" on *both* sides were on their way to transforming themselves into belligerents. Hanoi used the increasing American involvement as its justification for increasing its infiltration into the South. And the U.S. government pointed to the evidence of this increasing infiltration as the reason for bringing coercive pressure upon Hanoi and dispatching more men and materials to South Vietnam to redress the deteriorating military balance.

At Kennedy's death Johnson had inherited an American "advisory" force in Vietnam numbering somewhat short of 16,500. By August 1965, before the impact of the major increments ordered that year had been felt, there were already about 125,000 U.S. troops in the field. And decisions made in 1965 and 1966 meant that, barring a political settlement, the number of United States military personnel in South Vietnam could exceed half a million sometime in 1967.

The shift in the mission of these U.S. troops from "advisers" to the main offensive force also occurred between 1963 and 1966. U.S. advice to the South Vietnamese to make extensive use of the helicopter for reconnaissance, troop support, and troop transport required, at least at the outset, the establishment of training and maintenance bases staffed by Americans. But the existence of these bases also established a requirement for protecting them (they were obviously lucrative targets for the Vietcong). The South Vietnamese proved incapable of providing the kind of security needed, and so contingents of U.S. Marines were called to help, and eventually to take over, in the base security role. At this stage the United States became, willy-nilly, an active co-belligerent, albeit only in "defensive" situations. The next step, as the Communists increased their military units and their firepower, was for us to expand the perimeter of security for our bases. The actual operations involved in expanding the perimeter were, of course, very much the same as they would be in offensive combat missions. What was indistinguishable in operations easily became indistinguishable in purpose, and we swiftly drifted into a full participation in the "clear and hold" missions designed to reduce the proportion of South Vietnamese territory controlled by the Vietcong. Finally, as political instability in Saigon diverted the South Vietnamese military to political tasks, including the suppression of Buddhist civil disobedience, the United States found itself the dominant combat force in the Vietnam War.

When Johnson took the situation under intense scrutiny in late 1964, he found the commitments already entered into and the deployments already underway. To fail to approve the increased deployments now being asked for by the Secretary of Defense would be to fail to rectify the deteriorating military situation—it would mean accepting a humiliating military defeat. On the other hand, the increases in infiltration from North Vietnam, which paralleled the increased U.S. involvement during the past year, gave little hope that the increases in American troops would accomplish anything more than to drive the ground war to higher levels of intensity.

From what is known of Johnson-the-political-animal, it would be surprising to find that he would allow himself to be trapped into presiding over a slow war of human attrition on the Asian mainland and the long test of endurance it required. For one thing, we were likely to be hurt more than our adversaries, who (assuming China was drawn in) had a practically unlimited supply of expendable manpower. For another, the 1964 election results convinced Johnson that he embodied the great American consensus for getting on with the job of tending to the national welfare. The people were tired of the foreign entanglements the country had been sustaining since 1947, particularly those like Vietnam, where the connection with U.S. security was complicated and tenuous. Some means would have to be found for bringing a rapid conclusion to this war. Yet Johnson also sensed that the majority of people were overwhelmingly against Goldwater because he embodied the pugnacious aspect of American nationalism that risked further expenditure of blood and treasure in "confrontations" with adversaries around the globe. Goldwaterism, as the elections showed, was just not the dominant temper in 1964.

But here was LBJ, after having successfully made political capital out of Goldwater's pugnacity, ordering the very escalation strategies that Goldwater had been advocating. The contradiction is at least partially resolved by attributing to Johnson-the-electioneer the very real belief that bombing North Vietnam *would* lead to the larger war (possibly through the entry of the Chinese) that he knew the American public did not want. Whereas Johnson-the-Commander-in-Chief, looking in detail at the developing military situation in late 1964, saw that the United States was already heavily implicated in a rapidly expanding ground war which could easily lead to the intolerable and larger Asian land war unless some way was found to break out. Marginal increments to our forces in the South, then being recommended by the military command in Saigon and endorsed by McNamara in Washington, might not be sufficient to convince North Vietnam and China, and possibly even the Soviet Union, that an expansion of their commitments to Vietnam would involve them in a "deeply dangerous game."

But the way the decision to bring the North under aerial attack was announced and implemented obscured the underlying rationale, and possibly interfered with its utility as a signal to the Communist powers. The bombing raid across the 17th parallel following the Vietcong attack on Pleiku—like the air strike in response to the Tonkin incident—was defined as a reprisal. The implication was: don't do what you just did or we'll bomb again. But three days later, on February 10, the Vietcong again found their mark. This time a United States billet at Quinhon was blown up, killing 23 Americans. Now three times as many aircraft were used in our retaliation, and the targets were further north, but still in the southern part of North Vietnam. It could appear as if we were trying to establish a let-the-punishment-fit-the-crime pattern, with the crime being attacks on *our* installations. However, the White House attempted (probably deliberately) to blur this impression in its communiqué of February 11, which cited, in addition to the Quinhon incident, Vietcong ambushes, raids, assassinations, etc., against South Vietnamese personnel and installations as well as against Americans. It was these "continued acts of aggression by Communist Vietcong under the direction and with the support of the Hanoi regime," said the statements issued from Washington and Saigon, that were the reasons for the current air strike. This came a bit closer to displaying the central strategic rationale for commencing the bombing—namely, at least an "equalization" of the pain suffered by the North as compared to the suffering caused by their agents in the South, as a way of convincing Ho Chi Minh that if he continued the insurgency the price would henceforth be much higher than it had been. The selection of targets further north and the increase in intensity were also supposed to communicate that the first blows were only a harbinger of much more dangerous blows to come. Yet the full and explicit announcement of this rationale was evidently thought to sound too much like an "ultimatum," with all the risks that would involve of provoking counterultimatums, even by parties not yet involved. Consequently, in the coming months, as bombing of the North became a regular feature of the war, it was increasingly justified on the narrower grounds of its usefulness in "interdicting" the transport of men and material from the North to the South.

As the insurgency and terror in the South continued and the infiltration from the North increased, the administration was criticized heavily by domestic and foreign opponents of the bombing. The United States had expanded the war, it was charged, putting pressure on the Soviet Union to aid Hanoi with at least air defense equipment, and incurring the risk of an even greater direct clash with the giant Communist powers, and what did we have to show for it? An even higher level of warfare in the South. The flimsy argument that we had to bomb the North to buttress the shaky authority of each successive military junta in Saigon was even less convincing.

Meanwhile, with no discernible moves by the opponents to scale down their insurgency, the frequency, scale, and type of target we were bringing under aerial bombardment were increasing. The United States was, in this phase of the conflict too, using up its fresh options, and settling into a pattern of mutual injury, at a higher level of destruction than that of a few weeks ago. Hundreds of thousands of American boys were being sent overseas to fight Asian boys, the casualty lists were growing, the costs were in the billions, and still the end was no closer in sight.

Johnson's instinct to break out of the pattern now resulted in a series of flamboyant peace moves. Up to the spring of 1965 it had been his stance (in reply to promptings from de Gaulle, the UN Secretary General, Asian neutrals, and academic polemicists in this country) that there was nothing to negotiate except the cessation of the violent insurgency by the Communists, and—in any case—negotiations would have to follow a bona fide cease-fire. In April 1965 the White House appeared to be suddenly changing its tune, or at least to be willing to play the counterpoint of negotiations and planning for peace against the continuing din of bombs and mortar and the calls from "hawks" to expand our targets in the North. Some pundits suspected this was another Johnsonian ploy of playing off the hawks against the "doves" to preserve his options for tactical maneuver in the long and messy conflict that now seemed to stretch endlessly ahead. But the ring of sincerity in his Johns Hopkins address lends greater plausibility to the "break-out" hypothesis.

The case for "why we are there" was reiterated, with considerable eloquence, by the President at Hopkins on April 7. There were the references to the "deepening shadow of Communist China," presumably the real stage manager of the insurgency in Vietnam. "It is a nation which is helping the forces of violence in almost every continent. The contest in Viet-Nam is part of a wider pattern of aggressive purposes." There were the invocations of the promises made by "every American President" since 1954 "to help South Viet-Nam defend its independence." There was the catalogue of consequences that would befall the world from a failure to honor these promises now: around the world, "from Berlin to Thailand," the confidence of people "in the value of an American commitment and in the value of America's word" would be shaken. "The result would be increased unrest and instability, and even wider war." There were the homilies about appeasing the appetite of the insatiably hungry aggressor. "To withdraw from one battlefield means only to prepare for the next. We must stay in Southeast Asia—as we did in Europe—in the words of the Bible: 'Hitherto shalt thou come, but no further.' " And there was the posture of unflinching resolve: "We will not be defeated. We will not grow tired. We will not withdraw, either openly or under the cloak of meaningless agreement."

But once this is clear, said the President, "it should also be clear that the only path for reasonable men is the path of peaceful settlement." In a surprise formulation he suggested an acceptable outcome to such a settlement and a range of flexibility in negotiating formats—both a thawing from what seemed to be his preexisting frigid stance. The "essentials of any final settlement," he said, are "an independent South Viet-Nam—securely guaranteed and able to shape its own relationships to all others—free from outside interference—tied to no alliance—a military base for no other country."

This was a considerable departure by the White House from its scornful response to de Gaulle's suggestions for a "neutralization" solution. Moreover:

There may be many ways to this kind of peace: in discussion or negotiation with the governments concerned; in large groups or in small ones; in the reaffirmation of old agreements or their strengthening with new ones.

And we remain ready with this purpose for unconditional negotiations.

The peace we want, insisted the President, ought not to be incompatible with the desires of the North Vietnamese. "They want what their neighbors also desire . . . progress for their country, and an end to the bondage of material misery." Their Communist ideology and alignment with China were evidently not a bar to their peaceful association in regional economic development schemes: "We would hope that North Viet-Nam would take its place in the common effort just as soon as peaceful cooperation is possible."

Meanwhile, work could begin on projects for regional economic development with those nations among whom peaceful cooperation was now possible. To that end, reported the President, he would ask the Congress to contribute a billion-dollar investment to a program of Southeast Asian economic development to be organized initially by UN Secretary General Thant. Our participation would be inaugurated by a team of Americans headed by Eugene Black. "And I would hope," said Johnson, "that all other industrialized countries, including the Soviet Union, will join in this effort."

These hopes for the development of the rest of the world, and his dreams for an end to war, claimed the President, were deeply rooted in his childhood experiences. Rural electrification had brought cheer to the ordinary people along the Pedernales—was there any reason why it should not bring cheer to the sufferers along the Mekong? Why, that vast river could provide food and water and electricity "on a scale to dwarf even our own TVA." That would be impressive:

We often say how impressive power is. But I do not find it impressive at all. The guns and the bombs, the rockets and the warships, are all symbols of human failure. They protect what we cherish. But they are witness to human folly.
A dam built across a great river is impressive.

. . .

Electrification of the countryside—yes, that . . . is impressive.
A rich harvest in a hungry land is impressive.
The sight of healthy children in a classroom is impressive.
These—not mighty arms—are the achievements which the American nation believes to be impressive. And if we are steadfast, the time may come when all other nations will find it so. [13]

Meanwhile, the mighty arms, which were the symbols of human failure and the witnesses to human folly, had to be fully committed "to protect what we cherish." During the month of April the pounding of the North intensified, with 1500 air sorties against military targets recorded. [14] And in the month following the overture to peace at Johns Hopkins, 15,000 additional United States combat troops disembarked in South Vietnam, the largest increase yet for any month. The big buildup was proceeding apace.

This was precisely the wrong way to get Hanoi to the negotiating table, charged critics at home and abroad. To bargain with us while under increasing bombardment would look like surrender. Lester Pearson of Canada, Senator Fulbright, and numerous newspaper editors argued for a bombing pause to convince the Communists of our sincerity. The administration took counsel and decided to give this gambit a try.

From May 12 to May 18 the bombing raids ceased. Hanoi was informed in advance via diplomatic channels that the pause was coming and that we would be watching to see if there were "significant reductions" in actions by the Communist military units in South Vietnam. The message suggested that such reciprocal action would allow us to half our bombing, and thus meet what was assumed to be the essential North Vietnamese precondition for beginning peace talks. When the air attacks on the North were resumed on May 18, the administration claimed a disappointment that there had been no reaction from the other side.

But the critics were not silenced. Surely six days was not long enough to give Hanoi an opportunity to make a considered assessment of our intentions and arrange for an appropriate response. In June, Secretary Rusk told the Foreign Service Institute that all our government received from Hanoi and Peking were denunciations of the pause as a "wornout trick" and a "swindle." More recent reports, he said, contained clear proof that "Hanoi is not even prepared for discussions unless it is accepted in advance that there will be a Communist-dominated government in Saigon." [15] It was only in November that the State Department admitted it had received a negotiating offer from Hanoi via the French government just a few hours after the six-day May pause ended. The French government is reported to have suggested that the bombings should cease again after the message had been received but apparently the United States government did not regard the response as a sufficiently serious negotiating offer. The administration was now subject to the charge of being deficient in its credibility. [16]

The failure of the North Vietnamese to give a satisfactory response to our peace overtures in the spring of 1965 was stressed by the President in his July 28 "this is really war" speech, announcing an immediate 75 percent increase to our fighting strength in Vietnam. Fifteen efforts with the help of forty nations, he said, had been made to attempt to get the "unconditional discussions" started. "But there has been no answer." We were going to persist in our efforts to bring about negotiations, but meanwhile we would also persist on the battlefield, if need be, "until death and desolation have led to the same conference table where others could now join us at much smaller cost." [17]

The President was speaking at a time of extremely low morale in Saigon. Another civilian government had fallen on June 11, and Air Vice Marshal Ky had assumed the reigns of power in the face of increasing antigovernment and pro-"neutralism" agitation by the Buddhists. Support for neutralism, the new military junta announced, would be punishable by death. It was the beginning of a new time of political troubles in Saigon that would consume the energies of the South Vietnamese military while the United States began to assume the major combat functions. "We did not choose to be the guardians at the gate," said the American President, "but there is no one else." [18]

Thus, by the summer of 1965, the full character of the United States political–military involvement in Vietnam had matured, and its underlying premises had been revealed:

1. Global balance of power considerations demanded that the United States do all that was required to prevent the Communists from taking over South Vietnam. Failure to honor U.S. commitments to South Vietnam would weaken resistance to Communist expansion all around the globe—a resistance critically dependent upon the belief by the non-Communist societies that the United States, when called upon, would help them to prevail in their anti-Communist struggles.

2. If the Communist insurgency in South Vietnam were not defeated now, the Communist expansionary drive in the less developed countries, would very likely require a bigger war and possibly closer to our shores. For the Communist world, Vietnam was a test case for the strategy of expanding through "wars of national liberation." They had been pretty well convinced to abandon a strategy of direct military aggression by our stands in Europe and Korea. If this strategy of disguised aggression by paramilitary means were now allowed to succeed, those within the Communist camp who favored the coercive modes of expansion would be vindicated. If this "war of national liberation" were now convincingly defeated, however, those elements within the Communist world who believed in peaceful forms of competitive coexistence would be strengthened.

3. Those directing the insurgency in Vietnam could be induced to call it off only if they were convinced it would cost them too dearly to continue it and that, even with the higher-cost efforts, they would not succeed. The U.S. strategy in Vietnam, therefore, despite its turns and twists, had an underlying consistent objective: to increase the enemy's costs and diminish their prospects of success. Previous failures to adequately convince them (with only our *support* of South Vietnam) that their costs would be excessive and their prospects of success very low led to direct U.S. involvement, and this at increasingly higher levels of violence. The administration had no desire to have American soldiers again fight Asians or to widen the war to include the North, but as lower levels of conflict failed to convince the Communists that the United States was determined to frustrate their designs, the administration was compelled to make its determination even clearer.

4. The strategy of steadily increasing the costs to our opponents carried with it the need to increase our human and material costs; thus, American

staying power demanded, increasingly, a national consensus without which the President could not get the congressional majorities needed to provision the war. Consequently, a domestic dissent on the involvement in Vietnam became an ingredient in the test of strength and endurance with the enemy. Hanoi, it was feared, would exploit America's desires to negotiate an end to the violence with a view toward maximizing dissent in the United States. And the Vietnamese Communists would interpret such dissent as an indication that further persistence by them on the battlefield would soon bring about a condition in the United States where a majority could not be found to approve the continued high costs of the war.

THE EROSION OF DOMESTIC SUPPORT

As the buildup in Vietnam by the United States was met by increased Northern infiltration into the South, public criticism intensified. Students and professors held stop-the-war "teach-ins"; and artists, intellectuals, and religious leaders joined with standard peace-movement groups in petitioning the government, or marching on Washington to demonstrate against the bombing and for negotiations. Hanoi cooperated with hints through third parties that it might be willing to negotiate; and each of these were picked up in the press, sometimes some months after they had been made, and thrust at the administration as proof of official dishonesty in saying that we were constantly seeking to induce Hanoi to the conference table. The American leaders were uninterested in negotiations, charged the critics.

The administration's response to the domestic criticsm was at first testy and tight-lipped. But in the second half of 1965 the White House changed tactics and began to talk back to the critics, to take them seriously—some observers thought too seriously—and to send administration representatives to the teach-ins to present the full administration case. The case included the major premises summarized above, including the last one about the danger of too much dissent. This was a tactical blunder on the part of the administration, as it would be for any administration in the American democracy, particularly as the argument against too much argument was only valid if all of the other premises were valid. And serious critics disputed them all.

The President's worst fears of being driven to higher levels of warfare abroad without a sufficient consensus at home to support the greater resource drain seemed to be materializing. He and his aides were irritable and carping. But at the end of 1965, he resorted again to a brake-out-of-the-pattern move. This time it was a razzle-dazzle peace offensive the likes of which the diplomatic community had never seen. Prominent American officials made a whirlwind tour of world capitals while the military campaign was dramatically tuned down.

Responding to a Vietcong initiative for a Christmas Eve cease-fire, the United States halted air action over North Vietnam simultaneously with the start of the twelve-hour truce on the ground. A similar "natural" truce would be coming up on the Buddhist Lunar New Year (*Tet*), January 20–24.

The administration used the month-long interval of military escalation to press its diplomatic offensive, meanwhile not resuming the air attacks. This time the critics could not say the pause was too short for Hanoi to make serious contacts. Secretary Rusk issued publicly Washington's fourteen points for negotiation in response to Hanoi's four points, with the claim that the two positions were really not so far apart. Certainly, there was reason for negotiation on the basis of both positions. But the administration's credibility with its domestic critics, already seriously undermined by its past policy ambivalence and rhetorical excesses, was now injured even further by its frantic efforts, probably wholly sincere, to build a world consensus in back of unconditional discussions between the belligerents. Moreover, doubts were raised as to the "unconditional" nature of our appeals for discussions as it became clear that we were quite sticky on the point of *who* was a legitimate spokesman for the other side. "If the Vietcong come to the conference table as full partners," said Secretary Rusk, "they will . . . in a sense have been victorious in the very aims that South Vietnam and the United States are pledged to prevent."[19]

Claiming again to have received no serious offer from Hanoi to negotiate, the administration resumed the air attacks with even greater punch on January 28. The domestic critics, at least those who were patriotic in motive, must now finally realize there was no alternative but to rally in back of our military efforts. And certainly, if our boys *had* to be over there to hold the ground, who could criticize our efforts to negate as much of the danger as possible by destroying enemy power while it was still on the trails in Laos, on the bridges above the 17th parallel, or in the storage depots near the factories?

But the new jingoism in the administration's statements accompanying the resumption of bombings in January 1966, particularly the implication that anything less than enthusiastic support was unpatriotic, provoked patriotic men in the President's own party, like Senators Fulbright, Hartke, and Church, to an even greater attack on administration policies. Senator Fulbright's Foreign Relations Committee became the staging ground for this new phase of the domestic debate.

The most significant function of the Senate Foreign Relations Committee hearings in 1966 was to provide respectability for the serious criticisms—as distinguished from the emotional harangues of the so-called New Left. Ostensibly convened for the purpose of requiring the administration to justify its requests for supplemental foreign assistance monies (needed to finance the military and economic assistance to Vietnam over and above the amounts previously authorized in the fiscal 1966 budget), these hearings exposed the nation and the world to the profound doubts about U.S. Vietnam policy held by some of the country's most experienced former diplomats and military leaders and some of its most respected scholars.

General James Gavin testified before the Fulbright committee that he feared "the escalation in southeast Asia . . . [will] begin to hurt our world strategic position." This might have "tremendous significance" in the long run, he said. "When we begin to turn our back on what we are doing in world affairs . . . to support a tactical confrontation that appears to be escalating at the will of an enemy we are in a very dangerous position in my opinion."[20]

This policy, offered George Kennan, "seems to me to represent a grievous misplacement of emphasis in our foreign policies as a whole." Not only were great questions of world affairs not receiving the attention they deserved, said the author of the containment policy, but "assets we already enjoy and . . . possibilities we should be developing are being sacrificed to this unpromising involvement in a remote and secondary theatre." Elaborating, he claimed that

our relations with the Soviet Union have suffered grievously . . . at a time when far more important things were involved in those relations than what is ultimately involved in Vietnam. . . . And more unfortunate still, in my opinion, is the damage being done to the feelings entertained for us by the Japanese people. . . . As the only major industrial complex in the entire Far East, and the only place where the sinews of modern war can be produced on a formidable scale, Japan is of vital importance to us and indeed to the prospects generally of peace and stability in Asia. There is no success we could have in Vietnam that would warrant . . . the sacrifice by us of the confidence and good will of the Japanese people.

If we had kept our eye on these larger strategic considerations, Kennan suggested, we would have had no reason to become involved in Vietnam as we were today. And, challenging a central pillar of the administration's case, he contended that

. . . even in a situation in which South Vietnam was controlled exclusively by the Vietcong, while regrettable, and no doubt morally unwarranted, would not, in my opinion, present dangers great enough to justify our direct military intervention.

Given the situation that exists today in the relations among the leading Communist powers, and by that I have . . . in mind primarily the Soviet-Chinese conflict, there is every likelihood that a Communist regime would follow a fairly independent course.

Yet we were involved now, Kennan granted, and thus our prestige had become heavily implicated. This raised "new questions" which had to be taken into account. "A precipitate and disorderly withdrawal could represent in present circumstances a disservice to our own interests, and even to world peace." He did, however, feel that we should not rely on the "prestige" or "honor" excuse as a way of avoiding the search for fallback positions (possibly a retreat into coastal enclaves, as recommended by General Gavin) from which a more orderly reduction of our commitment and presence might take place. In a courageous statement for a man of Kennan's close establishment associations to make before a congressional committee in the full glare of the television cameras, Kennan confessed that

I . . . find it difficult . . . to believe that our allies, and particularly our Western European allies, most of whom themselves have given up great territories within recent years, and sometimes in a very statesmanlike way, I find it hard to believe that we would be subject to great reproach or loss of confidence at their hands simply because we followed a defensive rather than an offensive strategy in Vietnam at this time.

In matters such as this, it is not in my experience what you do that is mainly decisive. It is how you do it; and I would submit that there is more respect to be won in the opinion of this world by a resolute and courageous liquidation of unsound positions than by the most stubborn pursuit of extravagant and unpromising objectives.[21]

The President, anticipating what was in store in the February sessions of the Fulbright committee, felt it necessary to reassert once more his peace aims as well as his war aims for Vietnam. It was time to show that he meant business about the greater impressiveness of agricultural productivity, rural electrification, and schools than strike aircraft, flamethrowers, and the tremendous military logistics networks. It was also possible he wanted to take some of the spotlight away from the Fulbright hearings.

The television coverage of the administrator of the Agency for International Development, David Bell, before the Foreign Relations Committee was interrupted on February 4 for President Johnson's announcement of his trip to Honolulu to meet with Prime Minister Ky and President Thieu of South Vietnam. To emphasize that the main purpose of the meeting was to explore plans for the peaceful reconstruction of Vietnam, the President announced he was taking along John Gardner, Secretary of Health, Education and Welfare, and Orville Freeman, Secretary of Agriculture. There would of course be strategy huddles with General Westmoreland and the Vietnamese military, but the theme was to be socioeconomic development. And this was the emphasis in the Declaration of Honolulu issued by both governments from Hawaii on February 8. The government of South Vietnam pledged itself to "a true social revolution," to policies designed to "achieve regular economic growth," and to "build true democracy" through the formulation of a "democratic constitution" and subjecting it to ratification by popular ballot. The United States pledged itself to full support of these aspirations. And to demonstrate their seriousness of purpose, President Johnson persuaded the Vietnamese leaders to extend an immediate invitation to Secretaries Gardner and Freeman to survey the social and economic situation and suggest practical courses of action. Upon setting foot again on the continental United States on the evening of February 8, the President told of this reconstruction mission to Vietnam and announced that Vice President Humphrey was leaving immediately for Saigon to join the other Cabinet members and to meet with South Vietnamese officials to discuss these matters. The White House would be represented directly by McGeorge Bundy and Averell Harriman, both of whom would be going along with the Vice President.[22]

The President did get the headlines and the television coverage with this swoop into Asia with Health, Agriculture, and the idealism of Humphrey. But the image came across somewhat differently from what he had hoped. The tone of the television commentators and journalists who covered the event suggested rather strongly that this was Johnson hucksterism more than substance. Juxtaposed against the good-works backdrop was the indelible picture of LBJ embracing Prime Minister Ky as if he were a Democratic Party loyalist in the Texas statehouse. Ky, who had been installed recently by a military coup, was cracking down with authoritarian methods on the Buddhist agitators, and had been making asides to the effect that any negotiations with the Communists would be useless. Rather than Ky's endorsement of the Great Society, Saigon-style, the picture that critics chose to display was that of Johnson's committing himself to support Ky's irresponsible brand of jet-set militarism. Whatever Johnson did now his domestic critics would turn it against him.

THE DOMINICAN SIDESHOW

Juxtaposed with Johnson's swift resort to force in the Dominican Republic, the evolution of our Vietnamese strategy cast doubt on his protestations that he, in contrast to Mao Tse-tung, believed that power came from the pipes of an irrigation system rather than the barrel of a gun. The emerging popular view of Johnson—the militarist—was, of course, an unfortunate oversimplification. But, as an inspection of his public posturing at the time of the Dominican crisis shows, Johnson was himself somewhat responsible for perpetuating such gross popular caricatures of the reasons for his behavior.

The public rationale for the U.S. military intervention in the Dominican Republic in April and May of 1965 points to two distinct kinds of threats and, accordingly, two phases to our military response, each with a different objective.

The first threat was to the security and lives of United States citizens and other foreign nationals resulting from the civil violence which broke out in Santo Domingo on April 24. On April 28 Dominican law enforcement and military officials formally informed our embassy in Santo Domingo that the situation was out of control and that the police and the government could no longer guarantee the safety of United States or other foreign nationals.

We had "no desire to interfere in the affairs of a sister Republic," explained President Johnson, but on April 28 "there was no longer any choice for the man who is your President":

. . . when our entire country team in the Dominican Republic . . . said to your President unanimously: Mr. President if you do not send forces immediately, men and women—Americans and those of other lands—will die in the streets—well, I knew there was no time to talk, to consult, or to delay. For in this situation delay itself would be decision—the decision to risk and to lose the lives of thousands of Americans and thousands of innocent people from other lands.[23]

The President's prompt dispatch of 400 Marines on April 28, followed in the next three days by 1500 men from the 82d Airborne Division and additional Marine detachments, was an action—according to White House public statements of April 28, April 30, May 1, and May 2—dictated solely by the requirements of efficiently conducting the human rescue operation.[24] The limited objective, as stated, was impeccable, and presumably the means chosen were necessary (international machinery was simply too sluggish for such a swift ad hoc response), although there was already some wonderment expressed in the United States press at the size of the contingents dispatched for the rescue effort. President Johnson was acting properly within his executive responsibility of assuring protection to United States nationals and diplomatic missions abroad, just as President Eisenhower had done in ordering helicopters to rescue the Nixons' party from Caracas crowds in 1958.

However, the White House definition to the public of the objective of the intervention was rapidly expanded within the next few days as "Communist leaders, many of them trained in Cuba, seeing a chance to increase disorder, to gain a foothold, joined the revolution . . . and took increasing control." Almost overnight, therefore, the United States was openly intervening in force (with an additional 6500 men, and hints of more to come) to "prevent another Communist State in this hemisphere." We were not intervening to prevent change. Indeed, we were for major social transformations in the Dominican Republic. Nor were we intervening simply to prevent violent revolution, however much we were opposed to violent change. Maintaining his fidelity to the noninterventionist conventions of the inter-American system, the President reaffirmed the proposition that "revolution in any country is a matter for that country to deal with." But "it becomes a matter calling for hemispheric action only—repeat, only—when the object is the establishment of a Communist dictatorship."[25] In justifying his expanded military response to the situation, President Johnson felt impelled to show that he was acting in accord with our solemn obligations to our neighbors, and in defense of our own security, and therefore as any United States President, including Kennedy, would have acted:

> The American nations cannot, must not, and will not permit the establishment of another Communist government in the Western Hemisphere. This was the unanimous view of all the American nations when, in January 1962, they declared, and I quote: "The principles of Communism are incompatible with the principles of the Inter-American system."
> This is what our beloved President John F. Kennedy meant when, less than a week before his death, he told us: "We in this hemisphere must also use every resource at our command to prevent the establishment of another Cuba in this hemisphere."[26]

However, the last-quoted remark of President Kennedy was lifted out of a speech stressing the dire need for nations in the Alliance for Progress to take seriously the goals of social reform in order to avoid the kind of despair that led to Castroism.[27] It had quite a different connotation in Kennedy's speech than it did in the Johnson justification of his swift resort to *military* resources. Kennedy had talked of "every resource," as a way of stressing that military response to new Castroite or Communist possibilities was surely a last resort and, if anything, a confession of the failure by nations of this hemisphere to avail themselves of all the resources at their command to lessen the appeals of the Communists.

Johnson was undoubtedly correct in his identification of himself with Kennedy insofar as this referred to Kennedy's not ruling out the use of force if its use was necessary and likely to prevent another Communist takeover in the Caribbean. But the tricky concept here is that of "necessity"; its determination in any situation involves a set of premises about the political and social forces at work in the particular case, and the alternatives short of the use of force available for influencing them.

It is not at all clear that the premises Johnson availed himself of in determining the configuration and strengths of the various political and social forces in the Dominican Republic were similar to the premises with which Kennedy approached the analysis of instability in the contemporary Latin American context. There has been much speculation about the timing of Johnson's public announcement that he was intervening in the Dominican situation to prevent a Communist takeover in addition to protecting American lives, with prominent journalists and some members of Congress revealing evidence that suggests Johnson thought from the start that he was intervening against a leftist (and potentially Communist) takeover but used the rescue operation as a less controversial diplomatic pretext that would allow him to move troops in immediately.[28] The more significant question, however, is why in any case he thought it necessary for the United States to move in so quickly to prevent the leftist factions from winning in the civil conflict. A hint that he thought that Kennedy might not have intervened in the same way was contained in his defensive extemporaneous remark during a rally-round-the-flag speech on May 3 that "what is important is . . . that we know, and that they know, and that everybody knows, that we don't propose to sit here in our rocking chair with our hands folded and let the Communists set up any government in the Western Hemisphere."[29]

The dire consequences of a failure to act decisively continued to be the rationale invoked by administration spokesmen to exonerate those responsible for the United States decisions from their remarkable casualness with the facts and double-dealings with prominent Dominican leaders, as U.S. departures from international rectitude were exposed by respected journalists and by Senators Fulbright and Clark.[30] The presumably "unimportant" things, such as the credibility of the administration's public statements and private guarantees, just had to give way temporarily to the requirements of acting swiftly to prevent the Communists from coming to power in Santo Domingo. If that larger responsibility were fulfilled, history would absolve us of our smaller lapses.

But the administration's view of its larger responsibility also bears examination. That view rested on the following critical premises: (1) Another Communist regime in this hemisphere would be intolerable. (2) The Communists would very likely come to power in Santo Domingo without our military intervention. In invoking this rationale, what was the administration really saying about the reasons for its specific acts?

1. The establishment of another Communist regime in this hemisphere was intolerable. This oft-repeated assumption went unchallenged during both the Kennedy and Johnson administrations, but, as a result, also remained unelaborated. Presumably, the event of another Communist takeover would be dangerous to vital United States interests; but which interests?

Certainly the existence of Communist Cuba did not by the fact of its being Communist prevent the people of the United States from enjoying the blessings of liberty, except possibly for those few whose investments in pre-Castro Cuba were expropriated. There was no self-evident reason why one more small Communist nation in the Caribbean should constitute a threat to U.S. security. Of course, if the Soviets would try to make it into an offensive military base, that would be another matter entirely; but the United States had already demonstrated in October 1962 that it was a mistake for the Communists to try this gambit.

Was the denial of liberty to the Dominicans intolerable? If so, the value attributed to Dominican liberty had been suddenly inflated. For thirty years Washington acted indifferently to the harsh dictatorship of Trujillo, and only after he was assassinated in 1961 did the U.S. government throw its support, temporarily, behind democratic constitutionalists in Santo Domingo. Kennedy threatened a Marine landing to prevent an attempt by the Trujillo family to grab back power in November 1961; but when the democratically elected Juan Bosch was deposed by a military coup after having been in office only seven months, Kennedy's strongest actions were to suspend diplomatic relations and to halt economic aid. Diplomatic recognition and economic aid were reextended promptly by the new Johnson administration as the Dominican junta promised to hold general elections in the spring and summer of 1965. Self-determination by democratic choice for our Caribbean neighbors was a preference we might strongly indicate, but we were not about to take it upon ourselves to *assure* it to them.

Yet if the denial of political liberty was to come through the establishment of another Communist regime, that evidently *was* intolerable. To whom? Why? United States officials were not pressed to give an answer to this question—a phenomenon which is in part a clue to its answer: the nation generally still took for granted the premise that an extension of Communism is, by definition, an increase in the power of the opposing "bloc," or alliance, system, and, in proportion, a decrease in our power. Moreover, the inability of the United States once again to oppose such an extension in its traditional sphere of control, after Washington had been duped by Castro, would be taken as a fundamental failure of American capability and will to quarantine the Third World against Communist takeovers—with reverberations sure to be felt in Vietnam, among other places.

It was all a part of the same basic conflict, said the President to the congressmen he assembled at the White House on May 4, 1965, to plead for a $700 million supplemental military budget required now by the increase of our effort in Vietnam simultaneously with the Dominican intervention. By our actions in these two conflicts, he said, we will be signaling to the world that

. . . we are going to spend every dollar, we are going to take every action, we are going to walk the last mile in order to see that peace is restored, that the people of not only the Dominican Republic but South Viet-Nam have the right of self-determination and that they cannot be gobbled up in the 20th century and swallowed just because they happen to be smaller than some of those whose boundaries adjoin them.

I think it is well to remember that there are a hundred other little nations sitting here this moment watching what happens.[31]

The fusion, sometimes apparent confusion, by Johnson of Santo Domingo with Saigon during these weeks possibly reflected an intention to demonstrate to the world, particularly to the larger Communist powers who might be contemplating increased assistance to Ho Chi Minh, that despite our escalation by carefully modulated steps in Southeast Asia, our patience could wear thin, and we *might* even overreact.

2. If events in Santo Domingo were allowed to take their course during April and May 1965, without significant U.S. military intervention, the probability was very high that a Communist regime would quickly gain control of the Dominican Republic. In the official rhetoric, the simple fact of a rebellion against the civilian junta of Reid Cabral would not have been sufficient to justify a United States intervention. Indeed, President Johnson granted in his statement of May 2 that the April 24 uprising "began as a popular democratic revolution, committed to democracy and social justice." The threat to our interests came, he said, when this legitimate revolution "very shortly moved and was taken over and really seized and placed into the hands of a band of Communist conspirators."[32]

Critics, most prominent among them Senator Fulbright, charged that this was an inaccurate reconstruction of the real basis of our decision to intervene. The decision, he contended, was actually forced upon President Johnson by our diplomatic mission in Santo Domingo and conservative Latin Americanists in the State Department who were determined to prevent Juan Bosch's reinstallation by the "popular democratic revolution" but realized Johnson would not act to prevent the revolution from succeeding unless it was clear that the pro-Bosch forces had fallen under Communist control. "The principal reason for the failure of American policy in Santo Domingo," asserted Senator Fulbright, "was faulty advice given to the President by his representatives in the Dominican Republic at the time of the acute crisis. . . . On the basis of the information and counsel he received, the President could hardly have acted other than he did."[33] This was an assertion resting on more than speculation.

The detailed closed hearings conducted by the Senate Foreign Relations Committee during the summer of 1965 had corroborated a number of facts already placed in the public domain by journalists such as Szulc of the *New York Times,* Kurzman of the *Washington Post,* and Geyelin of the *Wall Street Journal:* namely, that the United States diplomatic mission on the scene in Santo Domingo had refused to mediate in the dispute between the violently contending factions of the Dominican military when the Bosch factions were losing (between April 26 and April 28). Then, as the pro-Bosch factions, under Colonel Caamano Deno, appeared to be turning the tide on April 28, the U.S. Embassy cabled Washington recommending that we furnish the anti-Bosch forces with communications equipment from Defense Department stocks in Puerto Rico. The administration was reluctant to grant this request so quickly on the heels of earlier reports that the "loyalists" were putting down the Bosch rebels. Ambassador Bennett persisted in his appeals to Washington, painting in more extreme colors with each cable the consequences of a failure to come to the help of the anti-Bosch military units.

Frantically, the embassy in Santo Domingo and the State Department now tried to find the proper legal formula for landing a contingent of U.S. Marines in time to prevent a rebel victory. Meanwhile, the President had asked the CIA to inform him concerning the extent of Communist infiltration in the pro-Bosch military and political leadership. The rescue operation rationale apparently got to Johnson before he had fully resolved his doubts about the credibility of the anti-Communist rationale, so he moved on the basis of the former; but added the Communist threat in a few days and made it the reason for his expansion of U.S. troops there to an eventual 20,000 and for his insistence upon a political solution satisfactory to the Organization of American States as a precondition for the withdrawal of our military forces.

What was the prospect of a Communist and/or Castroite takeover of the rebellion as perceived by the White House? On the basis of subsequent releases to the press and public statements by the President and the Secretary of State it would appear that these perceptions were fragmentary and uncertain even while the President was telling the nation unequivocally on May 2 that the "popular democratic revolution" had been "taken over" by "a band of Communist conspirators."

Clearly the President's May 2 statements were simplifications. However, the administration, while quickly backing off from its posture of fear of an imminent Communist takeover, rested its case on the argument that such a takeover was sufficiently probable as to warrant the intervention. Dean Rusk led the counterattack against the critics, dusting off another one of his famous Munich analogies. "I am not impressed," he said,

. . . with the remark that there were several dozen known Communist leaders and that therefore this was not a very serious matter. There was a time when Hitler sat in a beer hall in Munich with seven people. And I just don't believe that one underestimates what can be done in . . . a situation of violence and chaos, by a few highly organized, highly trained people who know what they are about and know they want to bring about.[34]

It was precisely this kind of reasoning by the administration that was the target of Senator Fulbright's criticism in his major speech of September 15, 1965:

Intervention on the basis of Communist *participation* as distinguished from *control* was a mistake in my opinion which also reflects a grievous misreading of the temper of contemporary Latin American politics. Communists are present in all Latin American countries, and they are going to inject themselves into almost any Latin American revolution and try to seize control of it. If any group or any movement with which the Communists associate themselves is going to be automatically condemned in the eyes of the United States, then we have indeed given up all hope of guiding or influencing even to a marginal degree the revolutionary movements and the demands for social change which are sweeping Latin America. (Emphasis added.)[35]

Pundits were now asking whether the Truman Doctrine of assistance to free peoples resisting subjugation by armed minorities or outside pressures had been supplemented by a Johnson Doctrine of military intervention to nip militant beer-hall crowds, or other embryos of insurgency, in the bud. The decisions regarding the Dominican Republic had to be made under great pressure and on the basis of inconclusive information, Fulbright offered. "In charity, this can be accepted as a reason why the decisions were mistaken." What especially galled the senator, however, were the administration's attempts to convert the rationalizations for its hasty action into a philosophy of contemporary statecraft.

But possibly there was a philosophy of sorts behind the action—a philosophy that was a carryover from the Dulles–Eisenhower period of U.S. foreign policy toward Latin America, now expressing itself in the person of a holdover from the Eisenhower period, himself a participant in the Guatemala affair of 1954, Johnson's key Latin America adviser, Under Secretary of State Thomas C. Mann. It was Mann's speech of October 12, 1965, before the Inter-American Press Association that henceforth served as the text of the basic administration defense of the Dominican intervention and, not incidentally, the rebuttal to Fulbright. The landing of troops in addition to the number required to protect and evacuate foreign personnel, contended Mann, was necessary in view of the "clear and present danger of the forcible seizure of power by the Communists." All of those in our government who had full access to official information were convinced of this, he maintained. And the evidence we now had, he argued, showed that we were right, since at the time of our intervention "the para-military forces under the control of known Communists exceeded in military strength the forces controlled by the non-Communist elements within the rebel movement." Equally important, claimed the Under Secretary, "is the fact that these non-Communist elements were working hand in glove with the Communists."[36] Thus, an injection of external military power, initially from the United States, was necessary, first, to rectify the balance of forces within the country, but also, presumably, to save the rebels from absorption by the Communists in their own ranks. This stands as the official elaboration of the premise that a division-size United States military contingent in the Dominican Republic was essential to the prevention of a Communist takeover of the country.

The philosophy articulated by Mann was simple: in dealing with a Communist insurgency situation (potential or actual) the really critical question is what is the immediate balance of coercive capabilities that can be exercised in the situation? If this is taken care of to our satisfaction, the more complicated political questions can then be attended to, and will eventually work themselves out in a not intolerable manner.

It is not at all clear that President Johnson himself thought he was buying such a stark philosophy in approving of the intervention in the Dominican Republic. But he did follow recommendations in the particular circumstances which implied such premises.

20

THE DISINTEGRATION OF THE FOREIGN POLICY CONSENSUS

There is division in the American house now. There is divisiveness among us all tonight.

LYNDON B. JOHNSON

Lyndon Johnson could legitimately claim that the resort to force to move men and nations was the exception, not at all the norm, of his foreign policies. His preferred mode of influence was that of the prophet Isaiah: "Come now and let us reason together."

It was reason, Johnson would insist, that brought about the solution of the Panama Canal crisis of 1964–65, and not simply the reason of the weak in accepting the dictates of the strong. The United States government, under Johnson, went further toward recognizing Panama's sovereignty over the Canal Zone, and in according Panamanians equitable treatment in United States zone installations than had any previous administration.

It was reason, the objective consideration of the advantages and disadvantages of alternative courses of action, that Johnson could claim to have brought to bear upon the Greeks and Turks to forestall their impending war over Cyprus, and upon the Indians and Pakistanis to persuade them to cease their war over Kashmir. The fact that the United States was in a position to affect the anticipations of advantage and disadvantage of the involved parties (the perquisites and protections of NATO membership to Greece and Turkey, the flow of military and economic assistance to the South Asian countries) was, of course, at the heart of the President's appeals to substitute reason for passion.

Johnson had also shown an ability to practice restraint in situations of extreme local instability, such as in Indonesia, Rhodesia, and the Middle East, where it might have been tempting for a great power to intervene. Rather than attempting to play the world policeman, he prudently allowed events to take their course in response to lesser influences.

The United States support for the Alliance for Progress had been extended indefinitely. Constructive development schemes had been sponsored from the Amazon to the Mekong. The Peace Corps continued to receive the wholehearted support of the White House. A nonproliferation treaty and other arms control accords had been spurred by the personal solicitude of the President. New economic and cultural bridges were being built to Eastern Europe. West Germany had been encouraged to depart from its rigid legalisms vis-à-vis the East. And not a harsh word had been heard to come from the President against the Soviet regime, despite the many opportunities to retaliate for anti–U.S. diatribes from the Kremlin.

The arts of conciliation and compromise, in the Johnson administration's self-image, were the facts of our power now, more so than at any time since the start of the cold war.

Yet an administration cannot escape the massive impressions created on domestic and foreign observers by its most dramatic actions. Regardless of intention, large doses of force in the international environment create a noise level that distorts the sound of other signals. And the effort to get conciliatory messages through the uproar of violence was virtually drowned out by a revival of the more histrionic aspects of postwar U.S. foreign policy—the resort to ideological hyperbole, to moralizing about the basis of our overseas commitments, to lecturing neutrals about *their* vital interests, and to threats of more violence to come if the enemy persisted in its course.

SECRETARY MCNAMARA JUMPS OFF THE VIETNAM ESCALATOR

By the middle of 1966, the military strategy for getting North Vietnam to call off the war in the South seemed to be producing just the opposite results. The more U.S. forces were deployed into

South Vietnam, the more units the North poured down the Ho Chi Minh trail and across the 17th parallel. Sustained bombing of the North only appeared to stiffen the will of Hanoi to persist. The studies Secretary of Defense McNamara called for were deeply shocking to him: although the bombing had destroyed major weapons storage sites, the flow of men and matériel into the South was undiminished. There was no feasible level of effort, concluded the studies, that would achieve the air war objectives. The only new proposal McNamara's experts could come up with was to build an electronic barrier across Vietnam below the 17th parallel. McNamara's memoranda to the President began to reflect pessimism and the beginning of despair, especially in view of the continual requests from General William Westmoreland for reinforcements that were pushing the number of U.S. troops in South Vietnam up to the 500,000 mark.

The President in turn became more and more suspicious of McNamara. The parting of the ways came in the spring of 1967, and was reflected in the Secretary of Defense's draft memorandum to the President of May 19 on the latest troop and air war requests from General Westmoreland. Because of the substance of its arguments and its pivotal role in crystalizing opposition to the war within the U.S. government, it warrants extensive quotation. Rejecting the next steps in the military escalation recommended by the Joint Chiefs of Staff as likely to be "counterproductive," McNamara argued that

there may be a limit beyond which many Americans and much of the world will not permit the United States to go. The picture of the world's greatest superpower killing or seriously injuring 1,000 non-combatants a week, while trying to pound a tiny backward nation into submission on an issue whose merits are hotly disputed, is not a pretty one. It could conceivably produce a costly distortion in the American national consciousness and in the world image of the United States—especially if the damage to North Vietnam is complete enough to be "successful."

. . .

Mining the harbors would . . . place Moscow in a particularly galling dilemma as to how to preserve the Soviet position and prestige. . . . Moscow in this case should be expected to send volunteers, including pilots, to North Vietnam; to provide some new and better weapons and equipment; to consider some action in Korea, Turkey, Iran, the Middle East or, most likely, Berlin, where the Soviets can control the degree of crisis better; and to show across-the-board hostility toward the U.S. (interrupting any on-going conversations on ABMs, non-proliferation, etc.).

. . .

To U.S. ground actions in North Vietnam, we would expect China to respond by entering the war with both ground and air forces.

Instead of the major new escalatory actions, McNamara recommended that the President "limit force increases to no more than 30,000; avoid extending the ground conflict beyond the borders of South Vietnam; and concentrate the bombing on the infiltration routes south of 20°."

With respect to one of the principal purposes of the bombing of North Vietnam—pressure on Hanoi to end the war—McNamara now contended that

it is becoming apparent that Hanoi may have already "written off" all assets and lives that might be destroyed by U.S. military actions short of occupation or annihilation. They can and will hold out at least so long as a prospect of winning the "war of attrition" in the South exists. And our best judgment is that a Hanoi prerequisite to negotiations is significant retrenchment (if not complete stoppage) of U.S. military actions against them.

And with respect to interdiction of men and matériel,

it now appears that no combination of actions against the North short of destruction of the regime or occupation of North Vietnamese territory will physically reduce the flow of men and matériel below the relatively small amount needed by enemy forces to continue the war in the South. . . . Our efforts physically to cut the flow meaningfully by actions in North Vietnam therefore largely fail. [1]

The President and his national security adviser, Walt Rostow, henceforth categorized McNamara as a "dove," which meant that he had to be effectively cut out of the most sensitive deliberations on the conduct of the war, since his rejection of the fundamental premises of the Vietnam strategy meant that he was no longer loyal to basic administration policy. In mid-October 1967, President Johnson informed McNamara that he was nominating him for the presidency of the World Bank, a post that had fallen vacant upon the retirement of the bank's previous president, Eugene Black.

To succeed McNamara as Secretary of Defense, LBJ appointed his friend Clark Clifford, the distinguished Washington lawyer and adviser to Presidents since Truman, who Johnson was confident would work well with him, Rostow, and Secretary of State Rusk to reunify the administration (and hopefully also the Congress) behind the Vietnam policy. But Clifford, to the surprise and eventual despair of Johnson, upon exposure to the data and studies that had turned McNamara against the existing strategy, soon turned out to be an even more effective mobilizer of dissent within the policy establishment against continuing the escalation policy than had McNamara.

Early in 1968 three developments converged and reinforced each other, culminating in Lyndon Johnson's withdrawal from the presidential race simultaneous with a change in grand strategy for ending the war in Vietnam, and, less visibly, in a willingness by some administration officials to challenge the heretofore sacrosanct premises about the U.S. world role. The first development was the upsurge of violence in the ghettos (1967 had been the worst summer ever), stimulated by and in turn stimulating popular discontent because more resources were being devoted to the war in a small Asian country than to the war on poverty at home. The second development was the transference of student militancy from civil rights to the issues of the war and the draft, and the ability of Eugene McCarthy and Robert Kennedy to convert student protest into the energizing force of a powerful antiadministration movement within the Democratic Party. The third development was the ability of Clark Clifford, succeeding McNamara as Secretary of Defense on March 1, 1968, to reach and move the President with evaluations of the military campaign in Vietnam that called into question critical assumptions under which the United States was fighting the war.

Clifford's eyes were opened during his first task as the President's chairman of an interagency task force to evaluate the latest request from General William Westmoreland, then American commander in South Vietnam, for 200,000 additional troops in the wake of the Communist Tet (lunar New Year) offensive. As later recounted by Townsend Hoopes, Under Secretary of the Air Force from October 1967 to February 1969, Clifford was stunned by the magnitude of the request and accordingly decided to broaden the task force's frame of reference to include the basic question of whether or not the United States was operating under a sensible strategic concept in Vietnam. Although the formal task force report to the President reaffirmed the existing policy, Clifford's doubts deepened during its deliberations, and in presenting the report to the President at the

White House on March 7, he felt impelled to express his own new-found reservations, questioning the efficacy of the ground and bombing strategies and wondering what the additional troop buildup would really accomplish. He said that he thought there should be further study before implementing the task force recommendations. The President granted his new Secretary of Defense this delay; but, as Hoopes recalls, "the longstanding friendship between the two men grew suddenly formal and cool." [2]

The President's insecurities were increased by the results of the March 12, 1968, New Hampshire Democratic primary election, which gave antiwar critic Senator Eugene McCarthy 42.2 percent of the vote, just a few percentage points behind Johnson's 49.2. And when on March 16, Robert Kennedy announced that he too would seek the presidency, LBJ's worst fantasies about the ambitions of the Kennedy clan's desire to recapture the White House themselves seemed to be materializing. Recalling these days for his biographer Doris Kearns, Johnson confesses that

I felt . . . that I was being chased on all sides by a giant stampede coming at me from all directions. On one side, the American people were stampeding me to do something about Vietnam. On another side, the inflationary economy was booming out of control. Up ahead were dozens of danger signs pointing to another summer of riots in the cities. I was being forced over the edge by rioting blacks, demonstrating students, marching welfare mothers, squawking professors, and hysterical reporters. And then the final straw. The thing I feared from the first day of my Presidency was actually coming true. Robert Kennedy had openly announced his intention to reclaim the throne in the memory of his brother. And the American people, swayed by the magic of the name, were dancing in the streets. The whole situation was unbearable for me. After thirty-seven years of public service, I deserved something more than being left alone in the middle of the plain, chased by stampedes on every side. [3]

But it was not only the dovish intellectuals and the people who had no knowledge of foreign affairs that were now challenging the wisdom of Johnson's Vietnam policies. Even veteran cold warriors with impeccable loyalty were calling for a fundamental reassessment. LBJ was particularly shaken by former Secretary of State Dean Acheson's judgment, which he voiced to the President privately on March 15, that the administration was operating under the grossest of illusions about what was possible in Vietnam, that no one believed Johnson's speeches any more, and that he had tost touch with the country which, as a whole, was no longer supporting the war. [4]

Clifford sensed that the time was ripe to assemble Johnson's Senior Advisory Group on Vietnam, of which Acheson was a member, along with some of the most distinguished former soilders, diplomats, and policy makers in whom Johnson had great respect. On March 25 they assembled at the White House to read recent background papers and receive briefings from various high government officials, and on March 26 met with the President himself to discuss the issue. Present were Dean Acheson, George Ball, McGeorge Bundy, Douglas Dillon, Cyrus Vance, Arthur Dean, John J. McCloy, General Omar Bradley, General Matthew Ridgway, General Maxwell Taylor, Robert Murphy, Henry Cabot Lodge, Abe Fortas, and Arthur Goldberg. According to Townsend Hoopes' account of this meeting, the President was "visibly shocked" and "stung" by the magnitude of the defection from the existing policy, and especially by the fact that sophisticated pragmatists like McGeorge Bundy and Cyrus Vance were now among those pressing for deescalation, negotiations, and disengagement ahead of being able to assure against a Communist takeover in South Vietnam.[5]

Clifford now apparently felt strengthened to intervene with Johnson's speechwriter Harry McPherson to help shape the speech on Vietnam the President was scheduled to deliver to the country on March 31, and through McPherson persuaded the now-demoralized LBJ to announce a unilateral deescalation of the bombing and to imply that there was more of the same to come if Hanoi would enter into serious negotiations. Clifford was gratified to see on his television screen the President finally coming around to the proposals he had been urging over the past weeks. What neither he nor the rest of the nation expected, however, was Johnson's dramatic closing remarks on March 31 that in order to devote all his time and energies to the quest for peace, "I do not believe I should devote an hour or a day of my time to partisan causes. . . . Accordingly, I shall not seek, and I will not accept, the nomination of my party for another term as your President."[6]

The President's personal démarche—his renunciation of further electioneering and of another term for himself—evidently was interpreted in Hanoi as a more credible bid for peace than were past efforts by the United States. Accepting the partial bombing halt as a basis for preliminary talks, the North Vietnamese also reciprocated on the military front by a temporary cessation of their shelling

of cities in the South and a substantial reduction of large unit operations in the demilitarized zone at the 17th parallel. Clifford and
his associates felt vindicated in their belief that a U.S. posture looking very serious about deescalating the conflict was better than mus-
cle-flexing for getting Ho Chi Minh to the bargaining table.

Johnson remained skeptical, however, still wanting to believe that
the real reason for Hanoi's willingness to negotiate was that they
had been hurt by the bombing more than they were willing to let
on, and that therefore a credible threat to resume full-scale bombing
was essential to induce them to accept an independent South Vietnam. Once again, in late October 1968, he decided against his own
instincts by ordering a total bombing halt, yielding to the insistences
of Clifford and the two U.S. negotiators in the Paris talks with the
North Vietnamese, Cyrus Vance and Averell Harriman. But LBJ
left office, chafing at the bit and full of self-doubts about whether
he had shown weakness or strength at the last.[7]

To be sure, there still were numerous unreconstructed Vietnam
interventionists in top policy-making posts in the fall of 1968, not
the least of whom were Secretary of State Dean Rusk and national
security adviser Walt Rostow. The change—which Clark Clifford
was particularly instrumental in bringing about—was that it was
now legitimate within the administration to debate the basic policy
premises underlying the Vietnam involvement. And the now debat-
able premises, it would emerge, were part and parcel of the *Weltanschauung* of forward containment of Communism that dominated official Washington's thinking since the late 1940s.

A fundamental tenet from Truman to Johnson was that the *irreducible national interest* ("securing the blessings of liberty to ourselves and our posterity") required that the Communists not be allowed to extend their sphere of control. This policy was based on a
set of interrelated assumptions, namely:

—The Soviets and the Chinese Communists are highly motivated to extend their rule to other areas.
—Soviet expansion alone, or the fruits of possible Chinese expansion if
added on to Soviet sphere, could eventually give the Communist nations a
preponderance of power globally that would enable them to dictate the
conditions under which the people of the United States should live.
—The establishment of additional Communist regimes, or the territorial

expansion by Communist countries other than Russia or China, would add to the global power of the Soviets and/or the Chinese and their capacities for expansion.

—The Soviets and the Chinese Communists would resort to military expansion if they were not checked by countervailing military power.

—In the crunch, against a determined attack by either of the two Communist giants, indigenous military power would be insufficient to deter or defend against the Communists, and United States military power would have to be brought in to redress the imbalance.

—A capability and clearly communicated will to defend whatever area the Communist powers might choose to attack, regardless of its intrinsic geopolitical weight in the overall balance, was necessary to prevent the Communists from picking and choosing easy targets for blackmail and aggression. Moreover, America's failure to defend one area would demoralize nationals in other such localities in their will to resist the Communists. Even in Western Europe and Japan, whose advanced industrialization made them critical weights in the global balance of power, people would wonder under what circumstances we might consider them dispensable.

—Even if the Soviets and the Chinese Communists were effectively deterred from direct military expansion, they would attempt to expand their spheres of control in the underdeveloped areas through support of subversive movements, insurgencies, and "wars of national liberation."

—(A group of assumptions prominent during the Kennedy-Johnson years). Economic underdevelopment and the political disorder that comes from unsatisfied aspirations for betterment provide easy opportunities for Communist takeover of subversive and insurrectionary movements; thus U.S. economic and political development programs, no less than counterinsurgency capabilities, must be prominent parts of the grand strategy of preventing adverse changes in the global balance of power.

Unavoidably, questioning of the nature of U.S. security interests in Vietnam, or even questioning—as Clifford did—whether the protection of our interests there were *worth* the high expenditures of human and material resources, would call into question the assumptions just enumerated.

U.S. policy makers had taken for granted that the Soviets and Chinese Communists had unrequited appetites for expansion. Did the record of the past two decades support this proposition? A serious body of "revisionist" history of the cold war period had emerged during the middle 1960s supportive of alternative propositions. The more extreme revisionists were arguing that the United States was more clearly the expansionist power since the Second World War, arrogantly attempting to reshape the world in the image of its ideological preconceptions, and that the Soviets and Chinese were only reacting defensively to this "encirclement." Moderate revisionists stressed the likelihood that both sides have been victims of tragic misperceptions of the other's real intentions, which were to assure themselves substantial, but limited, spheres of influence for legitimate reasons of economic and military security. Others, more agnostic with respect to the intentions of the Communists, nonetheless claimed that Russian and foreign actions as distinct from their rhetoric tended to be prudent if not conservative, that the Communist nations, like the Western countries, had difficult resource allocation problems and unmet domestic needs which placed weighty constraints on their inclinations for foreign adventure.

No less questionable were the forecasts of adverse consequences to the global balance of power that would result if the Communists were allowed to extend their area of control. Changes in the technologies of transportation, communication, basic materials production, and weaponry pointed to the need for a full-scale review of the strategic worth attributed to various peninsulas, straits, island outposts, and sources of raw materials.

Apart from obsolescent notions of geopolitics, the notion of a seamless web of U.S. commitments connecting and sustaining friendly nations of the non-Communist world was also in for hard scrutiny. The implication that United States security was tied vitally to the security of each nation (or was it to regimes?) to which it had made more or less equivocal pledges of protection from internal and external threats might have some utility as a *deterrent* if believed by Moscow and Peking; but what was its effect upon the behavior of the beneficiaries of U.S. protection? Where they tempted to provocative action themselves, confident we would bail them out? Were they stimulated to correct the deficiencies in their socioeconomic systems or, rather, were they only encouraged to perpetuate the very injustices and misallocations of resources that made them vulnerable in the first place?

Also due for skeptical examination was the idea that the Third World, especially its nonaligned elements, was up for grabs as between the two superpowers. Both the United States and the Soviet

Union had undergone the chastening experience during the first half of the decade of finding social, economic, and political forces in the less developed states nowhere nearly as malleable as hypothesized in Khrushchev's doctrine of "wars of national liberation" and Kennedy's "decade of development." Political movements and parties receptive to development models and tutelage offered by each of the superpowers often turned out to be politically discredited within their own countries and, if anything, cold war liabilities for their tutors. If this was indeed the emerging pattern, could not the United States afford to be more sanguine at the appearance of Soviet aid or trade missions in Third World countries? But would not such a relaxed attitude also seriously undercut the most politically salable rationale for the U.S. foreign aid program—namely, that it was essential for U.S. security because the Third World was now the new arena for conducting the global power competition?

The consensus underlying the constancy in foreign policy from Truman to Johnson was at an end. On January 20, 1969, there was no basic foreign policy to be handed over intact to the Nixon administration.

The period when policy changes could be attributed to changes in reliance on various tools of power, as distinct from changes in national interests and objectives, seemed to call for an analysis of contending programs and strategies. It now appeared, however, that the analysis of foreign policy choices would have to cut deeper, to contending concepts of national purpose and international order.

PART V

STATECRAFT UNDER NIXON AND FORD

Power used with good intentions, but ineptly, can be as destructive as power used with bad intentions. The greatest tragedy of all, however, occurs when those who have power fail to use it, and because of that failure lives and even freedom itself are lost.

RICHARD M. NIXON

The most onimous change that marked our period was the transformation in the nature of power. . . . As power had grown more awesome, it had also turned abstract, intangible, elusive.

HENRY A. KISSINGER

21

KISSINGER AND THE
CRISES OF POWER

If you act creatively you should be able to use crises to move the world towards the structural solutions that are necessary. In fact, very often the crises themselves are a symptom of the need for structural rearrangement.

HENRY A. KISSINGER

Any analysis of U.S. foreign policy during the Nixon and Ford administrations must focus primarily on the policies and diplomacy of Henry A. Kissinger. The earlier démarches of the period, when President Nixon was not yet consumed by Watergate and while Kissinger was still systematically enlarging his power within the administration, showed heavy presidential influence; and they are properly described as "Nixon administration" or "Nixon–Kissinger" policies. Even during the Ford administration, important presidential decisions were needed to resolve policy disputes between the Secretary of State and the Secretaries of Defense and Treasury. But only Kissinger strode commandingly across the full eight years of the period. It was his conceptual muscle and aggressive bureaucratic infighting that gave coherence to administration policies; and it was his diplomatic virtuosity and rhetorical artistry that became, for a considerable time, *the* foreign policy of the United States.

United States foreign policy was in crisis when Henry A. Kissinger assumed office in January 1969 as President Nixon's special assistant for national security affairs. Profound disorientation over the country's international purposes and the means to achieve them pervaded the foreign policy bureaucracy, Congress, and the elements of the public that are usually attentive to foreign policy matters. The bipartisan foreign policy consensus that had sustained vigorous executive action through two decades of the cold war had disintegrated. [1]

Many officials and analysts whose lives had been devoted to international relations were leaving the field to concentrate on domestic problems—race relations, urban affairs—having had their fill of attempting to reconstruct the world in the image of America. Among the exiles from the Kennedy and Johnson administrations who remained interested in foreign affairs, most seemed mainly anxious to prevent the United States from repeating the errors that had led to the Vietnam fiasco. Working through the Democratic-controlled Congress, nongovernmental think tanks, and public interest lobbies, the repentant global activists now constituted a loose but powerful coalition for a highly restricted definition of U.S. interests, low defense budgets, and close congressional control over executive actions that could involve the country in international conflict.

As Nixon and Kissinger saw it, nothing less than the power of the United States was at stake—which to them meant that virtually everything was at stake. The realpolitik approach to international relations views power itself as the most vital of national interests. Power, like the human body's central nervous system, provides the essential capacity to ward off threats, satisfy basic needs, and realize other purposes. Even survival itself is meaningless without power, for without it one is a mere vegetable for others to manipulate.

National "power" to Nixon and Kissinger was never simply military power (although some of Kissinger's preofficial writings might have appeared to establish such an equation). It was more generic than that, being the sum of the nation's capacities to act purposefully in international affairs and to resist being controlled by others. To be powerful, a country had to be able to provide or deny others what they wanted but could not obtain elsewhere.

The crisis of American power, as perceived by Nixon and Kissinger, was in large measure caused by psychological deficiencies rather than material ones. It emanated primarily from a collapse of confidence, both at home and abroad, in the U.S. government's capacity to effectively marshal this country's assets in support of its international interests. [2]

From this perspective the restoration of America's power required, first, a liquidation of the Vietnam conflict in a way that would avert a dangerous polarization of American society and still preserve the reputation of the United States as a country that sustained its commitments; second, a realistic reordering of the nation's priority interests so as to avoid squandering its resources in the service of idealistic goals peripheral to the central balance of military and geopolitical power; third, the development of a concept of international order that—while consistent with the priority interests of the United States—would provide a standard of legitimacy to which most nations could attach themselves; and finally, purposeful and dramatic action on global issues so that this country's leaders, once again, would be looked to as the main pacesetters in the international arena.

Nixon and Kissinger regarded the termination of U.S. military involvement in Vietnam as a prerequisite for fulfilling the other requirements for restoring U.S. power. While still trapped and bleeding in an Indochinese quagmire largely of its own making, the United States could hardly be considered as acting according to a rational strategy to implement its priority interests. Nor could it, while employing its advanced military equipment in a civil war in a remote poor country, credibly champion a standard of international order based on notions that the strong should not bully the weak and that force should not be employed across national boundaries to advance ideological objectives. The U.S. government, of course, still retained the capacity to act vigorously on various international matters of moment, and did so in some situations with effectiveness and flair; yet as long as U.S. leaders revealed profound impotence and irrationality in the face of the Vietnam conflict, their authority, and that of the U.S. government generally, would continue to erode at home and abroad.

The U.S. retreat from Vietnam, however, would have to be "honorable"—meaning that it would have to be a negotiated exit involving concessions by the North Vietnamese and their Soviet and Chinese backers. "However we got into Vietnam," Kissinger wrote in a January 1969 *Foreign Affairs* article outlining his terms for a settlement, "ending the war honorably is essential for the peace of the world. Any other solution may unloose forces that would complicate the prospects for international order."[3] Some of the forces feared by Kissinger and Nixon were international—militant revolutionaries emboldened to imitate Ho Chi Minh's defiance of the capitalist superpower; and Soviet and Chinese hardliners, now vindicated in their supposition that the West was too decadent, disorganized, and spineless to persist in foreign struggles that were protracted and costly. Some of the forces feared by the new administration were domestic—the anger of families whose sons had been killed or maimed for the patriotic objective of resisting the spread of Communism; the military and their hawkish supporters in Congress, who would blame the foreign policy "establishment" for putting paralyzing limitations on the capabilities of U.S. military forces to smash the enemy; and a general explosion of fierce resentment by ordinary proud Americans at leaders who could not save the country from a humiliating defeat. A wave of Marxist revolutions abroad and a neofascist backlash at home—the worst of all possible worlds.

Convinced that it was insane to continue wasting American blood and treasure in a remote war against an enemy fighting for what it believed to be its national integrity, but equally convinced that it was an act of political suicide to "bug out" of Indochina, the Nixon administration prolonged the bloodshed for four years while it engaged in a diplomatic charade to preserve American honor, whose ultimate result was to devalue the meaning of honor itself. To the extent that a country's power is in part dependent on the honor of its government, the Nixon administration's Vietnam withdrawal policy (described in chapter 23) was bound to leave the country less powerful than it was before 1969.

The second requirement for a restoration of America's power—a more realistic definition of U.S. international interests—was now recognized as necessary throughout the policy community in order to avoid future Vietnams, to avoid having U.S. actions controlled by commitments that were the products of an American universalism no longer appropriate to the complicated world of the 1970s.[4]

In the first of his four annual reports to Congress on U.S. foreign policy, President Nixon announced that his administration had instituted "a new approach to foreign policy, to match a new era of international relations." The approach bore the unmistakable imprint of its principal author, Henry Kissinger.

"The postwar period in international relations has ended," asserted the President. The ravages of World War II had been overcome. "Western Europe and Japan have recovered their economic strength, their political vitality, and their national self-confidence." The new nations too had less need to be as totally dependent on the United States, as previous administrations had assumed. "Once many feared that they would become simply a battleground of cold war rivalry and fertile ground for Communist penetration. But this fear misjudged their pride in their national identities and their determination to preserve their newly won sovereignty." In addition, the nature of the Communist world had changed—"The power of individual Communist nations has grown, but international Communist unity has been shattered . . . by the powerful forces of nationalism." Meanwhile, "a revolution in the technology of war has altered the nature of the military balance of power. . . . Both the Soviet Union and the United States have acquired the ability to inflict unacceptable damage on the other, no matter which strikes first. There can be no gain and certainly no victory for the power that provokes a thermonuclear exchange." [5]

If these trends were now taken fully into account, the foreign policy crisis inherited by the administration could be transformed into an opportunity to reformulate the international interests of the United States in a way that would match U.S. commitments to its capabilities. Kissinger had provided a broad-brush outline of the basis for a new concept of U.S. interests in his 1968 essay for the Brookings Institution. The essay was more precise in its characterizations of where we had been ("an undifferentiated globalism") than in its map of where we should be going, for as Kissinger put it, "in the years ahead, the most profound challenge to American policy will be philosophical: to develop some concept of order in a world which is bipolar militarily but multipolar politically." [6]

The new concept should relate U.S. interests to an understanding of historical trends, to an appreciation of the functions and limitations of national power in the international system, to the structural requirements for equilibrium in the contemporary setting. "But [this] philosophical deepening will not come easily to those brought up in the American tradition of foreign policy," wrote Kissinger. Foreign policy could no longer be based primarily on "enthusiasm, belief in progress, and the invincible conviction that American remedies can work everywhere." [7]

Anticipating what was soon to become the "Nixon Doctrine"— although, ironically, when Kissinger wrote it he was foreign policy adviser to Nelson Rockefeller, then Nixon's main opponent for the Republican presidential nomination—Kissinger argued that

the United States is no longer in a position to operate programs globally; it has to encourage them. It can no longer impose its preferred solution; it must seek to evoke it. In the forties and fifties, we offered remedies; in the late sixties and seventies our role will have to be to contribute to a structure that will foster the initiative of others. We are a superpower physically, but our designs can be meaningful only if they generate willing cooperation. We can continue to contribute to defense and positive programs, but we must seek to encourage and not stifle a sense of local responsibility. Our contribution should not be the sole or principal effort, but it should make the difference between success and failure. [8]

There were many target audiences for the Nixon Doctrine—allies, adversaries, and the U.S. public—but significantly, its first official enunciation was on the Pacific island of Guam, a stopover during the President's round-the-world trip in the summer of 1969. Here, between Hawaii and the Chinese mainland, a key staging area for the U.S. military effort in Vietnam, Nixon announced that the United States should not be expected to involve its own forces in future insurgency wars. The United States would furnish economic and military assistance where appropriate, but the nation directly threatened would have to provide the manpower for its own defense. However, the United States would provide a "shield" (presumably air power and naval support) if "a nuclear power threatens the freedom of a nation allied with us or of a nation whose survival we consider vital to our security and the security of the region as a whole." [9]

Kissinger's influence was evident here and was even more evident in the President's reiteration and explanation of the doctrine in his first State of the World message. Its "central thesis," Nixon told Congress, was "that the United States will participate in the defense and development of its allies and friends, but that America cannot—and will not—conceive *all* the plans, design *all* the programs, execute *all* the decisions, and undertake *all* the defense of the free nations of the world. We will help where it makes a difference and is in our interest." [10]

The United States would honor its existing commitments, said the President, but henceforth "our interests must shape out commitments, rather than the other way around." New commitments would be undertaken only in light of "a careful assessment of our national interests and those of other countries, of the specific threats to those interests and of our capacity to counter those threats at acceptable risk and cost." [11]

The promised "careful assessment of our own national interests," however, never surfaced in the form of an official statement available to Congress and the public at large so that there could be agreed-upon terms of reference for assessing the worth and means of sustaining particular commitments. Consequently, what was supposed to be a new conceptual basis for reforging the shattered foreign policy consensus turned out to be a plea to Congress and to the public to trust the executive's wisdom in understanding what the national interest required. This, of course, Congress and the public were increasingly unwilling to do, especially as the commitments and tactics they were asked to support seemed more and more to imply a continuation of the universalistic pretensions to American omnipotence that Kissinger and Nixon had so eloquently criticized in their early statements. If there was to be a *selective* involvement in international events, the basis of the selections was to be formulated in the executive with a minimum of congressional participation; moreover, tremendous leeway for ad hoc, improvisatory international maneuvers was to be retained by the executive. This the Congress, backed by public opinion, was in no mood to allow, so what started out as a "philosophical" or "conceptual" crisis, in Kissinger's formulation, came close to being a constitutional crisis over the authority to conduct foreign policy that, when compounded by the constitutional crisis surrounding Watergate, almost completely sapped the country's capacity to act purposefully and credibly abroad.

Grandiose promises of conceptual innovation coupled with a confusing record of delivery also affected the administration's third imperative for restoring U.S. power—the development of a structure of international order consistent with U.S. interests. "The greatest need of the contemporary international system," wrote Kissinger in 1968, "is an agreed concept of international order." [12] Again, the

Kissinger themes reappeared only slightly altered in President Nixon's first State of the World message:

> Peace must be far more than the absence of war. Peace must provide a durable structure of international relationships which inhibits or removes the causes of war. . . . We are working toward the day when *all* nations will have a stake in peace, and will therefore be partners in its maintenance. [13]

The "structure of peace," as sketched in this initial Nixon administration statement, was supposed to have three "pillars": (1) "partnership," a euphemism for the Nixon Doctrine's devolution of ground warfare and counterinsurgency responsibilities to U.S. allies; (2) "strength," a rationalization of U.S. military capabilities, particularly strategic forces, to preserve a global balance of military power and regional balances in the context of the Soviet Union's having attained essential strategic equality with the United States; and (3) "willingness to negotiate," a vague early formulation of what was soon to emerge as the triangular relationship of U.S.–Soviet détente on the one hand and the U.S.–China rapprochement on the other. [14]

The first two "pillars" hardly rated their advertisement as conceptual innovations, and the third—the promise of an "era of negotiation" to supplant the "era of confrontation"—remained little more than a tantalizing slogan until the surprising démarches toward China and the Soviet Union of 1971–72. The billing "*structure* of peace" was particularly mystifying, for there was no accompanying design, or even outline, of the essential characteristics of the international order that was supposed to be produced by these policies.

There was considerable talk by Kissinger of giving the Soviets "a stake in the international equilibrium" in connection with the U.S.–Soviet agreements in and surrounding the 1972 Nixon–Brezhnev summit. Journalists and academics speculated that the equilibrium was supposed to result from the interplay of forces in a "pentagonal" structure, a five-sided balance of power reminiscent of eighteenth- and nineteenth-century European balances that Kissinger was thought to want to reinstitute. Clues to the unrevealed grand design were sought in oblique formulations such as the President's statement to *Time* magazine that "it would be a safer world and better world if we have a strong, healthy United States, Europe, Soviet

Union, China, Japan; each balancing the other, not playing one against the other, an even balance." [15]

Kissinger appeared to know where he was helping the President sail the ship of state; but if there was a map in his head, he was reluctant to share it with the passengers or even the crew. They all were supposed to have faith in Henry the Navigator. Increasingly, however, as some of his almost magically fashioned international arrangements began to unravel—SALT, economic détente, the Vietnam peace accords, step-by-step diplomacy in the Middle East—a willing suspension of disbelief was no longer possible for many of his former admirers. Perhaps his most disparaging critics were right, that the Kissinger phenomenon had more flair than philosophy, more shuttle than substance.

Yet the performance did at least *imply* some major premises about the emerging international order and about what the United States (or Henry Kissinger) could and should do to help shape it. Significantly, the actions and the implied assumptions approximated rather closely the guidelines for statecraft that Kissinger had articulated in his historical writings, as distinct from his writings on military strategy and foreign policy during the cold war. This suggests that the international and domestic changes of the middle and late 1960s took Kissinger by surprise, as they did most of his contemporaries, and that for his intellectual retooling he relied on analysis by historical analogy much more than he cared to admit.

The pertinent analogies came mostly from the nineteenth-century Concert of Europe rather than from the classical eighteenth-century Balance of Power system—a point missed by much of the academic criticism of Kissinger's policies, which tried to score points on the former professor by showing how different the contemporary world is from Europe in the eighteenth century. To be sure, the contemporary world is also very different from nineteenth-century Europe, as Kissinger himself has often pointed out; [16] but the essential lessons Kissinger the historian drew from the successes and failures of the great diplomats of the post-Napoleonic period are amazingly similar to the premises of the *Weltanschauung* that can be inferred from Kissinger's own diplomacy. [17]

An international order that could contain the clash of national interests, power rivalries, and ideological antagonisms from engulfing world society in war, anarchy, and chaos had two structural imperatives, according to Kissinger: (1) an equilibrium of military power and (2) acceptance by the major powers of certain fundamental principles of legitimate and illegitimate state action in the international system. The substance of the requirements would vary in different historical epochs, but equilibrium and legitimacy would always be essential requisites for a civilized world. Neither was sufficient by itself. In the thermonuclear age they had become the twin conditions for the very survival of the human species.

History teaches, wrote Kissinger, "that no order is safe without physical safeguards against aggression."[18] States had to be ready and willing to apply military force to prevent any of their number from attempting to dominate the international system against the will of the others, or to violate its essential rules. Order thus required the capacity and the will, on the part of at least the major powers, to fight for more than one's immediate security. Commitments to weaker members of the system to help them fight against a country attempting to attain hegemony, and commitments to fight against aggression itself, were also necessary. To this extent at least, the lessons of history supported the basic containment and alliance policies of postwar U.S. administrations from Truman through Johnson.

For military containment to work, however, the will, on the part of those committed to order, to dispense with peace itself had to be made evident to those who might violate the rules of the system. There could be no military equilibrium—what in the contemporary period is called stable deterrence—without general confidence in its *psychological* as well as its physical components. As Kissinger put it,

Whenever peace—conceived of as the avoidance of war—has been the primary objective of a power or a group of powers, the international system has been at the mercy of the most ruthless member of the international community. Whenever the international order has acknowledged that certain principles could not be compromised even for the sake of peace, stability based on an equilibrium of forces was at least conceivable.[19]

This was precisely what was so worrisome about the present period, and why military containment might now be insufficient.

Faced with the prospect of thermonuclear extinction, alliance partners who were themselves not directly under attack might too readily alter their principles rather than join the fight. Sensing this, a revolutionary superpower—one anxious to dominate or overturn the existing system—could be tempted to coercively exploit the weak links in a containment chain on the assumption that even the rival superpower would retreat from military engagement. This assumption, though, might turn out to be a gross miscalculation, and could bring on the terrible holocaust whose anticipation was supposed to have eroded the will to resist the revolutionary superpower's aggression. Thus, the equilibrium system under today's conditions, if based almost entirely on a balance of military power, not only would be insufficient to prevent threats to the existing order but might prove to be too unstable to prevent the outbreak of central war.

Because central war could mean the destruction of civilization, it was more crucial than ever before to supplement the system of military equilibrium with a system of political "legitimacy." Once again, Kissinger defines the essence of such a system in his major historical work on the nineteenth-century Concert of Europe:

> "Legitimacy" as here used should not be confused with justice. It means no more than an international agreement about the nature of workable arrangements and about the permissible aims and methods of foreign policy. It implies the acceptance of the framework of the international order by all major powers, at least to the extent that no state is so dissatisfied that, like Germany after the Treaty of Versailles, it expresses its dissatisfaction in a revolutionary foreign policy.[20]

But just as the military equilibrium was insufficient to preserve the peace, so legitimacy—general international acceptance of the existing order—was hardly by itself an adequate basis for restraining a revolutionary state determined to smash that order. Indeed, if the revolutionary state is powerful enough, the conditions for a legitimate international order are negated, for in such situations "it is not the adjustments of differences within a given system that will be at issue, but the system itself. Adjustments are possible, but they will be conceived as tactical maneuvers to consolidate positions for the inevitable showdown, or as tools to undermine the morale of the protagonist."[21]

It was clear from Kissinger's historical and policy-oriented writings before he became a public official that he considered the Soviet Union and China to be "revolutionary states"—states whose aspirations could not be satisfied by the international order insisted on by the other major powers—and that the Soviet Union, at least, was powerful enough to make it impossible to restore a system of international legitimacy. Yet the Nixon–Kissinger "structure of peace" assumed a positive Soviet stake in the emerging international order.

The Declaration of Principles signed by Nixon and Brezhnev at their 1972 Moscow summit meeting included promises by both superpowers to base their relations on the principles of "sovereignty, equality, noninterference in internal affairs and mutual advantage"; to "always exercise restraint in their mutual relations; to negotiate and settle differences by peaceful means"; and to refrain from attempts to gain "unilateral advantage at the expense of the other, directly or indirectly." [22] A large package of interrelated U.S.–Soviet negotiations on specific issues—arms, control, economic and technological cooperation, a Middle East peace, and rules of mutual nonintervention in the other power's sphere of influence and in third-area conflicts—were supposed to provide a web of relationships, each linked to all of the others, that the Soviet Union would have strong incentives not to unravel. [23]

Not surprisingly, some of Kissinger's critics on the right pointed to this basic "contradiction" in Kissinger's "grand design." Warren Nutter, an Assistant Secretary of Defense for International Security Affairs during the Nixon administration, observed that whereas Kissinger had stressed in his scholarly writings that diplomacy vis-à-vis a revolutionary power could play only a symbolic role, "he now argues that negotiation with the Soviet Union will result in great substantive achievements." [24] Kissinger's main argument—that détente, even though it could not guarantee a modification of the Soviet Union's revolutionary aims, was a moral imperative in an age when thermonuclear war was the likely consequence of the failure to accommodate the conflicting aims of the superpowers—was lost on his critics.

Increasingly, during the Ford administration, the Reagan wing of the Republican Party attacked the Secretary of State for giving the Soviet Union more than the United States got in return—in the SALT negotiations, in East–West commerce, and in the Helsinki Final Act of the Conference on Security and Cooperation in Europe. So virulent was the right-wing criticism that in his 1976 campaign for the presidential nomination Ford explicitly renounced further official use of the word *détente;* and in the 1976 Republican National Convention the Reagan forces were able to insert anti-détente and anti-Kissinger planks in the platform.

Some liberals were angered by Kissinger's unwillingness to press the Soviet Union and other autocratic regimes on the subject of human rights. Kissinger's rationale for avoiding direct diplomatic pressure on the Soviet Union for its violations of human rights, and his opposition to the congressional refusal to grant commercial privileges and government credits to the USSR unless the Kremlin liberalized its restrictions on emigration, emphasized the risks to détente. Perhaps he was reluctant to voice the deeper conceptual basis for such restraint for fear of having his ideas appear too "classical" or European.

The result was not simply a conceptual void but also a tacit coalition among conservatives and liberals in opposition to Kissinger's alleged amoralism and supposed preference for negotiating with dictators rather than with genuine democrats. For Kissinger's critics on the left, this presumed moral deficiency was compounded by the blatant hypocrisy of professing noninterference in the domestic affairs of other states while authorizing antileftist activities by U.S. operatives in various countries—the most notorious being the Central Intelligence Agency's aid to anti-Allende forces in Chile.

In short, the world order concept, which was to provide a vision capable of rallying not only a new domestic consensus but also an international consensus, was revealed only in fragments, coyly and defensively. Those few who thought they caught a glimpse of the larger concept were not at all sure they liked what they saw. Others who listened to Kissinger's sonorous explanations of his policy initiatives doubted even the existence of a larger concept behind the hyperactive diplomacy. The need to restore confidence at home and abroad that the United States was again capable of acting purposefully in the world was passed on by Kissinger to his successors. Surely this must have been one of his keenest personal disappointments. It was equally a misfortune for the country, for he had correctly diagnosed the need for conceptual clarification but was unable to provide the remedy.

Because of Kissinger's reluctance to fully share the premises of his actions with his domestic and international audience, his performance during the eight years of the Nixon and Ford administrations came off more as a brilliantly executed series of improvisations than as a "mosaic" (one of Kissinger's favorite terms) in which each of the parts is integral to the whole conception. The best improvisations, of course, do emanate from a concept underneath the apparent spontaneity at the surface, and this was in fact the case with

Kissinger's most important moves: his negotiations with Le Duc Tho leading to the U.S. disengagement from Indochina; his simultaneous catering to Soviet and Chinese desires to increase their international respectability; his step-by-step diplomacy in the Middle East; his response to Third World economic demands at the Seventh Special Session of the United Nations; and his shift in the "tilt" of U.S. policy in Southern Africa, away from the support of white minority governments and toward the goal of black majority rule.

The fit of each of these tactical moves into Kissinger's grand strategy will be analyzed in subsequent chapters. Regardless of their substantive validity, however, they did serve as opportunities for Kissinger to "make waves," to re-create positive popular excitement around U.S. foreign policy, to restore America's existential leadership—characteristically based on the scope and momentum of this country's reaction to world events more than on depth of understanding. Although Kissinger had hoped to root U.S. foreign policy more deeply in a historically derived philosophy of international relations, he found himself turning into the arch-practitioner of the razzle-dazzle, "can do" American pragmatism that he had previously condemned. Instead of the Europeanization of America, the world was treated to the Americanization of Henry.

Innovation, surprising changes of direction, a ubiquitous presence, sheer momentum itself—these Kissinger knew were important aspects of power; but he also knew that such an activist diplomacy, unless "in the hands of a master," could become mindless and risky.[25] It was important, therefore, for the innovator to *institutionalize* the premises of his policy before he left office, or else they might be dissipated by his successors. However, as crisis cascaded upon crisis and the activist style eclipsed the philosophical, there was little left to institutionalize except Henry Kissinger himself—which he had to admit (humorously, but perhaps seriously) was a tragic impossibility.

Kissinger identified with the imposing statesmen he wrote about—with their success, but also with their failures. At the end of one of his most eloquent historical essays, he quoted from a poignant Bismarck letter: "That which is imposing here on earth . . . has always something of the fallen angel who is beautiful but without peace, great in his conceptions and exertions but without success, proud and lonely."[26]

22

THE INSUFFICIENCY OF
MILITARY CONTAINMENT

What in the name of God is strategic superiority? What is the significance of it,
politically, militarily, operationally, at these numbers? What do you do with it?
HENRY A. KISSINGER

Détente with the Soviet Union, rapprochement with China—both
of these early démarches of the Nixon administration were to a large
extent prompted by the realization that Soviet military power could
now neutralize the ability of U.S. military power to deter objectionable Soviet behavior short of direct threats to the United States itself. New means for affecting Soviet behavior were required to supplement military deterrence.

Military power was still considered necessary to induce the Soviet
Union to respect the range of U.S. interests abroad, for if the Soviet
Union, but not the United States, were able and willing to resort
to force when the secondary interests of the two superpowers
clashed, the Soviets could face down the United States in situation
after situation and ultimately achieve a position of global dominance. But U.S. military power was no longer deemed sufficient for
containing the Soviet Union within its current sphere of dominance, for military containment was based on confidence that the
United States would prevail in any major U.S.–Soviet war—a belief
that was eroding by the later 1960s.[1]

Confidence that the United States would prevail rested in some important cases on the credibility of U.S. threats to escalate a conflict to strategic levels—for example, in Berlin crises—where the Russians enjoyed a preponderance of locally applicable force. But now that the Soviet Union as well as the United States was supposed to have a strategic arsenal capable of assuring virtually total destruction of the attacker, no matter how large and well executed its first strike, it was highly unlikely that either superpower would seriously contemplate attacking the other for any purpose except retaliation for a direct attack on itself. With strategic deterrence thus restricted to the ultimate holocaust, lesser Soviet aggressive moves, even against loyal allies of the United States, could not be reliably prevented unless the United States and its allies developed other weighty levers on Soviet behavior.

The raw materials for fashioning such levers were sought by Nixon and Kissinger in the mutual paranoia between the Russians and the Chinese and in the Kremlin's desire to increase the Soviet Union's participation in the international economy. It was uncertain, however, that the contemplated triangular relationship—assuming that both Communist powers, for their own reasons, would latch on— would indeed operate to dissuade the Russians and the Chinese from attempting to take advantage of the new mood of isolationism growing in the United States. And the expectation that expanded commercial contacts would provide substantial U.S. leverage on the Soviets was also still only a hypothesis.

Meanwhile, congressional efforts to reduce U.S. defense expenditures were intensifying, and this, if successful in the context of the Soviet military buildup, could shift the global military balance in favor of the Russians. Nixon and Kissinger, neither of whom had been enthusiasts of arms control before 1969, now felt compelled to seriously negotiate limitations on the arms race.

Arms control thereupon was added to expansion of commercial relations with the USSR and normalization of relations with Peking as the cornerstones of the "structure of peace" that President Nixon spoke of in his 1969 Inaugural Address. For Kissinger they became essential elements of global order that otherwise—owing to the inherent weakness of containment based mainly on military deterrence—would become dangerously unstable.

THE ARMS CONTROL DILEMMA

Putting a cap on the strategic arms race proved to be the most difficult of the international restructuring tasks that Nixon and Kissinger set for themselves. It required that both sides abandon the goal of strategic superiority and that each give up attempting to protect its population against the other's nuclear attack. The concepts of parity and mutual deterrence went against the grain of many of the influential military and foreign policy elites in both countries. Moreover, the esoteric strategic doctrine that mutual deterrence required both sides to protect their missiles but not their people was hardly likely to be popular with the general public.

Nixon himself, having frequently rejected strategic parity as an acceptable context for conducting U.S.–Soviet relations, and having promised during the 1968 election campaign to restore "clear-cut military superiority" as a planning objective, was not about to frontally contradict hopes in the Pentagon (now free from the planning constraints of the McNamara years) to once again pull well ahead of the Russians. The new presidential assistant for national security affairs, however, provided just the right conceptual finesse. At his first presidential news conference, Nixon was asked by a questioner to distinguish between the planning goal of superiority over the Soviet Union being propounded by Secretary of Defense Melvin Laird and a notion being advanced by Kissinger called "sufficiency." [2] Nixon's answer, while leaving much to later elaboration, deftly chalked out the middle ground:

I think the semantics may offer an appropriate approach to the problem. I would say, with regard to Dr. Kissinger's suggestion of sufficiency, that that would meet certainly my guideline and, I think Secretary Laird's guideline with regard to superiority.

Let me put it this way: When we talk about parity, I think we should recognize that wars occur usually when each side believes it has a chance to win. Therefore, parity does not necessarily assure that a war may not occur.

By the same token, when we talk about superiority, that may have a detrimental effect on the other side in putting it in an inferior position and therefore giving great impetus to its own arms race.

Our objective in this administration . . . is to be sure that the United States has sufficient military power to defend our interests and to maintain the commitments which this administration determines are in the interests of the United States around the world.

I think "sufficiency" is a better term, actually, than either "superiority" or "parity." [3]

The new strategic planning concept, as elaborated in subsequent statements by the administration, was supposed to accomplish a number of purposes—not all of them compatible.

Sufficiency first and foremost required enough well-protected strategic forces to be able to inflict a level of damage on the Soviet Union that would deter the Soviet leaders from attacking. In this respect the Nixon administration incorporated the "assured destruction" criterion of former Secretary of Defense Robert McNamara. Assured destruction, however, was deemed insufficient as a force-planning concept, for, as interpreted by Nixon, it was "limited to the indiscriminate mass destruction of enemy civilians as the sole possible response to challenges." This would be an incredible response insofar as it involved "the likelihood of triggering nuclear attacks on our own population." As such, it was an inadequate strategic basis for preventing the Soviets from coercing the United States and its allies. [4]

It was also essential, explained the President, to maintain "a flexible range of strategic options." Given the variety of possible politico-military situations that could conceivably confront us, "our strategic policy should not be based solely on a capability of inflicting urban and industrial damage presumed to be beyond the level an adversary would accept. We must be able to respond at levels appropriate to the situation." [5]

The Nixon administration had three essential reasons for continuing such potentially destabilizing programs: (1) Deterrence *could* fail, and in such situations—however low their probability—the United States would want to disable as much of the Soviet war-fighting capability as possible, and to reduce the Soviet capacity to kill Americans. (2) The Soviets had been building an impressive counterforce capability that by the late 1970s or early 1980s might be able to destroy most of the U.S. land-based ICBMs; the clear strategic asymmetry that would be produced by the presence of such a Soviet capability and the absence of a comparable U.S. capability could be politically exploited by the Soviets in crisis confrontations between the superpowers. (3) The United States would be more effective in bargaining with the Soviets to alter and reduce the counterforce features of their strategic force programs if we too had counterforce elements that would need to be sacrificed; moreover, the existence of such U.S. programs would dramatize for the Soviets the consequences of a failure to agree to their limitation—namely, a counterforce arms race with the United States, whose technological abilities in this field were still far ahead of the Soviets.[6]

There was the persistent dilemma—once again unresolved though partially dissolved in a sea of ambiguous rhetoric—of how to keep the U.S. strategic deterrent umbrella extended over a broad range of U.S. alliance commitments and at the same time relinquish a strategic "first-strike" option against the Soviet Union. For, at base, the U.S. assurance to its allies that it would not allow them to be victimized by a Soviet threat to attack them with nuclear weapons rested on a readiness to issue a counterthreat to "retaliate" with a nuclear strike against the Soviet Union; such a "retaliation" would be in fact the first blow in a U.S.–Soviet war. Indeed, it was precisely the Soviet attainment in the late 1960s of an awesome intercontinental retaliatory capability that could absorb any first strike and still deliver a devastating response that seriously weakened the credibility of any U.S. threat to initiate a strategic nuclear war between the superpowers—even in response to a Soviet attack on western Europe. If the United States and the Soivet Union were now explicitly to renounce first-strike capabilities against each other, the central ribbing of the NATO umbrella would collapse and Western Europe would be an exposed target for nuclear blackmail by the Kremlin.

Consequently, in order to shore up the credibility of its commitments to NATO, the United States continued to deploy weapons with an impressive potential for destroying Soviet offensive strategic missiles and to justify these deployments with the broad "political" aspects of the sufficiency doctrine. This was, of course, at considerable tension with the self-limiting aspect of the doctrine—in particular U.S. official insistences that

sufficiency also means numbers, characteristics, and deployments of our forces which the Soviet Union cannot reasonably interpret as being intended to threaten a disarming attack.[7]

The Department of Defense seized upon Nixon's ambiguous concept of sufficiency to establish elastic definitions of what would constitute an adequate military balance of power vis-à-vis the Soviets.

During the Kennedy–Johnson years Secretary of Defense Mc-
Namara had held down the U.S. strategic force posture with an
increasingly strict application of the "assured-destruction" criterion,
which he defined as being able to destroy one-quarter of the Soviet
population and one-third of Soviet industry. No matter what the
Soviets might deploy, it was sufficient to be able to inflict this level
of damage in retaliation for a Soviet first strike in order to deter the
Kremlin from launching a strategic attack. Now, under Secretary of
Defense Laird, the military planning objectives were broadened to
ensure that (1) the Soviet forces could not inflict substantially more
damage in the United States than the U.S. forces could inflict on
the USSR; (2) that each leg of the strategic "triad" (bombers, land-
based ICBMs, and sea-based strategic missiles) would be independently able to survive a surprise Soviet attack and strike back with
a society-destroying level of destruction; and (3) that, in addition to
these war outcome criteria, the number of weapons deployed on
each side should not *appear* to give the Soviet Union an advantage. [8]

Ambiguous rhetoric might obscure the contradictions between the
Nixon–Laird notion of sufficiency as a defense planning concept and
the Nixon–Kissinger concept of sufficiency as an armament-limiting
concept; but when it came to actually negotiating a strategic arms
limitation agreement with the Russians, one or the other had to be
given the presidential nod. During the first Nixon administration,
1969–1972, Kissinger—partly through persuasion, partly through
deft bureaucratic infighting, partly by setting the proper international events into motion—was able to gain Nixon's endorsement of
his version at critical junctures. [9]

The climax of the first phase of the U.S.–Soviet strategic arms
limitation talks (SALT), culminating in the Moscow agreements of
1972—the treaty limiting antiballistic missile (ABM) systems and
the interim agreement on offensive strategic systems—came very
close to institutionalizing a "mutual assured destruction" relationship, dubbed MAD by its critics.

According to Article I of the ABM treaty, "Each party undertakes
not to deploy ABM systems for a defense of the territory of its country." [10]

The limited deployments allowed by the treaty (Article III) restricted each side to two sites of 100 launchers each, one site to
protect an offensive missile field and the other to protect the coun-

try's capital.[11] Clearly, the populations of both countries were to remain unprotected, consistent with the doctrine that if one's population were exposed to nuclear attack from one's enemy one would not dare to start a nuclear war.

The five-year interim agreement on offensive weapons allowed the Soviet Union to build up its ICBM force to 1618 while the United States would keep its existing level of 1054. The Soviets were allowed 950 submarine-launched ballistic missiles (SLBMs) and 62 submarines, while the United States was confined to 710 SLBMs and 44 submarines. Important weapon systems left out of the agreement—bombers, land mobile ICBMs, forward-based forces of less than intercontinental range, and multiple warheads—were to be the subject of the more comprehensive negotiations that were supposed to produce a completed treaty by October 1977.[12]

The allowance of a Soviet numerical advantage in ICBMs and SLBMs was not yet of serious concern to the U.S. Defense Department, for in the items not covered by the agreement the United States was well ahead of the Soviets. But the military preparedness coalition in Congress and the administration was determined to make the subsequent SALT negotiations more responsive to their interpretations of sufficiency. Senator Henry Jackson formulated a Senate resolution which the administration accepted, insisting that in any future strategic weapons agreements with the USSR the United States not accept provisions, such as those in SALT I, that would leave the United States with numerical inferiority.

Kissinger's achievement in satisfying Nixon's political need for a dramatic démarche in U.S.–Soviet relations was made possible by his ability to cater to Brezhnev's analogous political needs, and to make these even more intense by the acceleration of détente diplomacy with the U.S.–China rapprochement.[13]

The temporarily suppressed contradictions—in the administration's sufficiency concept and in the Soviets' analogous dilemma of simultaneously agreeing to stabilize the arms race while continuing to deploy strategic forces with impressive war-fighting characteristics—were bound to surface again even before the ink was dry on the SALT I agreements.

In the summer of 1972, the Defense Department asked Congress to provide funds for the development of strategic warheads with "hard-target kill capabilities," and programs were accelerated for installing accurate MIRVs on U.S. ICBMs and submarine-launched strategic missiles.[14]

In 1973 and 1974, under the new Secretary of Defense, James Schlesinger, the Pentagon further lifted the secrecy lid from its force-planning premises. In a series of candid news conferences, Schlesinger revealed the administration's intention to acquire "precision instruments that would be used in a limited counterforce role" and, in fact, that it was refining its strategic targeting doctrine to give the President a "broader range of options." In addition, the administration was prepared, on the basis of its ongoing research and development programs, to balance any Soviet attempt to obtain a major counterforce option ("We cannot permit the other side to have a relatively credible counterforce capability if we lack the same").[15] Schlesinger's annual defense posture statement to Congress for fiscal year 1975 provided a carefully worded justification for the renewed emphasis on counterforce options:

> To enhance deterrence, we may want . . . a more efficient hard-target kill capability than we now possess: both to threaten specialized sets of targets (possibly of concern to allies) with a greater economy of force, and to make it clear to a potential enemy that he cannot proceed with impunity to jeopardize our own system of hard targets. . . .

> To stress changes in targeting doctrine and new options does not mean radical departures from past practice. Nor does it imply any possibility of acquiring a first strike disarming capability. As I have repeatedly stated, both the United States and the Soviet Union now have and will continue to have large, invulnerable second strike forces. . . .

> We would be quite content if both the United States and the Soviet Union avoided the acquisition of major counterforce capabilities. But we are troubled by Soviet weapons momentum, and we simply cannot ignore the prospect of growing disparity between the two major nuclear powers. We do not propose to let an opponent threaten a major component of our forces without being able to pose a comparable threat. We do not propose to let an enemy put us in a position where we are left with no more than a capability to hold his cities hostage after the first phase of a nuclear conflict. And certainly we do not propose to see an enemy threaten one or more of our allies with his nuclear capabilities in the expectation that we would lack the flexibility and resolve to strike back at his assets.[16]

The main benchmarks previously outlined by President Nixon and Secretary Laird for establishing a sufficient U.S. strategic posture were thus elaborated by Schlesinger. However, particular stress was now accorded to "essential equivalence" with the Soviet Union in all the basic force characteristics ("throw-weight, accuracy, yield-to-weight ratios, reliability and other such factors") for reasons of military effectiveness *and* political appearances. The requirement was for "a range and magnitude of capabilities such that everyone—friend, foe, and domestic audiences alike—will perceive that we are the equal of our strongest competitors." [17] This meant that even though the Soviets might be exercising bad strategic logic in building forces that could destroy a large portion of the U.S. land-based ICBMs (bad logic in that the Soviet Union could still be destroyed by U.S. submarine-launched missiles and bombers), the United States—to preserve the appearance of symmetry—should also build such a counterforce capability.

Soviet defense programs were even more blatantly at cross-purposes with mutual strategic arms limitation. Consistent with the letter but not the spirit of the 1972 Moscow accords, the Russians continued to deploy heavy-payload ICBMs with substantial counterforce potential, and their military doctrine stressed the requirements of fighting and prevailing in a strategic war, more than deterrence. Evidence of continued Soviet reliance on heavy counterforce capabilities spurred U.S. defense planners to go ahead with new systems as a "hedge" against Soviet attempts to achieve strategic dominance. The major consequences were a full-speed-ahead program of retrofitting U.S. missiles with MIRV warheads, efforts to enhance the accuracy of all U.S. strategic systems (including submarine-launched missiles), and "next generation" bomber programs (the B-1 bomber and long-range cruise missiles for the modernized bomber force).

Kissinger and others who hoped to translate the 1972 interim agreement on offensive systems into a solid treaty by its expiration date of October 1977 were dismayed at the continued "qualitative" technological race proceeding on both sides. Not only was that race making a mockery of the quantitative limits agreed to in SALT I, but it was virtually precluding reliable verification of these or future limits. Kissinger's anxiety to put a cap on the accelerating competition before it was too late was reflected in his complaint at a Moscow press conference in connection with Nixon's 1974 visit that "both sides have to convince their military establishments of the benefits of restraint." [18]

The Secretary of State hastily arranged for Brezhnev and Ford to commit themselves, at their 1974 Vladivostok meeting, to negotiat-

ing a treaty that would at least freeze their arsenals at a specified
number of strategic missile launchers (2400 for each side), of which
only a subset (1320) could be MIRVed. Within the overall ceiling
of 2400, each side could deploy its own preferred mix of ICBMs,
submarine-launched ballistic missiles, or bombers; and there was no
specified limit on missile throw-weight.[19] The Vladivostok accord
was a political holding action at the top to keep the objective of a
mutual-deterrence treaty from being totally subverted by the combined pressures of technology and military doctrine, which, in the
United States as well as in the Soviet Union, were tending more
and more toward legitimating strategic counterforce and other war-
fighting capabilities. When it came down to attempts to convert the
Vladivostok principles into a stable and verifiable treaty, however,
the military experts on both sides—even those who were dedicated
to arms control—continued to be baffled by the increasing difficulty
of distinguishing offensive from defensive deployments, strategic from
tactical weapons, nuclear from conventional munitions, single from
multiple warheads, and by the virtual impossibility of determining
(in advance of its actually being used) whether a given weapon had
a city or a missile complex as its primary target.

Kissinger's skepticism about the stability over time of technical
limitations on military hardware led him to concentrate as much on
the symbolic benefits of negotiating constructively with the Russians
in the SALT arena as on the presumed military effects of any agreements that might be concluded. And his doubts that close attention
to the military balance itself would be sufficient for the purpose of
preventing the Russians from using military coercion against U.S.
interests reinforced this belief in the necessity of nonmilitary levers
on Soviet behavior. The China connection and the economic aspects
of détente diplomacy were supposed to compensate for the shortfalls
in military containment.

THE CHINA ANGLE

The Nixon–Kissinger construction of a new relationship with
China preceded and gave major impetus to the rapid elaboration of
the U.S.–Soviet détente relationship in the early 1970s. The China
connection, conceived of primarily as a means of pressuring the
Kremlin to be more accommodating to U.S. demands, was also de-

signed to serve other objectives of the administration: an early end to the Vietnam War; a reduction in overseas deployment of American troops; a dismantling of military commitments to Asian regimes that might be unstable or reckless; and simply the need to do something dramatic to convince the American public and international audiences that the government, under Nixon's leadership, did have the capacity to act impressively on the world stage. The new China policy, not incidentally, also could give concrete substance to Kissinger's vague concept of an emerging multipolar world.

However much administration spokesmen might publicly deny that gaining leverage on the Soviet Union was the central purpose of the China connection, this geopolitical *result* of the new triangular relationship was undeniable, and was never really denied. But Nixon and Kissinger apparently calculated that the leverage would be just as great if it was kept implicit, and that the Soviets might not have been able to bring themselves to be accommodating toward the United States in various fields if it looked to the world as if they were negotiating under coercive pressure.

As Washington and Peking drew toward each other across the hypotenuse of the triangle from 1969 to 1972, the theatrics of the démarche began to eclipse the geopolitics, but the former in no way undermined the latter. The show business staging of the Nixon visit seemed only to convince the Russians of the need to stage a more impressive summit spectacular of their own.

Historians will long debate whether this turn in U.S.–China policy was mainly the brainchild of Nixon or of Kissinger (not to mention Mao Tse-tung and Chou En-lai).[20] A resolution of this controversy matters little for the present analysis. More important is the fact that both men came to believe by early 1969 that a movement toward normalizing relations with Peking might now mesh with Chinese calculations and significantly reinforce the Soviets' incentive to explore their own common interests with the United States.[21]

China experts in and out of the government had been picking up signs during the late 1960s that Mao and Chou might be reading the tea leaves similarly. The Chinese condemned the Soviet invasion of Czechoslovakia in August 1968, and especially the doctrine of "limited sovereignty" of countries in the Socialist camp by which the Soviets justified their invasion. Tension was heightening along the Sino-Soviet border in the aftermath of Czechoslovakia. In November 1968 the Chinese Foreign Ministry proposed a convening of the Sino-American ambassadorial talks in Warsaw, which had been suspended since January.[22]

The Nixon administration, while indicating its willingness to resume the heretofore sterile exchanges in Warsaw, was searching for fresh ways to convince the Chinese that the White House might be open to an exploration of some fundamental improvements in the relationship. Early in 1969 Nixon began to hint strongly through French, Rumanian, and Pakistani intermediaries that he would like to visit China.[23] Meanwhile, an informal coalition of liberal members of Congress and China experts—perhaps sensing that the administration was exploring a shift in policy—tried to create public support for normalizing relations with the Communist regime. Senator Edward Kennedy, speaking on March 20, 1969, to a conference sponsored by the National Committee on United States–China Relations, urged that new initiatives be taken by the Nixon administration, such as the elimination of U.S. military bases in Taiwan and an offer to reestablish consular offices in the People's Republic. (The conference, chaired by former U.S. Ambassador to Japan Edwin O. Reischauer, took place two weeks after the outbreak of military conflict between Soviet and Chinese forces over a disputed island on the Ussuri River. China experts at the conference speculated that this development might provide an opportunity for a breakthrough in U.S.–China relations.)[24]

Starting in the summer of 1969, the Department of State began to announce various unilateral gestures of reconciliation. In July many travel and trade restrictions that had been applied to China since 1950 were relaxed. Americans traveling abroad would be permitted to bring back $100 worth of items produced in the People's Republic. Members of Congress, journalists, teachers, scholars, university students, physicians, and Red Cross representatives would automatically be cleared by the Department for travel to China. These moves were an effort to "relax tensions and facilitate the development of peaceful contacts," explained State Department spokesmen. These particular actions were chosen because they did not require Chinese reciprocation.[25]

Over the next year the administration continued to signal its intent to put U.S.–Chinese relations on a new basis: in November 1969, U.S. naval patrols in the Taiwan Strait (deployed by Truman at the start of the Korean War) were terminated, removing the most visible symbol of U.S. support for the Nationalist Chinese exiles. In December, the U.S. government partially lifted the embargo on trade by foreign subsidiaries of U.S. firms between China and third countries, again stating that the move was "strictly unilateral." In January 1970, the U.S. and Chinese ambassadors to Poland resumed their suspended talks in Warsaw and explored in a preliminary way the possibility of exchange visits by journalists, students, and scientists. On February 18, in the first of his four annual "State of the World" messages to Congress, President Nixon, reiterating the theme that "the Chinese are a great and vital people who should not remain isolated from the international community," revealed that it was administration policy to "attempt to define a new relationship" for the future. "We have avoided dramatic gestures which might invite dramatic rebuffs," explained the President. "We have taken specific steps that did not require Chinese agreements but which underlined our willingness to have a more normal and constructive relationship." [26] Two days later, at the ambassadorial talks in Warsaw, both sides discussed the possibility of moving the talks to Peking, and the Chinese hinted that they would welcome a high-ranking official to head the U.S. delegation. [27] This delicate courtship was set back somewhat during the spring and summer of 1970 as U.S. troops invaded Cambodia, while in China a struggle was played out between the Lin Piao faction, which favored a hard line toward Washington as well as Moscow, and the Chou En-lai faction, which favored a moderate policy at home and abroad, including better relations with the United States in order to put pressure on the Soviets.

Early in the fall of 1970 the atmosphere was suddenly alive with possibility. Mao evidently had thrown his weight decisively behind Chou and seemed to be sending his own signals to Washington that a new era in Sino-American relations might now be appropriate. Official Washington attached significance to Mao's having asked the prominent American chronicler of the Chinese Communist revolution, Edgar Snow, to join him on the reviewing stand for the National Day celebrations on October 1. Nixon and Kissinger, sensing that the time was ripe, intensified their efforts to communicate with the Chinese leaders via the Rumanians and Pakistanis. Secret notes, presumably dealing with the possibility of a high-level U.S. visit to

China, were carried back and forth through the winter months, except for a six-week hiatus in February and early March surrounding the invasion of Laos by South Vietnamese troops with U.S. air support.[28]

Nixon and Kissinger used all available diplomatic channels to reassure Mao that the Laos operation was not meant to threaten China in any way. And in the second annual State of the World Address to Congress the President reiterated his objective of drawing China into "a serious dialog." He invited the "People's Republic of China to explore the path of normalization of its relations with its neighbors and the world, including our own country." During the coming year, promised the President, "I will carefully examine what further steps we might take to create broader opportunities for contacts between the Chinese and American peoples, and how we might remove needless obstacles to the realization of these opportunities. We hope for, but will not be deterred by a lack of, reciprocity." This effort, the President explained, was part of the main foreign policy approach of his administration: "to create a balanced international structure in which all nations have a stake. We believe that such a structure should provide full scope for the influence to which China's achievements entitle it."[29]

The breakthrough occurred on April 27, 1971, when the Pakistani ambassador to the United States delivered a handwritten note from Peking, with no signature, inviting an "American envoy" to come to China for high-level talks. The note suggested either Kissinger or Secretary of State Rogers.[30] The invitation and the decision to send Kissinger to Peking were closely held secrets. The public was allowed the fantasy that the U.S. Ping-Pong team, touring China in April 1971 at the sudden invitation of Chou En-lai, was the vehicle through which the inscrutable Chinese were making known to the White House their willingness to explore an improvement in relations. While the Ping-Pong team was still in China, Nixon announced further relaxation of the twenty-year embargo on trade with the People's Republic. A Chinese Ping-Pong team was, of course, invited to tour the United States. And at the end of April Nixon began to hint unsubtly to journalists and foreign diplomats that he himself would like to be invited to visit China.

The Chinese cooperated in keeping under wraps Kissinger's secret July 1971 mission to Peking to arrange for the Nixon visit, so that the President himself could make a surprise announcement of the dramatic development after the fact. Nixon and Kissinger apparently felt they needed a fait accompli to overcome opposition to such a move from the Taiwan government and its U.S. supporters. In the playing out of this surprise, they knew they would cause anxiety in the Kremlin. The stratagem also shocked and angered the Japanese and other allied governments, but the affronts to established friends were presumed to be ultimately retrievable costs well worth the benefits of the new shift in global power relationships.

It was more than mere coincidence that Nixon's July 15 announcement that he would visit China was followed by his revelation in an August 4 press conference that he and the Soviet leaders had agreed that there should be a U.S.–Soviet summit meeting when there was something substantive to discuss that could not be handled in other channels. Nixon indicated that ongoing discussions with the Soviets were making progress in a number of fields—Berlin, SALT, the Mideast—and added pointedly that "if the time comes, as it may come, and both sides realize this, then the final breakthrough in any one of these areas can take place only at the highest level, and then there will be a meeting. But as far as the timing of the meeting before the visit to Peking, that would not be an appropriate thing to do."[31]

The Russians got the message and picked up on the cue. The early fall of 1971 was a particularly congenial season at various U.S.–Soviet negotiating tables. Agreements were reached on procedures for preventing nuclear accidents and on improving the emergency "hot line" between Washington and Moscow. And most significant, a preliminary accord was reached on the outlines of a Berlin settlement. President Nixon announced on October 12 that he had accepted Chairman Brezhnev's invitation to visit Moscow in May. Kissinger again traveled to Peking at the end of October—this time in the full glare of news media—to firm up plans for Nixon to visit China in February.

It was more than coincidental that Kissinger would be in Peking while the issue of China's representation in the United Nations was brought to a vote in New York. The latest U.S. position—ending twenty years of opposition to the Peking government's membership in the world organization, but still refusing to countenance the expulsion of Taiwan—was announced by Secretary of State Rogers on August 2 and stoutly defended in UN debates by Ambassador George Bush in the face of clear indications that the majority would take an unequivocal pro-Peking stand. In the key resolution on October 25, the General Assembly decided (by a vote of 76 to 35, with 17 abstentions) to recognize the representatives of the People's Republic as "the only legitimate representatives of China" and to "expell forthwith the representatives of Chiang Kai-shek from the place which they unlawfully occupy at the United Nations and in all the organizations affiliated with it." The White House immediately issued a statement accepting the will of the majority but regretting the explusion of Taiwan.

The year 1972 was to be, in effect, the Year of the Triangle: the year of maximum exploitation by the Nixon administration of its new China connection to pressure the Kremlin into accommodationist positions on SALT, European security issues, and the conflict in Southeast Asia; the year of maximum exploitation of the growing U.S.–Soviet détente to induce the Chinese to be patient with the United States for continuing to recognize the government of Taiwan and for its slow-paced disengagement from Southeast Asia; and the year of maximum exploitation of Nixon's popularity in both Moscow and Peking to induce the North Vietnamese to seriously negotiate an Indochina peace agreement with the United States. Not incidentally, the simultaneity of all this with the U.S. presidential election campaign was fortuitous, and was also exploited to the hilt.

Uncertain of the strength of the incentives of either Moscow or Peking to put good relations with the United States ahead of its other international and domestic objectives, the White House was anxious not to appear too blatant in playing on the Machiavellian triangle. Repeatedly, in statements preceding and following the President's trip to China, Nixon and Kissinger insisted that "our policy is not aimed against Moscow. The United States and the USSR have issues of paramount importance to resolve; it would be costly indeed to impair progress on these through new antagonisms." To attempt to use the opening to Peking "to exploit Sino-Soviet tensions . . . would be self-defeating and dangerous."[32]

The Chinese were more candid with respect to their own reasons for seeking a rapprochement with the United States. The official Peking journal *Hungchi* reprinted a 1940 article by Mao propounding the wisdom of "uniting with forces that can be united while isolating and hitting the most obdurate enemies."[33]

The Americans were successful, however, in keeping direct anti-Soviet statements out of the communiqué issued by President Nixon and Premier Chou En-lai in Shanghai at the conclusion of the Nixon visit. In the language of the communiqué, "The two sides state that . . . neither should seek hegemony in the Asia–Pacific region and each is opposed to efforts by any other country or group of countries to establish such hegemony." And, in a stroke of studied ambiguity, "Both sides are of the view that it would be against the interest of the peoples of the world for any major country to collude with another against other countries, or for major countries to divide up the world into spheres of interest."[34]

Even in the parts of the communiqué reserved for unilateral statements by each side, the Chinese, deferring to U.S. sensitivities, threw their barbs at the Russians in clever general formulations that could be applied to either the Americans or the Russians. Thus,

> The Chinese side stated: Wherever there is oppression, there is resistance. Countries want independence, nations want liberation and the people want revolution—this has become the irresistible trend of history. All nations, big or small, should be equal; big nations should not bully the weak. China will never be a superpower and it opposes hegemony and power politics of any kind. The Chinese side stated that it firmly supports the struggles of all the oppressed people and nations for freedom and liberation and that the people of all countries have a right to choose their social systems according to their own wishes and the right to safeguard the independence, sovereignty and territorial integrity of their own countries and oppose foreign aggression, interference, control and subversion. All foreign troops should be withdrawn to their own countries.[35]

For the most sensitive issue between the United States and China— the problem of Taiwan—the device of including two separate statements in the communiqué was indispensable. The Chinese reaffirmed their longstanding position that "Taiwan is a province of China . . .; the liberation of Taiwan is China's internal affair in which no other country has a right to interfere; and all U.S. forces and military installations must be withdrawn from Taiwan." The Americans attempted to finesse the issue as much as they could, declaring, in one of the most carefully crafted statements in the annals of diplomacy, that the United States acknowledges that all Chinese on either side of the Taiwan Strait maintain there is but one China and that Taiwan is a part of China. The United States Government does not challenge that position. It reaffirms its interest in a peaceful settlement of the Taiwan question by the Chinese themselves. With this prospect in mind, it affirms the ultimate objective of the withdrawal of all U.S. forces from Taiwan. In the meantime, it will progressively reduce its forces and military installations on Taiwan as the tension in the area diminishes.[36]

By granting the legitimacy of even this thin line of disagreement, however, Mao and Chou had made a substantial concession in the service of the higher goal they shared with Nixon and Kissinger of normalizing U.S.–China relations in order to gain new leverage on the Russians.

The most candid public exposition by a U.S. official of the connection between U.S. policies toward the Soviet Union and U.S. policies toward China was made by Winston Lord, director of the State Department's Policy Planning Staff (and Kissinger's closest aide on China policy). In a statement to a House subcommittee in March 1976, later published in a Department of State *Bulletin* under the title "The Triangular Relationship of the United States, the USSR, and the People's Republic of China," Lord put "improved prospects for global equilibrium" at the top of the list of benefits accruing to the United States from positive relations with China, and "a hedge against Soviet diplomatic and military pressures" as first among the advantages to be derived by the Chinese.

Lord's testimony reiterated the standard official position that an attempt by the United States to manipulate the Sino-Soviet rivalry, to meddle in it, or to take sides would be dangerous and self-defeating. "At the same time," he observed, "in a triangular relationship it is undeniably advantageous for us to have better relations with each of the other two actors than they have with one another." The United States has no desire to see the Sino-Soviet rivalry escalate into military conflict, said Lord, but "neither can we genuinely wish to see the two major communist powers locked once again in close alliance." In a meticulously formulated qualification, he granted that "a limited thaw in Sino-Soviet relations, however, would not automatically redound to our disadvantage, provided it was not based on shared opposition to the United States." An almost humorous understatement summed up the essence of the approach: "The record to date suggests that improvement in our ties with one does not harm our ties with the other." [37]

Kissinger himself would insist on this public rationale for the China rapprochement through the last days of his tenure as Secretary of State. In an interview with the *New York Times* on the eve of Jimmy Carter's inauguration, he once again stressed that "it is a mistake to define the Sino-Soviet relationship in terms of our exploiting their differences. . . . We didn't create them, we can't exploit them." But he went on, in a characteristic circumlocution, to place the triangular relationship at the center of his basic geopolitical strategy:

I believe it is important that the People's Republic of China continue to perceive us as interested in maintaining a world equilibrium. If they feel we have lost our interest in it or our comprehension of it, or our willingness to preserve it, then they will draw the inevitable conclusion, which will be to make whatever accommodation they can get [with the Soviet Union], or they will try to find some other means of protection, such as organizing the third world against both of us. [38]

THE COMMERCIAL LEVER

During the Kennedy and Johnson administrations, policy makers flirted with the idea of affecting Soviet behavior through commerce. The hope was to eventually stimulate consumer demands that would make it more difficult for the Kremlin to sustain high military budgets. Some champions of greater East–West commercial intercourse thought it might also encourage the Soviets to experiment with economic liberalization measures. Presidents Kennedy and Johnson each asked Congress to approve the sale of wheat to the Soviet Union as a step toward opening up limited commercial relations in other sectors. But such moves were tentative and peripheral to the main thrust of U.S. policy until the Nixon–Kissinger years.

It was not until well into the third year of the Nixon administration that the attempt to construct a commercial relationship between the two superpowers became an integral part of U.S. policy. But as with the change in policy toward China, the premises of this policy shift were only partly revealed to the public. Signs that the grounds of U.S. policy on East–West trade were being altered were picked up in the fall of 1971 by American firms, which suddenly began to experience success in obtaining previously denied licenses to export their products to the Soviet Union. The coincidence of the export license liberalization with the firming up of plans for Nixon to visit China and collateral progress toward a Nixon—Brezhnev summit was hardly accidental.

In the fall of 1971, the positive side of Kissinger's linkage strategy was in full swing. The Russians, woefully short of wheat for the coming winter as a result of a dismal harvest, were allowed to purchase $1 billion of American surplus food grains. The State Department indicated its readiness to reduce various discriminatory shipping regulations on Soviet vessels visiting U.S. ports. The Secretary of Commerce took a highly publicized trip to the Soviet Union surrounded by background stories from government ministries in both countries on the possibilities of pushing U.S.—Soviet trade to the $5 billion-a-year level by the mid-1970s. Appetites on both sides were whetted with visions of cooperative efforts to develop the oil, gas, and hard-mineral riches of Siberia. By the spring of 1972, progress on numerous bilateral commercial negotiations between subordinate levels of the governments was sufficiently advanced for the subject of a general U.S.—Soviet commercial rapprochement to be included as a major item on the agenda for the May summit meeting. Indeed, the Russians appeared to be more enthusiastic about normalizing economic relations than about any other aspect of détente, and this probably was the reason that they refrained from canceling the 1972 summit in the face of highly coercive U.S. actions against North Vietnam in the spring of 1972 (including the mining of Haiphong harbor, which, not incidentally, interfered with Soviet shipping).

The "basic principles" signed by President Nixon and General Secretary Brezhnev on May 29, 1972, affirmed that "The U.S.A. and the U.S.S.R. regard commercial and economic ties as an important and necessary element in the strengthening of their bilateral relations and will thus actively promote the growth of such ties. They will facilitate cooperation between the relevant organizations and enterprises of the two countries and the conclusion of appropriate agreements and contracts, including long-term ones."[39] By the end of the year, the accomplishments under this accord included an agreement by the Russians to pay back $722 million on their wartime Lend-Lease debt by the year 2001, in return for which President Nixon would now authorize the Export-Import Bank to extend credits and guarantees for the sale of goods to the Soviet Union; a commitment by the Nixon administration to seek congressional extension of most-favored-nation tariff rates to the Soviet Union; the delivery of 440 million bushels of wheat to the Soviet Union; a maritime agreement opening 40 ports in each nation to the other's shipping; provision for the United States to set up government-sponsored and commercial offices in Moscow to facilitate the work of U.S. business executives seeking contracts, and similar provisions for the Russians in Washington; and the establishment of a Joint U.S.–Soviet Commercial Commission charged with developing and guiding the elaboration of additional arrangements to encourage U.S.–Soviet commerce.

The new policy rested on a number of publicly stated premises, but also on some premises that remained unarticulated, apparently for fear of embarrassing the Kremlin. The openly articulated premises underlying the expansion of U.S.–Soviet commerce were the following:

—Recent progress on basic political issues (the framework and terms for SALT, and the status of Berlin) made it possible to initiate discussions on a wide range of projects for bilateral cooperation in nonpolitical fields.

—As cooperation in nonpolitical fields widened and deepened, they would reinforce the trend toward more constructive political relations.

—Bilateral economic arrangements, at first mainly involving trade, could later be broadened to include longer-term cooperative ventures that would "establish an interdependence between our economies which provides a continuing incentive to maintain a constructive relationship."

—As the nonpolitical relationships continued to expand, side by side with continuing progress on arms control and other political issues, there would be created on each side "a vested interest in restraint and in the preservation of peace."[40]

The most elaborate statement of the key premise that a growing web of economic arrangements could reduce political hostility between the United States and the Soviet Union was contained in a report to the President by Secretary of Commerce Peter Peterson, released to the public in August 1972:

Closer economic ties bear both cause and effect relationships to relaxation of political tension. Improvement in political relationships is a prerequisite for improved economic relationships, but, once in place, economic ties create a community of interest which in turn improves the environment for further progress on the political side.

Once set in motion, the cause-and-effect process can portend a downward spiral in political tension, a mutually beneficial economic foundation of the new relationship and tangible increases in the welfare and safety of the peoples of both countries. . . .

Our purpose is . . . to build in both countries a vested economic interest in the maintenance of an harmonious and enduring relationship. A nation's security is affected not only by its adversary's military capabilities but by the price which attends the use of those capabilities. If we can create a situation in which the use of military force would jeopardize a mutually profitable relationship, I think it can be argued that our security will have been enhanced.[41]

One who read between the lines of the public rationale and had occasion to discuss with U.S. policy makers their considerations at the time could ascertain a set of tougher assumptions underlying the effort to open up commerce with the Soviet Union—namely:

—The Kremlin leadership recognized that a continued modernization of the USSR would require a substantial shift of resources into many of the high technology, largely civilian areas that until recently had been low priority in comparison with military needs.
—But Brezhnev and his comrades also realized that, in order to close the modernization gap in the civilian economy and simultaneously maintain military parity with the United States, the Soviet Union would require substantial inputs from the West, especially in the fields of information technology and electronics.
—The needed Western economic and technological inputs could not be purchased without large credits from the United States and other advanced industrial countries and an improvement in the Soviet Union's export potential.
—Finally, the Russian leaders had come to believe, despite the Leninist dictum that capitalists would sell the hangman the rope to be used in their own executions, that only a fully credible Soviet policy of peaceful coexistence would stimulate the non-communist countries to extend sufficient credits, to liberalize their strategic lists, and otherwise let down their political barriers to East—West commerce.
—In short, the Soviet Union's *economic* need to open up commerce with the industrial countries was greater than the latter's need for commerce with the Communist countries; therefore, if the United States and its allies wisely bargained with the Soviet Union from this basic position of economic strength, the Russians, if not openly backed into a corner, might be willing to pay a *political* price for an expansion of East—West commerce.

Such, undoubtedly, were the unvarnished assumptions beneath the Kissinger gloss that "we have approached the question of economic relations with deliberation and circumspection and as an act of policy not primarily of commercial opportunity."[42] Apparently, the main political price Nixon and Kissinger wanted the Russians to pay was to stop aiding the North Vietnamese war effort in Indochina and to bring pressure on Hanoi to negotiate seriously with the United States to wind down the war.

The U.S. mining of Haiphong harbor took place just two weeks before President Nixon was due in Moscow for his first summit conference with Secretary Brezhnev. The Soviet Minister of Foreign Trade was in the United States at the time for an intense round of presummit commercial negotiations with Secretary of Commerce Peterson and other officials whose results were to be unveiled with much fanfare in Moscow. Nixon and Kissinger had doubts that the Moscow summit would be allowed to proceed on schedule, but they continued to remind the Russians of what was at stake. Kissinger's May 9 briefing to reporters on the Haiphong mining included a pointed reference to the negotiations in progress with the Soviet Union: "We are on the verge of a new relationship in which, on both sides, whenever there is a danger of crisis, there will be enough people who have a commitment to constructive programs so that they could exercise restraining influences."[43]

During the next few years, when the President or Kissinger publicly observed that détente itself was in jeopardy as a result of Soviet actions—for example, the threat to land Soviet paratroops in the Middle East in 1973 or the Soviet transport of Cuban forces to Angola—they clearly meant to play upon the Kremlin's presumed high motivation for commercial relations with the West. They did not, however, believe that the Kremlin's motivation for commercial relations was so high that U.S. credits and trading privileges could be used as a lever to directly induce changes *within* the Soviet system. This was their objection to the Jackson-Vanik Amendment to the Trade Reform Act of 1974, which sought to deny most-favored-nation trading status and credits to the Soviet Union if the Kremlin did not substantially remove restrictions on Jewish emigration. The administration claimed to be effectively representing the attitudes of the American people toward the denial of human rights in the USSR, but it regarded the Jackson-Vanik Amendment and the Stevenson Amendment (setting a $300 million limit on Export-Import Bank credits to the Soviet Union) as at best unhelpful and at worst likely to revive the bitterness of the cold war. "We have accomplished much," claimed Kissinger in 1974, "but we cannot demand that the Soviet Union, in effect, suddenly reverse five decades of Soviet, and centuries of Russian, history." [44]

The administration did, however, cooperate with the West Europeans in linking East–West economic cooperation to "basket three" human rights issues at the Helsinki Conference on Security and Cooperation in Europe. The Russians probably found it tolerable to go along with such linkage, since the Helsinki language was ambiguous and not explicitly directed at them, nor did the accords themselves contain any sanctions for noncompliance. From the standpoint of the administration, overuse or premature application of economic sanctions (denial of credits and trade) was in any case undesirable, for it would reduce the leverage the United States might obtain from ongoing arrangements.

On the other hand, the administration also belatedly came to the realization that, in the process of attempting to make the Soviet Union more dependent on the non-Communist world by removing political barriers to East–West trade, it may have, paradoxically, been creating some cumbersome interdependencies. This problem surfaced most clearly in the concession by both parties' 1976 presidential candidates to demands by U.S. agricultural interest groups that there be no further imposition of embargoes on grain shipments to the Soviet Union. The Ford administration's growing appreciation of the difficulty of operating a policy of economic leverage was reflected in the complaint by a high State Department official that "there has been a tendency in Western countries to let the legitimate quest for commercial advantage in Eastern markets overshadow the need to develop and pursue a purposeful strategy. This has tended to undercut the influences which the economic strength of the industrialized world could exert." [45]

All in all, Kissinger left office on January 20, 1977, with the nonmilitary levers on the Soviet Union that were central to his grand strategy having become objects of growing skepticism in the U.S. policy community. His own doubts about their efficacy, if not supported by a domestic consensus, were reflected in his renewed heavy emphasis in late 1976 (and in subsequent statements as a private citizen) on local balances of military power as essential for containing the Soviets.

23

AVOIDING HUMILIATION
IN INDOCHINA

Our defeat and humiliation in South Vietnam without question would promote recklessness in the councils of those great powers who have not yet abandoned their goals of world conquest.

RICHARD NIXON

By the time Richard Nixon assumed the presidency, few Americans still believed that Communist domination of the Indochinese peninsula would pose an intolerable threat to U.S. security. The main question was no longer *whether* the United States should slough off responsibility for preventing the North Vietnamese and the Vietcong from taking over South Vietnam, but *how* to liquidate this costly commitment.

Like Lyndon Johnson at the end of his presidency, the new President and his principal national security adviser believed the prestige of the United States still was heavily at stake in Vietnam, and they discerned a popular mandate that the United States exit from Vietnam "with honor." There were differences, however, between the administration and its critics, and even within the administration, over the ingredients of national honor.

To Nixon and Kissinger, as to Johnson, the nation's honor was bound up closely with its "credibility"—its reputation for keeping promises—and its refusal to be coerced by other nations. "The com-

mitment of 500,000 Americans has settled the issue of the importance of Vietnam," wrote Kissinger in 1968. "For what is involved
now is confidence in American promises. However fashionable it is
to ridicule the terms 'credibility' or 'prestige,' they are not empty
phrases; other nations can gear their actions to ours only if they can
count on our steadiness." [1]

But in view of many other Americans this country was being *dis-
honored* in Vietnam by its stubborn attempt to keep its promise to
stop a Communist takeover. An enlarging chorus of religious leaders, academics, students, media commentators, and politicians in
both parties tried to convince the administration of its folly. It was
dishonorable, they argued, for the United States to compel its young
men to kill and be killed in a small, faraway country in the vain
hope of helping a repressive and corrupt regime defeat the Communists in a civil war. It was dishonorable for the United States to
persist in trying to bomb North Vietnam into a submissive withdrawal of its forces in the face of clear evidence that the North
Vietnamese were deeply and unequivocally committed to the "liberation" of the South.

According to various accounts, Nixon and Kissinger both recognized, even before taking office, that the honor of the United States
was being sullied by its military involvement in Vietnam. They
understood that the war was unwinnable and that the United States
was being made to look foolish before the rest of the world as it
wasted more and more of its substance in a country of minor strategic importance. The trick was to withdraw from the war without
having it appear that the United States was giving up. "The basic
challenge to the new Administration," wrote Kissinger in *The White
House Years*, "was similar to de Gaulle's in Algeria: to withdraw as
an expression of policy and not as a collapse." [2] This policy had two
essential features: "Vietnamization" and a negotiated settlement with
Hanoi. The fighting itself was to be turned over to the South Vietnamese to continue on their own. Meanwhile, Hanoi would agree
to pull its forces back into North Vietnam and to support political
arrangements that would give the South Vietnamese Communists
(the National Liberation Front) a share in the governance of South
Vietnam. The negotiating agenda and process, as outlined in Kissinger's January 1969 article in *Foreign Affairs*, would take place on
two tracks: North Vietnam and the United States to effect military

disengagement, the National Liberation Front and the Thieu regime in Saigon to decide the political arrangement for South Vietnam.

As this became the Nixon administration's public posture, Hanoi presumably would see that what was being asked for was a "decent interval" to allow the United States to pull out with its honor intact, after which the North and South Vietnamese could settle the fate of their country without outside interference. Hanoi's maximum demand, of course, was an even larger capitulation by the United States and Saigon involving full withdrawal of U.S. forces, without a reciprocal pullback of the North Vietnamese, and the resignation of the Thieu government—prior to a cease-fire in South Vietnam and the start of processes to reconstitute a new government. But Kissinger apparently believed that Hanoi would understand Washington's need to avoid a humiliating exit and therefore could be persuaded to cooperate in choreographing an elaborate finale of mutual concessions.

Only a few days after Nixon's inauguration, the President and Kissinger moved to present their scheme directly to the North Vietnamese through Henry Cabot Lodge, their newly appointed head of the team negotiating with the North Vietnamese in Paris. The proposal Lodge carried to Paris was in essence the two-track process outlined in Kissinger's *Foreign Affairs* article, with the first step being a simultaneous *mutual* withdrawal of U.S. and North Vietnamese troops from South Vietnam—a change from the Johnson administration's position, which had held out for a withdrawal of North Vietnamese troops and a reduction of the level of violence in the South as the preconditions for U.S. troop withdrawal.

Nixon and Kissinger were determined that the Paris negotiations should stop being a charade, and accordingly they pulled out all the stops so as to maximize the incentives operating on North Vietnam to come to the negotiating table with an equally serious intent to conclude a settlement. They set in motion a series of phased, unilateral reductions in U.S. ground forces in Vietnam, but simultaneously revealed a capability and will to bomb North Vietnam and North Vietnamese staging areas in Cambodia and Laos with less squeamishness than the previous administration had shown. Meanwhile, they intensified pressure on Moscow and Peking to persuade Hanoi to negotiate an end to the war.

The administration pursued this multipronged strategy relentlessly for four years—continuing to make concessions in the U.S. negotiation position, gradually accelerating our unilateral troop withdrawals, applying larger doses of military coercion against North Vietnam, and attempting to thicken the links between Soviet and Chinese constructive influence on their North Vietnamese ally and U.S. responsiveness to Soviet or Chinese interests in other fields. With the signing of a mutually acceptable settlement in 1973, the strategy appeared to have worked, at least in the sense of providing an "honorable" cover for the U.S. military exit.

However, it took only two years for the cover itself to disintegrate completely. In the spring of 1975, with the Cambodian Communists (the Khmer Rouge) marching on Phnom Penh and the North Vietnamese armies closing in on Saigon, President Ford and Secretary Kissinger struck one last pose of support for their now-abandoned allies in Indochina. Knowing full well that the majority in Congress, reflecting a broad popular consensus, had no intention of diverting further national resources to a lost cause, the administration nevertheless asked for a supplemental military aid package for the anti-Communists in Cambodia and Vietnam. It was a transparent effort, at the last, to once again cast the blame for defeat on Congress in a desperate attempt to salvage the honor of the administration.

As the Vietcong raised their flag over Saigon and renamed it Ho Chi Minh City, the lack of any substantial popular interest in the outcome was, ironically, at least a partial vindication of the administration's strategy.

But this final denouement was a far cry from the Nixon–Kissinger script, which—more clearly in retrospect than during its unfolding—can be seen to have contained two fatal flaws: (1) the assumption that Hanoi would settle for anything less than a total victory over Saigon and (2) the assumption that the North Vietnamese would perceive that Nixon and Kissinger, while sincerely determined to pull U.S. military forces out of Vietnam, could not be party to the total defeat of the anti-Communist forces in Indochina. As it turned out, Hanoi's objectives were unequivocally total, and it remained unswerving in its conviction that the United States would give up even the ghost of a compromise settlement.

The dogged persistence of the belief that Hanoi's settling price was less than its repeated demands and that the positive and negative pressures on Hanoi would convince the Communists that they had to compromise prolonged the agony and brutality of the U.S. involvement four years longer than Kissinger originally promised it would take him to end it. The cost of the delays would continue to haunt all those associated with the effort: more than 15,000 Americans killed and 53,000 wounded from 1969 to 1973, not to speak of the far greater losses by the Vietnamese on both sides.

Overestimation of Hanoi's susceptibility to coercion and positive inducements distorted the U.S. peace efforts at virtually every benchmark along the way to the Communists' final victory. Distorted judgments were present in the basic approach of phasing in "Vietnamization" of the ground war while phasing out U.S. troops, in the graduated U.S. concessions to Hanoi's demands, in the dramatic escalations that followed in reaction to the Communists' rejection or ignoring of these concessions, and even in the Paris Peace Accords themselves.

The administration's unfounded views about the North Vietnamese were paralleled by its overestimation of the humiliation the U.S. government would suffer in the eyes of the American public and other nations if it "precipitously" gave up fighting in Vietnam. By 1971 opinion polls revealed that a substantial majority of U.S. citizens wanted to end the war, even at the risk of an eventual Communist takeover,[3] and most of the friends of the United States in Europe and Japan were embarrassed by their most powerful ally's irrational squandering of its human and material resources in a theater of secondary geopolitical significance.

Kissinger's attempt to dignify as a "tragedy" his and Nixon's prolongation of the bloodshed to gain an honorable peace in Indochina was transparent charlatanism. They had, primarily through their own rhetoric, backed themselves into a corner from which there was no escape except to admit that they were wrong. But such a noble course was evidently beyond these stubbornly proud men.

THE INVASION OF CAMBODIA: NIXON'S "SEVENTH CRISIS"

The invasion of Cambodia by U.S. troops on April 28, 1970, marked the end of the administration's ability to convince wide segments of the policy community that the White House really did have a workable "game plan" for ending the war. Clearly, Nixon and

Kissinger, no less than their predecessors, had little control over the significant events and actors in Indochina and had lost whatever intellectual or conceptual control over the situation they might have started out with in 1969, not to speak of the emotional control required to implement a strategy of deliberate, cool military disengagement. Nixon called his own agonizing over the invasion decision his "seventh crisis." [4] Kissinger found himself the object of intense animosity on the part of former academic colleagues and members of his own staff, four of whom resigned.

From the point of view of Nixon and Kissinger, the opposition to the Cambodian invasion was a typical expression of the naïveté and spinelessness of the liberal Eastern establishment. Cambodia's neutral status had already been systematically violated for more than a year by the belligerents on both sides: North Vietnamese soldiers had been using the Cambodian territory behind the South Vietnamese border as a base for troops and supplies for their operations in South Vietnam, and U.S. B-52s had been bombarding these staging areas since March 1969 with the acquiescence of the Cambodian ruler, Prince Sihanouk. The bombing had been concealed from the American public and even from many national security officials in the administration. William Beecher, the Pentagon correspondent of the *New York Times*, broke the story in early May; however, it was not until after the spring 1972 invasion of Cambodia that the bombing was officially acknowledged. [5]

Frustrated by the continuing refusal of Hanoi to discuss a mutual withdrawal of "foreign" forces from South Vietnam even as the United States began a good faith withdrawal of its own forces, and genuinely worried that the North Vietnamese might pounce on the South as soon as U.S. force levels got low enough, Nixon and Kissinger evidently felt by the spring of 1970 that they had no alternative but to break out of the pattern of weak signals they were transmitting to Hanoi.

Their opportunity came in March 1970 with the sudden rightwing coup in Phnom Penh that deposed Prince Sihanouk while he was out of the country. Marshal Lon Nol, the leader of the military coup, not only turned against the Cambodian Communists but also attempted to force the North Vietnamese contingents out of his country. The North Vietnamese, no longer constrained to respect the independence of Cambodia, now openly and vigorously supported the Cambodian Communists, who were building up their forces around Phnom Penh in preparation for a countercoup. Lon Nol's desperate plea for U.S. help could not be refused if the North Vietnamese were to be prevented from taking over Cambodia and completely outflanking South Vietnam. "If, when the chips are down," said Nixon, announcing the decision to attack the North Vietnamese sanctuaries in Cambodia,

the world's most powerful nation, the United States of America, acts like a pitiful, helpless giant, the forces of totalitarianism and anarchy will threaten free nations and free institutions throughout the world. It is not our power but our will and character that is being tested tonight. If we fail to meet this challenge, all other nations will be on notice that despite its overwhelming power the United States, when a real crisis comes, will be found wanting.[6]

Although the foray into Cambodia, like most of the dramatic escalations ordered by Nixon, was designed in part to shock Hanoi into willingness to compromise, the official public explanations stressed a limited military objective. "This is not an invasion of Cambodia," insisted the President. "The areas in which these attacks will be launched are completely occupied and controlled by North Vietnamese forces. Our purpose is not to occupy the areas. Once enemy forces are driven out of these sanctuaries and once their military supplies are destroyed, we will withdraw."[7]

Two months later, on June 30, 1970, the President proclaimed the Cambodian operation a complete success and announced that all American troops had been withdrawn from Cambodia on schedule. He reeled off the indicators of enemy's material and human losses, with a curious, if not spurious, exactitude: "22,892 individual weapons . . . 2,509 big crew-served weapons. . . . More than 15 million rounds of ammunition. . . . 14 million pounds of rice. . . . 143,000 rockets. . . . Over 199,552 antiaircraft rounds, 5,482 mines, 62,022 grenades, and 83,000 pounds of explosives, including 1,002 satchel charges. . . . Over 435 vehicles . . . over 11,688 bunkers and other military structures . . . 11,349 men killed and about 2,328 captured and detainees."

The "deeper meaning" of these "impressive statistics," said Nixon, was as follows:

We have eliminated an immediate threat to our forces and to the security of South Vietnam—and produced the prospect of fewer American casualties in the future.

We have inflicted extensive casualties and very heavy losses in material on the enemy—losses which can now be replaced only from the North during a monsoon season. . . .

We have ended the concept of Cambodian sanctuaries, immune from attack, upon which the enemy military had relied for five years.

We have dislocated supply lines and disrupted Hanoi's strategy in the Saigon area and the Mekong Delta. The enemy capacity to mount a major offensive in this vital populated region of the South has been greatly diminished.

We have effectively cut off the enemy from resupply by the sea. . . .

We have, for the time being, separated the Communist main-force units . . . from the guerrillas in the southern part of Vietnam. This should provide a boost to pacification efforts.

We have guaranteed the continuance of our troop withdrawal program. . . .

We have bought time for the South Vietnamese to strengthen themselves against the enemy.

We have witnessed visible proof of the success of Vietnamization as the South Vietnamese performed with skill and valor and competence far beyond the expectation of our commanders or American advisers. [8]

President Nixon understandably chose not to refer to the fact that after the sixty-day U.S. incursion into Cambodia the Communist forces occupied a larger portion of the country—about half of it. Some critics of the Nixon–Kissinger policies invoke this fact in attempting to show that the U.S. bombing and incursion into Cambodia *caused* its ultimate takeover by the Communists and the bloody decimation of its culture and civic order which followed. Kissinger effectively refutes this non sequitur in *The White House Years* ("Hanoi's insatiable quest for hegemony—not America's hesitant and ambivalent response—is the root cause of Cambodia's ordeal") [9]; but the "success" of the 1970 foray into Cambodia looks much less impressive when viewed in the context of these developments; and there can be no doubt that the U.S. military incursion lent a certain credibility to the North Vietnamese claim (however spurious in fact) that their own massive invasion of Cambodia was designed to prevent the "imperialists" from reimposing their domination of that country.

Although one immediate purpose of the operation was to shock Hanoi into facing up to the costs of continuing the war, it had the boomerang effect of finally shattering whatever confidence remained in the White House that the administration could revive popular faith in its competence to bring the war to an honorable end. As it turned out, Nixon and Kissinger were themselves shocked by the domestic reaction to their move, and the North Vietnamese leadership, apparently sensing this, only stiffened its intransigence at the negotiating table while intensifying its military efforts throughout Indochina.

The student protest movement, somewhat dormant since the election of Nixon, had been revived overnight by the news of the invasion of Cambodia. The combustible campus animosity toward the administration for its sluggish exit from Vietnam had been ignited into a firestorm of anger when four demonstrating students at Kent State University were killed by a trigger-happy Ohio National Guard unit. Efforts were intensified in Congress to limit the executive's war powers.

The Cambodian operation, conceived of as a means of widening U.S. options and limiting those of the North Vietnamese, had the opposite effect. Washington, not Hanoi, once again made the next concessions in the diplomatic arena—this time coming almost all the way toward the maximum demands of Hanoi.

Nixon now gave the go-ahead to propose a "cease-fire" even though the U.S. military and the U.S. Embassy in Saigon believed this would put the Thieu regime in great physical jeopardy and in an untenable political position. "Cease-fire-in-place" was a euphemism for what was, in effect, an agreement to allow Hanoi to keep its forces in South Vietnam and to legitimize their hold on the territory they had already conquered. Here, finally, was the abandonment of the U.S. insistence on a mutual withdrawal of U.S. and North Vietnamese forces from the South. "The decision to propose a standstill cease-fire in 1970," admits Kissinger, "implied the solution of 1972." [10] The U.S. forces alone would leave, being the only "foreign" forces there—a complete capitulation to Hanoi's insistence that the conflict in the South was a continuation of the civil war to liberate Vietnam from imperialism.

Even such a fundamental concession was insufficient for the North Vietnamese, who, more contemptuous than ever of their opponents, would settle for nothing less than an American renunciation of the legitimacy of the Thieu regime. This last demand, from the administration's point of view, was surely irrational, for the cease-fire-in-place and accompanying interim political arrangements proposed to the North Vietnamese were clearly only face-saving mechanisms to allow the United States to get out before the final deposition of Thieu and the participation of the Communists in the government in Saigon. Kissinger's military–diplomatic strategy from here on out was designed to convince Hanoi that (1) no matter how sick the United States was of the war, there was no possibility of persuading President Nixon to cooperate in the final humiliation of Thieu that Hanoi demanded, and (2) the United States was fully committed to a withdrawal of its own forces from Vietnam, and the cease-fire-in-place and interim political arrangements were not any kind of trick to put the North Vietnamese off balance.

THE MINING OF HAIPHONG HARBOR: ATTEMPTS TO WORK THE MOSCOW CONNECTION

From the summer of 1970 through the spring of 1971, terrible pessimism pervaded Washington over the capacity of Nixon and Kissinger to gain that "peace with honor" that would allow the administration to finally get out of Vietnam. With the failure of either the Cambodia invasion or the post-Cambodia negotiating concessions to move Hanoi, Nixon and Kissinger appeared to have used up most of their available carrots and sticks.

The U.S. air support for the South Vietnamese Army's 1971 incursion into Laos to cut the Ho Chi Minh trail network was a comparatively insignificant increment of coercion (Nixon was prevented by the Cooper-Church Amendment from using U.S. ground forces, as he had in Cambodia). Moreover, the South Vietnamese troops were beaten back without accomplishing their mission.

Kissinger once again reached deep into his bag for two further initiatives in his secret negotiations with Le Duc Tho during the spring and summer of 1971: a promise that President Thieu would resign prior to internationally supervised elections under comprehensive peace arrangements, and assurances to Hanoi that all U.S. troops would be out of Vietnam within six months following the signing of the peace agreement. Le Duc Tho countered with his own nine points as the basis for continuing to negotiate in detail. But by the fall of 1971, after six intense negotiating sessions in Paris, Kissinger and Le Duc Tho were still deadlocked over details—in essence, the inability of Kissinger and Nixon to agree to an unconditional surrender of South Vietnam. Le Duc Tho attempted to delegate the responsibility for further talks to his deputy.

Kissinger's insistence that Le Duc Tho himself continue were ignored, so the negotiations were suspended.

Meanwhile, events along the great power nexus had been maturing. It was during the summer and fall of 1971 that Kissinger had
arranged for Nixon's 1972 summit visits to Moscow and Peking; and
it might now be possible to induce the Communist giants, both of
whom were competing for U.S. favor, to lean hard on their Vietnamese comrades to compromise with the United States. But Hanoi,
perhaps sensing what was coming, began to lay the groundwork for
a massive new invasion of the South. U.S. and South Vietnamese
military commanders braced for an enemy offensive in February to
coincide with the President's trip to China. Instead, Hanoi launched
a major spring offensive across the demilitarized zone at the 17th
parallel on March 31, a month after the Peking summit and seven
weeks before the Moscow summit.

Nixon and Kissinger now moved to turn the screws on the Russians, to compel them to face the consequences for U.S.–Soviet relations of their continued support of the North Vietnamese war effort. State and Defense Department spokesmen began complaining
publicly about the heavy role of Soviet military supplies in the new
North Vietnamese offensive.

Meanwhile, North Vietnam was brought under heavy and sustained air bombardment for the first time since the Johnson administration. The port of Haiphong and storage depots around Hanoi
were raided by B-52s. Four Soviet merchant ships in Haiphong harbor were damaged by the bombings. U.S. officials hinted of still
more destructive escalations to come, including even the mining of
North Vietnamese ports which, by putting Soviet supply convoys in
jeopardy, would force the issue with the Kremlin.

While the risks of a direct U.S.–Soviet confrontation over Vietnam rose to dangerous levels during April 1972, Kissinger traveled
secretly to Moscow to firm up preparations for the May summit
between Brezhnev and Nixon. As recounted in the preceding chapter, the evident progress in SALT and commercial talks gave both
sides reason to hope for a major breakthrough in U.S.–Soviet relations to be unveiled at the summit as long as Vietnam did not ruin
it. Each side sensed that the other was most anxious for the summit
to take place. But as Kissinger was to find out in Moscow, since
both were aware of the other's real priorities, neither could use the

threat of postponing or canceling the summit as leverage on the other's role in Vietnam. Kissinger returned to Washington with plans for the May Nixon–Brezhnev meeting intact but with no meaningful Kremlin assurances to bring pressure on the Vietnamese to sign a compromise peace.

Two days after Kissinger returned from Moscow, Nixon went on nationwide television and radio to vent his frustration at the lack of progress in the peace negotiations and to explain the reasons for the resumption of the systematic bombing of North Vietnam. The Easter weekend military offensive of the North, argued Nixon, had stripped away "whatever pretext there was of a civil war in South Vietnam." Once again escalating his rhetoric on the enormity of the international crime being committed by Hanoi, the President made it more difficult to admit, finally, that the United States had no business continuing to participate in the war: "What we are witnessing here, what is being brutally inflicted upon the people of South Vietnam, is a clear case of naked and unprovoked aggression across an international border."[11] Curiously, this definition of the situation was revived after the United States had repeatedly offered to establish a cease-fire-in-place, to withdraw all its forces, and to establish interim political arrangements in the South based on the military status quo. Washington's willingness to legitimize the fruits of the war had thus already been established, even though at least ten regular North Vietnamese combat divisions were already in South Vietnam. Now Hanoi's movement of three additional combat divisions across the 17th parallel was pointed to as contradicting Hanoi's claim that the conflict was a civil war!

The reescalation of the U.S. stake in Vietnam was backed up by Nixon's promise to continue U.S. air and naval attacks on North Vietnam "until the North Vietnamese stop their offensive in South Vietnam."[12] Other officials hinted that more and more targets in the North would come under attack. Yet at the same time Nixon pledged to continue withdrawing American troops. He claimed to be able to do this because, according to reports he had received from the American commander in Vietnam, General Creighton Abrams, the South Vietnamese forces had demonstrated their ability to defend themselves on the ground against future enemy attacks. "I have decided," said the President, "that Vietnamization has proved itself sufficiently that we can continue our program of withdrawing

American forces without detriment to our overall goal of insuring South Vietnam's survival as an independent country."[13]

However, the military reports from the field during the next few days did not support the President's optimistic assessment of the fighting capabilities of the South Vietnamese army. Abandoning Quangtri City, south of the 17th parallel, the South Vietnamese forces virtually turned and ran southward to avoid the advancing North Vietnamese. Hue would be next, and the resulting demoralization of Saigon would bring on a humiliating collapse of the South's effort before the 1972 presidential elections. Something had to be done to break the downhill slide.

Kissinger, again meeting with Le Duc Tho in Paris, offered to accelerate the U.S. withdrawal (all U.S. troops would be removed before the November elections) if Hanoi would agree to a cease-fire and a return of U.S. prisoners of war. In effect, he was saying: Just give us a decent interval to get out under the cloak of an apparent compromise, and you can have the whole country. But riding high now, the North Vietnamese were evidently more confident than ever that they could have it entirely their way: The Americans would have to cooperate in immediately deposing the Thieu regime or else there would be no deal.

Nixon and Kissinger, still hoping to avoid wholesale capitulation to the Communist demands, now attempted to use their incompletely exploited indirect leverage on Hanoi through the Moscow connection. The Navy was authorized to implement one of the favorite options of the Joint Chiefs of Staff: mining Haiphong harbor and other ports in order to drastically increase the risks and costs to the Soviets of supplying North Vietnam. Presumably, this would compel the Kremlin to lean hard on Hanoi to bring the war to an end through diplomacy instead of attempting to win a total military victory. The order to execute the operation was issued on May 8, 1972, only two weeks before Nixon was scheduled to meet with Brezhnev in Moscow. In so forcing the issue of Vietnam with the Russians, Nixon and Kissinger clearly were risking Kremlin postponement, if not cancelation, of the summit. It was a gamble, but Nixon claimed that his back was against the wall and he was left with no alternatives.

In his May 8, 1972, address explaining this decision, Nixon

painted his options starkly: "immediate withdrawal of all American forces, continued attempts at negotiation, or decisive military action to end the war." The first course, he contended, "would mean turning 17 million South Vietnamese over to Communist tyranny and terror. It would mean leaving hundreds of American prisoners in Communist hands with no bargaining leverage to get them released." And it would "encourage . . . smaller nations armed by their major allies . . . to attack neighboring nations at will in the Mideast, in Europe, and other areas."

The alternative of negotiating an honorable settlement was his preferred course, said Nixon. But after four years during which "we have made every reasonable offer and tried every possible path for ending this war at the conference table, . . . the North Vietnamese arrogantly refuse to negotiate anything but an . . . ultimatum that the United States impose a Communist regime on 17 million people in South Viet-Nam."

It was plain, Nixon concluded, "that what appears to be a choice among three courses of action for the United States is really no choice at all. . . . There is only one way to stop the killing. That is to keep the weapons of war out of the hands of the international outlaws of North Vietnam"—in other words, a return to the first alternative, decisive military action:

All entrances to North Vietnamese ports will be mined to prevent access to these ports and North Vietnamese naval operations from these ports.

United States forces have been directed to take appropriate measures within the internal and claimed territorial waters of North Vietnam to interdict the delivery of any supplies.

Rail and all other communications will be cut off to the maximum extent possible.

Air and naval strikes against military targets in North Vietnam will continue. [14]

These acts of force would stop, promised the President, once U.S. prisoners of war were released by Hanoi and once an internationally supervised cease-fire had begun. At such time the United States would proceed to completely withdraw all its forces from Vietnam within four months.

Pointedly, Nixon began his address with special reference to the Soviet role. The present massive invasion of South Vietnam, he maintained, "was made possible by tanks, artillery, and other advanced offensive weapons supplied to Hanoi by the Soviet Union and other Communist nations." And he closed with remarks directed at the Soviet leadership:

> We expect you to keep your allies, and you cannot expect us to do other than help our allies. But let us . . . help our allies only for the purpose of their defense, not for the purpose of launching invasions against their neighbors. . . .
>
> Our two nations have made significant progress in recent months. We are near major agreements on nuclear arms limitation, on trade, on a host of other issues. Let us not slide back toward the dark shadows of a previous age. . . .
>
> We, the United States and the Soviet Union, are on the threshold of a new relationship. . . . We are prepared to build this relationship. The responsibility is yours if we fail to do so.[15]

In this pointed rhetoric as well as in the military action, the May 1972 escalation was the biggest gamble Nixon took in Vietnam, for it could have severely alienated the Russians on the eve of the Moscow summit and thereby in one blow shattered the larger diplomatic mosaic the administration was attempting to construct.

The talk around Washington at the time, possibly inspired by Kissinger himself, was that "Henry" opposed the President on this one, and it was the vigorous intervention of Secretary of the Treasury John Connally that stiffened the President's determination to up the ante despite the risks.[16]

It is not at all implausible that Kissinger, in order to keep his diplomatic channels open, felt that it was tactically necessary to separate himself somewhat from the administration's new belligerent posture. Kissinger would be the one who would have to reconstitute the summit plans if they were to fall apart temporarily, and it was Kissinger who still would have to meet face to face with his North Vietnamese counterparts when the negotiations resumed.

The basic escalatory ploy, however, was fully consistent with the Kissinger mode of coercive diplomacy. In any event the gamble worked, at least insofar as the Kremlin chose not to scuttle the larger détente relationship, and—to the surprise of most of the Washington policy community—the Russians indicated that the Nixon–Brezhnev summit was still on. But whether the gamble worked in its main objective of pressuring the Soviets to lean hard on the North Vietnamese to finally negotiate a compromise peace remains a question to be illuminated by further historical research.

Defenders of the Haiphong mining operation claim not only that it broke the back of North Vietnam's spring offensive but that in driving up the risks to the Soviets themselves of a prolongation of the war in Southeast Asia it was the key to a significant Kremlin decision to reduce arms deliveries to North Vietnam and to President Nikolai Podgorny's visit to Hanoi of June 15, presumably to tell the North Vietnamese that they must now negotiate seriously to end the war instead of banking on a total capitulation by their opponents.[17]

If the Soviets did indeed intercede with Hanoi in the spring and summer of 1972 on behalf of the United States, they probably did so in order to continue the momentum of détente expressed at the Nixon–Brezhnev summit. There is no evidence, or logic, in the argument that they did so *because* of the Haiphong mining. Moreover, at the summit Kissinger and Nixon, it has been reported, inched even closer to Hanoi's maximum demands, reaffirming their acceptance of a North Vietnamese military presence in South Vietnam, endorsing a tripartite electoral commission that would include neutralists and the Viet Cong, and conveying their willingness to call off the bombing of the North prior to a release of American prisoners.[18]

During the summer and fall, Kissinger exhibited great optimism that the long-sought agreement with Hanoi to end the war was imminent. In retrospective interviews he attributed the intensification of constructive negotiations with Le Duc Tho to the success of his leverage diplomacy in putting pressure on both Moscow and Peking (each afraid the other would be favored by the United States) to persuade Hanoi to allow the Americans to leave Vietnam "with honor."[19]

The sequence of events supports a contrary explanation—namely, that Nixon and Kissinger, fearful of being outflanked in the coming U.S. presidential elections by a Democratic peace candidate, conveyed to the Communist powers—more convincingly than ever before—their willingness to give in to Hanoi's demands on virtually all points. This interpretation is supported particularly by the evident reluctance of the White House to let the Thieu regime in Saigon know how completely the United States was now prepared to abandon South Vietnam. During the months following the Moscow summit, the problem of how to persuade Thieu to accept the inevitable became Washington's central preoccupation. White House military aide General Haig was dispatched to Saigon to persuade Thieu while Kissinger and Le Duc Tho labored through August, September, and October to dot the *i*'s and cross the *t*'s of what was now a basic Washington—Hanoi accord on most of the essential provisions of the peace agreement.

THE FINAL BRAVADO . . . AND DENOUEMENT

The hopes of Nixon and Kissinger to successfully conclude the peace negotiations on the eve of the November 1972 elections were dashed by Thieu's refusal to accept the terms agreed upon by Kissinger and Le Duc Tho. The South Vietnamese had numerous objections to the draft agreement, but their deepest grievances were over the establishment of a South Vietnamese coalition regime including the Communists, and over the failure to provide for a withdrawal of North Vietnamese troops from South Vietnam. Kissinger urged the President to authorize a separate peace between the United States and North Vietnam; but Nixon needed Saigon's acquiescence to preserve the fiction of an "honorable peace." Accordingly, he had Kissinger delay the final signing. Hanoi thereupon unilaterally disclosed the terms of the draft agreement, probably in an effort to force the issue between Washington and Saigon. Kissinger maintained a public air of optimism by insisting that "peace is at hand," but he surely feared a last-minute disintegration of all of his painstaking labors.

When Kissinger and Le Duc Tho met again a few weeks after the November 1972 election, in which Nixon had defeated George McGovern by an overwhelming margin, the North Vietnamese negotiator seemed to have toughened his stand. Not only did he reject all the points Kissinger presented on behalf of President Thieu, but according to Kissinger's subsequent press briefings he made additional demands to alter the texts he and Kissinger had agreed to in October. In retrospect the new intransigence on the part of the North Vietnamese is understandable, for they could easily have interpreted Nixon's procrastination prior to the elections as a cover for the massive military reinforcements the United States flew into South Vietnam immediately after the election. Although the White House's purpose in this new military infusion may have been to buy off Thieu rather than to alter the military balance of power in South

Vietnam before the cease-fire took effect, the North Vietnamese could well have suspected a ruse and decided to stall while engaging in their own compensatory reinforcements.

Nixon and Kissinger were more frustrated than ever. Had they slipped back on to a reverse track just as the opening at the end of the tunnel of war was immediately in front of them? Determined to break out at last, they tried one more dramatic set of moves. They now informed Hanoi that Nixon was ready to agree to a separate peace with North Vietnam if Thieu failed to agree to the October terms. They also informed Thieu of this decision and threatened to cut off all assistance to South Vietnam if Thieu persisted in being an obstructionist. Simultaneously, they delivered a 72-hour ultimatum to Hanoi that unless serious negotiations were resumed immediately they would bomb North Vietnam again with even less restraint than before. With the expiration of the ultimatum on December 18, U.S. bombers commenced a 12-day round-the-clock devastation attack on North Vietnam, including massive attacks on "military" targets in heavily populated areas of Hanoi and Haiphong.[20]

The 1972 Christmas bombing operation was nothing less than an effort to terrorize the North Vietnamese back to the negotiating table in a more contrite posture. Not incidentally, it would also impress President Thieu. After suffering a rain of bombs for nearly two weeks, the North Vietnamese said they had had enough; they were ready to resume serious negotiations. On December 30 Nixon ordered a halt to the attacks north of the 20th parallel and dispatched Kissinger to Paris for the diplomatic anticlimax.

On January 23, 1973, the Agreement on Ending the War and Restoring the Peace in Vietnam was initialed in Paris by Kissinger and Le Duc Tho. (On January 27 it was formally signed by Secretary of State William Rogers and the North Vietnamese Foreign Minister, Nguyen Duy Trinh, with the Foreign Minister of the Thieu regime and the Foreign Minister of the Communist "Provisional Revolutionary Government" in South Vietnam separately countersigning special copies so that their two names would not appear together on any one document.) "The people of South Vietnam have been guaranteed the right to determine their own future without outside interference," announced President Nixon. "Throughout these negotiations we have been in closest consultation with

President Thieu and other representatives of the Republic of South Vietnam. This settlement meets the goals and has the full support of President Thieu and the Government of the Republic of Vietnam, as well as that of our other allies who are affected."[21] Of course, neither the history of the negotiations nor the text of the 1973 agreement and attached protocols nor the subsequent fate of South Vietnam supported these claims by Nixon.

The Paris agreement and protocols were transparently a conditional surrender of the non-Communists to the Communists in Vietnam. Coequal status was henceforth to be given in South Vietnam to the "two parties"—the Government of the Democratic Republic of Vietnam (the Thieu regime) and the Provisional Revolutionary Government of South Vietnam (the Communists). The cease-fire would accordingly legitimize all Communist military gains to date, and their continuing military–administrative control of these areas, pending the establishment of a new government of South Vietnam. The new government was to be established through "free and democratic general elections," but the two parties would each have a veto in all transitional processes and institutions leading toward the establishment of the new government. Meanwhile, the armed forces of the United States were to be totally withdrawn, regardless of whether the political–governmental provisions of the agreement were working. There was no requirement, however, for the North Vietnamese to remove their forces. Some weak and ambiguous controls were provided on the military reinforcement by North Vietnam and the United States of their respective South Vietnamese allies, but the interpretation and enforcement of these controls would also be subject to the veto of both parties. Kissinger did succeed in getting the North Vietnamese to concede to most of the U.S. demands for the prompt return of all captured military personnel and foreign civilians; this was accomplished by putting the provision on the return of captured Vietnamese civilians in a separate article stipulating that the question "will be resolved by the two South Vietnamese parties."[22]

To the surprise of no one who knew the situation in Indochina, the paper peace began to crumble before its ink was dry. Both Vietnams violated the strictures against new military buildups; each blamed the other for the renewed outbreak of fighting and, of course, for the failure to set up institutions to govern the transition to free elections. The military balance of power in South Vietnam, Laos, and Cambodia continued to determine the future of these countries, given the prevailing political anarchy in each.

Kissinger, realpolitician that he was, could not have expected anything else. Yet in the first volume of his memories he insists that "I believed then, and I believe now, that the agreement could have worked. It reflected a true equilibrium of forces on the ground. . . . We believed that Saigon was strong enough to deal with guerrilla warfare and low-level violations."[23] This assessment proved false, for the violations during the early months of 1973 involved heavy infiltration of military personnel and equipment down the Ho Chi Minh Trail and across the demilitarized zone, including tanks and surface-to-air missiles. Witnessing this change in the balance of forces, and being prevented by U.S. domestic pressures from redressing the growing imbalance, Kissinger recalls, in his second volume, that "in my bones I knew that collapse was just a question of time."[24]

Kissinger denies any naïveté whatsoever about Hanoi's intentions. "I never believed," he recalls, "that Hanoi would reconcile itself to the military balance as it emerged from the Paris Agreement without testing it at least once more." However, Hanoi would be discouraged from actually attempting to topple the military balance because of its fear of U.S. retaliation. "American air power was thus always seen as an essential deterrent to the resumption of all-out war. Nixon gave assurances on this score to South Vietnamese President Nguyen Van Thieu to persuade Thieu to accept the Paris Agreement."[25]

The miscalculation in the White House, then, if we are to take Kissinger's published recollections at face value, was over the ability of the American political process to deliver on the military commitment that Nixon and Kissinger gave to Thieu and which Hanoi was supposed to have heard and believed. But how could Nixon and Kissinger have made such a gross miscalculation? Surely, by the fall of 1972, when the basic deal was being struck with Hanoi, the evidence was clear that the majority of the American people wanted an end to the sacrifice of American blood and treasure in Indochina, and that such sacrifice was not warranted to preserve a U.S. client state in South Vietnam. Kissinger still insists that "the people never chose abdication." He cites Nixon's huge electoral victory over

George McGovern in November 1972 and opinion polls as endorsements of the basic policy of "peace with honor." It is true, says Kissinger, that a majority of the American people came to believe that it had been a mistake to get involved in Vietnam in the first place and that that involvement should be brought to an end, "but an even larger majority rejected the peace movement's policy of immediate and unconditional withdrawal." This larger majority, claims Kissinger, was looking to the nation's executive for the leadership that would be so crucial in managing the transition to full peace in Indochina in a way that preserved the reputation of the United States as a country that honored its commitments and that did not tempt our adversaries to engage in new aggression.[26] But the required executive leadership was not to emerge. The principal reason, according to Kissinger, was Watergate.

During March and April 1973 Kissinger urged Nixon to order a three- or four-day sustained bombing of the North Vietnamese bases and trails in Laos and on both sides of the demilitarized zone separating North and South Vietnam. It was important "to give Hanoi a jolt" to make it clear to the enemy that "we may do something totally unexpected" if it continued to violate the Paris agreement. Kissinger could not get a clear and consistent set of orders out of his chief, however. He portrays Nixon during this period as "uncharacteristically indecisive," as "a distracted man." It was only later, when examining the records, that Kissinger found out the extent of Nixon's preoccupation with the Watergate investigations at the very time that it was most urgent to get him to act decisively to prevent the complete unraveling of the Indochina peace.[27]

"The normal Nixon would have been enraged beyond containment," offers Kissinger, at the mid-April reports that 35,000 fresh North Vietnamese troops had entered South Vietnam and nearby border sanctuaries; "but Watergate Nixon continued to dither."[28] The President did approve U.S. limited bombing of targets in Laos in a two-day retaliation for the North Vietnamese seizure of the Laotian town of Tha Vieng, and he also ordered the suspension of mine-clearing operations around North Vietnamese ports.

The "turning point" for Kissinger—the recognition that it would be futile to expect the beleaguered President to take the retaliatory actions required to deter Hanoi from further violations—came on April 14, 1973, when he heard from one of Nixon's legal advisers how Watergate was beginning to implicate the President himself. "I was appalled by the knowledge, seeing, for the first time clearly, how the Watergate challenges could reach to the heart of the Presidency and destroy all authority," recalls Kissinger. He could no longer urge Nixon to put his diminishing prestige behind a resumption of systematic bombing; the President no longer had the authority or the will to focus his energy on beating down the congressional opposition that was sure to be crystalized by such a renewal of coercive diplomacy.[29] In the following months, antiwar measures that had previously been blocked in the House of Representatives began to pass both houses, culminating in the "nail-in-the-coffin" legislation of June barring all further U.S. military action in Indochina. At the time, Kissinger railed against the Congress for denying him any significant sanctions to apply against Hanoi; but in *Years of Upheaval,* he is more candid, admitting that "the 'window' we had in those few months of early 1973 was closed by Watergate's enfeeblements."[30]

The Soviets, perceiving the paralysis of American will to respond, enlarged their flow of military supplies to the Vietnamese Communists over the next two years. Kissinger and President Ford made the obligatory pleas to a reluctant Congress to match the Soviet effort; but even as the final panic spread in South Vietnam in the spring of 1975 there were few Americans in political life who would define the raising of the Viet Cong flag over Saigon as sufficiently harmful to vital U.S. interests to justify still another futile pretense of honor.

24

THE MIDDLE EAST AND THE REASSERTION OF AMERICAN COMPETENCE ABROAD

We could not sit on the sidelines if the Middle East should rage out of control; the world would view it as a collapse of American authority, whatever alibi we might put forward. We had to protect our country's ability to play an indispensable role as the guarantor of peace and the repository of the hopes of free peoples.

HENRY KISSINGER

For Nixon and Kissinger the liquidation of the Vietnam War was the precondition for the restoration of American international power. They regarded détente with the Soviet Union and rapprochement with China as conducive to the revival of domestic and foreign belief in America's dedication to peace and world order, and in its "vision" (a favorite Kissinger word). It was in the Middle East, however, that Nixon and Kissinger could prove the capacity and will to *use* American power effectively during crises in the service of peace and order and, by so doing, re-create international respect for the United States as a constructive and competent superpower.

Their principal Middle Eastern challenges—countering the Soviet buildup of Egyptian military power, controlling the Jordanian crisis of 1970, and stage-managing the termination of the 1973 Arab–Israeli war—provided both men with the opportunity to manipulate the most awesome components of American power. Particularly in the 1973–74 crisis period, as Nixon became more preoccupied with Watergate, it was Kissinger who had to direct the major military as well as political moves; and by all accounts he loved it.

Kissinger had reason to rate his Mideast diplomacy as eminently successful: after the Israeli victories of 1967 the Russians had increased their influence with the Arabs, but the United States emerged from the crises of 1970–74 as the most influential external power. And in a situation that was widely regarded as the most likely tinderbox for igniting World War III, the Nixon and Ford administrations were instrumental in containing and terminating local conflagrations that could have exploded into global holocaust.

Credit must be given to the role played by the United States during the Kissinger years in defining the permissible bounds of action for all actors and providing external sanctions to the local antagonists to resolve their differences through diplomacy rather than war. When it came to a more permanent impact on the situation, however, in the sense of ameliorating the chronic sources of dangerous conflict in the Middle East or leaving intact a system of conflict controls that would reduce the prospects of major war, Kissinger had less basis for pride that he had made a historic contribution to international order.

THE FAILURE OF PEACE DIPLOMACY IN 1969 AND 1970

The Nixon administration inherited the basic dilemma of U.S. Middle Eastern policy: by guaranteeing Israel's security against Arab aggression, the United States had driven many countries into the arms of the Soviet Union and made it more difficult for pro-U.S. regimes in the area to sustain themselves in the face of radical domestic movements. But if the United States were to reduce its support for Israel, the Arabs, with Soviet backing, might soon come to believe they could overpower the small Jewish state. The crushing of Israel would be intolerable to the United States, and its prevention would require U.S. countermoves that would increase the likelihood of a U.S.–Soviet military clash.

Upon assuming the presidency, Nixon attempted to transcend this dilemma by making the United States the active catalyst of the peace process in the Middle East. New initiatives were taken on two levels simultaneously: (1) intense U.S.–Soviet consultations designed to lock the Russians into a joint approach toward an Arab–Israeli settlement and (2) a new "evenhanded" posture toward the demands of the Israelis and the Arabs. Both were reflected in what came to be known as the Rogers Plan—the U.S. draft outline of an Arab–Israeli settlement presented by Secretary of State William P. Rogers to the Soviets for Kremlin endorsement as agreed-upon terms of reference for more specific peace negotiations between Israel and Egypt.

In his memoirs Nixon recalls the thinking behind the new initiatives. "If the Soviets were committed to Arab victories and we were committed to Israeli victories, it did not require much imagination to see how both might be drawn in even against our wills—and almost certainly against our national interests." Whether or not the Kremlin could be enticed into a constructive diplomatic process, it was clearly in America's interest "to halt the Soviet domination of the Arab Mideast. To do so would require broadening American relations with the Arab countries. Within the first few weeks of my administration I began taking the first steps in this direction."[1]

The new approach rested on two assumptions that turned out to be untenable—or at least premature: (1) that the Kremlin too was increasingly apprehensive that the superpowers' competitive support of their respective Middle Eastern clients could lead to a direct U.S.–Soviet military clash, and therefore might be willing to trade the presence it was gaining from a polarization of the area in return for coequal status with the United States as joint peacemaker; and (2) that a posture of U.S. impartiality toward the Arabs and Israel would give the Nixon administration greater leverage over *both* sides than continuation of the past pro-Israel policies. The first assumption crumbled as evidence mounted in 1969 and 1970 of a continuing enlargement of the Soviet military presence in Egypt coupled with the buildup of the Russian Navy in the Mediterranean, and it was discarded when it became clear at the end of the year that the Kremlin was exerting little if any pressure on Nasser to negotiate a compromise peace. The second assumption, even though apparently contradicted by Israel's categorical rejection of the Rogers Plan as an "imposed" peace, was never adequately tested during this period. Soviet–Egyptian collusion in the military sphere, and then the Jordanian crisis, pushed the larger peace diplomacy aside and drove the United States back into the role of overt guarantor of Israeli security. In 1969 Russian military assistance was proceeding beyond simply replacing Egyptian losses in the Six Day War. The buildup now included modern surface-to-air missiles (SAMs) that might negate Israel's air superiority and thus shift the balance of power toward the Arabs, whose overwhelming military manpower advantage could eventually make the difference in a ground war. Indeed, the Egyptians were becoming more daring in the spring of 1969 in their military raids across the Suez Canal into Israeli-occupied territory along the East Bank, portending Nasser's flirtation with the idea of launching a major cross-canal invasion under the cover of Soviet antiaircraft sites on the West Bank. Israel, predictably, asked for additional U.S. fighter aircraft to compensate for the improvements in Egypt's air defense capabilities. To those who bought the premises of the Nixon–Rogers diplomatic initiatives, however, these military trends only underlined the urgency of efforts to get the Egyptians committed to negotiations with Israel and the Israelis committed to relinquishing most of the territory they had conquered in 1967.

The starting point for the proposed negotiations was United Nations Resolution 242, an ambiguous set of principles passed by the Security Council on November 22, 1967, that both Israel and Egypt said they accepted. Resolution 242 called for a settlement based on "withdrawal of Israeli armed forces from territories occupied in the recent June 1967 conflict" and "termination of all claims or states of belligerency and respect for and acknowledgement of the sovereignty, territorial integrity, and political independence of every state in the area and their right to live in peace within secure and recognized boundaries free from threats or acts of force."[2]

Implementation of Resolution 242 had stalled during the last fourteen months of the Johnson administration, primarily over differing interpretations of the sequencing of the Israeli withdrawals and the full recognition of Israel's legitimacy by the Arabs. The Arabs, backed by the Soviets, had been insisting on withdrawal first, then peace. The Israelis, supported at least implicitly by the United States, regarded Arab acceptance of Israel as the necessary precondition for relinquishment of territories conquered during the last round of the war. The two sides also disagreed over how much of the conquered territory Israel was obligated to give back.

President Nixon delegated Secretary of State Rogers to try to resolve the impasse through a series of diplomatic initiatives aimed at the Soviet Union, the Arabs, and Israel that would compress and dissipate the question of timing in a package of detailed provisions on the rights and duties of the local parties that would form the context for Israeli withdrawals. "To call for Israeli withdrawal as envisaged in the U.N. resolution without achieving agreement on peace would be partisan toward the Arabs," explained Secretary Rogers. "To call on the Arabs to accept peace without Israeli withdrawal would be partisan toward Israel. Therefore, our policy is to encourage the Arabs to accept a permanent peace based on a binding agreement and to urge the Israelis to withdraw from occupied territory when their territorial integrity is assured as envisaged by the Security Council resolution." [3]

The most fully worked out version of the Rogers Plan, as presented to the Soviets on October 28, 1969, provided for indirect negotiations between Israel and Egypt and outlined the key provisions of the agreement that should ensue: (1) a timetable, to be agreed upon during the negotiations, for withdrawal of Israeli forces from Egyptian territory occupied during the 1967 war; (2) a formal end to the state of war; (3) specification of the precise locations of the agreed-upon "secure borders," and the establishment of demilitarized zones; (4) freedom of navigation through the Strait of Tiran and an affirmation of its status as an international waterway; (5) nondiscriminatory navigation for the ships of all nations, including Israel, through the Suez Canal; (6) a final settlement of the Gaza strip issue; (7) participation in a process for resolving the Palestinian refugee problem; (8) mutual recognition of each other's sovereignty, political independence, and right to live in peace within secure boundaries free from threats of force; and (9) submission of the final document to the UN Security Council for ratification, and to the United States, the Soviet Union, Great Britain, and France, which would promise to help both sides adhere to the agreement. [4] In December the United States presented to the Big Four a parallel plan outlining a Jordanian–Israeli agreement, including provisions for Jordan's sharing in the administration of Jerusalem.

Despite the elaborate surrounding diplomacy—a preliminary series of meetings on earlier drafts with the Russians, U.S. soundings with Israel, and Soviet soundings with Egypt—the Rogers initiatives got nowhere. Israel flatly rejected the "attempt to impose a forced solution on her . . . [and] appease them [the Arabs] at the expense of Israel." [5] The Soviets, unable to deliver the Egyptians, also rejected the Rogers Plan.

In retrospect, Nixon claims to have known that the provisions for returning the occupied territories to the Arabs meant that "the Rogers Plan had absolutely no chance of being accepted by Israel." He also presents himself as being (privately) closer to the realistic persuasion of Kissinger, who not only predicted the Israeli rejection but also argued that the plan would encourage Arab extremists and naively play into the hands of the Soviets. "I knew that the Rogers Plan could never be implemented," writes Nixon,

> but I believed that it was important to let the Arab world know that the United States did not automatically dismiss its case regarding the occupied territories or rule out a compromise settlement of the conflicting claims. With the Rogers Plan on record, I thought it would be easier for the Arab leaders to propose reopening relations with the United States without coming under attack from the hawks and pro-Soviet elements in their own countries. [6]

Kissinger's influence on U.S. policy during the period of the Rogers Plan appears to have been shadowy but substantial. On the basis of Nixon's published recollections and detailed journalistic accounts, the popular notion that Kissinger took little interest in Middle Eastern affairs until the 1973 Yom Kippur War is unwarranted. [7] It is true, however, as Kissinger later recalled, that "I was not in the dominant position." [8]

The Nixon administration took office amid rumors that a new round of hostilities was imminent. A National Security Study Memorandum—NSSM-2—on the Middle Eastern situation was ordered by Kissinger early in January 1969 and delivered to him the day after inauguration. Nixon's decision to have the United States take an active role in the peace diplomacy was based on one of the main policy options in this document, the option reportedly favored by Kissinger. Moreover, while Secretary of State Rogers and Assistant Secretary Joseph Sisco began the process of sounding out all parties to a potential settlement, Kissinger, according to journalist Tad Szulc, was working with Soviet Ambassador Dobrynin to institute a secret top-level dialogue on the Middle East between the White House and the Kremlin, in keeping with the Nixon–Kissinger philosophy that a settlement required the exercise of substantial leverage by both the Soviet Union and the United States over their respective clients. Tangible leverage presumably existed on both sides in the form of controls over the transfer and witholding of military aid by Russia to Egypt and by the United States to Israel.[9]

From the point of view of Secretary of State Rogers and others who favored the policy of evenhandedness, the rejection by Israel and the Soviet Union of the Rogers Plan in late 1969 was due in part to the failure of President Nixon and his principal national security adviser to give it their firm backing. This was undoubtedly the case; but the more important question for the purposes of our analysis is why Nixon and Kissinger encouraged Rogers to proceed as far as he did while they themselves were only lukewarm toward the initiative.

One explanation is that the White House harbored no illusions about the Kremlin's motivation to oppose any real movement toward genuine peace as something that would reduce Soviet influence in the Middle East; yet the Rogers Plan was a vehicle for putting the Russians on the defensive and showing the Arabs that if there was to be any diplomatic leverage on Israel to return the conquered territories, it would have to come from Washington, not Moscow. Another explanation is that Nixon and Kissinger knew that Golda Meir's government would find the plan an unacceptable trade of Israeli physical security for Arab assurances, the latter being wholly unreliable so soon after the Arab humiliation of 1967; yet the initiative would give the policy of evenhandedness credibility with the Arabs—hence the elaborate efforts to keep the details of the U.S. proposals from the Israelis and the U.S. Jewish community. (This explanation is consistent with the White House's having let Rogers finally reveal the contents of his latest draft proposals in a major address in December 1969, with Nixon and Kissinger knowing full well that the outraged reaction from Israel and its U.S. supporters would consign the Rogers Plan to the State Department's file of misfired initiatives.) Another, even more cynical, explanation is that Nixon and Kissinger, knowing that the Arabists in the State Department had built up a full head of steam in preparation for implementing the policy of evenhandedness, saw the Rogers approach as a way of distracting the State Department from the real game of balance-of-power politics that the President wanted to play personally from the Oval Office.

White House actions surrounding the Rogers Plan are consistent with all of these explanations; and all of them, indeed, may accurately reflect the thinking of Nixon and Kissinger at the time. They are also consistent with Kissinger's retrospective remark to the Kalbs that "I always thought there had to be a period of stalemate in which the various parties recognize the limits of what they could achieve."[10] Kissinger's comment provides a context for understanding the most concrete element in U.S. policy toward the Arab–Israeli conflict during this period—namely, the Nixon administration's responses to the requests by the Meir government for new fighter aircraft to counter the Soviet buildup of Egyptian military capabilities.

The Israelis were asking for 80 A-4 Skyhawks and 25 F-4 Phantoms.[11] Some token deliveries, made in secret in the fall of 1969, were far short of previous Israeli requests and expectations; and the administration acted slowly in deciding how to respond to the new requests. The Israelis, of course, were anxious to maintain decisive military superiority; but for the Americans to substantially acquiesce to the Israeli requests would only mean that the Kremlin would feel compelled to respond to Arab requests to further enlarge Soviet deliveries in the area. From the White House perspective, it was important to maintain a deterrent balance, but at the lowest level of outside provisioning possible. A not incidental side benefit from the U.S. policy of maintaining a restrictive hand on the spigot controlling the flow of arms to Israel was the reminder it provided to the Israelis that it was necessary for them to act in consonance with Washington's basic Mideast policies if they wished to maintain an adequate military posture toward the Arabs.

Neither the Soviets nor the Arabs, however, chose to credit the restrained U.S. arms transfer policy in late 1969 as a genuine indication that the United States was ready to use its influence to compel Israel to give up the occupied territories. They focused primarily on the continuing role of the United States as Israel's military guarantor, and alleged that by helping to reduce Israel's military vulnerability the United States was reducing Israeli incentives to part with the conquered territory.

In January 1970, as the Israeli Air Force began to step up its raids on Egypt in retaliation for the persisting Egyptian forays across the canal, the process of polarization and competitive arming eclipsed the peace efforts. Raw balance-of-power calculations once again dominated the Middle Eastern scene and the deliberations in the White House. On January 31 Nixon received what Kissinger termed the "first Soviet threat" of his administration—a letter from Premier Kosygin stating that "we would like to tell you in all frankness that if Israel continues its adventurism, to bomb the territory of the UAR and other Arab states, the Soviet Union will be forced to see to it that the Arab states have the means at their disposal, with the help of which a due rebuff to the arrogant aggressor could be made." [12]

Nixon's reply to the threatening Kosygin letter was firm but, by his own characterization, "carefully low-keyed." He pointed out that the cease-fire was being violated by *both* sides, urged the Kremlin to be more positive in its response to the Rogers Plan, warned that increased Soviet arms shipments would draw the major powers more deeply into the conflict, and also proposed U.S.–Soviet discussions on limiting arms supplies to the Middle East. [13] Meanwhile, he continued to postpone responding to Israel's requests for new jet aircraft deliveries. But in the spring of 1970 the deterioration was advancing too rapidly both on the superpower level and on Israel's border to be arrested by benign pleas for cooperation. In April U.S. and Israeli intelligence sources were picking up signs not only that the Soviets were accelerating their deliveries of SAMs, supersonic jets, and tanks to Egypt but also that Russian military personnel were beginning to man some of the SAM sites and fly some of the planes. Nixon ordered a full investigation of the expanding Soviet role and quietly stepped up the flow of U.S. military supplies to Israel; but he still held back on approving delivery of the supersonic planes that the Israelis were now urgently demanding. [14]

As the situation along the Suez became more threatening to Israel, Nixon played on Israeli entreaties for a more forthcoming U.S. response to its military equipment requirements by asking the Israelis to exhibit more flexibility in their terms for a settlement. At the end of May, Prime Minister Meir reiterated Israel's acceptance of Resolution 242 and agreed that it should be the basis of indirect talks between Israel and the UAR. Washington next pressed for an Arab–Israeli cease-fire while talks between the Israelis and Egyptians were conducted under the auspices of UN Special Ambassador Gunnar Jarring. To overcome Israeli fears that a cease-fire would only be exploited by the Russians and Arabs to further strengthen

Arab military capabilities, Nixon assured Meir that the United States would continue its arms deliveries at whatever level was needed to prevent a shift in the local balance of power; to that end, in early July he authorized the shipment of electronic-countermeasure (ECM) equipment for Israeli jets to help Israel overcome the Soviet SAMs in the canal zone.[15]

The Israelis were not at all pleased with these marginalist and temporizing responses to their requests for decisive U.S. diplomatic and military backing at a time, as they saw it, of increasing peril to their very existence. And they continued to express deep skepticism about Arab motives in any cease-fire. The Israelis feared that the Arabs would use the cease-fire not, as the Americans hoped, as a transition to a negotiated peace but, rather, as additional time for completing their military buildup while forestalling a major new round of U.S. military supplies to Israel.

The strongest statement of American intentions during this period came from Kissinger in a June 26 background briefing at San Clemente. "We are trying to get a settlement in such a way that the moderate regimes are strengthened, and not the radical regimes," he told a group of newspaper editors. "We are trying to *expel* the Soviet military presence, not so much the advisers, but the combat pilots and combat personnel, before they become so firmly established."[16]

Egypt was the first to accept the American cease-fire proposal— on July 22, 1970, more than a month after Rogers proposed it. Jordan accepted on July 26. Israel reluctantly acquiesced on August 6. August 7 marked the first day of the cease-fire, which was supposed to last three months and to include a military standstill in a zone thirty-two miles wide on each side of the Suez Canal.

When the Israelis almost immediately began to report Egyptian violations of the truce, in the form of a continuing movement of SAM batteries into the standstill zone, the State Department was unimpressed and characterized the Israeli evidence as "inconclusive." But U.S. reconnaissance flights soon confirmed that the Egyptians were indeed systematically introducing new missile launchers into the prohibited area. On August 22 the administration informed the Soviet Union and Egypt that it had "incontrovertible evidence" of the violations, and it followed this up on September 3 by presenting the Russians and the Egyptians with evidence that at least fourteen missile sites had been modified between August 15 and August 27.[17]

Nixon now decided to sell Israel at least eighteen of the F-4 supersonic aircraft it had requested. He also ordered rush deliveries to Israel of the latest ECM equipment and conventional Shrike air-to-ground missiles so that the Israeli Air Force could neutralize the SAMs.

At least as important as the resumption of a major flow of U.S. military supplies to Israel was the impact of the Russian–Egyptian violations of the canal zone truce on the Nixon administration's general policy. At Kissinger's urging, and over the objections of Secretary of State Rogers, there was now a decided tilt toward the Israelis, and a new sympathy for the Meir government's reluctance to make territorial concessions in advance of public and tangible commitments from Egypt indicating plans to live in peace with the Jewish state. Nixon and Kissinger also were freshly determined to reduce Soviet influence over the Arabs and were on the lookout for opportunities to demonstrate American coercive power in the region. Such an opportunity came somewhat sooner than expected.[18]

THE JORDAN CRISIS

September 1970 was the month of maximum trauma for King Hussein, and the situation in Jordan presented Nixon and Kissinger with their first full-blown Middle Eastern crisis.

King Hussein was not only the most pro-Western of Arab leaders but also the most cooperative when it came to working for a compromise Arab–Israeli peace. As a consequence he was on the enemies list of the militant anti-Israelis in the region, particularly the Palestinian commando organizations that wanted to use Jordan's western border areas as a staging ground for raids into Israel. Moreover, many of the radical Palestinians living in Jordan were determined to destroy the Hussein regime and make Jordan the center of their drive to regain the Palestinian lands now controlled by Israel and to push the Jews into the sea.

On September 6, members of the Popular Front for the Liberation of Palestine (PFLP) hijacked a TWA plane and a Swissair plane and forced them to land on an airstrip in Jordan twenty-five miles from the capital, Amman. A third airliner was captured and flown to Cairo, where its passengers were unloaded just before the plane was blown up. Still another plane, a BOAC jet, was hijacked the next day and also flown to the Jordanian airstrip, giving the PFLP a total of 475 hostages, many of them Americans, in Jordan. The hijackers threatened to blow up the three planes with their passengers aboard unless all Palestinian and pro-Palestinian prisoners in Israel, West Germany, Britain, and Switzerland were released. Beyond this ostensible purpose, the PFLP motive seemed to be to humiliate the Jordan monarchy, paving the way for a Palestinian takeover of the government in Amman. King Hussein was in a double bind: if he failed to move decisively, the Jordanian army might take matters into its own hands, thereby undercutting his authority. Yet he was reluctant to order the army to storm the airstrip, apparently not so much out of fear that the hostages would be killed as out of anxiety that Syria or Iraq might move forces into Jordan on behalf of the Palestinians.[19]

Hussein's dilemma, however, meshed with Nixon's determination to show resolve and to inject the United States more directly into the Middle East scene as a counter to the increasing Soviet participation. U.S. paratroopers of the 82d Airborne Division were placed on semialert status; a fleet of C-130 air transports was dispatched to Turkey under an escort of F-4 jet fighters for possible use in evacuating the Americans from Jordan; and units of the Mediterranean Sixth Fleet were ordered to sail toward the coasts of Israel and Lebanon.

On September 12, six days after the hijacking began, the PFLP transferred the hostages to some of their camps and blew up the three empty planes. In exchange for an Israeli agreement to release 450 Palestinian prisoners, the hijackers began releasing the hostages but continued temporarily to hold 55 Jewish passengers.[20]

Three days later what had started out as an extortionary ploy exploded into a raging international crisis with the risk of a direct U.S.–Soviet clash. While holding the hostages in the desert, the PFLP stepped up terrorist attacks against the royal forces. On September 15 the King replaced his civilian officials with a military government, signaling his decision to move in force against the guerrilla strongholds. Jordan was now in a state of civil war.

The immediate question in Washington was whether Syria and

Iraq would intervene. The intelligence community tended to discount the likelihood of such intervention, but Nixon spoke and acted as if he considered it imminent. On September 16, in an off-the-record briefing to a group of Midwestern newspaper editors, he said that the United States might have to intervene if Syria or Iraq threatened Hussein. The *Chicago Sun Times* published some of the President's remarks and, surprisingly, was complimented by Nixon for breaking the ground rules. Clearly, Nixon wanted his implied warning to be picked up not only in Arab capitals but also in Moscow. Similar intense concern and hints of U.S. involvement were expressed by Kissinger and Assistant Secretary of State Sisco in background briefings that the press could attribute to "administration officials." [21] The verbal signaling was underscored by a set of military decisions: the aircraft carrier *John F. Kennedy* was ordered into the Mediterranean and the helicopter carrier *Guam,* loaded with 1500 marines, dispatched from Norfolk, Virginia, in the direction of the Middle East. Nixon also authorized half a billion dollars in military aid for Israel and an acceleration of fighter aircraft deliveries. [22]

Nixon recollects his considerations at the time as follows:

We would not allow Hussein to be overthrown by a Soviet-inspired insurrection. If it succeeded, the entire Middle East might erupt in war; the Israelis would almost certainly take pre-emptive measures against a Syrian-dominated radical government in Jordan; the Egyptians were tied to Syria by military alliances; and Soviet prestige was on the line with both Syria and the Egyptians. Since the United States could not stand idly by and watch Israel driven into the sea, the possibility of a direct U.S.–Soviet confrontation was uncomfortably high. It was like a ghastly game of dominoes, with a nuclear war waiting at the end. [23]

On September 18 Kissinger was informed by both the Israeli Ambassador, Yitzhak Rabin, and the Jordanian Ambassador, Abdul Hamis Sharaf, that some Syrian tanks had crossed into Jordan and were headed toward the city of Irbid. Kissinger had Sisco check with the Russians, who offered their assurances that the Syrians had not invaded Jordan. And the State Department received a communication from Moscow telling of the Kremlin's efforts to prevent any outside intervention by Jordan's neighbors.

The next day the White House received firmer evidence that the Syrians had indeed invaded, and it was not a small probe. Some hundreds of tanks were now rolling toward Irbid. Kissinger is reported to have been furious at the Russians for attempting to deceive him and the President. The Kremlin must have been aware of what was happening and perhaps had even urged the Syrians on, for Syrian tank units were known to have Soviet military advisers. Having spent a good part of the day presiding over an emergency meeting of the Washington Special Action Group in the White House Situation Room, Kissinger reported on the fast-breaking crisis to the President and recommended an alert of American forces. Nixon agreed and ordered a selective alert of American troops in the United States and Western Europe. The alert included the 82d Airborne Division at Fort Bragg and U.S. airborne units in West Germany— the latter crossing the Autobahn conspicuously on their way to the airfields. "We wanted to get picked up" by Soviet intelligence, Kissinger later told the Kalb brothers. The Sixth Fleet was also augmented, and the ships with Marine Corps fighting units aboard steamed ominously toward the coasts of Israel and Lebanon. These military moves were coupled with U.S. warnings to the Russians that if the Syrians did not withdraw from Jordan the Israelis might intervene and the United States itself might not be able to stay out.[24]

On September 20 and 21, the Syrians continued to pour military forces into Jordan. Either the U.S. countermoves had not registered or Damascus, with Moscow's backing, had determined that the Americans were bluffing. But in truth Nixon and Kissinger were deadly serious. The crisis edged further toward the brink of major international war as King Hussein requested Israeli air support and the Israelis in turn asked for U.S. protection in the event that such Israeli intervention provoked an Egyptian/Russian counterintervention. Additional U.S. military forces in Germany were placed on alert, and transport planes were readied to airlift them to the Middle East. The augmented Sixth Fleet moved in closer. As an indicator of U.S.–Israeli coordination, a small U.S. intelligence aircraft flew back and forth between the advance naval units and Tel Aviv, with the Russians obviously watching.

Finally, the Israelis and Jordanians got the presidential decisions they were waiting for: if Israel were attacked by Egyptian and Soviet forces in response to its military help to King Hussein, the United States would itself intervene militarily to oppose them. On September 22, emboldened by confidence that Israel would indeed join the battle and would be backed by the United States, Hussein threw his own ground and air forces fully against the Syrians. The crisis suddenly broke. Syrian tanks began turning around and moving back toward Syria. [25]

Triumphant, Nixon flew to Rome a few days later and spent a night on the aircraft carrier *Saratoga* in the Mediterranean to symbolize his renewed pride in the potency of American military power as a diplomatic instrument. Kissinger—prudently—did not share the limelight.

From their management of the Jordan crisis, Nixon and Kissinger apparently drew some lessons for the conduct of their subsequent Middle Eastern policy—lessons that turned them away from the evenhandedness associated with the Rogers Plan and back toward the more openly pro-Israel diplomacy of previous administrations. Indeed, until the 1973 Yom Kippur War and Arab oil embargo compelled them once again to reexamine the basic assumptions of this policy, Israel was treated as a virtual ally (along with Jordan, Iran, and Saudi Arabia) against a coalition of pro-Soviet states including Egypt, Syria, Iraq, and Libya. During this period, while the global pattern of international alignments was loosening under détente and rapid socioeconomic and political change was undermining any such simplistic division of the Middle East, the Nixon administration rather complacently trusted to regional polarization, backed up by Israeli and Iranian military superiority, to stabilize the area. Indications of divisions in the regional pro-Soviet coalition—most notably the decision of Anwar Sadat to expel some 10,000 Soviet military advisers from Egypt in July 1972—were seen not as evidence of the anachronism of the regional bipolar balance of power but, rather, as evidence of its success: Sadat was regarded as increasingly frustrated at the insufficient support he was getting from the Russians, who were presumably wary of backing him in further military adventures, given the new solidity of the U.S.–Israel political and military relationship.

THE YOM KIPPUR WAR

"The news of the imminent attack on Israel took us completely by surprise," recalls Nixon. [26] This admission itself would not be surprising if it simply referred to the jarring effect the news had on

Nixon personally. For the President was already up to his neck in the Watergate tapes by the morning of October 6, 1973, and was also trying to decide how to handle the legal charges of corruption being brought against Vice President Spiro Agnew. But the surprise went deeper, reflecting a massive intelligence failure in the U.S. government, which in turn was caused less by lack of hard information on the preparatory moves of Egypt and its allies than by the assumptions through which Kissinger and Nixon had processed all information coming out of the Middle East since 1970.

At the height of the crisis, Kissinger made a most revealing comment about the failure of both Israeli and U.S. intelligence (and therefore his own failure) to spot what was about to take place:

Nobody made any mistakes about the facts. There are always two aspects to intelligence. One is a determination of the facts; the other is the interpretation of these facts. And there is the tendency of most intelligence services—and indeed most senior officials and indeed of some newspapermen—to fit the facts into existing preconceptions and to make them consistent with what is anticipated. And if you start from the assumption that a war is probably unlikely—if you know that there have been Egyptian maneuvers every September over the last 10 years—then there is probably a tendency to make observed facts fit your preconceived theories.
. . .
   Over the years that I have been in this position, the possibility of a massive Arab attack was not considered among the most likely by any of the evaluators that I have talked to.[27]

The administration's bedrock assumption was that war was a wholly unattractive alternative to the Egyptians as long as Israel maintained effective superiority and there was a good prospect that it would return the occupied territories as a result of international political pressure. Egypt and Syria might threaten war from time to time, but this was only a ploy to intensify the international pressure on Israel to make concessions.

The premises may have been correct; but even so, they begged the question of how Egypt might assess the pertinent military balance at any time, which would include its judgments about the willingness of other countries to come to the aid of the belligerents in case of war. They also left as a variable the *degree* of Egyptian optimism concerning Israel's willingness to part with territory. In the final analysis the probability of a new Mideast war was to a large extent determined by highly subjective Egyptian judgments that could shift in response to the dynamic political and military situation.

Another unstable variable was Soviet policy. Kissinger and Nixon, however, assumed that the Soviets were firmly opposed to a new round of war between the Arabs and the Israelis. The Kremlin might still be attempting to gain influence among the Arabs from a no-war-no-peace situation, but a hot war could draw in the USSR and the United States on opposite sides, and this might spell the end of détente. Brezhnev was thought to have too much at stake in détente to put it at risk on behalf of his Middle Eastern clients. And being the military supplier of Egypt and Syria, he was in a position to pull the reins on any reckless action they might contemplate. The possibility that Soviet policy might be catalyzed by indigenous Middle Eastern factors, rather than the other way around, was presumably discounted in the White House, as was the possibility that the Soviet leaders might be so confident about the durability of the détente relationship in arms control and commerce that they could countenance a war between the Middle Eastern clients of the two superpowers.

Thus, it was the general orientation of those at the highest levels of the U.S. government that was responsible for the misreading and underweighting of a series of specific developments that, in retrospect, look like inexorable moves toward the October 1973 war: [28]

—On November 14, 1972, Anwar Sadat promised the Higher Council of his Arab Socialist Union party that Egypt would attack Israel sometime within the coming twelve months.

—During the winter of 1972–73, Egypt and the USSR seemed to be repairing their rift, which had led Sadat to expel all Soviet military advisers and experts the previous July and to place all Soviet bases and equipment in Egypt under exclusive Egyptian control. Egypt now invited back several hundred Soviet military advisers and allowed the Russians once again to use military facilities in Egypt. In return, Brezhnev agreed to substantially increase the flow of Soviet military equipment to Egypt, this time apparently in some categories that he was reluctant to include earlier, such as the advanced SAM-6 mobile antiaircraft missile. The deliveries also included bridge-building equipment.

—In the spring Sadat began a series of intensive consultations with King Faisal of Saudi Arabia, who in recent months had been hinting strongly that he was ready to use his oil assets as a political weapon against the friends of Israel, and with President Hafez Assad of Syria, the most prominent war hawk in the Arab camp.

—In June reports reached Washington of a massive acceleration of Russian arms deliveries to Syria, including late-model T-62 tanks, sophisticated antitank missiles, SAMs, and MIG-21 fighters.

—In the second week of September, King Hussein of Jordan flew to Cairo for a summit meeting with Sadat and Assad. Reports on the meeting indicated that war contingencies were discussed.

—During the last week of September, CIA reports to Kissinger spotlighted a number of unusual Egyptian, Syrian, and Soviet military movements. The annual Egyptian military maneuvers (which Kissinger later mentioned in his October 12 news conference) were being conducted with full divisions of Egyptian troops this time. Not only were the Egyptians stockpiling more ammunition and logistical support than ever before; they were also setting up a field communications network more complicated than mere maneuvers would require. The CIA analysts pointed to simultaneous suspicious deployments of Syrian tanks out of their normal defensive formations. U.S. surveillance also detected three Soviet freighters on their way to Egypt, possibly loaded with surface-to-surface missiles that could hit Israeli cities from Egyptian territory. Similar ominous movements were picked up by Israeli intelligence sources.

Then, suddenly, a Palestinian terrorist ambush of Soviet Jews headed through Austria for Israel made Kissinger jittery. He expressed great concern that the Israeli government—outraged and frustrated at the Austrian Chancellor's capitulation to the terrorists' demand that in return for releasing the hostages Austria close some facilities it had made available to transiting Jewish emigrés—might retaliate by attacking Palestinian camps throughout the Arab Middle East. This, Kissinger feared, could set off a cycle of violence that could expand quickly into all-out war; and he warned the Israeli Ambassador of the consequences.

As reports poured in on the intense military posturing now being undertaken by the potential belligerents, Kissinger feared, above all, a major Israeli preemptive strike, in the mode of its lightning raids at the outset of the 1967 war, to hobble the Syrian and Egyptian war machines; but Israeli officials assured him they were not going to strike first this time. The Secretary of State still refused to believe that Egypt and its allies might be planning to start a war as a deliberate act of policy. Even when Kissinger was informed on the night of October 4 that Russian dependents were being evacuated from Cairo and Damascus, he preferred to interpret the event as perhaps another indication of difficulties between the Soviets and their Arab hosts. His intelligence advisers, while disagreeing with this interpretation, still were not ready to predict war.

During the 48 hours preceding hostilities, with evidence from various sources confirming that the Syrian and Egyptian forward armored units were swinging into offensive formations, Kissinger received further assurances from Foreign Minister Abba Eban on the phone that Israel would not preempt. The American Ambassador to Israel, Kenneth Keating, allegedly underscored Kissinger's views in warning his hosts that only if there was irrefutable proof that the Arabs were the aggressors would the United States consider itself morally obligated to help the Israelis.[29] In his memoirs, Kissinger denies the allegation, by Golda Meir among others, that the United States brought great pressure against the Israelis not to preempt in October 1973. He admits having expressed the view in years past to Israeli officials that U.S. support would be impaired if Israel struck first. But as the Yom Kippur War approached, insists Kissinger, all the statements forswearing preemption were initiated by the Israelis themselves.[30]

Regardless of the exact nature of the intense conversations between American and Israeli officials on the eve of the Yom Kippur War, Prime Minister Meir evidently believed that if Israel struck a preemptive blow, it would have to fight alone; and, therefore, against the advice of the Israeli Chief of Staff, she decided to allow her country to accept the first blows. The Arabs struck massively and simultaneously from Syria in the north and Egypt in the south on Yom Kippur morning, October 6, while many Israelis were attending religious services. It was a well-planned, well-coordinated, and efficiently executed attack.

The immediate physical losses suffered by Israel for letting the Arabs strike first were large; but the ultimate gain was presumably of larger significance: namely, a clear moral claim on the United States for support of Israel as a victim of aggression. As it turned out, however, this moral claim had less currency in the White House than the Israelis had been led to believe.

The U.S. leaders, as should have been expected, would always put their own priorities first, and the resumption of hostilities once again made it plain that these were (1) to avoid a major war between the United States and the Soviet Union; (2) to ensure the survival of Israel (Nixon's and Kissinger's sentiments apart, they knew that it would be political suicide to allow Israel to be destroyed); (3) to prevent the Soviet Union from exploiting the conflict to enlarge its influence in the Middle East; and (4) to conduct U.S. diplomacy in the region in such a way as to enhance the regional and global prestige of the United States and to increase domestic support for the Nixon administration. None of these interests required unequivocal U.S. support for Israel's war aims or the underwriting of its military strategy. Rather, Nixon and Kissinger, in reassessing the new situation brought about by the onset of war, seemed—to the shock and dismay of the Israelis—to be moving back to the evenhanded approach they had flirted with prior to the 1970 Jordanian crisis.

The White House made no public condemnation during the 1973 war of either the Arabs or the Soviet Union. Kissinger articulated the objective of U.S. crisis diplomacy as follows:

First, to end hostilities as quickly as possible—but secondly, to end hostilities in a manner that would enable us to make a major contribution to removing the conditions that have produced four wars between Arabs and Israelis in the last 25 years.

We were aware that there were many interested parties. There were, of course, the participants in the conflict—Egypt and Syria on the Arab side, aided by many other Arab countries; Israel on the other. There was the Soviet Union. There were the other permanent members of the Security Council. . . .

It was our view that the United States could be most effective in both . . . tasks . . . if we conducted ourselves so that we could remain in permanent contact with all of these elements in the equation. . . .

Our position is . . . that the conditions that produced this war were clearly intolerable to the Arab nations and that in a process of negotiations it will be necessary [for all sides] to make substantial concessions.

The problem will be to relate the Arab concern for the sovereignty over territories to the Israeli concern for secure boundaries. . . .

We will make a major effort to bring about a solution that is considered just by all parties.[31]

Another premise—not publicly articulated—was that these objectives could not be attained if either side achieved a clear military victory in the hostilities. It was Kissinger's apparent adoption of this premise, particularly where it looked as if the Israelis might be attempting to conquer more territory than they obtained in 1967, that made him look anti-Israeli to many Israelis and their friends—not to mention the reputation he had gained with many Americans for perfidy and duplicity. Indeed, much of Kissinger's most controversial behavior—his procrastination in moving military supplies to Israel, the timing of his demands for a cease-fire-in-place, and especially his pressures on the Israelis to free the surrounded Egyptian Third Army—would seem fickle, if not irrational, without this premise.[32]

The most detailed account (other than Kissinger's own) of the considerations Kissinger brought to bear on the crucial decisions of the U.S. government during the 1973 war is provided by William Quandt. A member of the National Security Council staff, Quandt attended most of the Washington Special Action Group (WSAG) meetings that Kissinger used as the basic sounding board for exploring and choosing among his options. (The October 1973 crisis was managed in detail by Kissinger on behalf of the President, who was increasingly preoccupied by his personal crisis over Watergate.)

According to Quandt, at the outbreak of hostilities Kissinger expected a short war in which Israel would prevail. He was worried, however, that if the Israelis once again began to humiliate the Arabs the Soviets would find it difficult to stay out. Urgent diplomatic initiatives therefore were required to ensure that a cease-fire was reestablished on the basis of the territorial status quo prevailing before October 6. The cooperation of the Soviets would be essential in getting the Arabs to return to the status quo ante, so it was of vital importance that the Soviets understand that the United States would not countenance any new Israeli territorial expansion. Accordingly, Nixon sent Brezhnev a letter urging mutual restraint and the convening of the UN Security Council, while Kissinger pressed the case with his counterparts in the Soviet Union, Egypt, and Israel for a cease-fire based on the status quo ante. Otherwise, however, the United States kept a low profile during the first few days of the war.

Egypt and Syria, with major military units still in the territory they wished to reconquer, were not ready to accede to the cease-fire proposal. Kissinger was confident, however, that once the tide of battle turned against the Arabs they would change their tune, especially if Israel began to cross the canal into Egypt and move beyond the Golan Heights in Syria.

Between the third and sixth days of the war, the WSAG's assessments of the military prospects changed. Israel was finding it difficult to turn back the Arab assault. Suffering heavy losses of aircraft, the Israelis urgently appealed for more American arms and were informed that additional shipments had been approved, including a number of Phantom jets that would soon be on their way. It became impossible to ascertain who was gaining the upper hand as the Israelis launched a smashing counteroffensive on the Syrian front and began bombing Damascus. Assad and Sadat were putting great pressure on King Hussein of Jordan to open up a third front against Israel.

Kissinger's response to the rapidly developing military situation was to call for a cease-fire-*in-place*. Golda Meir immediately refused this revised proposal, insisting that any cease-fire must be tied to the restoration of the territorial dispositions prevailing before Yom Kippur. Sadat was cool to the Kissinger proposal, demanding concrete Israeli commitments to relinquish all land captured in 1967 as the condition for a cease-fire. The Russians, while not rejecting the cease-fire, and indicating willingness to cooperate with the United States on the diplomatic front, now began a major airlift of arms to the Syrians.

The Israelis pressed their case for accelerated U.S. arms deliveries with greater persistence. Kissinger seemed uncharacteristically slow in responding to the Israeli entreaties, and cited Defense Department objections to a massive resupply effort. Quandt suggests that the temporizing on the Israeli arms requests was consistent with the Kissinger strategy of (1) not having the United States emerge as Israel's ally in opposition to the Arabs and (2) pressuring the Israelis to accept a cease-fire-in-place. Kissinger, however, has denied any deliberate witholding of supplies to Israel for either purpose.[33]

Meanwhile, the shifting fortunes of the belligerents in the war itself were producing a shift in their attitudes toward a cease-fire-in-place. To the Israelis, who were once again on the military offensive and hopeful of more than regaining their lost ground, the idea began to look more attractive, especially if its actual implementation could be delayed for a few days, while to the Arabs it began to look more and more like a trap. On October 12 the Israeli government, still bargaining hard for maximum assurances of American arms supplies, accepted the principle of a cease-fire-in-place. Now it was Sadat who was unequivocally opposed.

Kissinger and Nixon, frustrated by the Egyptian leader's rejection of a cease-fire-in-place, suspecting that the Soviets were encourag-

ing him to dig in his heels, and feeling the need to counter the
Soviet airlift of supplies to Syria, were determined to change the
Soviet—Arab calculations of gains from allowing the war to continue.
Nixon authorized an acceleration and expansion of the delivery of
Phantoms and ordered the U.S. military to fly the aircraft and other
equipment directly into Israel. The principal purpose was to demonstrate to Sadat and the Kremlin that any prolongation of the war
could not possibly operate to the military advantage of the Arabs—
despite the flow of Soviet arms, which the United States could easily match. Nor could it be to their political advantage, for it would
make it more difficult for the United States to convince Israeli hawks
that the Arabs were sincerely interested in an equitable peace. A
collateral purpose undoubtedly was to show the Russians, once again,
that they would only be embarrassed if they attempted unilaterally
to change the balance of military power in the Middle East.

With the American airlift under way, the Israelis launched into
their climactic hard-driving offensive on both fronts. The Syrians
were decisively thrown off the Golan Heights and pushed back along
the Damascus road. To the south the Israeli troops crossed over to
the West Bank of the Suez Canal in a maneuver designed to encircle the Egyptian troops still in the Sinai peninsula and cut off their
line of retreat back over the canal into Egypt. In a matter of days,
Israel was decisively in control of the military situation around its
extended borders. Now it was the Russians who sent out anxious
calls for a cease-fire.

Brezhnev invited Kissinger to come to Moscow for "urgent consultations." The moment for a cease-fire might have arrived. Kissinger's premise that it would be counterproductive for the Israelis to
humiliate the Arabs had not altered. He left for Moscow on October
20 with his bargaining position strengthened by a presidential request to Congress for $2.2 billion in emergency military aid for Is-
rael.

While en route to Moscow, however, Kissinger received the news
of the momentous Saudi Arabian decision to embargo oil shipments
to the United States. Not only were the relative bargaining weights
on each side of the Arab—Israeli conflict changed thereby, but, as
Kissinger was to discover in the months and years ahead (see chapter 25), so was the overall world power equation out of which Kissinger had fashioned his realpolitik concepts.

The Kissinger—Brezhnev meeting in Moscow on October 21 produced an agreed-upon superpower approach to an Arab–Israeli truce: a cease-fire resolution, to be presented to the UN Security Council, that would call for a simple cease-fire-in-place and negotiations between the parties; and an eventual peace conference, to be chaired by both the United States and the Soviet Union. In effect, the superpowers were agreeing to act jointly to compel their respective clients to stop the fighting.

Despite the Israeli government's protest that it was not adequately consulted, the United States joined the Soviet Union in presenting their agreed-upon text of a cease-fire resolution to the United Nations the very next morning. And after less than three hours' deliberation by the Security Council, Resolution 338 was adopted by a vote of 14 to 0 (China did not vote). The October 22 resolution was a brief but specific statement:

The Security Council:

1. *Calls upon* all parties to the present fighting to cease all firing and terminate all military activity immediately, no later than 12 hours after the moment of the adoption of this decision, in the positions they now occupy;

2. *Calls upon* the parties concerned to start immediately after the cease-fire the implementation of Security Council resolution 242 (1967) in all of its parts;

3. *Decides* that, immediately and concurrently with the cease-fire, negotiations start between the parties concerned under appropriate auspices aimed at establishing a just and durable peace in the Middle East.[34]

The parties stopped shooting six hours after the Security Council passed its resolution, but not without some arm-twisting by both superpowers. Neither Israel nor Egypt was in a position to object too strongly. Israel was now in military control of more territory than before the war started, and thus was in a strong bargaining position. Egypt was reeling from the Israeli counteroffensive and would probably lose even more ground if a cease-fire were delayed any longer. Syria, too, recognized the new realities and accepted the cease-fire the next day.

Almost immediately after the formal cessation, however, there were charges and countercharges of violations of the truce. Who was responsible was of less concern to Kissinger, however, than the fact that the Israelis were exploiting the opportunity to extend their lines on the Egyptian side of the canal, putting them in a position to capture the city of Suez and completely encircle the 100,000-man Egyptian Third Army Corps.

The new Israeli military thrusts and their noose-tightening around the surrounded Egyptian Third Army precipitated a new crisis for Kissinger as the Soviets indicated an intention to intervene directly with their own forces to enforce the cease-fire. Kissinger's response—one of the most daring of his career—was to threaten counteraction against both the Israelis and the Russians. He would show the Russians that the United States could yet control the Israelis and that therefore Soviet intervention was unnecessary to prevent total humiliation of the Arabs; and he would show the Israelis (and the rest of the world) that the United States still had the will and the power to deter a direct Soviet intervention, but only if the Israelis themselves acted with reasonable restraint.

Kissinger's reasons for insisting on Israeli restraint went beyond the imperative of preventing Soviet intervention. Now, with the Arab oil embargo in effect, it was more than ever important for the United States to demonstrate the capacity to separate itself from the more extreme Israeli actions and to act as an honest broker in the region on behalf of an equitable peace. Accordingly, Kissinger had resolved to at least prevent the Israelis from strangling the Egyptian Third Army Corps, even before the Soviets threatened to intervene.[35] After the Soviet intervention had been deterred, Kissinger insisted that, at a minimum, the Israelis permit humanitarian convoys of food, water, and medical supplies to reach the surrounded Egyptian soldiers. He hinted that if the Israelis attempted to prevent this, the United States would itself convoy the supplies and threatened to vote in favor of an anti-Israeli resolution the Arabs had introduced in the UN Security Council. Still the Israelis were not about to give up their advantage. The impasse was finally overcome by Sadat's acceptance of direct military talks between Israeli and Egyptian generals at kilometer 101 on the Cairo–Suez road to implement U.N. disengagement resolutions—this in exchange for Israel's permission of a nonmilitary convoy to bring supplies to the Egyptian Third Army under UN and Red Cross supervision.[36]

The threat of Soviet intervention had emerged obliquely. On October 24 President Sadat appealed to the United States and the Soviet Union to send a joint U.S.–Soviet peacekeeping force to police the cease-fire. Kissinger immediately rejected the idea. Soviet troops in the Middle East could only spell additional trouble, with or without a U.S. counterpresence. That night Ambassador Dobrynin phoned Kissinger with a "very urgent" message from Secretary Gen-

eral Brezhnev to President Nixon–so urgent, said Dobrynin, that he
must read it over the phone to Kissinger. "Let us act together," said
Brezhnev, and "urgently dispatch Soviet and American contingents
to Egypt" in order to "compel the observance of the cease-fire without delay." The Soviet leader also went beyond the Sadat proposal
with a threat that Nixon later described as the most serious to U.S.–
Soviet relations since the Cuban missile crisis: "I will say it straight,"
Brezhnev warned, "that if you find it impossible to act together with
us in this matter, we should be faced with the necessity urgently to
consider the question of taking appropriate steps unilaterally. Israel
cannot be allowed to get away with the violations." [37]

U.S. intelligence agencies meanwhile were picking up signs of
Soviet military movements—"a plethora of indicators," according to
Secretary of Defense Schlesinger, that Soviet airborne divisions in
southern Russia and Hungary had been placed on alert. More Soviet
ships had entered the Mediterranean, and some unconfirmed reports suggested that they might be carrying nuclear warheads for
the missiles sent to Egypt earlier in the year. [38]

While unsure of what the Soviets were really up to—was it a
symbolic show of resolve? a bluff? an actual deployment of major
military units?—Kissinger acted swiftly to put the Kremlin on notice that any unilateral introduction of Soviet military force into the
area at this time would risk a dangerous confrontation with the
United States. A toughly worded presidential rejection of Brezhnev's proposals and demands was conveyed to the Kremlin. U.S.
forces around the world were put on an intermediate DEFCON
(defense condition) level, bringing the Strategic Air Command and
other units to a higher-than-normal state of readiness. The 82d Airborne Division was prepared for possible dispatch. And the aircraft
carriers *Franklin Delano Roosevelt* and *John F. Kennedy* were ordered
to move to the eastern Mediterranean.

The administration's momentous decisions on the night of October 24–25, involving the possibility of a direct military clash between the two superpowers, were made by Secretary of State Kissinger, Secretary of Defense James Schlesinger, and other *nonelected*
officials of the U.S. government. The President, emotionally consumed by the Watergate investigations, was indisposed or sleeping,
and the office of Vice President, in the interregnum between Spiro
Agnew's resignation and Gerald Ford's confirmation by the Senate,

was vacant. (Kissinger asked General Alexander Haig at 9:50 P.M. whether the President should have been awakened. The answer was negative: "Haig thought the President too distraught. . . . From my own conversation with Nixon earlier in the evening, I was convinced Haig was right.")[39]

Kissinger, still functioning also in his capacity as presidential assistant for national security affairs, convened the Washington Special Action Group to deliberate with him and Schlesinger in the White House Situation Room between 10:40 P.M. until 2 A.M. and to provide top-level unanimity for decisions taken in the President's name. The attendees included the Director of Central Intelligence, William Colby; Chairman of the Joint Chiefs of Staff, Admiral Moorer; presidential chief of staff Alexander Haig; deputy assistant to the President for national security affairs, Brent Scowcroft; and Kissinger's military assistant at the National Security Council, Commander John T. Howe. But for the absence of the President and Vice President, the group comprised the full statutory membership of the National Security Council. In chairing this crisis management group and making the key force-deployment and diplomatic decisions, Kissinger was, in effect, acting President. "It was a daunting responsibility to assume," he recalls.[40]

President Nixon's message to Brezhnev (which Nixon himself did not see until after it was sent) expressed some openness to the idea of having some American and Soviet noncombat personnel go into the area as part of an augmented UN observation team, but it categorically rejected "your proposal for a particular kind of action, that of sending Soviet and American military contingents to Egypt. It is clear," said the presidential reply, "that the forces necessary to impose the cease-fire terms on the two sides would be massive and would require the closest coordination so as to avoid bloodshed. This is not only clearly infeasible, but it is not appropriate to the situation." Moreover, "you must know . . . that we could in no event accept unilateral action. . . . Such action would produce incalculable consequences which would be in the interest of neither of our countries and which would end all we have striven so hard to achieve."[41]

In his October 25 press conference, Kissinger insisted that "we do not consider ourselves in a confrontation with the Soviet Union.

We do not believe it is necessary, at this moment, to have a confrontation. In fact, we are prepared to work cooperatively [with them]. . . . But cooperative action precludes unilateral action, and the President decided that it was essential that we make clear our attitude toward unilateral steps."[42]

CBS correspondent Marvin Kalb asked the Secretary of State whether the American alert might have been prompted as much by American domestic requirements as by the diplomatic requirements of the Middle Eastern situation—implying that the Nixon administration, reeling from the Watergate affair, needed its own "missile crisis" to reestablish its prestige with the American electorate. Kissinger's response was angry and defensive: "We are attempting to conduct the foreign policy of the United States with regard for what we owe not to the electorate but to future generations. And it is a symptom of what is happening in our country that it could even be suggested that the United States would alert its forces for domestic reasons." He was absolutely confident, said Kissinger, that when the record was finally made available it would show that "the President had no other choice as a responsible national leader."[43]

An hour after Kissinger's press conference, the Soviet Union joined the United States and the other members of the Security Council in voting affirmatively for Resolution 340, demanding an immediate and complete cease-fire and a return to the positions occupied by the belligerents prior to the recent round of violations, and setting up a UN emergency force composed of nonpermanent members of the Security Council (thus excluding the USSR and the United States) to oversee the cease-fire.[44] The guns fell silent on the Middle Eastern battlefields, and an intricate set of negotiations commenced to separate the forces, return prisoners of war, establish enforceable truce zones, and begin the long process toward an agreed-upon settlement of the underlying Arab–Israeli conflict.

Historians will long debate whether Kissinger played his cards with consummate skill or whether he (and the world) were miraculously lucky to have avoided World War III. Kissinger did, however, establish convincingly that he was neither pro-Israeli nor pro-Arab but genuinely of the conviction that vital U.S. interests required a durable Middle Eastern peace, and that this had to be based on specific political arrangements acceptable to all parties plus a local military equilibrium. This now-secured reputation served him well in the activist-mediator role that became the essence of his subsequent Middle East diplomacy.

KISSINGER'S NEW MIDDLE EAST DIPLOMACY

The brink of war, like the hangman's noose, disciplines the statesman's mind. Out of his practical experience in terminating the 1973 war, more than out of his realpolitik concepts, Kissinger finally put together a sophisticated Middle East policy for the United States that corresponded more closely to the complexity and volatility of the area than the administration's diplomacy following the Jordan crisis.

The code term for Kissinger's new Middle East diplomacy became "step by step"—a reference to Kissinger's method of (1) getting Egypt and Israel to disengage their forces in January 1974 from the dangerous overlapping dispositions in which they were left at the ceasefire the previous October; (2) getting Syria and Israel to reestablish a narrow demilitarized buffer zone between them in May 1974; and (3) getting Egypt and Israel to agree in September 1975 to the so-called Sinai II disengagement, which provided for the first substantial relinquishment by Israel of part of the territory it had conquered in the 1967 war, a thick demilitarized buffer zone comprising most of the relinquished territory, to be policed by the United Nations and a special observer team of U.S. civilians, as well as some limited Egyptian indicators of Israel's legitimacy, such as the allowance of nonmilitary cargoes bound for Israel to pass through the Suez Canal.

The step-by-step method separated tangible specific issues, on which there were incentives to achieve immediate agreement, from the larger issues in the Arab–Israeli conflict, which still generated high emotion on both sides. Rather than being asked to agree on a comprehensive set of principles for the settlement at the end of the road as the basis for the immediate specific negotiations, the parties would be induced to start down the road without an agreed-upon picture of their destination any more specific than the highly ambiguous UN Resolution 242. The process of working out an agreement, even on relatively minor matters, would have a salutary effect on the negotiating climate farther down the road. At every step vested interests would be built up on each side, which would not want to see the disintegration of what had already been achieved and therefore would act as a voice of moderation, possibly a peace lobby, for that side.

The step-by-step approach, however, could not be sustained for long if either side began to regard it as a ruse to prevent the attainment of highly valued objectives. This, indeed, soon emerged as a large problem for Sadat, who had to defend himself against militants in his own country and throughout the Arab world—especially against the Palestinians, who charged that he was selling out the goal of regaining the lost Arab territories in order to buy peace with Israel and the good will of the United States. As time went on, therefore, Kissinger was compelled to increase his pressure on the Israelis to make sufficiently meaningful concessions for Sadat to be able to demonstrate to his militant critics that substantial and rapid progress was being made toward the main Arab goal.

Another feature of the matured Kissinger diplomacy was to treat the Arab world not as "the other side" in the Arab–Israeli conflict but as a highly differentiated set of countries with which it was more productive to deal bilaterally on most issues, including relations with Israel. Even categorizing them into moderates and militants was too neat; and acting if such a division were valid might mean neglecting opportunities for the United States to build special lines of influence with each of the countries. Thus, Syria and Iraq, the leaders of the so-called militants, had their own historical enmities and divergent attitudes toward the Christian–Muslim conflict in Lebanon; and Egypt, Jordan, and Saudi Arabia, leaders of the so-called moderates, had played vastly different parts in the cold war, with Egypt becoming a Soviet client and maintaining a professedly "progessive" regime while the Jordanian and Saudi monarchies built their armed forces around American-supplied equipment. Then again, Saudi Arabia, which along with Iran was a dominant force in the oil producer cartel, was in a different class from Egypt and Jordan when it came to bargaining with the United States and other industrialized countries. Moreover, each of these countries had its own problems with displaced Palestinians and a different set of preferences and priorities when it came to the demands of the various Palestinian guerrilla organizations against Israel.

Of course, if U.S. bilateral diplomacy was conducted crudely, the

various Arab countries might see it as a divide-and-rule policy designed to advance Israeli interests and might join to present a united
front even if such unity would contradict important national interests. Even the subtle Kissinger found it impossible to sustain the
bilateral approach, which involved frequent "shuttling" between the
principal Middle Eastern capitals, without creating suspicion that
he was playing off one country against another. To mollify such
suspicions, especially near the end of his tenure, he began to weave
a tangle of complicated reassurances, often in the form of promises
of special economic and military-supply relationships, not all of which
were likely to be backed up by the Congress and some of which
required him to make compensatory promises to Israel.

A corollary to the strategy of building multiple relationships in
the Middle East was a somewhat more relaxed attitude toward the
Soviet role in the region than Kissinger had shown when he promised to "expel" the Soviets from Egypt. If it was now deemed counterproductive to polarize the Arabs into moderate and militant camps,
it was even more disadvantageous, from a global geopolitical perspective, to overlay this with pro-Soviet and pro-U.S. groupings.
This simply would give the Russians too many automatic clients. It
should not be because of U.S. policy that countries ran to the arms
of the Soviet Union or were reluctant to come to the United States
to satisfy needs that were not adequately attended to by the Russians. The evolution of Sadat's policy should serve as a model: let
events run their natural course and Arab nationalism would assert
itself against Soviet imperialism. The process might not take this
course, however, if the United States acted as if it were illegitimate
for Middle Eastern countries to have "peace and friendship" treaties
or client–patron relationships with the USSR, or as if in order to
build a relationship with the United States one must renounce relations with Moscow; for such an uncompromising U.S. policy would
itself cut against the grain of local nationalism and pride, and might
only further alienate some of these countries from the United States.

The more permissive U.S. attitude toward a Soviet Middle Eastern presence, however, might have its own pitfalls, particularly
where the easiest way for the Russians to get a local foothold was
through supplying military equipment. Increased flows of Soviet arms
into the area might produce adverse shifts in the local power balance, which the United States might need to counter by further

military buildups of Israel and/or other primary U.S. clients. Thus, what started out as a relaxed approach could result in a new spiral of competitive arming of military clients and even a rigid repolarization of the area.

In short, the new Kissinger strategy of defusing immediately combustible situations and weaving a web of positive relations with virtually all states in the region (regardless of their attitudes toward Israel) might not be sufficient to (1) prevent the expansion of Soviet imperialism in the Middle East, (2) reduce the prospects of a war between the superpowers starting in the region, and (3) ensure the continued survival of Israel. Moreover, the strategy could boomerang, resulting in another Arab–Israeli war with higher levels of armaments on both sides and with the Russians more ensconced in the area than ever; and unless in the interim the industrial world substantially reversed its growing dependence on Middle Eastern oil, the United States, Western Europe, and Japan might be severely divided among themselves and troubled by internal political dissension over the costs and risks of coming to Israel's assistance during its period of maximum peril.

Kissinger must have known, on the basis of his past historical studies and his baptism in the fire of Middle Eastern politics, that symptomatic firefighting and step-by-stp conflict resolution techniques were only surface ameliorants. If any region in the world required a "structure of peace" to prevent events there from severely undermining U.S. external security and internal stability, it was the Middle East. Kissinger had reestablished American competence in the area, but something more was required. Perhaps he had a grand design, some architecture, a "vision"; but this remained unarticulated and could not be inferred from his behavior.

25

THE ANACHRONISM OF CONSERVATIVE REALPOLITIK

In each period there exist anachronisms, states which appear backward and even decadent to those who fail to realize they are dealing with the most tenacious remnant of a disintegrating world order.

HENRY A. KISSINGER

The evolution of U.S. crisis diplomacy in the Middle East from 1969 to 1976 reflected the more general metamorphosis in U.S. foreign policy over which Henry Kissinger presided. What was once viewed as a protracted conflict between the forces of radicalism, revolution, and chaos (exploited by the Soviet Union) and the forces of moderation, stability, and order (led by the United States) showed itself to be a more complicated and many-sided interaction of ideological and material forces in which the natural and most effective role of the United States might often be that of sponsor of progressive reform. Similarly, the traditional stabilizing mechanism available to those who wanted to preserve the status quo—an advantageous balance of military power—was often insufficient for containing the forces of chaos and frequently inappropriate as a means through which the United States could exert influence on the side of constructive change.

The metamorphosis in U.S. policy was hardly smooth, however, and often found the Nixon and Ford administrations falling back on conservative realpolitik concepts and stances.

• Nixon and Kissinger discounted the humanitarian and moral implications of Pakistani President Yahya Khan's brutal suppression of the Bangladesh independence movement in 1971. They stressed rather the "illegitimacy" of India's reactive intervention and attempt to "dismember" the sovereign state of Pakistan. Reversing the standing U.S. policy of scrupulously avoiding taking sides in India–Pakistan conflicts, the administration aligned itself diplomatically with Pakistan in the Bangladesh conflict, threatened to call off the Nixon–Brezhnev summit scheduled for the spring of 1972 if the Kremlin did not put restraining pressure on India, and dispatched a Marine intervention task force, ostentatiously escorted by the nuclear aircraft carrier *Enterprise,* into the Bay of Bengal. This was a symbolic show of force, apparently with no real intention to directly participate in the fight. The administration was most worried that a decisive Indian victory over Pakistan (China's diplomatic ally in its own border conflicts with India), with the United States standing idly by, would destabilize the Asian balance of power—now viewed as subordinate level of the triangular U.S.–Soviet–Chinese balance, still being constructed—and might cause China to reconsider its opening to the United States. As it turned out, the Indians prevailed in effecting the separation of Bangladesh from East Pakistan despite the U.S. action. Nevertheless, Nixon and Kissinger claimed success in deterring India from pressing its advantage to the point of militarily attacking West Pakistan and occupying Pakistani-claimed areas of Kashmir.[1]

• In authorizing covert CIA programs to support Chilean opponents of the Marxist regime of Salvador Allende Gossens, and implicating the United States thereby indirectly in the violent military ouster and death of Allende in September 1973 (Kissinger denies allegations of active U.S. government complicity in or encouragement of the coup), Nixon and Kissinger reembraced the ideological anti-Communist definitions of U.S. interests that they claimed to be discarding in their "structure of peace" concepts. Kissinger himself had previously ridiculed claims by the U.S. military that Chile had vital strategic importance, and is reputed to be the originator of the quip that a Communist Chile would be a dagger pointed at the heart of Tierra del Fuego. But now he argued that "if Chile had followed the Cuban pattern, Communist ideology would in time have been supported by Soviet forces and Soviet arms in the southern core of the South American continent."[2]

• Kissinger's policy of politically quarantining Portugal—of acting as if that country had a contagious disease during the seventeen months of political turmoil following the April 1974 reformist coup in Lisbon—had the ostensible geopolitical rationale of insulating NATO military organs, especially the Nuclear Planning Group, from possible subversion by Portuguese leftists. The ruling Cabinet of the provisional government, although led by a popular general and a prominent liberal, included two leaders of the Portuguese Communist party as well as several Socialists. Actually, it was rather easy for the NATO organization to protect its essential functions against Communist subversion by setting up special subcommittees, excluding Portugal, to deal with sensitive matters. Kissinger's fears apparently went deeper: a Communist victory in Portugal would profoundly destabilize the European equilibrium, providing the Soviet Union for the first time with a major presence in Western Europe and on the strategically located Iberian peninsula. (The Portuguese Communists, under Alvaro Cunhal, were openly pro-Soviet and not part of the liberalizing "Eurocommunist" movement.) Accordingly, as the Communists intensified their efforts to take over the central and local governing apparatus of Portugal, Kissinger made it known that he intended to subject that country to virtually complete diplomatic and economic isolation from the West unless the Portuguese Socialists and liberals expelled the Communists from official positions of influence in Lisbon. Non-Communist leaders in Portugal, the U.S. ambassador in Lisbon, and some of America's European allies tried to dissuade Kissinger from such a coercive approach, arguing that it would only gain the Communists greater sympathy among the Portuguese people. (Kissinger's coercive diplomacy was never really put to the test. Cunhal impatiently overplayed his hand by attempting a military *putsch*. This rash Communist bid for total power was defeated by a coalition of moderate military officers and democratic Socialists, who now had sufficient grounds of their own for denying the Communists important positions in the government.)

• Kissinger's response to the phenomenon of "Eurocommunism" was also a product of a persisting cold war mind set. Kissinger was mistrustful of pledges by Communist Party leaders in Italy, France, and Spain to respect freedom of expression and association and democratic political processes, including the rights of opposition parties to openly oppose a Communist-controlled government and the obligation of governments to turn over power to other parties when the electorate so decides. He regarded such pledges as a deceptive stratagem to undercut the reluctance of the non-Communist parties in Western Europe to form electoral alliances and coalition governments with the Communists. Once the Communists were allowed to share power, argued Kissinger, they would have no scruples about reneging on their promises and, like the Communists in Eastern Europe in the late 1940s, would decisively suppress all opposition parties and deal brutally with anyone who cried foul. Moreover, the Western hope that, once in power, the European Communist parties would remain nationalist and pursue international policies distinct from those of the Soviet Union was regarded by Kissinger as a dangerously naïve basis for currently relaxing the barriers to their attaining power. It would be damaging enough, from Kissinger's viewpoint, if any of the key NATO countries turned initially neutralist. His strategy, therefore, was to allude openly to the international economic and political costs that would be incurred by any Western European country that turned toward Communism—a drying up of foreign investments of private capital, and second-class status in or expulsion from NATO—as a deterrent to any power-sharing experiments with the Eurocommunists.

• Kissinger's vacillation and delay in responding to the July 1974 Greek nationalist coup in Cyprus that deposed Archbishop Makarios was perhaps attributable in part to the Secretary of State's preoccupation with the Middle East crisis and the climactic traumas of Watergate. But the fact that, when preoccupied, Kissinger gave the benefit of the doubt to the Greek military junta that engineered the coup, and then remained aloof as Turkey, using U.S. arms in violation of congressional restrictions, invaded Cyprus to protect the island's Turkish minority, was revealing of his natural, almost instinctual, biases: suspicion, even contempt, of democratic reformers and populist politicans (into which category he placed Archbishop Makarios) and faith in the reliability of decisive, militaristic, disciplined leaders such as might be found in a Greek military junta or in NATO-loyal Turkish governments.

• In May 1975, two weeks after the final Communist takeover of Saigon, U.S. marines stormed a Cambodian Communist stronghold on Tang Island in the Gulf of Siam to rescue the American crewman from the freighter *Mayagüez*, which had been seized for penetrating what Cambodia claimed to be its territorial waters. Figher planes from the U.S. aircraft carrier *Coral Sea* bombed the Cambodian mainland. In this swift use of force, Kissinger and President Ford impatiently preempted their own diplomatic initiatives through the UN and neutral channels. They found out afterward that the Cambodian government had decided to release the crew before the marine and air assault had started. If that information had been in Ford's hands, the lives of the thirty-eight Americans who died in the operation, not to mention the larger number of Cambodians, could have been saved. But Kissinger and Ford, having just shown themselves unable to prevent the Communists from attaining total military victory in Vietnam in violation of the Paris agreements of 1973, were particularly anxious to demonstrate that the United States, under their leadership, was still not to be trifled with. By seizing the *Mayagüez*, puny Cambodia provided them with the opportunity for a show of the old machismo without the risk of major war.[3]

THE CRISIS IN THE WORLD ECONOMIC ORDER

The destabilization of international economic relations that resulted from the oil price increases and embargo imposed by oil-exporting countries in 1973 and 1974 was initially perceived and responded to by Kissinger mainly as an element in the East–West balance of power and as a critical variable in the Arab–Israeli conflict. To the extent that he regarded the economic and political actions of the Organization of Petroleum Exporting Countries (OPEC) as serious threats worthy of his attention, it was insofar as (1) the denial of oil to the Western industrialized nations or Japan might bring about the economic and political collapse of key members of the anti-Communist alliance, and (2) the Arab members of OPEC, using such a denial threat, could coerce the industrialized nations into supporting the Arab side in the Arab–Israeli conflict. The emergence of these threats in connection with the Arab–Israeli war of 1973 riveted Kissinger's attention on the economics as well as the politics of the global energy situation and, because the energy situation was now so closely linked with the overall workings of the international economy, compelled him to educate himself quickly on the structure and condition of the world economic order. ("From the start I had not expected to play a major role in international economics, which—to put it mildly—had not been a central field of study for me. Only later did I learn that the key economic policy decisions are not technical, but political.")[4] What he found significantly complicated his views on geopolitics and effected a transformation in his statesmanship. Global equilibrium, the structure of peace, the security of the United States itself—all of these depended as much on the distribution of economic power as on the distribution of military power and the pattern of political loyalties. It was therefore part of the art of high statesmanship to be able to manipulate the international economic variables, not simply as adjuncts to U.S.–Soviet Détente but as elements in the very essence of international power.

In this field too, it was in responding to crisis situations that Kissinger was able to seize the reins and perform most effectively while others were confused and demoralized. But during the first Nixon administration (1969–1972) the driver's seat for U.S. foreign economic policy was usually occupied by Secretary of the Treasury John Connally or the President himself.

The U.S. domestic economy was in deep trouble in 1971—"stagflation," it was called—in ways that could have damaging effects on Nixon's changes for reelection: unemployment was dangerously high, simultaneously with abnormally high increases in the prices of goods and services. U.S. labor unions had turned protectionist, arguing that a large part of the unemployment problem was due to the influx of foreign goods produced by cheap foreign labor, sometimes in foreign subsidiaries of U.S. multinational corporations. Trade and monetary experts were alarmed at the rapidly deteriorating U.S. balance of international payments, reflecting the lag of U.S. exports behind imports and the increasing outflow of U.S. dollars in the form of overseas investments. Monetarists claimed that the dollar was highly overvalued in relation to other currencies and that this was dangerous for the health of the U.S. economy; it artificially made U.S. goods more expensive than they should be on the world market, and made foreign goods cheaper in the United States. There was growing pressure in international financial circles for the United States to devalue the dollar, but this would mean that the domestic economy would have to absorb the first shocks of the international readjustment; moreover, such talk could cause a dangerous collapse of the whole monetary system as holders of U.S. dollars—the basic and most widely held of all currencies—rushed to cash them in for other currencies or, worse yet, demanded that the United States exchange their dollars for gold at the preestablished price of $35 per ounce. (There was nowhere near that amount of gold in the U.S. Treasury.)

Under these circumstances, argued Secretary of the Treasury Connally, the United States should begin to insist that others in the system assume some of the burdens of making the international economy work. The West Europeans and the Japanese, having recovered from World War II to become major competitors of the United States, should no longer be babied. Speaking in Munich in May 1971, Connally bluntly told the Europeans that the United States was losing patience with the other industrialized nations, which it was still protecting in the NATO alliance, for not pulling their weight in the economic system. Questions were beginning to arise in the United States, he warned, over how the costs of NATO and other mutual security arrangements should be allocated. "I find it an impressive fact, and a depressing fact, that the persisting underlying balance of payments deficit which causes so much concern, is more than covered, year in and year out, by our net military expenditures abroad." Financing the free world's military shield was part of the burden of leadership that the United States should not cast off, said the Treasury Secretary, but

the comfortable assumption that the United States should—in the broader political interests of the free world—be willing to bear disproportionate economic costs does not fit the facts of today.

. . .

No longer does the U.S. economy dominate the free world. No longer can considerations of friendship, or need, or capacity justify the United States' carrying so heavy a share of the common burdens.

And, to be perfectly frank, no longer will the American people permit their government to engage in international actions in which the true long-run interests of the U.S. are not just as clearly recognized as those of the nations with which we deal. [5]

Ten weeks after Connally delivered this stern lecture, President Nixon announced a "new economic policy" to "blaze the trail to a new prosperity." In addition to domestic measures to create new jobs (mainly tax breaks for industry to stimulate investment in new plants), to stimulate more consumer demand (a repeal of the 7 percent excise tax on automobiles and an increase in personal income tax deductions for dependents), and to control inflation (a temporary freeze on all wages and prices throughout the United States), Nixon ordered a set of measures designed to coerce the other industrialized nations into reconsidering their reluctance to allow the United States to openly compete with them in the international economy.

On the advice of Secretary Connally, he temporarily suspended the convertibility of the dollar into gold or other international reserve assets. This technical action, dubbed by journalists as "slamming the U.S. gold window," was taken, the President explained, to prevent the international money speculators from "waging an all-out war against the American dollar." Also on the advice of Connally, Nixon imposed a temporary tax of 10 percent on goods imported into the United States. This action was taken, he said, "to make certain that American products will not be at a disadvantage because of unfair currency exchange rates. When the unfair treatment is ended, the import tax will end as well." Now that the other nations have regained their vitality and have become our competitors, argued Nixon, "the time has come for them to bear their fair share of defending freedom around the world" and maintaining a stable international economic order.

The time has come for exchange rates to be set straight and for the major nations to compete as equals. There is no longer any need for the United States to compete with one hand tied behind her back.[6]

The European allies of the United States and Japan were shocked at Nixon's harsh tone and uncompromising posture. Kissinger and Nixon both had criticized the Kennedy and Johnson administrations for their arrogant unilateralism on matters of concern to the alliance and had pledged a more consultative approach. Now Washington, without prior consultation, not only was taking it upon itself to change key structural elements in the international monetary system but also was unilaterally imposing a special tariff (the 10 percent "import surcharge") on goods from its trading partners—in effect, twisting their arms until they gave in to U.S. demands to revalue their currencies.

The damaging effects of such coercive unilateralism to an overall system of mutual accountability among the economically advanced noncommunist countries alarmed the chairman of the Council on International Economic Policy, Peter Peterson, who implored Kissinger to intervene with Nixon against Connally's Texan shoot-it-out style. Kissinger, although almost totally preoccupied with Vietnam, and still unfamiliar with the intricacies of international economics, nonetheless weighed in in behalf of a less confrontationist approach.[7]

Nixon softened the U.S. position somewhat in subsequent negotiations with the Europeans and the Japanese by agreeing to devalue the U.S. dollar as the others up-valued their currencies. The result was the agreement concluded at the December 1971 meeting of the International Monetary Fund (IMF) to realign all major currencies and subsequently allow them to "float"—that is, to have their values set by suuply and demand on the world money markets within rather broad margins. Collaterally, the European Economic Community agreed to a new round of extensive trade negotiations with the United

States. Japan also exhibited a cooperative attitude in implementing the "voluntary" restraints on its exports to the United States and the import barrier liberalizations it had accepted earlier in the year in exchange for U.S. cooperation in returning Okinawa.

The official tone of mutual accommodation surrounding the December 1971 meeting of the IMF was capped by Nixon's personal appearance at the meeting to bless what he termed "the most significant monetary agreement in the history of the world." But this could not erase the fact that the United States had used not only economic coercion but also hints of a withdrawal of military protection to compel its allies to accede to its desires.

If the international system was now to feature intense competition and coercive bargaining within the anticommunist alliance as well as East–West rivalry, America's partners would make their own adjustments to this new reality. Perhaps General de Gaulle was right after all, and Europe (and even Japan) would have to seek a unique role in the system that would maximize its bargaining advantages vis-à-vis both superpowers. Kissinger would reap the bitter harvest of the seeds won in 1971 when, at the conclusion of the Vietnam war two years later, he turned his attention to the disintegrating "Atlantic community." The potentially disastrous geopolitical implications of the disintegrative trends would be driven home during the Yom Kippur War, when he tried to obtain allied cooperation against Arab oil blackmail and Soviet military threats.

By 1973 the differences in membership and purposes between the North Atlantic security community on the one hand and the West European economic community on the other hand were prominently exposed and crucially affecting relations between the United States and Europe. With the new era of détente reducing the immediacy of the common-defense purposes of NATO, the principle that everyone should do his part for the good of the whole was difficult to enforce. Those with the greatest military power did not automatically exercise the greatest authority, and conflicts within the community were harder to resolve than previously. Where nonmilitary matters were at issue—trade barriers, currency exchange rates, the terms of technological cooperation, access to energy supplies, environmental controls—there was now more opportunity for special-interest groups to press their demands on their own governments and on the deliberative assemblies and bureaucracies of the European and Atlantic communities. Even when it came to military issues, such as determining the size, composition, and strategy of NATO forces, the debates were less over how best to defend against military attack from the East than over the distribution of the economic burdens of alliance membership. Previously, when the United States had insisted that the economically thriving NATO countries provide more for their own defense and purchase military equipment from the United States to offset the U.S. balance-of-payments costs of American forces in Europe, it had been easier to compel agreement on the basis of the overriding imperatives of mutual security. But as the question of sharing military burdens became linked to monetary and trade issues (as had been done by Nixon and Connally in 1971), the United States found itself bargaining against a coalition of European countries in NATO.[8]

Against this background Kissinger proclaimed his "Year of Europe" in an address before Associated Press editors meeting in New York City on April 23, 1973. The formulation was remarkably patronizing, leading French wags to complain that it was as if an inconstant husband had suddenly announced a "year of the wife." Smarting from the insensitive and indifferent treatment they had been getting from top officials of the Nixon administration, European governments were predisposed to read the worst implications into the appeal for transatlantic cooperation, which Kissinger had meant as a sincere offer to make amends. His ringing call for a "new Atlantic charter" that would "strike a new balance between self-interest and the common interest, . . . identify interests and positive values beyond security in order to engage once again the commitment of people and parliaments, . . . [and set forth] a shared view of the world we seek to build" was received skeptically by the Europeans. They read his indelicately phrased observation—"The United States had global interests and responsibilities. Our European allies have regional interests"—as a reassertion of the hegemonic conceit that the United States had an obligation to consult with the Europeans only on specifically European matters but that the Europeans should consult with their superpower protector on all matters of significance. And they squirmed uncomfortably at the unintended irony of a Nixon administration official preaching to them that "we cannot hold together if each country or region asserts its autonomy whenever it is to its benefit and invokes unity to curtail the independence of others." [9]

As a realist, Kissinger understood the inevitability of such tensions, given the centrifugal forces pulling the international system away from the bipolar abnormalities of the early cold war period and back toward a more normal pattern of multiple and shifting coalitions. He was disappointed at the cool European response to his call for a new Atlantic charter, but not terribly surprised. Yet he still hoped that in times of profound challenge to their common values from the Soviet Union or some other source, at least the NATO nations would bond together to protect Western civilization. [10] He was therefore deeply dismayed at the Europeans' failure to rally around the alliance leader in the fall of 1973, when the very fabric of society was threatened by OPEC's quadrupling of the price of oil and the extortionist embargo imposed by the Arabs on oil exports to Israel's supporters. Not only did France, Britain, and Japan, conducting their own bilateral negotiations with the Arab producers, undermine Kissinger's efforts to organize a united front of the major consumer nations to break the producer cartel, but some of the NATO countries were so anxious to disassociate themselves from actions in support of Israel that they refused to allow U.S. planes to use their bases or even to overfly their territory to transport military supplies to Israel during the 1973 war. The American Secretary of State regarded such weakness in the face of Arab pressure as spineless and craven, reminiscent of the way European governments caved in to Hitler's demands on the eve of World War II.

Kissinger was able to adapt to this reality too, recognizing that the European and Japanese economies were more vulnerable to price changes and limited oil supplies than the United States, and that the Europeans had developed considerable experience, still lacking in the United States, in diplomatic dealings with the Arabs and other Third World raw materials producers on such matters. He also had to recognize how little he knew about the economic side of the world energy situation, and accordingly he quickly recast his staff to give it intense study and began personally to avail himself of governmental and nongovernmental counsel on the subject. This crash self-improvement course was paralleled by a series of urgent consultations with the major oil-consuming countries and with representatives of the producer countries so that, upon the termination of the Arab–Israeli war and the lifting of the oil embargo, the United States would be ready to propose a set of international rules for a rational and fair commerce in this vital resource. Failure to resolve the energy problem on the basis of international cooperation, Kissinger warned, would threaten the world with a vicious cycle of competition, autarchy, rivalry, and depression such as had led to the collapse of world order in the 1930s.

The basic approach to the energy problem that Kissinger would follow during the rest of his tenure as Secretary of State was presented by him in broad outline to a conference of major oil-consuming countries summoned by the United States in February 1974: [11]

1. *Conservation.* Kissinger called for a "new energy ethic" designed to promote the conservation and efficient use of energy supplies by all countries. The United States, being the world's most profligate country, bore a special responsibility in this regard, admitted Kissinger, and he pledged an expansion of this country's crisis-stimulated conservation measures and offered to collaborate in a mutual review by the energy-consuming countries of one another's programs.

2. *Alternate fossil energy sources.* Sources neglected during the era of low-cost oil now needed to be exploited—coal, of course, but also shale and offshore oil. The United States would be ready to coordinate its programs of new exploration and exploitation with the other consumer countries, and this might involve multilateral efforts to encourage the flow of private capital into new industries for producing energy, as well as governmental arrangements to accelerate the search for new energy sources.

3. *Research and development.* The United States was prepared, said Kissinger, "to make a major contribution of its most advanced energy research and development [technologies] to a broad program of international cooperation," including technologies to promote the use of nuclear reactors under controls to prevent the spread of nuclear weapons.

4. *Emergency sharing of petroleum.* The most generous of the Kissinger proposals, but also the most problematic in view of likely opposition in Congress, was his offer "to share available energy in times of emergency or prolonged shortages. We would be prepared to allocate an agreed portion of our total petroleum supply provided other consuming countries with indigenous production do likewise."

5. *International financial cooperation.* New international measures, but above all a spirit of international responsibility, were needed to cope with the accumulation of petrodollars and their "recycling" back into the con-

sumer countries. These measures, said Kissinger, should include "steps to facilitate the fuller participation of producing nations in existing international institutions and to contribute to the urgent needs of the developing countries."

As we look toward the end of this century, said America's archpractitioner and conceptualizer of conservative realpolitik,

we know that the energy crisis indicates the birth pains of global interdependence. Our response could well determine our capacity to deal with the international agenda of the future.

We confront a fundamental decision. Will we consume ourselves in nationalistic rivalry which the realities of interdependence make suicidal? Or will we acknowledge our interdependence and shape cooperative solutions? [12]

This was not simply posturing. Kissinger understood that the essence of statesmanship in the emerging international system was the ability to deal with the politics of economics and technology. He who had once dubbed such matters the province of second-rate minds now seemed to relish demonstrating his mastery of his new specialty. Confidently embodying a synthesis of finance minister and geopolitician, he grabbed the international ball back from the departments of Treasury and Commerce and made it clear once again to foreign governments that the President's principal adviser and spokesman on all matters of foreign policy—including economics— was Henry Kissinger.

This was a more complicated policy arena than Kissinger had written about or operated in during his first four years as a high government official. At home there were more players in the multiple legislative and bureaucratic games in the field of foreign economic policy making than there were in the field of national security policy and U.S.–Soviet relations. Kissinger was to find that the commanding position of the United States in the global economy was not readily cashed in for bargaining chips on the specific issues he wanted to deal with.

Even when the United States was a leading producer of goods for which there was high international demand, such as high technology and food, the international free market principles to which the United States was officially committed, combined with the opposition of domestic sellers to export controls, blocked Kissinger's efforts to convert these assets into flexible instruments of diplomacy. Kissinger flirted with using the position of the United States as the largest exporter of food grains to exert leverage against the oil producer cartel. But paradoxically, the 1974–75 famine conditions in India and the African Sahel removed this option. For to hold back food from the international market at a time of vast starvation, and by so doing further drive up world prices, would be regarded as an act of the grossest cruelty. Kissinger was resourceful, however, in turning U.S. dominance as a food producer into more general world political leadership by proposing a World Food Conference and, at its meeting in Rome in November 1974, offering a comprehensive scheme for nationally held but internationally coordinated stocks of surplus grain to stabilize grain prices and help the countries with the greatest need.[13]

Still, Kissinger's lack of tangible and effective leverage against the energy producers continued to bother him, and he found it hard to resist the temptation to reach for the familiar political–military bargaining chips.

At the end of 1974, Kissinger, unsuccessful in his effort to form a solid consensus among the major consumer countries for bargaining with OPEC, allowed himself to be quoted in *Business Week* on the pitfalls, but also the possibilities, of political and military power plays against the Arab oil producers. The only way to bring oil prices down immediately in the absence of consumer solidarity, Kissinger told his interviewers, would be to "create a political crisis of the first magnitude." When probed to describe what he meant, Kissinger talked of

massive political warfare against countries like Saudi Arabia and Iran to make them risk their political stability and maybe their security if they do not cooperate. That is too high a price to pay even for an immediate reduction in oil prices.

If you bring about an overthrow of the existing system in Saudi Arabia and a Qadaffi takes over or if you break Iran's image of being capable of resisting outside pressures, you're going to open up political trends which could defeat your economic objectives. Economic pressures or incentives, on the other hand, take time to organize and cannot be effective without consumer solidarity. Moreover, if we had created the political crisis that I described, we would almost certainly have had to do it against the opposition of Europe, Japan and the Soviet Union.

His interrogators persisited:

BUSINESS WEEK: One of the things we . . . hear from businessmen is that in the long run the only answer to the oil cartel is some sort of military action. Have you considered military action on oil?

KISSINGER: Military action on oil prices?

BUSINESS WEEK: Yes.

KISSINGER: A very dangerous course. We should have learned from Vietnam that it is easier to get into a war than to get out of it. I am not saying that there's no circumstance where we would use force. But it is one thing to use it in the case of a dispute over price, but it's another where there is some actual strangulation of the industrialized world.

BUSINESS WEEK: Do you worry about what the Soviets would do in the Middle East if there were any military action against the cartel?

KISSINGER: I don't think this is a good thing to speculate about. Any President who would resort to military action in the Middle East without worrying what the Soviets would do would have to be reckless. The question is to what extent he would let himself be deterred by it. But you cannot say you would not consider what the Soviets would do. I want to make clear, however, that the use of force would be considered only in the gravest emergency. [14]

When Kissinger's references to remote possibilities when force might be considered caused a stir in Arab and European capitals, he claimed to be "astonished." He insisted on public television that "no nation can announce that it will let itself be strangled without reacting. . . . I find it very difficult to see what it is that people are objecting to." He was simply saying that the United States would not permit itself or its allies to be strangled. "Somebody else would have to make the first move to attempt the strangulation. . . . There would have to be an overt move on an extremely drastic, dramatic and aggressive nature" before the United States would seriously consider using military forces against the oil producers. [15]

Only against economic actions that in their effects and intent would be akin to the use of force would the United States respond militarily; but in not totally ruling out such contingencies Kissinger obviously was attempting to warn the Arabs that at some point even their oil pricing policies, let alone another embargo, could seriously provoke the United States.

It was evident to Kissinger and other Western statesmen that an important shift in the global balance of power was taking place, in that key nations in the Third World were able to crucially affect the security and well-being of most of the countries in the non-Communist industrialized world. Nor was the multiplier effect of the changed power equation lost on the majority of Third World leaders, who now saw a chance—as long as they acted as a bloc with the OPEC countries—to make the West respond seriously to their longstanding demands for a better break in the world economy.

Kissinger was not at all pleased with the tacit bargain between the OPEC countries and other Third World countries to support one another's demands in international forums to maximize their bargaining leverage. Professedly nonaligned African, Latin American, and Asian nations now ganged up in the United Nations and its subsidiary organs to help the Arab countries pass anti-Israel resolutions. In return, the Middle Eastern Arab countries and Iran lent their support to some of the most radical demands emanating from the Third World for a restructuring of the international economic order and a global redistribution of income to the economically disadvantaged nations. "It is an irony," said Kissinger in an angry speech in July 1975,

that at the moment the United States has accepted nonalignment and the value of diversity, those nations which originally chose this stance to preserve their sovereign independence from powerful military alliances are forming a rigid grouping of their own. The most solid bloc in the world today is, paradoxically, the alignment of the nonaligned. This divides the world into categories of North and South, developing and developed, imperial and colonial, at the very moment in history when such categories have become irrelevant and misleading.

He warned those now in the majority in the UN General Assembly and its specialized bodies not to operate under the illusion that they could use their voting power coercively without paying a large price, "for the coerced are under no obligation to submit. To the contrary, they are given all too many incentives simply to depart the scene, to have done with the pretense." Those who abuse the procedures of the organization to isolate or deny the full privileges of the United Nations to members they dislike, as the majority, prodded by the Arabs, was now doing to Israel, "may well inherit an empty shell."

The United States has been by far the largest supporter of the United Nations, Kissinger reminded the Third World voting bloc; but

the support of the American people, which has been the lifeblood of the organization, will be profoundly alienated unless fair play predominates and the numerical majority respects the views of the minority. The American people are understandably tired of the inflammatory rhetoric against us, the all-or-nothing stance accompanied by demands for *our* sacrifice which too frequently dominate the meeting halls of the United Nations.[16]

As if to drive home his growing anger, Kissinger had President Ford appoint Daniel Patrick Moynihan as the new U.S. ambassador to the United Nations. Moynihan had recently published in *Commentary* a scathing attack on the Third World advocates of a new international economic order, whom he lumped together as the "Fabian socialist" international party of "equality," and their applogists in the United States. The United States should take the offensive, argued Moynihan, as the leader of the "liberty party" and speak out loudly against those who would sacrifice freedom and condone tyranny in the pursuit of professedly egalitarian ends.[17]

Kissinger's hardening rhetoric and the appointment of Moynihan raised apprehension in UN circles about the Seventh Special Session of the General Assembly, scheduled for the fall of 1975. The Special Session was to consider means of implementing the principles of the "new international economic order" formulated by the General Assembly majority in the Charter of Economic Rights and Duties of States voted the previous December. The Third World coalition was demanding

—international commodity agreements to assure the producers of the Third World of remunerative and "equitable" prices, perhaps by indexing commodity prices to prices of manufactured goods;
—debt relief in the form of cancellation or postponement of the repayment obligations of the poor countries to their international creditors;
—preferential treatment for developing-country exports in the markets of the industrialized world;
—increased official development assistance from the rich countries amounting to at least 0.7 percent of the gross national product of each rich country;
—increased allocations of special drawing rights (SDRs), the International Monetary Fund's reserve assets created to alleviate the balance-of-payments deficits of member countries;
—technology transfers from the technologically advanced countries to developing countries at concessionary prices;
—the right to nationalize and expropriate any foreign holdings within their territories without compensation (a demand directed at the current *bête noire* of the Third World militants, the multinational corporation);
—greater representation and voting rights for developing countries in international funding and lending institutions.

To the relief of all countries, save perhaps the Soviet Union, China, and some of the more intransigent Third World militants such as Algeria and Libya, the feared North—South confrontation failed to materialize. The big struggle took place before the convening of the Seventh Special Session, not between the diplomats of the industrial and developing nations but within the U.S. government, between State Department officials sympathetic to the demands of the Third World and Treasury officials anxious to protect the international economic status quo. Kissinger was converted to the reformist position sometime during the summer of 1975; and in the weeks immediately preceding the UN meeting he reportedly was engaged in a major dispute with Secretary of the Treasury Simon over the official U.S. posture toward the Third World's demands for a new international economic order. Kissinger won out and, with the blessing of President Ford, presented the new American policy to the United Nations in his historic address of September 1, 1975. It fell to Ambassador Moynihan, of all people, to deliver the Secretary of State's address to the General Assembly. (Moynihan, it became clear in subsequent months, never bought the philosophy he was now instructed to expound.)

The specific proposals put forward in Kissinger's address to the Seventh Special Session went only part way toward meeting the grievances of the developing-country coalition; but they did imply substantial acceptance of the legitimacy of international compensations to the poorer countries for their comparative disadvantages in the international market.[18]

Granting the obligation of the international community to protect vulnerable economies against dramatic drops in their export earnings, Kissinger proposed the creation of a new "development security facility" within the IMF with the mandate and financial resources to give concessionary loans and grants to developing countries to make up for their export shortfalls. (However, the United States rejected the standing demand of the Third World militants for an indexing system to peg the price of basic commodities to price changes in industrial goods.)

Conceding that many of the poor countries, in all fairness, did deserve special help in raising development capital, Kissinger urged expansion of the lending programs of the World Bank and the regional development banks as well as the creation of an international investement trust to mobilize portfolio investment capital for local enterprises. In addition, the United States would be willing to provide technical assistance and expertise to developing countries ready to enter long-term capital markets, and asked other developed countries to provide similar assistance.

On the touchy issue of the role of multinational corporations, Kissinger recognized the concerns of many host countries regarding the ability of foreign-controlled firms to dominate their economies, evade local laws, and intervene in their politics. He affirmed that "countries are entitled to regulate the operations of transnational enterprises within their borders." But, contended Kissinger, host governments had an obligation to treat transnational enterprises equitably and responsibly: "Governments and enterprises must both respect the contractual obligations that they freely undertake. Contracts should be negotiated openly, fairly, and with full knowledge of their implications. . . . Factfinding and arbitral procedures must be promoted as means for settling international disputes."

Finally, with respect to developing-country demands for a greater role in international institutions and negotiations, Kissinger agreed that "participation in international decisions should be widely shared, in the name of both justice and effectiveness. . . . No country or group of countries should have exclusive power in areas basic to the welfare of others. This principle is valid for oil. It also applies to trade and finance." [19]

Kissinger was to experience frustration in his attempts to implement these proposals in the form of specific agreements between the developed and developing countries. In part, this was because of the lack of enthusiasm in the departments of Treasury and Commerce for the whole approach of responsiveness to Third World demands. In part, it was because of the lingering suspicion among Third World leaders of Kissinger's motives, their fear being that he wanted to split the developing-country coalition from the OPEC countries and was attempting to co-opt the poor militants with cosmetic generosity. But as Kissinger's policies toward Africa in 1976 were to show, there was a shift taking place in his grand strategy that was both fundamental and genuine.

AFRICA AND THE REALPOLITIK OF CHANGE

On April 26, 1976, at a luncheon hosted by President Kenneth Kaunda of Zambia, Kissinger once again surpirsed the world with a bold recasting of U.S. policy on southern Africa, identifying the

United States for the first time as unequivocally on the side of black majority rule.

The new U.S. policy that Kissinger outlined comprehensively in Lusaka was clearly a dramatic turnabout from the assumptions of the so-called tar baby policy the Nixon administration had decided on during its first year in office. The policy had been nicknamed "tar baby" by its State Department opponents to express their judgment that it was a sticky policy that the United States would be unable to abandon if it did not work. (In the famous Uncle Remus story by Joel Chandler Harris, Brer Fox makes a tar baby and sets it by the side of the road to trick Brer Rabbit. Brer Rabbit falls into the trap and gets completely stuck.)[20] "Tar baby" had called for "selective relaxation of our stance toward the white regimes" while maintaining a public posture of "opposition to racial repression." The policy had been based explicitly on the premise that "the whites are here to stay and the only way that constructive change can come about is through them. There is no hope for the blacks to gain the political rights they seek through violence, which will only lead to chaos and increased opportunities for the communists." Increased U.S. economic aid would be provided to the black states "to focus their attention on their internal development and to give them a motive to cooperate in reducing tensions." The Republic of South Africa would also be encouraged to provide economic assistance to the black states of Africa. Concrete measures to implement the policy were to include a selective liberalization of the arms embargo against South Africa and the Portuguese territories, plus other relaxations of sanctions against the white regimes that had been imposed in conformity with U.N. resolutions; and flexible aid programs for the black states, including "nonsophisticated arms" in response to "reasonable requests" but opposition to the use of force by insurgent movements.[21]

In approving this policy, the President had set the direction for a U.S. course in southern Africa over the next five years that was to end ingloriously with the Angola crisis of 1975–76. The United States got stuck on the tar of its policy of improving relations with the white regimes while the Soviets were left to pick and choose among black clients. Kissinger's first response to this larger geopolitical consequence of "tar baby" was to counterintervene "covertly" against the Soviets and the Cubans in Africa; but in Angola this

only produced the further embarrassment of associating the United
States with the losing blacks.

Angola provided the shock of recognition for Kissinger that conservative realpolitik would no longer work in Africa. He resisted
learning this lesson, however, until U.S. incompetence in Angola
was exposed before the entire world.

Not that he wasn't warned. The Assistant Secretary of State for
African Affairs, Nathaniel Davis, saw the handwriting on the wall
and shared his judgment with the Secretary in no uncertain terms.
Davis had been asked by Kissinger to chair an interagency NSC
Task Force on Angola in the spring of 1975. The first job of the
Task Force was to evaluate the latest request from the Central Intelligence Agency for a substantial increase in the covert support
the agency was already providing to the opponents of Agostino Neto
and his Popular Movement for the Liberation of Angola (MPLA).

In January 1975 the CIA had been authorized by the Forty Committee (the top-level review board that controlled covert operations
abroad during the Nixon and Ford administrations) to funnel
$300,000 worth of assistance secretly to Neto's principal opponent,
Holden Roberto, the leader of the National Front for the Liberation
of Angola. The CIA was now back for more funds and for authorization to expand its political and economic assistance into covert
military aid to counter the growing Soviet shipments of military
equipment to Neto and his increasing reliance on Cuban military
advisers in the escalating civil war. It was also asking for authorization to initiate a new program of support for another of Neto's
opponents, Jonas Savimbi.

The CIA plan was strongly opposed by the NSC Task Force and
by Assistant Secretary Davis. The Task Force's report, submitted
to Kissinger in June 1975, pointed out that the covert military actions the CIA was recommending might lead to increased intervention by the Soviet Union and other foreign powers. The level of
violence in Angola would probably increase and, especially if there
were widespread tribal or racial massacres, U.S. support for one or
more of the indigenous rivals would become a major political issue
in the United States and an embarrassment internationally. It would
be impossible to ensure that the CIA operations could be kept secret, concluded the Task Force, and their exposure would have a
negative impact on US relations with many countries as well as with

large segments of the U.S. public and Congress. Moreover, the United States would be committing its prestige in a situation over which it had limited influence and one whose outcome was highly uncertain. If the MPLA did come to power, the chances for the United States to establish workable relations with it would have been greatly damaged.[22]

Assistant Secretary Davis weighed in with his own memorandum against the CIA plan. To have even a slight chance of success, he argued, the United States would have to intervene in Angola with a much higher level of visibility and resources than that envisioned in the proposals for covert military operations. The CIA paper itself admitted that the Soviets enjoyed greater freedom of action in the covert supply of military equipment and could escalate the level of aid more readily than the United States. Davis implored the Forty Committee to face the implications:

If we go in, we must go in quickly, massively and decisively enough to avoid the tempting, gradual, mutual escalation that characterized Vietnam during the 1965–67 period. . . . Unless we are prepared to go as far as necessary, in world balance of power terms the worst possible outcome would be a test of will and strength which we lose. The CIA paper makes clear that in the best of circumstances we won't be able to win. If we are to have a test of strength with the Soviets, we should find a more advantageous place.[23]

Davis' protestations were to no avail. The Forty Committee, with Kissinger's concurrence, endorsed the CIA Action Plan, and President Ford gave Kissinger and the CIA the go-ahead to implement it. Davis asked to be relieved of his position as Assistant Secretary of State for African Affairs. This was in July 1975. Over the next six months, virtually all of Davis' predictions came true. The Soviets transported over 10,000 Cuban troops into Angola by air and sea and flew in massive amounts of combat equipment for use by the Cubans and the MPLA, while South Africa and Zaïre intervened against Neto's forces. In December the Senate voted to prohibit all further covert aid to Angola. The Soviets and the Cubans pressed their advantage. Neto trounced his opponents in the northern regions of Angola, who had been aided by forces from Zaïre. The South Africans withdrew their forces from the southern regions of Angola. By the end of January 1876, it was all over except for the recriminations.

On January 29, 1976, Kissinger appeared before the Subcommit-

tee on African Affairs of the Senate Committee on Foreign Relations in one last defense of his Angola policies. The blame for their
failure, he insisted, lay not with the Ford administration but with
Congress for failing to provide the wherewithal for standing up to
the Russians in the crunch. His testimony was a string of castiga-
tions of the congressional majority for their naïveté and lack of spine:

Military aggression, direct or indirect, has frequently been successfully dealt with
but never in the absence of a local balance of forces. U.S. policy in Angola has
sought to help friends achieve this balance. Angola represents the first time since
the aftermath of World War II that the Soviets have moved militarily at long dis-
tances to impose a regime of their choice. It is the first time that the U.S. has
failed to respond to Soviet military moves outside their immediate orbit. And it is
the first time that Congress has halted the Executive's action when it was in the
process of meeting this kind of threat. . . .

If the United States is seen to emasculate itself in the face of massive, unprecedented Soviet and Cuban intervention, what will be the perception of leaders
around the world as they make decisions concerning their future security? . . .

I must note with some sadness that by its actions the Congress has deprived the
President of indispensable flexibility in formulating a foreign policy which we believe to be in our national interest. And Congress has ignored the crucial truth
that a stable relationship with the Soviet Union based on mutual restraint will be
achieved only if Soviet lack of restraint carries the risk of counteraction. . . .

Our diplomacy was effective so long as we maintained the leverage of a possible
military balance. African determination to oppose Soviet and Cuban intervention
was becoming more and more evident. . . .

By mid-December we were hopeful that the [Organization of African Unity]
would provide a framework for eliminating the interference of outside powers by
calling for an end to their intervention. At that point, the impact of our domestic
debate overwhelmed the possibilities of diplomacy. After the Senate vote to block
any further aid to Angola, the Cubans more than doubled their forces and Soviet
military aid was resumed on an even larger scale. The scope of Soviet—Cuban intervention increased drastically; the cooperation of Soviet diplomacy declined.[24]

Senator Dick Clark, chairman of the Subcommittee on African
Affairs, disagreed profoundly. The important lesson of Angola, he
maintained, is that we should not ignore the African black liberation movements until their victories against the minority regimes are
imminent and then back particular factions simply because their
opponents are backed by the Soviet Union. The United States, urged
Senator Clark, should make a new beginning in its African policy.
It should be directed toward establishing connections between U.S.
and African commitments to human rights and racial equality and
between the U.S. commitment to international pluralism and Afri-

can concepts of nonalignment. If the United States pursues such a new African policy, contended Clark, "our cold war interests in Africa may very well take care of themselves."[25]

In February the Organization of African Unity—the all-African regional association of black states—officially recognized the Neto regime as the legitimate government of Angola. Kissinger said little about Africa in public during the next two months. Only when he unveiled his new African policy in Lusaka at the end of April was it evident that he had taken to heart some of the criticism leveled at him by Senator Clark and others.

He had come to Africa, he said, "to usher in a new era in American policy." This new American policy endorsed the black African premise that racial justice and majority rule were the prerequisites for peace in Africa. This endorsement, however, was "not simply a matter of foreign policy but an imperative of our own moral heritage."

Specifically, with respect to Rhodesia, the United States unequivocally supported the British insistence that independence was illegal unless it was based on majority rule. "The Salisbury regime must understand," Kissinger warned, "that it cannot expect U.S. support either diplomatically or in material help at any stage in its conflict with African states or African liberation movements. On the contrary, it will face out unrelenting opposition until a negotiated settlement [to institute majority rule] is achieved." Accordingly, the United States was taking steps to insure its own and other nations' strictest compliance with UN resolutions on economic sanctions against Rhodesia. Consistent with U.S. nonrecognition of the Ian Smith regime in Salisbury, "American travelers will be advised against entering Rhodesia. American residents there will be asked to leave." In addition, the United States was ready to provide special economic assistance to countries bordering on Rhodesia that might themselves suffer economic hardship as a result of closing their borders to normal trade with Rhodesia. The Ford administration was prepared to immediately provide $12.5 million to Mozambique under this policy. Looking toward a successful transition to majority rule in Rhodesia and then full independence, Kissinger promised that the United States would join other nations in a program of economic and technical assistance to the "newly independent Zimbabwe." (Kissinger's use of the black African name for the country was symbolic of the basic shift in policy he was attempting to convey.) While essentially deferring to the blacks to establish their own regime in their own way, Kissinger nevertheless found it necessary to state "our conviction that whites as well as blacks should have a secure future and civil rights in a Zimbabwe that has achieved racial justice. A constitutional structure should protect minority rights together with establishing majority rule."

On the Namibia question, Kissinger strongly reiterated the standing U.S. position that the Republic of South Africa's continued occupation of its former mandate territory was illegal and that the South African government should withdraw and allow the United Nations to supervise the Namibian people's attainment of full self-determination and independent statehood.

On the matter of South Africa's internal racial policies, Kissinger associated the United States with the position of the black African states more clearly than any previous top U.S. official had. "The world community's concern with South Africa is not merely that racial discrimination exists there," said Kissinger. "What is unique is the extent to which racial discrimination has been institutionalized, enshrined in law, and made all-pervasive." The right of the white South Africans to live in their country was not being challenged by the world community, observed Kissinger. But the white South Africans must realize that the world will not tolerate the continued institutionalized separation of the races being enforced under the "apartheid" policy. Pretoria must heed the warning signals of recent years. "There is still time to bring about a reconciliation of South Africa's peoples for the benefit of all. But there is a limit to that time—a limit of far shorter duration than was generally perceived even a few years ago." In the immediate future the black African nations and the world community would be judging Pretoria's legitimacy as an African nation not only from its efforts to make constructive progress toward the elimination of apartheid but also from its behavior on the Namibian and Rhodesian issues. "The Republic of South Africa can show its dedication to Africa," advised Kissinger, "by using its influence in Salisbury to promote a rapid negotiated settlement for majority rule in Rhodesia."[26]

The Secretary of State backed up his new political orientation toward African issues by pledging to triple U.S. economic support for development programs in southern and central Africa over the next three years. And he gave this new stance additional credibility by stopping in Nairobi, Kenya, on the way back from his southern African tour to address the United Nations Conference on Trade and Development—the main UN forum through which the Third World countries had been pressing their demands—on how the United States was prepared to implement in detail the new approach to North–South economic issues that he had outlined the previous fall at the Seventh Special Session of the United Nations.

The evolution of Kissinger's North–South policy—now focused primarily on Africa—was remarkably analogous to the evolution in U.S. Latin American policy associated with the Kennedy administration's Alliance for Progress. It took the failure of a too-little, too-late intervention against the "communist threat" in Cuba (climaxed by the ill-fated Bay of Pigs invasion by Cuban exiles organized by the CIA) to convince the Kennedy administration that an entirely new approach that would put the United States on the side of progressive social change in Latin America was the only hope for arresting the growth of Soviet influence in the Western Hemisphere. Similarly, Kissinger's futile and tardy effort to salvage the Angola situation turned him in the direction of a type of alliance for progress in Africa as the best means of containing the expanding Soviet presence. In both cases a cold war motive lay in back of the programs, but the public definition of the program and its principal instrumentalities were cast in terms of economic and political development objectives. Kissinger would not like this analogy. He had vituperatively criticized Kennedy's Alliance for Progress as naïve in its premise that democratic socialists rather than the conservative military elite of the Third World would provide the best bulwark against instability and Soviet attempts to capture leftist movements. Now he was embracing movements and concepts that he had previously branded as romantic and soft, as insufficiently based on hard balance-of-power realities to be able to effectively counter the unsentimental and often brutal Marxist–Leninists.

"Has Henry lost his nerve?" asked critics on the right. "Is he merely up to his old deceptive tricks?" asked critics on the left. Perhaps both suppositions were wrong. Perhaps he believed it was time for a higher realpolitik: to advance, as he told the UN General

Assembly, "from the management of crises to the building of a more stable and just international order—an order resting not on power but on restraint of power, not on the strength of arms but on the strength of the human spirit." [27]

26

THE KISSINGER
CONTRIBUTION

The statesman is . . . like one of the heroes in classical drama who has had a vision of the future but cannot transmit it directly to his fellow men and who cannot validate its "truth." Nations learn only by experience; they "know" only when it is too late to act. But statesmen must act as if their intuition were already experience, as if their aspiration were truth. It is for this reason that statesmen often share the fate of prophets, that they are without honor in their own country, that they always have a difficult task in legitimizing their programs domestically, and that their greatness is apparent only in retrospect when their intuition has become experience.

HENRY A. KISSINGER

Kissinger's principal historical accomplishment was in helping the country adapt to the enlarging strategic power of the Soviet Union. He perceived, and got President Nixon to understand, that the Soviet Union's attainment of basic equality with the United States in strategic nuclear forces was probably irreversible and would have immense geopolitical consequences. The growing awareness in the United States, in the Soviet Union, and in other countries, that any war between the superpowers now carried high risks of enormous devastation to the United States as well as to the Soviet Union crucially undermined the inherited grand strategy of military containment of Soviet expansion. For if war between the Soviet Union and the United States was feared above all else save the surrender of the United States to the Soviet Union, then the Kremlin might be tempted to use military force against third parties—even those formally allied with the United States—confident that U.S. leaders would shrink from a direct superpower confrontation at the moment of truth.

Kissinger knew that if these emerging military realities were allowed to define the global balance of power, then the Soviet Union, as a revolutionary imperialist state determined to dominate the international system, would exploit U.S.–Soviet mutual deterrence as a cover for its own international power plays. He therefore saw the need to develop powerful nonmilitary levers on Soviet international behavior to compensate for the erosion of usable U.S. military superiority.

Kissinger's grand stragegy was to fashion two powerful new levers on the Kremlin out of the Soviet Union's need for economic modernization and its fear of China. Détente was in large part a response to the Soviet Union's domestic economic weakness. The Washington–Peking reconciliation was in large part an exploitation of Soviet international insecurity. With these two policies Kissinger hoped to continually remind the Kremlin that the USSR's economic well-being and political role in the world remained highly dependent on the good will and cooperation of the United States, despite the fact that the Soviet Union was now a military superpower.

The central purpose of this basic strategy, in Kissinger's own words, was to "give the Soviets a stake in international equilibrium." The stake was to be driven in deep by the levers in American hands: the capacity to help the USSR substantially in its lagging efforts at economic modernization and the capacity to destabilize the Soviet Union's security situation by tilting toward the Chinese in the Sino–Soviet conflict. In effect, Kissinger was offering the Kremlin a grandiose bargain: Soviet entry into the American (and global) markets of trade, investments, and credits, and full Soviet international "legitimacy" in a consultative, coequal superpower relationship with the United States, in exchange for Soviet international moderation and restraint (including Kremlin forbearance from attempting to exploit any power vacuums that might result during the period American international retraction following the Vietnam war). U.S.–Soviet arms control efforts, particularly the Strategic Arms Limitation Talks (SALT), were linked by Nixon and Kissinger to this grand strategy. SALT became the most visible and dramatic symbol—and test—of the Soviets' willingness to moderate their power competition with the United States and to be bound by mutually acceptable rules.

Kissinger's difficulties in getting his strategy to work are attributable less to its grand design than to the inability of the Nixon and Ford administrations to provide the domestic building blocks necessary to give the structure an immediate and secure foundation. The unsuccessful fight against congressional restrictions on trade privileges and credits to the USSR was, from Kissinger's perspective, almost as much of a setback as his failure to prevent Congress (in various "war powers" resolutions) from imposing restrictions on the administrations's use of force as an instrument of diplomacy.

Given the evident limitations on the administration's capacity to deliver carrots *or* sticks, the Russians found a number of new post-Vietnam opportunities too tempting to resist—in the Middle East, in southern Africa, and in Indochina. But by taking advantage of the domestic American confusion surrounding Watergate and the collapse of the Vietnam peace, the Kremlin reinforced the growing opinion in the United States that Kissinger's détente policies were based on unduly optimistic assumptions about Russian intentions and capabilities.

To the extent that strong popular and institutional support at home was necessary for Kissinger's diplomacy to succeed abroad, it did contain a deficiency in its essential concept. It was *too* geopolitical—in the realpolitik sense of the term—to sit comfortably with influential segments of the American polity. The previous cold war strategies, including containment, had combined ideology with clear balance-of-power imperatives: U.S. efforts centered on the organization and sustenance of a coalition of the "free world" nations against an expansionist totalitarian empire; negotiations with the adversary were mainly at the margins of diplomacy, confined largely to arms control efforts with the goals of "stabilizing" the military competition and avoiding inadvertent escalation of conflicts. Now the American public was being told that the totalitarian character of the Soviet Union (and of China) was no longer a barrier to relations with them. The aggressive expansion of the Communist imperialists could be contained by bringing them fully into the system of international interdependence and by superimposing complicated "multipolar" balances of political and economic power on the military balance.

As might have been predicted, opposition to the Kissinger strategy surfaced in groups with ethnic ties to oppressed populations within the Soviet camp (the American Jewish community and elements of organized labor with large East European memberships). And political factions that had made the cold war, anti-Communism, and military preparedness their stock in trade saw détente (negotiations instead of confrontation), with its stress on arms control and East–West commerce, as weakening the will and the material capacity of this country to succeed in the long-term conflict with an increasingly powerful enemy determined to impose its system on the world.

The human rights and military preparedness constituencies coalesced behind the Jackson-Vanik and Stevenson amendments holding back the U.S.–Soviet commercial normalization Nixon and Kissinger had promised. By linking trade and credits to Kremlin liberalization of restrictions of Jewish emigration and other civil liberties, some elements in the U.S. human rights constituency may have sincerely hoped to get the Russians to change their ways; others simply wanted to continue to punish the Kremlin for its wrongs. The military preparedness constituency, especially its more sophisticated members in Congress and the policy community, saw the human rights issue as a convenient means of scuttling détente; and Kissinger was justified in suspecting their motives.

Perhaps Kissinger could have done somewhat better by engaging in more consultation with influential members of Congress and less lecturing to them on the higher morality of avoiding thermonuclear war; but the liberal/ethnic/cold warrior backlash was probably an inevitable consequence of his effort to resurrect the classical diplomatic deference to the claim of governments to be completely sovereign within their own realms. Indeed, Kissinger almost lost Gerald Ford the Republican presidential nomination by locking the inexperienced new chief executive into a highly circumspect stance on human rights, capped by the denial of a White House reception for the exiled Russian author Alexander Solzhenitsyn. The Ford administration's reluctance to make a public fuss over the human rights violations of foreign countries undoubtedly contributed to Jimmy Carter's decision to make human rights the centerpiece of his foreign policy platform.

The Kissinger contribution, in no small measure, was to make a virtue out of necessity, to translate the tactical requirements of a postcontainment strategy into a world order vision, however coldly geopolitical. The vision remained cloudy in concept, however, and as Kissinger left office on January 20, 1977, the roadblocks on the path were more prominent than the destination.

The most embarrassing frustration of Kissinger's statesmanship came with the Soviet–North Vietnamese collusion, soon after the American withdrawal from Vietnam, to take advantage of the power vacuum in Indochina and the erosion of executive authority in Washington caused by Watergate. Kissinger ineffectually stomped and raged as the Vietnamese, Laotian, and Cambodian Communists, with new military supplies from their external Communist benefactors, proceeded to fully conquer the three Indochinese States. Kissinger's blaming of the U.S. Congress for this humiliating outcome—railing against the legislative branch's "spinelessness" in refusing to reopen the military supply pipeline to the remnants of the anti/Communist regime in Saigon in response to Hanoi's violation of the Paris Peace Accords—was a transparent attempt to deflect the embarrassment from the administration. There was, after all, not the slightest chance in 1975 that Congress would authorize any action implying recommitment of the United States to the fortunes of the anti-Communist elements in Indochina, and Kissinger surely knew it even while acting as if he was shocked. Brezhnev and the Hanoi leadership group also were confident that the United States would not reintervene in Vietnam at this point; the post-Watergate confusion apart, they saw Kissinger as a true realpolitician who had coldly calculated that Indochina was a peripheral interest of the United States and simply not worth the costs of a major military engagement or a collapse of the basic détente relationship.

By contrast, during the 1973 Arab–Israeli war Kissinger was operating from a position of credibility when he warned the Kremlin—in words, and by alerting the main U.S. military forces to deter a threatened Soviet military intervention—that Soviet moves to exploit the conflict were jeopardizing détente. The Middle East, because of its petroleum resources and central geopolitical position, was of prime strategic importance. Moreover, American governments, starting with the Truman administration, were irrevocably committed to the survival of Israel for deeply cutting domestic political reasons. Kissinger's stance against Soviet power plays in the area was based on established concepts of core U.S. interests and would be backed by Congress and public opinion. Once Kissinger had publicly defined Soviet machinations as threatening to these core security and political values, the Kremlin had no prudent choice but to adopt a posture of moderation.

It was in southern Africa, however, that Kissinger's détente policies were most starkly shown to be an inadequate supplement to military containment as a grand strategy for taming the aggressive inclinations of the Soviet Union. His blaming of Congress for not providing him the wherewithal to counter the heavy Soviet/Cuban involvement in the Angolan civil war was disingenuous. (Would he and President Ford really have thrust the country into another Third World quagmire prior to the 1976 elections, *even* if Congress had been willing?) Kissinger's suggestions to the Russians that Angola should be on the same agenda with SALT and U.S.–Soviet trade at high-level diplomatic meetings were disdainfully brushed aside by Brezhnev. The Soviet leaders shrewdly calculated that Angola just wasn't that salient for the American public; moreover, the Kremlin knew that influential American agribusiness interests, anxious to consummate long-term commercial deals in the USSR, were bringing pressure on the President to stop using them as political pawns.

The deeper causes of America's ineffectiveness in Angola were not lost on Kissinger, and led him to recognize what I have called "the anachronism of conservative realpolitik." He came to understand that neither efforts to exercise leverage directly on the Kremlin (whether through coercive deterrence or positive détente strategies), nor efforts to contain Soviet expansion with military assistance to anticommunist states or movements, were reliable means for countering Soviet power plays in politically unstable Third World countries. Rather, the United States would be more effective if it were (1) as a general policy, to identify with and funnel resources to states and groups that were broadly representative of the mainstream Third World movements of international nonalignment and egalitarianism, and (2) as a particular policy for Southern Africa, to exercise decisive U.S. leverage on the remaining white regimes to make rapid transitions to black majority rule.

The Kissinger shift in relation to Third World demands, from the oppositionist U.S. stance championed by UN Ambassador Daniel Patrick Moynihan to the generally constructive positive response of the West Europeans, emanated largely from realpolitik considerations: how best to compete with the Soviets for influence in the Third World and how best to prevent the oil-producing nations from organizing the Third World into a bloc that would play off the superpowers against each other, particularly in the Middle East and Africa, and undermine the economic strength of the West and Japan.

There was considerable sentiment emerging in the U.S. policy community and the public at large to have done with the UN (where the Arab countries lately had been organizing voting majorities in support of efforts to ostracize Israel) and to let an increasingly strident, insulting Third World fend for itself economically and politically. Kissinger would have fared better with the conservative wing of the Republican Party, and probably with the public at large, if he had continued to follow the Moynihan line of standing up to the "tyrannous majority" in the United Nations. But his ability to see beneath the surface of things led him to reject a U.S. stance that would have polarized international relations on a North–South basis. Instead, he now attempted to woo the Third World by embracing concepts of international justice and equality that he had earlier scoffed at as not rooted in the realities of power. To his credit he realized, however belatedly, that the realities of power were changing: The distribution of coercive power within the international system was making military force less usable as a U.S. trump card than previously. And the relative increase in the ability of countries to affect each other's domestic systems, deliberately or inadvertently, as a result of the expansion of material interdependence was making a wide variety of positive, associative relationships an essential attribute of international leadership.

In his latter-day "progressive" responses to the international populist demands for a global redistribution of wealth and political power, Kissinger still was acting essentially as a conservative. But in acting to conserve both American power and Western civilization he now adopted an international posture analogous to the progressive responses of Theodore Roosevelt and later of Franklin Roosevelt to the domestic populist and Marxist movements in the first half of the twentieth century—or indeed, analogous to the way one of his heroes, Otto von Bismarck, had responded to the liberal and egalitarian agitations in Germany in the 1870s.

Unfortunately, Kissinger conceived of the new statesmanship in

Bismarckian terms (as a maneuver to undercut the Marxists) rather than in terms of the ethos of American progressivism (which was dedicated to increased democratization), with the result that he was not as convincing as he needed to be to shape a domestic consensus in back of his foreign policy shift; and it was left to a neopopulist President less grounded in realpolitik to try to fashion a domestic consensus for a progressive foreign policy. (Kissinger, in exile, would later sneer at his successors' superficial articulation of *his* policies.)

Similarly, Kissinger's virtuosity in attempting to protect and enhance U.S. power through flexible multiple-relationship diplomacy was a bit too classical (in the mode of the nineteenth-century balance of power) to mesh well with the post Vietnam/post-Watergate insistence on openness and accountability. For the American Secretary of State to function as the indispensable middleman, as Kissinger did with such panache in his Middle Eastern shuttle diplomacy, required the ability to act as a sympathetic backer of the frequently incompatible demands of each of the hostile parties—a feat that did not always allow for public candor on the part of the middleman. Some of Kissinger's disappointed foreign counterparts and domestic confidants were bound to reveal the substance of the secret assurances they received from him; and when they did, the credibility of the Secretary of State and the American government once again would suffer at home and abroad, and somewhat diminish the power he had labored so hard to resurrect. In this respect too, the rather extreme insistence by candidate Jimmy Carter on openness and full public accountability—which soon proved to be an embarrassment to the new administration's diplomacy—was in part a reaction against Kissinger's having elevated double-dealing to a high art form.

Despite the shortcomings, Kissinger on balance played a weighty and constructive role in the necessary adaptation of U.S. policy to a world more complex and less responsive to simple exertions of American power than the one his predecessors had inherited after World War II. The historically significant drama of the Kissinger years was the turn in U.S. policy toward positively relating to, rather than pushing away, the new forces in world politics. For Kissinger this was a reluctant turn, and it exposed the extent to which he was a creature of the times rather than their master.[1]

PART VI

THE CARTER PERIOD

I was familiar with the arguments that we had to choose between idealism and realism, between morality and the exertion of power; but I rejected those claims. To me the demonstration of American idealism was a practical and realistic approach to foreign affairs, and moral principles were the best foundation for the exertion of American power and influence.

JIMMY CARTER

It is not a popular thing to remind people that power is important, that it has to be applied, that sometimes decisions which are not fully compatible with our concepts of what the world ideally ought to be like need to be taken.

ZBIGNIEW BRZEZINSKI

27

THE MANY FACES OF
JIMMY CARTER

*I am a farmer, an engineer, a father and husband, a Christian, a politician and
former governor, a planner, a businessman, a nuclear physicist, a naval officer,
a canoeist, and, among other things, a lover of Bob Dylan's songs and Dylan
Thomas' poetry.*

JIMMY CARTER

In his campaign for the presidency, Jimmy Carter latched on to
the popular discontent with Kissinger's realpolitik—a discontent
prominent on the ideological right as well as on the left, and which
nearly lost Gerald Ford the 1976 Republican nomination to Ronald
Reagan. Carter was more effective than any of his rivals for the
Democratic nomination, and more believable than Ford, in putting
himself forward as the embodiment of a revived national consensus
that U.S. foreign policy should reflect basic American values.

The divisions and bitterness of the period of Vietnam and Watergate would be overcome by giving fresh expression, at home and
abroad, to the country's traditional dedication to the achievement by
all of God's children of political self-determination, freedom from
oppression, and a decent material life. "World order" politics would
supplant "balance-of-power" politics. It was time to move beyond
arms control and toward the abolition of nuclear weapons. The bonds
of trust between the people of the United States and the officials
who conduct U.S. foreign policy would be restored, as would the

trust by other countries of the word of the United States, by avoiding secrecy in the formulation of policies and in negotiations with other countries.

Carter carried these themes forward into his early presidential pronouncements on foreign affairs—his Inaugural Address ("Our commitment to human rights must be absolute"; the ultimate goal of U.S. arms limitation policy is "the elimination of all nuclear weapons from this Earth"[1]); his maiden speech to the United Nations ("I have brought to office a firm commitment to a more open foreign policy. . . . No member of the United Nations can claim that mistreatment of its citizens is solely its own business"[2]); and his address at the 1977 commencement exercises of Notre Dame University:

I believe we can have a foreign policy that is democratic, that is based on fundamental values, and that uses power and influence, which we have, for humane purposes. We can also have a foreign policy that the American people support and, for a change, know and understand.

. . . Because we know that democracy works, we can reject the arguments of those rulers who deny human rights to their people. . . .

We are confident that the democratic methods are most effective, and so we are not tempted to employ improper tactics at home or abroad.

We are confident of our own strength, so we can seek substantial mutual reductions in the nuclear arms race.

And we are confident of the good sense of the American people, and so we let them share in the process of making foreign policy decisions. We can thus speak with the voices of 215 million, and not just an isolated handful.

. . . Being confident of our own future, we are now free of that inordinate fear of communism which once led us to embrace any dictator who joined us in that fear. . . .

For many years, we've been willing to adopt the flawed and erroneous principles and tactics of our adversaries, sometimes abandoning our own values for theirs. We've fought fire with fire, never thinking that fire is better quenched with water. This approach failed, with Vietnam the best example of its intellectual and moral poverty. But through failure we have now found our way back to our own principles and values.[3]

These idealistic aspects of Carter's world view were championed most vocally—inside the administration and to the public—by Andrew Young, protégé of Martin Luther King and devotee of his pacifist philosophy, formerly congressman for Georgia, early supporter of Carter's presidential candidacy, and Carter's ambassador to the United Nations.

But Zbigniew Brzezinski, Carter's principal tutor in world affairs during his campaign for the presidency, and his national security adviser in the White House, was always at Carter's elbow to insist that the idealistic impulses conform to the geopolitical realities of international relations—at least when it came to the actual conduct of policy. Brzezinski was a persistent advocate of the view that the necessary condition for the preservation of American values at home and their propagation abroad was the limitation of the power of the primary adversary, the Soviet Union. And he echoed Henry Kissinger's "linkage" approach to the Soviets in maintaining that the Kremlin could not expect the United States to sustain cooperative relationships with the USSR in some fields—arms control, trade, technology transfer—while the Soviets were engaging in aggressive power plays in Africa and the Persian Gulf area. Détente, insisted Brzezinski, "cannot be conducted on a selected and compartmentalized basis." [4] Indeed, Brzezinski was even more inclined than Kissinger to threaten a reduction in U.S.–Soviet cooperative arrangements as a punitive sanction for aggressive Soviet behavior, and to play upon Soviet fears of a Sino–American alliance against the Russians.

In contrast to Kissinger, however, Brzezinski advocated visible policies on behalf of human rights and Third World development as essential thrusts of an activist global policy that would be more than just a reaction to Soviet initiatives. In these respects he often could present himself as a "soul brother" to Andrew Young and other social-justice activists in the administration, even though he tended to shape his human rights and Third World policies to serve the geopolitical imperatives of the U.S.–Soviet competition rather than as ends in themselves.

A third approach was that of Carter's Secretary of State, Cyrus Vance. A former high government official (Secretary of the Army in the Kennedy administration, Deputy Secretary of Defense and then diplomatic trouble-shooter in the Johnson administration) and prominent New York lawyer, Vance was skeptical of grand designs, reformist or geopolitical, urging rather that each international situation be examined as a case-by-case basis to determine what U.S. interests might be implicated, and what policy options might best serve those interests. His preferred options, even with adversaries, usually were those stressing problem solving through negotiations aimed at narrowing points of difference and solidifying common interests instead of the pressure tactics of linkage and confrontation. Perceiving that vital U.S. interests would be served by limitations on the strategic arms race, he resisted all attempts in Washington to hold back on SALT negotiations and ratification unless the Soviets reversed their interventions in east Africa and Afghanistan. Nor did Vance believe that U.S. relations with most other countries should be determined with primary and explicit reference to the global power rivalry between the United States and the USSR. Rather, the United States should deal with countries "on the merits" of the particular needs of each country and the capacity of the United States to relate to these needs.

Jimmy Carter could be swayed by the world views and preferred style in each of these approaches; and at times during his campaign for the presidency and during his tenure in the White House he would appear to have adopted one or the other, and at times some confusing hybrid of all of them. An uncharitable explanation of Carter's apparent vacillation between these various approaches is that he had no deeply held views of his own and was simply a politician attempting to secure the support of diverse factions in the body politic and the policy establishment. A charitable explanation is that Carter, faithful to the country whose values he was attempting to embody, was a complex person, whose own deep impulses and commitments were sometimes at cross-purposes, particularly when it came to concrete policy implications, and that the various approaches he appeared to vacillate between were indeed facets of the real Jimmy Carter.

In an extensively researched biography of Jimmy Carter, Professor Betty Glad concluded that his "thought possesses a surface quality, and he lacks both creative ability and a basic philosophy to guide him in his political choices." [5] He frequently would quote the aphorism of Reinhold Niebuhr, whom he claimed as his favorite theologian, that "the sad duty of politics is to establish justice in a sinful world"; but he failed to articulate the substantive content of his justice concept, other than through his insistence that the United States must stand for "human rights" around the world and his egalitarian utterances echoing Jeffersonian themes that all persons have the right to life, liberty, and the pursuit of happiness, and that governments derive their just powers from the consent of the governed.

Carter's public campaign for the presidency had been unabashedly populist, claiming that the common people were his constituency and that it was their common sense which guided him in what was good or bad public policy, rather than the recommendations of experts or the calculations of Washington lawyers or power brokers.* Of course, having been Governor of Georgia, Carter knew as well as anyone else that "the people" are hardly unified in their common sense, and more often than not are divided into bitterly opposed self-seeking interests who themselves employ lawyers, power brokers, and experts to advance their demands.

His more private campaign had been a skillful effort to maintain and establish contacts in the world of the materially and politically powerful elites, and to engender in them confidence in his intelligence, worldliness, nonideological pragmatism, and sophisticated experience in dealing with corporate and governmental power. An important vehicle for Carter's establishmentarian campaign had been his membership in the Trilateral Commission, a nongovernmental organization of prominent influentials from North America, Western Europe, and Japan, to promote cooperation among the advanced industrialized countries. Founded by David Rockefeller and directed by Zbigniew Brzezinski, the Trilateral Commission included among its members many luminous exiles from past Democratic administrations (Cyrus Vance, George Ball, Paul Warnke, Harold Brown, Paul Nitze), media executives (Arthur Taylor of CBS, Hedley Donovan of *Time*), and prominent multinational corporation directors. It had been largely from his Trilateral Commission contacts that candidate Carter formed his Foreign Policy and Defense Task Force, and subsequently made his top-level and sub-Cabinet appointments to his administration.

*Carter himself was proud to apply the term "populist" to his political philosophy, calling his speech accepting the Democratic presidential nomination "a populist speech designed to show that I derived my political support, my advice and my concern directly from the people themselves, not from powerful intermediaries of special interest groups. 'Populist' is a word, as you know, that comes from *populus*—people—and I think the people have been the origin of my own political incentives and my political strength." Interview with Jimmy Carter, *U.S. News & World Report* (September 13, 1976). See also Jimmy Carter, *Keeping Faith: Memoirs of a President* (New York: Bantam Books, 1982), p. 74.

Carter's success as presidential candidate is largely attributable to his ability to present himself variously as populist and establishmentarian, human rights idealist and geopolitical realist, country boy and impeccably mannered dinner-party host, Bible-quoting "born-again Christian" and devotee of existentialism. He was credible in each of these roles, depending upon whom he was walking with, and—most remarkably—credible also in his professions of guileless honesty.* The aura of credibility undoubtedly was a reflection of the fact that all these facets were the real Jimmy Carter, that he indeed was an amalgam of all of them, and a true believer in the mystical ethos that this was the essence of the nation he felt called upon to represent. With Walt Whitman's America, he could proclaim: "Do I contradict myself?/Very well then I contradict myself, (I am large, I contain multitudes.)"

Some of Carter's main problems as President appear to have stemmed from his continuing to display in his executive role the all-things-to-all-people quality that got him elected. To continue in the Oval Office to give vent to the contradiction-laden instincts of Mr. Everyman was to fail to establish and stick to priorities among values and objectives without which consistent and credible policy is impossible to sustain. Each of Carter's most trusted advisers would sense that the chief was most sympathetic with one's own approach, and would carry back to subordinates and sometimes to the public such presidential guidance as one wanted to (and did) hear. Moreover, the President himself, often giving expression to the formulations of his different advisers, frequently would deliver himself in policies and pronouncements of a sequence of inconsistent moves and postures.

In foreign policy, the part of Jimmy Carter which was a Baptist preacher-politician was in tune with the moral sloganeering and simplifications of Andrew Young. But the engineer in Carter, always seeking structural principles and formulas to resolve problems, was particularly susceptible to the geopolitical grand designs and abstract formulations of Brzezinski, which provided a sense of in-

---

* Carter's promise never to lie catered to a people who, following the systematic lying at the highest levels of the U.S. government in connection with Vietnam and Watergate, wanted to trust their leaders again. His effort to demonstrate such credibility was taken to lengths unusual for a politician in his admission, near the end of the election campaign, to an interviewer for *Playboy* magazine that he had "looked on a lot of women [other than his wife] with lust." Interview with Jimmy Carter by Robert Scheer in *Playboy* (November 1976).

tellectual control over otherwise confusing events. Yet Carter was also a shrewd and pragmatic businessman, who understood the pitfalls of being carried away by emotion, ideology, or overly abstract logic. This part of Carter admired the case-by-case, corporate-lawyer approach of Cyrus Vance, who patiently and coolly could work through a complicated negotiating sequence with adversaries without getting trapped in a confrontation over general principles.

When it came to dealing with the Soviet Union, Carter's own paradoxical qualities and his susceptibility to the approaches of his various advisers would produce a confusing series of policy stances— confusing not only to the American public and allies but also to the Soviet leadership.

As a deeply religious man, Carter found strategies of polarization and alienation uncongenial; his preferred mode of dealing with adversaries was to discover with them bonds of common humanity as a context for attempting to harmonize, or at least reconcile, their conflicting interests. But such pacifist impulses were hardly as absolute for him, or even for Andrew Young, as they had been for their mutual hero, Martin Luther King. Carter would increasingly express in words as well as action an appreciation for maintaining an adequate arsenal of coercive power in order to defend one's interest against aggressive adversaries.

As a farmer and self-made millionaire, Carter apparently could switch as required to a stance of toughness and decisiveness in dealing with the Russians, especially when buoyed by Brzezinski's counsel that it is these qualities that the Russians respect most. Brzezinski's advice was that the President need not shirk from aggressively taking the diplomatic offensive against the Soviets, for they feared an America aroused and, despite their boasting, continued to admire our economic and technological prowess, and our military potential.

But when counseling with Secretary of State Vance, the latter's cool professionalism, the insistence on considering the manifold implications of any course of action, would appeal to Carter's self-concept as businessman-turned-chief-executive of the state of Georgia, and now sophisticated modernist statesman. He was particularly receptive to Vance's cautionary advice against unnecessarily provoking the Russians, of stimulating a full-blown arms race, of destroying the basis for the U.S.–Soviet cooperation—which was still new and fragile—by reviving a cold war psychology on both sides.

Carter's first major address devoted to U.S.–Soviet relations, delivered at the June 1978 Annapolis commencement, revealed his ambivalence so openly that it was an embarrassment to many in the administration.[6] It was widely believed, recalls Hodding Carter III, the State Department's press spokesman under Vance, that the President "took speech drafts offered by the State Department and the National Security Council and simply pasted half of one to half of the other. The result was predictably all over the lot, offering the Soviet Union the mailed fist and the dove's coo simultaneously."[7]

The Third World policies of the administration revealed a similar ambivalence at the top, once again reflecting the differing world views of the President's principal advisers. Brzezinski viewed the Third World much the way it was viewed in the Kennedy White House, as an arena of competition between the United States and the Soviet Union for influence over those demanding self-determination and equalization of wealth and power. To compete effectively, the United States should try to get on the side of the "new forces." However, the United States should not simply accept losses where the Soviets had already established a local power base; in such cases it was imperative to organize local balances of power against those within the Soviet camp, even it this meant the United States would have to back the more conservative or reactionary forces. Nor should the United States stand idly by and accept defection from the pro-U.S. camp toward nonalignment, for this, as viewed by Brzezinski, would weaken the global power position of the United States vis-à-vis the USSR. Especially in the case of important regional bulwarks against Soviet influence—most notably Iran—it was important to prevent a collapse of regimes friendly to the United States.

Brzezinski and Andrew Young were frequent allies on the importance of putting the United States on the side of movements for national self-determination and economic development in the Third World, even if their basic reasons for this posture differed. Their joint championing of U.S. support for the Marxist black liberation movement led by Robert Mugabe that took power in Zimbabwe was a notable case in point. Brzezinski saw that the real alternative was not a perpetuation of the more conservative black–white Rhodesian regime that had the backing of former white Rhodesian Prime Minister Ian Smith, but rather the Soviet-supported faction of the black liberation movement. By backing the dominant Mugabe group (also supported by China), the United States retained considerable influence with the new Zimbabwe government, while the Russians were left out in the bush. Andrew Young's reasons for supporting the black liberationists coverged here with Brzezinski's insofar as he too saw the Mugabe faction as the strongest among the liberationist forces. But Young was opposed to injecting cold war considerations prominently into decisions about whom to support or oppose in the Third World. U.S. support, rather, should go to the "progressive" forces, which in the South African context, meant those most capable of establishing and sustaining black majority rule in those areas still dominated by the white minority, and which in the Third World generally meant those attempting to redistribute wealth and political power to broader segments of the population. Young was against treating Third World countries and movements as pawns in the U.S.–Soviet rivalry—a policy he branded as a form of racist condescension—and argued instead for giving the benefit of the doubt to Third World "progressives" as people whose judgments about their own interests should be respected, even when this meant accepting help from the Russians and Cubans. Brzezinski, of course, regarded such a Third World policy as geopolitically naïve and dangerous.

Cyrus Vance, although as aware of the geopolitical realities as any of Carter's advisers, and hardly indifferent to Soviet expansionism, often differed with Brzezinski over the best means of limiting Soviet influence in the Third World. Vance held that Soviet expansion could be contained best by the development of strong, proud nations, unwilling to sacrifice their independence to the imperial purposes of a superpower. The United States should resist getting pulled into the game of competitive imperial expansion in the Third World. Rather, it should respond primarily to the development needs of Third World countries and in a way that conveyed respect for their own ability to define and deal with their indigenous problems. The problems of the Third World should not in the first instance be defined as cold war issues. The United States did not have to preach to the natives to save them from the Communist devil. American practical know-how and its pluralistic ideology would speak for itself. Influence would come by good works. The Russians would lose out in the larger competition by their crude power plays.

Carter, in part of his character, evidently wanted to be like Cyrus Vance, and even in some respects to share Andrew Young's compassion for the oppressed and poor peoples of the world. He wanted to be the kind, wise world leader who puts the human dignity of all God's children uppermost. But another part of him apparently wanted desperately to be admired as tough and unsqueamish in adversity, and perceived that the largest part of his domestic American audience identified with the machismo image more than the saint.

One of Carter's speechwriters during his first two years in office sums up the problems: "Carter has not given us an *idea* to follow. The central idea of the Carter administration is Jimmy Carter himself, his own mixture of traits, since the only thing that gives coherence to the items of his creed is that he happens to believe them all. . . . I came to think Jimmy Carter believes fifty things, but no one thing. . . . Values that others would find contradictory complement one another in his mind."[8]

Yet to blame the visible ambivalence and vacillation in U.S. foreign policy during Carter's presidency mainly on the character of Jimmy Carter is to miss the extent to which the Carter administration was an expression of a particular historical period rather than its creator.

Carter was perhaps all too faithfully a man of the season—the season of confusion in U.S. foreign policy goals following the country's misadventure in Vietnam; the season of popular moralistic backlash against the immorality of Watergate and against the amorality and elitism of Kissinger's brand of geopolitics; the season of realization that the Soviet Union, its arrogance revived by the attainment of full strategic equality with the United States and global military mobility, was not going to play détente according to the rules of mutual restraint; the season of adjustment to the dependence of the well-being of the people of the United States on the Middle Eastern oil producers, most of whom were hostile to this country for what they perceived as our past attempts to dominate them economically and politically and for our friendship with Israel.

Neither Carter nor Brzezinski nor any other influential official had the genius to translate the mood of confusion and apprehension which brought Carter to the presidency into a coherent foreign policy. A semblance of coherence developed out of the perceived need to more effectively prosecute the rivalry with the USSR, especially after the Soviet invasion of Afghanistan in late 1979—but haplessly this turn at the same time reinforced the larger impression of vacillation, for it appeared to contradict Carter's earlier pledges to reduce this country's preoccupation with the Soviet Union.

The departure from the administration of Andrew Young in August 1979 and finally Cyrus Vance in April 1980 was the necessary correlate of this shift by Carter toward the primary orientation of Brzezinski. Vance's resignation, especially, marked the ascendancy of the Brzezinski approach—the renewed preoccupation with the Soviet threat and the tendency to resort to confrontationist postures in dealing with adversaries. The Secretary of State said in resigning that he had been overruled in his objection to the attempt to rescue the American Embassy hostages in Iran by helicopter. This explicit reason, of course, was only the symptom of his more basic disagreement with the direction U.S. foreign policy was taking under Brzezinski's increasing influence. As Vance stated in his address at the 1980 Harvard commencement exercises: "Our real problems are long-term in nature. It will not do to reach for the dramatic act, to seek to cut through stubborn dilemmas with a single stroke." But it was also a "fallacy" to seek "a single strategy—a master plan" to yield "answers to each and every foreign policy decision we face. Whatever value that approach may have had in a bipolar world, it now serves us badly. The world has become pluralistic, exposing the inadequacy of the single strategy, the grand design, where facts are forced to fit theory." [9]

Ironically, it was Vance's patient, soft-spoken approach that was primarily responsible for most of the dramatic foreign policy success that Carter could claim for his administration: namely, the successful negotiation and ratification of the Panama Canal treaty; the Camp David accords between Israel and Egypt and their subsequent treaties; the husbanding of the installation of a black majority regime in Zimbabwe; and, finally, the deal with Iran to free the embassy hostages, consummated during the last hours of the Carter administration. The major accomplishments of the administration for which Brzezinski could sew chevrons on his sleeves were the establishment of full diplomatic relations with China and the revival of serious efforts in NATO to balance the Soviet military buildup; but these two elements were in the pipeline, so to speak, and it would have been surprising had they not materialized.

The largest disappointment of the Carter administration—its inability to gain congressional ratification of SALT II—can be blamed primarily on the Russians, who by invading Afghanistan on Christmas 1979 and brutally occupying that country thoughout 1980, ruined whatever chance Carter might have had to gain Senate concurrence to the treaties. A President with substantial political clout who believed, as Carter did, that SALT II was still in the national interest, despite Afghanistan, might have been able to successfully prosecute the ratification battle in 1980. Carter's international and domestic reputation as a statesman stayed too low to give him the kind of charisma that could convert wavering senators. Reluctantly, Carter backed away from a ratification fight which he was sure to lose.

Brzezinski would later complain that "SALT lies buried in the sands of Ogaden," a reference to the unwillingness of the United States to support the Somalians in 1978 in their war against the Ethiopians, who were being helped by Cuban troops and Soviet military advisers and equipment. In Brzezinski's view, SALT could have been ratified if the Carter administration had been able to sustain a reputation for toughness, that it was not "soft" toward the Soviets and was willing to "compete assertively" with them. "The argument that the phrase [about SALT and the Ogaden] is meant to capsulate," explained Brzezinski, "is that, unless we stand up to the Soviet drive by proxy soon enough, we'll not do well in the competition and will lose chances for effective cooperation." [10]

Vance, from retirement, would rebut Brzezinski's assertions and their implications. "The charge that some are making that there was an unwillingness to consider the use of force if necessary when our vital interests were concerned is hogwash," he declared. The trouble was, rather, that Brzezinski gave too much emphasis to "the use of military power or bluff, ignoring, in my judgment, the political, economic, and the trade aspects of our relationship with the Soviet Union." Brzezinski's epigram about SALT being "buried in the sands of Ogaden" was symptomatic of the grand strategy's neglect of the details of particular circumstances. It was "a catchy phrase without any substance," said Vance. Somalia had violated Ethiopian territory by invading the Ogaden in 1978, and the Soviet Union and Cuba had sent troops into Ethiopia to help an ally defend itself. The United States got what it wanted, Vance recalled, as the

Soviet Union and its allies, heeding the U.S. warning, held back from invading Somalian territory.[11]

Having lost the election to Ronald Reagan, Carter might at least have been spared further public altercations by those closely associated with his presidency. It was a measure of the weakness of his administration that his associates felt the need to absolve themselves of Carter's failures by blaming each other.

With such high-level divisiveness as a backdrop, Carter's lofty farewell address of January 14, 1981, was a sad reminder of how wide was the gap between the administration's aspirations and its achievements. Returning to the themes of his inaugural, Carter again pleaded for determination by the United States and all countries to "find ways to control and reduce the horrifying danger that is posed by the world's stockpile of nuclear arms." He reiterated the universalistic imperative of cooperation in husbanding and conserving the resources of the planet, given "the essential unity of our species." And he once again rang the bell for an enlargement of human rights at home and abroad.[12]

Carter's rhetoric was to blame more than anything else for the reputation his administration gained as being impotent. It was not that the United States during the Carter years failed to exercise international power; more often than not it did so effectively. Rather, Carter's idealistic professions on the way in and on the way out were so overblown that the administration was set up for the charge—largely valid—that U.S. power under Carter was grossly inadequate to the country's stated purposes. The story of the Carter administration's performance in world affairs reveals this shortfall in episode after episode. Yet with all the embarrassment at the rhetorical surface of events, there was no substantial backing away during the Carter years from vital interests of the United States.

28

IDEALISM AS THE HIGHER REALISM

*We seek these goals because they are right—and because we, too, will benefit.
Our own well-being, and even our security, are enhanced in a world that shares
common freedoms and in which prosperity and economic justice create the conditions for peace. . . . Nations, like individuals, limit their potential when they
limit their goals.*

CYRUS VANCE

The impulses to bring justice to the world reflected in Jimmy
Carter's campaign rhetoric were not the stuff that could be readily
translated into programs and actions. The diplomacy of the United
States had to be conducted in an international system of states, protective of their sovereignty, run by leaders no less proud than ours,
presiding over complex societies attempting to make their own adjustments to the often explosive confrontation of traditional ways of
life with technologically generated change. Many career foreign service officers who had lived and worked abroad, and experienced diplomats who had to negotiate with their counterparts around the
world, were not as ready as the Carter amateurs to label the policies
of other regimes morally "right" or "wrong," and were skeptical of
the ability of Americans whose experience was primarily in domestic
politics to adequately understand events in other lands, let alone to
effectively manipulate the indigenous social and political forces.
Wasn't *this,* after all, the lesson of Vietnam—not that we were on
the wrong side?

Secretary of State Vance, in particular—the most experienced foreign policy official at the top level of the new administration—was wary of the pitfalls in an ideologically crusading policy. It should not be the business of the United States, as Secretary of State John Quincy Adams used to counsel, to roam the world "in search of monsters to destroy."

But Vance, and other experienced hands, were also aware of the pitfalls in the realpolitik posture of aloofness from the "domestic" politics of countries the United States was supporting for geopolitical reasons. The manifestations of such support—generous financial credits, technology transfers, military and police training programs, a permissive weapons-sales policy—all constituted, in fact if not by design, a rather significant intervention into the domestic policy of the client country. Thus, in practice, the ideological neutrality that was supposed to underlie the realpolitik policy was vitiated, for the governments who came forward as the most willing clients were usually rightist regimes, dependent for their domestic political survival on domestic commercial and military classes, and resistant to egalitarian reforms.

In short, pure noninterventionism was a myth—and as a cloak for maintaining American "innocence" of the effects of U.S. material support on the domestic power of recipient governments, it was blatant hypocrisy. The United States government, while forswearing crusades to shape others in America's own image, did have a responsibility for assuring that this country at least not become an accomplice in the suppression, especially the brutal suppression, of the elementary human rights of other peoples.

Nonintervention as *respect* for other peoples, for their rights to self-determination of the form of government under which they chose to live, for their independence, was another matter. This the United States, true to its own early historical experience, could credibly champion. Such a neo-Wilsonian posture was consistent with the international pluralism that would be most advantageous to the United States in its competition with the Soviet Union for global influence. And a revival of the reputation of the United States as a champion of genuine self-determination would disallow the Soviets easy gains as sponsors of "national liberation" movements.

Thus the desire of the new President to bring morality back into U.S. foreign policy, to move away from the professed amoralism,

but actual immorality, of the Nixon–Kissinger period, was not necessarily inconsistent with a realistic pursuit of U.S. national interests. There were opportunities aplenty for translating the idealistic
impulses of the Carter amateurs into a sophisticated set of initiatives and instruments that would redound to this country's influence and power—for turning idealism into a higher realism. This
was the mission Vance set for himself within an administration well
populated with ideological crusaders and self-styled geopoliticians.
But it was his persistence in this mission that more than anything
else finally estranged the dedicated and self-effacing Secretary of
State from a President whose politically damaging reputation for
ambivalence and timidity made him more responsive to counselors
advocating bold postures and dramatic strokes.

FASHIONING A WORKABLE HUMAN RIGHTS POLICY

The earliest attempts by Carter to show the world that his human
rights posture was more than rhetoric were fashioned for him by
eager White House aides. A public letter by the President to the
Soviet dissident Andrei Sakharov and the media event of a White
House meeting with the recently exiled Vladimir Bukovsky por-
tended a resourceful cooptation of the human rights policy by Brzezinski and his staff of young activists. The Office of Human Rights
and of Humanitarian Affairs under Assistant Secretary of State Pa-
tricia Derian was slow in getting its act together, and its initiatives,
which would be just as much against oppressive right-wing oligarchies in the Third World, were eclipsed at the outset by what appeared to be a cold war revivalism in the White House. State Department officials spent much of the spring trying to reassure the
Russians that this was not the case, especially after Brezhnev and
Foreign Minister Gromyko insisted that serious negotiations on arms
control and other matters would be distorted, if not precluded, in
such an environment (see below, pp. 539–40).

A concerned President Carter asked Secretary Vance to sort things
out and to fashion a coherent and workable human rights policy.
The results of this first effort by the administration to think through
systematically the policy implications of the human rights posture
were presented in a major foreign policy address by Secretary Vance
at the University of Georgia Law School on April 30, 1977.

"In pursuing a human rights policy," said Vance, "we must always keep in mind the limits of our power and wisdom. A sure formula for defeat of our goals would be a rigid, hubristic attempt to impose our values on others. A doctrinaire plan of action would be as damaging as indifference." We must be realistic, he said. "Our country can only achieve our objectives if we shape what we do to the case at hand." In each reported case of a country violating basic human rights norms, therefore, the administration would ask a number of specific questions in determining whether and how to act:

First, what is the nature of the particular case?

What kinds of violations or deprivations are there? What is their extent?

Is there a pattern to the violations? If so, is the trend toward concern for human rights or away from it?

What is the degree of control and responsibility of the government involved?

And finally, is the government willing to permit outside investigation?

A second set of questions would concern the prospects for effective action.

Will our action be useful in promoting the overall cause of human rights?

Will it actually improve the specific conditions at hand? Or will it be likely to make things worse instead?

Is the country involved receptive to our interests and efforts?

Will others work with us, including official and private international organizations dedicated to furthering human rights?

Finally, does our sense of values and decency demand that we speak out or take action anyway, even though there is only a remote chance of making our influence felt?

A third set of questions would focus on the difficult policy dilemmas and tradeoffs.

Have we been sensitive to genuine security interests, realizing the outbreak of armed conflict or terrorism could itself pose a serious threat to human rights?

Have we considered *all* the rights at stake? If, for instance, we reduce aid to a government which violated the political rights of its citizens, do we not risk penalizing the hungry and the poor, who bear no responsibility for the abuses of their government?

The Secretary of State did not want to prejudge how such tradeoffs would be made in any specific case, for this might encourage some countries, for example, to repress political dissent for the ostensible reason of more effectively implementing an economic devel-

opment plan, or to rationalize draconian police tactics in the service
of security against terrorism. Yet in his listing of the types of human
rights the United States would work to advance around the world,
the placement of civil and political liberties third, behind

First, . . . the right to be free from governmental violation of the integrity of
the human person. . . . [such as] torture; cruel, inhuman, or degrading treatment
or punishment; and arbitrary arrest or imprisonment. . . .

Second, . . . the right to the fulfillment of such vital needs as food, shelter,
health care, and education. . . .

implied a rank ordering. The civil and political liberties generally
associated with liberal democracies, such as freedom of speech and
press and freedom to run for elective office, could not, realistically,
be insisted upon as universal rights that must be accorded equal
priority with the physical security and economic subsistence needs
of peoples. Elementary respect for the basic integrity of the human
person, however, was another matter, and the Carter administration was putting all, including its allies, on notice that this administration would not condone, and certainly not allow itself to be
associated with, violations of this fundamental norm of decent society.

In implementing this human rights policy, said Vance, the administration would avoid self-righteousness and stridency. This
country was not immune from criticisms. Our policy was to be applied in our own country as well as abroad. But as President Carter
emphasized in his speech to the UN General Assembly, "no member of the United Nations can claim that violation of internationally
protected human rights is its own affair."

Just as there were a variety of circumstances that had to be carefully assessed in determining when a country was indeed guilty of
human rights violations, so too were there a variety of possible responses whose appropriateness would have to be assayed on a case-
by-case basis. The means available ranged "from quiet diplomacy in
its many forms, through public pronouncements, to withholding assistance. Whenever possible, we will use positive steps of encouragement and inducement."

There could be no mechanistic formulas, no automatic answers.
"In the end, a decision whether and how to act in the cause of
human rights is a matter for informed and careful judgment." [1]

Opponents of giving human rights a central emphasis in U.S.

foreign policy were pleased to point out that, with all the qualifications, dilemmas, and tradeoffs in the Secretary of States exposition of the policy, the Carter administration could not really claim to be offering the country and the world anything new. And that was all to the good. Some opponents, however, continued to hold up the Carter administration's highly circumscribed performance in the human rights field to the standards of Carter's own earlier, more absolutist rhetoric, not to Vance's refinements, and, accordingly, took delight in villifying the administration for hypocrisy.

Many human rights idealists agreed, but with sadness, with the allegations of hypocrisy, as they witnessed Carter showering praise on dictators like the Shah of Iran and President Somoza of Nicaragua; continuing high levels of military support to the oppressive military regime in South Korea; taking a "hear no evil, see no evil, speak no evil" stance toward the People's Republic of China; and backing off quickly from his initial criticism of the Soviet regime for the way they treated dissidents in the USSR. It seemed as if the administration had the courage of its human rights convictions only when the violators were weak countries of little strategic value, like Haiti, Paraguay, Cambodia, and Uganda. But where there were costs and risks for taking a pro human rights stand, the administration was reluctant to show any spine.[2]

The impression of a chastened administration backing off from its promised strong stance on human rights in reaction to the opposition of strong international adversaries as well as friends was reinforced by the U.S. posture at the fall 1977 sessions of the Belgrade Review Conference on the Helsinki Accords. Rather than take the opportunity to publicly face the Soviet Union and other East European governments with the cases of human rights violations that had been compiled by the Congressional Commission on Security and Cooperation in Europe, the State Department instructed the U.S. delegation to politely raise the issue of compliance in general terms in the public sessions, saving the discussion of specific cases for private meetings closed to the press. The jounalists, however, could not be kept from filing reports on this decision, nor on the strong objections to it from the chief of the U.S. delegation to the Belgrade conference, former UN Ambassador and Supreme Court Justice Arthur Goldberg. The White House continued to back the State Department, whose principal argument in favor of the quieter approach was that our West European allies were anxious to preserve what little had been achieved at Helsinki by making the East accountable to a wider forum of governments on human rights issues, that results were being obtained on specific cases through careful negotiations, and that all this could be thrown overboard overnight if the Belgrade meetings degenerated into a shouting match.[3]

Despite the unpopularity of the pragmatic and quiet approach, the President remained committed to Vance's logic, with few exceptions, throughout his term of office, even though by following the approach favored by Goldberg and some of Carter's own domestic political advisers he would have been a more popular President. Behind the scenes, however, the President and the Secretary of State made it clear that they were dead serious about making human rights a central consideration in U.S. foreign policy, and that they expected the bureacracy to be resourceful in seeking and adapting policy instruments to give this commitment effect. Much legislation was already on the books, reflecting congressional attempts to get the executive to act in this field during the Kissinger years, so part of the effort would be simply to organize the administration to implement the law, particularly in foreign military and economic assistance programs.

The seriousness of the Carter–Vance commitment was reflected in the designation of Deputy Secretary of State Warren Christopher to head an Interagency Group on Human Rights and Foreign assistance. The group's mandate, backed by the authority of the National Security Council directive of April 1, 1977, which set it up, was to approve, delay, limit, or deny any proposed project on the basis of the recipient country's human rights record. Opponents within the bureaucracy of the new human rights emphasis might be able to box in or do end runs around the efforts of Assistant Secretary of State Derian and her newly enlarged Office of Human Rights and Humanitarian Affairs, but not the Secretary of State's most trusted second in command presiding over a powerful interagency group with members from the Departments of Defense, Treasury, Commerce, Labor, Agriculture, and the National Security Council. Decisions of the Christopher group were tantamount to an executive order, and were backed up by the appropriate White House and Cabinet-level endorsements when required.

As a result of the actions of the Interagency Group, assistance levels were lowered, on grounds of poor human rights performance, to Afghanistan, Guinea, the Central African Empire, Chile, Nicaragua, Paraguay, and El Salvador. And the group's findings of positive human rights developments resulted in increased levels of assistance for India, Sri Lanka, Botswana, Gambia, and the Dominican Republic, Peru, and Costa Rica.[4]

Under Carter, the U.S. government also opposed loans by international financial instituions to countries in gross violation of basic (especially "integrity of persons") human rights, but with much less consistency and automaticity than human rights zealots in the Congress wanted. Indeed, the Carter administration inherited a congressionally imposed requirement, denying it the case-by-case flexibility it thought essential, that the U.S. governors to both the Inter-American Development Bank and the African Development Fund must vote against loans to any country engaging in "a consistent pattern of gross violations of internationally recognized human rights unless such assistance will directly benefit needy people." This legislation, an amendment sponsored by Congressman Thomas Harkin of Iowa to the May 1976 bill authorizing funding to these regional banks, became the model for congressional attempts during 1977 to extend human rights provisos to development loans from the World Bank and other international lending institutions. The Carter administration lobbied hard against such legislation, arguing that it reflected an overly rigid approach, and that it would actually handicap U.S. efforts to encourage human rights improvements in other countries, since by making the U.S. votes against loans to specific countries automatic, it would weaken our bargaining power. A compromise bill passed the Congress on September 21, 1977, instructing U.S. officials to international financial institutions to "oppose" any loans to rights violators unless the loans directly benefited the needy. The requirement to "oppose" rather than to "vote no" was more consistent with the flexibility the administration wanted. Of course, one man's flexibility is another man's flabbiness, and the administration's efforts against the human rights riders to the multilateral-institution funding legislation were seized upon by critics as additional evidence of the hypocrisy of Carter's human rights stance.[5]

Despite dissatisfaction in the Congress and a public generally confused by the administration's pragmatic pullback from Carter's earlier rhetoric, the international atmosphere was significantly changed by the new policy, as governments around the world expected they would have to answer to the United States on their human rights records. After two years in office, the Carter administration could properly take some credit (as its spokesmen did) for positive human rights developments in several countries: substantial numbers of political prisoners were released in Bangladesh, the Sudan, Indonesia, South Korea, the Philippines, Brazil, Nepal, and Cuba. In Ghana, Nigeria, and Thailand significant steps toward the transfer of power from military to civilian democratic institutions were taken. More freedom was granted to the press in various countries. As put by one administration official in his congressional testimony, "Both dissidents and governments have acknowledged—the former favorably and the latter at times less so—our inclusion of human rights issues into U.S. foreign policy. The wall posters of China, the statements of Sakharov and others, and the declarations of groups concerned with political prisoners in Asia, Africa, and Latin America, demonstrate that the U.S. human rights policy is a constant reality."[6]

PANAMA, NICARAGUA, AND ZIMBABWE: TESTS OF THE REALISM OF THE NEW IDEALISM

In four situations during the period of the Carter administration, the United States was faced with challenges to the status quo that would have inevitable consequences for regional balances of power, and which provided this country with opportunities to put its ideals of self-determination and human rights in the service of its geopolitical interests. One of these, the revolution in Iran, because of the depth of the trauma it produced, and the consequences of its outcome for the global balance of power, will be treated in a separate chapter. The other three—the maturing of the negotiations on the Panama Canal treaties, the success of the Sandinista movement in Nicaragua, and the failure of half way measures toward black majority rule in Rhodesia/Zimbabwe—were not quite as traumatic for this country, nor as consequential in their immediate effects; yet their management by the Carter administration also sparked considerable domestic controversy over the power and purposes of the United States in the world.

The domestic controversy was most intense over the two treaties signed with great fanfare on September 7, 1977, by President Carter and Brigadier General Omar Torrijos Herrera ceding sovereignty over the Panama Canal and the Canal Zone to Panama and guaranteeing the United States future peacetime and wartime use of the canal.* For the treaties to become law, the Senate had to vote its consent with at least a two-thirds majority, or 67 votes; but at the outset of the Senate deliberations, a United Press International poll reported only 36 senators for or leaning toward approval, 27 against or leaning against, and 37 uncommitted.[7] Moreover, popular passion and organized pressures were running against approval. Carter found that his presumed electoral mandate to restore an idealistic content to U.S. foreign policy was rather thin and highly circumscribed. It was all right to be for self-determination and human rights if this meant the independence of Namibia from the Republic of South Africa, but not if it meant handing over one of the United States' proudest possessions to a small Latin American country.

The administration was able to win few converts by pointing out that technically the United States never had formal sovereignty over the canal and Canal Zone, but only a grant from Panama, through the original 1903 treaty, to act "as if it were sovereign," and that even this was extracted from Panama by a coercive power play which, by today's standards, would be universally condemned as imperialistic and illegitimate. The popular ground in the debate was occupied by those, like Ronald Reagan, who argued for a revival of the kind of American patriotism that took pride in Theodore Roosevelt's ag-

---

*The Panama Canal Treaty established a staged devolution of control of the canal and the zone to Panama, to be completed by the year 2000. Until then, the United States would retain its military base rights in the zone as well as full responsibility for the defense of the canal. The treaty also established schedules of fees to be paid Panama during this period and stipulated canal administrative procedures in detail. The Neutrality Treaty, which would take effect in the year 2000, was a guarantee by Panama to assure all nations the right to use the canal in peace and war, stipulating that only Panama was to operate the canal and to maintain any required military forces on its territory for the purpose, but implying a residual right of the United States to take matters into its own hands if Panama failed to live up to its treaty obligations. The United States also was given the status of first among equals by the provision that warships of the United States and Panama were entitled to transit the canal "expeditiously."

gressiveness in securing the canal, and by those, like Senator S. I. Hayakawa, who, with his quip "We stole it fair and square," gave vent to a cocky American jingoism pressing for release from the post-Vietnam restraints on such impulses.

Accommodating to the all-too-evident popular mood and senatorial reluctance to buck it, President Carter, during the seven-month battle for legislative approval of the treaties, shifted his own ground from the initial invocations of the country's traditions of fairness, nobility, and self-determination for all peoples, to predictions of disastrous geopolitical consequences for the United States if the treaties were rejected. And to assure senators that the United States was relinquishing neither any tangible military and commercial rights to use the canal in war or peace nor any real power to enforce these rights should Panama someday be hostile to the United States, the President accepted some ninety "reservations," "understandings," and "conditions" demanded by senators, as well as two amendments that required General Torrijos' consent, and in the process came perilously close to pushing the Panamanian into a repudiation of the whole effort.

Much of the dabate revolved around the issue of the effects of the treaties on the ability of the United States militarily to assure its use of the canal in wartime or when under terrorist siege—in many respects a false issue, since the canal, with or without U.S. sovereignty in the Canal Zone, was a highly vulnerable target; nor did the U.S. Navy anymore depend on navigating the canal to deploy main battle capabilities between the Atlantic and the Pacific. Nevertheless, the administration felt compelled to rebut all charges of the comparative military disadvantages under the treaties. Secretary of Defense Harold Brown, along with other military experts, reminded the Congress that "our armed forces now control and they will continue to control with overwhelming forces, the sea approaches to the canal" as well as to command the airspace in the region.[8] Brown, Brzezinski, and various State Department witnesses also made the more telling argument that with the treaties the likelihood of local terrorist acts and subversion of the canal would be reduced, for it would no longer be a symbol of U.S. power.

Despite the admendments and reservations—some (like the Deconcini reservation providing that if the canal were closed for any reason *either* the United States of Panama could take whatever steps were necessary, including military, to put it back into operation) almost killing both treaties—the President and all the heavies he could muster in the administration and outside (Kissinger included) were able to persuade the Senate to approve the treaties by only a slim two-vote margin over the required two-thirds.

In an address to the nation during the final weeks of the Senate's deliberations, President Carter, while emphasizing the geopolitical arguments he knew were the major points on which wavering senators wanted assurances, was not about to abandon the moral rationale that was still an important motive in his efforts, and which he believed was the face of America that was most important for regaining America's influence in the world. "When we talk about the Canal," he said, "whether we are for or against the treaties, we are talking about very deep and elemental feelings about our own strength."

Still, we Americans want a more humane and stable world. We believe in goodwill and fairness as well as strength. This agreement with Panama is something we want because we know it is right. This is not merely the surest way to protect and save the Canal, it's a strong, positive act of a people who are still confident, still creative, still great. [9]

It was also important at this time not to feed anti-American sentiments that were on the rise in Central America as a result of the Carter administration's guilt-by-association with the Somoza regime's harsh repression of the growing movement for political reform in Nicaragua.

In Nicaragua, the United States was unavoidably implicated in the challenges to the legitimacy of the oligarchical Somoza dynasty, which, because of its own staunch anti-Communism and record of tangible cooperation with U.S. anti-Communist interventions in Central America and the Caribbean, was heavily supported throughout the post–World War II period with U.S. economic and military assistance. Now, with the dictator Anastasio Somoza Debayle confronting a rapidly expanding revolution against his rule, the United States government—even with Carter's commitment to human rights—found itself trapped by its past obligations.

By the time of Carter's inauguration, opposition to Somoza had become broadly based in Nicaragua, with Managu's large and thriving middle classes organized in the Unión Democrática de Liberación, led by the respected editor of *La Prensa,* Pedro Joaquin Chamorro. The militant leftists, whose spearhead was the Frente Sandinista de Liberación Nacional, was still not the dominant force, but Somoza's strategy of focusing on the Sandinistas as the main threat to law and order, and his allegations that their Cuban and Russian connections (still rather thin) meant that an international Communist conspiracy was behind the effort to undermine his regime, gave the leftists more visibility and charisma in Nicaragua and internationally than they might have had otherwise. The Sandinistas thus became a partner with Somoza in polarizing Nicaragua between them, as their techniques of terrorism and hostage-taking led to increased brutality by Somoza's National Guard against suspected opponents of the regime. In the two years before Carter's election, the escalation of the brutal civil conflict had led Somoza to declare a state of siege, and with an elite "counterinsurgency force," supported by an 80 percent increase in U.S. military aid, launched a reign of terror in the countryside, featuring torture and mass executions, and the uprooting and forced resettlement of 80 percent of the rural population in the northern regions of the country.[10]

The gross and systematic brutality of the Somoza regime was brought to the attention of the Christopher Interagency Group and led to a restriction of military and economic aid to Nicaragua in April 1977, as one of the first acts by which the Carter administration could demonstrate its seriousness of purpose on human rights. It was a minor diminution of aid, however, a mere slap on the wrist to the Nicaraguan dictator who had over the years developed influential allies in the U.S. Congress and State and Defense Department bureaucracies. Somoza now banked on the efficiency with which his reign of terror had broken the back of the Sandinista resistance to reestablish his invulnerability and domestic order, and to allow him to dispense with those acts that offended the sensibilities of the Carter administration. And, indeed, in September 1977 the administration relaxed the restrictions it had imposed only five months before.

The moderates now stepped up their activities to mobilize support for peaceful electoral and constitutional change, and tried to forge links with some of the less fanatic elements of the Sandinista front. But the assassination of the moderate leader, Chamorro, in 1978 led to a new flareup of popular outrage and violence directed against

Somoza that drew in most elements of Nicaraguan society. The country's business leaders called a general strike to demand Somoza's resignation, and terrorists launched attacks throughout the country. The Sandinistas were revived, and so were the harsh, repressive tactics of the National Guard. The moderates placed their hopes in the Carter administration, anticipating a reimposition of sanctions on Somoza coupled with pressures for the institution of genuine constitutionalism and representative government.

But the severe deterioration of Somoza's ability to control events in 1978 posed a more stark dilemma for the Carter administration than did the 1977 situation. Sanctions at this time might further undercut Somoza's legitimacy at a time when the consequence would be the coming to power of the revolutionary elements. Yet no action in 1978, given the widespread knowledge that the situation was even worse now than in the previous year, would be an embarrassing retreat for the Carter human rights policy. The result was the Carter administration's 1978 decision to reimpose sanctions and to insist upon a "dialogue" between Somoza and the moderates. Once again, surface calm returned to the cities and countryside of Nicaragua, and by summer the Carter administration decided to reduce the sanctions. In addition Carter sent a letter to Somoza congratulating the dictator on his improved human rights record.[11]

The U.S. reconciliation with Somoza had just the opposite effect of that intended by Carter. Rather than stimulating movement toward the liberalization of the government in Nicaragua, it demoralized most of the moderates, and drove them in desperation into an alliance with the radicals under a new umbrella organization, the Broad Opposition Front.

With the country now polarized, the militant Sandinistas were able to set the pace and call the shots for the broad anti-Somoza coalition. In August 1978, they stormed the National Palace while Somoza's rubber-stamp Congress was in session and took 1500 hostages, in exchange for whom they were able to force Somoza to release 59 Sandinistas from his jails. The populace was electrified. Another general strike was called, and in September the Sandinistas launched attacks on National Guard garrisons in five provincial cities.[12] The National Guard, insecure now on the ground, retaliated from the air with bombing and strafing attacks on rebel strongholds in which thousands of innocent civilians were killed. By the end of the month Somoza had again established his power, but at the cost of totally losing his authority.

The events of bloody September 1978 finally convinced U.S. officials that Somoza must be persuaded to step down in favor of a constitutionalist regime. They still hoped, however, to accomplish this by a negotiation between Somoza and the moderates to arrange for a plebiscite, and in this way to prevent the Sandinistas from dominating the post-Somoza government. Somoza agreed to participate in such negotiations, but his attempts to manipulate and subvert them provoked even the moderate elements to walk out in protest. In the meantime the Sandinistas had been reorganizing and rearming for what was to become the final, successful stage of their insurrection.

The last, decisive anti-Somoza uprising began on June 4, 1979. Virtually the entire population of Managua cooperated in bringing to a halt all commercial and professional activity. The National Guard again retaliated with bullets and bombs, but this time the insurrection only spread. Well-equipped Sandinista forces that had been arming themselves and training in neighboring Costa Rica reentered the country. American and other foreign observers began to talk of an impending Sandinista victory.[13]

On July 21, 1979, Secretary of State Vance announced a change in United States policy during a meeting of the Organization of American States in Washington. "We must seek a political solution which will take into account the interests of *all* significant groups in Nicaragua," he told the assembled Latin American diplomats (emphasis added).

Such a solution must begin with the replacement of the present Government with a transition government of national reconciliation, which would be a clear break with the past. It would consist of individuals who enjoy the support and confidence of the widest possible spectrum of Nicaraguans.

· · ·

We propose that this meeting insist on a cease-fire within Nicaragua and on its borders and a halt to all shipments of arms and ammunition into Nicaragua.

· · ·

All of the member nations of this organization must consider on an urgent basis the need for a peacekeeping force, to help restore order and to permit the will of Nicaraguan citizens to be implemented in the establishment of a democratic and representative government.[14]

The Organization of American States almost unanimously rejected the U.S. proposals for a cease-fire and a regional peacekeeping force. It was clearly too little and too late, and—besides—the OAS was itself not well structured to perform this function.

The Sandinistas pressed forward, set up a provisional government, and Somoza, denied further U.S. backing, went into exile. The United States government, having lost virtually all credit with the Sandinista-dominated regime installed in Managua, proved no more capable of influencing events in that country during the remainder of the Carter presidency to prevent it from moving in a pro-Fidelista and pro-Soviet direction; if anything, it was the recent record of U.S. timidity in dealing with Somoza that made such a radicalization likely. In 1981, a new administration in Washington, staffed by advisers who had been pro-Somoza to the last, and who had regarded Carter's pressures on him as responsible for the success of the Sandinistas, had a ready-made target to add to their hit list of Soviet/Cuban clients in Central America. Carter could only shake his head at what happens to the best-laid plans of mice and men.

The Carter administration looked considerably more consistent and competent in dealing with the Rhodesia/Zimbabwe issue that it did with respect to the Panama Canal treaties or the Somoza ouster. Not that the policy dilemmas were less profound, or that a conservative opposition to a reformist policy was lacking, but rather that Carter's relatively impressive success on matters in southern Africa was largely the result of there being in the Congress and among his new appointees to high foreign policy positions an active constituency for change. The U.S. government was also lucky on the Rhodesia/Zimbabwe issue to be able to take a back seat to the British, who bore the principal international responsibility for bringing about a durable regime change in Salisbury.

The reformist constituency in the administration, a part of what UN Ambassador Andrew Young called "the new Africa coalition," consisted of Young himself, Assistant Secretary of State for Africa Richard Moose, and director of the Policy Planning Staff Anthony Lake. Building on the American black constituency support that Young was instrumental in bringing into the Carter camp in the 1976 campaign, and the emergence of African issues as a post-Vietnam foreign policy concern among American liberals, this group was instrumental in getting the Congress to repeal the Byrd Amendment (providing for U.S. imports of Rhodesian chrome), allowing Carter to fulfill one of his campaign promises, and to bring U.S. diplomacy back in concert with Britain's on the Rhodesia/Zimbabwe issue.[15]

The repeal of the Byrd Amendment, said Carter in signing the legislation, "puts us on the side of what is right and proper." By allowing the United States to join in the UN-authorized boycott of Rhodesian exports, to which the American delegation had originally subscribed, it "puts us back on the side of support for the United Nations. It puts us in the strategic position to help with the resolution of the Rhodesian question."[16]

Carter soon came under renewed pressure from conservatives in the Congress, however, to lift the reinstated boycott of Rhodesian materials as an indication of approval by the U.S. government for the racially mixed government Rhodesian Prime Minister Ian Smith had put together in 1978 and successfully submitted to electoral referenda in January and April of 1979. The President, following the advice of the African coalition in his administration, continued to concert U.S. policy with that of Britain, which even under the Conservative government of Margaret Thatcher refused to accord legitimacy to the new Muzorewa regime in Salisbury. The British urged a more deeply cutting change in Rhodesia/Zimbabwe that would bring the most popular and vigorous elements of the black liberationist movement, the Patriotic Front for the Liberation of Zimbabwe, into a new black-run government. If not, the British argued, the Marxist leadership of the Patriotic Front would come increasingly under the sway of the Soviet Union, and eventually stage a full-blown insurrection to install a pro-Soviet regime in Salisbury.[17]

It was thus essentially a realpolitik rationale of dealing with those who have the power (in this case potential power) that allowed Carter to sustain the embargo and to cooperate with Britain in inducing the Patriotic Front leader, Robert Mugabe, to lay down his arms and participate constructively in the formation of the new government of independent Zimbabwe. By so doing, the United States salvaged for itself in southern Africa, more than it had been able to do in Nicaragua or Iran, a position of influence with the ascending political forces. A not inconsiderable side benefit was the parallel diminution of Soviet influence.

The new regime in Salisbury would hardly be a model of liberal democracy, respecting human rights. But at least Carter could point to the outcome as, on balance, a large plus for the United States. He was properly pleased to find that the newly installed leader of Zimbabwe, "who was formerly looked upon as a Marxist and a hater of the United States—Mugabe—has now, I think, become one of our strong and potentially very good and loyal friends." [18]

29

CAMP DAVID: THE EXTENT AND LIMITS OF U.S. LEVERAGE IN THE MIDDLE EAST

We offer our good offices. I think it's accurate to say that of all the nations in the world, we are the one that's most trusted, not completely, but most trusted by the Arab countries and also by Israel. I guess both sides have some doubt about us. But we'll have to act kind of as a catalyst to bring about their ability to negotiate successfully with one another.

JIMMY CARTER

President Carter's foreign policy advisers, and Carter himself, had anticipated that the Middle East would provide the new administration with its greatest challenges *and* opportunities. The new directions in the U.S. international course that had been set during the Kissinger years required few major alterations, except for the restoration of a moral (human rights) content to U.S. policy. The disengagement from Southeast Asia had been fully accomplished. Soviet–American détente, though more precarious than Kissinger had hoped, was in need of husbanding, primarily through the vehicle of SALT II. The rapprochement with China had to be sealed through the extension of formal recognition. These were all in the nature of *implementations*. It was in the Middle East, however, that there was yet a need for a dramatic breakthrough. Kissinger had helped put the lid temporarily on a smoldering situation, and his role in arranging for a cease-fire in the Yom Kippur War and for the disengagement of Israeli and Egyptian forces from the Sinai had been feats of tactical brilliance.

But the momentum of Kissinger's shuttle diplomacy, after effectuating the Sinai II disengagement agreement, had begun to run down. Between Israel and each of her antagonists other than Egypt there were not the ingredients for the kinds of quid pro quo compromises that were needed to keep the peace process alive, nor did any of the other principal antagonists of Israel have that added incentive to play ball with the United States that President Sadat had after his falling out with the Soviets.

It was of the utmost importance to regain the lost momentum of the peace process, for in the Middle East the status quo itself was too dangerously volatile. The bitter resentments and impatience of the Arabs toward Israel and her deepening consolidation of the territories she captured in the 1967 war, plus the readiness of the Soviet Union to exploit Arab grievances in order to expand her own influence, would surely present Carter, like Nixon, Johnson, Eisenhower, and Truman before him, with another round of war in the Middle East. Renewed war would confront the United States with more profound dilemmas than ever: this time Israeli military superiority, if indeed she still maintained it, would be less than before, and the United States therefore would probably need to come to Israel's assistance more heavily than in the past rounds; but now there would be the clear prospect of the Arabs cutting off the flow of oil to Israel's supporters. Even short of a resumption of hostilities, continued high tension between the Arabs and the Israelis might at any time stimulate the Arab oil producers to use their resource as a political weapon.

A dramatic breakthrough from the status quo was required. Carter and Company thought they had a plan for bringing this about.

THE BROOKINGS REPORT AND THE OCTOBER 1977 INITIATIVE

The new administration's plan for getting the Middle East peace process moving again was brought with them into office, essentially made, in the form of the report of a 1975 Brookings Institution study group titled *Toward Peace in the Middle East*.[1] Co-directed by former U.S. Ambassador Charles Yost and Professor Morroe Berger of Princeton University, the Brookings study group included Zbigniew Brzezinski among its sixteen members.* It was Brzezinski who brought the report to candidate Jimmy Carter's attention and got him to endorse it during the 1976 presidential election campaign.

The Brookings study group concluded that the approach followed since the 1973 war, emphasizing interim steps designed to reduce tension and to move the parties gradually toward a comprehensive settlement, was no longer feasible. Rather, it was imperative, if a dangerous stalemate was to be avoided, that "peacemaking efforts should henceforth concentrate on negotiation of a comprehensive settlement, including only such interim steps as constitute essential preparations for such a negotiation." The negotiations should aim at a "package" of agreements on boundaries, the nature of a Palestinian entity, and the regime for Jerusalem, and should involve all the nations who would be affected, plus the principal external guarantors.

In exchange for Arab assurances to Israel of peaceful relations and the security of her territory and borders, said the Brookings group, Israel should withdraw to the boundaries prevailing prior to the start of the 1967 war, with only such modifications as might be mutually accepted. Israel also should accept the principle of Palestinian self-determination, and should not rule out the possibility that the Palestinian entity would be an independent state; but in return the Palestinians should recognize the sovereignty and integrity of Israel, and should accept whatever security arrangements, mutual guarantes, demilitarized zones, or UN presence is embodied in the peace settlement. The Brookings group felt it was premature to stipulate the precise nature of the regime for Jerusalem, and granted that it might be wise to leave this question, particularly the issue of Israel's sovereignty over the whole city, to a late stage in the negotiations. But it was not too early to obtain agreement on the minimum criteria for governing the city—namely, that there should be unimpaired access to all the holy places and that each would be under the custodianship of its own faith; that there should be no

---

* The complete membership of the Brookings Middle East study group was Morroe Berger (co-director), Robert R. Bowie, Zbigniew Brzezinski, John C. Campbell, Najeeb Halaby, Rita Hauser, Roger Heyns (chairman), Alan Horton, Malcolm Kerr, Fred Khouri, Philip Klutznick, William Quandt, Nadav Safran, Stephen Spiegel, A. L. Udovich, and Charles W. Yost (co-director).

barriers to the free circulation of populations throughout the city; and that each national group, if it so desired, should have substantial political autonomy within the area of the city where it was predominant.

Some of the elements of the proposed comprehensive Arab–Israeli peace settlement could be implemented in stages. But, advised the Brookings study group, "In order that a settlement be sufficiently attractive to all the parties to induce them to make the necessary compromises, all aspects of the settlement will have to be spelled out explicitly in an agreement or agreements that will be signed more or less simultaneously as part of a 'package deal.' " [2]

Such a comprehensive package would, of course, have to be considered and approved, if not actually negotiated, in a general "Geneva"-style conference at which all of the parties directly involved were represented along with the pertinent big-power guarantors of the settlement. The "Geneva" format refers to the December 1973 conference in Geneva co-chaired by the United States and the Soviet Union and attended by Israel, Egypt, and Jordan, which broke up after only two days. If Geneva were to be reconvened, perhaps with a larger membership, Israel could obtain her objective of negotiating face to face with her Arab neighbors. It would again commit the USSR to the negotiating process in a way that would make it difficult for the Kremlin to reject the settlement that would emerge. Moreover,

since there is no question but that the USSR has had a considerable capacity for obstructing a general settlement, and any settlement which it opposed would be likely to prove unstable, its involvement in the negotiating process and in the arrangements and guarantees following a successful negotiation would seem on balance to be an advantage rather than a disadvantage of a general conference. [3]

The idea of a general conference also had inherent difficulties: How would the Palestinians be represented, and would they first have to recognize Israel and its right to exist in peace and security? How could such a general conference be structured and conducted so as not to degenerate rapidly into a polarized polemical debating arena, with the Soviet Union playing to the militant Arab galleries?

Such obstacles to a successful general conference are serious, admitted the authors of the Brookings report, but they should not be insurmountable if the nations involved could be persuaded that there is no viable alternative to a comprehensive settlement.

These were the assumptions underlying the initiative early in the Carter administration to get the Soviets committed to the broad principles in the Brookings report as the terms of reference for a reconvened Geneva conference. The Soviets were more than willing to be brought back into the picture as a partner in the Middle East peace process, and jumped at the chance of joining the United States in a call to reconvene the Geneva conference.

In their formal joint statement of October 1, 1977, issued simultaneously in Moscow and Washington, the United States and the Soviet Union, as co-chairmen of the Geneva conference, maintained that "a just and lasting settlement of the Arab–Israeli conflict . . . should be comprehensive, incorporating all parties concerned and all questions." The settlement should resolve

such key issues as withdrawal of Israeli armed forces from territories occupied in the 1967 conflict; the resolution of the Palestinian question, including insuring the legitimate rights of the Palestinian people; termination of the state of war and establishment of normal peaceful relations of the Palestinian people; termination of the state of war and establishment of normal peaceful relations on the basis of mutual recognition of the principles of sovereignty, territorial integrity and political independence.

The only right and effective way to achieve a fundamental solution to these issues, said the U.S.–Soviet statement, was through

negotiation within the framework of the Geneva Peace Conference, specifically convened for these purposes, with participation in its work of the representatives of all the parties involved in the conflict, including those of the Palestinian people.[4]

Although the statement departed somewhat from the standard Arab formulations (it did not name the Palestine Liberation Organization as the representative of the Palestinians, and it did not insist on Israeli withdrawal from *all* territories occupied in the 1967 war), it outraged the government of Israel and its supporters in the United States by referring to the "legitimate rights" of the Palestinian people, the code words for the claim to statehood, rather than their "legitimate interests"—the more innocuous phrase which Israel over the years had been willing to accept. The joint statement also alarmed Egypt's President Answar Sadat, who wanted least of all to bring the Soviet Union back heavily into the peace process. Sadat had only recently made his historic shift away from being a principal client of the USSR and did not trust Soviet motives; and now here was the Carter administration unwittingly becoming an accomplice of the Kremlin in subordinating Egypt's interests to Russia's geopolitical designs in the Middle East.

The negative reactions by Israel and Egypt to the October 1, 1977, joint statement were no real surprise to the Carter administration's Middle East experts, for Prime Minister Begin and President Sadat each had previously voiced objections to reconvening the Geneva forum and suspicions of Soviet designs. Nevertheless, Brzezinski and Carter were determined to shake loose the logjam that had developed out of the step-by-step approach, were convinced that Soviet leverage was needed to get the recalcitrant Arabs to negotiate with Israel, and felt that they could keep the Russians honest by making it clear to the Kremlin that Soviet cooperation in bringing about a Middle East peace was an essential link in the overall détente relationship. Begin and Sadat, as well as the rest of the parties in the region, could be brought along if the two superpowers were operating in concert.

What the Carter administration did not know, however, was that simultaneously with the dialogue between the Russians and the Americans that produced the October 1 statement, the highest levels of the Begin and Sadat governments were in secret dialogue to explore the prospects of a direct and substantial accommodation between Israel and Egypt. (The secret Israeli-Egyptian dialogue during the fall of 1977 had grown out of the decision by Begin to share Israeli intelligence information with Sadat about a Libyan terrorist plot to assassinate the Egyptian leader, which allowed Sadat's secret police to capture the terrorists in Cairo. Sadat was doubly grateful when Begin announced to the Knesset that Sadat could go ahead with a military attack across the Egyptian–Libyan border without fear that Israel would take advantage of the situation on the Sinai front while Sadat's forces were preoccupied with the situation on Egypt's western front).[5] Sadat's dramatic decision to accept Begin's rhetorical invitation to come to Jerusalem to talk peace could not have been predicted (even Sadat's closest associates were surprised); but it is doubtful that the Carter administration would have so easily discounted the anticipated Israeli and Egyptian objections to the concerted Soviet–American move to reconvene the Geneva conference if they had been aware of the rapport that was developing between Begin and Sadat.

Sadat's historic visit to Israel on November 9, 1977, completely pulled the rug out from under the U.S.–Soviet October 1 démarche. In some measure, however, it may have been provoked by that démarche, which is ironic, for the resulting negotiations between Israel and Egypt gave Jimmy Carter the opportunity to play his sought-for role as peacemaker.

CARTER AS MEDIATOR

Israeli Prime Minister Menachem Begin, in taking up Sadat's offer of direct negotiations leading toward a peace settlement, offered his own terms for such a settlement. Not surprisingly, Begin's terms differed substantially from those Sadat had proposed in his personal appearance before the Israeli Parliament. Whereas Sadat had offered full peace and diplomatic relations in exchange for the end of Israeli occupation of the Arab territories she conquered in 1967 *and* the achievement by the Palestinians of the right to establish their own state, Begin, in return for Egypt's willingness to normalize relations with Israel, offered to relinquish Israeli control of the Sinai and to provide the Palestinians on the West Bank and the Gaza Strip with limited local "autonomy" side by side with the continuation of Israeli settlements and troop deployments in these areas.

The United States government, temporarily knocked off balance by the decision by Sadat and Begin to begin a dialogue themselves, once again was able to resume the role of provider of good offices to Egypt and Israel in their efforts to overcome the still-wide divergence in their terms for peace. Now, however, this mediating role would be played less through the peripatetic shuttling of high U.S. officials, à la Kissinger, between Cairo and Jerusalem, than through the President of the United States encouraging the leaders of each country to visit with him personally in the United States to work out, at the highest level, ways of consumating real peace.

Begin came first, in mid-December 1977, to talk with Carter, and the following week traveled to Ismailia, Egypt, to negotiate directly with Sadat. Still, neither the two Middle Eastern leaders nor their technical working groups were able to resolve the impasse.

Next it was Sadat's turn to visit with Carter. Meeting at Camp David in early February 1978, the two Presidents of humble rural beginnings and deeply religious sentiments apparently established an easy rapport (in contrast to the reportedly poor chemistry between each of them and Begin), with Sadat commenting that the United States was no longer simply a "go-between" but was now a "full partner" in the peace process. There was more than personal rapport involved, however. This first Carter–Sadat meeting marked a return to the geopolitical understanding which Kissinger and Sadat had developed that the United States and Egypt shared a priority interest in reducing the Soviet Union's influence in the Middle East; and that momentum in achieving an Arab–Israeli settlement was crucial for this purpose, but so was the assumption by the United States of the role, previously played by the Soviets, of Egypts's principal arms supplier.

Four days after Sadat left the United States, the Carter administration proposed that Congress authorize sales of $4.8 billion worth of military jet aircraft to Israel, Saudi Arabia, and Egypt. The Egyptian portion of the package (Cairo could purchase fifty F-54E short-range fighter bombers) would be the first transfer of U.S. weapons to Egypt since the 1950s. Speaking for the administration, Secretary of State Vance argued that "Egypt, too, must have reasonable assurance of its ability to defend itself if it is to continue the peace negotiations with confidence." [6]

Prime Minister Begin came to the White House again at the end of March 1978; but this time President Carter gave him a deliberately cool reception. The administration was now growing impatient with what it regarded as Israel's increasing intransigence on the West Bank and Gaza Strip issues. Begin had stated on March 4 that his government did not regard U.S. Resolution 242 as obligating Israel to withdraw from the West Bank and Gaza. Moreover, the White House was especially irked at the Begin–Sharon* policy of encouraging Israeli settlements on the West Bank to give corporeal substance to Begin's biblical and ancient legal claims of Israeli sovereignty over this area. Carter himself apparently was also miffed at the Israelis for their mid-March invasion of southern Lebanon in retaliation for a PLO terrorist raid near Tel Aviv.

Sadat too was growing more and more impatient, and by the sum-

---

* Begin's Minister of Agriculture, the flamboyant hawk General Ariel Sharon, was the principal architect of the settlements policy, even pushing Begin to more substantial and even irreversible colonization of the occupied areas than apparently was the Prime Minister's preference.

mer of 1978 was calling Begin "an obstacle to peace," and on July 30, citing the "negative" and "backward" moves of Israel, opposed resuming their bilateral peace talks.

President Carter now interjected himself even more actively into the bargaining. In early August 1978 he dispatched Secretary of State Vance to Cairo and Jerusalem with handwritten notes inviting Begin and Sadat to meet with him in a three-way summit at Camp David to work out a peace agreement they all wanted. The Egyptian President and the Israeli Prime Minister accepted immediately and without conditions.

The negotiations at Camp David between September 5 and 17, 1978, were more like a compressed version of Kissinger's shuttle diplomacy than the famous summits between the leaders of the United States, the USSR, and Britain during World War II, where important bargaining took place in face-to-face sessions among the Big Three. Carter and his aides "shuttled" between the cabins of his two guests at the Maryland mountain retreat to hammer out a mutually acceptable agreement. And representatives of Begin and Sadat held working sessions with Carter in his cabin. Vice President Mondale, Secretary of State Vance, and National Security Adviser Brzezinski were also actively involved in the cabin-to-cabin shuttle. Carter, Begin, and Sadat met together only twice during the thirteen-day marathon before they appeared together on September 17 to announce their success. [7]

It was an extremely difficult and delicate task of mediation for the Americans, for in the ten months since Sadat's visit to Israel, Sadat and Begin had retreated back to positions the other found offensive, and it was with these positions that they opened the Camp David negotiations. Begin came prepared to return all of the Sinai to Egypt (with the proviso that some Israeli settlements be allowed to remain there), but Israel would not, he said, cede sovereignty over the West Bank and Gaza, nor the right to maintain Israeli forces and settlements in these areas. Moreover, Israel could not agree to an independent Palestinian state. Sadat's opening demands were that Israel withdraw totally from all the territory occupied during the 1967 war (which implied, in addition to the Sinai, the West Bank, and Jerusalem, the Gaza Strip and the Golan Heights) and recognize the right of full self-determination for the Palestinians on the West Bank and in Gaza. In short, Israel was bargaining for a separate peace with Egypt—the only Arab country willing to negotiate with her—but Egypt was insisting on linking any bilateral agreement to a broader Arab–Israeli settlement, without which Sadat knew he would be branded throughout the Arab world as a traitor to their common cause.

The central impasse was overcome by separating, for the time being, the Sinai issues, on which explicit and detailed agreements were immediately possible, from the West Bank and Gaza issues, on which agreement still seemed remote. The Sinai agreement would constitute the core of a peace treaty between Egypt and Israel to be concluded before the end of the year, whereas only general principles for settlement of the West Bank and Gaza issues would have to be agreed upon at this time. Both sets of issues, however, would be linked by virtue of their being two parts of an agreed "framework for Peace in the Middle East" to be issued by the three governments as the fruit of their Camp David meetings, and by having the Egyptian–Israeli peace treaty preamble commit both parties to work diligently toward a comprehensive settlement of the Arab–Israeli conflict in all its aspects. [8]

Even given this crucial breakthrough, there were still numerous difficulties to be worked out in each part of the draft Camp David "Framework" over which Begin and Sadat each threatened to walk out on the negotiations and return to a confrontationist, coercive relationship. The thorniest obstacle to agreement on the draft Egyptian–Israeli peace treaty was the issue of Israeli settlements in the Sinai—a pet project of the popular General Sharon. Carter, however, was adamant in supporting Sadat's demand that the Sinai settlements be removed, and reportedly painted for Begin the stark consequences of a refusal by the Israelis to acquiesce on this one: a renewal of war in the Sinai in which Israel could not count on U.S. help. [9] Begin's backdown in agreeing to dismantle the Sinai settlements, if the Knesset approved, broke the final serious logjam, and allowed for a full-speed-ahead drafting of the final Camp David accords that were announced by the smiling trio of Carter, Sadat, and Begin at the White House on September 17, 1978.

The Camp David accords were published as two documents—the "Framework for Peace in the Middle East," and the "Framework for Conclusion of a Peace Treaty Between Egypt and Israel"—each signed by President Sadat and Prime Minister Begin as the parties and by President Carter as the witness. The first, more general document included the agreed principles for negotiating "autonomy" and a "self-governing authority" for inhabitants of the West Bank and Gaza. The second document stipulated the key points of agreement on the Sinai that would constitute the core of the peace treaty to be concluded within three months.

The framework for settling the West Bank and Gaza issues outlined a negotiating process to establish a "self-governing authority" to last a period of not longer than five years—"the transitional period." During this transitional period negotiations were to be undertaken among Egypt, Israel, and Jordan and elected representatives of the inhabitants of the West Bank and Gaza "to agree on the final status" of these areas.

The transitional "self-governing authority" for the West Bank and Gaza was to be established by negotiations to begin immediately between Egypt, Israel, and Jordan and "representatives of the Palestinian people." The Palestinians could be included in the Egyptian and Jordanian delegations. The resulting "self-governing authority" would be an "administrative council" that would be "freely elected by the inhabitants of these areas to replace the existing military government." A local police force would be established which could include Jordanian citizens. Israeli armed forces would be withdrawn, but there could be a redeployment of some remaining Israeli forces into specified "security locations." During the five-year "transitional period," "representatives of Egypt, Israel, Jordan and the self-governing authority will constitute a "Continuing Committee" to decide by agreement on the modalities of admission of persons displaced from the West Bank and Gaza in 1967, together with the necessary measures to prevent disruption and disorder."

Thus, while granting the right of eventual self-determination to the Palestinians, the terms of the "Framework" preserved basic Israeli sovereignty over the West Bank and Gaza for at least the five-year transitional period: no devolution of authority to the Palestinian administrative council would take place beyond what it would be granted in the yet-to-be-undertaken "autonomy talks" to institute the period of limited self-government; some Israeli forces would remain in the area, albeit at specially designated locations; and Israel would retain a veto over any developments in the area she did not like, through her membership in the Continuing Committee along with Egypt and Jordan. The other side of the coin was that these provisions could be interpreted by the Egyptians (as Sadat tried to do to the other Arabs who accused him of selling out the Palestinians in order to achieve his separate peace with Israel) as a significant erosion of Israeli sovereignty over the West Bank and Gaza. Israel was more answerable than ever before to others—the United States, Egypt, and Jordan (if King Hussein would agree to participate in the process)—for how she dealt with the inhabitants of the West Bank; the burden of proof would be on Israel to demonstrate why she could not move toward granting full self-determination and statehood to the Palestinians; real, tangible, increases in administrative (including police) powers were to be given to the resident Palestinians during the transitional period; and although the tripartite Continuing Committee would give Israel a veto over major changes in the status of the area, it also would give Egypt and Jordan vetoes over attempts by Israel to reassume local powers she had already relinquished.

The Camp David "Framework" for the peace treaty between Egypt and Israel was a much briefer, yet more specific, document, committing the parties to a continuation and rapid conclusion of the treaty negotiations begun at Camp David, and recording details already agreed, including the withdrawal of Israeli armed forces from the Sinai; limitations on deployments of Egyptian and Israeli military units on their respective sides of their common border; limitations on Egyptian armed forces to be stationed in the Sinai immediately east of the Suez; provision for United Nations forces adjacent to the Egyptian–Israeli border near the Strait of Tiran; and guarantees of rights of free passage to Israeli ships through the Gulf of Suez, the Suez Canal, the Strait of Tiran, and the Gulf of Aqaba. The Israeli troop withdrawals would be phased over a period of two to three years, but the two countries would establish full diplomatic and economic relations three to nine months after the signing of the peace treaty and upon the completion of an "interim withdrawal" of Israeli troops from the Sinai to lines yet to be determined.[10] The decade-long impasse between the two countries in implementing Resolution 242 had been overcome at last—truly an historic achievement. But between the raising of the goblets of peace and being able to drink their wine there was still much to be worked out.

There was the overarching issue of the degree of linkage between the Egyptian–Israeli peace treaty and the negotiations over the status of the West bank and Gaza. Sadat, anxious to counter the intensifying drumbeat of charges by other Arab leaders that he was a traitor to their cause, wanted a stronger link to be stated explicitly in the preamble to the treaty than did the Israelis, who were worried that the preambular linkage could be interpreted to mean that the provisions in the body of the treaty were inoperative until substantial progress had been achieved in the autonomy talks. The Israelis were doubly worried as the Carter administration, in the months following Camp David, was even more insistent than Sadat that collateral progress on the Palestinian autonomy arrangements was an essential context for a durable Egyptian–Israeli peace. Assistant Secretary of State Harold Saunders was dispatched on a mission in October to convince King Hussein of Jordan to join the negotiations, and to persuade Palestinian leaders in the West Bank that the "autonomy" promised in the Camp David accords was only an interim step toward more complete self-determination. While on his trip Saunders angered Begin by saying that Israel would dismantle its settlements in the West Bank—there had been no such commitment at Camp David—and by calling East Jerusalem "occupied territory." [11] A provoked Israeli government hardened its opposition to what looked like new American pressures for a comprehensive peace and announced plans to "thicken" the Israeli settlements on the West Bank.

It began to appear as if Begin had never really intended to transfer substantial power to the Arabs in the West Bank and Gaza, and that even his limited concessions on the matter at Camp David were only for the purpose of getting the Egyptian–Israeli peace treaty moving, and need not ever have to be concretely delivered. Sadat could not allow the rest of the Arab world to gain the impression that he had been diddled by Begin, and began to toughen his stands on various details in the draft bilateral peace treaty. And when Carter suggested in February 1979 that Begin and Sadat come again to Camp David for a second summit to resolve their differences, both leaders declined. Begin himself saw Carter in Washington in March, but left complaining that the Americans were now supporting Egyptian proposals that were totally unacceptable to Israel.

Carter now decided to inject himself even more weightily into the bargaining than he had done through the means of the Camp David summit. He personally would fly the shuttle between Jerusalem and Cairo in the type of mediational diplomacy Kissinger had pioneered, but with an immense difference—the prestige of the President of the United States was now implicated in the success or failure of the effort. This indeed was Carter's daring gamble, and was what would give his insistences on constructive negotiation added weight, for now Carter would be viewed in the media worldwide as a principal participant in the negotiations, with high political values of his own immediately at stake, not just as a detached go-between providing "good offices." Carter was gambling on the assumption that the Israelis and Egyptians were fundamentally committed to a consummation of the peace between them essentially on the terms outlined at Camp David, and that the outstanding disagreements were negotiable details which, as part of the end game of the bargaining, had been inflated into matters of "principle" by each side.

In Jerusalem and Cairo, Carter created the impression that his failure to bring home peace was intolerable to him and that noncooperation at this point by either Sadat or Begin could therefore result in a deterioration of relations between the United States and whichever country was most responsible for preventing final agreement. Any deterioration in relations with the United States was a particularly fearsome prospect for the Israelis, given the enlarging strategic interest of the Americans in securing access to Persian Gulf oil and therefore in cultivating friendly relations with many of Israel's hostile neighbors. The West Europeans and the Japanese had already put good relations with their Middle East oil suppliers ahead of friendship with Israel; it thus would be suicidal for the Begin government to alienate the American President at this time. Sadat too was in a bind that could be manipulated by Carter: increasingly isolated from other Arab governments, most of whom had broken diplomatic relations with Egypt in reaction to his trip to Jerusalem and subsequent negotiation of the Camp David accords, Sadat had no place to turn but to the United States for economic credits to rescue the faltering Egyptian economy and for arms to maintain a military balance not only against Israel but against his Soviet-armed enemy on Egypt's western border, Libya's Muammar Qaddafi. Sadat, of course, did retain the option of another dramatic turnaround to embrace the Pan-Arab cause and to junk his Nobel

Prize–winning peace initiatives with Israel, and therefore Carter
could not push him to accept terms that would sacrifice vital Egyptian interests, or that would personally humiliate the proud Egyptian President. But Carter also could see that Sadat would be doubly
humiliated if he were to crawl back to the militant Arab fold; and
that therefore any implied threat to do so in response to reasonable
Israeli demands backed by the United States was a bluff.

By purposefully inflating his own, and thus the United States
government's, stake in an Israeli–Egyptian settlement, and thereby
maximizing the pressure on Begin and Sadat to converge on the
terms of their treaty, Carter's Middle-Eastern shuttle of March 8–
13, 1979, should be ranked as one of the most impressive démarches
in the annals of diplomacy—less infused with emotional drama than
Sadat's 1977 trip to Jerusalem, but, as it turned out, the crucial
element in transforming Sadat's initiative from simply an act of political theater into a major branch point in world history.

The terms of the "Treaty of Peace Between the Arab Republic of
Egypt and the State of Israel" signed in Washington on March 26,
1979, by President Sadat and Prime Minister Begin and by President Carter as "witness" were remarkable as peace treaties go. Usually peace treaties codify the results of war, giving international legitimacy to control over territory established by battle, and attempting
to give de jure durability to the new de facto situation and to resolve
marginal issues not settled by war that could provoke new hostilities. The Egyptian–Israeli treaty, by contrast, changed substantially
territorial dispositions established twelve years previously by war,
and instituted a fundamentally new status quo, effecting a revolutionary change in the thirty-year-old situation in the Middle East in
which the leading Arab country, among others, had refused to grant
legitimacy to the State of Israel.

As anticipated in the Camp David framework, Israel agreed to
evacuate its military forces and civilians from the Sinai Peninsula
in a phased withdrawal over a three-year period; the state of war
between Egypt and Israel was terminated; and the parties agreed to
establish normal and full diplomatic relations after the initial nine
months of Israeli military withdrawal; Israeli ships were accorded
the right of free passage through the Suez Canal and its approaches,
and all normal international navigational rights through the Strait
of Tiran and the Gulf of Aqaba. The parties agreed to negotiate
special security arrangements, including the emplacement of United

Nations forces, to monitor the implementation of the peace treaty. They also agreed "not to enter into any obligation in conflict with this treaty."

On the controversial issue of the linkage of the Egyptian–Israeli peace treaty to the negotiations on the regime for the West Bank and Gaza, as provided for in the Camp David framework, the text of the treaty itself was mute, except for a vague clause in the preamble committing the parties to continue "the search for a comprehensive peace in the area and for the attainments of the settlement of the Arab–Israeli conflict in all its aspects." The Israelis won their determined fight to keep all clauses out of the treaty that might make its implementation conditional on the settlement of the Palestinian problem. Sadat's need to demonstrate to the other Arab countries and the Palestinians that his peace with Israel was only the opening move in a larger strategy of getting the Israelis to give back all of the territories conquered in 1967 was catered to, on the insistence of President Carter, in the form of a "Joint Letter" to Carter signed by Begin and Sadat in which they agreed to continue good faith negotiations according to the Camp David framework for "the establishment of the self-governing authority in the West Bank and Gaza in order to provide full autonomy to the inhabitants."

It was more than politeness or the requirements of protocol that were reflected in the accolades paid by Sadat and Begin at the signing ceremony to Carter's role in the negotiations. As put by Sadat, "the man who performed the miracle was President Carter. Without any exaggeration, what he did constitutes one of the greatest achievements of our time. . . . There came certain moments when hope was eroding and retreating in the face of pride. However, President Carter remained unshaken in his confidence and determination. . . . Before anything else, the signing of the peace treaty *and the exchange of letters* is a tribute to the spirit and ability of Jimmy Carter." [12] (Emphasis added.) Begin agreed.

But the scope of the Carter "miracle" was limited, as was his power to enlarge it.

THE PALESTINIAN ISSUE: THE LEAST TRACTABLE PROBLEM

One of the assumptions on which there had been consensus among President Carter's principal foreign policy advisers at the start of his administration was that the Palestinian issue was an integral part of the Arab–Israeli conflict and that its resolution, accordingly, had to be an integral part of any durable settlement of that conflict. The assumption was central to the Brookings Institution study group's proposals that Jimmy Carter endorsed during his election campaign. Moreover, it seemed to fit neatly into Carter's religio-emotional enthusiasm for a foreign policy built around human rights. Certainly the self-determination of peoples, the idea that nations had a right to their own states, was a basic human right that the United States should champion. And after all, wasn't President Truman's support for the establishment of the State of Israel, and the commitment of all subsequent U.S. administrations to the survival of Israel in the face of Arab hostility, a product of that deep American belief in national self-determination? Now it was the Palestinians who were demanding their place in the sun. It seemed only elementary and right that a new administration pledged to restore a concern for human rights as an animating principle of U.S. foreign policy should be politically responsive to the Palestinian demand. But as Carter was soon to learn, the issue was considerably more complicated than when looked at either through the abstract prism of the Brookings report or through the neo-Wilsonian *Weltanschauung* that underlay Carter's own initial foreign policy impulses.

Carter's initial impulses were expressed as a March 16, 1977, town meeting at Clinton, Massachusetts, where he endorsed the idea of a "homeland" for the Palestinians. The immediate and vociferous protests this provoked in the American Jewish community and from Israeli spokesmen provided only the beginning of his baptism in the fire of this bitter conflict of peoples contending for primary jurisdiction over the same land. It was to flare up again in response to the U.S.–Soviet joint statement of October 1, 1977, in which the superpowers called, among other things, for "the resolution of the Palestinian question, including insuring the legitimate rights of the Palestinian people."

"Legitimate rights" or any other surrogate term for statehood for the Palestinians would be summarily rejected by the Israelis, and they would resfuse—absolutely—to participate in any negotiations in which such statehood was one of the terms of reference. As the Israelis saw it, full political self-determination for the Palestinians was tantamount to self-liquidation for the Jewish state, since a Palestinian state, particularly if it were controlled by the current dominant element among the Palestinians, the Palestinian Liberation Organization (PLO), would be a garrison bristling with Soviet arms, pledged to push the Israelis into the sea. Carter, in hearing these reasons for Begin for Israel's intransigent opposition to any suggestion of the legitimacy of a Palestinian state or even to negotiations with the PLO, was driven, like each of his predecessors, to the realization that this was truly a nonnegotiable stance by the Israeli government, and not simply a maximalist bargaining position.

But by the time of Carter's presidency, Palestinian self-determination had become *the* Pan-Arab cause, an emotional rallying point around which the Arabs could gather to overcome their intense nationalistic and religious rivalries with one another—a noble-sounding surrogate for the cause that could not be so openly advocated without alienating the United States and other friends of Israel— namely, the destruction of the Jewish state. This was why Sadat was so adamant on linking the Palestinian issue to his accommodation with Israel. It was essential for him to show that peaceful coexistence with Israel, which was now genuinely an Egyptian national interest, was a necessary conditon for securing self-determination for the Palestinians. Indeed, the justification Sadat used when appealing to other Arabs to join with him (or at least not condemn him) in making peace with Israel was that Israeli security was the means by which Palestinian self-determination could be achieved; that the Israelis would moderate their opposition to a Palestinian state only when they felt assured that the Palestinian cause was not being used as a vehicle to undermine the Jewish state; and that an Arab-controlled Palestine on Israel's eastern and southwestern borders would not be used as a base for attacking her during another Arab–Israeli war.

Sadat was giving Egyptian national interests primacy in making peace with Israel, but he could not afford to dispense with Pan-Arabism as a larger cause through which to energize Egyptian nationalism, as Nasser had done. An Egyptian statesman had to be regarded as an international leader of the Arabs in order to sustain the charisma that was necessary for him to lead at home.

Brzezinski in particular felt he understood Sadat's situation and motives and accordingly was insistent within the counsels of the administration that the United States pressure the Israelis to give Sadat meaningful commitments pointing toward eventual Palestinian self-rule for the West Bank and Gaza. For Brzezinski and also the State Department's principal official in charge of Middle Eastern affairs under Cyrus Vance, Assistant Secretary of State Harold Saunders, it was not Wilsonian idealism that led them to urge Carter to tilt toward Sadat's position on the Palestinian issue, but realpolitik—the recognition of the intractable forces working on Sadat, and his need to deliver something impressive to the Pan-Arabists in order for him to sustain the bilateral peace process he initiated with Israel. Thus by the time of the Camp David summit, the President's own sentiments, now well buttressed with the rationale of practical statesmanship, were manifested in very strong personal interventions on the Palestinian issue in critical moments in the negotiations—which the Israelis regarded as either ignorance of, or an insensitivity to, *their* problems.[13] But Carter by this time was neither ignorant nor insensitive to the problems of either side. He was fixed now, with dogged determination, on a path that he was convinced was the only way to bring to fruition even the Egyptian–Israeli peace treaty, let alone the next steps in resolving the broader Arab–Israeli conflict.

The result, was indicated above, was the Camp David framework for West Bank autonomy negotiations and the commitments in the 1979 peace treaty and associated letters to pursue these negotiations. Without Carter's weighing in heavily to support Sadat's insistences on these linkages between the Egyptian–Israeli peace and the larger Arab cause, Sadat's dramatic trip to Jerusalem and the Camp David summit meeting of Begin, Sadat, and Carter would have been interesting footnotes to history, but not the momentous turning points they have become.

The Carter administration's success in getting the Israelis to recognize that moving toward Palestinian self-determination was an essential corollary to an Egyptian–Israeli peace led inexorably to the need for the U.S. government, as the next phase of its active role in the peace process, to deal directly with the dilemmas the Israelis themselves had been dealing with over the years: how Israel was to make secure arrangements for peaceful coexistance, let alone for eventual statehood, with a movement that was insistent that Israel itself was an illegitimate entity and had to be removed from the Middle East; how Israel was to respond to terrorist attacks on her people by Palestinians operating out of bases in neighboring countries.

Israel's established responses to these threats were clear and understandable: nonrecognition of the Palestine "liberationists" and reprisal against the terrorist bases in neighboring countries. The Begin government also pursued a policy of enlarging Israeli settlements on the West Bank and making unequivocal declarations of Israeli sovereignty over the West Bank and Gaza.

The Carter administration, embarrassed by the Begin government's intransigence, and anxious to give Sadat something to demonstrate to the other Arab countries that his peace moves had indeed opened up new possibilities for a resolution of the Palestinian issue, began to alter, subtly, the U.S. government's previous policy backing the basic Israeli positions on the issue.

Carter administration officials, somewhat heady from their success in pulling off the Egyptian-Israeli treaty, now attempted, through indirect contacts with the PLO (using Europeans and Third World diplomats as informal conduits), to discern whether the PLO might be ready to drop its standing claim that Israel was an illegitimate state in return for being themselves recognized by the United States (and eventually Israel) as a legitimate bargaining agent for the Palestinians.* However, when the American UN ambassador, Andrew Young, was discovered to have been meeting with some PLO representatives, albeit "informally" and "without authorization," the protests from members of Congress and Jewish organizations compelled Young's resignation from the Carter administration in July 1979. And as the 1980 presidential election campaign neared, all U.S. governmental efforts that might imply some shift toward acceptance of an independent Palestinian state or toward recognizing the PLO were put on hold.

But the deepening ambivalence within the Carter administration toward Israel's policies in the West Bank and Gaza was revealed in March 1980 by the embarrassing vote by the U.S. delegation for a

---

* The United States and Israel were holdouts against a near international consensus to deal with the PLO as the bargaining agent for the Palestinians. In October 1974, the UN General Assembly voted 105 to 4, with 20 abstentions, to recognize the PLO, and in November 1974, Yasir Arafat addressed the General Assembly. In 1978 the PLO opened a Washington office, but the U.S. government still refrained from direct contact with the organization.

Security Council resolution "deploring the decision of the Government of Israel to officially support Israeli settlements in the Palestinian and other Arab territories occupied since 1967"; stating that "all measures taken by Israel to change the physical character, demographic composition, institutional structure or status of the Palestinian and other Arab territories occupied since 1967, including Jerusalem, or any part thereof, have no legal validity"; calling upon Israel to dismantle the existing settlements and to rescind its plans for such settlements; and calling upon all states not to provide Israel with assistance to be used specifically in connection with settlements in the occupied territories.[14] Ambassador Donald McHenry's vote in favor of the Security Council resolution followed intensive but hurried consultations by him with Secretary Vance, and by Vance with Carter and Brzezinski, in which it was decided that McHenry should vote for the resolution provided that various references to Jerusalem were deleted. But precisely what language was offensive and what was acceptable was apparently left vague, and upon McHenry's assurances that the unacceptable phrases had been deleted, Vance gave him the go-ahead to vote affirmatively.[15]

The Sunday morning *New York Times* headlined the seeming change of direction by the Carter administration: "u.s. votes at u.n. to rebuke israelis—A Major Stiffening of Policy." And Carter's opponents for the Democratic nomination, especially Senator Edward Kennedy, joined spokesmen for Jewish organizations in immediately pouncing on the administration for caving in to the Arab oil producers and "jeopardizing the security of Israel."

The White House quickly constructed a retreat, disavowing support for the resolution as finally passed, but explaining Ambassador McHenry's vote as the result of "the failure to communicate" the President's understanding that "*all* references to Jerusalem" would be deleted from the UN resolution. Presumably, McHenry would not have voted affirmatively if Vance had clearly communicated this policy.

Critics were quick to find out and reveal, however, that there indeed had been intensive communication between the UN delegation and the State Department, and between Vance, Brzezinski, and Carter over successive drafts of the resolution; and that if McHenry still had to be specifically instructed to prevent him from voting the wrong way, then, clearly, the thrust of the discussions within the highest counsels of the U.S. government must have been generally in favor of the UN rebuke to Israel on its settlement's policy.* Then, after the fact, to apologize for the vote as a communications faux pas was to do little to assuage the Israelis while at the same time freshly antagonizing the Arabs.

In the fashionable phrase of the day, Carter was caught between a rock and a hard place: he could no longer simply stand pat on the Palestinian issue without being left behind in the post–Camp David shift of international opinion toward granting the inhabitants of the West Bank and Gaza full self-determination, and without further undermining Sadat, which in turn could even negate the conditions for a durable Egyptian–Israeli peace. But any movement to join the emerging international consensus on this issue would cause a political crisis in Israel, which might well turn not only Begin but the majority of Israelis against all commitments made during the Camp David process, including provisions in the peace treaty to pull out of the Sinai, since it would lend credibility to the charge by Israeli rightists that the United States had trapped Begin into admitting, willy-nilly, that all the territories occupied in the 1967 war really belonged to the Arabs and should be returned to them, and that their continued control by Israel was illegal; and would alienate groups in the United States whose support was essential for Carter's reelection in 1980.

The aura of the dedicated and effective peacemaker that Carter had all of a sudden acquired for his mediation between Sadat and Begin at Camp David and subsequently in putting together the Egyptian–Israeli peace treaty was now just as suddenly dissipated, as the charges of vacillation, ambivalence, and inconstancy were driven home by his political opponents. Carter's successor in the White House would soon get his opportunity to attempt to prove that a less ambivalent U.S. policy toward the Middle East was in the national interest and capable of being implemented.

---

* Supporting the impression that the administration really meant to separate itself from Israel on the settlements issue was Vance's refusal, in his March 20, 1980, appearance before the Senate Foreign Relations Committee to discredit the bulk of the UN resolution. See Terrence Smith, "Vance Rebuffs Call to Disavow Full U.N. Move on Israel," *New York Times,* March 21, 1980.

30

HOSTAGES IN IRAN: PARALYSIS AND PRUDENCE IN THE USE OF AMERICAN POWER

America will continue the careful and considered use of its power. We shall pursue every, and I repeat, every legal use of that power to bring our people home, free and safe.

JIMMY CARTER

The public face of United States policy toward Iran throughout Jimmy Carter's first presidential year was one of unwavering support for the Shah, despite growing concern within the administration and in the Congress over the vulnerability of the Shah's regime and his use of his secret police, SAVAK, to brutally suppress political opposition. On November 15, 1977, the President and the Shah stood together on the White House south lawn, exchanging expressions of mutual admiration and respect while blinking and wiping their eyes from the tear gas cloud produced by the Washington police in their charge to break up a fierce riot north of the White House between 4000 anti-Shah and 1500 pro-Shah demonstrators. And on January 2, 1978, U.S. news media carried reports of Carter New Year's Eve toast in Teheran to the Shah's regime as "an island of stability" in one of the more troubled areas of the world. "This is a great tribute to you, Your Majesty, and to your leadership and the respect, admiration and love which your people give to you." [1]

Critics of the policy of continuing to support the Shah with mawkish flattery and lavish arms sales wondered how an administration professing dedication to human rights and arms control could justify these actions. However, the reasons for special support to the Shah, especially during his time of troubles, were convincing to the new President, just as they had been convincing to Carter's predecessors: Iran was a crucial asset for the West to be able to count on in the geopolitically vital rimland of Eurasia—not only because of its oil, but also because of its size and location in the center of the containment line between Russian and the Persian Gulf— and the Shah had proven himself over three decades to be a willing and reliable partner in this task. The Shah's Iran was the most important of the "regional influentials" (Brzezinski's phrase) upon which the United States had to rely, particularly in the post-Vietnam era of opposition to overseas U.S. military deployments, to provide an adequate forward defense against Soviet impulses to expand the Russian sphere of control. Both the human rights and the conventional arms transfer policies of the Carter administration provided explicitly for geopolitically determined exceptions such as this. The legacy of past commitments, and the lack of current alternatives, to the Shah continued to tilt sentiment in the administration, including Carter's, in favor of supporting the Shah—until the foundational premises of the policy had already crumbled beyond repair.

THE LEGACY OF PAST POLICIES

The Carter administration inherited the dominant view in the U.S. policy establishment of the Shah as "our man in the Persian Gulf." In the Nixon and Ford policies toward Iran, human rights were overlooked in favor of the presumed geopolitical imperative of sustaining in southwest Asia an indigenous anti-Soviet and antiradical bulwark, whose two principal pillars were supposed to be Iran and Saudi Arabia. "Under the Shah's leadership," recalls Kissinger, "the land bridge between Asia and Europe, so often the hinge of world history, was pro-American and pro-West beyond any challenge. . . . The Shah's view of the realities of world politics paralleled our own. . . . Iran under the Shah, in short, was one of America's best, most important, and most loyal friends in the world." [2]

Nixon and Kissinger had themselves built upon a legacy of U.S.– Iranian relations that went back to World War II and that had been elaborated during the Truman, Eisenhower, and Johnson administration.

President Roosevelt perceived it to be the American mission to prevent the USSR and Britain from transforming their wartime zones of military occupation in Iran into a permanent postwar partition of the country. It was on U.S. insistence that the two occupying powers signed a treaty with Iran in January 1942 to withdraw their troops from Iranian territory within six months after the end of the war. Roosevelt was animated partly by anti-imperialist sentiments and his ever-present hope for perpetuating Big Three wartime cooperation into the postwar peace. But he also was concerned, with Britain no longer able to perform her historic geopolitical role of containing Russian expansion into the oil-rich Persian Gulf, to solidify within Iran a posture of determined independence—a substitute, as it were, for the traditional British presence.[3] In any event, by being simply in favor of an independent Iran, the United States would not have to assume an anti-Soviet posture.

The geopolitical, rather than the idealistic, basis for U.S. attempts to assure Iranian independence took over U.S. diplomcy during the first year of the Truman administration when, in the first major U.S.–Soviet altercation of the postwar period, the United States brought maximum diplomatic pressure on the Soviets to get Stalin to honor his commitment to withdraw Russian occupation troops from northern Iran after the cessation of hostilities. (see chapter 3). The geopolitical considerations henceforth dominated U.S. policies toward Iran; but the assessments of the best means for keeping Iran out of the Soviet sphere kept fluctuating between efforts to induce the Shah to liberalize his regime and efforts to bolster his internal and external power by aiding him to build up his security forces and his military establishment.

The larger movement of U.S. policy, however, was toward catering to the Shah's preferences for a powerful military establishment and other trappings of monarchical, even imperial, grandeur and for glamorous industrialization projects and away from insistences on basic socioeconomic and political reforms.

The Truman–Acheson policy of trying to convince the Shah that he needed to modernize and democratize Iran lest it suffer a fate analogous to Chiang's China, and of making loans and arms transfers at least partly contingent upon a sincere effort by the Shah to institute domestic reforms, gave way to the Eisenhower–Dulles policy of relying on the Shah to make Iran the centerpiece of the U.S. anti-Communist alliance system in the Middle East and of intervening to help the Shah combat his domestic enemies.[4] The Eisenhower administration feared that Mohammed Mossadegh, the nationalistic Prime Minister of Iran appointed by the Shah in 1951, was by 1953 demogogically catering to extremist and pro-Soviet elements, especially the Marxist Tudeh Party, and that Mossadegh's nationalization of the Anglo-Iranian Oil Company was only the first step toward a complete radicalization of Iran's political economy and a turn toward alignment with the Soviet Union. As Mossadegh moved in 1953 to dissolve the Parliament and to assume dictatorial powers, the Eisenhower administration felt justified in authorizing the CIA to proceed with its plan to topple Mossadegh and reinstate the Shah, who already had fled to Italy. Although, at the time, the overthrow of Mossadegh and the restoration of the Shah was more popular than unpopular in Iran, the recollection by Iranians of the CIA-engineered coup, more than any event in the relationship between the two countries, provided the source of the hysterical charges during the 1979–1980 hostage crisis that the United States was a full accomplice in all of the crimes committed by the Shah against his countrymen.

While the restoration of the Shah in 1953 hardly produced the reign of terror that the 1978 revolutionary leaders in retrospect alleged was the immediate result, and while many participants in the Mossadegh government willingly went to work for the Shah, the 1953 coup did severely decimate the sociopolitical infrastructure that was gradually maturing in Iran, and which, given time and encouragement, might have provided a stable structure for a moderate democracy. In the post-Mossadegh period all political authority was concentrated in the monarchy; the bureaucracy and Parliament became rubber stamps for the Shah's decrees, and in the name of securing the regime against a resurgence of Tudeh radicalism from the left and Muslim fundamentalism from the right, the Shah delegated more and more enforcement powers to the armed forces and SAVAK. With the Shah less inclined than ever to accept foreign advice on the basic structure of his regime, the bargaining between

Washington and Teheran tended to concentrate during the remaining years of the Eisenhower administration on the material inputs and technical assistance the United States could contribute to Iran's economic, administrative, and military modernization and on the role Iran should play in the regional "mutual security" network being constructed in the Near East by John Foster Dulles. The Shah shrewdly calculated, as did other leading U.S. clients in the Third World, that by catering to Dulles' preoccupation with the U.S.–Soviet rivalry he could get maximum support from the United States for building up his own domestic and regional power, even though this was targeted more against the Shah's local adversaries than against hypothetical Soviet aggression.

Actually, the Eisenhower administration was not at all sanguine about Iran's future stability and pro-Western orientation; and in the White House in particular there was concern that the Shah's emphasis on expensive military projects was dangerously retarding the evolution of a balanced domestic economy capable of supporting his attempts to rapidly industrialize the country. But Eisenhower and Dulles were loath to threaten a reduction in military or economic assistance as a lever on Iranian domestic reform for fear of undercutting the Shah's authority and stimulating the anti-Shah groups.

Iran's top-heavy economic and military programs went even more against the grain of the economic development philosophies influential among John F. Kennedy's New Frontiersmen in the White House and in the Agency for International Development. So too did the Shah's reputation as a ruthless autocrat. The President's own determination to move away from the previous administration's policy of deference to the Shah was apparently crystalized by Khrushchev's prediction at the Vienna summit in 1961 that the Shah would fall victim to a popular uprising. In 1962 the Kennedy administration conditioned its contributions to Iran's economic plan and military modernization upon the Shah's agreement to reduce his army from 240,000 to 150,000 men and to institute various economic and political reforms. Displeased with such meddling, the Shah nevertheless went along with most of the new U.S. insistences, but meanwhile attempted to increase his bargaining power vis-à-vis the United States by accepting Soviet economic and military aid, and by exploiting the increasing dependence of the United States, Western Europe, and Japan on Iranian oil.

During the Johnson administration the Shah, perhaps sensing the opportunity arising out of the U.S. preoccupation with Vietnam, became increasingly manipulative of his U.S. patrons, and at the same time more successful in keeping the Americans from placing reform stipulations on their aid and arms sales. U.S. financial aid, in any event, was being rapidly phased out due to Iran's soaring oil revenues, and therefore provided virtually no leverage by the late 1960s. The Shah's main requests now were that he be permitted to purchase the most sophisticated military equipment: ground-to-air missile systems and radars, supersonic aircraft, and even surface-to-surface missiles. The Shah perceived that many top U.S. officials, alarmed at Soviet arms deliveries to Iraq and Egypt, were ready to go to bat for his requests before congressional committees and within the bureaucracy, despite growing skepticism about the Shah's purported needs and worries about the distortions the arms transfers would produce in Iran's economic and social system. Whatever opportunities there might have been for U.S. officials to capitalize on the divisions in Washington by way of hard bargaining with the Shah were bypassed in the latter years of the Johnson administration; instead the President and Secretary of State followed the counsel of Under Secretary of State Eugene Rostow that the Shah not be "alienated," lest he turn to the Soviets to satisfy his desires.[5]

The Shah's star in the Washington sky reached its zenith during the Nixon-Kissinger years. The "Nixon Doctrine" (see above, pp. 326–27) devolving the frontline containment and regional stabilization tasks to selected U.S. allies, who would be well supplied with U.S. military equipment, was precisely suited to the role of Iran as conceived of by the Shah. Southwest Asia, in the wake of the British military withdrawal from the Persian Gulf at the end of 1971, was seen by Nixon and Kissinger as a particularly tempting target for Soviet power plays. Kissinger recalls that "there was no possibility of assigning any American military forces to the Indian Ocean in the midst of the Vietnam war and its attendant trauma." But with Iran as a willing military client, "the vacuum left by British withdrawal, now menaced by Soviet intrusion and radical momentum, would be filled by a local power friendly to us. . . . And all of this was achievable without any American resources, since the Shah was willing to pay for the equipment out of his oil revenues."[6]

Despite this mutuality of interests between Washington and Teheran, the Shah was not averse to playing hardball diplomacy to extract the maximum possible out of the American arsenal. In 1971 he indicated a willingness to join with the Arab majority in OPEC in its threat to use the oil cartel as an instrument of international leverage against Israel unless the United States was fully responsive to Iran's security needs. The result was Nixon's promise in Teheran in May 1972 to allow the Shah to buy virtually any and all nonnuclear weapons he wanted.[7] Kissinger objects to journalistic characterizations of the 1972 arms transfer agreement as "open ended," branding these accounts "hyperbole."[8] But the fact of a nearly totally open spigot on the American arms pipepline to Iran after 1972 is indisputable.

From 1973 to 1977 more than a third of all U.S. military sales were to Iran, whose military budget rose fourfold during this period, consuming over a quarter of the Iranian government's expenditures. The increase in the value of arms exports from $1 billion annually in the early 1970s to $10 billion annually in the mid-1970s was attributable in large part to the Shah's insatiable appetite for new weapons.

BELATED REASSESSMENT OF THE SHAH'S STAYING POWER

The Carter administration inherited more than the arms sales contracts of its predecessors; it also inherited career bureaucrats in the departments of State and Defense who, in approving the sales, had made judgments about the basic viability of the Shah's rule, and about his regime's suppression of political opposition. The prevailing consensus among the careerists was that the Shah was without peer among Middle Eastern leaders in his ability to maintain domestic order while instituting major socioeconomic reforms of a traditional society, and that the draconian measures he sometimes used were hardly unusual among regimes in the region or indeed throughout the Third World. The careerists had to contend against Carter appointees who were committed to helping the President implement his campaign promises to reduce arms sales and promote human rights, but the old hands found a powerful ally in Zbigniew Brzezinski, who accepted the Kissingerian argument that a constriction of weapons transfers to Iran, especially if it were an expression of discontent with the monarchy's human rights record, would be against our interests, since it could only alienate the Shah and turn him toward other arms suppliers.

As evidence mounted during the first half of 1978 that opposition to the Shah's regime was spreading in Iran, this bureaucratic coalition in Washington continued to successfully resist a fundamental reassessment of U.S. policy by arguing that any criticism of the Shah at this time would play into the hands of his opponents and exacerbate the turmoil, and this in turn could only increase the Shah's tendency to rely on SAVAK's brutal techniques of repression. Consistent with Secretary of State Vance's cautionary guidelines on implementing the President's human rights policy (see above, pp. 466–72), pressures exerted on other governments should be constrained by the realization that in some circumstances our good intentions may produce pernicious results.

In the fall of 1978, when it began to be evident that the growing instability in Iran was more serious than anything that had been seen since the Mossadegh period, Brzezinski himself began to argue that the overthrow of the Shah was a real possibility. Strikes were endemic in essential public service industries; the economy was near collapse; wealthy Iranians were sending their money out of the country; and the Ayatollah Khomeini was calling from Paris for civil war. Carter's national security adviser's response to the impending crisis was predictable: back the Shah all the way and let him and his opponents know that this was U.S. policy. [9]

The view from the American Embassy in Teheran was quite different. Ambassador William Sullivan sent a message to Washington on November 9, 1978, recommending that since the Shah's regime might collapse, the United States should begin to look for alternative means to preserve its interests. The unity of the armed forces and their willingness to support a post-Shah regime would be crucial to preserving the territorial integrity and independence of Iran, and therefore the United States should attempt to use its influence to "broker an arrangement" between the Khomeini group and the leading military officers on the makeup of the new regime and on the role of the armed forces under it. Receiving no reply to his message, and believing his views were no longer welcome at the White House, Ambassador Sullivan, through talks on his own with the revolutionary leaders and the military, began to explore the possibility of acceptable post-Shah arrangements. [10]

By the end of the first week of December 1978, reports reaching
the White House on the disastrous crumbling of the Shah's support
in Iran moved Carter to publicly urge the Shah to broaden the base
of his government in an effort to restore its legitimacy. And the
President, in response to questioning by the press, allowed himself
to express some doubt about the Shah's ability to hang on to power
unless he instituted a major effort to transform his regime into a
constitutional monarchy with free elections and a decentralization
of power. [11]

Behind the scenes, a fierce debate raged among Carter's inner
council of top foreign policy and national security advisers.

Brzezinski and James Schlesinger (Carter's Energy Secretary, and
formerly Secretary of Defense under Nixon and Ford) wanted the
President to make clear to the Shah that the United States encouraged and would back him in a major mobilization of the Iranian
armed forces to put down civil disturbances, take over the provision
of essential services, and root out and incarcerate subversive groups—
in short, anything that was necessary to decisively smash the revolution.

Secretary Vance, on the other hand, felt the time had come for
the President to separate the United States from the Shah. There
was no saving him anymore, and he should be urged to leave the
country. The United States should back a transition government
that would be backed by the armed forces and could rely on them
to restore public order and establish procedures for instituting a
constitutional, popularly legitimized regime.

By the end of December, events in Iran itself appeared to validate
the Vance approach. The Shah appointed Shahpour Bakhtiar, an
opposition leader and former deputy minister in the Mossadegh government, to the post of Prime Minister. Bakhtiar's conditions were
that he be allowed to release political prisoners, dissolve SAVAK,
and reinstitute freedom of the press—also that the Shah should leave
the country.

The announcement on December 29, 1978, of the shah's appointment of Bakhtiar as Prime Minister was followed by great confusion
and near chaos: the militant National Front, heady with the developing revolutionary situation, expelled Bakhtiar for being too willing
to compromise. The Shah's spokesman denied that Reza Pahlevi had

actually consented to leave Iran. Rumors were rife, and seemingly credible, about coups being hatched by the right, the left, and various factions of the armed forces. And increasing attention—Iranian and international—was focused on the charismatic Ayatollah Khomeini to determine to whom he might throw his support. Ambassador Sullivan urged a meeting between U.S. officials and Khomeini, but Brzezinski vetoed the idea. Khomeini rejected the Bakhtiar government and himself named a shadow government with a religiously oriented leader of the National Front, Mehdi Bazargan, as its Prime Minister. Meanwhile the United States government had declared its support for Bakhtiar. Finally, on January 16, 1979, the Shah left for Egypt, telling Bakhtiar that his departure would result in a worsening of the situation and that the people would soon call him back to rule.

In the midst of all this confusion, the White House, taking up some of the suggestions made by Ambassador Sullivan, appointed its own emissary to the Iranian military to negotiate their cooperation with the new Bakhtiar regime. Brzezinski's designee for this mission was General Robert Huyser, a deputy to General Alexander Haig, then Supreme Allied Commander in Europe, who knew little about Iran. Ambassador Sullivan, however, continued to urge to no avail that Bakhtiar was despised by the Khomeini group, and that the crucial negotiations should be with them.

Ambassador Sullivan's recollections of this chaotic period reveal the gap between White House and Embassy perspectives about what was actually happening in Iran:

I received terse instructions telling me that the policy of the U.S. government was to support the Bakhtiar government without reservation and to assist its survival. I replied . . . that the Bakhtiar government was a chimera that the shah had created to permit a dignified departure, that Bakhtiar himself was quixotic and would be swept aside by the arrival of Khomeini and his supporters in Tehran. Moreover, I argued that it would be feckless to transfer the loyalty of the armed forces to Bakhtiar because this would cause the destructive confrontation between the armed forces and the revolutionaries that we hoped to avoid. It would result in the disintegration of the armed forces and eventually in the disintegration of Iran. [12]

Sullivan's warnings were discounted, and he soon was relieved of his ambassadorship. The revolutionaries worked assiduously to develop converts in the armed forces, and as Sullivan had predicted, there were mutinies and defections as confrontations between junior officers and loyal Army elements began to occur. SAVAK was also riddled with defections.

In the midst of this crumbling of the Bakhtiar regime, the Ayatollah Khomeini finally landed in Iran on February 1, 1979, and appointed Medhi Bazargan *his* (meaning Iran's) Prime Minister. On February 11, the Army declared itself neutral. As revolutionary machine gunners began to close in around the official prime ministerial office, Bakhtiar made good his escape and soon afterward fled the country. The Khomeinists were exultant, but obsessed with the idea that the United States was yet plotting a counterrevolution to reinstall the Shah.

ATTEMPTING TO CONTROL THE UNCONTROLLABLE

Despite the extreme hostility against the United States being whipped up in Iran by the Marxists and the Khomeinists, U.S. officials in Teheran and Washington remained optimistic during the first ten months of 1979 that the Khomeinists, who seemed to have the upper hand, would realize that now the main threat to their being able to turn Iran into a fundamentalist Islamic state was from the Marxists and their external patron, the Soviet Union, and that therefore after the Khomeinists consolidated their power they would soon move to reestablish cordial relations with the United States. An early sign that the Khomeinists knew where their real interests lay was their denunciation of the February 14, 1979, armed attack and capture of the United States Embassy by the radical Fedayeen-i-Khalq group, many of whom had been trained by Palestinian guerrillas. The armed militants were persuaded to release their control of the embassy and the American officials they had taken prisoner by the intervention of the new regime's Deputy Premier, Ibrahim Yazdi, and its foreign minister, Karim Sanjabi.

On February 21, 1979, the United States officially recognized the Bazargan government, and Ambassador Sullivan met with the regime's military and political leaders to facilitate the resumption of American arms transfers to Iran. The United States would also continue its oil purchases and business activities in Iran to the extent desired by the new regime.

But revolutions have their own dynamics—the compulsion to wipe the slate clean, to get revenge for past wrongs, and to find scape-goats for the inability to restore order—which often drown out the voices of those who want to move rapidly to put a new regime on a responsible domestic and international course. First there would have to be a full catharsis.

It would have been best if the United States could have com-pletely extracted itself from the scene during the period of Iran's postrevolutionary catharsis. Indeed, this was the policy of the Carter administration at least with respect to Iran's *internal* affairs (al-though the Americans could never get the Iranian militants to be-lieve that Washington was not plotting a counterrevolutionary coup to restore the Shah). But as the revolution, in the classic mold of revolutions, began to take revenge on members and supporters of the old regime, voices were raised in the U.S. Congress against the retributive brutality; and in May the Senate passed a resolution de-ploring the executions. Khomeini and his followers were furious and vilified the United States for its double standard of indifference to the brutalities of the Shah's regime.

The Khomeinists now competed with the leftist militants in stir-ring the Teheran street crowds into mobs of screaming frenzy against the Americans; and moderates who wanted to preserve cordial con-tact with U.S. diplomatic and commercial representatives in Iran had to defend themselves against allegations of conspiring with American CIA agents who allegedly, as in the time of Mossadegh, were posing as embassy officials, journalists, and corporate repre-sentatives but were really organizing a countercoup for the Shah. When Khomeini was warned that the anti-American hysteria might endanger Iran's long-term relationship with the United States, he replied: "May God cause it to be endangered. Our relations with the United States are the relations of the oppressed with the op-pressor, they are the relations of the plundered with the plun-derer." [13]

However, it was the *deus ex machina* of the Shah's cancer that more than anything else pulled the Carter administration and the Khomeinists into the confrontation that nearly led them into war against each other and damaged severely the relations between Iran and the United States for many years to come.

It was President Carter's decision to let the Shah come to the United States for medical treatment—a decision Carter recalls having taken in mid-October 1979 because of being told by State Department officials that the treatment the Shah needed was available only in New York and that the Shah was at the point of death—that provoked the takeover of the U.S. Embassy on November 4 by the revolutionaries and their holding as hostages the American officials for more than fourteen months. The ranking embassy official in Teheran, chargé d'affaires L. Bruce Laingen, had warned several times that the admission of the Shah to the United States would endanger the security of the embassy and had asked for an augmentation of the U.S. military guard; but Laingen's warnings were discounted and his requests deferred.

The decision to admit the Shah for cancer treatment and the *non*-decision on strengthening protection of the embassy, being the immediate precipitants of the hostage crisis, warrant close analysis.

The question of whether or not to grant the deposed Shah *political* asylum in the United States had been decided in the negative, but not without intense controversy at the top levels of the Carter administration. Predictably, Brzezinski was for inviting the Shah, Vance was opposed. "It was my view from the beginning," a *New York Times* interviewer quotes Brzezinski as recalling, "that we should make it unambiguously clear that the Shah was welcome whenever he wanted to come. Our mistake was to ever let it become an issue in the first place." [14]

When the Shah left Iran in January 1979, he apparently felt he had a firm invitation from the United States. Walter Annenberg, the wealthy publisher and former U.S. Ambassador to England during the Nixon administration, was to have let the Shah use his estate in Rancho Mirage, California. But while in transit in Egypt, the Shah was informed that there had been a cooling of enthusiasm in the United States for his arrival. The Beverly Hills home of his mother had been stoned, and the U.S. government was getting worried about its ability to provide adequate protection for the Shah and his family. Offended by this as yet unofficial rebuff, the Shah himself cut off further discussion for the time being of his residing in the United States and decided to go instead to Morocco, where he would be more welcome. After two months in Morocco, however, the Shah was again a man without a country, for demonstrations against the Shah by university students had reached such a pitch that his embarrassed host, King Hassan, felt compelled to request him to find another place of exile before the forthcoming Islamic summit conference in Marrakesh. Humiliated, the Shah now inquired whether the United States was ready to receive him, and was told by the U.S. Ambassador in Morocco that the United States government was concerned for the safety of Americans in Iran if the Shah came to the United States. The embassy in Teheran was particularly vulnerable. There would be demonstrations in the United States itself, and there would be various legal complications. In short, it would no longer be "convenient" for the Shah to come.[15]

David Rockefeller and Henry Kissinger now got to work on the Shah's behalf and found him temporary refuge at a resort in the Bahamas, and then in Cuernavaca, Mexico. Rockefeller and Kissinger also stepped up their efforts to get the Carter administration to reconsider the decision to refuse the Shah's request to come to the United States, and enlisted a senior member of the policy establishment who was highly respected by the Democrats, John J. McCloy, to join them in personal interventions with Vance, Vice President Mondale, and Carter himself (Brzezinski needed no persuading). Rebuffed by the President, Kissinger took to the public podium to voice his outrage at the Carter administration's treatment of the Shah as reducing the monarch to "a Flying Dutchman looking for a port of call."[16]

Another try was made by the Shah's twin sister, Princess Ashraf, in an August 10, 1979, letter to President Carter in which she stressed "the quite noticeable impairment of his [my brother's] health" as a consideration Carter should take into account. The administration was still not apprised of the Shah's cancer, however. Its response, conveyed by Deputy Secretary of State Warren Christopher, expressed concern for the welfare of the Shah and his family, but once again denied the request on grounds of there being "a reasonable chance that the United States can in the months ahead improve the relations with the new government [in Iran] on the basis of mutual respect and cooperation." Christopher's letter referred to "the still serious risks to the safety of our people in Iran" with the clear implication that admitting the Shah to the United States would exacerbate those risks. When relations with Iran were established again on a better course, "we will be reviewing our position on the best timing of your brother's move to the United States."[17]

Reports that the Shah's health was indeed deteriorating alarmingly prompted aides to David Rockefeller to dispatch a medical specialist, Dr. Benjamin Kean, to examine the Shah in late September 1979. Dr. Kean's examinations and consultations with the Shah's French and Mexican physicians revealed that the Shah had been suffering from cancer for the past seven years, but had kept it a secret from the world, and that extensive tests and diagnoses were required by cancer specialists to determine how far the disease had progressed and what further treatment was needed. Dr. Kean was put in telephone contact with the State Department's medical officer, Dr. Eben Dustin, who in turn reported to his political superiors in the Department what Dr. Kean had told him.

It was the report from the State Department's medical officer that apparently convinced Secretary Vance that, despite the political difficulties it would cause, the Shah should be admitted to the United States, not to take up residence, but only for the required emergency medical observation and treatment. Carter agreed, and on October 22 the Shah flew from Mexico to the United States, where he was taken immediately to New York Hospital. Retrospective interviews by *New York Times* reporters have discovered that the key link in this chain of decision—the State Department medical report on the Shah's medical needs immediately precedent to his being allowed to come to the United States—may have overly narrowed the options for Vance and the President. Dr. Kean, the physician tending to the Shah in Cuernavaca upon whom the department's medical officer relied for his information, recalls telling the medical officer that it would be *preferable* to have the Shah treated in the United States but that the required examinations and treatment could be performed in Mexico or elsewhere, if necessary by specialists and equipment flown in from the United States.[18]

The decision to bring the Shah to New York for medical reasons was cabled to the American chargé d'affaires in Teheran on October 20, 1979, and he who immediately informed the Bazargan government.

Although angry at Washington's decision, the Iranian officials promised that the embassy would be protected against assaults by militants, such as the armed attack the previous February. After the February assault on the embassy, U.S. personnel had been reduced from over 1000 to less than 100, a few extra Marine guards had been assigned to the embassy, and steel doors had been installed. It was obvious that these new security measures would be insufficient to defend the embassy from a determined siege by armed militants, but the assumption in Washington was that the Iranian government, as it did in February, would provide timely intervention with its own police forces in case of a serious threat to the premises or to U.S. officials.

The failure to reinforce embassy security was part and parcel of the lack of awareness in Washington of the depth, pervasiveness, and essential characteristics of the revolutionary impulses that swept the Shah from power, and that these impulses had not yet had their full catharsis. By the time of the Shah's arrival in the United States for medical treatment, the Bazargan regime, for the very reasons that Secretary Vance and others thought it could be trusted—its moderation and desire to normalize the situation—had lost its revolutionary legitimacy not only with the left but, more importantly, with the Muslim fundamentalists. Khomeini's continuing authority over the revolution required him to separate himself from the Barzagan government that he had originally installed and blessed, and thus to even further undermine its crumbling authority.

Inadvertently, the Carter administration, by deciding to work with the Bazargan government, was only contributing to its increasing illegitimacy with the Khomeinists. And when top U.S. officials made special efforts to enlarge cordial relations with Bazargan to show that the admission of the Shah to the United States was entirely an *apolitical* "humanitarian" act, they were—unintentionally, of course—playing right into the hands of the anti-Bazargan militants for whom the new "satan" had become Jimmy Carter. Zbigniew Brzezinski, by meeting with Bazargan in Algiers on October 31 on the anniversary of Algerian independence, and allowing a photograph to be taken of them, inflicted the proverbial kiss of death on his regime. The next day, the Ayatollah Khomeini broadcast an appeal to the Iranian people to take to the streets on November 4 to demonstrate and to "expand with all your might your attacks against the United States and Israel."

The November 4 demonstration had originally been the idea of the Society of Islamic Students (the date being the first anniversary of an invasion by the Shah's troops of Teheran University resulting in the killing of several students) to demand that the Shah be re-

turned to Iran to stand trial for torturing his political opponents and
other crimes. Khomeini was now taking over the demonstrations,
but the students would yet force the pace of events, for they had
decided, apparently without Khomeini's knowledge, to seize the
American Embassy. [19]

THE TEST OF AMERICA'S HUMANITARIANISM:
STRENGTH OR WEAKNESS

In making their basic initial demand, backed by Khomeini, that
the Shah be returned to Iran to stand trial, the young militants in
control of the embassy were gambling on the humanitarianism of
the American leadership they had been charging was heartless and
vicious. If the Carter government were more concerned with demonstrating its noncoercibility and finding a pretext for counterrevolutionary intervention than with protecting the lives of some sixty
Americans, then the next step in the drama would be a bloodbath
of unknown dimensions—an attempt by the Americans of a com-
mando-style rescue of the embassy captives or a bombing of the embassy, and/or some other swift, lethal reprisal against Iran—in which
many or all of the embassy employees but also many Iranians would
be killed.

In fact, the militants came close to losing their gamble. But apparently martyrdom in the cause of the fundamentalist Muslim revolution was an outcome they were willing to court; and this stance—
that they would be willing to die with the captives if necessary in
the service of Allah—was a crucial element in their power over
Carter.

Carter did place a very high value on freeing the hostages un-
harmed, higher than some of his advisers and many of his political
opponents thought was prudent. But Carter denied at the time, and
afterward, that he thereby sacrificed America's honor and power to
his humanitarian impulses. Rather, he argued that the humanitarian valuation of individual lives was a part of America's essential
strength and honor, and that his management of the hostage crisis
was designed precisely to avoid forcing the issue to the point where
in order to prevent a real loss of U.S. power, it would be necessary
to sacrifice the lives of the hostages.

Demonstrators started circling the embassy early in the morning of November 4. In midmorning some of them began scaling the gate, at which time the guards locked the recently installed steel door to the chancellery. But the mob broke open the steel door. The few Marine guards present held off the Iranians by pointing shotguns at them while allowing the embassy employees to gather on the second floor, access to which was barred by a second steel door. On the second floor of the embassy, employees began to shred secret documents and destroy computer circuits. Meanwhile the embassay's security officer attempted to talk with the leaders of the intruding militants, but was taken captive and apparently forced to order a marine to open the steel access door to the second floor. The militants rushed upstairs and immediately took all the Americans captive, except three officials who had locked themselves in a steel vault to complete the shredding of documents. The officials within the vault were coerced into surrendering before they had finished their shredding job as the militants held a knife to the throat of one of their American captives before a television monitor on view within the vault.

Sixty-three American officials were now at the mercy of a group of young Iranian militants in physical control of the embassy; and three more—including chargé d'affaires Laingen—who had been on a visit to the Iranian Foreign Ministry blocks away and were in telephone contact with the embassy during its siege, were also taken captive. The militants, a small group of hitherto virtually unknown radical Muslim activists, mostly university students, suddenly found themselves at the center of the world political arena, in a position to bargain with one of the global superpowers—that is, as long as they kept their American captives alive and as long as Jimmy Carter continued to place a high value on the lives of these American officials. The hostage drama had begun.[20]

"I listened to every proposal, no matter how preposterous," recalls Carter, "all the way from delivering the Shah for trial as the revolutionaries demanded to dropping an atomic bomb on Tehran."[21] One proposal was a rescue attempt in emulation of Israeli methods of freeing hostages held by airplane hijackers, such as the famous rescue at Entebbe, Uganda. The Joint Chiefs of Staff pointed out the pitfalls of such an attempt in the present situation: Tehran was not like the Entebbe airport; there was no way to pull off such a commando raid in the middle of the city without getting the hostages killed in the process. Even so, this option might yet have to be used, and thus the military was ordered to prepare for such a rescue effort and to put their people most knowledgeable about this kind of operation to work in devising ways of minimizing injury to the hostages in case a rescue was decided upon. A "show of force" in the form of amassing naval units near Iran was discussed, but dismissed as premature, for to work as a coercive ploy it would have to be a visible and dramatic deployment and this might provoke the militants into either a wholesale slaughter of the hostages or a countercoercive ploy of killing them one at a time to pressure the United States to give in to their demands while there was still some chance of saving the remainder.

Carter early on decided to shift the responsibility for bloodshed onto the captors: "I am not going to take any military action that would cause bloodshed or arouse the unstable captors of our hostages to attack or punish them," he announced, *as long as they were not harmed or put on trial*. The clear implication was that he would feel compelled to take military action under such circumstances, but yet this kind of formulation stopped short of an ultimatum which locked the United States into a military response. On the other hand, it left open the definition of "harmed," and "put on trial" so that he would not have to tolerate the hostages' being tortured or otherwise abused, and the captors would be put on notice not to push their luck. [22]

Carter's initial restraint on the use of any force that would endanger the lives of the hostages was consistent with the dominant public sentiment at the time, as reflected in public opinion polls and editorial opinion, which in turn was shaped by media attention given to the families of the hostages, their anguish, and their fears. The President himself met periodically with these families and thereby helped create a national empathy with their plight, so that it was not a group of faceless U.S. diplomats and embassy guards whose lives were at risk, but the sons and daughters of one's neighbors.

Having rejected a military move against Iran or a rescue operation as immediate responses to the taking of the hostages, the Carter administration moved quickly to exploit the nonlethal forms of pressure at its disposal that might sway those in control in Iran to induce the militants to release the hostages. Who those in control were, apart from Khomeini himself, was not at all clear; and Khomeini was still an enigma. Would the international diplomatic and economic pressures being organized really make any difference to him? It was decided to try anyway, under the assumption that there were large segments of Iranian society that did want Iran to be an accepted member of the larger society of nations, and did realize that their own material well-being was dependent upon the government of Iran and Iranian citizens being able to buy and sell normally in the international market. If most of the internationally connected and internationally sensitive elements in Iran could be made to realize that the hostage-holding would hurt them, then perhaps even the xenophobic Khomeinists could be prevailed upon to intercede to get the hostages released.

On November 7, the President prohibited U.S. companies from buying oil from Iran—a move of questionable effect, given the prevailing sellers' market for oil, and probably of greater inconvenience to American oil importers than to the Iranian exporters. A week later the President enlarged the scope of proscribed economic transactions to include various other imports as well as certain U.S. exports to Iran. But these too, to have any real pinch in Iran, would require concerted action by other countries so that Iran could not simply shift its commerce elsewhere; and such cooperation with the United States proved hard to induce.

The most important economic sanction was a freeze on Iranian assets on deposit in U.S. banks in this country and abroad—some $12 billion in all, which at the time was estimated to be about $5 billion less than this. Postponed a few days while the risks to the United States were being assessed, the freeze order was precipitated by an announcement on November 14 by the new Iranian Foreign Minister, Bani-Sadr, that Iran was going to withdraw all its assets from American banks. The U.S. government received this information on the Iranian move at 5 A.M., and acted quickly to order the freeze before the banks opened that morning. In reporting the freeze to the Congress that day, Carter stated two purposes: getting the hostages released and protecting the property claims of U.S. individuals and corporations against Iran.[23]

How important the desire to get back the frozen assets was in eventually motivating the Iranian government to free the hostages is unclear. The unfreezing of the assets did, however, figure importantly in the final *negotiations* over the hostages' release, as a way of giving the Iranians something substantial to take home on their side.

On the diplomatic front, the Carter administration, now defined by the Khomeinists as the enemy, had to rely on intermediaries to press its case that normalized U.S.–Iranian relations would be of substantial benefit to the post-Shah regime; that the United States had no plans or intentions to reinstate the Shah; that the United States was willing to hear the claims of the Iranians against its own alleged crimes in Iran, and even to discuss the Shah's future, but not with a knife at the throats of American officials. Carter himself contacted as many as thirty foreign leaders personally, among them Leonid Brezhnev, to request such intercession.[24]

To the surprise of most Americans, but not to Carter and his advisers, one of the early intermediaries, and probably the most effective, was the PLO leader Yasir Arafat. The Palestinian guerrilla chief was not asked directly by the Carter administration to use his influence with Khomeini, but Carter was apprised of the initiative of Congressman Paul Findley (Republican of Illinois), a known champion of Palestinian causes, to get Arafat to intercede, and that Arafat wanted the U.S. leadership to know that he was engaging in an action that might be politically costly for him. On November 19 and 20, thirteen hostages—the women and blacks—were released upon Khomeini's orders, evidently as a result of Arafat's intercession. As far as is known, however, after his November contacts with Khomeini, the PLO leader played no further role in the hostage affair.

The diplomatic intercessions were also for the purpose of finding out precisely what the Khomeinists now running the government would settle for to release all of the hostages. In mid-November, in secret "proximity talks" at the United Nations between Vance and an envoy of the Iranian government (Vance and the Iranian, Ahmad Salmatian, sat in separate rooms and passed papers to each other through Secretary General Kurt Waldheim), it was determined that the Iranian government would no longer insist on the extradition of the Shah. The hostages might be released if three conditions were met: (1) the U.S. government would arrange for the Shah's wealth to be returned to Iran; (2) the U.S. government would pledge never to interfere again in the internal affairs of Iran; and (3) the U.S. government would agree to participate in an international forum in which Iran could present its charges against both the Shah and the United States and have these examined before the world. Vance indicated his desire to pursue negotiations on each of these demands and his hope of reaching a settlement with the Iranian Foreign Minister, Bani-Sadr, at the time of the Security Council meetings on the crisis scheduled for the end of November.[25]

Before the delicate negotiations could resume, however, there was another shakeup in the government in Teheran. Khomeini denounced the forthcoming UN Security Council meetings as staged by and for the United States. Foreign Minister Bani-Sadr was dismissed and replaced by Sadegh Ghotbsadeh—a vocal proponent of forcing the extradition of the Shah. The Carter administration was disheartened by this regression, but surmised it might be a part of the Byzantine political maneuverings among the Khomeinists, and that the real settling price had been revealed by Bani-Sadr's representative in New York. Patience and further diplomatic skill might yet return the Iranians to this more reasonable bargaining posture.

Carter had his domestic political problems too. Each passing day of the hostages' captivity was being counted off on the TV evening news. Opposition politicians were demanding a reassertion of American will and power to protect this country's honor. Editorial writers were complaining that the President had drastically weakened the U.S. bargaining power by making the lives of the hostages the highest national interest and thereby giving the world to believe that we were an easy target for blackmail.

Then, to make matters worse, the Mexican government announced that it could not allow the Shah to return to Mexico upon completion of his medical treatment in New York. Medical reports issued from New York Hospital indicated the Shah was ready to leave at the start of December. If he remained in the United States beyond then, the credibility of Carter's original rationale for admitting him would be destroyed with Teheran and efforts to free the hostages might collapse.

The Shah was flown to Lackland Air Force Base in Texas—"temporarily" and "en route" to his next place of residence outside the United States—while the White House and State Department frantically attempted to locate another country for his exile. Panama's General Torrijos, who had developed a close rapport with the

White House during the successful negotiations on the canal treaty, bailed out the administration by inviting the Shah to reside in Panama.

The Iranians now, in January 1980, focused their diplomatic activity on Panama, attempting to get the Panamanian government to extradite the Shah to Iran. This allowed issues between the United States and Iran to return to the points in the November proximity talks at the UN, but it was difficult to get the Iranians to give this negotiating track the required attention while they were concentrating their efforts on Panama. Presidential assistant Hamilton Jordan, who had been responsible for managing the Shah's move to Panama, seized on the opportunity to establish contact with a couple of French and Argentinian intermediaries, Christian Bourguet and Hector Villalón, whom the Iranians were using to press Torrijos on the extradition issue. Jordan got them to serve simultaneously as a conduit for the White House in transmitting to Iran the President's desire to resume discussion of Teheran's other demands.

Meanwhile, UN Secretary General Waldheim intruded himself into the situation, announcing on December 30, 1979, that he was going personally to Teheran to attempt to negotiate a release of the hostages. In Teheran, Waldheim was told that his effort would have to be restricted to fact-finding, since only the United States, not the UN, had the power to make things right. Khomeini refused even to meet with the Secretary General. But Waldheim's inquiries in Teheran did convince him that what the Iranians wanted most from the United States now as a condition for the release of the hostages was an admission of past complicity in the Shah's crimes, and that this might be accomplished through an international commission of inquiry whose findings the United States would agree to accept. Exploiting this information, the White House, through the Jordan/Bourguiet–Villalón conduit, attempted to get things moving again by indicating a receptivity to the commission idea and by trying to institute specific discussions about the modalities: Would the hostages be released simultaneously with the formation of the commission? Upon the commencement of its hearings in Teheran? Or only after it had reported its findings? The intermediaries converged with Jordan on the outlines of a partial scenario: an independent distinguished-persons commission would go to Iran before the hostages were released, and this commission, in addition to hearing charges about the Shah and the United States, would be able to talk with the hostages. The President of the United States and the President of Iran (now Bani-Sadr) would deposit statements with the United Nations expressing understanding of the particular grievances of the other. The United States by agreeing to this scenario hoped to set in motion a dynamic process in which the Iranian government itself would take over control of the hostages from the young militants, and a quick release would follow before the publication of the commission's report. But would the regime in Teheran so commit itself?

Despite the remaining uncertainties on the precise tasks of the commission when it arrived in Teheran and the timing of the hostages' release in relation to the commission's report, Iran and the United States agreed in early February to the appointment of the five-member commission by UN Secretary General Waldheim and to its membership: Andrés Aguilar Mawdsley of Venezuela, Mohammed Bedjaoui of Algeria, Adib Daoudy of Syria, Hector Wilfred Jayewardene of Sri Lanka, and Louis-Edmond Pettiti of France. But the artful drafting of ambiguous terms defining the commission's role thrust its five members into an embarrassing situation when they discovered that the Iranians and the Americans had not resolved their essential differences over what the commission was supposed to do. The visit with the hostages, according to the Americans, was to determine their well-being; but according to the Iranians, it was to interrogate the hostages to assist the commission in determining the extent of the U.S. "crimes" in Iran. Efforts of some of the commissioners to gain further clarification of their mission made the Iranians angry and almost resulted in their canceling its visit at the last moment. And while the commission was flying to Teheran on February 23, 1980, the Ayatollah Khomeini announced that he had never been in accord with the idea of the commission and that anyway the fate of the hostages would be determined by the new Majlis, the Iranian Parliament, after it was formed.[26]

As it turned out, the Iranians stage-managed the scenario in Iran largely to their satisfaction, providing hundreds of victims of brutal treatment by the Shah's government and police for the commission to interview. By the end of the first week in March, the investigation of the past having been performed, the Iranian government, to implement its end of the bargain, was supposed to take control of the hostages from the militants. But the young militants at the embassy refused and the Iranian government claimed to be in no better position than the United States to use force against them without provoking a slaughter of the hostages. The Iranian officials appealed to Khomeini to attempt to salvage the affair without great international embarrassment to Iran, whereupon the Ayatollah proposed that the commission be allowed to see the hostages at the embassy without the students having to relinquish control; but as a condition for being able to interview the hostages, the commission should *first* make a declaration of its findings about the brutality of the Shah's regime and the past interference by the United States in the internal affairs of Iran.

The commissioners properly refused to be manipulated so crassly and, despite frantic appeals from the United States and the UN Secretariat to stay on, refused to continue their work under such terms, nor would they publish their report. It now looked as if the Ayatollah's timetable—no action on the hostages until the new parliament was convened in the spring and decided what to do—would prevail. In the meantime, it would take great diplomatic skill to restore a climate for resuming negotiations on the hostages' release, for now all parties were again angry and highly suspicious of one another.

Another complication arose in March, with the apparent maturing of the bilateral negotiations between Iran and Panama on the extradition of the Shah, and a worsening of his medical condition. This was a risky time to have the Shah readmitted to the United States for further medical treatment; but to insist that he stay in Panama would mean that the Iranians would get hold of him. Actually, General Torrijos was himself playing a tough bargaining game with the Iranians, holding out the possibility of extradition as a way of getting the hostages released and having the United States deeply in his debt. And, fortunately, Egypt's Anwar Sadat came forward with the offer of domicile for the Shah plus acceptable medical treatment in Egypt, which relieved the United States from the need to again provoke the Iranians.

Now Carter's own domestic political troubles (Senator Kennedy won the New York presidential primary on March 26), coupled with his anger at the Iranians' sabotage of the UN commission's work, began to erode his patient and meticulous approach. On March 29, he sent a warning to Bani-Sadr that if the hostages were not transferred to the control of the government in Teheran within 48 hours, the United States would inflict new and harsh sanctions on Iran. With the failure of this ultimatum to produce results, Carter was in a corner. Graduated diplomatic and economic sanctions were no more likely to work now than before; but, given the ugly mood in Iran at not being able to get at the Shah or have his and the American "crimes" revealed by the UN commission, a major escalation, such as a naval blockade of Iran, might provoke the Iranians into staging a "show trial" of the hostages and demands for their execution.

THE ABORTIVE RESCUE MISSION

Administration hints that the use of force was now seriously contemplated punctuated a stiffening of diplomatic and economic sanctions during the first half of April 1980. On April 7 the United States formally broke diplomatic relations with the government of Iran; and on April 17 the President announced a ban on all exports to Iran and the U.S. government's seizure of the Iranian assets frozen in U.S. banks.

The members of the European Economic Community reluctantly voted sanctions of their own under the assumption, reinforced by their conversations with U.S. officials, that such concerted U.S.–European action would make it unnecessary for the United States to resort to force at this time, and that the resulting international isolation of Iran should be the basic pressure on Teheran for a while; the failure of the Europeans to join the United States in applying diplomatic and economic sanctions, the U.S. officials had strongly suggested, would compel a resort to military action before the summer.

Behind the scenes, however, Carter was closely reviewing his military options and, even before the EEC had voted to cooperate in the nonmilitary sanctions, he decided, at an April 11 National Security Council meeting with Brzezinski, Harold Brown, Deputy Secretary of State Warren Christopher (Vance was in Florida on a four-day vacation), General David Jones (Chairman of the Joint

Chiefs of Staff), Stansfield Turner (Director of the CIA), Vice
President Mondale, and White House aides Hamilton Jordan and
Jody Powell, to go ahead with the helicopter rescue of the hostages.

Upon his return from Florida, Secretary Vance, in a private
meeting with Carter, objected to the rescue plan, arguing that even
if it succeeded with minimal injury to the hostages (which he thought
improbable), the raid would place at risk the approximately two
hundred other Americans still living in Iran, who could themselves
be seized as hostages, and it would jeopardize U.S. relations with
other countries in the region, and also U.S. relations with the EEC
countries, who were under the impression that we had deferred any
military moves as a result of their joining us in the diplomatic and
economic sanctions. A follow-up meeting of the National Security
Council was convened to hear out Vance's objections, but with little
debate, for Carter already had made up his mind to go ahead
with the rescue. On April 17, Vance told Carter that even if the
raid succeeded he wanted to resign.[27]

Why did the President feel he had to resort to the rescue raid
just then? Couldn't he have waited so as to satisfy Vance and the
Europeans that all other options short of force had been exhausted?
Evidently, a few key details determined the timing: the hostages
were still being held in the embassy compound (once they were dispersed to other places of incarceration it would be almost impossible
to try a rescue); the desert nights were getting longer and the desert
temperatures hotter as summer approached; thus each passing week
would degrade the efficiency of the helicopter operation and reduce
nighttime concealment—two crucial elements of the plan. Carter
was convinced it was now or never.[28]

The President was strengthened in his conviction that this was
the time to try a more dramatic option by reports of a shift in public
attitudes toward the use of force against Iran. A *Washington Post*
nationwide poll conducted from April 9 to 13 showed nearly a two-
to-one majority in favor of military action even if it imperiled the
lives of the hostages (this in contrast to a similar poll taken in January showing 51 percent rejecting the use of force on grounds that
it could result in harm to the hostages).[29]

The rescue scheme authorized by the President on April 11 had
been carefully worked out to minimize the chances of its being dis-

covered by the Iranians in time for them to first move or kill the hostages. Early in the evening of April 24, 1980, six C-130 Hercules transport planes carrying 90 commandos, helicopter fuel, and weapons-jamming equipment took off from Egypt. At the same time eight Navy RH-53D "Sea Stallion" helicopters took off from the aircraft carrier *Nimitz* in the Arabian Sea and headed for a a rendezvous with the six C-130s in the Dasht-i-Kavir salt desert 200 miles southeast of Teheran. The commandos who had been flown in on the transports were then to have been carried in the helicopters to a staging site just outside of Teheran, where they were to be met by other commandos who had been infiltrated into Iran over recent months, and had obtained local trucks in which they would drive the raiding party, unnoticed, blending with Teheran city traffic, to the embassy compound. In the middle of the night, the force, equipped with nonlethal chemical weapons, was to scale the compound wall, cut telephone and electricity lines, incapacitate the Iranians, and evacuate the hostages in helicopters that meanwhile had landed on the embassy grounds. The helicopters would escape to another desert rendezvous with the C-130s, which would then fly the hostages and the raiding party out of the country, leaving the helicopters behind. Some Americans would be likely to lose their lives in the operation.*

The mission was aborted in midcourse, however, after three malfunctioning helicopters reduced the fleet of those that would have been available for the final evacuation efforts from the embassy to five, instead of the original eight helicopters. Receiving this information and an evaluation from the mission commanders at the desert airstrip that at least six operational helicopters would be required to implement the rescue plan, Carter had no choice but to call off the attempt. No one had yet been killed; but, tragically, while the helicopters were refueling for their return flight, one of them collided with a C-130 on the ground, igniting both planes and killing eight men. Knowing that the failed raid could no longer be kept secret, the President sadly informed the nation on television of the abortive rescue operation and freak desert collision that killed the eight men. But he expressed no regrets for attempting the mis-

---

* A CIA evaluation of the plan estimated that most probably 60 percent of the hostages would lose their lives in the rescue attempt. See Salinger, pp. 237–38.

sion, and thereby implied that this was not the last of such efforts,
or of other military moves contemplated against Iran, especially if
the hostages were now harmed by the angry Iranians.[30]

To the relief of the Carter administration and the American public, the Iranians contented themselves with verbal anger and ridicule at the desert debacle, including a warning to Carter from the
Ayatollah "that if he commits another stupid act we won't be able
to control the youths now holding the . . . spies and he will be
responsible for their lives," and a statement from President Bani-
Sadr that to make a second rescue attempt impossible, the hostages
were being transferred outside the embassy.

THE DIPLOMATIC DENOUEMENT

Domestic politics in Iran and the United States preoccupied both
countries for four and one half months after the abortive rescue
attempt. The Shah died in an Egyptian military hospital on July 27,
and no high official of the U.S. government attended his funeral
(Former President Nixon did attend, but only in a private capacity).
The Iranians were electing their first parliament since the revolution. The United States was in the final stages of the nominating
process for the fall's presidential elections. The hiatus on the diplomatic front was an opportunity for Carter to follow the strategy,
recommended by European diplomats and some professionals within
the State Department, of turning the spotlight off the hostages and
thus to reduce the bargaining leverage the Iranians could gain from
their incarceration. The American press, with its tendency for sin-
gle-minded emphasis on the issue of the day, obliged by indulging
in its typical obsession with the presidential election.

The Iranian parliamentary elections, completed in August, were
a popular victory for the Khomeinists, legitimizing their revolution
and making it less important for them to show their power and curry
favor with the masses by exploiting the hostage issue. Moreover,
electoral success gave the Islamic leaders a new set of imperatives
beyond providing Iran with an emotional catharsis—namely, restoring civic order and peace, giving economic stability to the country
for which they were now officially responsible, and resurrecting its
international respectability. The role of "kidnapper" served none of
these purposes, and Khomeini, still titular leader and elder states-

man of the revolution, sensing this, now blessed serious negotiations to free the hostages for the first time since the embassy takeover the previous November.

The Carter administration was made aware of this devaluation of Iran's interest in the hostages in early September when German diplomatic intermediaries informed Secretary of State Edmund Muskie (Vance's successor) that the Khomeinists now wanted to meet urgently to work out a deal to release the hostages. A close associate of the Ayatollah, Sadegh Tabatabai, met in Bonn with Deputy Secretary Warren Christopher to get down to specifics; and at these meetings it was immediately apparent that Iran's demands were now within the range of negotiability. There was no mention of ransom, or even of an apology from the United States. The Iranians still wanted a U.S. pledge of noninterference in Iran; but the principal talking points were over the release of Iran's financial assets that had been seized by the United States and the size and repayment modalities of Iran's obligations to its U.S. creditors. The credibility of the negotiating positions Tabatabai represented to Christopher was established in a speech by the Ayatollah stating essentially the same conditions.

From here on out, the negotiations, which took place mainly in Algeria, with the Algerians acting skillfully as mediators, resembled complicated international commercial negotiations rather than the highly charged political encounters of the earlier stages in the crisis. High politics was an ever-present background factor, but now the political context worked to reinforce Iran's incentives to settle with the United States. Iraq's attack on Iran on September 22, and the ensuing border war between them, made it all the more urgent for Iran to establish international respectability with its Western arms suppliers (especially the United States) to counterbalance the new arms Iraq had been receiving from the Soviet Union. Ronald Reagan's election in November also increased the incentives in Tehran to settle before January 20, for the President-elect had revealed himself during the campaign to be a more confrontationist type than Carter, unwilling to grant that Iran had any legitimate cause whatsoever for its actions over the past year. Reagan, moreover, had pledged to freeze the negotiations when he assumed office and to reassess the whole strategy of dealing with the hostage issue. The Carter administration played on the Iranians' fears of Reagan by convincing them that a finalized official agreement with the Carter government, capped by a return of the hostages before Reagan was inaugurated, would very likely be honored by the new administration, whereas an uncompleted agreement could be easily torn up.

The negotiating end game, typically, involved efforts by both sides to extract maximum face for themselves, as well as some nontrivial differences over the financial settlement. As late as December, the bargaining almost got derailed by Teheran's surprise insistence that its frozen assets plus the wealth removed from Iran by the Shah required $25 billion to be handed over to Iran by the United States. Patient negotiation by Christopher, with helpful intercessions by the Algerians, moved the Iranian demands back to the more reasonable level of approximately $8 billion in exchange for the hostages which appeared in the final agreement of January 20. After setting aside $5.1 billion that Iran owed in debts to American banks, some $3 billion in cash was to be released to Iran simultaneously with the freeing of the hostages. The $3 billion was to be held in escrow until the hostages were safely airborn in a U.S. Air Force plane. This final exchange of fifty-two live bodies for cash, as the two Air Force planes carrying the hostages cleared Iranian airspace, was consummated just after 12:30 P.M. on January 20, 1981. Ronald Reagan had become President at noon.

31

SALT VS. MOVING
BEYOND "MAD"

From the beginning of human history combat was often the measure of courage.
Willingness to risk war was the mark of statecraft. My fellow Americans, that
pattern . . . must now be broken forever.

JIMMY CARTER

The strategic arms controllers Carter appointed to the offices that
would have primary responsibility for reenergizing the stalled SALT
II negotiations were all, at the outset of the Carter presidency, committed to the logic of mutual strategic deterrence reflected in the
SALT I accords and to assuring that the SALT II treaty perpetuated that logic. Cyrus Vance at State, Harold Brown at Defense,
and Paul Warnke at the Arms Control and Disarmament Agency
(ACDA) had each reendorsed the mainline arms control logic during
their confirmation hearings in early 1977, saying that a thermonuclear war would be suicide for both superpowers, that the concept
of "limited" strategic nuclear warfare was a fantasy, and that the
only purpose of each side's strategic nuclear arsenal should be to
deter a strategic nuclear attack by the other.

In reasserting the deterrence-only criterion for the strategic arsenal Vance, Brown, and Warnke were self-consciously restoring
the strategic planning concepts they had helped develop in the 1960s
when they were all high officials in the Defense Department under
Secretary of Defense Robert McNamara. Along with McNamara

they had flirted during the first two years of the Kennedy administration with notions of limited strategic war (McNamara's doctrine
of "controlled counterforce"; see above, pp. 169–70) and with the
possibilities for limiting damage to the United States during a strategic conflict with the Soviet Union by a combination of civil defense preparations, antiballistic missiles, and offensive forces designed to knock out Soviet retaliatory forces. But by the end of 1963,
they had discarded these strategic "war fighting" notions as both
wasteful and dangerous. Forces designed to limit the damage the
Soviet Union could inflict upon the United States in a strategic war
were wasteful because the Soviets would never accept the implied
elimination of their ability to deter a strategic attack by the United
States, and would spend at very high levels to negate any of the
contemplated improvements in the U.S. damage-limiting capabilities—the result being only to push the arms race into increasingly
expensive levels of competition. Such forces and their doctrines for
use were at the same time dangerous, for their prime targets were
the other side's offensive forces, which meant that the opponent in
a brink-of-war situation might have a high incentive to fire off his
strategic forces before they would be knocked out; and if both sides
were operating with such counterforce doctrines and weapons, there
would be dangerous temptations present in intense crises for strategic preemptive attacks. On the basis of this elemental analysis,
McNamara and his Pentagon brain trust had decided, over howls of
protest from the Air Force, to make "assured destruction" of Soviet
society both the *necessary and sufficient* criteria for the design of the
strategic forces and to attempt to persuade the Russians to adopt a
similar logic for their strategic arsenal. Thus Vance, Brown, and
Warnke were present at the creation of Mutual Assured Destruction (MAD) and were among those originally responsible for formulating and disseminating its rationale.

In exile during the Nixon and Ford administrations, Vance,
Brown, and Warnke watched doctrines and weapons programs antithetical to the MAD concept gain acceptability within the administration and the policy community. SALT I, signed by Nixon and
Brezhnev in 1972, still was based on MAD premises (see above, pp.
339–40). But the negotiations within the government to develop
SALT II proposals, and then the start of the dialogue with the Rus-

sians on SALT II, were infused with intense debates—most notably between Secretary of Defense James Schlesinger and Secretary of State Kissinger—over how to make SALT compatible with the coming generation of counterforce weapons and with intelligence analyses purporting to show that the Soviets, despite SALT I, were engaged in a major buildup of strategic "war-fighting" capabilities.

Vance and Warnke took up their new posts in the Carter administration convinced of the urgency of restoring a consensus in the government and the policy community on the wisdom of the MAD premises, and on this basis to get the negotiations with the Russians back on track. Brown, however, as he got into his new job, was immediately faced with the complications, and with sophisticated arguments from Brzezinski over at NSC, that MAD was a woefully insufficient basis for strategic force planning and arms control policy in the late 1970s and early 1980s. If we were really serious about a mutual-deterrence strategic balance between ourselves and the Russians, argued Brzezinski, then we would have to turn around the arms programs on both sides much more dramatically than was called for in the SALT II proposals inherited from the previous administration.

THE "DEEP CUTS" PROPOSAL OF MARCH 1977

President Carter was responsive to Brzezinski's plea for bold moves in the arms control field that would break out of the pattern established in SALT I and the Ford–Brezhnev agreement at Vladivostok in 1974 allowing the Soviets to build up to equality in numbers of missile launchers and missile launchers capable of carrying multiple warheads (MIRVs), and then to cap the strategic arms race at this high level of "parity." Carter wanted a *reversal* of the strategic arms race and movement *toward* the goal of nuclear disarmament stated in his inaugural address. And he listened appreciatively to the Pentagon briefings showing how under the cover of formal numerical equality, the Soviets, with their heavier missile throw-weight and MIRVing and accuracy improvements, would soon be achieving a capacity to knock out as much as 90 percent of the U.S. ICBM force in a first strike, using only a portion of their force. This was potentially a dangerously unstable situation, which could be rectified either by a major augmentation in the U.S. strategic arsenal, which in turn would mean the end of SALT, or by getting the Soviets to agree to deep cuts in their heavy ICBM force.

Vance and Warnke agreed with the objective of moving toward a mutual reduction in counterforce weapons, but considered that this would be more appropriately tackled at the SALT III stage. The Russians were ready to resume the SALT II negotiations to establish essential quantitative equivalence across most categories of strategic weapons. Perhaps some "qualitative" controls could be built in at this time; but if we wanted to get the SALT process back on track, it was best to continue for the time being to negotiate within the terms of reference the Russians had already accepted. However, sensing that the President was smitten by the idea of starting out boldly and strong with the Russians, and was willing to have compromise proposals prepared as a fallback position in case the Russians proved too stubborn, Vance and Warnke did not press their case and the Brzezinski/Brown approach was translated into a detailed proposal for Vance to show Soviet Foreign Minister Gromyko in Moscow.

The new draft U.S. position that Vance and Warnke carried to Moscow provided for a reduction of each side's total strategic launchers to a level of 1800 to 2000 (the Vladivostok guidelines had stipulated 2400), of which 1100 to 1200 could carry multiple warheads (compared with 1320 in the Vladivostok guidelines). Neither side could MIRV more than 550 of its ICBMs, however; and the Soviets would have to cut their heavy missle force in half—down to about 150 launchers. Flight testing of existing ICBMs would be limited and there would be a total ban on the development, testing, and deployment of new ICBMs or mobile modes of deploying existing ICBMs.

The Secretary of State and his chief SALT negotiator also carried fallback positions, but the existence of these was kept secret from all but the highest members of the National Security Council (Vance and Warnke were ordered by the President, on Brzezinski's suggestion, to keep this negotiating strategy secret even from their most senior aides). [1]

Presented to the Soviet leaders in Moscow on March 28 and 29, 1977, the new proposal was immediately rejected by the Soviet leadership. They were visibly angry not only at the substance but also at the way the Carter administration attempted to mold public opinion behind the initiative before the Russians had an opportunity to review it in detail and discuss it in private with American officials. (In his March 24 news conference, President Carter had indicated that Secretary Vance would be taking "new proposals" on strategic arms limitations to Moscow, the first of which would be for an "actual substantial reduction," so as to get away from the previous pattern of agreeing only to "ground rules for intensified competition.")[2]

Following the official Soviet rejection, Secretary Vance held a news conference in Moscow on March 30, at which he revealed the details of the two proposals the American delegation put forward. The first, a "deferral proposal," would formalize the Vladivostok accord and defer the issues that, more than any other, had held up agreement on the SALT II treaty—whether to count U.S. cruise missiles and the Soviet Backfire bomber under the numerical limits on strategic weapons. The second, which the Americans said they preferred, was the "comprehensive proposal," which Vance now revealed in considerable detail.

Foreign Minister Gromyko retaliated with a news conference of his own on March 31, the first such performance in years in Moscow by a top Soviet leader, in which he assailed the Carter proposals as "a dubious, if not a cheap, move." The Americans, in demanding that the Russians eliminate half of their "heavy" missiles, he charged, were engaged in a "shady maneuver" to put the Soviets at a strategic disadvantage, in violation of the equality assumptions that had governed the negotiations since 1972 and were reflected in the Vladivostok accords. "What are we to do," Gromyko asked, "if a new administration comes to office and throws aside what was positive and what went before? We want stability in our relations. . . . We might well ask, is that the way to reach an accord? What has changed since Vladivostok to dictate the necessity for such a demand? Nothing. Absolutely nothing has changed. This is not the way to reach a solution of problems. This is the way of mounting one unresolved problem on top of another."[3] Gromyko was asked at this press conference whether President Carter's public support of the human rights of Soviet dissidents had conditioned the Kremlin's reactions to the American arms proposals. His response was revealing. It had not figured directly, responded Gromyko, but it "poisons the atmosphere." The interests of both sides were properly defined in 1972 with the advancement of the thesis of noninterference in the two countries' internal affairs. "This thesis is all the more correct today. No kind of noise, squeal or screech addressed from abroad to the Soviet Union will detract us from this road." [4]

Administration spokesmen put the best face on the flat and unequivocal Soviet rejection of their approach; and, indeed, Brzezinski advised the President to "hang tough," that the Soviet tantrum was a negotiating tactic, and that before too long *their* interest in a strategic arms agreement would lead them to move toward the new comprehensive proposal. Moreover, the proposal was more consistent with U.S. security needs than those inherited from the previous administration; and it had support of important hardliners in the Senate, including Senator Henry Jackson. Vance and Warnke, however, maintained that both the substance and style of the démarche had miscalculated Soviet sensitivities and perceptions of their own security needs. It was important to convey to their Soviet counterparts that the new administration was concerned to understand Soviet perceptions of the kind of strategic balance they could live with, and to resume quiet negotiations toward achieving a mutually acceptable treaty.

Both sides in the internal administration controversy over the debacle in Moscow turned out to be right in part. The Russians were anxious to negotiate and probably were overreacting with some calculated anger. But conducting the negotiations in public as a kind of high drama in superpower bargaining was not the way to get them to take *our* new strategic concerns seriously. Carter in particular was responsive to Vance's counsel to lower the decibel level, with respect both to SALT issues and to human rights, so that when Secretary Vance and Foreign Minister Gromyko met again in Geneva in May, there could be serious and detailed discussions between them on guidelines for resuming, in secret, the stalled strategic arms negotiations. In April, public statements by Carter and Brezhnev helped to restore an appropriate atmosphere. Brezhnev talked of the possibility of "a reasonable accommodation" if the United States abandoned its "one-sided position." And Carter indicated that his administration was "reassessing some of the objections the Soviets had raised to see if there is some alternative that would be equally fair to both sides. . . . If during this reanalysis we show that there is any inequity there, we would be very eager to change it." [5]

FINESSING THE DIFFERENCES

Where there is a will there is a way, Carter felt, and made sure that the national security bureaucracy knew that he was determined both to get SALT back on track *and* to move toward substantial cuts in the most dangerous weapons. The bureaucracy came up with a way in the so-called "Three-Tier Proposal" developed by the Director of the Office of Political Military Relations in State, Les Gelb, and a temporary holdover from the Kissinger years at the NSC, William Hyland. Gelb and Hyland proposed that Tier One should be the draft SALT II *treaty,* which, catering to the insistences of the Soviets, would retain the essential features of the Vladivostok accords plus elements that had been worked out in the formal and informal negotiations before the United States presented its deep cut proposal. Tier Two would be U.S. suggestions for a *three-year protocol* to the treaty, covering contentious new systems not yet deployed which both sides would refrain from deploying during the period of the protocol (particularly cruise missiles, mobile missiles, and new Soviet ICBMs). Tier Three would be a *statement of principles to govern future negotiations* on SALT III.

The top levels of both the Soviet and U.S. governments liked this three-tier approach as a vehicle for resuming serious negotiations. The Americans, of course, would be free once negotiations resumed to attempt to move up some of the Tier Three items into SALT II, as, for example, limitations on Soviet heavy missiles and even some reductions. The Soviets, for their part, could attempt to get certain of the protocol measures, such as limitations on cruise missiles, extended in the form of commitments to continue them in SALT III. The bargaining would be tough; but it would again be between the strategic experts and not in front of the press. Announcements would be made by the top political leadership on both sides about agreements, with minimal and only general statements about negotiating positions.

Within these agreed boundary conditions, negotiations between the Soviets and Americans—between Vance and Gromyko; between

the chief SALT negotiators on each side, Paul Warnke and Vladimir Semyonov and their deputies; and between various technical
working groups—inched along for two full years, with fits and starts,
impasses and breakthroughs, and oscillations between pessimism and
optimism, until June 18, 1979, when Presidents Carter and Brezhnev signed the SALT II treaty in Vienna, and an exultant Jimmy
Carter flew back to Washington to present it to a joint session of
Congress that very night.

At about midpoint from the start of negotiations in Geneva in
May 1977 until the summer 1979 signing, Secretary of State Vance,
to counter numerous press leaks and attacks from anti-SALT lobbies like the Committee on the Present Danger, revealed the principal features of the agreement that was still being refined. In an
address to the American Society of Newspaper Editors on April 10,
1978, anticipating the ratification debate, he stated the criteria for
any SALT agreement the Carter administration would find acceptable: (1) It had to clearly maintain or improve the overall security
of the United States as compared to the situation without an agreement; (2) it had to take into account fully the interests of the NATO
allies; and (3) it had to be independently verifiable by the United
States to assure ourselves that the Soviets were complying with its
terms and to provide timely detection of any Soviet efforts that could
leave the United States at a strategic disadvantage. The agreement
they were now working toward, explained Vance, would fulfill these
criteria in the following ways:

First, it would establish equal limits for both sides on the overall number of strategic missile launchers and strategic bombers. As you know, under the first SALT
agreement, the Soviets maintained greater numbers than the United States. . . .

Second, the agreement would reduce the number of strategic weapons below the
level that the Soviets now have—and very much below what they could have without the agreement. It would require the Soviets to destroy several hundred weapons. We would not be required to destroy any weapons currently operational.

Third, the agreement would establish sublimits on those systems we see as most
threatening and destabilizing, such as ICBMs equipped with MIRV'd warheads,
and on MIRV'd ballistic missiles more generally.

Fourth, we are trying to impose restraints on the improvement of existing weapons
and the development of new and more sophisticated systems.

Fifth, the agreement we are negotiating would permit the United States to preserve
essential options for modernizing our forces. Specifically, it would allow us to con-

tinue our major development programs, such as the cruise and MX missiles and Trident program.[6]

For those who had been following the course of the dialogue on SALT since 1972, such a treaty, if actually negotiated, would be a considerable achievement, and—remarkably—would incorporate many of the features of the comprehensive proposal of March 1977 that the Russians had so vociferously rejected.

THE GREAT DEBATE BEGINS

As negotiations proceeded along these lines, and the administration become confident that a treaty would soon be signed, the Department of State and the Arms Control and Disarmament Agency, anticipating many of the objections that opponents would raise to its provisions, issued a 2600-word brochure in November 1978 for wide public distribution summarizing and presenting the rationale for what had already been agreed. (The Russians were informed and raised no objections to the publication of such a document at this time.)

The State–ACDA brochure indicated that the basic agreement, which would run to 1985, would set a comprehensive ceiling, for each side, of 2400 strategic nuclear launchers, to be reduced to 2250 during the lifetime of the agreement. Within that ceiling, each side would be allowed 1320 launchers equipped for delivering multiple warheads (namely, MIRVed ICBMs and submarine-launched ballistic missiles, as well as airplanes equipped to carry cruise missiles); and within that 1320 sublimit, each side was further limited to how many of each type of launcher could be MIRVed. The brochure claimed that these "equal limits on the overall U.S. and Soviet strategic forces" would require the Soviets to dismantle or destroy "up to 300 strategic systems" (compared with none of ours). Soviet strategic forces under the agreement, said the brochure, would be "well below what they could deploy in the absence of an agreement."[7] The agreement also would have an attached protocol setting forth certain limitations to last only for three years, while it was determined whether or not to include them in a SALT III treaty. One of these was to be a prohibition on the deployments on ground-launched and sea-launched cruise missiles with ranges in excess of 600 kilometers. Another of the three-year prohibitions was to be on the deployment of mobile ICBM launchers.

Immediately, critics in the Committee on the Present Danger hollered "sellout," and got to work preparing a counterbrochure. Written largely by Paul Nitze (who had served as a high-level strategic planner in the administrations of Truman, Kennedy, Johnson, and Nixon, and who had resigned, disgruntled, from the SALT I delegation), this counterbrochure, published in March 1979, two months before Carter and Brezhnev signed SALT II, was a harbinger of the tough going the treaty would have in the Senate.

The government's claim that "essential equivalence" would be maintained by SALT II was false, argued the Committee on the Present Danger. The supposed "equal numerical limits" were derived from a preoccupation with only a portion of the relevent dimensions of strategic power. The strategic power balance could only be accurately assessed by taking into account a wide array of factors, including, in addition to those highlighted in the ACDA/State brochure, throw-weight (the size of payloads that could be projected to enemy targets); accuracy of delivery systems; power to knock out hardened sites such as missile silos and command-and-control communication centers; relative vulnerability of such vital strategic centers; gross area-destruction capabilities; and relative protection or vulnerability of populations and industrial plants. Taking all these factors into account, said the committee, would reveal "a large imbalance in Russia's favor." The government's claim that the Soviets would have to destroy up to 300 missiles was disingenuous, for the contemplated treaty would allow the Soviets to retain 308 launchers for their largest and newest types of MIRVed ICBMs. The United States had not yet built such systems, and would not be permitted to under the treaty. "As a result of progress in MIRVing and accuracy, the Soviet Union's warheads will, within the life span of the treaty, surpass ours in gross numbers, destructive power, and versatility." The committee also found it inexcusable that the treaty provisions as revealed by the government appeared to excuse the Soviet Union from counting its Backfire bombers against the prescribed limits, notwithstanding the capability of these bombers to reach targets in the continental United States. Finally, the Committee on the Present Danger challenged the verifiability of the forthcoming SALT accord, and claimed that the U.S. SALT negotiators were evidently willing to substitute trust in the Soviet Union's good faith compliance with certain provisions as a substitute for stringent verifiability requirements. [8]

By the time Leonid Brezhnev kissed Jimmy Carter on the cheek in Vienna on June 18, 1979, to celebrate their signing of the SALT II treaty, the sharp attacks the treaty had already received in the public debate had severely weakened the prospects of its gaining Senate approval. To the cognoscenti in the policy community, the final treaty text itself and its protocol contained nothing that had not already been revealed in newspaper reports and advance State and ACDA briefings. There was some suspense, however, over exactly what kind of an appended statement the Soviets would make on the Backfire bomber, and what its formal relationship would be to the treaty (treaty supporters in the administration and the Congress knew that unless the President were able to get some meaningful guarantees from Brezhnev on this issue, the hopes for ratification would be slim).

Appended to the treaty formally submitted to the Senate by the President on June 22 was a copy in typescript of the handwritten statement Brezhnev handed to President Carter on June 16 in Vienna, stating that the Soviets "will not increase the radius of this airplane in such a way as to enable it to strike targets on the territory of the USA. Nor does it intend to give it such a capability in any other manner, including in-flight refueling. At the same time, the Soviet side states that it will not increase the production rate of this airplane." And immediately below the letter was a statement signed by Secretary of State Vance recounting that "President Carter stated that the United States enters into the SALT II Agreement on the basis of the commitments contained in the Soviet statement and that it considers the carrying out of these commitments to be essential to the obligations assumed under the Treaty." [9]

Administration spokesmen defended the weak form of the guarantee on the Backfire on the grounds that the choice was between excluding Backfire from the terms of the treaty text or not having the treaty at all. This admission added fuel to the charge of critics that the Carter administration had been negotiating from weakness rather than from strength. The Democratic majority on the Senate Foreign Relations Committee was able to beat back an amendment sponsored by Senate Minority Leader Howard Baker requiring that the Backfire be counted against the Soviet Union's ceiling for strategic vehicles; but the Foreign Relations Committee did adopt an amendment, asking for a further affirmation by the Soviet Union that it was legally bound by its written and oral statements to Carter about the Backfire bomber.

Although most of the substantive issues in the SALT ratification debate had been anticipated in the past year's debate-of-the-brochures between the administration and the Committee on the Present Danger, there was considerable uncertainty over how the senators would align themselves in their own debate, and then what the final lineup would be on the advise and consent vote. One of the potentially crucial "swing" votes was that of former astronaut John Glenn, now a Democratic senator from Ohio, and a respected member of the Foreign Relations and Government Operations committees. Glenn was particularly concerned over potential weaknesses in the verification provisions of the treaty, and presented two strong amendments designed to make the verification more reliable. The first Glenn amendment would have required both sides to use radio telemetry to relay flight data from their test missiles back to earth, thereby allowing the intelligence agencies on each side to monitor the other's compliance with treaty limits on the weight and other characteristics of the missiles. The second Glenn amendment would have removed as asymmetrical a provision in the treaty text which, as it stood, required the United States to give the Soviet Union prior notification of all ICBM flight tests while requiring the Soviets to give prior notification of only 5 to 10 percent of its ICBM flight tests. Both of these amendments were rejected by the Senate Foreign Relations Committee, and weaker ones substituted which Senator Glenn found insufficient. When the committee voted 9 to 6 on November 9, 1979, to recommend the treaty to the Senate, Glenn cast his vote with the anti-SALT minority. [10]

Another big question mark was whether or not former Secretary of State Henry Kissinger would support the treaty. Kissinger had been a strong supporter of the SALT process, and his opinion would not only influence the vote of liberal Republicans and quite a few middle-of-the-road Democrats, but it would also powerfully shape the way the debate was conducted in the media and the newspapers. Testifying before the Senate Foreign Relations Committee on July 31 with full media coverage, Kissinger indicated only conditional support for the treaty. He did not believe it would be wise for the Senate to approve the treaty until the administration had proposed and the Congress approved a beefed-up five-year defense plan that would include an MX missile with effective counterforce capability against Soviet hardened ICBMs; antibomber defenses effective against the Soviet Backfire bomber; the deployment of intermediate-range strategic missiles in Europe that could hit the USSR; a stronger Navy; and an improved airlift and sealift for emergency overseas deployment of U.S. forces in crises. The Carter administration had not done enough in any of these categories, and had allowed an "ominous tilt" to emerge in the U.S.–Soviet balance which had to be corrected before the United States accepted the limitations on its strategic buildup contemplated in SALT II. Assuming such a unilateral correction to its own defense programs, the United States should not insist on renegotiating SALT II with the Russians, but should attach to its ratification a number of reservations and understandings—the most important of which were an explicit termination in 1981 of the protocol limiting the ranges of cruise missiles to 600 kilometers, and a stipulation that SALT III would have to allow the United States to possess any weapon the Soviet Union was permitted to have.[11]

The administration was severely disappointed and sorely wounded by Kissinger's decision to damn the SALT II treaty with faint praise and loud criticism of the Carter/Brown military-preparedness policies. Defensively, the Pentagon chief attempted to rebut such charges, in detailed testimony showing that the United States was building substantial counterforce capabilities, was prepared to deploy the MX missile, was making ready the theater nuclear forces that could strike the USSR from Western Europe, and was ready to match across-the-board any augmentations the Soviets might make in their arsenal. There was virtually nothing in the treaty to prevent us from doing what we might want to do on grounds of military cost-effectiveness. Such administration argumentation swayed few SALT opponents, who were convinced that the U.S. had been negotiating from weakness, and it began to sour dedicated arms controllers, who now began to view the treaty as perhaps more of a

channeling of the arms race into new, and potentially very dangerous, fields, rather than as a way station to substantial reductions.

Thus the ratification of SALT II was already in deep trouble when
on January 3, 1980, a week after the Soviet Union had invaded
Afghanistan, President Carter asked the Senate to defer its action
on the treaty. It was unlikely now that the Senate would take up
formal consideration again until after the 1980 presidential election,
which, from the point of view of the treaty's supporters, was probably just as well, since it had become too hot to handle for any
candidate with an insecure constituency.

FROM MAD TO NUTS

The controversy over SALT reflected a deeper strategic controversy—as indicated at the beginning of this chapter—between the
proponents of a deterrence-only strategic force posture and the proponents of a war-fighting capability. But by the time the SALT negotiations were well underway in 1978, the deterrence-only camp
had already lost out in the administration. Contrary to the allegations of the Committee on the Present Danger, the Carter administration had not altered strategic policy to fit the requirements of a
deterrence-only arms control philosophy that was to be manifested
in SALT II; rather, the administration's arms control policy and
SALT II negotiating positions had been altered to fit the adoption
by Secretary of Defense Brown of the deterrence logic premised on
the need to have a credible strategic war-fighting capability.

Dubbed "NUTS" by some of its critics, for the concocted title
Nuclear Utilization Target Selection,[12] the strategic war-fighting
logic was revealed in detail in the February 1978 Defense budget
presentations of Secretary Brown to the Congress, but not formally
adopted by Carter until the spring of 1980 in Presidential Directive
No. 59.

The doctrine was really nothing new. After having been discarded by Secretary of Defense MacNamara in 1963, it was revived
by the Republican Secretaries of Defense under Nixon and Ford,
and governed U.S. strategic weapons planning in fact if not in formal doctrine (especially since it contradicted the arms control logic
Kissinger was trying to get the Russians to accept during the early

1970s). What was new was the adaptation Harold Brown made in his own thinking to the war-fighting logic (after having rejected the notion of a "limited strategic war" during his confirmation hearings), and then his conversion of Jimmy Carter to accept his belief that it was the most prudent policy.

Brown had not altered his view that the assured destruction mission of U.S. strategic forces—their capability, at all times, regardless of the size of a Soviet attack, to inflict unacceptable damage on Soviet centers of population and industry—must be maintained as a retaliatory option in order to confidently deter the Soviets from a large-scale strategic attack on U.S. strategic forces. But with the expansion and increasing sophistication of the Soviet strategic arsenal, he argued, we have to take other possibilities into account as well:

The Soviets, among other options, could avoid attacking our main population centers. They could withhold some of their offensive capabilities for follow-on strikes. They could attack a wide range of military and economic targets in addition to our strategic forces. They could even use their forces selectively against a small number of targets. In short, the Soviets are acquiring capabilities that will give their nuclear forces some of the flexibility that we have associated previously with only the more traditional military capabilities. All of these characteristics of flexibility are increasingly present in our forces as well.

None of this potential flexibility had changed his view that a thermonuclear exchange would be an unprecedented disaster for both the Soviet Union and the United States, said Brown. Moreover, the odds were high, whether the weapons were used against tactical or strategic targets, that control would be lost on both sides and the exchange would become unconstrained, with fatalities running into scores of millions. Even so, he remained quite uncertain as to how an adversary with increasingly sophisticated strategic weapons might consider employing them in a desperate crisis.

The uncertainties left us with only one sound basis on which to design the U.S. strategic forces, said Brown. They had to be made *militarily* effective—that is, they had to be designed on the basis of two assumptions: (1) deterrence might fail, and (2) the U.S. strategic forces "must have the capability to respond realistically and effectively to an attack at a variety of levels." In other words, "we cannot afford to make a complete distinction between deterrent forces and what are so awkwardly called war-fighting forces."

Assured destruction should not be the only response available to the President.

Credibility cannot be maintained, especially in a crisis, with a combination of inflexible forces (however destructive) and a purely retaliatory counter-urban/industrial strategy that frightens us as much as the opponent.

. . .

We want to be capable at all times of responses that are deliberate, controlled, and in precise compliance with the directives of the President. It is not our policy to limit his choices to a single option, and they are not so limited.

As a part of the required flexibility,

we must be able to launch controlled counterattacks against a wide range of targets—including theater and conventional forces, lines of communication, war-supporting industry, and targets of increasing hardness: from aircraft runways and nuclear storage sites to command bunkers and ICBM silos.

Though the probability of escalation to a full-scale thermonuclear war would be high in the circumstances of even an intendedly controlled strategic exchange, cautioned Brown, we must avoid making that probability a certainty. At the same time, "we must ensure that no adversary would see himself better off after a limited exchange than before it." [13]

The contradictions between these force-planning doctrines and the assumptions underlying SALT I were fundamental, for the 1972 ABM Treaty and the Interim Agreement on Offensive Weapons (see above, pp. 339–41) were based on the assumptions (1) that weapons designed to destroy the other side's strategic deterrent forces were dangerously provocative and must be banned; and (2) that other strategic nuclear war-fighting capabilities were at best superfluous to the deterrence-only, assured-destruction function of strategic nuclear forces and therefore could be negotiated away at the SALT bargaining table. The new deterrence logic advanced by Brown from 1978 on, and promulgated in the Presidential Directive of 1980, assumed, on the contrary, that both sides would maintain capabilities for striking at each other's main strategic forces and at a whole range of military targets during various phases of a strategic war.

Under the new logic, then, how would it be possible to agree on the criteria for dangerous and unnecessary weapons? The answer, quite simply, was that there was no longer any way to derive the arms control requirements from the strategic logic now accepted as legitimate.

Bargaining on limits and reductions henceforth, as reflected in SALT II, would be almost entirely a kind of horse-trading—we'll give up (or retain) X if you give up (or retain) Y—to maintain "essential equivalence" in strategic power. But there was no necessary reason why the force balances achieved through this bargaining process would be any less dangerous or less expensive to maintain than the force balances that would result from allowing the strategic rivalry to proceed entirely outside of the SALT process.

Whether the strategic arms competition between the United States and the USSR would be restrained or become an irrational race to Armageddon would depend from here on out largely on the overall climate of relations between the two superpowers. In a period of confrontation and deep mistrust each would view the strategic weapons deployed by the other as potential "first strike" weapons, and would accelerate its own compensatory programs to retain at least a MAD/NUTS equivalence. It would now be more difficult than ever to insist that strategic arms control be "unlinked" from the overall atmosphere of Soviet–American relations on grounds that it was essential to accomplish in and of itself. Negotiations like SALT would function more as a barometer of the climate than as a means of avoiding the holocaust.

Thus it was a foregone conclusion that an event like the Soviet invasion of Afghanistan would sign the death warrant for SALT II. But there were few deep mourners, even within the Carter administration, for by this time the treaty itself appeared to have become a rather peripheral policy instrument for managing the balance of power—and perhaps even a liability for Carter's reelection.[14]

32

AFGHANISTAN AND THE
REASSERTION OF
GEOPOLITICAL IMPERATIVES

*We need to increase the speed with which we can deploy our forces—through
increased airlift and sealift capabilities, through the further prepositioning of
material, and through the assurance of basing and transit rights in emergencies.*
SECRETARY OF DEFENSE HAROLD BROWN

More than any other event, the Soviet military invasion of Afghanistan at the end of December 1979 appeared to bring Jimmy
Carter's view of the Russians into congruence with Zbigniew Brzezinski's and to cause the President finally to discard his election
campaign promise to supplant balance of power politics with world
order politics. "It's only now dawning on the world the magnitude
of the actions that the Soviets undertook in invading Afghanistan,"
said Carter in a New Year's Eve television interview. "This action
of the Soviets has made a more dramatic change in my own opinion
of what the Soviets' ultimate goals are than anything they've done
in the previous time I've been in office." [1]

The President's admission of being moved to reassess his views of
the Soviet Union was jumped at by critics as evidence of Carter's
shallowness and naïveté when it came to the hard facts of geopolitics and Soviet strategy, and the inevitability of Soviet–American
rivalry all around the Eurasian rimland, or what Brzezinski had

been calling the "arc of crisis." Actually, the President already had
moved considerably toward adopting Brzezinski's geopolitical views
well before the Soviet action on the eve of his last year in office
provided a provocation of sufficient weight and drama to justify a
formal resurrection of a U.S. foreign policy directed centrally at
containing Soviet expansion.

THE TOUGHENING STANCE IN 1978 AND 1979

Brzezinski had pushed for a tough stance against Soviet expansion
during the first year of the Carter administration in response to the
open Soviet support of Ethiopia in its border war with Somalia, and
the Kremlin's exploitation of this conflict as an opportunity to move
Soviet naval and air power and a hefty contingent of Cuban troops
into the strategically significant Horn of Africa. At the time, however, Carter was more swayed by Secretary of State Vance's arguments that this was the wrong place to draw the line against the
Soviets, since it was the Somalis, not the Ethiopians, who were
widely regarded by other Africans as the expansionary aggressors in
the border conflict. The strongest statements in opposition to the
Soviet–Cuban activities in Africa came from Brzezinski, not the
President, as did the administration's warnings to the Kremlin that
such Soviet power plays might threaten the negotiating climate for
SALT II and that the Senate, in response to public anger at Soviet
behavior, might be reluctant to ratify whatever agreement was negotiated. [2]

The fact that Carter could have muzzled Brzezinski and didn't
was taken by the administration's critics as evidence of a leadership
gap at the top of the administration. A more plausible explanation
is that Carter found it useful to have the stern-faced Brzezinski
surface the hawkish impulses within the administration without the
President yet having to adopt this demeanor himself—thus preserving room to maintain the cordial relations with Brezhnev that might
be crucial for progress on SALT and other matters, such as the
Arab–Israeli conflict, where the administration was anxious to gain
Soviet cooperation.

Carter did accept the need to display credible capabilities and
intentions to oppose Soviet moves to take advantage of their military

prowess and mobility, and to disabuse the Kremlin of any beliefs that this administration had a "soft" approach to world order and might be squeamish about employing military counters to Soviet aggression. The capacity to act tough if driven to it was conveyed in two major presidential addresses in 1978—the March 17 speech at Wake Forest University calling for increased defense spending, and the June 7 commencement address at the Naval Academy in Annapolis on U.S.–Soviet relations.

Reiterating the doctrine that a Russian strategic nuclear attack on the United States "would amount to national suicide for the Soviet Union," the President took cognizance, from the podium at Wake Forest, of impending improvements in Soviet missiles that could make U.S. ICBMs increasingly vulnerable to a Soviet first strike during the coming decade. However remote their attempting to launch such a first strike, cautioned Carter, "it is a threat on which we must constantly be on guard." He used the occasion of this university speech to point to the accelerated development and deployment of cruise missiles for U.S. strategic bombers and decisions to work on the MX intercontinental ballistic missile and Trident II submarine-launched ballistic missile "to give us more options to respond to Soviet strategic deployments. If it becomes necessary to guarantee the clear invulnerability of our strategic deterrent, I shall not hesitate to take actions for full-scale development and deployment of these systems."

The President also pointed to the enlargement and modernization of Soviet theater deployments in Western Europe, charging that these were "beyond a level necessary for defense," and indicating that in response the United States was developing new force augmentation and modernization plans with its NATO allies, focusing on efforts for speedy reinforcements in wartime and to plug specific gaps in deployed NATO defenses. Additionally, announced the President, "the Secretary of Defense, at my direction, is improving and will maintain quickly deployable forces—air, land, and sea—to defend our interests throughout the world."[3]

Paralleling this concern with Soviet military capabilities, the President's remarks at the June commencement exercises at the Naval Academy were hardly a sanguine characterization of Soviet intentions:

To the Soviet Union, détente seems to mean a continuing aggressive struggle for political advantage and increased influence. . . . The Soviet Union apparently sees military power and military assistance as the best means of expanding their influence abroad. Obviously, areas of instability in the world provide a tempting target for this effort, and all too often they seem ready to exploit any such opportunity.

As became apparent in Korea, in Angola and also, as you know, in Ethiopia more recently, the Soviets prefer to use proxy forces to achieve their purposes.

. . .

The Soviet Union attempts to export a totalitarian and repressive form of government.

. . .

The Soviet Union can choose either confrontation or cooperation. The United States is adequately prepared to meet either choice.[4]

Carter's acknowledgment that the containment of Soviet expansion still required a visible readiness and impressive capability to use force was reflected in a number of programs and actions during the second and third years of his administration:

• Reversing his campaign promise to reduce defense expenditures by as much as 7 percent from the last Ford administration budget, Carter now pledged to increase the real level of defense spending by some 3 percent each year and persuaded most of the NATO allies to make the same pledge.

• The administration initiated and gained alliance cooperation in a new NATO Long Range Defense Program to rectify European theater deficiencies in a number of fields—especially the growing Soviet tank superiority (against which NATO now planned to deploy a new generation of conventional and nuclear antitank weapons); and the Soviet deployment of new intermediate-range missiles such as the multiple-warhead SS-20 in western Russia targeted on Western Europe (against which the United States would deploy on the Continent two new intermediate-range nuclear missiles of its own, the Pershing II and the ground-launched cruise missile).

• The Defense Department was authorized to improve the U.S. strategic arsenal in two major respects: reducing the vulnerability of the ICBMs to a Soviet strategic first strike (the preferred vulnerability-reducing option was a mobile deployment of the new MX missile); and improving the accuracy and other effectiveness characteristics of U.S. strategic weapons so as to give them a capability for rendering *Soviet* ICBMs more vulnerable. Without these improvements, maintained Secretary of Defense Brown, the Soviet Union might appear to have a "war-fighting" strategic arsenal while the United States was prepared only for a mutual-suicide type of strategic war, and this might give the Soviets an intimidating edge in a future intense U.S.–Soviet confrontation.*

• The military services were ordered to organize a Rapid Deployment Force (RDF) for quick military intervention in crises outside the NATO area. When finally fleshed out in the 1980s, the RDF was supposed to be ready to inject up to 150,000 troops with fighting equipment into a trouble spot, say, in the Persian Gulf, with the leading contingents arriving in a matter of days from the "go" order. (This idea, popular with military strategists as far back as the Eisenhower administration, was thought to have been buried by the post-Vietnam antipathy to U.S. military interventions in the Third World; but it had been revived in a classified study of the country's global military requirements directed by Samuel P. Huntington out of Brzezinski's office in 1977, and Brzezinski himself became one of the strongest backers of an RDF. Brzezinski argued that without such a capability, the Soviets could present the United States with local military faits accomplis in areas of strategic importance like the Horn of Africa or the Persian Gulf.)

• In the aftermath of the fall of the Shah's government in Iran, the Carter administration announced in March 1979, without waiting for congressional review, that it would sell $400 million worth of advanced military equipment to North Yemen, including jet aircraft, tanks, and antitank guided missiles, to help that country—an ally of Saudi Arabia— defend itself in its ongoing war against South Yemen, a Soviet client state. To punctuate U.S. support for the North Yemenis and the Saudis, the aircraft carrier *Constellation* and associated escort ships set sail from the Philippines toward the Arabian Sea. Administration spokesmen explained that this was part of a larger strategy to demonstrate that stability in the Middle East and the Arabian peninsula was a vital U.S. interest, and that the decisions involving Yemen were only the first steps toward an enlarged U.S. military presence in the region. (By the end of March 1978, the two Yemens agreed to a cease-fire, the South having been strongly pressured by the Soviets to call off the war. Although the administration would have liked to be able to claim that its tough stance was decisive in stopping the war, the more weighty consideration with the Soviet Union seems to have been the embarrassment its backing of South Yemen was causing other Soviet clients in the area, especially Syria and Iraq.)

* The flexible targeting doctrine for U.S. strategic forces was formulated in the summer of 1979 in Presidential Directive 59, but the go-ahead for the associated improvements in U.S. strategic forces to make them at least equivalent to the Soviets' in "war-fighting" capability was obtained by Brown in late 1977 and was featured in his unclassified budget presentations to the Congress in January and February of 1978. See above, pp. 545–51, for additional discussion of the Carter administration's strategic force planning premises and their relationship to SALT.

Carter was not about to be pushed, however, into an indiscriminate confrontationist stance against all Soviet international actions he disliked. In the late summer of 1979, prominent members of Congress began to point with alarm to intelligence information on the presence of a Soviet combat brigade in Cuba, and the Democratic chairman of the Senate Foreign Relations Committee, Frank Church of Idaho, announced that the Senate's consideration of SALT II would be deferred until the problem was resolved. Recalling the way congressional pressures of a similar sort moved President Kennedy to confront the Kremlin in the Cuban missile crisis of 1962, Carter was persuaded that he had best take a tough stand early if he wanted to keep control over the issue and preserve a political climate in which the SALT treaty could be ratified.

The Brzezinski faction wanted the President to demand that the Soviets dismantle its brigade in Cuba and for Carter to define his stance as part of the global U.S. policy contesting Soviet and Cuban interventionary behavior in the Third World and the Middle East. But Carter's inclinations this time were closer to those of the Vance faction, which was urging isolation of the issue of the Soviet brigate, for fear that a generalized tough response would whip up an anti-Soviet psychology in the Congress and the public that might make it impossible to gain ratification of the SALT treaty.

In his television address to the nation on the Soviet combat brigade in Cuba, Carter tried to cool down the atmosphere. "I want to reassure you at the outset that we do not face any immediate, concrete threat that could escalate into a war or a major confrontation," said the President. The particular combat unit, he revealed, had existed in Cuba for several years; what was new was our own intelligence analysis, which only recently was able to determine the nature of that unit—a brigade of two or three thousand men, armed with about forty tanks and other modern military equipment, engaging in combat training exercises. "This is not a large force, nor an assault force. It presents no direct threat to us. It has no airborne or seaborne capability. In contrast to the 1962 crisis, no nuclear threat to the U.S. is involved."

Nevertheless, said the President, the Soviet brigade in Cuba is "a serious matter." It "contributes to tension in the Caribbean and the Central American region." And along with the increasing delivery of modern arms to Cuba in recent years, and the presence of Soviet naval forces in Cuban waters, the brigade has "added to the fears of some countries that they may come under Soviet domination." In a concession to Brzezinski's desire to connect the issue with the broader problem of Soviet expansion, the President complained that because of the Soviet military aid, Cuba now has one of the largest, best-equipped armed forces in the region and that "these forces are used to intrude into other countries in Africa and the Middle East." The Brigade thus "raises the level of the responsibility that the Soviet Union must take for escalating Cuban military actions abroad."

Having defined the threat, and shown himself to be fully aware of its implications, the President then went on to show how the issue was being rather simply resolved. The administration was in contact with the Soviet government at the highest levels, and the Soviets, while not granting that the brigade was in fact a combat unit, gave certain assurances which the United States could now interpret as an agreement to prevent the force being used in a combat role—namely, that the unit in question could and would do no more than operate as a training center; that it would not be enlarged or given additional capabilities; and that the Soviet personnel in Cuba would not be used against the United States or any other nation.* The administration was not simply relying on these Soviet assurances, however. A stepped-up surveillance of Cuba would monitor the status of the brigade. Moreover, U.S. military maneuvers in the Carribbean were being expanded and would be conducted regularly from now on.

The President was anxious for the country to put the Cuban threat in perspective:

I have concluded that the brigade issue is certainly no reason for a return to the Cold War. A confrontation might be emotionally satisfying for a few days or weeks for some people, but it would be disastrous to the national interest and the security of the United States.

We must continue the basic policy that the United States has followed for 20 years under six administrations of both parties—a policy that recognizes that we are in competition with the Soviet Union in some fields, and that we seek cooperation in others—notably maintaining the peace and controlling arms.

My fellow Americans, the greatest danger to American security tonight is certainly not two or three thousand troops in Cuba. The greatest danger to all nations

* These assurances had been obtained in an exchange of letters between Carter and Brezhnev between September 25 and 27, 1979. See Hedrick Smith, "Carter Feels Certain Soviets Will Alter Brigade in Cuba," *New York Times*, October 3, 1979.

of the world—including the United States and the Soviet Union—is the breakdown of a common effort to preserve the peace, and the ultimate threat of a nuclear war.[5]

Carter's cautious defusing of the Cuban issue and his subordination of it to the requirements of maintaining good relations with the Kremlin during the SALT ratification process would come back to haunt him in the form of opposition party charges that the Soviet invasion of Afghanistan three months later was in large part the product of Kremlin calculations that if the United States was now afraid to confront the Soviet Union only 90 miles from the American mainland, surely the Russians could discount any substantial U.S. counteraction to their move against this underdeveloped Eurasian country. Though Carter took what appeared to him at the time to be the most responsible course of action on the Cuban issue, when he received the news of the Christmas Eve airlifting of Soviet troops and armored vehicles into Kabul, Carter could not help wondering if those in his administration who counseled stronger action had been right.

REDRAWING THE CONTAINMENT LINE

The sudden and swiftly executed Soviet military takeover of their Muslim neighbor in the last week of 1979 and first week of 1980 was the kind of fait accompli about which Brzezinski had been warning. Once it had been substantially accomplished (the Russians had difficulty in completely subduing fierce Afghan tribesmen in the mountainous parts of the country), there was little the United States could do to retrieve the situation. The immediate question was whether or not the Soviet move (the first combat use of Soviet troops outside of the immediate Warsaw Pact area in Eastern Europe since World War II) was only the first phase of a larger plan of aggressive expansion targeted on the oil-rich Persian Gulf. The answer was a large question mark. The rest of the states in the region, even unstable Iran, were apparently not in immediate jeopardy of military attack; the Soviets were concentrating tens of thousands of troops in their Afghanistan operation; these troops would be pinned down as an army of occupation for months if not years; and it was highly unlikely that the Soviets could afford to make additional major diversions from their primary military deployments in Eastern Europe and along the China border. But the longer-term threat posed to other states in the region by a consolidated Soviet military presence on Iran's eastern border and Pakistan's northwestern border could not be discounted; and a failure of the United States to react strongly now to the invasion of Afghanistan would undoubtedly shake the confidence of those Persian Gulf countries who depend ultimately on U.S. protection against an imperially expanding Russia and would vindicate those who had signed peace and friendship treaties with the USSR.

An immediate military countermove by the United States was not a seriously considered option. Afghanistan itself was simply not that important a geopolitical prize to deny the Soviet Union, and it therefore would have been grossly imprudent to climb on to an escalation ladder of military threat and counterthreat that would dangerously commit the prestige of the United States to a Soviet military withdrawal. A regime in Afghanistan friendly to the Soviet Union, one that would not allow that country to be used as a base for building anti-Soviet links into the Muslim populations of the USSR, was, after all, a more substantial interest to the Soviet Union than a free Afghanistan was to the United States, if that's as far as things went.*

Thus the current Soviet military takeover, while illegitimate, shocking, and even outrageous, was itself not really intolerable to the United States. However, the reverberations of an obviously ineffectual U.S. response would be intolerable. As put by President Carter, "If the Soviets are encouraged in this invasion by eventual success, and if they maintain their dominance over Afghanistan and then extend their control to adjacent countries, the stable, strategic, and peaceful balance of the world will be changed. This would threaten the security of all nations including, of course, the United States, our allies and friends. Therefore, the world cannot stand by and permit the Soviet Union to commit this act with impunity." [6]

Accordingly, the administration immediately applied a wide range of punitive but nonlethal sanctions: the President asked the Senate to delay further consideration of the SALT II treaty; licensing of high-technology items for sale to the USSR was suspended; fishing

---

*The United States had already indicated its willingness to tolerate the Soviet Union's conversion of Afghanistan from a nonaligned country to a client state by acquiescing, without much visible diplomatic protest, to the Soviet-engineered coup in 1978 that installed a pro-Soviet Marxist regime in Kabul.

privileges for Soviet ships in U.S. waters were severely curtailed; an embargo was placed on 17 million tons of grain already purchased by the Russians but not yet shipped to them; planned openings of new American and Soviet consular facilities were canceled; and most of the Soviet–American cultural and economic exchanges then under consideration were deferred. The President also announced that he was considering asking U.S. athletes not to participate in the Olympic Games scheduled for Moscow in the summer.

Critics charged that the sanctions were too little and too late to effect a reversal of the Soviet aggression, but they were unable to propose stronger alternatives that were feasible. Collateral moves to shore up the region against *further* Soviet encroachments were feasible, however; and the administration made it a point to leave no stone unturned in its determination to redraw the containment line deeply in the sands of Southwest Asia. Pakistan was offered $400 million in military aid. Discussions with Kenya, Oman, Somalia, and Egypt were intensified to arrange for the establishment of service facilities for U.S. naval units deployed in the region.

The President firmed up his public rationale for these actions in his State of the Union address of January 23, 1980. "The implications of the Soviet invasion of Afghanistan could pose the most serious threat to world peace since the Second World War," said the President.

The Soviet effort to dominate Afghanistan has brought Soviet military forces to within 300 miles of the Indian Ocean and close to the Strait of Hormuz—a waterway through which much of the free world's oil must flow. The Soviet Union is now attempting to consolidate a strategic position that poses a grave threat to the free movement of Middle East oil.

And he then voiced the warning that was labeled by journalists, with the approval of the White House, as the Carter Doctrine:

Let our position be absolutely clear: Any attempt by any outside force to gain control of the Persian Gulf region will be regarded as an assault on the vital interests of the United States. It will be repelled by use of any means necessary, including military force. [7]

The administration's two-pronged response—imposing current economic and diplomatic sanctions on the Soviet Union; and building up, over the next five years, a military capability to confront future Soviet power plays in the Persian Gulf region—was designed

Kremlin, the world, and not incidentally the American
that the Soviet invasion of Afghanistan was based on a
tion of the American will to resist Soviet aggressive ex-
especially in the geopolitically crucial "rimland" area be-
1e Mediterranean and China. It was generally a popular
response in this country, despite the grumblings of wheat farmers
and some Olympic athletes at their having to bear more of the burdens of applying the sanctions than would other Americans. And it
virtually assured that the 1980 elections would be contested in a
post-détente atmosphere, with candidates competing over who could
best stand up to the Russians.

Afghanistan also—more than any event in Carter's tenure in the
White House—reordered the priorities in the Carter foreign policy
from those indicated at the outset of the administration. Human
rights, global economic development, reducing arms sales, preventing the spread of nuclear weapons, even the Soviet–American strategic arms agreements, were all subordinated to the imperative of
preventing the Soviet Union from gaining global dominance. Allies
with dubious human rights records, like Pakistan, would be courted
and built up; economic aid would be allocated selectively on grounds
of the consequences for East–West alignment; conventional arms
transfers would be increased to countries opposed by arms clients of
the Soviet Union; adherence to the nuclear nonproliferation treaty
and safeguards would not be rigidly imposed as a precondition for
military or economic aid when such insistences might alienate an
anti-Soviet ally; and, finally, the Russians would be put on notice
that we were prepared to resume the arms race in all categories of
weapons if driven to it, and that the USSR would be substantially
worse off at the end of the next round.

Ironically, a national consensus was being created by the Carter
administration's new rhetorical and policy preoccupations with the
Soviet threat that appeared to legitimize the complaints of the unreconstructed cold warriors in the Reagan camp. The Reaganites,
who had never accepted even Kissinger's détente approach, had been
charging that the Carter foreign policy was inexcusably naïve in its
emphasis on human rights and world order, and had contributed to
the decline of the West's ability and will to stand up to the Soviet
Union. It was time, argued the Reaganites—with impressive success first in their own party and then in the November 1980 general

election—to install in Washington a group of leaders who never had been duped by Soviet professions of peaceful coexistence, who had always understood the crucial relevance of military power to the security of the American way of life, and who had been willing all along to bite the bullet of higher defense expenditures and a confrontationist policy toward the Soviet Union and its allies. Thus the Carter administration, now adopting many of the foreign policy views of its earlier critics, helped reinforce the backlash which removed it from office.

PART VII

THE REAGAN ADMINISTRATION

The foreign policy of the United States should reflect a national strategy of peace through strength. The general principles and goals of this strategy would be:

- *to inspire, focus, and unite the national will and determination to achieve peace and freedom;*
- *to achieve overall military and technological superiority over the Soviet Union;*
- *to create a strategic and civil defense which would protect the American people against nuclear war at least as well as the Soviet population is protected;*
- *to accept no arms control agreement which in any way jeopardizes the security of the United States or its allies, or which locks the United States into a position of military inferiority;*
- *to reestablish effective security and intelligence capabilities;*
- *to pursue positive nonmilitary means to roll back the growth of communism. . . .*

Our strategy must encompass the levels of force required to deter each level of foreseeable attack and to prevail in conflict in the event deterrence fails.

—REPUBLICAN NATIONAL PLATFORM OF 1980

33

THE NOT-SO-GRAND
STRATEGY OF THE
REAGAN ADMINISTRATION *

In our approach to foreign affairs, we have sought to distinguish between the symptom of the problem and the problem itself, the crisis and its cause, the ebb and flow of daily events and the underlying trend.

ALEXANDER M. HAIG

Ronald Reagan was convinced that his election victory, in addition to being a popular mandate to reduce the role of government in the domestic economy, was a mandate on foreign policy: to reverse the decline of U.S. power relative to the Soviet Union's; to regain for the United States the reputation of a country that could not be pushed around; to reestablish the United States as the leader of the "free world" anti-Communist coalition; and to organize the required policies and programs under a Grand Strategy that would bring U.S. power into balance with U.S. interests, that would establish priorities among these interests and determine choices among means—in contrast to the "let-it-all-hang-out" ambivalence of the Carter years.

Assembling a formidable phalanx of experienced national security

* Some of the material in this chapter is taken from my essay "The Reagan Administration's Not-So-Grand-Strategy," a commentary on Robert E. Osgood's *Containment, Soviet Behavior, and Grand Strategy* (Berkeley: Institute of International Studies, University of California, 1981) that was included in that publication, pp. 29–33.

and international relations experts, recruited largely from the Committee on the Present Danger (which had been the most influential lobby against the SALT II Treaty), Reagan's immediate circle of defense and foreign policy advisers worked during the pre-inaugural transition to spell out the policy and organizational implications of the President-elect's views, and to narrow down the list of appointees to the Departments of State and Defense who would implement these policies. From the perspective of Reagan's immediate aides—those like Richard Allen and William Van Cleave, who had been with him throughout the campaign—the President-elect's views already amounted to a Grand Strategy; and from their new positions on the White House staff or National Security Council, they, the inner core of loyalists who knew him best, could assure that the policy options presented to the President were consistent with the Strategy.*

The men Reagan appointed to head the departments principally responsible for carrying out the Grand Strategy were in basic accord with its philosophy and, despite some embarrassing contests over bureaucratic "turf," appeared to be working in tandem during the first few months of the administration to give the framework flesh and bones. While no single document was produced spelling out the premises and major policy implications of the Grand Strategy, the assumptions, explicit and implicit, in the various pronouncements and initiatives made from January to March 1981 by President Reagan, Secretary of State Alexander Haig, and Secretary of Defense Caspar Weinberger cumulatively expressed a rather coherent view of the U.S. role in the world, remarkably in consonance with stances Reagan had taken on the way to the White House:

• The containment of Soviet power and influence, once again, as from the late 1940s through the early 1960s, would unambiguously top the list of U.S. international objectives, followed only by the objective of maintaining access to Persian Gulf oil. But even the oil-access requirement could be best tended to "in the East–West context" (as Haig put it), for if the oil-producing countries in the geopolitically crucial Persian Gulf rimland around the USSR could be made to realize that the main threat to their independence comes from the Soviets, they would want to maintain good

---

*Richard Allen did land a job close to the President as national security adviser. William VanCleave, however, reportedly alienated the new Secretary of Defense, Caspar Weinberger, and was given only a token appointment to the Foreign Intelligence Advisory Board.

relations with the United States. The United States would make it known that it did indeed intend to play favorites among the countries of every continent: those countries governed by regimes which inclined more toward the Kremlin's positions on international issues and toward the Soviet model for structuring domestic society would not be treated as well by the United States as those who resisted Soviet influence.

• Military power would provide the principal means for asserting U.S. influence and limiting Soviet expansion. The Soviets were assumed by the Reaganites to be truly impressed by little in international relations other than who has the military capability and the will to use it. Force for the Soviets, and also therefore for those who would stand up to them, was not simply the *ultima ratio* of world politics, but the everyday determinant of who gets what, when, and how. Similarly, it was assumed that the outcome of civil wars with an East–West dimension would be determined by the effectiveness of the military supply pipelines to the locals from the superpowers and by the credibility of commitments of more direct help from the United States and the USSR to their respective allies and clients. Ultimately, the long-term contest for political influence in most regions of the world would be won by whichever superpower had demonstrated the most active and reliable support for those who had joined its camp.

• However, local balances of military power between U.S. allies and clients on one side and Soviet allies and clients on the other were to be tied into the overall global U.S.–Soviet balance. In this way, the potential gaps between U.S. interests and power in the global containment policy could be transcended. "We must not," said Weinberger, "pursue a defense strategy that anticipates a point by point response to [Soviet aggressive] actions, but rather one which permits us to take full advantage of Soviet vulnerabilities." [1] The Rapid Deployment Force and other capabilities for projecting U.S. military power into local situations were to be designed to establish a "credible presence" which would put the United States in the line of potential Soviet or Soviet-proxy attack, and thereby commit the United States to belligerency in case the Soviets attacked, but did not lock it into fielding its main counterattacks on terrain chosen by the Soviets. (The United States seemed to be returning full circle to the requirement for a capacity to strike "at times and places of our own choosing"—if no longer in "massive retaliation," then at least in strategic reprisal.)

• Military planning and budgeting—as a function of this Grand Strategy—could now proceed according to a clear set of priorities: pride of place would go to the strategic nuclear arsenal, to close the "window of vulnerability" (jargon for the period in the mid-1980s when the bulk of U.S. ICBMs presumably could be destroyed in a Soviet first strike) and other gaps at the top of the escalation ladder, and, if possible, to provide the

United States with escalation dominance. The second highest priority would be accorded mobility capabilities to enhance the options available to the President to establish a U.S. military presence in crises threatening to U.S. overseas interests—a presence that would make U.S. escalatory threats credible, not necessarily overwhelm enemy capabilities on the spot. Finally, the war mobilization capacity of the country would be enlarged to allow for rapid expansion of military manpower and equipment in crises, and to allow for protracted warfare if that became necessary.

In short, the Reagan foreign policy was to be oriented around a Grand Strategy for containing the Soviet Union, premised on a starkly bipolar view of geopolitics, placing great reliance on the military components of power, and relying on advanced strategic and tactical systems to punish the Soviets and other adversaries "where it hurts them," both for deterrence and for war-fighting when deterrence failed.

On this much there was a basic consensus at the top levels of the administration, and also at the sub-Cabinet levels staffed by Reagan loyalists. The tests of the soundness of a basic foreign policy, however, are not so much in its internal self-consistency and its appeal to true believers. Rather, its validity is determined by its consistency with the facts of domestic and international life, and the ability of the programs and actions it spawns to service the security and well-being of the people of the United States. Measured against these criteria of realism and efficacy, the Reagan Grand Strategy ran into trouble from the start, and was faced in one policy area after another with the need to sacrifice ideological consistency and support from true believers in order not to be foolishly and even dangerously insensitive to the complexities of the contemporary world.

THE STRATEGIES OF CONFRONTATION AND REPOLARIZATION

In his first news conference as President, Ronald Reagan reiterated the assumptions about Soviet aims and behavior he had been expressing over the years and that now would govern his administration's approach to U.S.–Soviet relations. It was evident, said Reagan, not only from the behavior of the USSR but also from the statements of every Russian leader since the revolution, that "their goal must be the promotion of a world revolution and a one world

Socialist or Communist state—whichever word you want to use."
The Soviet leaders had also made it clear that

the only morality they recognize is what will further their cause, meaning they
reserve unto themselves the right to commit any crime, to lie, to cheat, in order to
obtain that . . . , and we operate on a different set of standards. I think when
you do business with them, even at a détente, you keep that in mind.[2]

Such shrill words about Soviet lying and cheating in the service
of their goal of world domination had not been heard from the presidency since the Truman administration (they were, however, heard
from the office of Secretary of State during John Foster Dulles' tenure). Perhaps these were only off-the-cuff remarks by the new President, somewhat unnerved by the format of the White House news
conference. But when given a chance to elaborate or refine his ideas
two weeks later in a less-pressured discussion with five reporters in
his office, the President stuck to his guns. The Soviets "don't sub-
scribe to our sense of morality," he explained. "They don't believe
in afterlife; they don't believe in God or a religion. And the only
morality they recognize, therefore, is what will advance the cause
of socialism."[3]

The consequences of this view of the Soviet Union for U.S.–
Soviet relations were clear—and these too Reagan had voiced frequently during the campaign. They were now being reaffirmed by
him as President, and by other high foreign policy officials of the
administration. The Soviets must be dealt with primarily as the enemy, as "the threat," to be deterred, confronted, contained. Negotiations were not to be ruled out, even though the Soviets were
confirmed liars and cheats, as long as it was understood by U.S.
diplomats that negotiation was the continuation of confrontation by
other means. "Negotiation from strength" was the only acceptable
posture, and therefore before resuming the SALT process or other
arms control negotiations, the United States would have to rectify
the adverse trends in the U.S.–Soviet military balance that the Reagan administration inherited from its predecessors.

Accordingly, the rectification of the U.S. military deficiencies
would have to take priority over all other policy imperatives (save
reinvigorating the domestic economy, which was a necessary condition for the required rearmament).

Secretary of State-designate Haig, in his confirmation hearings, put the situation facing the United States in the "worse case" frame as he had learned to do during his military career. Haig warned that "the central strategic phenomena [*sic*] of the post-World War II era" was the recent "transformation of Soviet military power from a continental and largely land army to a global offensive army, navy and air force, fully capable of supporting an imperial foreign policy." Because of the "episodic nature of the West's military response," said the former Supreme Allied Commander in Europe,

this tremendous accumulation of armed might has produced perhaps the most complete reversal of global power relationships ever seen in a period of relative peace. . . . Unchecked, the growth of Soviet military power must eventually paralyze Western policy altogether.[4]

He was not advocating a unilateral arms race, insisted Haig, nor strategic "superiority," which he regarded as a not particularly useful term. "I would hope that the policy [of rearmament] . . . would be one which would contribute to the lessening of the arms race. But in that context, it's very very important that we not pursue policies which we think are contributing to that, but which are really providing an incentive for a lack of breakthrough in arms control negotiations."[5]

The way to provide the Soviets the proper incentives to negotiate seriously on arms control was to face them with the prospect of a full-blown arms race with the United States which they would be sure to lose. This, in addition to rectifying currently dangerous imbalances, was one of the reasons for the go-ahead being given to many force-expansion programs. In response to the angry reactions from Moscow to the new anti-Soviet toughness in Washington, Reagan could only chortle, "They're screaming like they're sitting on a sharp nail simply because we now are showing the will that we're not going to let them get to the point of dominance where they can someday issue to the free world an ultimatum of surrender or die. And they don't like that."[6]

Although the administration was pressured by its NATO allies into an early commencement of negotiations with the Soviets on "Euro-strategic" medium-range missiles, it continued to adhere to its stated intentions to refurbish American strategic power before resuming SALT (or START, which Arms Control and Disarmament Agency Director Eugene Rostow said would be the new name to emphasize that they would be Strategic Arms *Reduction* Talks). As put by Secretary of Defense Weinberger, "The Soviets will respond seriously to proposals for meaningful and equitable reductions in strategic forces only if they have a real need to do so. Thus, they must become convinced of our commitment and resolve to take the steps necessary to meet our deterrent needs, regardless of what actions they might take." [7]

The intention was clear, and there was a solid consensus at the top levels of the Reagan administration for a massive buildup in U.S. military strength as an essential context for the new confrontationist stance toward the USSR. The consensus broke down when it came to the evaluation of competing force-planning options (particularly for deploying the new MX intercontinental missile) and, as will be discussed below (pp. 590–94), the effects of the astronomical price tag—estimated at \$1.6 trillion over the next five years—on Reagan's commitments to reduce the federal budgetary deficit and to reduce taxes.

The resumption of a confrontationist approach toward the Soviet Union, however, did not have to wait for the fruition of rearmament plans. There were plenty of opportunities all around the globe to draw the line and lower the threshold against their expansionary moves.

Under the Carter administration, the Reaganites maintained, the Soviets, in cooperation with Cuba, had been allowed to dangerously enlarge their influence in our own hemisphere, and right under our noses in Central America. The first order of business was to recognize this fact, and then to do something about it.

El Salvador was the immediate flash point, where the U.S.–backed civilian-military regime headed by José Duarte was opposed by a leftist insurrection aided through Nicaragua, presumably with Cuban and other Soviet bloc active support. The State Department in early February 1981 issued an elaborate White Paper on "Communist Interference in El Salvador," which laid the groundwork not only for a series of emergency aid requests for the Duarte regime but also for possible moves against those countries in the Caribbean and Central America—particularly Cuba and Nicaragua—giving support to the rebel forces. The White Paper purported to show conclusively—on the basis of captured guerrilla documents and weapons—that "over the past year, the insurgency in El Salvador has been progressively transformed into a textbook case of indirect armed aggression by Communist powers through Cuba." The external Communist powers had been attempting to "cover" their involvement, said the State Department, by providing mostly arms of Western manufacture. But U.S. intelligence organizations apparently had been able to determine that the weapons, transshipped through Nicaragua, were procured from diverse sources of captured Western weapons, including Vietnam and the Marxist government in Ethiopia. The evidence was "definitive," according to the White Paper, that

Cuba, the Soviet Union, and other Communist states . . . are carrying out . . . a well-coordinated covert effort to bring about the overthrow of El Salvador's established government and to impose in its place a Communist regime with no popular support

. . .

By providing arms, training, and direction to a local insurgency and by supporting it with a global propaganda campaign, the Communists have intensified and widened the conflict, greatly increased the suffering of the Salvadorian people, and deceived much of the world about the true nature of the revolution.

Special U.S. government emissaries were being sent to various capitals along with the White Paper to assure that the world was alerted to the gravity of this international Communist threat.[8]

That the Duarte government in San Salvador was itself highly unpopular, and was unable to restrain the Salvadorian military from brutal, repressive tactics against the insurgents and their supporters in the general population, was somewhat beside the point to the Reagan administration. The battle lines had been drawn between East and West, between the clients of the Soviet Union and the clients of the United States. If this country were lost to the Communists, right on the heels of the loss of Nicaragua, then the dominoes would indeed have begun to fall throughout the hemisphere. Ronald Reagan had not become President to preside over the liquidation of the U.S. sphere of influence. This was neither the time nor the place to be overly squeamish about the expediential human rights violations of a friendly authoritarian regime, for here was exactly the kind of contest between the authoritarians and the "totalitarians" that the ideological gurus in the Reagan administration

(most prominently U.N. Ambassador Jeane Kirkpatrick) had pointed
to as the essence of the East–West struggle, and a clear-headed
leadership with its eye on the larger geopolitical consequences ought
to have no trouble in knowing where to throw its support.

The basic choice had been made during the first few weeks of
the administration to support the anti-Communists in El Salvador
and to undermine the Communists and their supporters. Gratuitous
suggestions from the French and the Mexicans to attempt to bring
the revolutionaries into a coalition government were flatly rejected.
El Salvador was not Zimbabwe. U.S. military assistance and economic assistance would continue to flow to the Duarte regime. And
the administration, especially through statements from Secretary of
State Haig and White House counselor Edwin Meese, began as early
as February 1981 to talk of more direct action by the United States
against the hemispheric suppliers of the Salvadorian insurgents, especially Nicaragua and Cuba, to arrest the flow of weapons at "the
source." The President and his spokesmen ruled out no military
options. The menu of contemplated options leaked to the press included, for example, a naval blockade of the waters adjacent to Nicaragua and El Salvador but also a blockade of Cuba. Even with
respect to the possible deployment of U.S. troops to El Salvador, the
President, when pressed at news conferences, was not willing to
totally foreclose his options, and resorted to the standard circumlocution that there were no "plans" for the use of U.S. combat troops.

None of this, administration spokesmen took pains to make clear,
was a knee-jerk reaction to the chronic indigenous political instability in the hemisphere, which from time to time and place to place
exhibited a leftist, even Marxist, coloration. This was high geopolitics—the Grand Strategy in action.

Testifying before the House Foreign Affairs Committee on March
18, 1981, Secretary of State Haig dwelt on what he called a "four-
phased operation" of the Soviet Union in Central America. The first
phase, "the seizure of Nicaragua," had already been completed.
"Next is El Salvador," he said, "to be followed by Honduras and
Guatemala." This was not necessarily a domino theory, said Haig.
"I would call it a priority target list—a hit list, if you will—for the
ultimate takeover of Central America." 9

The threat in Central America was in turn a part of the global
threat from the Soviet Union against which, Haig emphasized—to

congressional committees, domestic and foreign journalists, TV interviewers, anyone who would talk with him—the United States was organizing a global response. The threat could take any number of forms: Soviet troops marching across international borders (Afghanistan); proxy wars, as between Ethiopia and Somalia in the Horn of Africa, and between North and South Yemen; Marxist-Leninist civil wars, as currently manifested in El Salvador; and, perhaps the most insidious threat, one which could crop up almost anywhere, international terrorists' efforts to shatter public confidence in the ability of authorities in the non-Communist world to maintain public order. Much of the terrorism in the world today was not simply the expression of desperate, frustrated individuals or disenfranchised groups trying to get the world's attention. The Secretary of State claimed to be in possession of reports showing the Soviet Union to be behind a great deal of the training, funding, and equipping of terrorists. "They today are involved in conscious policy, in programs, if you will, which foster, support and expand this activity which is hemorrhaging in many respects throughout the world today."[10]

The problem of terrorism, with or without Soviet sponsorship, was a major problem in its own right, said Haig. "It is a subject which will be high on the priority of our national security and foreign policy agenda." Those concerned with human rights ought to be concerned first with terrorism. Indeed, "the greatest problem to me in the human rights area today is the area of rampant international terrorism." The Secretary of State obviously spoke less carefully than he intended in one of his remarks on the subject: "International terrorism will take the place of human rights in our concern because it is the ultimate abuse of human rights." But the basic message was loud and clear. A struggle was being waged across the globe between those countries and movements committed to order and stability and those countries and movements attempting to disrupt and overthrow the established order. Under Reagan, the United States was resuming its historically determined contemporary role—taken on at the time of the Truman Doctrine, but sloughed off in recent years—of leader of the forces of order against the forces of disorder led by the Soviet Union. On every continent it was therefore essential to seek out and forge a coalition of the forces of order against the forces of disorder. The struggle for human rights only had meaning within this context.[11]

Even in the Middle East, divided along another axis by the Arab–Israeli conflict and numerous ethnic and nationalistic rivalries, the United States would be working to establish "a consensus of strategic concerns" focused on the Soviet threat. Presumably when the countries in the region got their priorities right, they would find ways of ameliorating and even resolving their conflicts among themselves.

The vigorous articulation of this global vision earned Haig a flashy *Time* magazine cover story in the March 16, 1981, issue, with the title "The 'Vicar' Takes Charge" (the ecclesiastical analogy was Haig's own for his relationship to the President) and a handsome macho-stance cover photo, hands on hips in front of a large bronze eagle, and across this heroic photograph the words TAKING COMMAND: THE WORLD ACCORDING TO HAIG. Reagan's inner circle of advisers at the White House resented this attempt to embody and take credit for the Reagan foreign policy, as did Secretary of Defense Weinberger, who was still learning the ropes over at the Pentagon and assimilating the esoterica of military strategy. But no one in the administration challenged the substance of Haig's analyses or prescriptions—at least not just yet. Within weeks, however, the lack of correspondence between Haig's abstractions and the more complicated realities of world politics, plus the desire of other officials to step forward with their own analyses and policy initiatives, began to shatter the surface coherence of even the anti-Soviet planks of the Grand Strategy.

Haig's efforts to take center stage as the high official with the most knowledge and experience in foreign affairs suffered an early embarrassment with the circulation of a draft report by the CIA in March 1981 concluding that there was insufficient evidence behind the Secretary of State's charges that the Soviet Union was systematically aiding and abetting terrorism around the globe. Yes, there were a number of cases in which there was evidence of Soviet direct help to terrorist groups, but in many instances of terrorism in recent years the evidence of such Soviet involvement was either lacking or not at all clear.[12] Reagan's Director of the CIA, William Casey, not wanting to undercut Haig and the newly enunciated pol-

icy of combating terrorism, called for a review of the CIA estimate
(which Casey himself evidently had not reviewed in its draft form).
But follow-up studies by the intelligence agencies in State and Defense, as well as continuing studies in the CIA, were unable to find
many significant direct links between the Soviet Union and terrorist
activities in the Third World. On occasion, as with the PLO, terrorists were able to obtain weapons and training from the Soviet
Union and other Warsaw Pact countries; but hardly ever was there
direction or control of the terrorist groups by the Soviets.[13]

Similarly, Haig's charges that the Soviets were engaged in a determined bid to establish satellites in this hemisphere, which he
inferred from State Department findings of gun-running by Soviet
client states to the Salvadorian rebels, were disputed by Latin
American experts in the United States, by the Mexican government, and by non-Communist political leaders in Europe who had
contact with the leftists. These critics charged this administration
with advancing self-fulfilling hypotheses about the prospects of "another Cuba" by its refusal to recognize the indigenous core of the
Salvadorian rebellion against the ruling civilian-military junta, and
by enlarging U.S. military and economic assistance to the junta.

Nor was Secretary of Defense Weinberger pleased with Haig's
public allusion to U.S. readiness for military confrontations in the
Caribbean and Central America in ways that might force the Pentagon's hand and require diversions of military capabilities from
higher-priority missions in Western Europe, the Middle East and
Persian Gulf, and northeast Asia.

Reagan himself, however, consistent with the *mare nostrum* attitudes he had expressed over the years toward the Caribbean and the
Panama Canal, his fixation with the Marxist–Leninist threat in the
hemisphere, and his pre-presidential advocacy of coercive moves
against Castro (Reagan had suggested blockading Cuba in response
to the Soviet invasion of Afghanistan), was rather solidly in the Haig
camp on El Salvador and other Latin American issues—at least with
respect to the alarmist definition of the threat. And, indeed, over
the first year of his presidency, his remarks became more and more
shrill on the "Communist conspiracy" to take over El Salvador, and
bordered on the hysterical in his February 1982 warnings to the
organization of American States against attempts by "Cuba and its
Soviet backers" to arm and direct "extremists in guerrilla warfare

and economic sabotage as part of a campaign to exploit troubles in Central America and the Caribbean." Their goal was "to establish Cuban-style Marxist–Leninist dictatorships" throughout the region.[14] Nor did the President rule out the use of U.S. military power to counter this perceived threat, reiterating frequently in press conferences Haig's formulations about the United States having to take steps to interrupt "at the source" (meaning, presumably, Cuba and/or Nicaragua) the flow of Communist-bloc military assistance to the El Salvadorian insurgents.

Reagan had been counseled by President José Lopez Portillo of Mexico, with whom he had developed good rapport even before inauguration, not to take such a polarizing approach to hemispheric affairs—that this was the surest road to the "other Cubas" which Reagan said he was trying to prevent. Mexico itself, while antithetical to Castro's variety of Socialism, felt that the Cuban dictator had to be worked with and induced through positive incentives to return Cuba to constructive participation in the inter-American system. Moreover, Mexico's own nonaligned diplomacy, and her attempt to lead the fight for a new international economic order were not consistent with her support for an East–West/right–left polarization of the region. El Salvador was not yet in the Soviet camp, and need not go that way even under a post-Duarte leftist regime if Mexico and other moderate progressives in the hemisphere did not force their Soviet/Cuban satellization by isolating and alienating the leftists. Reagan could not easily discount the Mexican objections to his policies, as Mexico was one of the most influential members of the Third World coalition, was emerging as a major source of marketable oil, and was expected to be one of the essential pillars of support for the visionary Caribbean development scheme Reagan was attempting to bring to life (see below, pp. 601–2). Yet the obsession with the Communist conspiracy to take over the hemisphere, and the evident itch to bloody Castro's nose, were apparently too strong to be subordinated to the requirements of building a solid consensus with the most important of our southern neighbors.

From the point of view of Haig and Reagan, the consensus that had to be forged was one about the nature of the most important global struggle—the East–West, totalitarian vs. anti-Communist struggle—which required a reconstitution and solidification of a worldwide anti-Soviet coalition. It was like 1947 all over again.

Especially in North Africa, the Middle East, and Southwest Asia, and despite the deeply cutting animosities between the Israelis and the Arabs and between shifting coalitions of rivalrous Arab states and Muslim movements, it was absolutely imperative to forge a strategic consensus among most of the countries against the increasingly obvious Soviet thrust to dominate that whole geopolitically crucial and oil-rich "rimland" area. On this there were no substantial disagreements at the top levels of the administration, except, perhaps, on the corollary issues of how to manage the delicate business of Arab–Israeli relations within the context of the intensified East–West struggle.

The principal instrumentality for forging this strategic consensus was to be an enlargement of U.S. weapons sales to cooperative countries. With the loss of Iran from the center of the anti-Soviet containment line, Saudi Arabia would now receive new and very special attention by the arms salesmen of the Reagan administration. Just after inauguration, Reagan and his advisers decided to carry forward Carter's recommendation to the Congress that the Saudis be allowed to purchase equipment for the sixty F-15 fighter aircraft they bought from the United States in 1978 that would enable these warplanes to conduct offensive missions. This decision was made public on April 3, 1981, along with the disclosure that the administration intended to sell Saudi Arabia five Airborne Warning and Control System (AWACS) airplanes. The announcement, on the eve of Secretary of State Haig's first official mission to the Middle East to convince Israeli and Arab leaders to join his strategic consensus against Soviet expansion, touched off a storm of protests in Israel and among her supporters in the United States, which Haig, with an eye toward getting the peace process moving again, and Reagan, with an eye on domestic politics (especially lining up Congress behind his economic programs) felt compelled to mollify. The Israelis had been offered the right to buy an additional forty F-15s (they already owned twenty-five) to compensate for the Saudi sale, and Haig was now sympathetic to the Begin government's contention that these should be provided on a grant basis, since otherwise the Israeli economy would be disastrously strained by the need to buy the new arms.

During the summer and early fall of 1981, AWACS became the symbol of the debate in the United States over Reagan's Mideast policy. Was the new arms package for the Saudis symptomatic of an historic "tilt" in U.S. policy toward the Arabs? Or was it merely a component of the new strategic consensus policy? The Saudis themselves obliged the critics by admitting publically that, as far as they were concerned, their principal opponent was Israel, not the Soviet Union.

The assassination of Egyptian President Anwar Sadat on October 6 only intensified the AWACS debate. The administration argued that now, more than ever, with Iran having seceded from the West and the future of Egypt highly uncertain, it was crucial that the United States solidify its ties with "moderate" Saudi Arabia. Critics argued that, to the contrary, the lesson of Sadat's murder was the instability of all regimes in the Arab Middle East and the dangers, therefore, of relying heavily on any of them to provide important links in the containment chain around the Soviet Union. Administration planners, in response to the latter criticism, insisted that they were not so foolish as to allow any *crucial* links in the U.S. defense strategy for the region to be located in any one country. The new Saudi surveillance and air defense capabilities would be useful in countering Soviet, or Soviet-proxy, expansionary moves, but not all that important. The United States was therefore engaged also in negotiations with Kenya, Somalia, and Oman to provide staging and servicing facilities for the U.S. Rapid Deployment Force. Turkey to the northwest, Sudan to the southwest, Pakistan to the east, the U.S. Navy in the Indian Ocean—all of these were part of the strategic plan for organizing a regional balance of power against any contemplated Soviet aggressive moves. Saudi Arabia was less important as a military bulwark than as a source of oil and as a financier for her fellow Arab nations to allow them to buy into the new arrangements; and it was primarily for this reason that it was necessary to keep the Saudis happy.

To reassure the Israelis and thereby to persuade members of Congress, who were being heavily lobbied by Jewish organizations, that the Saudi weapons package could not be used in ways that would endanger Israel's security, the President, in October 1981, during the thirty-day Senate debate, sent Majority Leader Howard Baker a letter indicating that the Saudis had agreed to a set of restrictions on the use of the AWACS and that they had granted the United States the right of continual inspection of the air and ground security arrangements for the use of the equipment. "The Saudi AWACS," said the President's letter, "will be operated solely within the boundaries of Saudi Arabia except with the prior, explicit mutual consent of the two Governments, and solely for defensive purposes as defined by the U.S."[15]

Meanwhile, the President and Weinberger negotiated a Memorandum of Strategic Understanding with Prime Minister Begin and Israeli Defense Minister Ariel Sharon, pledging military cooperation between the two countries to counter Soviet threats to the region. The accord was far short of what the Israelis had been angling for—namely, substantial prepositioning of U.S. combat capabilities so as to create a strategic interdependence between the two countries that the United States could not lightly throw overboard in a future Arab–Israeli crisis—but it did constitute a reaffirmation by the United States government of its special relationship with Israel.[16]

With these new assurances to Israel and heavy lobbying of wavering senators by the President himself, the administration, by a four-vote margin in the Senate on October 28, 1981, was able to prevent Senate rejection of the Saudi arms package. The administration claimed a major foreign policy (and domestic political) victory for its basic "strategic consensus" approach. But it would quickly find that the victory was not all that it had been trumped up to be.

No sooner had the deal passed the Senate than the Saudis denied that they had accepted binding restrictions on their use of the military equipment. It was a simple commercial deal between two sovereign states, and the Kingdom of the House of Saud retained its prerogatives to do what it pleased with its own military forces. Secretary of Defense Weinberger made efforts over the next six months to work out specific arrangements: for the AWACS transfers to Saudi Arabia, for the training of Saudi crews, for the maintenance of the complicated equipment, and for the sharing of intelligence information obtained by the planes that would not be unacceptable to the Saudis and at the same time would restore the credibility of promises the President made to the Senate and to Israel. His endeavors, however, produced at best ambiguous general statements of agreement which each government could interpret its own way. The more serious consequence of both the sale and the compensatory accords with Israel, which in turn required equal special treatment for Egypt and Jordan, was to stimulate a new phase of the multifaceted arms race in the region, where all countries, under the newly legitimized rationale of arming to preserve an East–West balance, were making themselves more threatening to one another. Since all the countries would be coming to the United States to have their requests filled, there was no built-in mechanism to translate the so-called strategic consensus into a means of regional conflict resolution; and the bilateral dependencies with the United States that were to be enlarged would turn out to be two-way levers—more like separate seesaws in which the United States could have its own balance disrupted on any of them by the defection or foot-dragging of a partner. Rather than putting itself in a stronger position to control regional affairs, the United States by the strategic consensus policy had entrapped itself into a set of contradictory dependencies that would allow the regional actors to play the superpowers off against each other in ways that could increase the chances not only of new Middle Eastern wars but also of World War III.

At the same time, the heavy courtship of Arab clients now being undertaken by the Reagan administration only stimulated unilateralist tendencies on the part of the Israelis. Feeling pressure from the United States government to accede to the standard Arab demands that Israel should return *all* of the Arab lands conquered during the 1967 war, the Begin government moved in December 1981, without consulting the United States, to extend Israeli civil law to the Golan Heights (the strategic high ground between Israel and Syria that the Israelis had captured in 1967). The Reagan administration, charging this was inconsistent with the consultation clauses in the just-concluded Memorandum of Strategic Understanding, suspended further negotiations with Israel to implement the terms of the memorandum. All that this produced, however, was a vitriolic lecture by Begin to the American ambassador in Jerusalem, Samuel Lewis, on the unacceptability of Israel's being treated like a vassal state. As with other attempts to reprimand or sanction Israel for unilateral acts during the Reagan administration (Israel's bombing of the Iraqi nuclear reactor in the spring of 1981, and her air raid on PLO concentrations around the city of Beirut, Lebanon, in the summer, in response to which the transfers of some of the fighter aircraft Israel had ordered were temporarily held back), this slap on the wrist only served to convince the Israelis of the need to clarify the fact that the strategic consensus between them and the Americans did not give the United States a veto on Israeli foreign or domestic policy any more than it gave the United States a veto on Saudi policy. Moreover, the Memorandum of Strategic Understanding required accountability and consultation only with respect to the Soviet threat, not with respect to issues between Israel and her Arab neighbors.

In short, the promulgation of the strategic consensus policy for the Middle East, rather than providing a basis for the reassertion of U.S. power in the region, demonstrated—indeed dramatized—the extent of U.S. impotence over the region's indigenous political forces.

The policy of reminding others that they needed to come to the United States for military protection against the Russian bear proved no more effective in the North Atlantic area as a magnet against growing centrifugal tendencies. Despite Afghanistan, despite Poland, and despite the impressive augmentation of Soviet military capabilities over the past decade, the West Europeans and the Canadians had not given up entirely on détente and arms control as important means of restraining Soviet aggressive impulses. The continuation by the continental West European countries of their negotiations with the Soviet Union on the natural gas deal (see below, p. 608–12) and on other economic and technology exchanges in defiance of Reagan administration pleas for a tightly coordinated alliance-wide restriction on economic intercourse with the Russians was symptomatic not only of the reduced economic power of the United States vis-à-vis its allies, but also of its declining reputation as the Grand Strategic leader of the alliance.

The NATO partners were rather resentful of being pressured to subordinate their alleged "domestic" reasons for making long-term energy supply arrangements with the Russians to the geopolitical imperative of weakening the Soviet economic base for its military buildup, while the Reagan administration, fulfilling its election campaign promise to agricultural lobbies, denied itself the most powerful American economic sanction on the Russians by rescinding the embargo Carter had imposed on grain shipments to the USSR in response to the Afghanistan invasion. Nor did the United States warrant being deferred to as a leader in the field of North–South relations, given the Reagan administration's embarrassing preachments to the developing countries about becoming prosperous through hard work and private enterprise in the free market (see below, pp. 594–602).

Even on matters of military strategy and force planning, however, in which the great preponderance of American military capability and the sophistication of American defense intellectuals usually made the United States the leader and the West Europeans the followers in the councils of NATO, the Reagan administration was not showing itself to be worthy of the normal deference.

In the midst of an already confusing intra-alliance debate on the timing and priority to be given the deployment of new U.S. nuclear missiles in Europe, high officials in the Reagan administration, including the President himself, began to deliver themselves of pronunciamentos on nuclear weapons and strategy that demonstrated the lack of adequate deliberation and guidance within the administration, let alone adequate consultation with the allies.

The Reagan administration had inherited the "two-track" decision of the NATO Council in 1979 to respond to the continuing buildup of Soviet intermediate-range missiles targeted on Western Europe by (1) preparing to station some 572 U.S. missiles on European soil capable of striking the USSR, and (2) attempting, in the three-year interim before the actual deployment, to engage the Soviets in negotiations to limit, reduce, or eliminate these Euro-strategic missiles on both sides. In its early months, the Reagan administration gave highly equivocal indications of its seriousness about proceeding along the second track. It would be more consistent with a negotiation-from-strength posture to first have the new missiles in hand, either already deployed or ready for deployment, before entering into actual negotiations with the Russians. The evident procrastination of the Reagan administration on the second track put West European leaders, especially Helmut Schmidt of Germany, in an awkward position for resisting the growing demands of lay disarmament groups to have the West European governments unilaterally renounce the stationing of the new U.S. nuclear missiles on European soil.

Secretary of State Haig, the former SACEUR, was tuned in to these West European concerns and gave them voice within the Reagan administration. Haig wanted to have the administration recommit itself to the simultaneous two-track approach, which meant sincerely pursuing negotiations while the missiles were still being developed. The Pentagon and the National Security Council staff were not so anxious to please Schmidt and the other Europeans at this point, considering it more important to get U.S. strategic planning and NATO programs in order before beginning a serious arms control dialogue with the Russians. Then in August 1981, Weinberger got the President to authorize production of neutron weapons, over Haig's objections and without NATO consultations, ignoring the fact that during the Carter administration the intra-alliance controversy over the potential deployment of neutron weapons in Western Europe nearly tore NATO apart. A damaging renewal of this controversy was narrowly avoided by Haig's assurance to the Europeans that the actual deployment of the weapons would, of course, be subject to their approval.

Now it was the President's turn to muddy the waters even more. In an impromptu response to a question in an October 16, 1981, meeting with out-of-town newspapers editors in which he was asked if there could be a limited exchange of nuclear weapons in Europe or whether any use of nuclear weapons in a European war would inevitably lead to a full-scale nuclear war between the United States and the Soviet Union, Reagan replied that "I don't honestly know." And he went on to offer the observation that "I could see where you could have the exchange of tactical weapons against troops in the field without it bringing either one of the major powers to pushing the button." [17]

The furor which this candidly agnostic remark set off in Europe, and the grist it provided to the Soviet's propaganda mill, led to urgent meetings in the administration to devise a clarificatory statement for the President to issue. The statement, read to reporters on Air Force One while the president was en route to Cancún, Mexico, on October 21, 1981, was designed to counter inferences from his October 16 statement that the United States might in some circumstances consider confining a nuclear war to European territory while preserving the homelands of the Soviet Union and the United States as sanctuaries from nuclear attack. "The suggestion that the United States could even consider fighting a nuclear war at Europe's expense is an outright deception," said Reagan.

The essence of United States nuclear strategy is that no aggressor should believe that the use of nuclear weapons in Europe could reasonably be limited to Europe.

Indeed, it is the joint European-American commitment to share the burden of our common defense which assures the peace. Thus, we regard any military threat to Europe as a threat to the United States itself. Three hundred seventy-five thousand United States servicemen provide the living guarantee of this unshakable United States commitment to the peace and security of Europe.[18]

The President hoped to be able to leave it at this standard reiteration of the American NATO commitment; but two weeks later, Secretary of State Haig, testifying before the Senate Foreign Relations Committee, attempted to defend the President's earlier statement that a limited nuclear exchange in Europe was possible. President Reagan had been correct in what he said, observed Haig, because "NATO's strategy is premised on the concept that we will conduct ourselves in response to an attack in such a way as to seek to limit the level of that attack to the lowest level possible." Haig went on to cite an example of what he meant: "There are contingency plans in the NATO doctrine," he recalled, "to fire a nuclear weapon for demonstrative purposes to demonstrate to the other side that they are exceeding the limits of toleration in the conventional area, all designed to maintain violence at the lowest level possible."[19] Then the next day Secretary of Defense Weinberger, testifying before the Senate Armed Services Committee, appeared to be flatly contradicting Haig on the possibility of a nuclear demonstration-shot warning. "There is nothing in any plan that I know of that contains anything remotely resembling that, nor should it," said Weinberger. Later that day, to negate the impression that the Secretary of State and the Secretary of Defense were working at cross-purposes, a joint statement was issued by the White House, the State Department, and the Defense Department explaining that "Secretary Haig was correct in noting that a demonstrative use is an option that has been considered by NATO. Secretary Weinberger is correct in saying that it has never been transferred into a military plan."[20]

Five days later, in his November 10, 1981, press conference, the President returned to the original point of confusion and enlarged upon it: "I suppose it's hypothetical where you're talking about is it possible to even use a nuclear weapon without this spreading automatically to the exchange of the strategic weapons. . . . [On October 16] I gave what I thought was something that was possible, that the grave difference between theater nuclear weapons—the artillery shells and so forth that both sides have—that I could see where both sides could still be deterred from going into the exchange of strategic weapons if there had been battlefield weapons troop-to-troop exchanged there." And finally, as if to make sure that nothing was left out of the circle of confusion, the President responded to a question on the nuclear warning shot by saying, in contradiction of the previous week's White House/State/Defense attempt to reconcile the Haig and Weinberger statements, "There seems to be some confusion as to whether that is still a part of NATO strategy or not. And so far I've had no answer to that."[21]

All this publicly exposed dialogue between the highest officials of the U.S. government about the way a nuclear war might be fought in Europe had the inadvertent effects of galvanizing anti–nuclear war demonstrations on both sides of the Atlantic, reviving anti-American and pro-neutralist pressures on the West European members of NATO, and allowing Brezhnev to take the arms control high ground with his proposal for a freeze on nuclear weapons deployments in Europe. Germany's Chancellor Schmidt was particularly disturbed over these developments, which could well result in parliamentary majorities in various European countries against stationing the new American missiles in Europe, while the Soviets kept their menacing Euro-strategic missiles in place. The only way to counter this potentially disastrous shift in the East–West balance of power, argued Schmidt, was for the Americans to come forward with a bold initiative for Euro-strategic arms control that would shift the focus of popular concern to the Russian military threat. Reagan's strategic advisers, while very negative to the Ostpolitik features in other elements of current West German foreign policy, could see at least the "tactical" wisdom in the Chancellor's suggestions for countering Brezhnev's freeze proposals.

The result was President Reagan's dramatic arms reduction proposal of November 18, 1981. Building on one of the options proposed by Schmidt, himself a former Defense Minister and strategic expert, the President announced that "the United States is prepared to cancel its [planned] deployment of Pershing II and ground-launched missiles if the Soviets will dismantle their SS-20, SS-4, and SS-5 missiles. This would be an historic step. With Soviet agreement, we could together substantially reduce the dread threat of nuclear war which hangs over the people of Europe. This, like the first footstep on the moon, would be a giant step for mankind." [22]

President Reagan's arms control and strategy advisers could have had no illusions that the Russians would accept this so-called zero option for Euro-strategic missiles on the Continent. It was a longstanding position of the Soviet government that its intermediate-range systems deployed in the western USSR were necessary counters to the American nuclear bombers based in Britain, the submarine-carried nuclear missiles in the waters around Europe, and the French nuclear strike force—all capable of delivering nuclear attacks on Russia itself. The nuclear balance in Europe was *now* in rough equilibrium, argued the Soviets; it was the 572 missiles the Americans planned to emplace on the continent in 1983 and 1984 that would destabilize the balance. Indeed, Brezhnev, having gotten wind a few weeks before Reagan's announcement that the administration was toying with the idea of making Schmidt's zero option the official U.S. position at the arms control negotiations previously planned to commence in Geneva on November 30, had already publicly rejected it in an interview with a West German magazine. "Most probably the authors of such 'proposals' do not really want talks, let alone successful talks," said the Soviet leader. "What they need is a breakdown of the talks, which they can use as a sort of justification for continuing the planned arms race." [23]

Brezhnev's allegations were given a certain amount of veracity by the fact that the details of the new American proposal had been worked up in the Arms Control and Disarmament Agency, directed by Eugene Rostow, formerly chairman of the board of the Committee on the Present Danger, in close collaboration with Assistant Secretary of Defense Richard Perle, a long-time foe of U.S.–Soviet arms control, and by Reagan's appointment of Paul Nitze, the guru of the anti-SALT forces, to head the U.S. negotiating team in Geneva. Nevertheless, Chancellor Schmidt and his West European colleagues were very pleased with the Reagan démarche, letting it be known that they considered it a serious opening bid in what would, of course, have to be a complicated bargaining process—an interpretation of U.S. intentions that the Reagan administration did not go out of its way to deny. In any event, for the time being at least, the pressure on the pro-NATO governments in Western Europe to rescind the 1979 decision accepting the new American missiles would be deflected. Moreover, there were reasons to believe that the Reaganites might become serious about arms control after all, given the havoc the expensive new rearmament programs were inflicting on the administration's economic and fiscal programs.

PROVIDING A MARGIN OF MILITARY SAFETY AT TOLERABLE COST

The revival of the policy of global, all-continents, coercive containment of the USSR and its proxies, and of negotiation from strength, presumed credible capabilities for brandishing military power anywhere and at any level—from paramilitary through strategic confrontations. One of Reagan's central and most repeated charges during the election campaign being that the military programs of previous administrations, Carter's in particular, had undermined such a national security policy, the new administration was committed to demonstrate from the outset that it was willing to spend whatever was necessary to bring U.S. military power rapidly up to the required levels.

Not surprisingly, when Secretary of Defense Weinberger presented the rest of the administration with the bill for the buildup—$1.6 trillion over the next five years, amounting to a real (after inflation) average increase of 7 percent a year—Reagan's budget director, David Stockman, raised the obvious objection: these massive new outlays were not compatible with the President's overall fiscal and economic program for bringing the government's expenditures into balance with its revenues, and at the same time reducing taxes.

Something had to give. Even without reduced taxes, Stockman argued, Reagan's contemplated reductions in the government's domestic programs would not free sufficient financial resources to sustain Weinberger's buildup. The implications were stark: more and even increased government deficit spending during the Reagan presidency; embarrassingly unbalanced budgets each year; domestic and international economies whipsawed by high rates of inflation and high interest rates to control the inflation—all of this compounded by the President's resolve to stick by his commitment to lower federal taxes. Shouldn't the Secretary of Defense, therefore, go back to his budgeteers with requests to allocate cuts under a specified ceiling (as President Eisenhower had required the Pentagon to do in the 1950s during an analogous Republican effort to balance the budget), especially in light of the fact that Weinberger's $1.6 trillion five-year plan was, by his own admission, a rough estimate?

Weinberger's adamant response—from all reports on the administration's budgetary deliberations during the spring of 1981—was that the $1.6 trillion was a minimum estimate, and that the more systematically analyzed requirements that would be presented to the President in the fall might just as well produce an even higher figure! Moreover, a backdown from that initially publicized gross estimate now, because of domestic economic considerations, would send our adversaries and allies the wrong signal. They would question the resolve and national commitment of the United States to negate the Soviet drive for global military superiority—the renewed resolve and commitment that Reagan's election was supposed to represent.

Weinberger's insistence on not sacrificing defense was buttressed by some of Reagan's economic advisers, including the Chairman of the President's Council of Economic Advisers, Murray Weidenbaum. Their argument was that the fears expressed by Stockman and others were short-sighted and based on an incorrect analogy with the effects of the Vietnam War buildup on the domestic economy and federal budget during the Johnson administration. The country's economy in the 1980s had more slack than it did in the 1960s; the military budget could expand at this time without straining the productive capacity of the country. The initial inflationary pressures would be kept under control by the tight money policies of the Federal Reserve Board. And, most important, all good "supply-side" economists should keep their cool, for the administration's tax cut program was designed to stimulate an average annual economic growth rate of 4.4 percent, which would close the budget gap by the next presidential election.[24]

Of course, the administration's senior economists were fully aware that they were engaged in an optimistic gamble; and the Pentagon, therefore, was asked to do what it could, while the President and the Secretary of Defense continued to deny publicly that any substantial cuts in the defense budget were contemplated.

An early test of the President's commitment to the military buildup despite its risk to his fiscal program would come in the fall of 1981, when he would be asked to authorize in more detail the military program requirements the Defense Department would be submitting to Congress in early 1982 as a part of the new budget cycle. Three new strategic weapons that had been the subject of considerable debate over the past few years—the MX missile system, the B-1 bomber, and the Trident II missile for submarines—now needed presidential endorsement for their development and deployment programs to continue. Together, these programs would consume about $25 billion in the projected fiscal 1983 budget, and would total over $200 billion in outlays over the coming five years—or as much as 15 percent of the whole military budget.

Weinberger had wanted all of these programs. He got two out of the three: the B-1 bombers and the new Trident missiles for the submarines were approved. But the President in his fall 1981 review turned down perhaps the most expensive part of the MX missile program—a scheme to deploy a portion of the new ICBMs in a "mobile" mode, dispersing them continuously among thousands of specially built shelters so that the enemy would not be able to destroy a significant portion of them without using up a significant portion of its own missiles in the attack. In rejecting this scheme (which Weinberger had inherited from Secretary of Defense Brown), the White House statement relied on the basic criticism that had been voiced by arms controllers in and out of government: "The more shelters or holes we build, the more Soviet missiles will be built. They can build missiles as fast as we can build shelters, at about the same cost to both countries." [25] Acceptance of this criticism was a considerable departure from the earlier stance of Reagan that we would in such matters challenge the Soviets to an arms race, and *they* would back off.

The administration was not dropping the MX missile program, however. For they regarded its accuracy as an essential improvement over the existing ICBMs, a feature that would give the United States as much of a capability to knock out Soviet land-based missiles as the Soviets were presumed to soon have against ours. Initial deployment of the MX would be in the existing ICBM silos, while the Pentagon gave urgent study to better, less expensive ways of protecting it.

Arms controllers were appalled at this interim fallback decision on the MX. For a period of a few years, from its initial deployment in 1986, the most lethal and accurate missile in the U.S. strategic arsenal, the one the Soviets would know was targeted on their best strategic weapons, would be sitting in stationary sites, highly vulnerable to Soviet missile attack (the marginal "hardening" the administration was ordering for these sites would not, according to the Pentagon itself, substantially reduce their vulnerability). This meant that to assure the usability of these prime strategic assests in wartime, they would have to be launched out of their silos upon early warning of a Soviet attack. If both sides were operating with such launch-on-warning programs for their prime strategic offensive forces, the prospects would be dangerously increased that each side would feel compelled to launch a preemptive first strike in an intense crisis. The administration was not closing the so-called window of vulnerability. It was simply opening one on the Soviets too— and, paradoxically, with *both* sides' ICBMs vulnerable to a first strike, the security of both from a thermonuclear war by miscalculation would be less than if only one side's ICBMs were vulnerable.

If budget director David Stockman was heartened by the postponement of the costly MX deployment, he was soon to discover that Weinberger would retrieve all of the monies thus saved and allocate them to other Pentagon programs anyway. As it turned out, the President had not been moved from his hard-as-a-rock stance that this administration would spend all that was necessary to provide the United States with a "margin of safety" in the U.S.–Soviet military balance of power. And the Secretary of Defense would now go back to his weapons system analysts, strategists, and budgeteers to firm up tighter rationale for each of the specific items in the comprehensive Defense Department budget that would be due for presidential authorization by the end of the year.

The result, unveiled in the President's budget message of February 6, 1982, was a military spending request to the Congress of $216 billion for fiscal year 1983, a $33 billion increase from fiscal 1982, with even larger increases projected for the next four annual budgets, amounting, as previously anticipated, to $1640 billion over the course of five years. The new strategic systems authorized by the President in October were going forward, thereby increasing the strategic forces budget from the $16.2 billion in Carter's last budget to $23.1 billion for fiscal 1973. An even larger increase was proposed for the general purpose forces budget, raising it to $106.2 billion for fiscal 1983, with the most dramatic augmentations occurring for "mobility" forces—airlift, sealift, and equipment for the

Rapid Deployment Force and a nearly 20 percent increase in naval combat ships over the coming decade. (The emphasis on seapower and maritime transport capabilities represented the ascendency of "realist" unilaterist assumptions that the United States should be able to project its power onto any continent without having to rely on the willingness of allies to provide staging bases for U.S. aircraft or troops.)[26]

National defense, the largest and most expanded part of the federal budget would help swell the deficit for fiscal 1983 alone to $91.5 billion—even under the administration's most optimistic assumptions about growth-producing revenue. Reagan had made his choice. The cuts would come in government-supported domestic programs, including welfare, food stamps, health care, and housing. The tax cuts he pushed through the Congress in 1981 would not be rescinded. If obtaining the required margin of military safety for the country meant continued inflation and an unbalanced budget contradictory of Reagan's fiscal philosophy, so be it. These were tolerable costs for the achievement of his highest priority: making this nation Number One again. At least this was the outcome of the crucial first round in what promised to be an increasingly bitter series of annual budget battles.

KEEPING THE WORLD SAFE FOR FREE ENTERPRISE

It would no longer be necessary for the United States, as a superpower with regained respect, to give in to Third World demands for "Socialistic" interferences with the international economy. Reagan and his advisers on foreign economic policy believed that the rhetorical concessions Kissinger had made to the Third World at the Seventh Special Session of the United Nations (see above, pp. 430–32), and which were adopted as U.S. policy by the Carter administration, were economically unsound. Kissinger was wrong, they believed, in justifying his 1976 responsiveness on grounds of the realpolitik imperative of countering Soviet influence in the Third World. The Soviets had very little in the form of economic resources and technologies that the developing countries were anxious to obtain. It was U.S. investments, financial credits, and technological know-how that most of the modernizing elites of the Third World wanted, as well as opportunities to sell their goods in the

U.S. market, and therefore the United States should "keep its cool" and not be blackmailed by developing-country threats to jump in bed with the Russian bear.

This being his administration's basic stance, Reagan initially saw no reason to attend the North–South economic "summit" meeting that was scheduled for the late summer or fall of 1981 in Cancún, Mexico, especially since the Cancún summit was the brainchild of the German ex-Chancellor Willy Brandt and was supposed to implement the socialistic proposals for a global redistribution of wealth contained in the recently issued Brandt Commission Report.[27]

The proposals of the Brandt Commission were anathema to the "classical" economists, like Milton Freidman of the University of Chicago, on whom Reagan depended for advice concerning international economic issues. This classical view held that global development was distorted by most man-made barriers to the free exchange of goods in the international market. Anything that prevented individuals and private firms from buying as cheaply as possible and selling to the highest bidder anywhere in the world was both inefficient and unjust. International free trade—or as close an approximation to it as possible—supposedly would result in the greatest good for the greatest number of people. According to the classical theory, it would induce producers to locate where the factors of production (natural resources, labor, capital, managerial skills) can be obtained most efficiently and therefore would result in goods that can be sold more cheaply, Everyone benefits. Moreover, this basic free market process would tend toward a global distribution of production and income-earning opportunities on the basis of the comparative advantage of various societies to provide the factors of production more efficiently for certain kinds of products. This dynamic in turn was supposed to produce a specialization of production by particular countries and presumably thereby provide them each with secure sources of income.

In holding to this classical academic model of international economics, the Reagan administration was out of step with the governments of the other advanced industrial countries, especially the newly elected socialist government in France under Mitterrand and the reformed socialism of the Schmidt government in Germany, but also to a certain extent with Margaret Thatcher's Conservative government in Britain. These governments, the Canadians, and other members of the European Economic Community granted the need for a more regulated global economy, with special protections and subsidies for the weaker competitors in the ex-colonial world to allow them to diversify their industrial bases and to overcome deficiencies (unskilled labor, poorly developed financial systems, and the like) during the development process, after which—perhaps—some of them might be in a position to compete in a more open global market.

Reagan consequently found himself a minority of one on North–South issues in his first seven-nation summit meeting with the leaders of Britain, Canada, France, Italy, Japan, and West Germany in Ottawa on July 20–21, 1981. The allies were unable to budge him on the economics of the problem, but did, evidently, convince him of the political importance of a less rigid rejection of Third World demands, and convince him that he could go to the Cancún meeting in the fall without thereby conceding to any demands the United States found unacceptable.*

Largely to avoid an open break with the allies on North–South and international economic issues, Reagan agreed to language in the formal Ottawa communiqué that departed somewhat from his real views. He joined them in expressing support for the "stability, independence, and genuine nonalignment of the developing countries," and in stating that the seven looked forward to substantive discussion on North–South economic issues at Cancún and to participation "in preparations for a mutually acceptable process of global negotiations." And he surprised many of his economic advisers by agreeing to Point 14 of the Ottawa communiqué: "We are committed to maintaining substantial and, in many cases, growing levels of official development assistance and will seek to increase public understanding of its importance. We will direct the major portion of our aid to the poorer countries, and will participate actively in the United Nations conference with the least developed countries."[28]

These were tactical concessions made for the purpose of avoiding an open split with the allies. His summit partners made some too, of more importance to Reagan—namely, soft-pedaling their own

---

*Between his inaugural and the summit at Ottawa, Reagan had made a deal with President José Lopez Portillo of Mexico, who would be co-chairman at Cancún with Prime Minister Elliot Trudeau, that he, Reagan, would attend on condition that Cuba's Fidel Castro was not present.

criticisms of the domestic economic policies of the administration, particularly those resulting in high interest rates, that were exacerbating recessionary economic trends in Western Europe.

Back on home ground, however, Reagan and other high officials of the administration responsible for international economic matters made sure that their positions on North–South relations would not be misunderstood. The position the President would be taking at Cancún, said Myer Rashish, the Under Secretary of State for Economic Affairs, "is fully consistent with the philosophy of this administration from the beginning"—the belief in "enterprise and the allocation of resources through the free market." The Reagan administration did not accept the proposals of the "Group of 77" developing countries and the Brandt Commission Report for "instruments for getting resources out of the rich for the so-called poor" in order to implement notions of "distributive justice and equality." The betterment of the poor would come, rather, from viable growth, and this would be the result of removing the barriers to enterprise. The Third World was moving in the opposite direction by its demands for cartel-like agreements to raise the price of commodities it produces. "Our philosophy does not stop at the waterfront," said Rashish. "The market place . . . [has] a crucial role to play in allocating resources. Governments cannot annul that law." The Under Secretary also said the U.S. government under Reagan was against conducting negotiations on North–South economic issues in forums like the UN General Assembly, where the Third World has a voting majority. The best place to deal with these issues was in the established international economic institutions, where those who controlled the resources had comparable decision-making authority, such as the General Agreements on Tariffs and Trade, the International Monetary Fund, and the World Bank. Nor should the 21 leaders coming to Cancún in October to meet with the President be under the illusion that he was prepared to "negotiate" with them in this forum. He was coming only to exchange views.[29]

On September 21, 1981, in his address before the UN General Assembly, Secretary of State Haig took a considerably more moderate line, recognizing that "many of the poorer developing countries must continue to rely heavily on concessional assistance for some time to come," and that "certain kinds of development programs will not pay the quick and direct financial returns needed to attract private capital." For this reason, he said, the United States would continue to provide development-assistance financing at concessional rates and to support various multilateral development banks. However, "given today's economic conditions and the limitation on aid budgets in many countries," it should be understood that "a strategy for growth that depends on a massive transfer of resources from developed to developing countries is simply unrealistic." The best basic strategy for generating the development process in the have-not nations was to create an environment in the developing countries attractive to domestic and international private investment. This the United States had learned from its own experience. "But our goal is not to impose either our economic values or our judgments on anyone." The President would be coming to Cancún in October to engage in a "reasoned dialogue." [30]

A week later, President Reagan stated the free market philosophy in less equivocal terms at the annual meeting of the Board of Governors of the World Bank and the International Monetary Fund. The post–World War II system of international economic institutions, of which the World Bank and the IMF were a part, were established, he said, "to facilitate individual enterprise in an open international trading and financial system." It was important to recommit the world to that philosophy:

We who live in free market societies believe that growth, prosperity, and ultimately human fulfillment are created from the bottom up, not the government down.

. . .

The societies which have achieved the most spectacular, broad-based economic progress in the shortest period of time . . . believe in the magic of the marketplace.

Everyday life confirms the fundamentally human and democratic ideal that individual effort deserves economic reward. . . . So let me speak plainly: we cannot have prosperity and successful development without economic freedom. Nor can we preserve our personal and political freedoms without economic freedom.

This too was the requirement for a properly functioning and just international order:

My own Government is committed to policies of free trade, unrestricted investment and open capital markets. The financial flows generated by trade investment and growth capital flows far exceed official development assistance funds provided to developing countries.

This, of course, was the goal. Concessions did have to be made to the facts of uneven development:

. . . we are sensitive to the needs of the low-income countries. They can benefit from international trade and growth in the industrial countries because they export many raw materials and primary products the industrial world needs. But they also depend upon our aid to strengthen their economies, diversify their exports and work toward self-sufficiency.

Accordingly, said the President, the United States government, taking into account its budgetary restraints, will continue to provide the World Bank with resources allowing them to contribute to the development needs of the poor. But it was unmistakable from the thrust and emphasis of his remarks that it was private investment that should be assuming an ever-increasing role in the stimulus to economic development, and the U.S. government, under a renewed commitment to the free enterprise philosophy, would be evaluating the success of the international institutions in terms of their ability to improve the opportunities for private investment. It was this vision—of worldwide prosperity through private enterprise in a global free market—that the United States would be championing at the Cancún conference.[31]

At Cancún itself, however, meeting with the leaders of twenty-one other countries from October 22 to 24, the politician in Reagan evidently influenced him, as it had at Ottawa, to modulate the pontifical insistences that the world be made safe for private enterprise. But his presence there also had the political effect of preventing the conference from turning into a forum for demands on the United States and other industrialized countries that they simply were not ready to accommodate. The United States joined in accepting the idea of global negotiations designed to aid the poor nations, but, along with Britain and West Germany, refused to become a part of the consensus that such negotiations should be under the aegis of UN bodies, where each country has one vote. As far as at least these three were concerned, no substantive international decisions by the General Assembly-type forums could overrule the policies of the IMF, the World Bank, or the GATT. The final conference communiqué reflected this fundamental impasse. And the outcome left considerable doubt in the minds of the original conveners of Cancún as to what, if anything, had been accomplished. Reagan and his economic advisers were not at all displeased with this result.

On another front, too, the Reagan administration could congratulate itself for holding the fort of the global free market against the assaults of international socialism. On March 3, 1981, just days before the 150-country Law of the Sea Conference was about to reconvene its seven-year deliberations to finalize work on a comprehensive treaty to regulate the use of the oceans and its resources, the Reagan administration instructed its delegates to the conference "to seek to insure that the negotiations do not end at the present session of the Conference, pending a policy review by the United States."[32]

The State Department explained that a preliminary interagency review had determined that the Law of the Sea treaty text being prepared for signature might compromise important U.S. security interests and would inhibit U.S. companies in their exploitation of the seabed for its mineral resources. Particularly objectionable to some of the important U.S. industries involved in the mining were treaty provisions under which an international organization with a voting majority of Third World countries would develop seabed resources in parallel with private companies, and also have a share in the profits. U.S. negotiators, through five administrations, had engaged in tough and protracted negotiations to achieve this compromise with the conference majority, who had held out originally for an international public ownership of all the deep seabed mineral resources. Now the new administration was rejecting the whole thing, including some 320 articles and annexes on navigation, fishing, use of straits, and ocean pollution.

The basic posture on North–South issues, in short, was not particularly well designed to enlarge U.S. influence in the South *or* in the North among allies more responsive to the grievances of their former colonial wards. The Third World countries and movements most ready to rally round the flag of free enterprise (or at least anti-Marxism) were not necessarily the most important countries to have on our side. The most influential Third Worlders were advocates of economic and social reform (international as well as domestic) founded at least in part on Socialist, sometimes Marxist, premises. The most respected leaders of the developing-country coalition— Venezuela, Mexico, Nigeria, Tanzania, Algeria, India—while covering a wide spectrum of regimes, were in this "progressive" camp.

Reagan, however, had his own vision. The wealth and energies of private capital of the United States, if mobilized under an idealistic cause to promote economic development and—not incidentally—lucrative investment and trading opportunities in previously depressed areas of the globe, could give the lie to the nay-sayers who had lost faith in the American dream of economic freedom. The place to start was in our own hemisphere, close to home in Central America and the Caribbean Basin. Addressing the Organization of American States on February 24, 1982, the President offered what he called "an integrated program that helps our neighbors help themselves, a program that will create conditions under which creativity, private enterpreneurship and self-help can flourish. The Caribbean Basin Initiative was built on six planks: (1) no protective tariffs by the United States against Caribbean products exported to the United States for the next twelve years (the only exceptions being textiles and apparel products); (2) special tax incentives in the United States to American private investors in the area; (3) some $660 million in official U.S. development assistance to countries in the region; (4) technical assistance and training programs for the private sectors of the Caribbean countries: (5) efforts to induce other foreign investors, including some of the better-endowed hemispheric countries like Canada, Venezuela, and Mexico, to cooperate with the United States in developing the region; and (6) special provisions to see that Puerto Rico and the United States Virgin Islands would benefit from the program.[33]

As the Carribean Basin Initiative was juxtaposed with his plea to the OAS to cooperate with the United States in opposing the advances of Soviet-sponsored and Cuban-led Marxist–Leninist movements in the hemisphere, some of the Central American and Caribbean governments would have difficulty in associating themselves too closely with that Initiative. The juxtaposition suggested a polarized, two-camps regional policy by the United States that was inconsistent with the basic international stance of most Latin countries of nonalignment on East–West issues, and might cut too much against the grain of their mixed, Socialist/capitalist philosophies of national development. Finally, the central energizer of the whole scheme, U.S. private investment, might shy away from an area which, by the President's own characterization, was a hotbed of revolutionary anti-American, anticapitalist activity. Was there a simple dilemma of priorities here—political stability being the precondition for private enterprise–led economic development vs. economic development being the precondition for political stability? Or was the design even more profoundly flawed in its premises of both the attractive power and the coercive power of the United States in the 1980s?

34

IDEOLOGY VS. THE
REAL WORLD

*We must recognize the complex and vexing character of this world. We should
not indulge ourselves in fantasies of perfection or unfullfillable plans, or solutions gained by pressure. It is the responsibility of leaders not to feed the growing
appetite for easy promises and grand assurances. The plain truth is this: We face
the prospect of all too few decisive breakthroughs.*

GEORGE P. SHULTZ

More ideological than any of its predecessors, the Reagan administration would need to modify its initial stances, even more than its
predecessors had to alter theirs, to avoid placing the country in embarrassing or unnecessarily dangerous international situations. By
the midterm congressional elections of 1982, some adaptation to the
realities of world politics was discernible—particularly in the State
Department—but this was still at tension with a determination in
the White House not to become "Carterized" (the insider's code-
word for looking overly ambivalent and inconstant).

The bipolar worldview was proving to be grossly incongruent with
the complexities of Middle East politics, and also an unhelpful oversimplification when it came to devising policies toward Africa and
Latin America. The ideological definition of who's on who's side in
the global struggle could not be squared with the efforts to continue
to play on the triangular relationship with the USSR and China.
The effort to build up a margin of military superiority over the So-

viet Union, and from that vantage point to "negotiate from strength" on arms control and other East–West issues, had run up against the rock-solid determination of the Soviets to maintain at least military parity with the United States; the resulting arms race would be inconsistent with Reagan's domestic economic policies. Meanwhile, the policy of military buildup first, arms control negotiations second, and in particular the rhetoric on nuclear war strategies, had stimulated the broadest-based anti-nuclear movement yet in this country and abroad, which the politician in Ronald Reagan could not ignore. And, most embarrassingly, in many of the essentials of their initial grand strategy, the Reaganites were finding themselves at cross-purposes with the NATO allies and Japan. If a "strategic consensus" could not be fashioned even with the principal NATO allies, how realistic were the prospects of a strategic consensus between the United States and countries in the Middle East, Africa, and Latin America?

The Reagan administration was, of course, no exception to the norm in which a new team in Washington promises more than it can deliver. Eisenhower and Dulles created expectations that they would help "liberate" Eastern Europe from communism. They also were committed to provide a leaner, less expensive military establishment—the so-called New Look—which would rely primarily on strategic and tactical nuclear weapons, firepower rather than manpower, "more bang for a buck." As it turned out, "liberation" was buried in 1956 along with the corpses of Hungarian anti-Soviet revolutionaries who took the rhetoric seriously and consequently were shot down by Russian tanks on the streets of Budapest, while the United States looked on helplessly. Eisenhower's lean military policy also had to be discarded during his second term, when its strategic centerpiece—the threat of massive nuclear retaliation to attacks at any level of warfare—was neutralized by the Soviet Union's impending attainment of an equivalent nuclear arsenal.

John F. Kennedy was going to close the "missile gap"—the margin of Soviet superiority in ICBMs that supposedly loomed in the early 1960s because of the negligence of the Eisenhower administration. He was also going to shift the United States to the side of progressive change in the Third World, in contrast to the Eisenhower-Dulles policy of propping up conservative oligarchies. Upon assuming office, Kennedy discovered the "missile gap" to have been a myth and authorized only minimal alterations in the strategic weapons programs already begun by the Eisenhower administration. Offers of support for social reform found few sincere takers in the Third World, where many countries were ruled by elites which were either part of or relied for their power on profoundly inegalitarian social structures; nor was the reformist policy more than indifferently implemented by career bureaucrats within the pertinent U.S. agencies. Tragically, the Kennedy administration involved itself deeply in Vietnam under the illusion that it would reform the narrowly based and rigidly conservative regime in Saigon. Eventually that folly sent 500,000 U.S. troops to Vietnam, 50,000 of whom were killed before the United States withdrew ten years later.

In 1968 Richard Nixon promised to restore U. S. strategic superiority—the only proper base, in his view, from which to negotiate with the Russians—but ended up institutionalizing strategic parity in SALT I. He and Henry Kissinger articulated a grand strategy of "linkage" between issues for gaining leverage on the USSR. However, they found that the links in trade that Congress (concerned with Soviet restrictions on Jewish emigration) would allow were too thin to provide substantial leverage on Soviet behavior, and the Soviet military buildup simultaneous with neoisolationist pressures in the United States denied the United States the capacity to negotiate from strength. It was only Kissinger's tactical brilliance that rescued U. S. diplomacy from the embarrassment of speaking loudly while carrying a small twig.

Jimmy Carter promised to end our preoccupation with the Soviet Union and to supplant balance-of-power politics with world-order politics, centered around a renewed commitment to human rights. By the end of his administration there was a virtual obsession with Soviet designs on the Horn of Africa and the Persian Gulf, while human rights were relegated to the fringes of policy.

But whereas Reagan's predecessors were proud of their ability to adapt pragmatically to the realities of world politics, the Reaganites are proud of the extent to which they have been able to resist compromising their ideological stance. President Reagan has been apologetic to those on his right flank, like Senator Jesse Helms of North Carolina, for whatever accommodations his administration has been compelled to make with international and domestic forces opposed to the cold war policies Reagan championed on his way to the White

House. These accommodations have been rationalized as only tactical retreats in the service of the overriding grand strategy of weakening the main enemy (totalitarian socialism) and strengthening the causes of political and economic freedom all around the globe.

THE "FULL-COURT PRESS" AGAINST THE SOVIETS

In agreeing to undertake arms control negotiations with the Soviet Union on three fronts—the theater nuclear force negotiations, the Strategic Arms Reduction Talks (START), and the Mutual and Balanced Force Reduction (MBFR) discussions—*before* the Kremlin had shown any inclination to remove Soviet troops from Afghanistan or to reduce the repression in Poland, and *before* his rearmament policy had materialized in important new deployments, Reagan did back off somewhat from his early embrace of the doctrines of "linkage" and "negotiation from strength." It became clear to the Reaganites that unless they looked serious about controlling the arms race, their rearmament programs would be frustrated by the enlarged anti-nuclear movement in this country and by an uncooperative attitude on the part of key NATO allies on the deployment of new weapons in Europe; moreover, the Russians would be allowed to gain the high ground in the international peace propaganda contest.

Administration spokesmen explained that it would not be inconsistent with the "negotiation from strength" posture to start START and the theater arms negotiations before the "window of vulnerability" on the U.S. ICBMs had been closed by the deployment of the new MX missile, before the presumed superiority of the Soviets in the Eurostrategic balance had been rectified by the deployment of Pershing IIs and Ground Launched Cruise Missiles, and before U.S. strategic-war–fighting capabilities had been enhanced by the deployment of the new B-1 bomber. Rather, the continuing *development* of these and other weapons would provide U.S. arms control negotiators with powerful bargaining chips and, more importantly, would provide the country with the needed "margin of safety" in the event the negotiations failed to produce an acceptable agreement.

The unlinking of arms control negotiations with restrained Russian behavior could be compensated for by a tighter linking of East–West trade and credit arrangements to Soviet actions in Afghanistan, Poland, and elsewhere. Contrary to journalistic speculation and allegations from some of Reagan's more conservative constituency, the administration was not abandoning its grand strategy for globally confronting the Soviets. The adaptations were only tactical.

The public restatement of the marginally revised grand strategy was made by William Clark, Richard Allen's successor in the post of National Security Adviser, in a May 21, 1982, address at Georgetown University's Center for Strategic and International Studies. The Reagan strategy, explained Clark, included "diplomatic, political, economic, and informational components built on a foundation of military strength." Its objective was to "convince the Soviet leadership to turn their attention inward" instead of engaging in aggressive international moves. It included a buildup of military forces for confronting the Soviet threat throughout the world, and contemplated "counteroffensives on other fronts" than those chosen by the Soviets. Other high officials (speaking anonymously) amplified on the National Security Adviser's remarks. One called it a "full-court press against the Soviet Union." It was designed to take advantage of Soviet political and economic weaknesses, and included "an active but prudent campaign aimed at internal reform in the Soviet Union . . . and a shrinkage of the Soviet empire." As put by Clark himself, "We must force our principal adversary, the Soviet Union, to bear the brunt of its economic shortcomings." [1]

The Clark speech was only a mild public distillation of a 125-page planning document issued by the Office of the Secretary of Defense called "Fiscal Year 1984–1988 Defense Guidance." Leaked to the *New York Times*, the guidance included requirements for fighting a "protracted" nuclear war that could last for many weeks. In such a war, American nuclear forces were supposed to "prevail" and be able "to force the Soviet Union to seek earliest termination of hostilities on terms favorable to the United States." U.S. strategic forces would be expected to destroy Soviet military bases around the world and to "decapitate" the Soviet military system by destroying its leadership group and its central lines of communication. To provide the array of strategic capabilities needed to perform these missions, U.S. planners were directed to speed up their development of space-based weaponry and anti-ballistic missile systems, even though the latter might require abrogating the SALT I limitations on ABM deployments. A more powerful conventional war-fighting posture was called for, "capable of putting at risk Soviet interests all around the world, including the Soviet homeland."

The rationale for the new U.S. military buildup was not simply one of military effectiveness. It was part and parcel of the "full-court press" strategy to make life difficult for the Soviets during peace as well as war. The guidance document, accordingly, urged the development of weapons that "are difficult for the Soviets to counter, impose disproportionate costs, open up new areas of military competition and obsolesce previous Soviet investment." [2]

Moreover, the military aspects of the "full court press" were to be paralleled by economic and political warfare on the Soviet system short of actual hostilities. One aspect of this comprehensive thrust at Soviet vulnerabilities was the Reagan policy of restricting the sale of technologies to the USSR that could help it overcome its economic difficulties. The restrictions on the sale of equipment for the Soviet pipeline for transporting Soviet natural gas to Western Europe—originally announced by President Reagan as a sanction against the Soviets for their repressive policies in Poland—were now integrated into the grand strategy for bringing long-term pressure on the Soviet system.

Even more than the policy of challenging the Russians to a full-blown arms race, the policy of bringing maximum pressure against the Soviet economic system produced a major altercation with America's principal NATO allies, Germany, England, France, and Italy. Centered on the arrangements to provide technology and financing for the Soviet pipeline and commitments to purchase the gas that would be transported through it, the issue reflected and exacerbated deep-seated transatlantic differences on East–West relations.

The issue of the gas pipeline was brought to a head by the U.S. decision, announced by President Reagan on December 29, 1981, to impose economic sanctions on the Soviet Union for its "heavy and direct responsibility for the repression in Poland." The list of oil and gas equipment requiring export licenses was being extended to include pipelayers, said the President, and the issuance of such licenses was now suspended. The embargo on gas pipeline equipment was one of a number of new sanctions announced at the time, including suspension of Aeroflot service to the United States; closing the Soviet Purchasing Commission; suspension of issuance or renewal of export licenses for electronic equipment, computers, and other high technology materials; suspension of negotiations on a new U.S.–Soviet maritime agreement; nonrenewal of various exchange agreements on energy and technology; and a postponement of negotiations on a new U.S.–Soviet long-term grains agreement (significantly, there was no postponment or suspension of short-term agreements for Soviet purchases of U.S. grains).[3]

The Department of Commerce, in spelling out more precisely the export license suspensions, indicated that the affected equipment included air and gas compressors, gas turbine engines for compressors, sensors, meters, and mixing equipment, and pipeline-laying equipment.[4]

The problem in implementing these controls was that to be effective they required similar export controls by the West Europeans, since some of the components on which the Russians were crucially dependent were manufactured in Europe by subsidiaries of U.S. corporations or by European firms. But the relevant European governments—France, the Federal Republic of Germany, the United Kingdom, and Italy—would not go along with the embargo. Particularly in a time of economic recession in the Western industrialized countries, and with the United States having recently cut back on its steel imports from the European community, the Europeans were in no mood to forego the job-generating orders for the pipeline equipment.

The Reagan administration tried to persuade its European counterparts that their assistance to the Soviets in building the gas pipeline had geopolitical considerations transcending immediate economic considerations: The U.S. call for an embargo was part of the grand strategy of denying the Soviet Union goods and technology that contribute to its warmaking capacity. Yes, the White House, in lifting the embargo on grain sales to the Soviet Union that had been imposed by President Carter, had responded to domestic economic considerations; but the grain made no contribution to Soviet military capabilities. And in purchasing the grain the Russians would deplete their hard currency reserves and thereby, presumably, restrict their overall ability to play a large role in the global economy. From the gas delivery deals the Soviets had negotiated with the West Europeans, however, the USSR would earn over $10 billion a year in hard currency, and this would free it from economic pressures that otherwise might restrict its capacity to continue its dangerous military buildup and to pursue an aggressive foreign policy. Moreover, the Western countries participating in the pipeline deals would become highly dependent on the gas they would be receiving through the pipeline, and thus would be vulnerable to Soviet threats to turn off the spigot in East–West crises.

The West Europeans rejected all of the Reagan administration arguments. Economic coercion of the Soviet Union had not worked in the past and would not work now; if the USSR were denied hard currency earnings in the West, and if this produced a constriction of the Soviet development plans, the Kremlin would take it out of the hides of the Soviet people, by deferring the satisfaction of ordinary consumer needs in housing and other amenities; it would not arrest Soviet military developments, but it would revive Moscow's paranoid suspicions of the West as seeking to destroy the socialist experiment in Russia—the probable result of all this being a *more* aggressive foreign policy. The West Europeans also contested the allegation that they were making themselves vulnerable to Soviet political pressures by becoming dependent on the USSR for energy. At most the supplies from Russia would constitute 5 percent of their total energy consumption, a gap that could be filled from other sources in the event of a cutoff from the East. Furthermore, the West's ability to obtain substantial supplies of energy from the USSR would make them just that much less dependent on Persian Gulf oil.

Rebuffed by the NATO allies, Reagan, over the objections of Secretary of State Alexander Haig, but responsive to the get-tough approach of Secretary of Defense Caspar Weinberger, decided to move unilaterally. In the spring and summer of 1982, the President issued directives prohibiting U.S. companies from participating in the construction of the Soviet natural gas pipeline, barring foreign subsidiaries of U.S. corporations from selling or delivering equipment to the USSR for the pipelines, and banning the use of American equipment and/or technology in the pipeline project by foreign companies themselves. The West Europeans were particularly adamant in their opposition to the last of these prohibitions, claiming that their companies were manufacturing equipment and using technology under American licenses obtained before President Reagan's December 1981 imposition of sanctions against the USSR and that, moreover, it was an infringement of the sovereign authority of their governments for the United States now unilaterally to impose such controls on these West European companies.

The State Department, attempting to deflect the White House from this collision course with the allies, urged that the administration modify its stance to one of persuading the NATO countries to help squeeze the Soviet economy by restricting the financial credits they offer the USSR. But the President dug in his heels and at the end of June 1982 escalated the confrontation with the West Europeans by directing the Commerce Department to prohibit the export of goods and data from the United States to foreign companies who continued to provide equipment and technology to the Soviet gas pipeline project.[5]

One by one the governments of France, Italy, West Germany, and the United Kingdom, defying the President's demands, announced that they had instructed their companies to honor the pipeline equipment contracts they had already negotiated with the Soviet Union. "The question," explained Prime Minister Margaret Thatcher, "is whether one very powerful nation can prevent existing contracts from being fulfilled. I think it is wrong to do that."[6]

As the embarrassing interalliance altercation continued during the fall of 1982, hopes for a resolution centered on the ability of the new Secretary of State, George Shultz, to moderate the President's machismo-like determination. One avenue being explored was an allied agreement to enlarge the list of technology and equipment that the NATO countries would define as having military applications, and which therefore should be prohibited. The United States indicated it wanted the NATO allies to join it in restricting the export of semiconductors and other microelectronic devices used in the computers of advanced weapons systems. State and Commerce department officials were hinting to their West European counterparts that their agreement to tougher controls on such exports might make the President more relaxed about the pipeline.[7]

The Europeans countered with suggestions for a full-blown consulation and review of Western commercial intercourse with the East. Reagan authorized George Shultz to participate in this review, and the sanctions against the allies were lifted. But given the fundamental clash in premises for dealing with the Soviet Union the resulting consensus would simply paper over an agreement to disagree. This was a considerable retreat by the Reagan administration, since it was precisely its unwillingness to tolerate independent East–West commercial strategies by other members of NATO that led to the embarrassing transatlantic row.

CONFRONTING THE COMPLEXITIES OF THE
MIDDLE EAST IN LEBANON

The Reagan administration's attempt to reforge a worldwide coalition united around a "consensus of strategic concerns"—namely, the growth of Soviet military power and Soviet international aggressiveness—ran into early difficulties in the Middle East. As recounted in the previous chapter, the Saudis publicly refused to accept the definition of the purpose of their new arms purchases, including the AWACS aircraft, as one of enhancing the regional balance against the USSR and its local proxies; and the Israelis, despite the explicit pledges of mutual consultation in their November 1981 Memorandum of Strategic Understanding with the United States, appeared to be determined, more than at any time since the Suez crisis of 1956, to pursue their own national interests as they saw fit, unhampered by accountability to even their superpower protector.

Nowhere was the primacy of local rivalries over the global East–West competition between the United States and the Soviet Union more dramatically evident than in the Lebanon crisis of 1982. On the surface the Lebanon crisis could be fit into the East–West paradigm through which the Reaganites tried to view the Middle East. The administration, of course, had to deal with the very real risk of the United States and the Soviet Union being drawn into a dangerous confrontation by their respective clients. The Syrians, armed with Soviet surface-to-air missiles and Soviet fighter aircraft, were protecting the PLO guerrillas in Southern Lebanon against retaliatory attacks by an Israeli air force armed with advanced U.S. planes and anti-missile weapons. In 1981 the Israelis were threatening to destroy the Syrian air bases if they continued to shield PLO attacks across the border into Israel. The Syrians were requesting additional Soviet help to beef up their air defense capabilities. The Israelis were asking for additional material assistance and political backing from the United States to counter the Soviet-supported buildup of the Syrians in Lebanon and the continuing supply of the PLO units with arms, including tanks and rockets, from Warsaw Pact sources, North Korea, and Libya.

The temporary ceasefire obtained in the summer of 1981 by U.S. special ambassador Philip C. Habib was due in no small measure to Habib's being able to convince the antagonists that the United States itself had a direct and vital interest in preventing further escalation of the conflict. But the fragility of the ceasefire reflected the fact that the dangerous situation in Lebanon had a life of its own which was not subject to firm control by either superpower.

Indeed, Syria's military presence in Lebanon had more to do with intra-Arab conflicts than with the Arab-Israeli conflict per se, let alone the Soviet-American rivalry; and the Soviet Union's need to be the benefactor and protector of the Syrian presence caused the Kremlin considerable difficulty with other Arab clients who are Syria's rivals. The Syrian army had come into Lebanon in force during the mid 1970s civil war and had remained as the largest unit in the Arab peacekeeping force after 1976. The Syrians continued to meddle directly in the Lebanese civil strife, switching from alliance with the Lebanese Christians (which had put them in a tacit alliance with Israel) against the Palestinians to support for the Muslims against the Christians, and latterly as military defender of the PLO against Israel. The main concern in Damascus during this period was the hegemonic assertiveness of its neighbor Iraq (also a major Soviet client in the area)—a concern exacerbated by Iraq's 1980 attack on Iran. Syria, by providing diplomatic backing and military supplies to Iran, not only risked being drawn into a direct confrontation with Iraq, but also made it more embarrassing for the Kremlin to be generously responsive to Syria's new demands for military equipment.

Israel's 1982 invasion of Lebanon, ostensibly to clear the Palestinian guerrillas out of a 25-mile-thick border area, was prompted more by the opportunity to pull off a fait accompli against its divided Arab opponents than by immediate needs to protect its northern settlements in the Galilee against PLO violations of the ceasefire. And the Begin government's decision to push on to Beirut to decisively smash the main PLO bastions was understandably the result of being confirmed in its supposition that the Syrians would hold back from a main-force engagement with the Israelis in Lebanon, and that neither the Russians nor the other Arab countries would run high risks to defend the Palestinians.

The Reagan White House thus would learn—to its surprise—that it was the *weakness* of the Soviets and their clients in the Middle East, not their strength, that precipitated the new round of devastation and violence; and that the deeper political causes were hardly amenable to control by a resurrected John Foster Dulles-style system of U.S. alliances and military bases in the region.

Once again, as during the previous year's unilateral moves by Israel—the bombing of the Iraqi nuclear reactor, the air raid on Beirut, and the extension of Israeli civil law to the disputed Golan Heights—the assumption of a convergence of U.S. and Israel strategic interests was shown to be inoperative at crucial junctures. The Arabs could hardly be expected to join a strategic consensus which gave the Americans no leverage over the Israelis. Post-Sadat Egypt, in particular, considering that Sadat in the Camp David peace process had gambled on the ability of the United States to "deliver" Israel's future compromises on territorial issues and on the regime for Palestinian autonomy in the West Bank, was put in a most vulnerable position vis-à-vis the other Arab states. The Soviets, though immediately shown up as ineffectual in backing their clients (or in getting the United States to sit on Israel) to prevent Jerusalem from pulling off its power play, would reap the longer-term rewards of Arab lack of confidence in the ability of the United States to control Israel.

Within the administration, these shocking realizations galvanized a consensus behind the views of Secretary of Defense Weinberger that the Israelis had to be publicly brought to heel while the Arabs were given fresh assurances that the United States was truly committed to an "evenhanded" approach to the still-outstanding issues between them and Israel. With only Secretary of State Haig objecting, President Reagan insisted that the Israelis lift their siege of Beirut and allow the Palestinians to be escorted out of Lebanon safely by a multinational force including U.S. units, and that the Israelis commit themselves to withdraw from Lebanon as soon as either a multinational presence or a reconstituted Lebanese government was able to restore order.*

---

* Secretary of State Haig's position was closer to that of the Begin government's view that only if Israel demonstrated the capability and will to decisively destroy all the PLO strong-

The crisis peaked in mid-August as the Israelis, interrupting the ceasefire that was supposed to provide Ambassador Habib with the context for negotiating the evacuation of the Palestinians, launched a new round of air attacks on PLO strongholds in West Beirut. President Reagan arranged for himself to be photographed making an angry phone call to Prime Minister Begin from the Oval Office, with the newly appointed Secretary of State Shultz standing nearby. The photograph appeared in the newspapers on August 13, accompanied by a White House news release explaining that "The President was shocked . . . when he learned of the heavy Israeli bombardment of West Beirut. As a result, the President telephoned Prime Minister Begin . . . [and] expressed his outrage over this latest round of massive military action. He emphasized that Israel's action halted Ambassador Habib's negotiations for the peaceful resolution of the Beirut crisis when they were at the point of success. The result has been more needless destruction and bloodshed. The President made it clear that it is imperative that the cease-fire in place be observed absolutely in order for negotiations to proceed."[8]

A denouement of sorts came a month later when Israeli troops occupied West Beirut to restore order in response to the assassination of the newly elected Christian president of Lebanon, Bashir Gemayel. Once again the Begin government acted unilaterally, and once again the Reagan administration demanded Israeli withdrawal. Identical statements by the White House and State Department said "There is no justification in our view for Israel's continued military presence in West Beirut and we call for an immediate pullback."[9] A few days later, on September 18, in Palestinian detention camps within the area controlled by the Israeli army, Lebanese Christian militiamen massacred scores of Palestinian men, women, and children in retaliation for the murder of President-elect Gemayel. The Reagan administration now turned the screws even harder on the Begin government. President Reagan summoned the Israeli ambassador to "demand that the Israeli government immediately withdraw its forces from West Beirut," and announced that an enlarged con-

---

holds in Lebanon could the international community get the PLO leadership and their Arab friends in neighboring countries to agree to a full evacuation of the PLO guerillas from Lebanon. According to this reasoning, a U.S. insistence that the Israelis not complete their military strangulation of Beirut would prematurely reduce the pressure on the PLO to agree to such evacuation, and might lead to a longer and bloodier war of attrition.

tingent of U.S. marines was being dispatched to Lebanon to join other elements of the multinational peacekeeping force. U.S. defense department officials hinted that U.S. aid levels to Israel might have to be reappraised if Israel did not comply with the President's demand. The Israeli government, stunned by the barbarity that had been allowed to take place in an area where its army was supposed to be maintaining public order, stung by popular and opposition party cries of moral responsibility and demands for a judicial inquiry, was for the first time on the defensive for its role in Lebanon. A beleaguered Prime Minister Begin now ordered his troops out of Beirut and its environs.[10] The more nearly complete pacification of Lebanon and arrangements for an evacuation of all Palestinian units from the country coupled with a withdrawal of Syrian and Israeli forces would still have to be worked out.

One major impact on the Reagan foreign policy from the Lebanon crisis was that it allowed the State Department and other experts on the Middle East to instruct the President and his immediate advisers in the White House on the intricacies of the Arab–Israeli conflict and, in particular, the Palestinian issue. A usual vehicle for this (especially with Ronald Reagan), a planned presidential speech on the Middle East, was moved up to September 1, 1982 from its projected delivery date in the fall.

The Reagan speech of September 1, under the slogan of "a fresh start," marked a return to the policy directions set by President Carter during the Camp David negotiations with Prime Minister Begin and President Sadat: first, that there should be full safeguards for Israeli security, both internal and external; second, that there should be a homeland established for the Palestinians on the West Bank and Gaza; third, that the transition to this goal of a Palestinian homeland should take five years, during which Israel should relinquish its claim to sovereignty over the West Bank and Gaza, and accept instead the controlling authority of U.N. Security Council Resolution 242; but fourth, that the United States continues to support Israel in her opposition to the creation of an independent Palestinian state in these territories; fifth, the preferred U.S. solution is for "self-government by the Palestinians of the West Bank and Gaza in association with Jordan"; sixth, that there should be an immediate "freeze" on Israeli settlements in these disputed areas;

and seventh, that "Jerusalem must remain undivided, but its final status should be decided through negotiations."[11]

This new diplomatic emphasis by the Reagan administration was a "fresh start" for Reagan rather than for U.S. foreign policy as it had been evolving before 1981. It marked a return by Reagan to the wisdom of the Carter–Sadat understanding that a preoccupation with the Soviet threat was insufficient for bringing either peace to the Middle East or a limitation of Soviet influence. Sadat's dramatic trip to Jerusalem in 1977 showed Carter that he could make more progress toward peace without directly involving the Soviets. Lebanon showed Reagan that attention to the details of the indigenous political rivalries and conflicting nationalisms of the Middle East would produce relevant mediational efforts, and that attempts to repolarize the region on an East–West basis would only enlarge Soviet influence.

THE "CRUSADE FOR FREEDOM"

The Reagan administration's earlier more simplified view of the international interests of the United States as sufficiently defined by the fight against the Soviet Union and Marxism-Leninism also steered the United States into an embarrassing confrontation with reality off the coast of South America, in the form of a cluster of hard rocks called the Falkland Islands by the British and the Malvinas by the Argentinians.

The neo-Dullesian good-guys–bad-guys world view had been given intellectual respectability by political scientist Jeane Kirkpatrick, whose influential *Commentary* article "Dictatorships and Double Standards" brought her to the attention of candidate Reagan and led to her appointment as Ambassador to the United States. Under the Kirkpatrick formulation, which was adopted by Reagan and fit rather well with Alexander Haig's own predilections, the "authoritarian" Argentine junta, led by General Leopoldo Galtieri, was perceived as a key ally of the United States in its campaign to counter the efforts of the Marxist-Leninist "totalitarians" to take over Latin America.[12] The courtship of the Galtieri junta by Reagan, Haig, Weinberger, and Kirkpatrick, and their citations of human rights "progress" by the regime in order to reverse congressionally imposed restrictions on arms sales to the Argentinians, undoubtedly was a major factor in Galtieri's calculation that his April 1982 invasion of the Falklands to wrest them away from Britain would be allowed to stand as a fait accompli. The junta's presumption was that the United States would not countenance, let alone help, the British resort to force to retake the islands.

Indeed, for almost a month after the invasion by Argentina, the Reagan administration acted to bear out Galtieri's confidence. The United States refrained from taking sides on the competing claims of sovereignty and even on the more limited grounds of the peaceful settlement of international disputes. As the British naval task force sailed toward the Falklands, Secretary of State Haig tried to act as mediator, hoping to avert a shooting war between two allies of the United States by commiting Britain to negotiate with Argentina over the future political status of the islands in return for a pullout of Argentina's military forces, followed perhaps by some kind of an international presence to administer the islands during the period of negotiations on their future political status. But neither side was willing to compromise its claim to be the controlling sovereign. Haig could not persuade Prime Minister Thatcher to rescind her demands that the status quo be restored as a precondition for negotiations, nor could he persuade Galtieri that he should pull out his occupying troops before a recognition by Britain of Argentinian sovereignty over the Malvinas.[13]

As the British task force reached the immediate vicinity of the Falklands on April 30, Secretary Haig announced that because his mediation efforts had failed, and since Argentina had violated the international rules against the use of force to settle political disputes between countries, the United States had no choice but to back the United Kingdom. This, of course, reflected Haig's real preferences for the British, as well as Reagan's unwillingness to offend Margaret Thatcher, who was thus far his most cooperative and ideologically compatible ally in NATO. It also appeared to reflect popular sentiment in the United States and the dominant consensus of editorial opinion.

But the U.S. shift to the ground of higher principle at the end of April 1982 had been too late to avert the bloody battle. The generals in Buenos Aires apparently had miscalculated that the British were only bluffing when they dispatched a naval task force, and further miscalculated that even if it came to a clash of arms, a respectable fight at the outset by Argentina would quickly convince the Thatcher government, and the friendly administration in Washington, that this was just one more colonial anachronism that wasn't worth holding on to.

In June, while the British troops tightened the noose on the beleaguered Argentine garrisons still holding out on the islands, President Reagan warmly embraced the British effort before a cheering Parliament in London as part of the great "crusade for Freedom." Voices had been raised, said the President, protesting the sacrifice of British young men "for lumps of rock and earth" so far away in the South Atlantic. "But those young men aren't fighting for mere real estate. They fight for a cause, for the belief that armed aggression must not be allowed to succeed and that people must participate in the decisions of government under the rule of law." [14] The last phrase was an endorsement of the British position, undoubtedly correct, that in a free plebiscite the Falkland Islanders would show an overwhelming preference for retaining British sovereignty.

The British would of course have to work out among themselves later the question of whether their current victory of principle was really worth the human sacrifices and the continuing costs of attempting to sustain this legacy of empire.

However, some of the larger consequences of this unnecessary war would be borne by the United States, for not only did it demonstrate the bankruptcy of the administration's ideological framework for dealing with the Third World, but it also disastrously contributed to the isolation of the United States in the hemisphere brought on by Reagan's alignment of the United States with the oligarchic and anti-reform elements in Central America.

The "East–West" framework for reconsolidating the U.S. (hemi)sphere of influence in the Americas simply disintegrated in the face of the "North–South" pressures brought to a boil by the Falkland crisis. The Argentinians, who previously had been elevated by the Reagan administration to the status of principal cohorts of the United States for fighting Marxist-Leninist subversion throughout Latin America, and who had been providing material help and training to anti-Sandinista and anti-Cuban groups in Central America, were no longer inclined to make Argentina available as a spear-carrier in the crusade for freedom. Argentina would, for a considerable time to come, tend first to the repair of its own security relationships and prideful standing in the hemisphere, and attempt to strengthen bonds with new "friends" who had stood by her (at least diplomatically) during the confrontation with Britain—particularly, Mexico, Venezuela, Nicaragua, and, most shockingly to the ideological preconceptions of the Reaganites, Castro's Cuba. Sorely disappointed at the U.S. support of Britain against them, the Argentinians would now more openly cultivate and expand their growing relationship with the USSR (Argentina had been an important supplier of grain to the Soviets), possibly including the purchase of military equipment from the Russians. More ominously, Argentina would move systematically to reoutfit its armed forces with the most sophisticated weapons available, thus stimulating regional arms races with Chile and Brazil—including perhaps further development of the capacity to produce nuclear weapons by all three of the South American powers.

All in all, U.S. efforts to assert political and economic leadership in Latin America, symbolized by Reagan's Caribbean Basin Initiative, were set back seriously. Embarrassingly, the Reagan administration's attempt to revive a broad cold war coalition in the hemisphere was shown to be a naïve, if not dangerous, illusion.

On the rebound from the setback to the Reagan crusade in the Americas, the administration would only reassert the ideological basis of its grand design—as a global effort to combat Soviet-style totalitarianism and to promote democracy. In ideologically combative cold war rhetoric, the likes of which had not been prominent in the pronouncements of high American officials since the period of John Foster Dulles, the President told the British Parliament that

the Soviet Union runs against the tide of history by denying human freedom and dignity to its citizens. It is also in deep economic difficulty. . . .

Overcentralized, with little or no incentives, year after year the Soviet system pours its best resources into the making of instruments of destruction. . . .

What we see here is a political structure that no longer corresponds to its economic base, a society where productive forces are hampered by political ones. The decay of the Soviet experiment should come as no surprise to us. Wherever the comparisons have been made between free and closed societies—West Germany and East Germany, Austria and Czechoslovakia, Malaysia and Vietnam—it is the democratic countries that are prosperous and responsive to the needs of the people. And one of the simple but overwhelming facts of our time is this: of all the millions of refugees we've seen in the modern world, their flight is always away from, not toward, the Communist world. Today on the NATO line, our military forces face East to prevent a possible invasion. On the other side of the line, the Soviet forces also face East—to prevent their people from leaving.

Throughout the world, intoned Reagan, "man's instinctive desire for freedom and self-determination surfaces again and again" and is now manifest not only in Poland, but also, though less visibly, in the Soviet Union itself.

We cannot ignore the fact that even without our encouragement, there have been and will continue to be repeated explosions against repression in dictatorships. The Soviet Union itself is not immune to this reality. Any system is inherently unstable that has no peaceful means to legitimatize its leaders. In such cases, the very repressiveness of the state ultimately drives people to resist it—if necessary, by force.

Particularly in light of these difficulties in the Communist world, the United States should not hold back from responding actively to Brezhnev's claim that the competition of ideas as systems is fully consistent with the relaxation of tensions and peace.

While we must be cautious about forcing the pace of change [within the Communist world and in other dictatorships], we must not hesitate to declare our ultimate objectives and to take concrete actions to move toward them. . . .

The objective I propose is quite simple to state: to foster the infrastructure of democracy—the system of a free press, unions, political parties, universities—which allows a people to choose their own way, to develop their own culture, to reconcile their own differences, through peaceful means.

The new "crusade for freedom" would include enlarging the information-disseminating capabilities of the Voice of America and its regional affiliates, and getting Congress to remove the post-Vietnam, post-Watergate legislative restrictions on covert operations by U.S. intelligence agencies. "This is not cultural imperialism," argued the President. "It is providing the means for genuine self-determination and protection for diversity."[16]

Hearing Reagan charge in March 1983 that the Soviet Union is "the focus of evil,"[16] many veterans of the early postwar period of foreign policy experienced a sense of déjà vu. It seemed as if the country had returned full circle to the universalistic containment imperatives of the Truman Doctrine and the Dullesian pretensions to liberate the communist world from tyranny.

Critics saw in the revived ideological thrust to American foreign policy a romanticism incompatible with current domestic and international circumstances. Sophisticated defenders of the Reagan crusade saw it as an appropriate and necessary set of myths for mobilizing the resources and will required to maintain an international balance of power against a Soviet Union anxious to exploit its newly arrived status as a global superpower.

THE RESIGNATION OF ALEXANDER HAIG: CAUSES AND EFFECTS

In resigning as Secretary of State on June 25, 1982, Alexander Haig wrote President Reagan that "it has become clear to me that the foreign policy on which we embarked together was shifting from that careful course which we laid out." [17] Unlike former Secretary of State Cyrus Vance, who also claimed to have resigned on principle, and who elaborated on this in a commencement address at Harvard University and in press interviews, (see above, pp. 461–63), Haig did not publicly elaborate on his cryptic formal resignation statement. The President refused to provide a public explanation for Haig's resignation even when pressed by reporters at press conferences—a refusal which lent credence to the widespread speculation, fueled by leaks to the press by White House aides, that the proud and ambitious ex-general and aide-de-camp of Nixon and Kissinger had been frustrated more in his power drives than in his policies.

According to Haig's rivals in the White House and National Security Council, the "beginning of the end" started even before the inauguration of President Reagan, when the Secretary-designate met with the President-elect to define the authority the Secretary of State would have in the new administration. Haig was reported to have asked for control of virtually everything touching on foreign affairs, from crisis contingency planning to food policy to arms control negotiations to all administration contacts with foreign officials and any official contacts with the press. After Haig's resignation in the summer of 1982, the *Washington Post* obtained a copy of the "talking paper" Haig used to prepare for this meeting with Reagan, which confirmed the allegations of the White House officials. Validated by Haig's associates as authentic, the "talking paper" has Haig telling the President-elect that within the area of foreign affairs, Reagan's expressed concept of "Cabinet Government" required that "the Secretary of State be your Vicar for the community of Departments having an interest in the several dimensions of foreign policy." To manage the development of policy alternatives in the wide range of fields he enumerated, Haig would inform Reagan that "you must have a single manager who can integrate the views of all your Cabinet Officers and prepare for you the range of policy choices." To assure this, "I propose to establish a number of interdepartmental groups which will include representation from all of the Departments who have a role to play. All of these NSC subcommittees will be chaired by State except where there is a clear prevailing interest as, for example, at Treasury or Defense." And the Secretary-designate would indeed ask for tight control over all external contacts:

All contacts with foreign officials must be conducted at the State Department—otherwise, allies and adversaries will exploit the opportunity to drive a wedge between us on matters of policy.

In the same vein, there must be no independent press contact with the office of your National Security Adviser. I must be your only spokesmen on foreign affairs.[18]

Not surprisingly, Reagan was persuaded by his close associates from California and the presidential election campaign—most of whom would now staff the White House and the National Security Council—to deny Haig such a centralization of power. And from that point on, according to Haig's perspective, they did not let up on their "guerrilla campaign" to undercut his authority with the President. Both sides in this rivalry were confirmed in their suspiciousness of one another by a series of incidents that took place over the next eighteen months—some petty, some having to do with the organization of the government, some involving disagreements over high policy: Haig's impromptu, but constitutionally wrong, "I'm in charge" statement while the President was receiving emergency hospital treatment after the attempt on his life; the Secretary of State's tantrum at being informed that Vice President Bush was being put in charge of "crisis management"; Haig's strong representations of State Department positions opposing the administration's lifting of the embargo on grain sales to the USSR, opposing sanctions against the West Europeans for fulfilling their gas pipeline equipment contracts with the USSR; briefings to reporters by White House aides about Haig's threats to resign; real and imagined slights to the Secretary and his wife on accommodations and travel arrangements during the President's European "summit" trip in the summer of 1982; the whispering campaign inspired by some of Haig's opponents in the government that he had conspired with the Begin government on the Israeli invasion of Lebanon in 1982; Secretary of Defense Weinberger's trip to Saudi Arabia and statements there undercutting Haig's statements from Jerusalem in support of Israel during the Lebanon crisis. What was surprising in all of this, however, was that Haig, a long veteran of Washington intrigue (and a protege of that master bureaucratic infighter, Henry Kissinger) should have taken this all quite so personally.

Haig's mistake, as the *New York Times*'s James Reston put it, "was to take these incidents as an affront to him personally and the authority of his office. It is a very old tragedy in Washington: people here fail in politics and the press when they begin to think they *are* what they, for a short while, merely *represent*." [19]

Haig's tragedy was also the nation's, however. By allowing himself to fall into the trap of petty bickering that undercut his authority, he helped contribute to the hold of amateurs in international relations over the country's foreign policy during the first half of the Reagan administration, and thereby retarded the education of the President out of his ideological simplicities. [20]

Perhaps the President would take instruction better from his new Secretary of State, George Shultz. Reagan personally knew and had great respect for the soft-spoken former professor, economic policy maker, and corporation executive. Some of the modifications in the administration's foreign policy stance in the fall of 1982—a more nuanced approach to the Arab-Israeli conflict, a less confrontationist reaction to NATO allies who insisted on implementing the gas pipeline deals they had negotiated with the USSR, a tamping down of the shrill alarms about the Marxist-Leninist threat in Central America—reflected at least the style of the pragmatic Shultz. [21]

But in crucial issues of grand strategy having to do directly with the Soviet–American military balance, Shultz, unlike Haig, could not claim any professional expertise. Thus the departure of Haig left high-level policy-making in the defense and arms control fields almost totally in the hands of three amateur geopoliticians: Secretary of Defense Weinberger, National Security Adviser Clark, and the President himself.

To be sure, there was military expertise aplenty in the Pentagon,

the National Security Council staff, the CIA, the Arms Control
and Disarmament Agency, the career foreign service, and on the
delegations to the various Soviet–American arms-control negotiations. However, when it came to resolving the inevitable policy disputes within and between these agencies, and to making controlling
budgetary decisions on defense expenditures, the geopolitical philosophy and knowledge (or lack of it) of those at the very top would be
determinative.

THE POWER OF FACE

Was the occasional glimmer of moderation halfway through
Reagan's 1981–85 term a portent of a more basic adaptation to complexity? The line between style and substance in foreign policy is
always blurry. The public postures struck by American presidents
create expectations in the domestic body politic which then cannot
be easily contradicted without a loss in credibility—a vital factor in
a politician's power. Foreign statesmen, aware of the central role of
public opinion in the American democracy, also clearly mark the
stance and demeanor of the President. He does indeed, as John F.
Kennedy said, "sit on a conscpicuous stage."

No one could be more conscious of the power of worlds and appearances than Ronald Reagan. The screen actor first got his name
on the national political marquee by virtue of The Speech—his
spellbinding, flawlessly delivered endorsement of the Republican
1964 presidential candidate, Barry Goldwater, and the free-enter-
prise, anti-government brand of conservative populism that Goldwater represented—which Reagan repeated to thousands of audiences across the country. The newly acquired political charisma
served him well in his own successful 1966 campaign for the gov-
ernorship of California—a state in which image is virtually synon-
omous with politics. But as governor, realizing that the state legislature was unwilling to allow him to put his ideology into practice,
he adapted his programs rather substantially and appropriately
changed his image to cater to the California electorate's preferences
for pragmatism on the part of its public officials.

Now as President, feeling that the broad public shared his basic
ideology, Reagan was considerably less willing to alter direction. "Stay
the course!" became his favorite motto. When frustrated in his pol-

icy initiatives he preferred to draw on his skills and reputation as The Great Communicator to create an aroused public opinion that would pressure reluctant congressmen to fall into line behind his programs.

The most determined attempts to substitute rhetoric for reassessment of basic policies came in the defense and arms control fields. Casper Weinberger's easy talk of fighting and winning ("prevailing in") nuclear wars was scaring the American people and U.S. NATO allies more than the Russians. In the 1982 congressional elections, a ballot initiative proposing a "freeze" on all further testing, production, and deployment of nuclear weapons was passed by the voters in eight out of nine states and in municipal and county elections throughout the country, despite a campaign blitz against the measure by the President and his lieutenants charging that such a freeze would perpetuate Soviet strategic superiority, and that voter approval of the ballot measures, while not binding on the government, would weaken the U.S. hand in its arms control negotiations with the Russians. The congressional elections also provided a pro-freeze majority in the House of Representatives. The Catholic bishops were formulating a pastoral letter challenging the morality of the administration's nuclear war doctrines.

In response to the growing opposition, the President and his spokesmen purged the most militaristic phrases from their public pronouncements. References to fighting and prevailing in nuclear war were kept to a minimum. The essential purpose of U.S. arms was to *deter* war, and, as Reagan neatly put it, "to preserve freedom" in case deterrence failed. But despite the intensifying pressures from the Congress and the administration's own economists to cut back on military expenditures, the White House continued to endorse most of the Pentagon's requests for new weapons, many of which were designed to enhance nuclear war-fighting capabilities.*

A credible nuclear war-fighting capability was the primary rationale for the controversial MX missile, the highly accurate, ten war-

---

*The President's fiscal 1984 budget proposals to the Congress showed a token $8 billion reduction from the Pentagon's original requests, but, even so, contemplated spending $239 billion on military programs in 1984, a 14 percent increase over 1983. Almost all of the reductions reflected a manpower and wage freeze. Virtually every weapon on Secretary Weinberger's initial shopping list survived the administration's own internal budgetary review. Whether they would survive the scrutiny of an increasingly skeptical Congress remained a big question mark as this book went to press.

head ICBM to replace the existing Minuteman missiles—"the right missile at the right time," argued the President. The MX had a basing problem (how to prevent it from being destroyed by a Soviet first strike with comparable missiles) that might yet prevent Congress from funding its production and deployment. It also had an image problem—one of its principal targets being unlaunched Soviet missiles still in their silos, wasn't the MX itself a first-strike weapon? (See above, p. 592).

Reagan would take care of the image problem: In a detailed statement endorsing a clustered ("Dense Pack") basing option for the MX—the kind of detailed statement usually reserved for the Secretary of Defense—Reagan intoned that the new missile was "absolutely essential to maintain America's deterrent capability to deter war and protect our nation." Accordingly, he was giving the MX the name of "Peacekeeper." [22]

Ironically, the critics of the MX were the ones most delighted by this Presidential intervention. By mid-term, having stumbled numerous times in press conferences over the intracacies of strategic policy, Reagan, by taking it upon himself to elucidate the rationale for the new missile, reinforced impressions in the Congress that "political" rather than objective strategic considerations lay in back of this and other administration proposals in the military and arms control fields. And in christening the monster ICBM "Peacekeeper" Reagan handed media pundits an irresistible opportunity to comment on the similarity of rhetoric to the doublespeak which novelist George Orwell had predicted would be the stock-in-trade of the world's rulers in 1984. A skeptical Congress sent Reagan's latest MX proposal back for further study.

Nor did the President do much to erase the impression that for him face was the essence of power, when, early in 1983, in response to growing alarms from U.S. embassies in Western Europe that the Soviets were gaining the propaganda advantage in the battle of arms control proposals, he appointed a set of high-level interdepartmental coordinating committees to work on—not the substance or negotiability of the U.S. proposals—but their public relations aspects. [23] Meanwhile, Vice President Bush was dispatched to Europe to "sell" the NATO allies on the President's sincerity about arms control. And in a proposal calculated to be rejected by the Soviets, Reagan said he would be prepared to meet with General Secretary

Andropov anytime, any place "to sign an agreement banning U.S. and Soviet intermediate-range, land-based nuclear missile weapons from the face of the earth." [24]

Similarly, it was quintessential Hollywood showmanship when Reagan, pre-empting the cold water his own review commission was about to throw on the MX, called at the end of March 1983 for crash development of laser and particle-beam weapons to be stationed in outer space with the mission of vaporizing enemy ICBMs minutes after launch. "I know this is a formidable technical task," said the President, "one that may not be accomplished before the end of the century. But isn't it worth every investment necessary to free the world from the threat of nuclear war?" [25]

It would take more than public relations campaigns to restore international credibility both to the country's negotiating stances and to its deterrent threats. Neither professions of peaceful intent nor machismo rhetoric, nor an artful mix of the two, would be sufficient. Appearances are a necessary ingredient of a nation's power, but they count for little if disembodied from a substantive base. Thus Reagan's grand strategy of building up "real" power—the military arsenal—so as to be able, once again, to negotiate from strength. However, the goal of negotiating from strength, if that required military *advantage* over our principal rival, was romanticism, not realism.

If the United States yet retained a potential power advantage, it was in the attractiveness of the still-noble American purpose of liberty and justice for all. The contagious conviction that right makes might could still be the essence of America's international influence. Sensing this, Reagan returned in 1983 to the good guys versus bad guys worldview of the Truman doctrine to mobilize support for the deepening U.S. intervention in Central America. [26]

But power needed to be more strongly grounded in purposes, policy in political philosophy, and international action in respect for other peoples' values. Slogans and star-wars fantasies could not reduce the urgent need for new and deeper thinking about U.S. foreign relations.

NOTES

1. THE IRREDUCIBLE NATIONAL INTEREST AND BASIC PREMISES ABOUT WORLD CONDITIONS

1. Preamble, *Constitution of the United States.*
2. Lyndon B. Johnson, quoted in the *New York Times,* April 22, 1965.

2. MORAL PURPOSES AND THE BALANCE-OF-POWER CONSIDERATION

1. John F. Kennedy, Inaugural Address, January 20, 1961; *Department of State Bulletin,* February 6, 1961, pp. 175–76.
2. Jimmy Carter, question-and-answer session with a group of publishers, editors, and broadcasters, May 20, 1977, in *Public Papers of the Presidents of the United States: Jimmy Carter, 1977,* 1:147.
3. For the period from McKinley to Franklin Roosevelt, see Robert E. Osgood, *Ideals and Self-Interest in American Foreign Relations* (Chicago: University of Chicago Press, 1953).

3. THE SHATTERING OF EXPECTATIONS

1. A thorough scholarly account of the wartime diplomacy of Franklin D. Roosevelt and the first two years of the Truman administration is provided by John Lewis Gaddis, *The United States and the Origins of the Cold War, 1941–1947* (New York: Columbia University Press, 1972). See also James MacGregor Burns, *Roosevelt: The Soldier of Freedom* (New York: Harcourt Brace Jovanovich, 1970); and Daniel Yergen, *Shattered Peace: The Origins of the Cold War and the National Security State* (Boston: Houghton Mifflin, 1977), pp. 3–137.
2. See Harry S. Truman, *Memoirs: Year of Decisions* (New York: Doubleday, 1955), 1:332–412.
3. *Ibid.,* p. 70.
4. *Ibid.,* p. 71.
5. William D. Leahy, *I Was There* (New York: McGraw Hill, 1950), pp. 351–52.
6. Truman, *Memoirs,* 1:85–87.
7. See especially Gar Alperwovitz, *Atomic Diplomacy: Hiroshima and Potsdam* (New York: Simon and Schuster, 1965).
8. The quotations are from Truman's letter to Byrnes of January 5, 1946. Truman, *Memoirs,* 1:551–52.
9. Truman, *Memoirs: Years of Trial and Hope* (New York: Doubleday, 1956), 2:11.

10. Walter Mills, *The Forrestal Diaries* (New York: Viking, 1952), p. 102.

11. *Ibid.*, p. 129.

12. *Ibid.*, pp. 135–40.

13. Truman, *Memoirs*, 2:95.

14. *Ibid.*, pp. 96–97.

15. Truman, *Memoirs*, 1:551–52.

16. John C. Campbell, *Defense of the Middle East: Problems of American Policy* (New York: Praeger, 1960), p. 33.

17. Truman, *Memoirs*, 2:100. Actually, the Greek Communists and their local allies were prosecuting their insurrection against the Greek monarchy contrary to the wishes of Stalin. The Greek Communists were aided by Tito, with whom Stalin was having an altercation; and, in any event, Stalin preferred to keep his spheres-of-influence agreement with Churchill, consigning Greece to British control. On this, see Yergin, *Shattered Peace*, pp. 288–95.

18. Address by the Secretary of State at Princeton University, February 22, 1947.

19. Joseph M. Jones, *The Fifteen Weeks* (New York: Viking, 1955), pp. 138–41. Dean Acheson's account of the February 27, 1947, meeting in the White House is in his *Present at the Creation* (New York: Norton, 1969), p. 219.

20. Jones, pp. 157, 162.

21. Address by President Truman to Congress, March 12, 1947.

22. W. W. Rostow, *The United States and the World Arena* (New York: Harper, 1960), p. 209.

23. *Department of State Bulletin* (May 11, 1947), 16:410, 920–24.

24. Quoted by Harry Bayard Price, *The Marshall Plan and Its Meaning* (Ithaca: Cornell University Press, 1955), p. 22.

25. Jones, pp. 251–52. See also George F. Kennan, *Memoirs 1925–1950* (Boston: Atlantic, Little, Brown, 1967), pp. 335–45.

26. *Department of State Bulletin*, June 15, 1947, pp. 1159–60.

27. Price, pp. 24–29; Rostow, pp. 209–13.

28. X (George Kennan), "The Sources of Soviet Conduct," *Foreign Affairs* (July 1947), pp. 566–82.

29. *Ibid.*, passim.

4. 1948–1950: INTERNAL DIALOGUE ON THE COMPONENTS OF THE BALANCE OF POWER

1. Walter Millis, *The Forrestal Diaries* (New York: Viking, 1951), p. 341.

2. This interpretation of Marshall's views relies heavily on Warner R. Schilling's thorough study, "The Politics of National Defense: Fiscal 1950," in Warner R. Schilling, Paul Y. Hammond, and Glen H. Snyder, *Strategy, Politics, and Defense Budgets* (New York: Columbia University Press, 1962), pp. 5–266, passim.

3. Millis, pp. 240, 350.

4. *Ibid.*, 350–51.

5. This review is the subject of a detailed monograph by Paul Hammond entitled "NSC-68: Prologue to Rearmament," and published in Schilling, Hammond, and Snyder, *Strategy, Politics, and Defense Budgets*, pp. 271–378. My account of the substance of arguments and activities surrounding NSC-68 relies heavily on the Hammond monograph.

6. See Edward S. Flash, Jr., *Economic Advice and Presidential Leadership: The Council of Economic Advisers* (New York: Columbia University Press, 1965), pp. 39–52.

7. Coral Bell, *Negotiations From Strength* (New York: Knopf, 1963), pp. 6–10.

5. THE PRIMACY OF BALANCE-OF-POWER CONSIDERATIONS DURING THE KOREAN WAR

1. Samuel P. Huntington, *The Common Defense: Strategic Programs in National Politics* (New York: Columbia University Press, 1961), pp. 59–61.

2. Harry S. Truman, *Memoirs: Years of Trial and Hope* (New York: Doubleday, 1956), 2:341.

3. *Ibid.*, p. 380.

4. *Ibid.*, pp. 387–88.

5. *Ibid.*, pp. 397–98.

6. *Ibid.*, p. 403.

7. *Ibid.*, p. 408.

8. *Ibid.*, p. 432.

9. U.S. Senate, Committee on Armed Services and Committee on Foreign Relations, *Hearings: Military Situation in the Far East*, 82d Congress, 1st session, 1951, pp. 731–32, 1219.

10. Truman, *Memoirs*, 2:437.

11. See Robert E. Osgood, *NATO: The Entangling Alliance* (Chicago: University of Chicago Press, 1963), pp. 78–79.

12. *Ibid.*, pp. 70–71.

13. *Hearings: Military Situation in the Far East.*

14. For the full text of Acheson's remarks see his January 12, 1950, speech before the National Press Club, Washington, D.C., in *Department of State Bulletin*, January 23, 1950, pp. 111–18.

15. Department of State, *United States Relations With China* (Washington: GPO, 1949), p. 383.

16. Quoted by Tang Tsou, *America's Failure in China, 1941–1950* (Chicago: University of Chicago Press, 1963), p. 363. Dr. Tsou thoroughly documents the prevailing U.S. consensus of the late 1940s that the stakes on the China mainland were not worth a U.S. military combat intervention.

17. Quoted by John C. Sparrow, *History of Personnel Demobilization* (Washington: Dept. of Army, 1951), p. 380. See also Tang Tsou, p. 366.

18. Harry S. Truman, Press conference of November 30, 1950; see Truman, *Memoirs*, 2:395–96.

6. A NEW LOOK FOR LESS EXPENSIVE POWER

1. Paul Y. Hammond, in Warner R. Schilling, Paul Y. Hammond, and Glenn H. Snyder, *Strategy, Politics, and Defense Budgets* (New York: Columbia University Press, 1962), pp. 359–61; Glenn H. Snyder, in *ibid.*, p. 407.

2. Dwight D. Eisenhower, *Mandate for Change: The White House Years 1953–1956* (New York: Doubleday, 1963), p. 74.

3. *Ibid.*, pp. 172–73.

4. *Ibid.*, p. 535.

5. *Ibid.*, pp. 535, 541.

6. Edward S. Flash, Jr., *Economic Advice and Presidential Leadership: The Council of Economic Advisers* (New York: Columbia University Press, 1965), pp. 100–2.

7. The period of the formulation of the New Look is described in detail by Snyder, 386–456; Charles J. V. Murphy in a series of *Fortune* articles (January 1953, September 1953, November 1953, December 1953, January 1956, February 1956, and March 1956); and in Robert J. Donovan, *Eisenhower: The Inside Story* (New York: Harper, 1956), pp. 17–19, 55–59. The following discussion is a brief amalgam of these various accounts.

8. Eisenhower, radio address, March 19, 1953, in *New York Times,* May 20, 1953.

9. See Robert E. Osgood, *NATO: The Entangling Alliance* (Chicago: University of Chicago Press, 1963), pp. 89–90.

10. For details on the formulation and contents of NSC-162, see Snyder, pp. 406–10.

11. Snyder, in *Ibid.,* pp. 414–15.

12. *Ibid.,* pp. 436–38.

13. John Foster Dulles, "The Evolution of Foreign Policy," address to the Council on Foreign Relations, January 12, 1954, in *Department of State Bulletin,* January 25, 1964, pp. 107–10.

14. John Foster Dulles, "Policy for Security and Peace," *Foreign Affairs* (April 1954), pp. 353–64.

7. COMMITMENTS AND COERCION: DULLES' PSYCHOLOGY OF POWER

1. On Dulles' *Weltanschauung,* see Michael A. Guhin, *John Foster Dulles: A Statesman and His Times* (New York: Columbia University Press, 1972).

2. John Foster Dulles, "Report on the Near East," in *Department of State Bulletin,* June 15, 1953, pp. 831–35.

3. John C. Campbell, *Defense of the Middle East: Problems of American Policy* (New York: Praeger, 1960), pp. 49–62.

4. Eisenhower, press conference, April 7, 1954, in *New York Times,* April 8, 1954.

5. From Eisenhower letter to Churchill, April 4, 1954. Quoted by Eisenhower in *Mandate for Change: The White House Years 1953–1956* (New York: Doubleday, 1963), p. 346.

6. *Ibid.,* 354.

7. See Chalmers Roberts, "The Day We Didn't Go To War," *The Reporter* (September 14, 1954).

8. Eisenhower, *Mandate for Change,* p. 352.

9. *Ibid.,* p. 354.

10. Dulles, radio-TV address, March 8, 1955, in *Department of State Bulletin,* March 21, 1955, p. 463.

11. In *Department of State Bulletin,* March 28, 1955, pp. 526–27.

12. Eisenhower, *Mandate for Change,* pp. 476–77.

13. Quotes are from February 1955 Eisenhower letters to Churchill, appearing in *Mandate for Change,* pp. 470–75.

14. Emmet John Hughes, *The Ordeal of Power: A Political Memoir of the Eisenhower Years* (New York: Atheneum, 1963), p. 208.

15. James Shepley, "How Dulles Averted War," *Life* (January 16, 1956), pp. 70ff.

16. *Ibid.*

8. WAGING PEACE: THE EISENHOWER FACE

1. Eisenhower's role in controlling the less temperate members of his administration is well described in Robert A. Divine, *Eisenhower and the Cold War* (New York: Oxford University Press, 1981).

2. Emmet John Hughes, *The Ordeal of Power: A Political Memoir of the Eisenhower Years* (New York: Atheneum, 1963), pp. 343–44.

3. Quoted by Sherman Adams, *Firsthand Report: The Story of the Eisenhower Administration* (New York: Harper, 1961), p. 89.

4. Dwight D. Eisenhower, *The White House Years: Waging Peace, 1956–1961* (New York: Doubleday, 1965), 2:365.

5. Adams, *Firsthand Report,* p. 89.

6. Hughes, p. 109.

7. Dwight D. Eisenhower, *Mandate for Change: The White House Years 1953–1956* (New York: Doubleday, 1963), p. 149.

8. "The Chance for Peace," address by the President, April 16, 1953, to the American Society of Newspaper Editors, in *Department of State Bulletin*, April 27, 1953, pp. 599–603.

9. Eisenhower, *Mandate for Change*, p. 251.

10. *Ibid.*, p. 252.

11. *Ibid.*, pp. 251–55.

12. Adams, *Firsthand Report*, p. 112.

13. Quoted by Andrew Berding, *Dulles On Diplomacy* (Princeton: Van Nostrand, 1965), p. 24.

14. See Roscoe Drummond and Gaston Coblentz, *Duel at the Brink: John Foster Dulles' Command of American Power* (New York: Doubleday, 1960), pp. 134–39, for a vivid description of Dulles' reactions to the cheering throngs and Soviet embraces during the May 15, 1955, signing ceremonies in Vienna.

15. See Coral Bell, *Negotiation from Strength: A Study in the Politics of Power* (New York: Knopf, 1963), p. 127.

16. *Ibid.*, pp. 111–23, passim.

17. Adams, pp. 176–77.

18. Eisenhower, *Mandate for Change*, p. 506.

19. Radio-Television address by the President, July 15, 1955, in Department of State, *American Foreign Policy, 1950–1955: Basic Documents* (Washington: GPO, 1955), 2:2005–8.

20. Robert J. Donovan, *Eisenhower: The Inside Story* (New York: Harper, 1956), pp. 345–46.

21. Adams, pp. 177–78.

22. Donovan, pp. 348–49.

23. James Reston, *New York Times*, July 22, 1955.

24. Proposal by the President at the Geneva Conference of Heads of Government, July 21, 1955, in Department of State, *American Foreign Policy 1950–1955, Basic Documents*, 2:2842–43.

25. Statement by the President at the Geneva Conference of Heads of Government, July 23, 1955, *ibid.*, p. 2014.

26. Adams, pp. 178–79.

27. Eisenhower, *Mandate for Change*, p. 530.

9. COMPLICATING THE PREMISES: SUEZ AND HUNGARY

1. John Robinson Beal, *John Foster Dulles: 1888–1959* (New York: Harper, 1959), p. 228.

2. See Walt W. Rostow, *The United States in the World Arena* (New York: Harper, 1960), pp. 364–65.

3. Robert J. Donovan, *Eisenhower: The Inside Story* (New York: Harper, 1956), p. 388.

4. Sherman Adams, *Firsthand Report: The Story of the Eisenhower Administration* (New York: Harper, 1961), p. 245.

5. Anthony Eden, *Full Circle* (London: Cassell, 1960), pp. 374–75.

6. Dwight D. Eisenhower, *The White House Years: Waging Peace, 1956–1961* (New York: Doubleday, 1965), 2:33, 34 n; and Townsend Hoopes, *The Devil and John Foster Dulles* (Boston: Atlantic, Little, Brown, 1973), pp. 330–44.

7. Eisenhower, *Waging Peace*, p. 50.

8. *Ibid.*, p. 38.

9. *Ibid.*, p. 53.

10. *Ibid.*, p. 80.

11. *Ibid.*, appendix, p. 680.

12. *Ibid.*, p. 91.

13. *Ibid.*, p. 91.

14. *Ibid.*, p. 90.

15. Dulles, speech to Council on Foreign Relations, October 6, 1952. Quoted by Beal, *John Foster Dulles*, p. 312.

16. Quoted by Beal, pp. 311–12.

17. Dulles, radio-television address, in *Department of State Bulletin*, February 9, 1953, 28:711, pp. 207–16.

18. Message from the Allied Commandants in Berlin to the Representative of the Soviet Control Commission, June 18, 1953, and letter from the Allied Commandants in Berlin to the Soviet Military Commander in Berlin, June 24, 1953; texts in Department of State, *American Foreign Policy 1950–1955: Basic Documents* (Washington: GPO), 2:1744–45.

19. Dulles, press conference, June 30, 1953, in *American Foreign Policy 1950–1955: Basic Documents*, pp. 1745–46.

20. *American Foreign Policy 1950–1955: Basic Documents*, p. 1750.

21. Warren R. Schilling, Paul Y. Hammond, and Glenn H. Snyder, *Strategy, Politics, and Defense Budgets* (New York: Columbia University Press, 1962), pp. 407–9.

22. Eisenhower, *Waging Peace*, pp. 87–89.

23. Roscoe Drummond and Gaston Coblentz, *Duel at the Brink: John Foster Dulles' Command of American Power* (New York: Doubleday, 1960), pp. 180–81.

24. *Ibid.*, p. 181. See also Andrew Berding, *Dulles on Diplomacy* (Princeton: Van Nostrand, 1965), pp. 115–16.

10. SPUTNIK: NEW ATTENTION TO MATERIAL FACTORS OF POWER

1. See Arnold L. Horelick and Myron Rush, *Strategic Power and Soviet Foreign Policy* (Chicago: University of Chicago Press, 1966).

2. Dwight D. Eisenhower, *The White House Years: Waging Peace, 1956–1961* (New York: Doubleday, 1965), 2:205.

3. Radio-Television address by the President, November 7, 1957; see *Waging Peace*, pp. 223–25.

4. The most complete description, compiled from numerous open sources, is by Morton H. Halperin in his "The Gaither Committee and the Policy Process," *World Politics* (April 1961), pp. 360–84.

5. Eisenhower, *Waging Peace*, pp. 219–23.

6. Halperin, passim.

7. Samuel P. Huntington, *The Common Defense: Strategic Programs in National Politics* (New York: Columbia University Press, 1961), p. 94.

8. From Eisenhower's account of November 1957 NSC deliberations, *Waging Peace*, pp. 221–22.

9. Quoted by Huntington, p. 101.

10. Eisenhower, *Waging Peace*, p. 222.

11. Reply by the Secretary of State to a question at a news conference, February 11, 1958, in *Department of State Bulletin*, March 3, 1958, p. 335.

11. CONDITIONED RESPONSES TO NEW CHALLENGES

1. Department of State, *American Foreign Policy: Current Documents* (Washington: GPO, 1957), pp. 784–85.

2. *Ibid.*, p. 790.

3. *Ibid.,* pp. 787–90, passim.

4. Statement by the Secretary of State before the Committees on Foreign Relations and Armed Services of the Senate, January 14, 1957, in *ibid.,* pp. 796–97.

5. *Ibid.,* p. 800.

6. Public Law 85–87, Congress, 1st session, H.J. Res. 117, *American Foreign Policy: Current Documents,* 1957, pp. 816–17.

7. Documents Nos. 298–303, in *ibid.,* pp. 1023–28. See also John C. Campbell, *Defense of the Middle East: Problems of American Policy* (New York: Praeger, 1960), pp. 127–31.

8. Dwight D. Eisenhower, *The White House Years: Waging Peace, 1956–1961* (New York: Doubleday, 1965), 196.

9. White House news conference of August 21, 1957, in *American Foreign Policy: Current Documents,* 1957, p. 199.

10. *Current Digest of the Soviet Press,* 9(2):23.

11. Department of State press release, September 10, 1957, in *Department of State Bulletin,* September 30, 1957.

12. Address by President Eisenhower to the nation, July 15, 1958. Also Special Message of President Eisenhower to the Congress, July 15, 1958. Both in Department of State, *American Foreign Policy: Current Documents,* (Washington: GPO, 1958), pp. 965–67, 969–72.

13. Campbell, *Defense of The Middle East,* pp. 142–44.

14. Eisenhower, *Waging Peace,* p. 290.

15. *Ibid.,* pp. 290–91.

16. Address by the President to the Third Emergency Session of the UN General Assembly, August 13, 1958, in *American Foreign Policy: Current Documents,* 1958, pp. 1032–39.

17. Res. XCIII, Tenth Inter-American Conference, Caracas, Venezuela, March 1–28, 1954, in Department of State, *American Foreign Policy, 1950–1955: Basic Documents* (Washington: GPO), 1:1300–2.

18. *Ibid.*

19. Edwin Lieuwen, *U.S. Policy in Latin America: A Short History* (New York: Praeger, 1965), pp. 88–92.

20. Eisenhower's candid discussion of the intervention in his *Mandate for Change: The White House Years 1953–1956* (New York: Doubleday, 1963), pp. 504–11, details most of the essentials.

21. *Ibid.,* p. 511.

22. Lieuwen, p. 113.

23. Eisenhower, *Waging Peace,* p. 525.

24. Radio-television address by the President, February 21, 1960, in *Department of State Bulletin,* March 7, 1960, pp. 351–53.

25. Address by President Eisenhower to the nation, March 8, 1960, *Department of State Bulletin,* March 28, 1960, pp. 471–74.

26. Eisenhower, *Waging Peace,* p. 530.

27. Statement by the President, July 11, 1960, in *Department of State Bulletin,* August 1, 1960, pp. 318–19.

28. Statement by Under Secretary of State Dillon, September 6, 1960, in *Department of State Bulletin,* October 3, 1960, pp. 533–37.

29. Eisenhower, *Waging Peace,* p. 539.

30. *Ibid.,* p. 533.

31. Arthur M. Schlesinger, Jr., *A Thousand Days: John F. Kennedy in the White House* (Boston: Houghton Mifflin, 1965), p. 222.

32. Eisenhower, *Waging Peace,* pp. 293–94.

33. Memorandum re Formosa Strait Situation, dated September 4, 1958, appendix O, *Waging Peace,* pp. 691–92.

34. For an analysis of the way the Eisenhower administration went about limiting its own options, see Morton H. Halperin and Tang Tsou, "United States Policy Toward the Offshore Islands," *Public Policy* (1966), pp. 119–38.

35. *Ibid.*, p. 304.

36. For a description of the U.S. responses to procedural harassments on the access routes to Berlin during the spring and summer of 1958, see Jean Edward Smith, *The Defense of Berlin* (Baltimore: Johns Hopkins University Press, 1963), pp. 157–60.

37. Note from the Soviet Foreign Ministry, November 27, 1958, in *Department of State Bulletin,* January 19, 1959, pp. 81–89.

38. *New York Times,* November 27, 1958.

39. Quotations are from Eisenhower, *Waging Peace,* pp. 334–49, passim.

40. *Ibid.*, p. 342.

41. *Ibid.*, p. 341.

42. Western Proposal on Berlin (Draft Agreement), June 16, 1959, Department of State account of the Geneva Foreign Ministers' Meeting, May–August, 1959, pp. 312–13.

43. See, for example, Smith, *The Defense of Berlin,* p. 204.

44. Eisenhower's own paraphrase of his confidential letter to Macmillan (sent sometime between July 15 and 20, 1959), in *Waging Peace,* p. 402.

45. *Ibid.*, pp. 405–12.

46. Text in *New York Times,* September 29, 1959.

12. PERCEIVED DEFICIENCIES IN THE NATION'S POWER

1. N. S. Khrushchev, "For New Victories for the World Communist Movement," *World Marxist Review: Problems of Peace and Socialism* (January 1961), pp. 3–28.

2. Arthur M. Schlesinger, Jr., *A Thousand Days: John F. Kennedy in the White House* (Boston: Houghton Mifflin, 1965), p. 302.

3. See Theodore C. Sorensen, *Kennedy* (New York: Harper, 1965), pp. 629–33; and Schlesinger, pp. 340–42.

4. See Schlesinger, pp. 585–91.

5. Address by the President, March 13, 1962, in *Department of State Bulletin,* April 2, 1962, pp. 539–42.

6. State of the Union Message by the President, January 30, 1961.

7. *Ibid.*

8. *Ibid.*

9. Quoted by Sorensen, p. 408.

10. Address by President Kennedy to the Congress, January 25, 1962, in House Document 314, 87th Congress, 2d session.

11. See early sections of the 1961 State of the Union Message for this catalogue of domestic deficiencies.

12. John F. Kennedy, *The Strategy of Peace,* edited by Allan Nevins (New York: Harper, 1960), p. 4.

13. *Ibid.*

14. Quoted by Sorensen, p. 528.

13. ATTENDING TO THE MILITARY BALANCE

1. See Seymour E. Harris, *Economics of the Kennedy Years, and a Look Ahead* (New York: Harper, 1964).

2. Quoted by William W. Kaufmann, *The McNamara Strategy* (New York: Harper, 1964), p. 48.

3. General Maxwell Taylor recounts these doctrinal battles and advances the doctrine of "flexible response" in his *The Uncertain Trumpet* (New York: Harper, 1960).

4. See William W. Kaufmann, ed., *Military Policy and National Security* (Princeton: Princeton University Press, 1956); Robert E. Osgood, *Limited War* (Chicago: University of Chicago Press, 1957); Henry A. Kissinger, *Nuclear Weapons and Foreign Policy* (New York: Harper, 1957); and Bernard Brodie, *Strategy in the Missile Age* (Princeton: Princeton University Press, 1959).

5. *Public Papers of the Presidents of the United States: John F. Kennedy, 1961*, p. 231.

6. See Henry A. Kissinger, *The Troubled Partnership: A Reappraisal of the Atlantic Alliance* (New York: Anchor Books, 1966), especially pp. 106–28. See also Raymond Aaron, *The Great Debate* (New York: Doubleday, 1965).

7. *Public Papers of the Presidents: John F. Kennedy, 1961*, p. 385.

8. See Seyom Brown, "An Alternative to the Grand Design," *World Politics* (January 1965), pp. 231–42.

9. See Theodore C. Sorensen, *Kennedy* (New York: Harper, 1965), p. 567; and Arthur M. Schlesinger, Jr., *A Thousand Days: John F. Kennedy in the White House* (Boston: Houghton Mifflin, 1965), pp. 872–73.

10. Remarks of Secretary of Defense Robert S. McNamara at Commencement Exercises, University of Michigan, Ann Arbor, June 16, 1962, in Department of Defense News Release No. 980-62.

11. *Ibid.*

12. *Ibid.*

13. Press conference of the President of France, November 10, 1962, in *New York Times*, November 11, 1962.

14. I am indebted to Herbert Dinerstein for the domestic analogy.

15. *Public Papers of the Presidents: John F. Kennedy, 1963*, pp. 174–75.

16. Sorensen, *Kennedy*, p. 564; Henry Kissinger, *The Troubled Partnership*, pp. 82–83.

17. Joint statement following discussions with Prime Minister Macmillan—the Nassau Agreement, December 21, 1962, *Public Papers of the Presidents: John F. Kennedy, 1962*, pp. 908–10.

18. Schlesinger, *A Thousand Days*, pp. 865–66.

19. Testimony of the Secretary of Defense before the Senate Committee on Armed Services, February 20, 1963.

20. Testimony before the House Subcommittee on Appropriations, 1963; quoted by Kaufmann, *The McNamara Strategy*, p. 95.

21. Testimony before House Committee on Armed Services, February 1, 1963.

22. Speech to American Society of Newspaper Editors, April 20, 1963.

23. Testimony before subcommittee of Senate Committee on Appropriations, April 24, 1963.

24. *Ibid.*

25. Testimony before Senate Committee on Armed Services, February 21, 1963.

26. Testimony before House Armed Services Committee, January 30, 1963.

27. Testimony before House Armed Services Committee, February 1, 1963.

28. "McNamara Thinks About the Unthinkable," *Saturday Evening Post* (December 1, 1962), pp. 13–19.

29. Testimony before Senate Committee on Armed Services, February 21, 1963.

30. *Ibid.*, February 20, 1963.

31. *Public Papers of the Presidents: John F. Kennedy, 1963*, pp. 890–94.

14. NEW TOOLS FOR THE NEW ARENA: OPPORTUNITIES AND OBSTACLES

1. From an address at La Grande, Oregon, November 9, 1959, in John F. Kennedy, *The Strategy of Peace,* edited by Allan Nevins (New York: Harper, 1960), pp. 107–8.

2. The most comprehensive policy-oriented statement to come out of this group was the book by Max Millikan and Walt Rostow, *A Proposal—Key to an Effective Foreign Policy* (New York: Harper, 1957). A more theoretical treatise is Rostow's *The Stages of Economic Growth: A Non-Communist Manifesto* (London: Cambridge University Press, 1960). Some refinements are added by John Kenneth Galbraith, "A Positive Approach to Foreign Aid," *Foreign Affairs* (April 1961), pp. 444–57.

3. Arthur M. Schlesinger, Jr., *A Thousand Days* (Boston: Houghton Mifflin, 1965), p. 592.

4. Task force quotations are taken from Schlesinger, pp. 195–96.

5. Address by President Kennedy at a White House Reception, March 13, 1961, in *Department of State Bulletin,* April 3, 1961, pp. 471–74.

6. *Ibid.*

7. *Ibid.*

8. Address by Secretary of the Treasury Douglas Dillon to the Inter-American Economic and Social Conference, Punta del Este, Uruguay, August 7, 1961, in *Department of State Bulletin,* August 28, 1961, pp. 356–60.

9. Title I, Charter of Punta del Este, signed August 17, 1961.

10. Theodore C. Sorensen, *Kennedy* (New York: Harper, 1965), p. 535.

11. Tad Szulc, *The Winds of Revolution: Latin America Today—and Tomorrow* (New York: Praeger, 1963), pp. 243–44.

12. Quoted by Sorensen, p. 535.

13. Address by President Kennedy at the White House, March 13, 1962, in *Department of State Bulletin,* April 2, 1962, pp. 539–42.

14. Evaluation of the First Year of the Alliance for Progress by the Ministerial Representatives of the Inter-American Economic and Social Council, meeting in Mexico City, October 22–27, 1962, in *Department of State Bulletin,* December 10, 1962, pp. 897–901.

15. *Ibid.*

16. Address by President Kennedy to the Inter-American Press Association, Miami Beach, Florida, November 18, 1963, in *Department of State Bulletin,* December 9, 1963, pp. 900–4.

17. Millikan and Rostow, *A Proposal,* p. 151.

18. Address by President Kennedy to the Congress, March 13, 1962, House Document 362, 87th Congress, 2d session.

19. Schlesinger, *A Thousand Days,* p. 597.

20. Department of State, *Report to the President of the United States from the Committee to Strengthen the Security of the Free World: The Scope and Distribution of United States Military and Economic Assistance Programs,* March 20, 1963. (Washington: GPO).

21. Address in Salt Lake City at the Mormon Tabernacle, September 26, 1963, in *Public Papers of the Presidents of the United States: John F. Kennedy, 1963,* pp. 733–38. (Emphasis added.)

15. CASTRO, LAOS, THE CONGO: LIMITS ON THE COERCIVE POWER OF THE SUPERPOWERS

1. Address in Seattle at the University of Washington's 100th Anniversary Program, November 16, 1961, *Public Papers of the Presidents of the United States: John F. Kennedy, 1961,* pp. 725–26.

2. Theodore C. Sorensen, *Kennedy* (New York: Harper, 1965), p. 644.

3. Quoted by Arthur M. Schlesinger, Jr., *A Thousand Days: John F. Kennedy in the White House* (Boston: Houghton Mifflin, 1965), p. 339.

4. See Schlesinger, pp. 240–43; and Sorensen, p. 297.

5. Press conference, April 12, 1961, in *Public Papers of the Presidents: John F. Kennedy, 1961,* pp. 258–59.

6. Peter Wyden, *Bay of Pigs: The Untold Story* (New York: Simon and Schuster, 1979).

7. For a perspective on how large the gap was between what competent U.S. journalists knew about Cuba and the assumptions underlying official moves, see Tad Szulc and Karl E. Meyer, *The Cuban Invasion: The Chronicle of a Disaster* (New York: Ballatine Books, 1962).

8. Schlesinger, pp. 252–95.

9. Schlesinger, p. 276.

10. Quoted by Schlesinger, p. 251.

11. Sorensen, pp. 297, 307.

12. Address to the American Society of Newspaper Editors, April 20, 1961, *Public Papers of the Presidents: John F. Kennedy, 1961,* pp. 204–6.

13. Press conference, March 23, 1961, in *ibid.,* pp. 213–20.

14. See Schlesinger, p. 339.

15. See Arthur J. Dommen, *Conflict in Laos: The Politics of Neutralization* (New York: Praeger, 1965), pp. 194–95.

16. Press Conference, March 23, 1961, *Public Papers of the Presidents: John F. Kennedy, 1961,* p. 214.

17. My reconstruction of the conversation at Vienna, as it relates to the Laotian conflict, is an amalgam of the accounts of Schlesinger, pp. 358–74, and Sorensen, pp. 543–50.

18. Sorensen, p. 643.

19. Schlesinger, p. 339.

20. Sorensen, p. 645.

21. Schlesinger, p. 516.

22. Department of State, *American Foreign Policy: Current Documents* (Washington: GPO, 1962), pp. 1072–85.

23. *Public Papers of the Presidents: John F. Kennedy, 1962,* pp. 18–19.

24. Dwight D. Eisenhower, *The White House Years: Waging Peace, 1956–1961* (New York: Doubleday, 1965), 2:574.

25. Statement by the Secretary of State before the Subcommittee on African Affairs of the Senate Committee on Foreign Relations, January 18, 1962, in *American Foreign Policy: Current Documents,* 1962, pp. 820–21.

26. Schlesinger confesses to siding with his White House colleagues, approvingly quoting the remark, "Every nation has a right to its own War of the Roses," Schlesinger, p. 577.

27. Sorensen, p. 638. Schlesinger, p. 578, says that Kennedy had decided to approve the fighter planes, if they were requested.

16. BERLIN AND CUBAN MISSILES: DEFINING SPHERES OF CONTROL

1. Jean Edward Smith, *The Defense of Berlin* (Baltimore: Johns Hopkins University Press, 1963), p. 230.

2. Theodore C. Sorensen, *Kennedy* (New York: Harper, 1965), pp. 584–86.

3. Quotations are from the text of the *aide-mémoire,* handed by Chairman Khrushchev to President Kennedy at Vienna on June 4, 1961, in Department of State, *American Foreign Policy: Current Documents* (Washington: GPO, 1961), pp. 584–86.

4. The full text of the President's address of July 25, 1961, appears in *Public Papers of the Presidents of the United States: John F. Kennedy, 1961,* pp. 533–40.

5. Quoted by Smith, pp. 254–55.

6. *American Foreign Policy: Current Documents,* 1961, pp. 619–20.

7. *Ibid.,* pp. 620–21.

8. Sorensen, p. 594.

9. General Clay's virtuosity in brilliantly staging a "confrontation" to counter attempted Communist "salami slices" is well described in George Bailey's "The Gentle Erosion of Berlin," *The Reporter* (April 26, 1962), pp. 15–19.

10. Quoted by Arthur M. Schlesinger, Jr., A *Thousand Days: John F. Kennedy in the White House* (Boston: Houghton Mifflin, 1965), p. 399.

11. See Arnold L. Horelick, "The Cuban Missile Crisis: An Analysis of Soviet Calculations and Behavior," *World Politics* (April 1964), pp. 363–89.

12. *Public Papers of the Presidents: John F. Kennedy, 1962,* pp. 897–98.

13. *Ibid.,* p. 898.

14. *Ibid.,* pp. 808–9.

15. Quoted by Elie Abel, *The Missile Crisis* (New York: Lippincott, 1966), pp. 64–65.

16. Sorensen, pp. 684–85.

17. Abel, pp. 80–81.

18. Quoted by Abel, in footnote p. 64.

19. Robert F. Kennedy, *The Thirteen Days: A Memoir of the Cuban Missile Crisis* (New York: W. W. Norton, 1969).

20. The title of an insightful essay on the missile crisis by Albert and Roberta Wohlstetter. See their "Controlling the Risks in Cuba," *Adelphi Papers* (April 1965), Institute for Strategic Studies, London.

21. Robert Kennedy continued to maintain that his brother could not order an air strike because the contemplated attack without warning against a small nation would offend the American conscience. See Abel, p. 88.

22. Abel, p. 101.

23. *Public Papers of the Presidents: John F. Kennedy, 1962,* p. 808.

24. Sorensen, p. 715; see also Abel, p. 201.

25. Sorensen, p. 710.

26. Abel, p. 174; Sorensen, p. 710.

27. Sorensen, p. 717.

17: THE TEST BAN: STABILIZING THE BALANCE

1. N. S. Khrushchev, "The Present International Situation and the Foreign Policy of the Soviet Union," Report at the December 12, 1962, session of the Supreme Soviet, in *Current Digest of the Soviet Press* (January 16, 1963), pp. 4–8; (January 23, 1963), pp. 3–10, 56.

2. For text, see *Current Digest of the Soviet Press* (December 12, 1963), pp. 2–8, 14.

3. Letter from Chairman of the Council of Ministers to the President of the United States, December 19, 1962, Department of State, *American Foreign Policy: Current Documents* (Washington: GPO, 1962), pp. 1306–8.

4. For an account of the Soviet negotiating positions on the test ban from late 1962 through the summer of 1963, see Lincoln P. Bloomfield, Walter C. Clemens, Jr., and Franklin Griffiths, *Khrushchev and the Arms Race: Soviet Interests in Arms Control and Disarmament 1954–1964* (Cambridge: Massachusetts Institute of Technology Press, 1966), pp. 185–200.

5. Arthur M. Schlesinger, Jr., A *Thousand Days: John F. Kennedy in the White House* (Boston: Houghton Mifflin, 1965), p. 900.

6. Theodore C. Sorensen, *Kennedy* (New York: Harper, 1965), pp. 730–31.

7. John Kennedy, Commencement Address at American University, Washington, June 10,

1963, in *Public Papers of the Presidents of the United States: John F. Kennedy, 1963,* pp. 459–64.

8. See *Current Digest of the Soviet Press* (July 31, 1963), pp. 3–9.

9. "Open Letter of CPSU Central Committee to All Party Organizations and All Communists of the Soviet Union, July 14, 1963," *Two Major Statements on China* (New York: Cross Currents Press, 1963), pp. 3–49.

10. Kennedy, Address to the American People on the Nuclear Test Ban Treaty, July 26, 1963, *Public Papers of the Presidents: John F. Kennedy, 1963,* pp. 601–6.

11. Robert S. McNamara, testimony of August 13, 1963, before Senate Committee on Foreign Relations, Committee on Armed Services, and Senate members, the Joint Committee on Atomic Energy, *Hearings: Nuclear Test Ban Treaty,* 88th Congress, 1st Session, pp. 97–100. (Hereafter cited as *Hearings.*)

12. Preparedness Investigating Subcommittee of the Committee on Armed Services, U.S. Senate, *Interim Report on the Military Implications of the Proposed Test Ban Treaty,* 88th Congress, 1st Session, 1963.

13. McNamara, *Hearings,* p. 101.

14. *Ibid.,* pp. 102–3.

15. John Foster, Jr., *Hearings,* p. 637.

16. Harold Brown, Senate Committee on Foreign Relations, *Report on the Nuclear Test Ban Treaty,* 88th Congress, 1st Session, 1963, pp. 15–16.

17. General Maxwell B. Taylor, *ibid.,* p. 16.

18. Harold Brown, *ibid.,* pp. 14–16.

19. McNamara, *Hearings,* p. 104.

20. See September 19, 1963, speech by Barry Goldwater explaining his vote against the treaty, in *New York Times,* Sept. 20, 1963.

21. McNamara, *Hearings,* pp. 104–5.

18. THE BREAKUP OF BLOCS: THE DECLINE OF IDEOLOGY AND CONTROL

1. John F. Kennedy, Special Message to Congress, May 25, 1961, in Department of State, *American Foreign Policy: Current Documents* (Washington: GPO, 1961), p. 31.

2. Press conference of the President of France, May 15, 1962, in Department of State, *American Foreign Policy: Current Documents* (Washington: GPO, 1962), pp. 544–45.

3. Press conference, May 17, 1962, in *Public Papers of the Presidents of the United States: John F. Kennedy, 1962,* pp. 401–2.

4. Address at Independence Hall, Philadelphia, July 4, 1962, in *ibid.,* pp. 537–39.

5. Television and radio interview, December 17, 1962, in *Public Papers of the Presidents: John F. Kennedy, 1962,* pp. 889–904, at 903.

6. Quotations from press conference by President Charles de Gaulle, January 14, 1963; pertinent excerpts are reprinted in the Council on Foreign Relations publication *Documents on American Foreign Relations 1963* (New York: Harper, 1964), pp. 168–80.

7. Theodore C. Sorensen, *Kennedy* (New York: Harper, 1965), p. 572.

8. Philip L. Geyelin, *Lyndon B. Johnson and the World* (New York: Praeger, 1966), pp. 167–74.

9. Dean Rusk, statement to North Atlantic Council, May 12, 1964, in *Department of State Bulletin,* June 1, 1964, pp. 850–52.

10. See George F. Kennan, *On Dealing with the Communist World* (New York: Harper), 1964.

11. Marshall D. Shulman, *Beyond the Cold War* (New Haven: Yale University Press, 1966).

12. Zbigniew Brzezinski, *Alternative to Partition: For a Broader Conception of America's Role in Europe* (New York: McGraw-Hill, 1965).

13. Kennedy, Press conference, October 9, 1963, in *Public Papers of the Presidents: John F. Kennedy, 1963*, pp. 767–75.

14. "United States Policy and Eastern Europe," address by Secretary of State Rusk, February 25, 1964, in the Council on Foreign Relations, *Documents on American Foreign Relations 1964*, pp. 144–49.

15. Lyndon B. Johnson, address of May 23, 1964, in the *Department of State Bulletin*, June 15, 1964, pp. 922–24.

19. THE VIETNAM AND THE DOMINICAN INTERVENTIONS

1. Arthur M. Schlesinger, Jr., *Robert Kennedy and His Times* (Boston: Houghton Mifflin, 1978), pp. 709–11.

2. President Kennedy's interview with Walter Cronkite, *Public Papers of the Presidents of the United States: John F. Kennedy, 1963*, p. 652.

3. For details of the U.S. government's cooperation in the coup against Diem see *The Pentagon Papers: The Defense Department's History of United States Decisionmaking on Vietnam*, Senator Mike Gravell, ed. (Boston: Beacon Press, 1971), 2:212–20, 239, 253–54, 257–62, 734, 738, 789–92.

4. *Ibid.*, 3:3.

5. *Ibid.*, 3:141–52. See also Leslie H. Gelb and Richard Betts, *The Irony of Vietnam: The System Worked* (Washington: Brookings Institution, 1979), p. 102.

6. *The Gulf of Tonkin: The 1954 Incidents, Hearings Before the Senate Committee on Foreign Relations*, 90th Congress, 2d Session (Washington: GPO, 1968).

7. U.S. Congress, Joint Resolution of August 7, 1964.

8. Address to the American Bar Association, August 12, 1964, in *Public Papers of the Presidents of the United States: Lyndon B. Johnson, 1963–64*, 2:953.

9. Remarks in Manchester, New Hampshire, September 28, 1964, in *ibid.*, p. 1164.

10. October 21, 1964, in *ibid.*, p. 1391.

11. Press conference by Secretary of Defense McNamara and Under Secretary of State Ball, February 7, 1965, in *New York Times*, February 8, 1965.

12. State Department Publication 7839, February 1965.

13. Address by President Johnson at Johns Hopkins University, April 7, 1965, in *Department of State Bulletin*, April 26, 1965, pp. 606–10.

14. See the President's message to Congress, May 5, 1965.

15. In *Department of State Bulletin*, July 12, 1965.

16. *New York Times*, November 18 and 19, 1965.

17. In *Department of State Bulletin*, August 16, 1965, pp. 262–65.

18. *Ibid.*

19. In *New York Times*, January 29, 1966.

20. James Gavin, testimony before Senate Committee on Foreign Relations, *Hearings: Supplemental Foreign Assistance Fiscal Year 1966—Vietnam*, pp. 230–31.

21. George Kennan in *ibid.*, pp. 331–36.

22. The Declaration of Honolulu and accompanying statements are published in *Weekly Compilation of Presidential Documents*, February 14, 1966.

23. From President's statement of May 2, 1965, in *Department of State Bulletin*, May 17, 1965, pp. 744–45.

24. *Ibid.*, pp. 738–48.

25. President's statement of May 2, 1965, in *ibid.*, pp. 745–47.

26. *Ibid.*, p. 746.

27. See *Public Papers of the Presidents of the United States: John F. Kennedy, 1963*, pp. 872–77.

28. Most of the evidence is documented in Theodore Draper's detailed account, "The Dominican Crisis: A Case Study in American Policy," *Commentary* (December 1965), pp. 33–68.

29. *Public Papers of the Presidents: Lyndon B. Johnson, 1965,* p. 480.

30. See Dan Kurzman, *Santo Domingo: The Revolt of the Damned* (New York: Putnam, 1965); Tad Szulc, *Dominican Dairy* (New York: Dell edition, 1966); Barnard Collier's articles in the *New York Herald Tribune* during late April and May, 1965; James Goodsen's article in the *Christian Science Monitor,* May 19, 1965; and Philip Geyelin's article in the *Wall Street Journal,* June 25, 1965. Senator Fulbright's major speech on the Dominican crisis appears in the *Congressional Record,* September 15, 1965, as does Senator Clark's on September 17, 1965.

31. Senate Committee on Foreign Relations, *Background Information Relating to the Dominican Republic,* July 1965, p. 63.

32. In *Department of State Bulletin,* May 17, 1965, p. 745.

33. *Congressional Record,* September 15, 1965.

34. Rusk, Senate Committee on Foreign Relations, *Background Information Relating to the Dominican Republic,* July 1965, p. 78.

35. Fulbright, *Congressional Record,* September 15, 1965.

36. Address by Under Secretary of State Thomas C. Mann, San Diego, October 12, 1965, Department of State Press Release, No. 241.

20. THE DISINTEGRATION OF THE FOREIGN POLICY CONSENSUS

1. Draft memorandum for the President from the Secretary of Defense ("The Mc-Naughton Draft Presidential Memorandum"). May 19, 1967, *The Pentagon Papers,* 4:477–89.

2. Townsend Hoopes, *The Limits of Intervention* (New York: McKay, 1969), p. 181.

3. Doris Kearns, *Lyndon Johnson and the American Dream* (New York: Signet edition, 1977), p. 357.

4. Hoopes, p. 205.

5. *Ibid.,* p. 217.

6. *Ibid.,* p. 222, for background. President Johnson's March 31, 1968, radio-TV address is in *Public Papers of the Presidents of the United States: Lyndon B. Johnson, 1968,* I:469–476.

7. Kearns, pp. 351–68, passim.

21. KISSINGER AND THE CRISIS OF POWER

1. Henry Kissinger, *The White House Years* (Boston: Little, Brown, 1979), pp. 55–58.

2. *Ibid.,* p. 65.

3. Henry Kissinger, "The Vietnam Negotiations," *Foreign Affairs* (January 1969), 47(2):234.

4. Kissinger, *The White House Years,* p. 57.

5. Richard M. Nixon, *U.S. Foreign Policy for the 1970s: A New Strategy for Peace,* Report to Congress, February 18, 1970 (Washington: GPO, 1970), pp. 2–3.

6. Henry Kissinger, "Central Issues in American Foreign Policy," in Kermit Gordon, ed., *Agenda for the Nation* (Washington: Brookings Institution, 1968), p. 602.

7. *Ibid.,* pp. 602, 612.

8. *Ibid.,* p. 612.

9. Nixon, *U.S. Foreign Policy,* pp. 5–6.

10. *Ibid.,* p. 6.

11. *Ibid.,* p. 7.

12. Kissinger, "Central Issues," p. 588.

13. Nixon, *U.S. Foreign Policy*, pp. 4–5.

14. *Ibid.*, pp. 5–14.

15. Interview of President Nixon, *Time* (January 3, 1972), p. 11.

16. In a 1973 address Kissinger insisted that "there is no parallel with the nineteenth century. Then, the principal countries shared essentially similar concepts of legitimacy and accepted the basic structure of the existing international order. Small adjustments in strength were significant. The 'balance' operated in a relatively confined geographic area. None of these factors obtains today." Henry A. Kissinger, "The Nature of the National Dialogue in Foreign Policy," in *Pacem in Terris III: The Nixon-Kissinger Foreign Policy: Opportunities and Contradictions* (Santa Barbara, Calif.: Center for the Study of Democratic Institutions, 1973), 1:15.

17. My finding that, despite his denials, Kissinger's world order desiderata are essentially derived from his studies of nineteenth-century statesmanship is buttressed by two excellent pieces of scholarship: Frank A. Burd, "World Order as a Final Cause in the Foreign Policy of Henry Kissinger," Paper delivered at the Annual Meeting of the International Studies Association, Washington, D.C., 1975; and Stephen A. Garret, "Nixonian Foreign Policy: A New Balance of Power—or a Revived Concert?" *Polity* (Spring 1976), 8:389–421.

18. Henry A. Kissinger, *A World Restored: Metternich, Castlereagh, and the Problem of Peace* (Boston: Houghton Mifflin, 1957), p. 318.

19. *Ibid.*, p. 1.

20. *Ibid.*

21. *Ibid.*

22. Declaration of Principles signed by President Richard Nixon and General Secretary Leonid Brezhnev, Moscow, May 29, 1972.

23. The policy of détente is analyzed in more detail in chapter 22.

24. G. Warren Nutter, *Kissinger's Grand Design* (Washington: American Enterprise Institute, 1975), p. 13.

25. See Kissinger's essay, "The White Revolutionary: Reflections on Bismarck," *Daedalus* (Summer 1968), 97(3):888–924.

26. *Ibid.*, p. 922.

22. THE INSUFFICIENCY OF MILITARY CONTAINMENT

1. Henry Kissinger, *The White House Years* (Boston: Little, Brown, 1979), pp. 62, 66–67.

2. *Ibid.*, p. 217.

3. President Nixon's news conference on January 27, 1969, *Department of State Bulletin*, no. 1547 (February 17, 1969), 143.

4. Richard M. Nixon, *U.S. Foreign Policy for the 1970s: Building for Peace* (Washington: GPO, 1971), pp. 170–71.

5. Richard M. Nixon, *U.S. Foreign Policy for the 1970s: The Emerging Structure of Peace* (Washington: GPO, 1972), p. 158.

6. From Melvin Laird and James Schlesinger defense posture statements.

7. Nixon, *U.S. Foreign Policy* (1971), p. 170–71.

8. See Jerome Kahan, *Security in the Nuclear Age: Developing U.S. Strategic Arms Policy* (Washington: Brookings Institution, 1975), pp. 142–96.

9. The skirmishing over strategic arms policy inside the U.S. government is described in rich detail by Kissinger in *White House Years*, pp. 215–18, 539–51; and by John Newhouse, *Cold Dawn: The Story of SALT* (New York: Holt, Rinehart, and Winston, 1973), esp. pp. 133–65.

10. Treaty Between the United States of America and the Union of Soviet Socialist Republics on the Limitation of Anti-Ballistic Missile Systems (signed in Moscow May 26, 1972).

11. *Ibid.*

12. Interim Agreement Between the United States of America and the Union of Soviet Socialist Republics on Certain Measures With Respect to the Limitation of Strategic Offensive Arms (signed in Moscow May 26, 1972).

13. Newhouse, *Cold Dawn*, pp. 234–36.

14. See Kahan, *Security in the Nuclear Age*, pp. 189–92.

15. Secretary of Defense James L. Schlesinger's news conferences on August 17, 1973; January 10, 1974; and January 24, 1974, Department of Defense texts (processed).

16. Secretary of Defense James R. Schlesinger, *Annual Defense Department Report, FY 1976 and Transition Budgets* (Washington: Department of Defense, February 5, 1975), pp. 1–14.

17. *Ibid.*

18. Kissinger's news conference in Moscow on July 3, 1974, *Department of State Bulletin*, no. 1831 (July 29, 1974), 71:210.

19. See Thomas W. Wolfe, *The SALT Experience: Its Impact on U.S. and Soviet Strategic Policy and Decisionmaking* (Santa Monica, Calif.: RAND, R-1686-PR, September 1975), pp. 164–71, for the specifics of the Vladivostok agreement, many of which were left out of the cryptic summit communiqué and dribbled out in subsequent press conferences and background news stories.

20. Kissinger's version of the early moves toward China is in *The White House Years*, pp. 163–94. The Kalb brothers, reflecting Kissinger's pre-Watergate deference to Nixon, give the nod to the President and cite his 1967 article in *Foreign Affairs* as evidence. Marvin Kalb and Bernard Kalb, *Kissinger* (New York: Dell, 1975), p. 250.

21. Kissinger, *The White House Years*, pp. 163–65.

22. A. Doak Barnett, *China Policy: Old Problems and New Challenges* (Washington: Brookings Institution, 1977), pp. 4–5.

23. Kissinger, *The White House Years*, p. 180.

24. Kalb and Kalb, *Kissinger*, pp. 259–60.

25. *Department of State Bulletin*, no. 1573 (August 18, 1969), 61:126.

26. Richard M. Nixon, *U.S. Foreign Policy for the 1970s: A New Strategy for Peace*, Report to Congress, February 18, 1980 (Washington: GPO, 1970), pp. 140–41.

27. Kalb and Kalb, *Kissinger*, pp. 263–64.

28. *Ibid.*, pp. 266–70.

29. Nixon, *U.S. Foreign Policy* (1971), pp. 105–10.

30. Kalb and Kalb, *Kissinger*, p. 272. See also John G. Stoessinger, *Henry Kissinger: The Anguish of Power* (New York: Norton, 1976), p. 120; and William Safire, *Before the Fall: An Inside View of the Pre-Watergate White House* (Garden City, N.Y.: Doubleday, 1975), p. 372.

31. President Nixon's news conference on August 4, 1971, in *Department of State Bulletin* no. 1678 (August 23, 1971), 65:191.

32. Nixon, *U.S. Foreign Policy* (1972), p. 35.

33. Tillman Durdin, "Peking Explains Warmer U.S. Ties," *New York Times*, August 22, 1971.

34. Text of joint communiqué issues at Shanghai, February 27, 1972, in *Department of State Bulletin*, no. 1708 (March 20, 1972), 66:435–38.

35. *Ibid.*

36. *Ibid.*

37. Winston Lord, statement before the Subcommittee on Future Foreign Policy Research and Development, House Committee on International Relations, March 23, 1976. Full text in *Department of State Bulletin*, no. 1921 (April 19, 1976), 74:514–18.

38. Excerpts from "Interview with Kissinger: Eight Years in Washington Evaluated," *New York Times*, January 20, 1977.

39. "Basic Principles of Relations Between the United States of America and the Union of Soviet Socialist Republics," in *Department of State Bulletin*, no. 1722 (June 26, 1972), 66:898–99.

40. Richard M. Nixon, *U.S. Foreign Policy for the 1970s: Shaping a Durable Peace*, Report to Congress, May 3, 1973, pp. 31–35.

41. Peter G. Peterson, *U.S.–Soviet Commercial Relations in a New Era* (Washington: U.S. Department of Commerce, August 1972), pp. 3–4.

42. See Seyom Brown, *New Forces in World Politics* (Washington: Brookings Institution, 1974), pp. 67–78.

43. *Department of State Bulletin*, no. 1718 (May 29, 1972), 66:755. Kissinger also arranged a special meeting between the Soviet Trade Minister and President Nixon and key U.S. trade officials at the White House three days after the Haiphong mining was announced. The Kremlin kept its cool, denouncing the U.S. threats to Soviet shipping as a gross violation of freedom of navigation and demanding that the blockade be lifted immediately, but continuing its preparations for the Moscow summit. See Kalb and Kalb, *Kissinger*, pp. 352–53.

44. Kissinger, September 19, 1974. *Department of State Bulletin*, no. 1842 (October 14, 1974), 71:505–19.

45. Helmut Sonnenfeldt, "U.S.–Soviet Relations in the Nuclear Age," *Department of State Bulletin*, no. 1923 (May 3, 1976), 84:581.

23. AVOIDING HUMILIATION IN INDOCHINA

1. Henry Kissinger, "The Vietnam Negotiations," *Foreign Affairs* (January 1969), 47(2):218–19; and Henry Kissinger, *The White House Years* (Boston: Little, Brown, 1979), pp. 227–29, 298.

2. Kissinger, *The White House Years*, p. 298. See also Richard Whalen, *Catch the Falling Flag* (Boston: Houghton Mifflin, 1972); and Marvin Kalb and Bernard Kalb, *Kissinger* (New York: Dell, 1975), pp. 142–50.

3. Albert H. Cantril and Charles W. Roll, Jr., *Hopes and Fears of the American People* (New York: Universe Books for Potomac Associates, 1971), pp. 37–38.

4. Nixon's autobiography, published by Doubleday in 1962, was called *Six Crises*.

5. For Kissinger's defense of the legality and morality of the secret bombing of Cambodia see *The White House Years*, pp. 239–54.

6. President Nixon, radio-TV address to the nation, April 30, 1970, in *Department of State Bulletin*, no. 1612 (May 18, 1970), 62:620.

7. *Ibid.*, p. 619.

8. Richard M. Nixon, "A Report on the Conclusion of the Cambodian Operation," *Department of State Bulletin*, no. 1621 (July 20, 1970), 63:65–74.

9. See William Shawcross, *Sideshow: Kissinger, Nixon and the Destruction of Cambodia* (New York: Simon and Schuster, 1979) for the most elaborate version of the charge that the United States was to blame for Cambodia's tragedy. Kissinger's refutation is in *The White House Years*, pp. 433–521.

10. Kissinger, *ibid.*, p. 974.

11. Richard M. Nixon, "A Report on the Military Situation in Vietnam and the Role of the United States," *Department of State Bulletin*, no. 1716 (May 15, 1972), 66:684.

12. *Ibid.*, p. 685.

13. *Ibid.*, p. 684.

14. Richard Nixon, address of May 8, 1972, in *Department of State Bulletin*, no. 1718 (May 29, 1972), 66:747–50.

15. *Ibid.*

16. See Roger Morris, *Uncertain Greatness: Henry Kissinger and American Foreign Policy* (New York: Harper & Row, 1977), pp. 184–86.

17. Kalb and Kalb, *Kissinger,* pp. 352–54.

18. Morris, p. 186.

19. Kalb and Kalb, p. 384.

20. In *The White House Years* Kissinger unequivocally endorses the Christmas 1972 bombing: "Nixon chose the only weapon he had available. His decision speeded the end of the war; even in retrospect, I can think of no other measure that would have" (p. 1461).

21. Address by President Nixon, January 23, 1973, in *Department of State Bulletin,* no. 1755 (February 12, 1973), 68:153.

22. "Texts of Agreements and Protocols on Ending the War and Restoring the Peace in Vietnam," *ibid.*, pp. 169–88.

23. Kissinger, *The White House Years,* p. 1470.

24. Kissinger, *Years of Upheaval* (Boston: Little, Brown, 1982), pp. 369–70.

25. *Ibid.*, pp. 301–35.

26. *Ibid.*, pp. 306–308.

27. *Ibid.*, pp. 318–19.

28. *Ibid.*, p. 324.

29. *Ibid.*, pp. 332–37.

30. *Ibid.*, p. 327.

24. THE MIDDLE EAST AND THE REASSERTION OF AMERICAN COMPETENCE ABROAD

1. Richard M. Nixon, *RN: The Memoirs of Richard Nixon* (New York: Grosset & Dunlap, 1978), pp. 467–77.

2. UN Security Council Resolution 242 (1967).

3. Secretary of State William R. Rogers, "A Lasting Peace in the Middle East: An American View," address delivered December 9, 1969, in *Department of State Bulletin,* no. 1593 (January 5, 1970), 62:8.

4. William B. Quandt, *Decade of Decisions: American Policy Toward the Arab–Israeli Conflict, 1967–1976* (Berkeley: University of California Press, 1977), pp. 89–90.

5. Israeli Cabinet statement, December 22, 1978, quoted by Quandt, p. 91.

6. Nixon, *RN,* pp. 478–79. Nixon's claim of advance skepticism about the prospects for the Rogers Plan is borne out by the fact that the President failed to identify himself with the plan at the time either publicly or within the counsels of government. See Tad Szulc, *The Illusion of Peace: Foreign Policy in the Nixon Years* (New York: Viking, 1978), pp. 97–98.

7. Kissinger portrays his role in Middle East policy as relatively less active than on other matters in the first year or so of the Nixon administration. Assigning principal responsibility for Middle East affairs to Secretary of State Rogers was Nixon's way of comforting his old friend, who was otherwise frustrated at being left out of the action. Moreover, Nixon calculated that in the Middle East almost any U.S. policy would fail, and would incur the wrath of Israel's supporters; so it was good to get the White House out of the direct line of fire. "He also suspected," recounts Kissinger, "that my Jewish origin might cause me to lean too much toward Israel" (*The White House Years* [Boston: Little, Brown, 1979], p. 348).

8. *Ibid.*, 567.

9. Szulc, pp. 90–94.

10. Marvin Kalb and Bernard Kalb, *Kissinger* (New York: Dell, 1975), p. 217.

11. *Quandt, Decade of Decisions,* p. 88.

12. Nixon, *RN,* p. 479.

13. *Ibid.* See also Kissinger, *The White House Years*, p. 560–61.

14. See Kalb and Kalb, *Kissinger*, p. 215; Quandt, *Decade of Decisions*, pp. 97–99.

15. Quandt, pp. 100–101.

16. Kissinger, as quoted by Kalb and Kalb, *Kissinger*, p. 222.

17. Szulc, *Illusion of Peace*, pp. 317–20; Quandt, *Decade of Decisions*, pp. 106–8; Kalb and Kalb, *Kissinger*, pp. 225–26.

18. Kissinger, *White House Years*, pp. 567–91.

19. See Quandt, p. 113.

20. Szulc, *Illusion of Peace*, pp. 324–25.

21. Kalb and Kalb, *Kissinger*, pp. 228–29.

22. Quandt, *Decade of Decisions*, p. 114.

23. Nixon, *RN*, p. 483.

24. Kissinger, *The White House Years*, pp. 594–631, provides the most complete account of White House actions and considerations in the Jordan crisis. Nixon devotes only a few cryptic paragraphs of his memoirs to the crisis.

25. Kalb and Kalb, *Kissinger*, pp. 236–38; Quandt, *Decade of Decisions*, pp. 116–19; Szulc, *Illusion of Peace*, pp. 329–31.

26. Nixon, *RN*, p. 920.

27. Kissinger's news conference on October 12, 1973, *Department of State Bulletin*, 69, no. 1792 (October 29, 1973):537.

28. Kissinger, *Years of Upheaval* (Boston: Little, Brown, 1982), and Kalb and Kalb, *Kissinger*, pp. 510–19, provide most of the material on the indications of impending war. See also Szulc, *Illusion of Peace*, pp. 726–27, and Nadav Safran, *Israel: The Embattled Ally* (Cambridge, Mass.: Belknap-Harvard, 1978), pp. 467–75.

29. John Stoessinger, *Henry Kissinger: The Anguish of Power* (New York: Norton, 1976), p. 179.

30. Kissinger, *Years of Upheaval*, p. 477.

31. Kissinger's news conference on October 25, 1973, *Department of State Bulletin*, no. 1794 (November 12, 1973), 69:583–94.

32. See Edward R. F. Sheehan, *The Arabs, Israelis, and Kissinger: A Secret History of American Diplomacy in the Middle East* (New York: Readers Digest Press, 1976). Kissinger "recognized instinctively," says Sheehan, "that . . . if he allowed neither side to win decisively, then he might manipulate the result to launch negotiations, and—ultimately—to compose the Arab-Israeli quarrel. All of Kissinger's ensuing moves must be understood in this perspective" (p. 32).

33. Some critics allege that the excuse of Defense Department objections was wholly contrived by Kissinger, that Secretary of Defense Schlesinger was actually in favor of a forthright response to Israeli requests, and that Kissinger had fabricated this ploy to make the Israelis feel that though he personally was on their side, he would have difficulty helping them out unless they provided him with leverage—in the form of a more compromising stance on the cease-fire—over Schlesinger and the growing coalition of pro-Arab sentiment in the U.S. government. See esp. Szulc, *Illusion of Peace*, pp. 735–39. Kissinger's detailed rebuttals to all such allegations are in *Years of Upheaval*, pp. 491–96, 513–15.

34. UN Security Council Resolution 338, October 22, 1973, in *Department of State Bulletin*, no. 1974 (November 12, 1978), 69:604.

35. Kissinger, *Years of Upheaval*, pp. 570–71, 602–11.

36. Kalb and Kalb, *Kissinger*, pp. 550–51.

37. Kalb and Kalb, p. 553; Quandt, *Decade of Decisions*, p. 196; Szulc, *Illusion of Peace*, p. 745; Nixon, *RN*, p. 938.

38. James Schlesinger's news conference on October 26, 1973, in *Department of State Bul-*

letin, no. 1796 (November 19, 1973), 69:617–26. See also Kissinger, *Years of Upheaval,* p. 584.

39. Kissinger, *Years of Upheaval,* p. 585.
40. *Ibid.,* 585–86.
41. Nixon, *RN,* pp. 939–40.
42. Kissinger's news conference on October 25, 1973, p. 588.
43. *Ibid.,* p. 589.
44. *Department of State Bulletin,* no. 1974 (November 12, 1973), 69:604–5.

25. THE ANACHRONISM OF CONSERVATIVE REALPOLITIK

1. Henry Kissinger, *The White House Years* (Boston: Little, Brown, 1979), pp. 842–918.
2. Henry Kissinger, *Years of Upheaval* (Boston: Little, Brown, 1982), pp. 374–413; but see Seymour M. Hersh, "The Price of Power," *Atlantic Monthly* (December 1982) 250(6):31ff.
3. Gerald R. Ford, *A Time to Heal* (New York: Harper & Row and Readers Digest, 1979), pp. 275–84.
4. Kissinger, *The White House Years,* p. 950.
5. John B. Connally, remarks at the International Conference of the American Bankers Association, Munich, May 28, 1971 (Department of the Treasury news release).
6. Richard M. Nixon, television and radio address on August 15, 1971, in *Department of State Bulletin,* no. 1680 (September 6, 1971), 65:253–56.
7. Kissinger, *The White House Years,* pp. 955–62.
8. See Seyom Brown, *New Forces in World Politics* (Washington: Brookings Institution, 1974), pp. 29–44.
9. Kissinger, address delivered to the annual meeting of the Associated Press editors, April 23, 1973, in *Department of State Bulletin,* no. 1768 (May 14, 1973), 68:593–98. See also Alvin Shuster, "Europe Cool to U.S. Design for New Ties," *New York Times,* May 22, 1973.
10. Kissinger, *Years of Upheaval,* pp. 128–94.
11. For details on the consultations prior to and during the Washington energy conference of 1974, see *ibid.,* pp. 896–934.
12. Kissinger, address delivered February 11, 1974, to the opening session of the International Oil Conference, Washington, excerpts in *New York Times,* February 12, 1974.
13. See address by Kissinger at the World Food Conference in Rome, November 16, 1974, in *Department of State Bulletin,* no. 1851 (December 16, 1974), 71:821–29.
14. Interview with Secretary of State Kissinger, *Business Week,* January 13, 1975; full text reprinted in *Washington Post,* January 3, 1975.
15. Bernard Gwertzman, "Threat of Force Serves as U.S. Weapon," *New York Times,* January 20, 1975.
16. Kissinger, address delivered in Milwaukee, July 14, 1975, in *Department of State Bulletin,* no. 1884 (August 4, 1975), 73:149.
17. Daniel P. Moynihan, "The United States in Opposition," *Commentary* (March 1975), pp. 31–44.
18. See Seyom Brown, "The New Legitimacy," *International Journal* (Winter 1975–76), 31(1):14–25.
19. Kissinger, address read by Daniel P. Moynihan to the General Assembly of the United Nations, September 1, 1975, in *Department of State Bulletin,* no. 1891 (September 22, 1975), 73:425–41.
20. Anthony Lake, *The "Tar Baby" Option: American Policy Toward Southern Rhodesia* (New York: Columbia University Press, 1976).
21. National Security Council Interdepartmental Group for Africa, *Study in Response to*

National Security Study Memorandum 39: Southern Africa, Document (AF/NSC-IG 69—August 15, 1969, reprinted in full in Mohamed A. El-Khawas and Barry Cohen, eds., *National Security Study Memorandum 39: The Kissinger Study of Southern Africa* (Westport, Conn.: Lawrence Hill, 1976).

22. The report of the NSC Task Force on Angola is summarized by Nathaniel Davis, "The Angola Decision of 1975: A Personal Memoir," *Foreign Affairs* (Fall 1978), 57(1):109–24.

23. *Ibid.,* pp. 113–14.

24. Kissinger, statement made January 19, 1976, before the Subcommittee on African Affairs of the U.S. Senate Committee on Foreign Relations, *Hearings on U.S. Involvement in Civil War in Angola,* 94th Congress, 2d session (Washington: GPO, 1976), pp. 14–23.

25. Statement by Senator Dick Clark, February 6, 1976, in *ibid.*

26. Kissinger, address delivered in Lusaka, Zambia, April 27, 1976, in *Department of State Bulletin,* no. 1927 (May 31, 1976), 74:672–79.

27. Kissinger, "Toward a New Understanding of Community," address delivered to the 31st session of the UN General Assembly, September 30, 1976, in Department of State Press Release no. 485.

26. THE KISSINGER CONTRIBUTION

1. Two of Kissinger's former university colleagues have published thoughtful evaluations: Stanley Hoffmann, in *Primacy and World Order: Foreign Policy Since the Cold War* (New York: McGraw-Hill, 1978), and John G. Stoessinger, in *Henry Kissinger: The Anguish of Power* (New York: Norton: 1976). My study traces more closely the unfolding of particular policies than Hoffmann's does, and is more sweeping in its appraisal than Stoessinger's is. A philosophically penetrating analysis of the intellectual sources of Kissinger's concepts is provided by Peter Dickson in *Kissinger and the Meaning of History* (New York: Cambridge University Press, 1978).

27. THE MANY FACES OF JIMMY CARTER

1. *Public Papers on the Presidents of the United States: Jimmy Carter, 1977* (Washington: GPO, 1977), 1:3–4.

2. *Ibid.,* pp. 444–50.

3. *Ibid.,* pp. 955–56.

4. Interview with Zbigniew Brzezinski, *U.S. News & World Report* (May 30, 1977), pp. 35–36.

5. Betty Glad, *Jimmy Carter, In Search of the Great White House* (New York: Norton, 1980), pp. 485–86.

6. Jimmy Carter, Address at the United States Naval Academy, June 7, 1978, *Weekly Compilation of Presidential Documents,* 14 (23):1052–57.

7. Hodding Carter III, "Life Inside the Carter State Department," *Playboy* (February 1981), p. 215.

8. James Fallows, "The Passionless Presidency, *Atlantic,* May, 1979, pp. 33–46f.

9. Cyrus Vance, Commencement address at Harvard University, June 4, 1981, *New York Times,* June 5, 1981.

10. Richard Burt, "Brzezinski Calls Democrats Soft Toward Moscow," *New York Times,* November 30, 1980.

11. Bernard Gwertzman, "Vance, Looking Back, Lauds Pact on Arms and Retorts to Brzezinski," *New York Times* December 3, 1980.

12. *Vital Speeches* (February 1, 1981), 47(8):226–28.

28. IDEALISM AS THE HIGHER REALISM

1. Cyrus Vance, "Human Rights and Foreign Policy," address at the Law Day Ceremonies at the University of Georgia Law School at Athens, April 30, 1977, in *Department of State Bulletin*, no. 1978 (May 23, 1977), 76:505–8.

2. See Arthur Schlesinger, Jr.'s account of the first two years of the Carter administration's human rights policy in his article "Human Rights and the American Tradition," *America and the World 1978* (special issue of *Foreign Affairs*), 57(3):503–26.

3. Michael Dobbs, "Goldberg and Aides Differ on Tactics at Belgrade Parley," *Washington Post*, October 17, 1977; Flora Lewis, "Amid Debate at Belgrade, Quiet Change of Aims and Style," *New York Times*, October 16, 1977.

4. Information on the role and decisions of the Interagency Group on Human Rights and Foreign Assistance is from Neil J. Kritz, "The Carter Human Rights Policy: An Analysis," manuscript, Brandeis University, 1981.

5. *Ibid.*

6. Mark L. Schneider, Acting Assistant Secretary of State for Human Rights and Humanitarian Affairs, statement to the Subcommittee on International Organizations of the House Foreign Affairs Committee, February 28, 1979 (processed).

7. Cecil V. Crabb, Jr., and Pat M. Holt, *Invitation to Struggle: Congress, the President, and Foreign Policy* (Washington: Congressional Quarterly Press, 1980), p. 71.

8. Senate Committee on Foreign Relations, *Senate Debate on the Panama Canal Treaties: A Compendium of Major Statements, Documents, Record Votes and Relevant Events*, 96th Congress, 1st session (February 1979), p. 97.

9. Carter, address to the nation, February 1, 1978, in *Public Papers of the Presidents of the United States: Jimmy Carter, 1978*, 1:262.

10. See William M. LeoGrande, "The Revolution in Nicaragua: Another Cuba?" *Foreign Affairs* (Fall 1979), 58(1):28–50.

11. *Ibid.*, pp. 32–33.

12. Richard R. Fagen, "Dateline Nicaragua: The End of the Affair," *Foreign Policy* (Fall 1979), no. 36, p. 184.

13. Fagen, pp. 185–86; LeoGrande, "The Revolution in Nicaragua," p. 35.

14. Cyrus R. Vance, address to the Organization of American States in Washington, June 21, 1979, excerpts in *New York Times*, June 22, 1979.

15. Andrew Young, "The United States and Africa: Victory for Diplomacy," *America and the World 1980* (special issue of *Foreign Affairs*, 1981), pp. 649–66.

16. Carter, remarks on signing H.R. 1746 into law, March 18, 1977, in *Public Papers of the Presidents: Jimmy Carter, 1977*, 1:451–53.

17. David Ottaway, "Africa: U.S. Policy Eclipse," *America and the World 1979* (special issue of *Foreign Affairs*, 1980), pp. 640–41.

18. White House briefing by the President for civic community leaders, April 30, 1980, in *Public Papers of the Presidents: Jimmy Carter, 1980–1981*, 1:801.

29. CAMP DAVID: THE EXTENT AND LIMITS OF U.S. LEVERAGE IN THE MIDDLE EAST

1. Brookings Middle East Study Group, *Toward Peace in the Middle East* (Washington: Brookings Institution, 1975).

2. *Ibid.*, p. 13.

3. *Ibid.*, p. 18.

4. *Department of State Bulletin* (November 7, 1977), 77(2002):639–40.

5. Sidney Drell and Uri Dan, "Untold Story of the Mideast Talks," *New York Times Magazine,* January 21, 1979, p. 20ff.

6. Secretary of State Cyrus Vance, Statement of February 14, 1978.

' 7. Jimmy Carter, *Keeping Faith: Memoirs of a President* (New York: Bantam, 1982), pp. 327–403.

8. Drell and Dan claim that the bifurcation of the Sinai issues into a treaty and the other aspects of the Arab–Israeli conflict into a set of guidelines for future negotiations was at first opposed by Brzezinski and the State Department as too much a separate peace between Israel and Egypt which would alienate the rest of the Arab world; and that Carter had to overrule his advisers to save the Camp David process from failure. *New York Times Magazine,* January 28, 1979, p. 38.

9. *Ibid.*

10. Camp David accords, Sept. 17, 1978, *Weekly Compilation of Presidential Documents,* 114(38):1523–28.

11. Drell and Dan, p. 38.

12. Treaty signing ceremony, *Weekly Compilation of Presidential Documents,* 15(13):518–22.

13. See Moshe Dayan, *Breakthrough: A Personal Account of the Egypt-Israel Peace Negotiations* (New York: Knopf, 1981).

14. U.N. Security Council Resolution 465

15. Thomas N. Betheil, "Incidentally, The U.N. Vote Was Right," *The Washington Monthly* (May 1980), pp. 32–41.

30. HOSTAGES IN IRAN: PARALYSIS AND PRUDENCE IN THE USE OF AMERICAN POWER

1. Jimmy Carter, in *Keeping Faith: Memoirs of a President* (New York: Bantam, 1982) quotes from his New Year's Eve toast to the Shah (p. 437), but leaves out the embarrassing phrase about the "respect, admiration, and love" of the Shah by the Iranian people. For this part of the toast, see the *New York Times,* January 2, 1978.

2. Henry Kissinger, *The White House Years* (Boston: Little, Brown, 1979), p. 1262.

3. For U.S. policies toward Iran during World War II see Bruce R. Kuniholm, *The Origins of the Cold War in the Near East: Great Power Conflict and Diplomacy in Iran, Turkey, and Greece* (Princeton: Princeton University Press, 1980), pp. 130–208.

4. See Barry Rubin, *Paved With Good Intentions: The American Experience in Iran* (New York: Oxford University Press, 1980), especially pp. 29–90.

5. *Ibid.,* pp. 116–23.

6. Kissinger, *The White House Years,* p. 1264.

7. Michael Ledeen and William Lewis, *Debacle: The American Failure in Iran* (New York: Knopf, 1981), p. 51.

8. Kissinger, *The White House Years,* p. 1264.

9. Zbigniew Brzezinski, *Power and Principle: Memoirs of the National Security Adviser 1977–81* (New York: Farrar, Strauss, 1983), pp. 358–78.

10. William H. Sullivan, "Dateline Iran: The Road Not Taken," *Foreign Policy* (Fall 1980), no. 40, pp. 175–86. Compare with Brzezinski, pp. 376–82.

11. Jimmy Carter, news conference, December 7, 1978, in *Weekly Compilation of Presidential Documents,* 14(49):2171–83.

12. Sullivan, "Dateline Iran," p. 184. Compare with Carter, *Keeping Faith,* pp. 443–49.

13. Quoted by Rubin, *Paved With Good Intentions,* p. 290.

14. Terrence Smith, "Why Carter Admitted the Shah," *America in Captivity: Points of Decision in the Hostage Crisis* (special issue of *New York Times Magazine,* 1981), p. 42.

15. Pierre Salinger, *America Held Hostage: The Secret Negotiations* (New York: Doubleday, 1981), pp. 15–17. See also Carter, *Keeping Faith*, p. 452.

16. Henry Kissinger, speech of April 9, 1979, at Harvard Business School dinner, quoted by Terrence Smith, "Why Carter Admitted the Shah," p. 42.

17. Warren Christopher, letter of August 18, 1979, quoted by Salinger, p. 18.

18. Smith, "Why Carter Admitted the Shah," p. 47. See also Carter, *Keeping Faith*, pp. 454–55.

19. See Salinger, pp. 26–27.

20. The details of the takeover, unknown by Washington at the time, were reconstructed by journalists on the basis of interviews with the released hostages in early 1981. I have relied principally on the account by Charles Mohr, "Events That Led Up to Takeover of U.S. Embassy on November 4, 1979," *New York Times*, January 21, 1981.

21. Carter, *Keeping Faith*, p. 459.

22. See Carter statement on the American hostages, December 7, 1979, *Weekly Compilation of Presidential Documents*, 15(49):2205.

23. Carter's message to the Congress, November 14, 1979, *Weekly Compilation of Presidential Documents*, 19(46): No. 46, p. 2118. On the technicalities of implementing the freeze and other economic sanctions, see Robert Carswell, "Economic Sanctions and the Iranian Experience," *Foreign Affairs* (Winter 1981/82) 60(2):247–65.

24. Terrence Smith, "Putting the Hostages' Lives First," *America in Captivity* (special issue of *New York Times Magazine*, 1981), p. 78.

25. The secret proximity talks of mid-November 1979 are described in Smith, "Putting the Hostages' Lives First," pp. 81–82.

26. Salinger, *America Held Hostage*, pp. 169–81.

27. Robert Shaplen, "Eye of the Storm" *The New Yorker* (June 9, 1980), 2:48–49.

28. See Drew Middleton, "Going the Military Route," *America in Captivity* (special issue of *New York Times Magazine*), pp. 103–12; also the accounts in *Time* and *Newsweek* of May 5 and 12, 1980.

29. "Poll: Use of Force in Iran Favored," *Washington Post*, April 20, 1980.

30. The story of the Rescue mission has been reconstructed from the material in Carter's *Keeping Faith*, pp. 506–21, Brzezinksi's *Power and Principle*, and from numerous journalistic accounts based on Pentagon briefings in the days following the raid. Particularly useful accounts appeared in the *New York Times*, April 27, 1980; *Time* and *Newsweek* April 5, 1980; and the Middle article in *America in Capacity*.

31. SALT VS. MOVING BEYOND "MAD"

1. Strobe Talbott, *Endgame: The Inside Story of SALT II* (New York: Harper & Row, 1979), pp. 39–67.

2. Jimmy Carter, news conference of March 24, 1977, in *Weekly Compilation of Presidential Documents*, 13(13):439–45.

3. Quotations of Gromyko from reports of his press conference in *Washington Post* and *New York Times*, March 31, 1977.

4. *Ibid.*

5. Carter, question-and-answer session with reporters at Dobbins Air Force Base, Georgia, April 8, 1977, in *Weekly Compilation of Presidential Documents*, 13(16):515–18.

6. Cyrus Vance, address to the American Society of Newspaper Editors, April 10, 1978, in Department of State Press Release no. 154.

7. Department of State and Arms Control and Disarmament Agency, SALT and American Security (Washington: GPO, November 1978).

8. Committee on the Present Danger, *Does the Official Case for the SALT II Treaty Hold Up Under Analysis?* (Washington: Publication of the CPD, March 14, 1979).

9. *SALT II Agreement: Vienna, June 1979* (Washington: Department of State, 1979), Selected Documents no. 12a.

10. For the Senate's deliberations see *U.S. Defense Policy: Weapons, Strategy and Commitments,* 2nd ed. (Washington: Congressional Quarterly, 1980), pp. 15–29.

11. Summary of Kissinger testimony in *U.S. Defense Policy,* p. 23.

12. Spurgeon M. Keeny, Jr., and Wolfgang K. H. Panofsky, "Mad Versus Nuts: Can Doctrine or Weaponry Remedy the Mutual Hostage Relationship of the Superpowers?" *Foreign Affairs* (Winter 1981/82), 60 (2):287–304.

13. Secretary of Defense Harold Brown, *Department of Defense Annual Report, Fiscal Year 1979* (Washington: Department of Defense, February 2, 1978), pp. 53–60.

14. Carter himself was sincerely one of the deep mourners. His failure to make significant progress on arms control, he says in his memoirs, "was the most profound disappointment of my Presidency." *Keeping Faith,* p. 265.

32. AFGHANISTAN AND THE REASSERTION OF GEOPOLITICAL IMPERATIVES

1. Jimmy Carter, interviewed by Frank Reynolds of ABC News, December 31, 1979; text of interview in *New York Times,* January 1, 1980.

2. The strongest hint of a "linkage" between U.S. support for SALT and Soviet good behavior in the Horn of Africa were Brzezinski's in February 1978. See Strobe Talbott, *Endgame: The Inside Story of SALT II* (New York: Harper and Row, 1979), pp. 146–47.

3. Carter, address at Wake Forest University, March 17, 1978, in *Weekly Compilation of Presidential Documents,* 14(12):529–35.

4. Carter, commencement address at the United States Naval Academy, Annapolis, Maryland, June 7, 1978, in *Weekly Compilation of Presidential Documents,* 14(23):1052–57.

5. Carter, speech of October 1, 1979, in *Weekly Compilation of Presidential Documents,* 15(40):1802–6.

6. Carter, nationwide television address, January 4, 1980, in *Weekly Compilation of Presidential Documents,* 16(2):25–27.

7. Carter, State of the Union Address, January 23, 1980, in *Weekly Compilation of Presidential Documents,* 16(4):194–203. Quote at p. 197.

33. THE NOT-SO-GRAND STRATEGY OF THE REAGAN ADMINISTRATION

1. Caspar Weinberger, statement before the Senate Armed Services Committee, March 4, 1981. Department of Defense (processed) 1981.

2. Ronald Reagan, news conference of January 29, 1981, in *Weekly Compilation of Presidential Documents,* 17(5):66–67.

3. Reagan, interview with five reporters, February 2, 1981, in *New York Times,* February 3, 1981.

4. Alexander M. Haig, Jr., statement before Senate Foreign Relations Committee, January 9, 1981, in *New York Times,* January 10, 1981.

5. *Ibid.*

6. Reagan, question-and-answer session with reporters, August 13, 1981, in *Weekly Compilation of Presidential Documents,* 17(33):868–877.

7. Weinberger, testimony before Senate Foreign Relations Committee, November 3, 1981, quoted in Richard Halloran, "Weinberger Calls Arms Buildup 'a Necessary Prerequisite' to Talks," *New York Times,* November 4, 1981.

8. "Special Report on Communist Involvement in the Insurrection in El Salvador," in *Department of State Bulletin,* no. 2048 (March 1981), 81:1–11.

9. Alexander Haig, testimony before House Foreign Affairs Committee, March 18, 1981; excerpts and report in *New York Times,* March 19, 1981.

10. Haig, news conference, January 28, 1981, in *New York Times,* January 29, 1981.

11. Quotations from Haig's January 28, 1981, news conference, *ibid.*

12. Judith Miller, "Soviet Aid Disputed in Terrorism Study," *New York Times,* March 29, 1981.

13. See Philip Taubman, "U.S. Tries to Back Up Haig on Terrorism," *New York Times,* May 3, 1981.

14. Reagan, address to the Organization of American States in Washington, February 24, 1982, U.S. Department of State, *Current Policy,* No. 370.

15. Letter from Reagan to Howard Baker, *Weekly Compilation of Presidential Documents.*

16. Text of Memorandum of Understanding Between the United States and Israel, *New York Times.*

17. Reagan, impromptu remarks to newspaper editors, text in *New York Times,* October 17, 1981.

18. Reagan, statement to reporters, text in *New York Times,* October 22, 1981.

19. Haig testimony before Senate Foreign Relations Committee, excerpts in *New York Times,* November 5, 1981.

20. Richard Halloran, "Haig Is Disputed by Weinberger on A-Blast Plan," *New York Times,* November 6, 1981.

21. Reagan, news conference, text in *New York Times,* November 11, 1981.

22. Reagan, address to the National Press Club, Washington, November 18, 1981, in *Weekly Compilation of Presidential Documents,* 17(47):1273–78.

23. Leonid Brezhnev, interview with *Der Spiegel,* November 2, 1981, quoted by Hedrick Smith, "Reagan Arms Plan: A New Tone Toward Moscow," *New York Times,* November 19, 1981.

24. See articles in *Newsweek,* June 8, 1981, an issue devoted to the first Weinberger defense budget.

25. Background statement from the White House on the MX missile and B-1 bomber, *New York Times,* October 3, 1981.

26. Text of President Reagan's budget message to the Congress, *New York Times,* February 7, 1982. See also the accompanying commentary on the military portion of the budget by Leslie H. Gelb.

27. *North–South: A Programme for Survival—Report of the Independent Commission on International Development Issues* (Cambridge: MIT Press, 1980). In addition to endorsing the standard Third World demands for commodity price stabilization agreements, preferential marketing agreements with the industrial countries, special balance-of-payments supports, debt forgiveness, and the like, the Brandt Commission proposed international taxes on world trade and travel to raise revenues for redistribution to the poor countries.

28. Text of the communiqué issued after the Ottawa conference, *New York Times,* July 22, 1981.

29. Bernard D. Nossiter, "Haig Aide Says U.S. Opposes Sharing the Wealth," *New York Times,* August 8, 1981.

30. Haig, address before the UN General Assembly, September 21, 1981, in Department of State, *Current Policy,* no. 314.

31. Reagan, address to the Board of Governors of the World Bank and the International Monetary Fund, September 29, 1981, in *Weekly Compilation of Presidential Documents,* 17(40):1052–55.

32. *New York Times,* March 4, 1981.

33. Ronald Reagan, address to the Organization of American States, February 24, 1982, U.S. Department of State, *Current Policy,* no. 370.

34. IDEOLOGY AND THE REAL WORLD

1. Richard Halloran, "Reagan Aide Tells of New Strategy on Soviet Threat," *New York Times,* May 22, 1982; Saul Friedman, "Reagan Calls for Pressure on USSR," *Boston Globe,* May 22, 1982.

2. The Defense Department's guidance document was summarized and quoted in detail by Richard Halloran, "Pentagon Draws up First Strategy for Fighting a Long Nuclear War," *New York Times,* May 30, 1982.

3. Ronald Reagan, statement on sanctions being applied to the Soviet Union, *Weekly Compilation of Presidential Documents,* 17(53):1429–30.

4. Letter from Secretary of Commerce Malcolm Baldrige to Henry Reuss, Chairman of the Joint Economic Committee, in *East–West Commercial Policy: A Congressional Dialogue with the Reagan Administration* (A study prepared for the Joint Economic Committee by the Congressional Research Service of the Library of Congress) February 16, 1982 (Washington: GPO, 1982).

5. Clyde H. Farnsworth, "U.S. Threatens Strict Penalties for Soviet Sales," *New York Times,* June 24, 1952.

6. Margaret Thatcher, remarks to the British House of Commons, July 1, 1982, quoted by James Feron, "Mrs. Thatcher Faults U.S. on Siberia Pipeline," *New York Times,* July 2, 1982.

7. Judith Miller, "Curb Sought on Equipment for Soviet," *New York Times,* October 2, 1982.

8. Photograph of President Reagan angrily phoning Begin on August 12, 1982, and the accompanying White House press release, *New York Times.* August 13, 1982.

9. Bernard Gwertzman, "U.S. Calls Israeli Act a 'Violation' and Demands Immediate Pullout," *New York Times,* September 17, 1982.

10. See various reports in the *New York Times* on September 19, 20, and 21, 1982 for the reactions in Israel, the United States, and other countries to the September 18 massacre of the Palestinian civilians.

11. Ronald Reagan, address to the nation broadcast from Burbank, California, September 1, 1982, Department of State, *Current Policy,* no. 417. See also, George Shultz, address before the United Jewish Appeal, New York City, September 12, 1982, Department of State, *Current Policy,* No. 419.

12. Jeane Kirkpatrick, "Dictatorships and Double Standards," *Commentary* (November 1979), 68(5):34–45.

13. Laurence Freedman, "The War of the Falkland Islands, 1982," *Foreign Affairs* (Fall 1982) 61(1):196–210.

14. Ronald Reagan, Address Before the British Parliament, June 8, 1982, Department of State, *Current Policy,* no. 399.

15. *Ibid.*

16. Ronald Reagan, speech of March 8, 1983, *New York Times* March 9, 1983.

17. Transcript of remarks by Reagan and Haig, *Boston Globe,* June 26, 1982.

18. Talking Paper for Meeting Between President-Elect Reagan and Secretary Designate Haig, 10 A.M., January 6, 1981. Text published in the *Washington Post,* July 13, 1982.

19. James Reston, "Who's Now in Charge," *New York Times,* June 30, 1982.

20. Some perceptive observations on how the self-defeating paranoid style of Secretary of State Haig left a large vacuum in foreign policy-making during Reagan's first two years are offered by Lou Cannon, *Reagan* (New York: Putnam, 1982), esp. pp. 294–401.

21. Bernard Gwertzman, "The Shultz Method: How the New Secretary of State Is Trying to Stabilize Foreign Policy," *New York Times Magazine*, January 2, 1983, pp. 13ff.

22. Ronald Reagan, "Paths Toward Peace: Deterrence and Arms Control," Department of State, *Current Policy*, No. 435, November 22, 1982.

23. Bernard Gwertzman, "Reagan Intensifies Drive To Promote Policies in Europe," *New York Times*, January 20, 1983.

24. John Vinocur, "Reagan Suggests Session on Arms with Andropov," *New York Times*, February 1, 1983.

25. Ronald Reagan, "Peace and National Security," Address to the nation, Washington, D.C., March 23, 1983, Department of State, *Current Policy*, No. 472.

26. Ronald Reagan, Address to Joint Session of Congress, April 27, 1983, *New York Times*, April 28, 1983.

INDEX